Communication
Principles for a Lifetime
Third Edition

STEVEN A. BEEBE
Texas State University–San Marcos

SUSAN J. BEEBE
Texas State University–San Marcos

DIANA K. IVY
Texas A&M University–Corpus Christi

PEARSON

Boston New York San Francisco
Mexico City Montreal Toronto London Madrid Munich Paris
Hong Kong Singapore Tokyo Cape Town Sydney

Editor-in-Chief: Karon Bowers
Editor: Brian Wheel
Senior Development Editor: Carol Alper
Editorial Assistant: Heather Hawkins
Vice President, Director of Marketing: Tim Stookesberry
Production Supervisor: Beth Houston
Editorial Production Service: Quica Ostrander/Lifland et al., Bookmakers
Composition Buyer: Linda Cox
Manufacturing Buyer: Megan Cochran
Electronic Composition: Publishers' Design and Production Services, Inc.
Interior Design: Glenna Collett
Photo Researcher: Helane Prottas
Cover Administrator: Joel Gendron

For related titles and support materials, visit our online catalog at www.ablongman.com.

Between the time Website information is gathered and then published, it is not unusual for some sites to have closed. Also, the transcription of URLs can result in typographical errors. The publisher would appreciate notification where these errors occur so that they may be corrected in subsequent editions.

Library of Congress Cataloging-in-Publication Data

Beebe, Steven A., 1950–
    Communication : principles for a lifetime / Steven A. Beebe, Susan J. Beebe, Diana K.
Ivy. — 3rd ed.
    p.   cm.
    Includes bibliographical references and index.
    ISBN 0-205-46702-4
    1. Communication.   I. Beebe, Susan J.   II. Ivy, Diana K.   III. Title.

HM1206.B44 2007
302.2—dc22
                                                            2005057483

Printed in the United States of America

10 9 8 7 6 5 4 3   10 09 08 07

Credits appear on page 483, which constitutes a continuation of the copyright page.

For our teachers . . . and our students

Brief Contents

UNIT ONE Principles of Communication

CHAPTER 1 Foundations of Human Communication 1
CHAPTER 2 Self-Awareness and Communication 29
CHAPTER 3 Understanding Verbal Messages 57
CHAPTER 4 Understanding Nonverbal Messages 79
CHAPTER 5 Listening and Responding 105
CHAPTER 6 Adapting to Others: Bridging Culture and Gender Differences 135

UNIT TWO Interpersonal Communication

CHAPTER 7 Understanding Interpersonal Communication 165
CHAPTER 8 Enhancing Relationships 191

UNIT THREE Communicating in Groups and Teams

CHAPTER 9 Understanding Group and Team Performance 219
CHAPTER 10 Enhancing Group and Team Performance 245

UNIT FOUR Presentational Speaking

CHAPTER 11 Developing Your Presentation 281
CHAPTER 12 Organizing and Outlining Your Presentation 313
CHAPTER 13 Delivering Your Presentation 335
CHAPTER 14 Speaking to Inform 363
CHAPTER 15 Speaking to Persuade 383

APPENDIXES

APPENDIX A Interviewing 412
APPENDIX B Communication and Technology 433
APPENDIX C Sample Speeches for Discussion and Evaluation 446

Contents

Preface   xv

UNIT ONE
Principles of Communication

1 Foundations of Human Communication   1

Communication Defined   2
Communication Competence   4
The Message Should Be Understood   5
The Message Should Achieve Its Intended Effect   5
The Message Should Be Ethical   5
■ Ethics and Communication: What Are the Sources of Your Ethical Views?   7
Why Study Communication?   8
▨ On the Web   8
To Improve Your Employability   8
To Improve Your Relationships   9
To Improve Your Health   9
Communication Models   10
Communication as Action: Message Transfer   11
Communication as Interaction: Message Exchange   12
Communication as Transaction: Message Creation   13
Communication Characteristics   15
Communication Is Inescapable   15
Communication Is Irreversible   15
Communication Is Complicated   15
Communication Emphasizes Content and Relationships   17
Communication Is Governed by Rules   17
Communication Principles for a Lifetime   17
Principle One: Be Aware of Your Communication with Yourself and Others   19
Principle Two: Effectively Use and Interpret Verbal Messages   19
Principle Three: Effectively Use and Interpret Nonverbal Messages   20

Principle Four: Listen and Respond Thoughtfully to Others   21
Principle Five: Appropriately Adapt Messages to Others   21
■ Diversity and Communication: Principles for a Lifetime: Principles for All Cultures?   22
Communicating with Others: Three Situations   23
Interpersonal Communication   23
Group Communication   24
Presentational Communication   25
Principles for a Lifetime: Enhancing Your Skills   26
Summary   26
Discussion and Review   27
Putting Principles into Practice   27

2 Self-Awareness and Communication   29

Self-Awareness: How Well Do You Know Yourself?   31
Self-Concept: Who Are You?   32
Self-Concept Components   32
One or Many Selves?   33
■ Technology and Communication: Exploring Self-Concept through Computer-Mediated Communication   34
How the Self-Concept Develops   35
■ Ethics and Communication: Cyber Selves   36
Self-Esteem: What Is Your Value?   38
Gender   38
▨ On the Web   38
Social Comparisons   39

■ Diversity and Communication: Self-Esteem and
Ethnicity   40
Self-Expectations   41
Self-Fulfilling Prophecy   41
**Communication and the Enhancement of
Self-Esteem   42**
Engage in Positive Self-Talk   42
Visualize   43
Reframe   44
Develop Honest Relationships   44
Surround Yourself with Positive People   44
■ On the Web   45
Lose Your Baggage   45
The Perception Process   46
Stage One: Attention and Selection   47
Stage Two: Organization   48
Stage Three: Interpretation   48
**Communication and the Enhancement of
Perceptual Accuracy   49**
Increase Your Awareness   50
Avoid Stereotypes   51
■ On the Web   52
Check Your Perceptions   52
**Principles for a Lifetime: Enhancing Your
Skills   53**
Summary   53
Discussion and Review   54
Putting Principles into Practice   54

3   Understanding Verbal
Messages   57

Why Focus on Language?   59
■ On the Web   60
The Nature of Language   60
■ Diversity and Communication: Words across the
Country   61
People Use Words as Symbols   61
People Attach Meaning to Words   61
People Create Denotative and Connotative Meanings
for Words   61
People Convey Concrete and Abstract Meanings
through Words   62
Meanings Are Culture Bound   62
Meanings Are Context Bound   63
The Power of Words   63
The Power to Create and Label Experience   63
The Power to Affect Thoughts and Actions   64
■ Technology and Communication: Minding Your
Manners, Even on the Net   64
The Power to Shape and Reflect Culture   65
The Power to Make and Break Relationships   65
Confronting Bias in Language   66
■ Ethics and Communication: Ebonics or "Standard"
English?   66

Biased Language: Race, Ethnicity, Nationality, and
Religion   67
■ On the Web   68
Biased Language: Gender and Sexual Orientation   68
Biased Language: Age, Class, and Ability   71
**Using Words to Establish Supportive
Relationships   72**
Describe Your Own Feelings Rather Than Evaluate
Others   73
Solve Problems Rather Than Control Others   73
Be Genuine Rather Than Manipulative   74
Empathize Rather Than Remain Detached from
Others   74
Be Flexible Rather Than Rigid toward Others   74
Present Yourself as Equal Rather Than Superior   74
■ On the Web   75
Avoid Gunny-Sacking   75
**Principles for a Lifetime: Enhancing Your
Skills   76**
Summary   76
Discussion and Review   77
Putting Principles into Practice   77

4   Understanding Nonverbal
Messages   79

Why Focus on Nonverbal Communication?   81
Nonverbal Messages Communicate Feelings and
Attitudes   81
■ Technology and Communication: Conveying Emotions
Online   82
Nonverbal Messages Are More Believable Than Verbal
Ones   82
Nonverbal Messages Are Critical to Successful
Relationships   82
Functions of Messages   83
The Nature of Nonverbal Communication   84
The Culture-Bound Nature of Nonverbal
Communication   85
The Rule-Governed Nature of Nonverbal
Communication   85
The Ambiguous Nature of Nonverbal
Communication   86
The Continuous Nature of Nonverbal
Communication   86
The Nonlinguistic Nature of Nonverbal
Communication   87
The Multichanneled Nature of Nonverbal
Communication   87
Codes of Nonverbal Communication   88
Appearance   88
Body Movement, Gestures, and Posture   88
■ Ethics and Communication: Lie Detectors   91
Eye Contact   91

■ On the Web   92
Facial Expressions   92
Touch   93
The Voice   94
■ Diversity and Communication: Cultural Meanings of
   Silence   95
Physical Environment, Space, and Territory   95
**How to Interpret Nonverbal Cues More
   Accurately   98**
Immediacy   99
Arousal   100
Dominance   100
**Principles for a Lifetime: Enhancing Your
   Skills   101**
Summary   102
Discussion and Review   102
Putting Principles into Practice   103

5   Listening and Responding   105

How We Listen   107
Selecting   107
Attending   108
Understanding   108
Remembering   109
Responding   109
Listening Styles   109
People-Oriented Listeners   110
Action-Oriented Listeners   110
Content-Oriented Listeners   110
Time-Oriented Listeners   110
Adapting to Your Listening Style   111
■ Diversity and Communication: East and West
   Listening Styles   111
Listening Barriers   112
Self Barriers   112
Information-Processing Barriers   115
Context Barriers   116
Improving Your Listening Skills   118
Stop: Turn Off Competing Messages   118
Look: Listen with Your Eyes   119
Listen: Understand Both Details and Major
   Ideas   119
■ Diversity and Communication: Who Are Better
   Listeners, Men or Women?   120
Responding Skills   123
Be Descriptive   124
Be Timely   124
Be Brief   124
Be Useful   124
Responding with Empathy   124
Understand Your Partner's Feelings   125
Ask Appropriate Questions   125

■ Ethics and Communication: Honest Listening   126
Paraphrase Message Content   126
■ Technology and Communication: Can Computers
   Listen Empathically?   127
Paraphrase Emotions   127
■ On the Web   127
**Principles for a Lifetime: Enhancing Your
   Skills   129**
Summary   130
Discussion and Review   130
Putting Principles into Practice   130

**6   Adapting to Others: Bridging Culture
       and Gender Differences   135**

**Ethically Adapt Your Communication to
   Others   137**
Culture and Communication   138
■ Diversity and Communication: Diversity
   Almanac   138
Defining Culture   139
■ Technology and Communication: Adapting to
   Cultural Differences When Communicating
   Electronically   140
Cultural Contexts   141
Cultural Values   141
■ On the Web   145
Gender and Communication   146
The Importance of Gender in Culture   146
Why Women and Men Communicate Versus
   How   147
**Barriers to Bridging Differences and Adapting to
   Others   149**
Assuming Superiority   150
Assuming Similarity   150
Assuming Differences   151
Stereotyping and Prejudice   152
■ Ethics and Communication: Stereotyping
   Others   153
Different Communication Codes   153
**Adapting to Others Who Are Different from
   You   154**
Seek Information   154
Ask Questions and Listen   155
Tolerate Ambiguity   156
Develop Mindfulness   156
Become Other-Oriented   156
Adapt to Others   159
**Principles for a Lifetime: Enhancing Your
   Skills   161**
Summary   161
Discussion and Review   162
Putting Principles into Practice   163

UNIT TWO
Interpersonal Communication

7 Understanding Interpersonal Communication   165

What Is Interpersonal Communication?   167
Interpersonal Communication Involves Quality   167
Interpersonal Communication Involves Mutual Influence   168
Interpersonal Communication Helps Manage Relationships   168
Initiating Relationships   169
Interpersonal Attraction: Why We Like Whom We Like   169
■ Ethics and Communication: The Harmless Crush?   170
■ Diversity and Communication: What Attracts You?   171
▥ On the Web   172
Communicating Our Attraction   174
Getting That First Conversation Going   174
■ Technology and Communication: Gender and Online Communication   175
Maintaining Relationships   179
Self-Disclosure: Revealing Yourself to Others   180
▥ On the Web   181
Two Models of Self-Disclosure   182
Expressing Emotions   184
Principles for a Lifetime: Enhancing Your Skills   186
Summary   187
Discussion and Review   188
Putting Principles into Practice   188

8 Enhancing Relationships   191

The Importance of Friendship   192
Communication Principles for a Lifetime: Enhancing Friendships   194
The Importance of Family   194
Communication Principles for a Lifetime: Enhancing Family Relationships   195
The Importance of Colleagues   196
Communication Principles for a Lifetime: Enhancing Workplace Relationships   196
Stages of Relationship Development   197
Relational Escalation   198
Relational De-Escalation   199
■ Ethics and Communication: Making Breaking Up Easier to Do?   200
■ Technology and Communication: Cheating in Cyberspace   201
Managing Interpersonal Conflict   202
A World of Conflict   202
How Conflict Functions in Relationships   203
■ Diversity and Communication: Conflict and Culture   204
Styles of Managing Conflict   208
Conflict Management Skills   210
▥ On the Web   211
Principles for a Lifetime: Enhancing Your Skills   214
Summary   215
Discussion and Review   216
Putting Principles into Practice   217

UNIT THREE
Communicating in Groups and Teams

9 Understanding Group and Team Performance   219

Groups and Teams Defined   220
Communicating in Small Groups   221
▥ On the Web   222
Communicating in Teams   222
Understanding Types of Groups and Teams   224

Primary Groups   224
Study Groups   224
■ Ethics and Communication: Ethically Achieving a Team Goal   225
Therapy Groups   225
Problem-Solving Groups   225
■ Technology and Communication: Does Virtual Group Communication Improve Decision Making?   226

Focus Groups   226
Social Groups   226
Understanding Group and Team Dynamics   227
Roles   227
Rules   228
Norms   231
Status   231
Power   232
Cohesiveness   234
Communication Interaction Patterns   235
Understanding Phases of Group and Team Development   236
Orientation   237
Conflict   237
Emergence   238
Reinforcement   238
On the Web   239
The Process Nature of Group Phases   239
Diversity and Communication: The Impact of Individualism and Collectivism on Groups and Teams   239
Principles for a Lifetime: Enhancing Your Skills   240
Summary   241
Discussion and Review   241
Putting Principles into Practice   242

10 Enhancing Group and Team Performance   245

What Effective Group Members Do   246
Identify and Implement Key Functions to Achieve Results   247

Identify a Clear, Elevating Goal   247
Develop a Results-Driven Structure   248
Gather and Use Information Effectively   248
Develop Options   248
Evaluate Ideas   249
Develop Sensitivity toward Others   249
When Not to Work in Groups and Teams   250
Structuring Group and Team Problem Solving   251
Step 1: Identify and Define the Problem   252
Step 2: Analyze the Problem   253
Step 3: Generate Creative Solutions   254
Technology and Communication: E-Brainstorming   256
Step 4: Select the Best Solution   257
Ethics and Communication: Managing Conflict in Groups and Teams   259
Step 5: Take Action   260
Enhancing Group and Team Leadership   262
Trait Approach   262
Functional Approach   262
Styles Approach   263
Situational Approach   264
Transformational Leadership   266
Diversity and Communication: Differences in the Use of Time in Groups and Teams   266
Enhancing Group and Team Meetings   267
Manage Meeting Structure   268
On the Web   269
Manage Meeting Interaction   271
Principles for a Lifetime: Enhancing Your Skills   274
Summary   275
Discussion and Review   275
Putting Principles into Practice   275

UNIT FOUR
Presentational Speaking

11 Developing Your Presentation   281

An Overview of the Presentational Speaking Process   283
Developing Your Presentation Step by Step: Consider Your Audience   284
Understanding Speaker Anxiety   284
Managing Speaker Anxiety   285
Know How to Develop a Presentation   285
Be Prepared   285
Focus on Your Audience   286
Focus on Your Message   286

Give Yourself a Mental Pep Talk   286
Use Deep-Breathing Techniques   287
Take Advantage of Opportunities to Speak   287
Seek Professional Help   287
Selecting and Narrowing Your Topic   287
Who Is the Audience?   288
What Is the Occasion?   288
What Are My Interests and Experiences?   288
Silent Brainstorming   288
On the Web   289
Scanning Web Directories and Web Pages   289
Listening and Reading for Topic Ideas   289

■ Developing Your Presentation Step by Step: Select and Narrow Your Topic   290

Identifying Your Purpose   290
General Purpose   291
Specific Purpose   291

Developing Your Central Idea   292
■ Developing Your Presentation Step by Step: Determine Your Purpose   293
Audience-Centered   293
A Single Topic   293
■ Developing Your Presentation Step by Step: Develop Your Central Idea   294
A Complete Declarative Sentence   294
Direct, Specific Language   294

Generating Main Ideas   294
Does the Central Idea Have *Logical Divisions?*   295
Can You Think of Several *Reasons* the Central Idea Is True?   295
Can You Support the Central Idea with a Series of *Steps* or a *Chronological Sequence?*   295
■ Developing Your Presentation Step by Step: Determine Your Main Ideas   296

Gathering Supporting Material   296
Sources of Supporting Material   297
■ Technology and Communication: A New Kind of Search Engine   297
■ Ethics and Communication: The Question of Speechwriting   301
■ Developing Your Presentation Step by Step: Gather Supporting Material   301
Types of Supporting Material   302
Acknowledgment of Supporting Material   306
■ Diversity and Communication: Adapting to Diverse Audiences   307

Principles for a Lifetime: Enhancing Your Skills   309
Summary   310
Discussion and Review   310
Putting Principles into Practice   311

12 Organizing and Outlining Your Presentation   313

Organizing Your Main Ideas   314
Organizing Ideas Chronologically   315
Organizing Ideas Topically   315
Organizing Ideas Spatially   316
Organizing Ideas to Show Cause and Effect   316
Organizing Ideas by Problem and Solution   316

Organizing Your Supporting Material   317
■ Diversity and Communication: Acknowledging Cultural Differences in Organizing Messages   318
■ Developing Your Presentation Step by Step: Organize Your Speech   318

Organizing Your Presentation for the Ears of Others   319
Previews   319
■ Ethics and Communication: The Ethics of Primacy and Recency   319
Verbal and Nonverbal Transitions   320
Summaries   320

Introducing and Concluding Your Presentation   321
Introductions   321
■ On the Web   322
Conclusions   323

Outlining Your Presentation   324
Preparation Outline   324
■ Technology and Communication: Using Outlining Software   325
■ Sample Preparation Outline   326
Delivery Outline   329
■ Sample Delivery Outline   329

Principles for a Lifetime: Enhancing Your Skills   332
Summary   333
Discussion and Review   333
Putting Principles into Practice   333

13 Delivering Your Presentation   335

Methods of Delivery   336
Manuscript Speaking   336
Memorized Speaking   337
Impromptu Speaking   337
Extemporaneous Speaking   338

Effective Verbal Delivery   339
Using Words Well   339
Crafting Memorable Word Structures   340

Effective Nonverbal Delivery   343
Eye Contact   343
Physical Delivery   343
■ Diversity and Communication: The Academic Quarter   345
Facial Expression   345
■ On the Web   346
Vocal Delivery   346
■ Developing Your Presentation Step by Step: Rehearse Your Presentation   347
Appearance   348
■ Technology and Communication: Rehearsing on Videotape   349

Effective Presentation Aids   349
Types of Presentation Aids   349
Computer-Generated Presentation Aids   353
Guidelines for Preparing Presentation Aids   354
■ Ethics and Communication: Profanity in an Audio Presentation Aid   354

Guidelines for Using Presentation Aids   355

Some Final Tips for Rehearsing and Delivering Your Presentation   357
■ Developing Your Presentation Step by Step: Deliver Your Presentation   358

Principles for a Lifetime: Enhancing Your Skills   358

Summary   359

Discussion and Review   360

Putting Principles into Practice   361

14 Speaking to Inform   363

Types of Informative Presentations   364
Presentations about Objects   364
■ Ethics and Communication: Confidential or Potentially Dangerous Information   365
Presentations about Procedures   365
Presentations about People   366
Presentations about Events   366
Presentations about Ideas   367

Strategies for Organizing Your Informative Presentation   367
Organizing Presentations about Objects   367
Organizing Presentations about Procedures   368
Organizing Presentations about People   368
Organizing Presentations about Events   368
Organizing Presentations about Ideas   368

Strategies for Making Your Informative Presentation Clear   370
Simplify Ideas   370
Pace Your Information Flow   370
Relate New Information to Old   370
■ Diversity and Communication: Using an Interpreter   371

Strategies for Making Your Informative Presentation Interesting   371
Relate to Your Listeners' Interests   371
Use Attention-Catching Supporting Material   372
Establish a Motive for Your Audience to Listen to You   373
■ On the Web   373
Use Word Pictures   373
■ Technology and Communication: Using an Electronic Thesaurus   374
Create Interesting Presentation Aids   374
Use Humor   375

Strategies for Making Your Presentation Memorable   375
Build in Redundancy   376
Use Adult Learning Principles   376
Reinforce Key Ideas Verbally   376
Reinforce Key Ideas Nonverbally   376

■ Sample Informative Presentation: The Power of Music   377

Principles for a Lifetime: Enhancing Your Skills   379

Summary   380

Discussion and Review   381

Putting Principles into Practice   381

15 Speaking to Persuade   383

Persuasion Defined   384
■ Ethics and Communication: Hidden Agendas   385

Motivating Your Audience: The Psychology of Persuasion   386
Motivating with Dissonance   386
Motivating with Needs   387
Motivating with Fear Appeals   388
Motivating with Positive Appeals   388

Selecting and Narrowing Your Persuasive Topic   389

Identifying Your Persuasive Purpose   389

Developing Your Central Idea as a Persuasive Proposition   391
Propositions of Fact   391
Propositions of Value   391
Propositions of Policy   391

Supporting Your Presentation with Credibility, Logic, and Emotion   392
Ethos: Establishing Your Credibility   392
■ Diversity and Communication: "Elementary Reasoning, My Dear Watson"   393
Logos: Using Evidence and Reasoning   394
■ On the Web   397
Pathos: Using Emotion   397

Organizing Your Persuasive Message   398
Problem and Solution   399
Cause and Effect   399
Refutation   400
The Motivated Sequence   400
■ Technology and Communication: The Motivated Sequence in Television Advertising   402

How to Adapt Ideas to People and People to Ideas   402
The Receptive Audience   402
The Neutral Audience   404
The Unreceptive Audience   404
■ Sample Persuasive Presentation: Cruisin' Out of Control   406

Principles for a Lifetime: Enhancing Your Skills   408

Summary   410

Discussion and Review   410

Putting Principles into Practice   411

APPENDIX **A**   **Interviewing**   **412**

The Nature and Types of Interviews   413
Information-Gathering Interview   413
Appraisal Interview   413
Problem-Solving Interview   413
Persuasion Interview   414
Job Interview   414
Interview Structure   415
The Opening   415
The Body: Asking Questions   416
The Conclusion   419
How to Be Interviewed for a Job   420
Be Aware of Your Skills and Abilities   420
Prepare Your Resumé   421
▧ Sample Resumé   422
Identify the Needs of Your Employer   423
Listen, Respond, and Ask Appropriate
   Questions   424
Follow Up after the Interview   425
■ Technology and Communication: Tips for
   E-Resumés   426
**How to Be Interviewed in an Information-
   Gathering Interview   427**
Prepare for the Interview   427
Listen Effectively   427
Respond Appropriately   427
▧ On the Web   428
The Responsibilities of the Interviewer   428
Be Aware of Biases and Prejudices   429
Adapt to an Interviewee's Behavior   429
Deal Wisely with Sensitive Content   429
Listen Effectively   429
Record Information   429
Ask Appropriate Questions   430
**Principles for a Lifetime: Enhancing Your
   Skills   430**
Summary   431

APPENDIX **B**   **Communication and
   Technology   433**

**Technology and Interpersonal
   Communication   434**
An Impersonal Technological Innovation   434
The Role of Technology in Relationship
   Initiation   435
The Role of Technology in Relationship
   Maintenance   437
Technology and Group Communication   439
The Technological Formation of Small Groups   439
Teleconferencing   440
The Effects of Technology on Group Interaction   441
**Technology and Presentational
   Communication   442**
Source Material for Presentations   442
Technological Innovations and Presentation
   Aids   442
Technology and Enhanced Speech Delivery   443
**Principles for a Lifetime: Enhancing Your
   Skills   444**
Summary   445

APPENDIX **C**   **Sample Speeches for
   Discussion and
   Evaluation   446**

Informative Speech   446
Persuasive Speech   453

Notes   455

Index   475

Credits   483

Boxed Features

Ethics and Communication

CHAPTER 1   What Are the Sources of Your Ethical Views?   7

CHAPTER 2   Cyber Selves   36

CHAPTER 3   Ebonics or "Standard" English?   66

CHAPTER 4   Lie Detectors   91

CHAPTER 5   Honest Listening   126

CHAPTER 6   Stereotyping Others   153

CHAPTER 7   The Harmless Crush?   170

CHAPTER 8   Making Breaking Up Easier to Do?   200

CHAPTER 9   Ethically Achieving a Team Goal   225

CHAPTER 10   Managing Conflict in Groups and Teams   259

CHAPTER 11   The Question of Speechwriting   301

CHAPTER 12   The Ethics of Primacy and Recency   319

CHAPTER 13   Profanity in an Audio Presentation Aid   354

CHAPTER 14   Confidential or Potentially Dangerous Information   365

CHAPTER 15   Hidden Agendas   385

Diversity and Communication

CHAPTER 1   Principles for a Lifetime: Principles for All Cultures?   22

CHAPTER 2   Self-Esteem and Ethnicity   40

CHAPTER 3   Words across the Country   61

CHAPTER 4   Cultural Meanings of Silence   95

CHAPTER 5   East and West Listening Styles   111

              Who Are Better Listeners, Men or Women?   120

CHAPTER 6   Diversity Almanac   138

CHAPTER 7   What Attracts You?   171

CHAPTER 8   Conflict and Culture   204

CHAPTER 9   The Impact of Individualism and Collectivism on Groups and Teams   239

CHAPTER 10   Differences in the Use of Time in Groups and Teams   266

CHAPTER 11   Adapting to Diverse Audiences   307

CHAPTER 12   Acknowledging Cultural Differences in Organizing Messages   318

CHAPTER 13   The Academic Quarter   345

CHAPTER 14   Using an Interpreter   371
CHAPTER 15   "Elementary Reasoning, My Dear Watson"   393

Technology and Communication

CHAPTER 2   Exploring Self-Concept through Computer-Mediated Communication   34
CHAPTER 3   Minding Your Manners, Even on the Net   64
CHAPTER 4   Conveying Emotions Online   82
CHAPTER 5   Can Computers Listen Empathically?   127
CHAPTER 6   Adapting to Cultural Differences When Communicating Electronically   140
CHAPTER 7   Gender and Online Communication   175
CHAPTER 8   Cheating in Cyberspace   201
CHAPTER 9   Does Virtual Group Communication Improve Decision Making?   226
CHAPTER 10   E-Brainstorming   256
CHAPTER 11   A New Kind of Search Engine   297
CHAPTER 12   Using Outlining Software   325
CHAPTER 13   Rehearsing on Videotape   349
CHAPTER 14   Using an Electronic Thesaurus   374
CHAPTER 15   The Motivated Sequence in Television Advertising   402
APPENDIX A   Tips for E-Resumés   426

Developing Your Presentation Step by Step

CHAPTER 11   Consider Your Audience   284
             Select and Narrow Your Topic   290
             Determine Your Purpose   293
             Develop Your Central Idea   294
             Determine Your Main Ideas   296
             Gather Supporting Material   301
CHAPTER 12   Organize Your Speech   318
CHAPTER 13   Rehearse Your Presentation   347
             Deliver Your Presentation   358

Preface

Students may take only one course in communication during their entire college career. Yet we want students to remember essential communication principles and skills for the rest of their lives. In our third edition of *Communication: Principles for a Lifetime*, our goal remains the same as in the first and second editions: to provide a cogent presentation of what is fundamental to human communication by organizing the study of communication around five principles that are inherent in the process of communicating with others. Communication is essential for life. We want students to view this course on communication not as simply another course in a string of curricular requirements or options but as a vital, life-enriching course that will help them enhance their communication with others. To remember and apply these essential communication principles, we believe students need a digest of classic and contemporary research and practice that will help them with both the mundane and the magnificent, the everyday and the ever-important communication experiences that constitute the fabric of their lives.

THE CHALLENGE OF TEACHING A FUNDAMENTALS OF COMMUNICATION COURSE

Most introductory communication courses cover a vast terrain of communication concepts, principles, and skills. In fact, there may be too much of a good thing. The barrage of ideas, contexts, theories, and skills can leave students and instructors overwhelmed by a hodgepodge of sometimes unrelated information. Besides learning about several theories of communication, students are also presented with what may appear to them to be abbreviated courses in interpersonal communication, group communication, and public speaking. In addition to a conceptual understanding of communication, students are expected to master a patchwork of communication skills, including group discussion and problem-solving skills, listening and paraphrasing skills, conflict management skills, and informative and persuasive public speaking competencies. When a typical hybrid or introductory communication fundamentals course is over, both students and instructors have covered an astounding amount of information and skills; they may not, however, appreciate the coherent structure of what is fundamental about human communication. They may end the course viewing communication as a fragmented area of study that includes a bushel basket full of concepts and applications but having little understanding of what is truly fundamental about how we make sense out of the world and share that sense with others.

OUR SOLUTION TO THE CHALLENGE: AN INTEGRATED APPROACH TO TEACHING AND LEARNING COMMUNICATION PRINCIPLES AND SKILLS

To help students remember and integrate essential information, we've organized the study of human communication around five fundamental communication principles. Organizing communication content using these five principles is helpful not only for students but also for instructors. These principles can help stitch together the plethora of ideas and information typically found in an introductory communication course. They provide a framework for understanding the importance of communication in our lives. We don't claim that everything students need to know about communication is embedded in our five organizing communication principles. These principles do, however, synthesize essential research and wisdom about communication. They are designed to help introductory communication students see the "big picture" of the role and importance of communication, both as they sit in the classroom and as they live their lives.

The communication principles we highlight should look familiar. However, although they are included in some way in most introductory communication texts, they are not often used as a scaffolding to provide coherence to the entire course. In most texts, principles are typically presented in the first third of the book and then abandoned, as material about interpersonal, group, and public communication is presented. We don't use a hit-and-run approach. Instead, using examples and illustrations students can relate to, we carefully discuss each principle early in the book. Throughout the latter two-thirds of the book we gently remind students how these principles relate to interpersonal relationships, group and team discussions, and public presentations. In other words, we cover classic communication content but organize it around five principles so the information has coherence.

What are the five fundamental principles?

Principle One: Be aware of your communication with yourself and others.
Principle Two: Effectively use and interpret verbal messages.
Principle Three: Effectively use and interpret nonverbal messages.
Principle Four: Listen and respond thoughtfully to others.
Principle Five: Appropriately adapt messages to others.

A subtext for these five principles is the importance of communicating ethically with others. Throughout the book we invite students to consider the ethical implications of how they communicate with others, in a feature entitled Ethics and Communication. As we discuss in Chapter 1, we believe that to be effective, a communication message must achieve three goals: It must be understood, achieve its intended effect, and be ethical. Our five communication principles for a lifetime are designed to help students achieve these three goals.

The relationship among the five communication principles is illustrated with a pentagon model. When each principle is introduced or discussed, the corresponding segment of the model is highlighted.

In addition to identifying five communication principles, we want students to see how these principles relate to the classic communication contexts of interpersonal communication, group and team communication, and presentational speaking. We link the five communication principles with specific content by using a margin icon to identify a discussion of a skill, a concept, or an idea related to one or more of the five communication principles. The icon, de-

Appropriately adapt messages to others

Be aware of your communication with yourself and others

Listen and respond thoughtfully to others

Effectively use and interpret verbal messages

Effectively use and interpret nonverbal messages

scribed in Chapter 1 and illustrated in the margin here, first appears in Chapter 7, Understanding Interpersonal Communication, which is the first context chapter of the book.

Aware
Verbal
Nonverbal
Listen and Respond
Adapt

Overview of the Book

Overall, the book retains the structure of the two previous editions. The book is organized into four units. In Unit One the five principles are introduced (Chapter 1), and then each principle is discussed and illustrated in a separate chapter. These chapters help students see the value of each principle and its centrality in their lives. Chapter 2 discusses the principle of being self aware. Chapter 3 focuses on using and interpreting verbal messages. The focus of Chapter 4 is on using and interpreting nonverbal messages. Chapter 5 includes a discussion of the interrelated processes of listening and responding, giving special attention to the importance of being other-oriented and empathic. The last principle, appropriately adapting to others, is presented in Chapter 6; we use this principle to illustrate the importance of adapting one's behavior to accommodate to culture and gender differences among people.

Unit Two links concepts and strategies for understanding interpersonal communication with our five communication principles for a lifetime. Chapter 7 presents information to help students better understand the nature and function of communication in relationships. Chapter 8 identifies strategies that can enhance the quality of our interpersonal relationships with others.

Unit Three discusses how the five communication principles can help us understand and enhance communication in small groups and teams. Chapter 9 explains how groups and teams work. In Chapter 10 we offer practical strategies for collaboratively solving problems, leading groups and teams, and running and participating in meetings.

The final unit, Unit Four, presents classic content to help students design and deliver a speech, with references to contemporary research and using the latest technological tools. Our popular audience-centered approach to developing a presentation emphasizes the importance of adapting to listeners while also being an ethical communicator. Chapters 11 through 15 offer information and tips for developing presentation ideas, organizing and outlining messages, delivering a presentation (including using various kinds of presentational aids), crafting effective informative presentations, and developing ethically sound persuasive messages.

We conclude the book with three appendixes designed to supplement our instruction about communication fundamentals. Appendix A includes practical strategies for being interviewed and for interviewing others. As in the text, we relate our discussion of interviewing to the five communication principles for a lifetime. Appendix B helps students apply communication principles to their technology-punctuated lives. The Internet has changed the way we connect to other people, and in Appendix B, we examine applications of technology and media in light of our five communication principles to help students see that, even with new technology, people's interactions are governed by classic principles of human communication. Finally, Appendix C includes two examples of recent presentations to illustrate what effective, well-planned presentations look like.

Our Partnership with Instructors Helps Students Learn

As authors, we believe we are in partnership with instructors to help students master the course content. A textbook is essentially a "distance learning" tool. When we write the book, we are separated by both time and space from the learner. But to help shorten the distance between author and reader and engage students in the learning process, we've incorporated a variety of learning resources and pedagogical features. As we note in the text, information alone is not communication. Communication occurs when the receiver responds to information. Our special features help turn information into a communication message that can affect students' lives.

Aware
Verbal
Nonverbal
Listen and Respond
Adapt

Principles Model and Icon   Our pentagon model and margin icons help students see connections among the various communication concepts and skills we present. Throughout the book we provide an integrated framework to reinforce what's fundamental about human communication. We want students to remember the five fundamental principles long after the course is over and they have forgotten the facts they memorized for exams. The principles can also help them remember strategies and concepts to enhance their interpersonal relationships, improve group and team meetings, and design and deliver effective presentations.

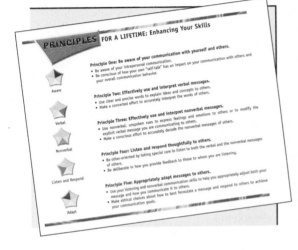

Principles for a Lifetime: Enhancing Your Skills   In addition to the margin icon that highlights material related to one or more communication principles in the text, we conclude each chapter with Principles for a Lifetime: Enhancing Your Skills, a summary of the chapter content organized around the communication principles. In the first six chapters these summaries distill essential information about the individual principle we present in a given chapter. Starting in Chapter 7, we summarize the chapter content using all five communication principles for a lifetime as a framework. Miniature versions of our principles icon highlight the five fundamental principles. The purpose of this chapter-end feature is to help students integrate the material related to the context discussed with the five principles that undergird the descriptive and prescriptive information presented in the chapter. Principles for a Lifetime will help students connect the variety of ideas and skills with the five communication principles.

Ethics and Communication   To help students apply ethics to what they learn about human communication, we include in each chapter a feature called Ethics and Communication. In this revised and expanded ethics feature, we present a case study and then pose ethical questions for students to consider, asking them to ponder how they would respond to a specific ethical dilemma. The questions we pose are designed to be thought-provoking illustrations that can spark insightful class discussion or be used in combination with a journal assignment or other learning method to help students see connections between ethics and communication.

Technology and Communication   Because of the importance of technology in our lives, in each chapter we include a feature entitled Technology and Communication. This feature is intended to help students become sensitive to the sometimes mind-boggling impact of new technology on our communication with others. We also discuss the importance and role of technology in several chapters throughout the book as well as in a revised and expanded Appendix B. The prevalence of technology in students' lives offers powerful teachable moments to help students learn and apply communication principles.

On the Web   We do more than just talk about technology. We encourage students to reach out to the vast array of learning resources on the Internet by including Web resources that link to the topic of each chapter. These annotated Web links, many of which are new to this edition, provide background, context, and activities to help students apply course content. All Internet addresses are included in the Companion Web site that supports this book. If Web addresses change, we update them periodically on the Web site at www.ablongman.com/beebe.

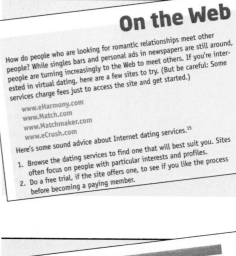

Diversity and Communication   Each chapter includes a Diversity and Communication feature to help students see the importance of diversity in their lives. Yet we don't relegate diversity only to a boxed feature. Because we believe diversity is such an important communication topic in contemporary society, we discuss it not only in a comprehensive chapter on our fifth principle of communication (appropriately adapt messages to others), but throughout the book as well.

Developing Your Presentation Step by Step   The chapters in Unit Four, Presentational Speaking, contain a series of boxes that follow one student through the steps of preparing and giving a presentation. Students learn tips that they can readily apply as they prepare their own presentations.

Comprehensive Pedagogical Learning Tools   To help students master the material, we've built in a wealth of study aids:

- Learning objectives
- Chapter outlines
- Concise Recap boxes that distill key content
- Boldface key terms with margin definitions
- Chapter-end narrative summaries of each chapter
- Chapter-end summaries of the five communication principles
- Chapter-end questions for discussion and review
- Skill-building activities and collaborative learning exercises

New to the Third Edition

Reviewers, instructors, and our students have given us feedback about the two previous editions. This feedback has helped us make the third edition the best possible teaching and learning resource. Following our own Principle Four, we listened and responded to their suggestions. In every chapter we have made the following improvements:

- Updated and expanded references to research to incorporate the latest findings about human communication principles and skills
- Provided new, contemporary examples and illustrations to which students can relate
- Added new cartoons and other illustrations to amplify the content of our message
- Revised and expanded the Ethics and Communication feature and augmented our discussion of ethics in the text
- Revised and expanded the Diversity and Communication feature and added new research about diversity
- Revised and expanded the Technology and Communication feature and included an expanded discussion of the role of online communication in relationships
- Updated the On the Web feature with new references to interesting information, activities, and self-tests
- Added new Principles for a Lifetime summaries to Chapters 1–6
- Revised all Principles for a Lifetime summaries in Chapters 7–15
- Added a new feature to the presentational speaking chapters, Developing Your Presentation Step by Step, in which we walk a student through the process of designing and delivering a speech
- Added a new appendix (Appendix B), Communication and Technology

We've made many other specific changes to chapter content throughout the book. Here's a brief list of selected revisions and additions that we've made to specific chapters:

- Expanded our discussion of ethics and communication in Chapter 1
- Provided new information about self-concept and self-esteem and added a discussion of ethical issues related to identity exploration online in Chapter 2
- Presented new information on the use of language that refers to race, ethnicity, and gender in Chapter 3
- Added new material about gestures, posture, and other nonverbal codes in Chapter 4
- Incorporated the latest research findings about listening styles in Chapter 5
- Added to our discussion of barriers to intercultural communication in Chapter 6
- Significantly augmented our discussion of the implications of online communication for interpersonal relationships in Chapter 7
- Provided new material about relationship development and role formation in families and friendships in Chapter 8
- Provided new and updated information about developing effective team communication as well as new research about managing conflict in diverse groups in Chapter 9
- Added a new section on when not to work in groups and augmented our discussion of leadership in Chapter 10
- Updated the section on Web-based research and the use of electronic indexes and full-text databases in Chapter 11
- Offered a new, alternative strategy for drafting the overall organization of a presentation in Chapter 12
- Presented new ideas for developing visual aids in Chapter 14
- Presented a new and complete annotated persuasive speech in Chapter 15
- Included videotaped versions of several of the student speeches from the text on the accompanying MySpeechLab Web site
- Updated and expanded Appendix A on interviewing
- Presented a new Appendix B on communication and technology, which includes information about the role of technology in interpersonal communication, group and team communication, and presentational speaking
- Provided new sample speeches, including one that provides information about speech development and delivery, in Appendix C

OUR PARTNERSHIP WITH INSTRUCTORS

A textbook is only one tool to help teachers teach and learners learn. We view our job as providing resources that teachers can use to augment, illustrate, and amplify communication principles and skills. As part of our partnership with instructors to facilitate learning, we offer an array of print, electronic, and video resources to help teachers do what they do best: teach. We also offer an array of materials designed for students, to help them enrich their learning experience. Combined with the vast array of learning resources we've built into the text, this dazzling package of additional resources will help instructors forge both intellectual and emotional connections with their students.

Instructor Supplements

Print Resources

- **Instructor's Resource Manual** by Travis Russ, Rutgers University. For each chapter in the text, the *Instructor's Resource Manual* provides At-a-Glance grids that link text objectives to the manual's content as well as to other supplements. Additionally, each chapter includes outlines, discussion and journal questions, classroom activities and assignments, and Internet suggestions. Free on request to adopters; available in print and electronically through the Allyn and Bacon/Longman Instructor's Resource Center.
- **Test Bank** by Sue Stewart, Texas State University–San Marcos. This *Test Bank* contains over 1,500 questions in multiple-choice, true/false, matching, fill-in-the-blank, short answer, and essay formats. Free on request to adopters; available in print and electronically through the Allyn and Bacon/Longman Instructor's Resource Center.
- **A Guide for New Teachers of the Basic Communication Course: Interactive Strategies for Teaching Communication**, Third Edition, by Susanna G. Porter. This guide helps new instructors teach an introductory course effectively. It covers such topics as preparing for the term, planning and structuring your course, evaluating speeches, utilizing the textbook, integrating technology into the classroom, dealing with challenges, and much more. A resource matrix at the end of the guide outlines how best to utilize it in conjunction with *Communication: Principles for a Lifetime*, Third Edition. Available in print and electronically through the Allyn and Bacon/Longman Instructor's Resource Center.
- **Blockbuster Approach: Teaching Interpersonal Communication with Video**, Third Edition, by Thomas Jewell, Marymount College. This guide provides lists and descriptions of popular videos that can be used in the classroom to illustrate complex concepts of interpersonal relationships. Sample activities are also included. Available in print and electronically through the Allyn and Bacon/Longman Instructor's Resource Center.
- **ESL Guide to Public Speaking**, by Debra Gonsher Vinik, Bronx Community College of the City University of New York. This guide provides strategies and resources for instructors teaching in bilingual or multilingual classrooms. It also includes suggestions for further reading and a list of related Web sites.
- **Great Ideas for Teaching Speech (GIFTS)**, Third Edition, by Raymond Zeuschner, California Polytechnic State University. This book provides descriptions and guidelines for assignments successfully used by experienced public speaking instructors in their classrooms.

Electronic Resources

- **Computerized Test Bank**. The print *Test Bank* is also available through Allyn and Bacon's computerized testing system, TestGen EQ. This fully networkable test-generating software is available on a multiplatform CD-ROM for Windows and Macintosh. The user-friendly interface allows instructors to view, edit, and add questions, transfer questions to tests, and print tests in a variety of fonts. Search and sort features allow instructors to locate questions quickly and to arrange them in a preferred order. Free on request to adopters; also available electronically through the Allyn and Bacon/Longman Instructor's Resource Center.

- *MySpeechLab* is a state-of-the-art interactive and instructive online solution for introductory speech and communication courses. Designed to be used either as a supplement to a traditional lecture course or as a complete online course, MySpeechLab combines video, activities, speech preparation tools, research support, tests, and quizzes to make teaching and learning fun. Video footage of several of the student speakers mentioned in the text are included in MySpeechLab. Contact your Allyn and Bacon representative for additional details and ordering information.

- *Video Workshop for Introduction to Communication*, Version 2.0, by Kathryn Dindia, University of Wisconsin; *Video Workshop for Interpersonal Communication*, Version 2.0, by Christine North, Jamestown College; *Video Workshop for Public Speaking*, Version 2.0, by Tasha Van Horn of Citrus College and Marilyn Reineck of Concordia University. *VideoWorkshop* is a way to bring video into your course for maximized learning in introductory communication, interpersonal communication, and public speaking courses. This total teaching and learning system includes quality video footage on an easy-to-use CD-ROM, plus a *Student Learning Guide* and an *Instructor's Teaching Guide*—both with textbook-specific Correlation Grids. The result? A program that brings textbook concepts to life with ease and that helps students understand, analyze, and apply the objectives of the course. *VideoWorkshop* is available for several course areas and can be ordered only when value-packaged with participating Allyn and Bacon textbooks. Visit www.ablongman.com/videoworkshop for more details.

- *Allyn and Bacon Classic and Contemporary Speeches DVD*. This DVD presents a collection of over 120 minutes of video footage of speeches in an easy-to-use format. Each speech is accompanied by a biographical and historical summary that helps students to understand the context and motivation behind each speech. Contact your Allyn and Bacon representative for additional details and ordering information.

- *Allyn and Bacon Digital Media Archive for Communication,* Version 3.0. This CD-ROM contains electronic images of charts, graphs, maps, tables, and figures, along with media elements such as video, audio clips, and related Web links. These media assets are fully customizable and can be used with our pre-formatted PowerPoint outlines or imported into the instructor's own lectures. The images are available for both Windows and Mac platforms. Contact your Allyn and Bacon representative for additional details and ordering information.

- *Allyn and Bacon PowerPoint Presentation for Introduction to Communication*. This PowerPoint presentation includes approximately 50 slides that cover a range of communication topics: public speaking, interpersonal communication, group communication, mass media, and interviewing. Available electronically through the Allyn and Bacon/Longman Instructor's Resource Center.

- *PowerPoint Presentation for Principles of Communication*, Third Edition, by James R. Smith, State University of New York, New Paltz. This text-specific package consists of a collection of lecture outlines and graphic images keyed to every chapter in the text. Available electronically through the Allyn and Bacon/Longman Instructor's Resource Center.

- The *Allyn and Bacon Public Speaking Transparency Package,* Version II contains 100 transparencies of images and text from our current public speaking texts. The transparency package can provide visual support for classroom lectures and discussion on a full range of course topics. Contact your Allyn and Bacon representative for ordering information.

- ***Course Compass for Introduction to Communication***. *Course Compass*, powered by Blackboard and hosted nationally, is the most flexible online course management system on the market today. By using this powerful suite of online tools in conjunction with Allyn and Bacon's preloaded textbook and testing content, you can create an online presence for your course in under 30 minutes. The Introduction to Communication course features quiz questions, video clips, instructor's manuals, PowerPoint presentations, still images, course preparation guidance, *Video Workshop for Introduction to Communication*, Web links, and much more! To find out how you can get the most out of this dynamic teaching course, log on to www.coursecompass.com. The content is also compatible with Blackboard and WebCT.

Video Resources

- The ***Allyn and Bacon Student Speeches Video Library*** includes three 2-hour American Forensic Association videos of award-winning student speeches and three videos of student speeches delivered in the classroom. Contact your local Allyn and Bacon representative for ordering information; some restrictions apply.
- The ***Allyn and Bacon Public Speaking Video*** includes excerpts of classic and contemporary speeches as well as student speeches to illustrate the public speaking process. One speech is delivered two times by the same person under different circumstances to illustrate the difference between effective and ineffective delivery, based on appearance, nonverbal communication, and verbal style. Contact your local Allyn and Bacon representative for ordering information; some restrictions apply.
- The ***Allyn and Bacon Student Speeches Video III*** includes student speeches covering a variety of topics that illustrate informative, persuasive and after-dinner speeches and eulogies. Contact your Allyn and Bacon representative for ordering information; some restrictions apply.
- The ***Allyn and Bacon Public Speaking Key Topics Video Library***. Adopters of Allyn and Bacon communication texts may receive one video from this series. Video topics include Critiquing Student Speeches, Addressing Your Audience, and Speaker Apprehension. Contact your local Allyn and Bacon representative for ordering information; some restrictions apply.
- The ***Allyn and Bacon Communication Video Library*** contains a collection of communication videos produced by Film for the Humanities and Sciences. Topics include Business Presentations, Great American Speeches, and Conflict Resolution. Contact your local Allyn and Bacon representative for ordering information; some restrictions apply.
- ***Allyn and Bacon Small Group Communication Video***. New! Allyn and Bacon offers a 40-minute video that contains twelve scenarios illustrating key concepts of small group communication. An accompanying *User Guide* features transcripts, teaching activities, and class discussion questions for each episode. Contact your local Allyn and Bacon representative for ordering information; some restrictions apply.
- ***Allyn and Bacon Interpersonal Communication Videos***. Allyn and Bacon offers three interpersonal communication videos, ranging from 30 to 50 minutes long, that present scenarios illustrating key concepts in interpersonal communication. The accompanying *User Guides* feature transcripts, teaching activities, and class discussion questions for the episodes. Contact your Allyn and Bacon representative for ordering information; some restrictions apply.
- ***Interpersonal Movie Library***. This collection contains popular feature films dealing with a range of interpersonal communication topics. Contact your Allyn and Bacon representative for ordering information; some restrictions apply.

Student Supplements

Print Resources

- The **Study Guide**, prepared by Richard J. Sabatino, Texas State University–San Marcos. For every chapter in the text, the *Study Guide* contains learning objectives, chapter outlines, key terms, application activities, Web activities, and self-test questions in multiple-choice, true/false, and fill-in-the-blank formats. An answer key is provided for all questions.

- **Research Navigator Guide for Speech Communication**, by Terrence Doyle, Northern Virginia Community College, and Linda R. Barr, University of the Virgin Islands. This resource guide is designed to teach students how to conduct high-quality online research and document it properly. The guide provides access to Research Navigator (www.researchnavigator.com), which contains exclusive databases of credible and reliable source material, including EBSCO's ContentSelect Academic Journal Database and the New York Times Search by Subject Archive. This product is available free when packaged with this text. Contact your Allyn and Bacon representative for ordering information, some restrictions apply.

- **Speech Preparation Workbook** by Jennifer Dreyer and Gregory H. Patton, San Diego State University. This workbook takes students through the various stages of speech creation—from audience analysis to writing the speech—and provides supplementary assignments and tear-out forms. Contact your Allyn and Bacon representative for ordering information, some restrictions apply.

- **Preparing Visual Aids for Presentations**, Fourth Edition, by Dan Cavanaugh. This 32-page booklet provides a host of ideas for using today's multimedia tools to improve presentations and includes suggestions for planning a presentation, guidelines for designing visual aids, storyboarding, and a PowerPoint presentation walkthrough. Contact your Allyn and Bacon representative for ordering information; some restrictions apply.

- **Public Speaking in the Multicultural Environment**, Second Edition, by Devorah A. Lieberman, Portland State University. This booklet helps students learn to analyze cultural diversity within their audiences and adapt their presentations accordingly. Contact your Allyn and Bacon representative for ordering information; some restrictions apply.

- **Outlining Workbook** by Reeze L. Hanson and Sharon Condon, Haskell Indian Nations University. This workbook includes activities, exercises, and answers to help students develop and master the critical skill of outlining. Contact your Allyn and Bacon representative for ordering information; some restrictions apply.

Electronic Resources

- The **Companion Web Site Plus with Online Practice Tests**, which can be accessed at www.ablongman.com/beebe, was prepared by Diana Murphy. This text-specific site provides a wealth of activities and Web links to enrich your course. The site also contains online learning objectives, flashcards, crossword puzzles, and a fully expanded set of practice tests for each chapter containing multiple-choice, true/false, and essay questions.

- **Allyn and Bacon Communication Studies Web Site,** by Terrence Doyle, Northern Virginia Community College, and Tim Borchers, Minnesota State University at Moorhead, and **Allyn and Bacon Public Speaking Web Site,** by Nan Peck, Northern Virginia Community College. These Web sites contain modules of enrichment materials, Web links, and interactive activities designed to enhance students' understanding of key concepts. The Communication Studies Web Site covers topics related to interpersonal communication, small group communication, and public speaking. Students can access this site at www.ablongman.com/commstudies. The Public Speaking Web Site helps students build, organize, and research speeches while learning about the process of public speaking. Students can access this Web site at www.ablongman.com/pubspeak.

- *Interactive Speechwriter Software*, Version 1.1 by Martin R. Cox. This interactive software package provides supplemental material, writing templates (for informative, persuasive, and motivated sequence speeches, as well as for outlines), sample student speeches (text only), and more. This software enhances students' understanding of key concepts discussed in the text and is available for Windows and Mac platforms. Contact your Allyn and Bacon representative for ordering information; some restrictions apply.

- *Speech Writer's Workshop CD-ROM*, Version 2.0. This interactive software will assist students with speech preparation and will enable them to write better speeches. The software includes four separate features: (1) a speech handbook with tips for researching and preparing speeches plus information about grammar, usage, and syntax; (2) a speech workshop that guides students through the speechwriting process and includes a series of questions at each stage; (3) a Topics Dictionary containing hundreds of speech ideas, divided into subcategories to help students with outlining and organization; and (4) a citation database that formats bibliographic entries in MLA or APA style. Contact your Allyn and Bacon representative for ordering information; some restrictions apply.

- *VideoWorkshop for Introduction to Communication*, Version 2.0, by Kathryn Dindia, University of Wisconsin; *Video Workshop for Interpersonal Communication*, Version 2.0, by Christine North, Jamestown College; and *VideoWorkshop for Public Speaking*, Version 2.0, by Tasha Van Horn of Citrus College and Marilyn Reineck of Concordia University. *VideoWorkshop* includes quality video footage on an easy-to-use CD-ROM plus a *Student Learning Guide* with textbook-specific Correlation Grids. The result is a program that brings textbook concepts to life with ease and that helps students understand, analyze, and apply the objectives of the course. *VideoWorkshop* is available to accompany Introduction to Communication, Interpersonal Communication, and Public Speaking courses. Visit www.ablongman.com/videoworkshop for more details.

- *Communication Tutor Center*, www.aw.com/tutorcenter (access code required). The Tutor Center provides free, one-on-one interactive tutoring from qualified public speaking instructors on all material in the text. The Tutor Center can help students understand major communication principles and offers help with study methods. In addition, students have the option of submitting self-taped speeches for review and critique by Tutor Center instructors to help prepare for and improve their speech assignments. Tutoring assistance is offered by phone, fax, Internet, and e-mail during Tutor Center hours. For more details and ordering information, contact your Allyn and Bacon representative.

ACKNOWLEDGMENTS

Although our three names appear on the cover as authors of the book you are holding in your hands, in reality hundreds of people have been instrumental in making this book possible. Communication scholars who have dedicated their lives to researching the importance of communication principles, theories, and skills provide the fuel for the book. We thank each author we reference in our endnotes for the research conclusions that have led to our contemporary understanding of communication principles. We thank our students who have trusted us to be their guides in a study of human communication. They continue to enrich our lives with their enthusiasm and curiosity. They have inspired us to be more creative by their honest, quizzical looks and have challenged us to go beyond textbook answers with their thought-provoking questions.

We are most appreciative of the outstanding editorial support we continue to receive from our colleagues and friends at Allyn and Bacon. We thank Joe Opiela for helping us keep this project moving forward when we wondered if the world needed another communication book. Vice President Paul Smith has been exceptionally supportive of our work since we've been members of the Allyn and Bacon publishing family. Karon Bowers, Executive Editor, has continued to provide valued support and encouragement. Brian Wheel, Acquisitions Editor, has also provided outstanding support at every stage of the development and revision of this book. Our thoughtful and talented development editor, Carol Alper, helped us polish our ideas and words. Karen Black, Diana Ivy's sister, who conducted permissions research, was a true blessing, providing skilled assistance with important details and administrative support. We acknowledge and appreciate the ideas and suggestions of Mark Redmond, a valued friend, gifted teacher, and skilled writer at Iowa State University. His co-authorship with us on *Interpersonal Communication: Relating to Others* significantly influenced our ideas about communication, especially interpersonal communication.

We are grateful to the many educators who read the manuscript and both encouraged and challenged us. We thank the following people for drawing on their teaching skill, expertise, and vast experience to make this a much better book:

Reviewers of the Third Edition

Dom Bongiorni, Kingwood College
Jo Anne Bryant, Troy University
Cherie Cannon, Miami–Dade College
Thomas Green, Cape Fear Community College
Gretchen Harries, Austin Community College
Xin-An Lu, Shippensburg University of Pennsylvania
Sara L. Nalley, Columbia College
Kristi Schaller, University of Hawaii
David Shuhy, Salisbury University
John Tapia, Missouri Western State College

Reviewers of the First and Second Editions

Lawrence Albert, Morehead State University
Leonard Assante, Volunteer State Community College
Michael Bruner, University of North Texas
Diana O. Cassagrande, West Chester University
Dan B. Curtis, Central Missouri State University
Terrence A. Doyle, Northern Virginia Community College
Dennis Dufer, St. Louis Community College
Julia F. Fennell, Community College of Allegheny County, South Campus
Annette Folwell, University of Idaho
Mike Hemphill, University of Arkansas at Little Rock
Teri Higginbotham, University of Central Arkansas
Phil Hoke, The University of Texas at San Antonio
Lawrence Hugenberg, Youngstown State University
Stephen Hunt, Illinois State University
Carol L. Hunter, Brookdale Community College
Dorothy W. Ige, Indiana University Northwest
A. Elizabeth Lindsey, The New Mexico State University
Robert E. Mild, Jr., Fairmont State College
Timothy P. Mottet, Texas State University–San Marcos
Alfred G. Mueller II, Pennsylvania State University, Mont Alto Campus
Kay Neal, University of Wisconsin–Oshkosh
Penny O'Connor, University of Northern Iowa

Kathleen Perri, Valencia Community College
Evelyn Plummer, Seton Hall University
Charlotte C. Toguchi, Kapi'olani Community College
Beth M. Waggenspack, Virginia Tech University
Gretchen Aggert Weber, Horry-Georgetown Technical College
Kathy Werking, Eastern Kentucky University
Andrew F. Wood, San Jose State University
Debra Sue Wyatt, South Texas Community College

We have each been influenced by colleagues, friends, and teachers who have offered support and inspiration for this project. Happily, colleagues, friends, and teachers are virtually indistinguishable for us. We are each blessed to know people who offer us strong support.

Steve and Sue thank their colleagues at Texas State University–San Marcos for their insights and ideas that helped shape key concepts in this book. Cathy Fleuriet and Tom Burkholder, who served as basic course directors at Texas State, influenced our work. Tim Mottet, currently a basic course director at Texas State, is a valued, inspirational friend and colleague who is always there to listen and freely share his ideas and experience. Richard Cheatham, Dean of the College of Fine Arts and Communication, continues to provide enthusiastic encouragement for this project. Kosta Tovstiadi, from the University of Oklahoma, provided skilled research assistance to help us draw on the most contemporary communication research. Michael Hennessy and Patricia Margerison are Texas State English faculty who have been especially supportive of Sue's work. Finally, Steve thanks his skilled and dedicated support team at Texas State. Administrative Assistant Sue Hall, who continues to be Steve's right hand, is a cherished friend and colleague. Manuscript typist Sondra Howe and technical support expert Bob Hanna are two other staff members who provide exceptional support and assistance for this project and many others.

Ivy is grateful to her students, colleagues, and friends at Texas A&M University–Corpus Christi for their patience and unwavering support for her involvement in this book project. In particular, Michelle Maresh, Jason Pruett, Kelly Quintanilla, Flicka Rahn, Nada Frazier, Chair Don Luna, Deans Paul Hain and Richard Gigliotti, and Provost Sandra Harper constantly reaffirmed the value of a well-written, carefully crafted book—one that speaks to students' lives. Their support of Ivy's research efforts, along with constant "fueling" from her wonderful students, has made this project a real joy. Ivy's deepest thanks also go to Steve and Sue Beebe for their generosity in bringing her into this project, and for their willing mentorship.

Finally we express our appreciation to our families. Ivy thanks her ever-supportive family, parents Herschel and Carol Ivy, sister Karen Black (who supplied the permissions research and constant encouragement), and nephew Brian Black (whose humorous e-mails provided great comic relief). They have been constant and generous with their praise for her writing accomplishments. Ivy is especially grateful to her father, Herschel Ivy, for lovingly offering many lessons about living the highly ethical life.

Sue and Steve especially thank their parents, Herb and Jane Dye and Russell and Muriel Beebe, who taught them much about communication and ethics that truly are principles for a lifetime. They also thank their sons, Mark and Matthew Beebe, for teaching life lessons about giving and receiving love that will remain with them forever.

Steven A. Beebe
Susan J. Beebe
San Marcos, Texas

Diana K. Ivy
Corpus Christi, Texas

Good communication is as stimulating as black coffee and just as hard to sleep after.
Anne Morrow Lindbergh

Jean Dubuffet, "Visage rouge et visage bleu" from the series "Le Metro," gouache on paper, 1943. Photo: Philippe Migeat.

Foundations of Human Communication

CHAPTER OUTLINE

Communication Defined

Communication Competence

Why Study Communication?

Communication Models

Communication Characteristics

Communication Principles for a
   Lifetime

Communicating with Others: Three
   Situations

Summary

CHAPTER OBJECTIVES

After studying this chapter, you should be able to:

1. Define communication and explain why it is an important course of study.

2. Describe three criteria that can be used to determine whether communication is competent.

3. Compare and contrast communication as action, interaction, and transaction.

4. Identify five characteristics of communication.

5. List and explain five fundamental principles of communication.

6. Define and describe communication in interpersonal, group, and presentational communication situations.

Communication is essential for life. Communicating is a fundamental aspect of being human. Even if you live in isolation from other people, you talk to yourself through your thoughts. Like life-sustaining breath, communication is ever-present in our lives. Understanding and improving how we communicate with others is a basic life skill.

Human communication is inescapable. Consider the number of times you have purposefully communicated with someone today, as you worked, ate, studied, shopped, or went about your daily duties. Most people spend between 80 and 90% of their waking hours communicating with others.[1] It is through the process of communication that we convey who we are, both to ourselves and to others; it is our primary tool for making our way in the world.

This book presents fundamental principles that undergird all aspects of communicating with others when both sending and receiving messages. In the course of our study of human communication, we will discuss a myriad of skills, ideas, concepts, and contexts. The number of terms, ideas, skills, and competencies that you'll encounter in this discussion can be overwhelming. To help you stitch together the barrage of ideas and information, we will organize our study around five fundamental communication principles. Together, these five principles will provide a framework for our discussion of the importance and pervasiveness of human communication.

Principle One: Be aware of your communication with yourself and others.
Principle Two: Effectively use and interpret verbal messages.
Principle Three: Effectively use and interpret nonverbal messages.
Principle Four: Listen and respond thoughtfully to others.
Principle Five: Appropriately adapt messages to others.

These five principles distill decades of research as well as the wisdom of those who have taught communication during the past century. We don't claim that everything you need to know about communication is covered by these five principles. They do, however, summarize considerable knowledge about the communication process and what constitutes effective and ethical communication.

We will provide an overview of these principles later in this chapter and devote a separate chapter to each principle. This book examines each fundamental principle in the context of three prevalent communication situations:

- interpersonal interactions
- group and team communication
- presentational speaking

Our goal is to present both classic and contemporary research conclusions about the role and importance of communication in our lives. In addition to discussing live, face-to-face human communication, we will highlight the increasing importance of technology in our communication with others in a feature called Technology and Communication that will appear throughout the book.

Before we elaborate on the five fundamental communication principles, it is important to provide some background for our study of communication. The purpose of this first chapter is to provide that background. We will define communication, discuss why it is important to study, examine various models of or perspectives on communication, and identify characteristics of human communication. Having offered this prelude, we then discuss the five foundational principles of human communication that we will use throughout the book to help you organize the concepts, skills, and ideas we present in our discussion of interpersonal, group, and presentational speaking situations.

COMMUNICATION DEFINED

Communication is one of those words that seems so basic you may wonder why it needs to be formally defined. Yet scholars who devote their lives to studying communication don't always agree on its definition. One research team counted more than 126 published definitions.[2]

In its broadest sense, **communication** is the process of acting on information.[3] Someone does or says something, and others think or do something in response to the action or the words as they understand them.

Communication is not unique to humans. It is possible, for example, for you to act on information from your dog. She barks; you feed her. This general definition also suggests that your dog can act on information from you. You head for the pantry to feed her; she wags her tail and jumps in the air, anticipating her dinner. Although researchers study communication between species as well as communication systems used by particular animal species, these fields of study are beyond the scope of this book. The focus of our study is human communication: people communicating with other people.

To refine our definition of communication, we can say that **human communication** *is the process of making sense out of the world and sharing that sense with others by creating meaning through the use of verbal and nonverbal messages.*[4] Let's look at the key components of this definition.

- *Communication is about making sense.* We make sense out of what we experience when we begin to interpret what we see, hear, touch, smell, and taste with sensations, feelings, thoughts, and words. Identifying patterns and structure in what we experience is a key part of making sense out of what happens to us. Although we often think that "making sense out of something" means rationally and logically interpreting what we experience, we also make sense through intuition, feelings, and emotions.[5]

- *Communication is about sharing sense.* We share what we experience by expressing to others and to ourselves what we experience. We typically use words to express our thoughts, but we also use music, art, clothing, and a whole host of other means to convey what we are thinking and feeling to others.

- *Communication is about creating meaning.* It's more appropriate to say that meaning is *created* through communication rather than sent or transmitted. To say that we send or transmit messages is to imply that what we send is what is received. In human communication, however, what is expressed by one person is rarely interpreted by another person precisely as intended. In reality, meaning is *co-created* by both the speaker and the listener. By this we mean that all individuals who are involved in the communication process shape how a message is understood by drawing on their own experiences while attempting to make sense out of the message. Meaning is created in the heart and mind of both the message source and the message receiver, based on such things as the characteristics of the message, the situation, and the perceptions and background of the communicators.

- *Communication is about verbal and nonverbal messages.* One way we communicate is by using words that trigger meaning in others symbolically. **Symbols** are words, sounds, gestures, or visual images that represent thoughts, concepts, objects, or experiences. The words on this page are symbols that you use to derive meaning that makes sense to you.

    Not all symbols are verbal; some are nonverbal. You use gestures, posture, facial expression, tone of voice, clothing, and jewelry to express ideas, attitudes, and feelings. Nonverbal messages primarily communicate emotions—our likes and dislikes, whether we're interested or uninterested, and our feelings of power or lack of power.

Some scholars assert that *all* human behavior is really communication. When you cross your arms while listening to your friend describe her day, she may conclude that you're not interested in what she's talking about. But it could just be that you're cold. While all human expression has the potential to communicate a message (someone

communication
The process of acting on information.

human communication
The process of making sense out of the world and sharing that sense with others by creating meaning through verbal and nonverbal messages.

symbol
A word, sound, gesture, or visual image that represents a thought, concept, object, or experience.

may act or respond to the information they receive from you), this does not mean you *intentionally* are expressing an idea or emotion. Presenting information to others does not mean communication has occurred: Information is not communication. "But I told you what to do!" "It's there in the memo. Why didn't you do what I asked?" "It's in the syllabus." These exasperated communicators assumed that if they sent a message, someone would receive it. However, communication does not operate in a simple, linear, what-you-send-is-what-is-received process. People don't always accurately interpret the messages we express—and this unprofound observation has profound implications. One reason we have communication courses, academic departments that focus on communication, and people who earn Ph.D.s in communication is because of the challenge we encounter in understanding one another.

Because of the ever-present potential for misunderstanding, communication should be *other-oriented*—it should acknowledge the perspective of others, not just the creator of the message. Communication that does not consider the needs, background, and culture of the receiver is more likely to be misunderstood. We'll emphasize the importance of considering others or considering your audience throughout the book. Knowing something about the experiences of the person or persons you're speaking to can help you communicate more effectively and appropriately.

Human communication is complex and varied. It also emerges in many different forms: face-to-face conversations, speeches, radio and television programs, e-mail, Web sites, letters, books, and articles.

COMMUNICATION COMPETENCE

What does it mean to communicate competently? Does it mean you are able to present a well-delivered speech? Or that you are able to carry on a brilliant conversation with someone? Is the fact that you are usually asked to chair a committee meeting because you are so organized evidence of your communication competence? Being a competent communicator is more than just being well liked, glib, able to give polished presentations, or able to interact smoothly with individual people or in groups and teams. Although it is difficult to identify core criteria that define competent communication in all situations, we think certain goals of communication serve as measures of competence regardless of the setting. We suggest the following three criteria:[6]

- The message should be understood as the communicator intended it to be understood.
- The message should achieve the communicator's intended effect.
- The message should be ethical.

The Message Should Be Understood

A primary goal of any effective communication transaction is to develop a common understanding of the message from both the sender's and the receiver's perspectives. You'll note how the words *common* and *communication* resemble each other. We acknowledge the challenge of communicating with others; differences in culture, language, experience, gender, education, and background all are sources of misunderstanding. One of the aims of the principles we discuss in this book is to create clarity of expression and a common understanding.

Message clarity is missing in the following headlines that have appeared in local U.S. newspapers:

Panda Mating Fails: Veterinarian Takes Over

Drunks Get Nine Months in Violin Case

Include Your Children When Baking Cookies

Police Begin Campaign to Run Down Jaywalkers

Local High School Dropouts Cut in Half

Meanings are fragile, and messages can be misunderstood. An effective message is one that the receiver understands.

The Message Should Achieve Its Intended Effect

When you communicate intentionally with others, it is for a specific purpose: to achieve a goal or to accomplish something. Because different purposes require different strategies for success, being aware of your purpose can enhance the probability of your achieving it.

Typical goals of speaking in public are to inform, to persuade, or to entertain. In small groups we often communicate to solve problems and make decisions. In our interpersonal relationships we interact to build trust, develop intimacy, or just enjoy someone's company. Thus, another criterion for judging the effectiveness of communication is to gauge whether the intent of the message is achieved.

Whether you are attempting to close a sale, get a date, give directions to the mall, or tell a joke, you should consider your goal. The purpose of our communication with others is not always to give or receive something tangible. Sometimes it is simply to make human contact, to establish a relationship, or just to be with someone. But one way to assess whether your communication was effective, regardless of the purpose, is to determine whether the outcome you sought is the outcome you got.

The Message Should Be Ethical

Communication can be used to achieve good or bad objectives. A message that is understood and achieves its intended effect but that manipulates listeners, unfairly restricts their choices, or uses false information may be effective, but it is not appropriate or ethical. **Ethics** are the beliefs, values, and moral principles by which we determine what is right or wrong. Ethics and ethical behavior have long been considered critical components of human behavior in a given culture.

Philosophers have debated for centuries whether there is such a thing as a universal moral and ethical code.[7] British author and scholar C. S. Lewis suggests that there is a universal ethical code that serves as the basis for interpreting the "goodness" or "badness" of human behavior; evidence for such a code can be found, says Lewis, in the teachings of cultures throughout the world and through time.[8] In their book *Communication Ethics and Universal Values*, communication scholars Clifford Christians and

ethics
The beliefs, values, and moral principles by which we determine what is right or wrong.

The Dalai Lama teaches an ethical code that provides guidance for successful communication whether or not you believe in the Tibetan Buddhist religion.

Michael Traber make the following claim: "Every culture depends for its existence on norms that order human relationships and social institutions."[9] What are these universal norms—these beliefs and behaviors that describe what is normal, appropriate, or inappropriate? Christians and Traber suggest there are three universal cultural norms: (1) the value of truth, (2) respect for another person's dignity, and (3) the expectation that innocent people should not suffer harm.[10]

Scholars and philosophers who suggest that a universal code of ethics exists do not claim that people in all cultures always behave in ways that are true to universal standards. Proponents of a universal ethical code do suggest that a universal moral code is the ideal basis for evaluating what is right and wrong behavior, including communication behavior.

All religions of the world have a moral code that provides guidance for how people should treat others.[11] The Ten Commandments serve as ethical guidelines for those who adhere to Judeo-Christian ethical principles. In Christianity the Golden Rule— "Do unto others what you would have others do unto you"—is a fundamental value. Buddhism teaches a similar value: "One should seek for others the happiness one desires for oneself." Hinduism asks adherents to live by the precept "Do nothing to others which would cause pain if done to you." Judaism teaches, "What is hateful to you, do not do to others." Islam suggests, "No one of you is a believer until he desires for his brother that which he desires for himself." The underlying ethic of how to treat others can clearly be seen across most of the world's religions.[12]

Our purpose is not to prescribe a specific religious or philosophical ethical code, but rather to suggest that humans from a variety of cultures and traditions have sought to develop ethical principles that guide their interactions with others.

Philosophy and religion are not the only realms that focus on ethical behavior. Most professions, such as medicine, law, and journalism, have explicit codes of ethics that identify appropriate and inappropriate behavior. The National Communication Association has developed a Credo for Communication Ethics to emphasize the importance of being an ethical communicator:

Ethical communication is fundamental to responsible thinking, decision making, and the development of relationships and communities within and across contexts, cultures, channels, and media. Moreover, ethical communication enhances human worth and dignity by fostering truthfulness, fairness, responsibility, personal integrity, and respect for self and others.[13]

Ethics and Communication

What Are the Sources of Your Ethical Views?

Many people think that success means achieving what they want to achieve. Success is often equated with acquiring money, power, position, and influence. But when communicating with others, we've suggested, we achieve success if the communication message is understood as intended, achieves its intended effect, and satisfies a third criterion: It is ethical. Success is based not only on the communication outcome, but also on the methods and approaches used to communicate. If you lie, knowingly withhold key information, or use force to achieve your communication goals, then your message has not been successful, even if you are understood perfectly and you get what you want.

The question of who gets to decide what constitutes ethical behavior is one that arises often. Ethics are the beliefs, values, and moral principles by which we determine what is right or wrong. But where do your ethical beliefs, values, and principles come from? What are the sources of your sense of what is right and wrong?

Use the checklist below to identify the key sources of your ethical views.

INSTRUCTIONS: First, rate the influence of each factor listed below on a scale of from 1 (a minor influence on your ethical beliefs and practices) to 5 (a major influence on your ethical beliefs and practices).

_____ Grandparents
_____ Other family members (e.g., brothers, sisters, aunts, uncles)
_____ Friends
_____ Parents
_____ The Internet
_____ Government officials and public figures
_____ Laws and the legal system
_____ Music
_____ Works of art
_____ Sacred and inspired writing (e.g., the Bible)
_____ Religious beliefs
_____ Clergy and religious leaders
_____ Fiction and poetry
_____ TV and radio
_____ Newspapers and magazines
_____ Teachers
_____ Other sources

After you have rated the sources of influence, circle the sources of ethical influence that you rated the highest. (Perhaps you rated several sources a 5.) Of those items you circled, rank-order the top three. Assign a rank of 1 to the most important ethical influence, a 2 to the second most important, and a 3 to the third most important.

- What connection can you make between the sources of ethical influence in your life and the way you communicate with others?
- Can you think of specific ways in which the sources of your ethical beliefs and practices have directly influenced your communication with others?

Often we are unaware of the underpinnings of our ethical beliefs. This activity invites you to consciously examine the link between the sources of your perceptions of what is right and wrong and your communication behavior toward others.

Echoing the wisdom offered by others, we suggest that competent communication is grounded in an other-oriented ethical perspective that is fundamental to all human interactions.

For most people, being ethical means being sensitive to others' needs, giving people choices rather than forcing them to behave a certain way, keeping private such information as others wish to remain private, not intentionally decreasing others' feelings of self-worth, and being honest in presenting information. Unethical communication does just the opposite: It forces views on others and demeans their integrity.

Being honest is a key element of ethical communication. If you knowingly withhold key information, lie, or distort the truth, then you are not communicating ethically or effectively. For example, after Paul missed the test in his communication class, he mournfully told his professor that his grandmother had died and he had to attend the funeral. Paul's professor allowed him to make up the test. Paul's professor understood the message, so Paul achieved the effect he wanted. Paul's grandmother, however, is alive and well. According to our criteria for effective communication, Paul's dishonesty made his communication inappropriate and unethical.

Throughout the book we will offer opportunities for you to examine ethical issues in a feature called Ethics and Communication.

WHY STUDY COMMUNICATION?

Why are you here? No, we don't mean "Why do you exist?" or "Why do you live where you do?" What we mean is, "Why are you taking a college course about communication?" Perhaps the short answer is, "It's required." Or maybe your advisor, parent, or friend encouraged you to take the course. If it is a required course, what's the rationale for that requirement? And required or not, what can a systematic study of human communication do for you?

Communication touches every aspect of our lives. To be able to express yourself to other people is a basic requirement for living in a modern society. From a practical standpoint, most of you will make your living with your minds rather than your hands.[14] Even if you do physical labor, you will need communication skills to work with others. When you study communication, you are developing leadership skills. "The art of communication," says author Daniel Quinn, "is the language of leadership."[15]

Although the value of being a competent communicator is virtually undisputed, there is evidence that many people struggle to express themselves clearly or to accurately understand messages from others. One study estimated that one-fifth of the students in the United States were not successful with even elementary communication tasks; in addition, more than 60% of the students could not give clear oral directions for someone else to follow.[16] When leaders in major corporations were asked to specify the most important skills for workers to have, 80% said listening was the most important work skill; 78% identified interpersonal communication skill as the next most important. However, the same leaders said only 28% of their employees had good listening skills and only 27% possessed effective interpersonal communication skills.[17] In support of these leaders' observations, another national study found that adults listen with 25% accuracy.[18] In addition to lacking communication skill, there is also evidence that the majority of adults are fearful of speaking in public; about 20% of the population is acutely apprehensive of presentational speaking.[19]

Aren't some people just born to be better communicators than others? If so, why should you work to develop your communication skill? Just as some people have more innate musical talent than others, there is evidence that some people may have an inborn biological ability to communicate with others.[20] This does not mean you should not work to develop your communication ability. Throughout the book we will offer ample evidence that if you work to improve your skill, you will be rewarded by enjoying the benefits of enhanced communication competence. What are these benefits? Read on.

On the Web

Most colleges and universities offer courses in communication and allow students to major or minor in communication, speech communication, or communication studies. The study of human communication may also be among the offerings of a department that focuses on mass communication, speech communication, and theatre. Students who select communication as a major or a minor pursue a wide variety of careers and professions, including business, law, government, education, and social services.

There are several professional academic communication organizations that offer a wealth of resources, information, and ideas about human communication. Chances are that the instructor for your communication course is a member of one or more of these organizations. The following Web sites offer you a panoramic view of the communication discipline from an academic perspective.

www.natcom.org is the Web address for the National Communication Association.

http://facstaff.uww.edu/wca/ is the Web address for the World Communication Association.

www.icahdq.org/ is the Web address for the International Communication Association.

www.americancomm.org/ is the Web address for the American Communication Association.

www.cios.org/encyclopedia/comlinks/websites.htm is a comprehensive Web site that lists dozens of Web sites on a variety of communication topics.

To Improve Your Employability

Regardless of your specific job description, the essence of what you do when working at any job is to communicate; you talk, listen, relate, read, and write, whatever your job title. People who can communicate effectively with others are in high demand. As noted by John H. McConnell, CEO of Worthington Industries, "Take all the speech and communication courses you can because the world turns on communication."[21] McConnell's advice is supported by research as well as by personal observations. As shown in Table 1.1, a survey of personnel managers revealed that they consider communication skills the top factor in helping graduating college students obtain employment.[22]

TABLE 1.1
Factors Most Important in Helping Graduating College Students Obtain Employment[23]

Rank/Order	Factors/Skills Evaluated
1	Oral communication (speaking) skills
2	Written communication skills
3	Listening ability
4	Enthusiasm
5	Technical competence
6	Work experience
7	Appearance
8	Poise
9	Resume
10	Part-time or summer employment
11	Specific degree held
12	Leadership in campus/community activities
13	Recommendations
14	Accreditation of program activities
15	Participation in campus/community activities
16	Grade-point average
17	School attended

In addition to the practical, work-related rationale, enhancing your communication skill can significantly improve the quality of relationships with others in a variety of situations.

To Improve Your Relationships

We don't choose our biological families, but we do choose our friends. For unmarried people, developing friendships and falling in love are the top-rated sources of satisfaction and happiness in life.[24] Conversely, losing a relationship is among life's most stressful events. Most people between the ages of 19 and 24 report that they have had from five to six romantic relationships and have been "in love" once or twice.[25] Understanding the role and function of communication can help unravel some of the mysteries of human relationships. At the heart of a good relationship is good communication.[26]

Virginia Satir, a pioneer in family enrichment, described family communication as "the largest single factor determining the kinds of relationships [we make] with others."[27] Learning principles and skills of communication can give us insight into why we relate to other family members as we do. Our early communication with our parents had a profound effect on our self-concept and self-worth. According to Satir, people are "made" in families. Our communication with family members has shaped how we interact with others today.

Many of us will spend as much or more time interacting with people in our places of work as we do at home. And although we choose our friends and lovers, we don't always have the same flexibility in choosing those with whom or for whom we work. Increasing our understanding of the role and importance of human communication with our colleagues can help us better manage stress on the job as well as enhance our work success.

To Improve Your Health

Life is stressful. Research has clearly documented that the lack or loss of close relationships can lead to ill health and even death. Having a social support system—good friends and supportive family members—seems to make a difference in our overall

Communication can improve the quality of life for people of any age.

health and quality of life. Good friends and intimate relationships with others help us manage stress and contribute to both physical and emotional health. For example, physicians have noted that patients who are widowed or divorced experience more medical problems, such as heart disease, cancer, pneumonia, and diabetes, than do married people.[28] Grief-stricken spouses are more likely than others to die prematurely, especially around the time of the departed spouse's birthday or near their wedding anniversary.[29] Terminally ill patients with a limited number of friends or social support die sooner than those with stronger ties.[30] Without companions and close friends, our opportunities for intimacy and stress-managing communication are diminished. Studying how to enrich the quality of our communication with others can make life more enjoyable and enhance our overall well-being.

So again, we ask the question: Why are you here? We think the evidence is clear: People who are effective communicators are more likely to get the jobs they want; have better quality relationships with friends, family, and colleagues; and even enjoy a healthier quality of life.

COMMUNICATION MODELS

Communication researchers have spent a considerable amount of time trying to understand precisely how communication takes place. In the course of their study, they have developed visual models that graphically illustrate the communication process.

By reviewing the development of communication models, you can see how our understanding of communication has evolved over the past century. Early models viewed communication as a transfer or exchange of information, but this view evolved to include a more interactive, give-and-take approach. Researchers' understanding then progressed even further to today's view that communication is a process in which meaning is co-created simultaneously among people. The three models of the communication process that we show here begin with the simplest and oldest perspective and then move to more contemporary models.

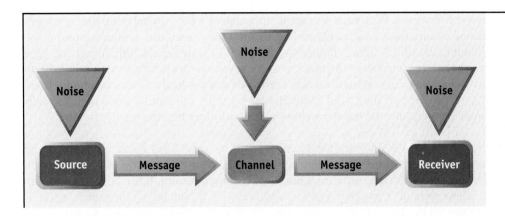

FIGURE 1.1
A Model of Communication as Action

Source: From *The Mathematical Theory of Communication*. Copyright 1949, 1998 by the Board of Trustees of the University of Illinois. Used with permission of the University of Illinois Press.

Communication as Action: Message Transfer

"Did you get my message?" This simple sentence summarizes the communication-as-action approach to human communication. In this model, communication takes place when a message is sent and received. Period. Communication is a way of transferring meaning from sender to receiver. In 1948, Harold Lasswell described the process as follows:

Who (sender)
Says what (message)
In what channel
To whom (receiver)
With what effect[31]

Figure 1.1 shows a simplified representation of the communication process developed by communication pioneers Claude Shannon and Warren Weaver, who viewed communication as a linear input/output process consisting of a source, a message, a channel, a receiver, and noise. Today, although researchers view the process as more complex, they still define most of the key components in this model in basically the same way that Shannon and Weaver did.

Source   The **source** of communication is the originator of a thought or an emotion that expresses ideas or feelings. The source, the developer of that thought or emotion, puts a message into a code that can be understood by a receiver. Translating ideas, feelings, and thoughts into a code is called **encoding**. Vocalizing a word, gesturing, and establishing eye contact are means of encoding our thoughts into a message that can be decoded by someone. **Decoding,** the opposite process of encoding, occurs when the words or unspoken signals are interpreted by the receiver.

Receiver   The **receiver** is the person who decodes the signal and attempts to make sense out of what the source encoded. Think of a TV station as a source broadcasting to a receiver (your TV) that picks up the station's signal. In human communication, however, there is something in between the source and the receiver: We filter messages through past experiences, attitudes, beliefs, values, prejudices, and biases.

Message   **Messages** are the written, spoken, and unspoken elements of communication to which we assign meaning. You can send a message intentionally (talking to a friend before class) or unintentionally (falling asleep during class); verbally ("Hi. What's up?"), nonverbally (a smile and a handshake), in written form (this book); or through any number of electronic channels.

Channel   A message is communicated from sender to receiver via some pathway called a **channel.** With today's technological advances, we receive messages from a va-

source
Originator of a thought or emotion, who puts it into a code that can be understood by a receiver.

encoding
A process of translating ideas, feelings, and thoughts into a code.

decoding
A process of interpreting ideas, feelings, and thoughts that have been translated into a code.

receiver
Person who decodes a message and attempts to make sense out of what the source has encoded.

message
Written, spoken, and unspoken elements of communication to which people assign meaning.

channel
Pathway through which messages are sent.

riety of channels. With your phone, the Internet, or a fax transmission, the communication channel may be a telephone line. Cellular telephones use a wireless channel. Ultimately, communication channels correspond to your senses. When you call your mother on the telephone, the message is conveyed via an electronic channel that activates auditory cues. When you talk with your mother face-to-face, the channels are many. You see her: the visual channel. You hear her: the auditory channel. You may smell her perfume: the olfactory channel. You may hug her: the tactile channel.

Noise   **Noise** is interference. Noise keeps a message from being understood and achieving its intended effect. Without noise, all of our messages would be communicated with considerable accuracy. But noise is always present. It can be literal—the obnoxious roar of a gas-powered lawn mower—or it can be psychological, such as competing thoughts, worries, and feelings that capture our attention. Instead of concentrating on your teacher's lecture, you may start thinking about the chores you need to finish before the end of the day. Whichever kind it is, noise gets in the way of the message and may even distort it. Communicating accurate messages involves minimizing both literal and psychological noise.

It may appear that scholars have neatly identified the components of communication, such as source, message, channel, receiver, and noise, and can prescribe precisely what is needed to make communication effective. While the communication-as-action approach is simple and straightforward, it has a key flaw: Human communication rarely, if ever, is as simple a matter as "what we put in is what we get out." Others cannot automatically know what you mean just because you think you know what you mean. Although by Lasswell's and Shannon and Weaver's time communication scholars had already begun identifying an array of key elements in the communication process, the action approach overlooked their complexity.

Communication as Interaction: Message Exchange

The communication-as-interaction perspective uses the same elements as the action model but adds two new ones: feedback and context. **Feedback** is the response to the message. Without feedback, communication is less likely to be effective. When you order your pepperoni pizza and the server says in response, "That's a pepperoni pizza, right?" he has provided feedback to ensure that he decoded the message correctly.

Think of a Ping-Pong game. Like Ping-Pong balls, messages bounce back and forth. We talk; someone listens and responds; we respond to this response. This perspective can be summarized using a physical principle: For every action there is a reaction.

Feedback can be intentional (applause at the conclusion of a symphony) or unintentional (a yawn as you listen to your uncle tell his story about bears again); verbal ("That's two burgers and fries, right?") or nonverbal (blushing after being asked for a date).

A second component recognized by the interaction perspective is **context**—the physical, historical, and psychological communication environment. All communication takes place in some context. As the cliché goes, "Everyone has to be somewhere." The literal or psychological "somewhere" of communication is the context. A conversation with your good friend on the beach would likely differ from one the two of you might have in a funeral home. Context encompasses not only the physical environment but also the number of people present, their past relationship with the communicators, the communication goal, and the culture in which the communicators are steeped. The psychological context includes the impact of what is going on in the minds of the communicators; the speaker's and listener's personalities and styles of interacting with others influence how messages are understood.

The communication-as-interaction model, as shown in Figure 1.2, is more realistic than the communication-as-action model, but it still has limitations. Although it emphasizes feedback and context, it does not quite capture the complexity of the com-

noise
Interference, either literal or psychological, that hinders the accurate encoding or decoding of a message.

feedback
Response to a message.

context
Physical, historical, and psychological communication environment.

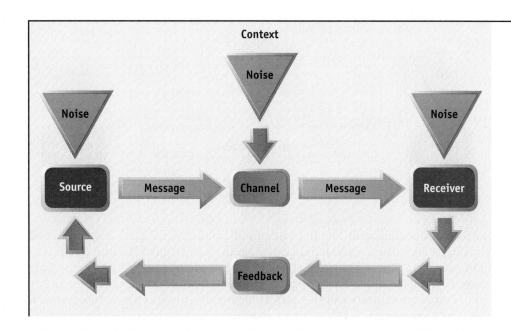

FIGURE 1.2
A Model of Communication as Interaction
Interaction models of communication include feedback as a response to a message sent by the communication source and place the process in a context.

munication process if the communication takes place *simultaneously*. The interaction model of communication still views communication as a linear, step-by-step process. But in many communication situations, both the source and the receiver send and receive messages at the same time.

Communication as Transaction: Message Creation

The communication-as-transaction perspective, which evolved in the 1960s, acknowledges that when we communicate with another, we are constantly reacting to what our partner is saying and expressing. Most scholars today view this perspective as

RECAP

Components of the Human Communication Process

Term	Definition
Source	Originator of an idea or emotion
Receiver	Person or group toward whom a source directs messages and who decodes the message
Message	Written, spoken, and unspoken elements of communication to which we assign meaning
Channel	Pathway through which messages pass between source and receiver
Noise	Any literal or psychological interference with the clear encoding or decoding of a message
Encoding	Translation of ideas, feelings, and thoughts into a code
Decoding	Interpretation of ideas, feelings, and thoughts that have been translated into a code
Context	Physical, historical, and psychological communication environment
Feedback	Verbal and nonverbal responses to a message

FIGURE 1.3
A Model of Communication as Transaction
The source and the receiver of a message experience communication simultaneously.

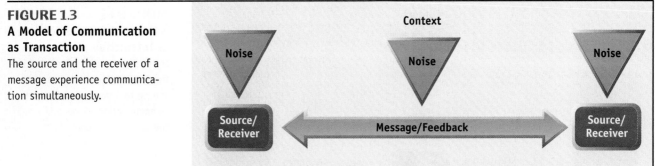

the most realistic model of communication. Although it uses such concepts as action and interaction to describe communication, in this model, all of the interaction is simultaneous. As Figure 1.3 indicates, we send and receive messages concurrently. Even as we talk, we are also interpreting our partner's nonverbal and verbal responses. Transactive communication also occurs within a context, and noise can interfere with the quality and accuracy of our encoding and decoding of messages.

As we send messages, we monitor the degree to which the other person understands each message. We mutually define the symbols we use. If one partner misunderstands a message, both can work to clarify the meaning. For example, if I ask you to hand me the book off my desk and you hand me a pad of paper, we have failed to create a shared meaning. I might then say, "No, not the pad of paper, the red book next to the phone"; you then would hand me the book. Your action would require me to explain and be more specific. We would not simply transfer or exchange meaning; we would create it during a communication transaction.

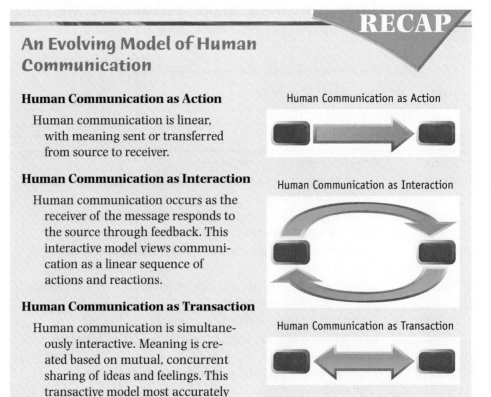

RECAP

An Evolving Model of Human Communication

Human Communication as Action

Human communication is linear, with meaning sent or transferred from source to receiver.

Human Communication as Interaction

Human communication occurs as the receiver of the message responds to the source through feedback. This interactive model views communication as a linear sequence of actions and reactions.

Human Communication as Transaction

Human communication is simultaneously interactive. Meaning is created based on mutual, concurrent sharing of ideas and feelings. This transactive model most accurately describes human communication.

Human Communication as Action

Human Communication as Interaction

Human Communication as Transaction

One research team says that communication is "the coordinated management of meaning" through episodes during which the message of one person influences the message of another.[32] Technically, only the sender and receiver of those messages can determine where one episode ends and another begins. We make sense out of our world in ways that are unique to each of us.

COMMUNICATION CHARACTERISTICS

Now that we have defined communication, noted its importance, and seen how our understanding of it evolved over the last half of the 20th century, we turn our attention to describing how it works by examining the characteristics of communication. The following characteristics are evident when communication occurs: Communication is inescapable, irreversible, and complicated; it emphasizes content and relationships; and it is governed by rules.

Communication Is Inescapable

Opportunities to communicate are ubiquitous—they are everywhere. Even before we are born, we respond to movement and sound. With our first cry, we begin the process of announcing to others that we are here. And once we make contact with other humans, we communicate and continue to do so until death. Even though many of our messages are not verbalized, we nonetheless intentionally, and very often unintentionally, send them to others. As we noted earlier, some communication scholars question whether it is possible to communicate with someone unintentionally. What experts do agree on is this: Communication with others plays an ever-present role in our life. We spend most of our waking hours sending messages to or interpreting messages from others.[33] Even as you silently stand in line at a supermarket checkout line, your lack of eye contact with others waiting in line suggests you're not interested in striking up a conversation. Your unspoken messages may provide cues to which others respond. Even when you don't intend to express a particular idea or feeling, others may try to make sense out of what you are doing—or not doing. Remember: People judge you by your behavior, not your intent.

Communication Is Irreversible

"Disregard that last statement made by the witness," instructs the judge. Yet the clever lawyer knows that once her client has told the jury that her husband gave her a black eye during an argument, the client cannot really "take back" the message. In conversation we may try to modify the meaning of a spoken message by saying something like, "Oh, I really didn't mean it." But in most cases, the damage has been done. Once created, communication has the physical property of matter; it can't be uncreated. As the helical model in Figure 1.4 suggests, once communication begins, it never loops back on itself. Instead, it continues to be shaped by the events, experiences, and thoughts of the communication partners. A Russian proverb nicely summarizes the point: "Once a word goes out of your mouth, you can never swallow it again."

Communication Is Complicated

Pick up any newspaper this morning, and you will see that there is conflict brewing or erupting in some part of the world. Perhaps there is conflict and disagreement in your own home or in a relationship with someone you care about. Communicating with others is not simple. If it were, we would know how to reduce dramatically the number of misunderstandings and conflicts in our world. This book could also offer you a list of simple techniques and strategies for blissful management of your communication hassles. You won't find that list in this book or any other credible book. Human communication is complicated because of the number of variables and unknown factors involved

FIGURE 1.4
A Helical Model of Communication

Interpersonal communication is irreversible. This helical model shows that communication never loops back on itself. Once it begins, it expands infinitely as the communication partners contribute their thoughts and experiences to the exchange.

Source: Copyright © F. E. X. Dance in *Human Communication Theory* (Holt, Rinehart and Winston, 1967), 294. Reprinted with permission.

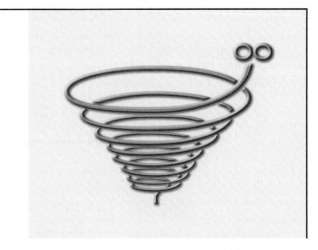

when people interact. To illustrate the complexity of the process, communication scholar Dean Barnlund has suggested that whenever we communicate with another person, there are really at least six "people" involved: (1) who you think you are; (2) who you think the other person is; (3) who you think the other person thinks you are; (4) who the other person thinks he or she is; (5) who the other person thinks you are; and (6) who the other person thinks you think he or she is.[34] Whew! And when you add more people to the conversation, it becomes even more complicated.

Life is not only complicated, it's also uncertain. There are many things we do not know. We seek information about such everyday things as the weather or about such questions as what others may think about us. Several communication theorists suggest that we attempt to manage our uncertainty through communication.[35] In times of high uncertainty (when there are many things we do not know) we will communicate more actively and purposefully so as to manage our uncertainty. For example, we are likely to ask more questions, seek information, and listen intently when we are uncertain.

Adding to the complexity of communication and the problem of our own uncertainty is the fact that messages are not always interpreted as we intend them. Osmo Wiio, a Scandinavian communication scholar, points out the challenges of communicating with others when he suggests the following maxims:

1. If communication can fail, it will.
2. If a message can be understood in different ways, it will be understood in just the way that does the most harm.
3. There is always somebody who knows better than you what you meant by your message.
4. The more communication there is, the more difficult it is for communication to succeed.[36]

Although we are not as pessimistic as Professor Wiio, we do suggest that the task of understanding each other is challenging.

THE FAR SIDE® BY GARY LARSON

"The wench, you idiot! Bring me the *wench*!"

Communication Emphasizes Content and Relationships

What you say—your words—and how you say it—your tone of voice, amount of eye contact, facial expression, and posture—can reveal much about the true meaning of your message. If one of your roommates loudly and abruptly bellows, "HEY, DORK! CLEAN THIS ROOM!" and another roommate uses the same verbal message but more gently and playfully suggests, "Hey, dork. Clean this room," both are communicating a message aimed at achieving the same outcome. But the two messages have different relationship cues. The first shouted message suggests that your roommate may be grumpy and frustrated that the room still harbors the remains of last night's pizza party, while roommate number two's more calmly expressed request suggests he or she may be less frustrated and simply wants the room tidied up a bit.

The **content** of communication messages is the new information, ideas, or suggested actions that the speaker wishes to express. The **relationship dimension** of a communication message is usually more implied; it offers cues about the emotions, attitudes, and amount of power and control the speaker feels toward the other.[37]

Another way of distinguishing between the content and relationship dimensions of communication is to consider that the content of a message refers to *what* is said. The relationship cues are provided in *how* the message is communicated. For example, when you read a transcript of what someone says, you can get a different meaning than you would if you actually heard the person's words.

The rules of both formal and informal play often call for a high five between teammates or friends.

Communication Is Governed by Rules

When you play Monopoly, you know that there are explicit rules about how to get out of jail, buy Boardwalk, or pass "Go" and get $200. The rules are written down. When you play a game with others, there may even be some unwritten rules, such as "When you play Monopoly with Grandpa, always let him buy Boardwalk. He gets grumpy as a bear before breakfast if he doesn't get to buy it." There are also rules that govern how we communicate with others. Most of the rules are imbedded in our culture or discussed verbally rather than written in a rulebook.

According to communication researcher Susan Shimanoff, a **rule** is a "followable prescription that indicates what behavior is obligated, preferred, or prohibited in certain contexts."[38] The rules that help define appropriate and inappropriate communication in any given situation may be explicit or implicit. For a class, explicit rules are probably spelled out in your syllabus. But your instructor has other rules that are more implicit. They are not written or verbalized because you learned them long ago: Only one person speaks at a time; you raise your hand to be called on; you do not pass notes.

Communication rules are developed by those involved in the interaction and by the culture in which the individuals are communicating. Most people learn communication rules from experience, by observing and interacting with others.

COMMUNICATION PRINCIPLES FOR A LIFETIME

As you saw on page 2, underlying our description of human communication are five principles that provide the foundation for all effective communication, whether we are

content
The part of a message that focuses on the new information, ideas, or suggested actions that a communicator wishes to express; *what* is said.

relationship dimension
The aspect of a communication message that offers cues about the emotions, attitudes, and amount of power and control the speaker directs toward others; *how* something is said.

rule
A followable prescription that indicates what behavior is expected or preferred and what behavior is prohibited in a specific situation.

FIGURE 1.5
**Communication Principles
for a Lifetime**

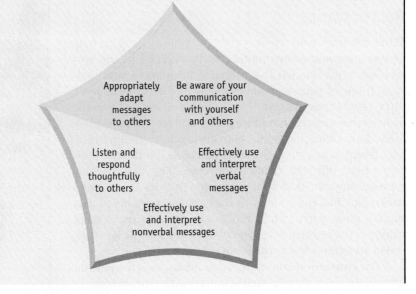

communicating with others one-on-one, in groups or teams, or by presenting a public speech to an audience. Throughout the book we will emphasize how these principles are woven into the fabric of each communication context. We will expand on the discussion here with a brief introduction and then will provide a more comprehensive discussion in the following five chapters to describe and illustrate the scope and power of these principles. Recall the five communication principles for a lifetime that we presented at the beginning of this chapter:

Principle One: Be aware of your communication with yourself and others.
Principle Two: Effectively use and interpret verbal messages.
Principle Three: Effectively use and interpret nonverbal messages.
Principle Four: Listen and respond thoughtfully to others.
Principle Five: Appropriately adapt messages to others.

These five principles operate together rather than independently to form the basis of the fundamental processes that enhance communication effectiveness. The model in Figure 1.5 illustrates how the principles interrelate. Moving around the model clockwise, the first principle, being aware of your communication with yourself and others, is followed by the two principles that focus on communication messages, verbal messages (principle 2) and nonverbal messages (principle 3). The fourth principle, listening and responding, is followed by appropriately adapting messages to others (principle 5). Together, these five principles can help explain why communication can be either effective or ineffective. A violation of any one principle can result in inappropriate or poor communication.

Throughout this book we will remind you of how these principles can be used to organize the theory, concepts, and skills we offer as fundamental to human communication. Chapters 2 through 6 will each be devoted to a single principle. Chapters 7 through 15 will apply these principles to the most prevalent communication situations we experience each day—communicating with others interpersonally, in groups and teams, and when giving a talk or presentation.

To help you see relationships among the five communication principles for a lifetime and the various skills and content we will present in Chapters 7 through 15, we will place in the margin a small version of the model presented in Figure 1.5 like the one that appears in the margin here. We will also label which principle or principles we are discussing. Refer to the principles pentagon in Figure 1.5 as we introduce the principles.

Aware
Verbal
Nonverbal
Listen and Respond
Adapt

Principle One: Be Aware of Your Communication with Yourself and Others

Aware

The first foundation principle is to be aware of your communication with yourself and others. Effective communicators are conscious, or "present," when communicating. Ineffective communicators mindlessly or thoughtlessly say and do things that they may later regret. Being aware of your communication includes being conscious not only of the present moment, but also of who you are, your self-concept, your self-worth, and your perceptions of yourself and others. Being aware of your typical communication style is also part of this foundation principle. For example, some people realize that their communication style is to be emotional when interacting with others. Others may be shy.

As noted, self-awareness includes being conscious of your intrapersonal communication messages. By **intrapersonal communication,** we mean the communication that occurs within yourself, including your thoughts, your emotions, and your perceptions of yourself and others. Talking to yourself is an example of intrapersonal communication. Although our intrapersonal communication is often the focus of psychologists, our intrapersonal messages also form the basis of our communication with others.[39]

Competent communicators are aware of the choices they make when they communicate both intrapersonally and with others; incompetent communicators react to others' messages with thoughtless, quick, knee-jerk responses. Because they do not mindfully censor themselves, they may blurt out obscene, offensive, or profane words. Ineffective communicators operate in an unthinking "default" mode. Being aware of our communication is a foundation principle because all of the choices we make when communicating rest on our ability to make conscious choices when we respond to others.

Earlier in this chapter we noted that human communication is the process of making sense out of the world and sharing that sense with others. Being aware of who we are and how we perceive, or "make sense" of, what we observe is a fundamental principle that helps explain both effective and ineffective communication. In the next chapter we develop this principle and foreshadow how it relates to a variety of communication situations.

Principle Two: Effectively Use and Interpret Verbal Messages

Verbal

The second principle we introduce here and elaborate on in Chapter 3 is to use and interpret verbal messages effectively. Verbal messages are created with language. A **language** consists of symbols and a system of rules (grammar) that make it possible for people to understand one another.

As we noted earlier, a symbol is a word, sound, gesture, or other visual signal that represents a thought, concept, object, or experience. When you read the words on this page, you are looking at symbols that trigger meaning. The word is not the thing it represents; it simply symbolizes the thing or idea.

Your reading skill permits you to make sense out of symbols. The word *tree,* for example, may trigger a thought of the tree you may be reading under now, a tree in your own yard or a nearby park, or a great sequoia you saw on your family vacation in Yosemite National Park. Effective communicators use appropriate symbols to create accurate meaning. Author Daniel Quinn once commented, "No story is devoid of meaning, if you know how to look for it. This is as true of nursery rhymes and daydreams as it is of epic poems."[40] Meaning is created when people have a common or shared understanding.

The effective communicator both encodes and decodes messages accurately; he or she selects appropriate symbols to form a message and interprets carefully the messages

intrapersonal communication
Communication that occurs within yourself, including your thoughts and emotions.

language
The system of symbols (words or vocabulary) structured by rules (grammar) that makes it possible for people to understand one another.

of others. The process of using and interpreting symbols is the essence of how we make sense out of the world and share that sense with others.

Words have power. The words we use to describe ourselves and our world have considerable influence on how we perceive what we experience. Any good advertising copywriter knows how to use words to create a need or desire for a product. Political consultants tell politicians how to craft sound bites that will create just the right audience response. And words can hurt us. Words have the ability to offend and create stress. For example, derogatory words about someone's gender or race can do considerable harm. Throughout this book we will present strategies and suggestions for selecting the best word or symbol to enhance your listeners' understanding.

Nonverbal

Principle Three: Effectively Use and Interpret Nonverbal Messages

Messages are also nonverbal. Nonverbal communication is communication by means other than written or spoken language that creates meaning for someone. Nonverbal messages can communicate powerful ideas or express emotions with greater impact than mere words alone. An optimistic hitchhiker's extended thumb and an irate driver's extended finger are nonverbal symbols with clear and intentional meaning. But not all nonverbal symbols are clearly interpreted or even consciously expressed. You may not be aware of your frown when someone asks if he or she may sit next to you in a vacant seat in a restaurant. Or your son may excitedly be telling you about his field trip to the fire station while you stare into the pages of your newspaper. You have no intention of telling your son he is not important, but your lack of nonverbal responsiveness speaks volumes.

One of the most important reasons our unspoken messages are significant is that they are the primary way we communicate feelings and attitudes toward others. With someone whom you like or love very much, you may spend a very small percentage of your time verbalizing your affection and friendship. The other person can discern your interest and admiration based on your nonverbal expressions and the amount of time you spend together. Your eye contact, facial expression, and tone of voice communicate your pleasure in his or her company. You may also know someone who doesn't like you. This less-than-friendly person may never have to come right out and say, "I don't like you." But you know you're not on friendly terms based on nonverbal cues: A scowl, an uninterested tone of voice, and a lack of eye contact signal that you're not held in high esteem. Our nonverbal messages communicate how we feel toward others.

When there is a contradiction between what you say and what you do, your nonverbal message is more believable than your verbal message. When asked how your meal is, you may tell your server that the meal is "great," but your nonverbal message—facial expression and tone of voice—clearly communicates your unhappiness with the cuisine. As we noted when we discussed the concept of content and relationship messages, our nonverbal cues often tell people how to interpret what we are saying.

Effective communicators develop skill in interpreting nonverbal messages of others. They also monitor their own messages to avoid unintentionally sending contradictory verbal and nonverbal messages. It's sometimes hard to interpret nonverbal messages because they don't have a neat beginning and ending point—the flow of information is continuous. It may not be clear where one gesture stops and another begins. Cultural differences, and the fact that so many different nonverbal channels (such as eye contact, facial expression, gestures, posture) can be used at the same time, make it tricky to "read" someone's nonverbal message accurately. We amplify our discussion of the power of nonverbal messages in Chapter 4.

Principle Four: Listen and Respond Thoughtfully to Others

So far, our list of principles may appear to place much of the burden of achieving communication success on the person sending the message. But effective communication with others also places considerable responsibility on the listener. As we explained earlier in the chapter, because communication is a transactional process—both senders and receivers are mutually and usually simultaneously expressing and responding to symbols—listening to words with sensitivity and "listening between the lines" to nonverbal messages join our list of fundamental principles.

Listening can be hard because it looks easy. You spend more time listening than performing any other communication activity—probably more than any other thing you do except sleep.[41] Despite spending the greatest portion of our communication time listening, there is evidence that many if not most of us do not always listen effectively. What's tricky about listening? Both psychological, or internal, noise (our own thoughts, needs, and emotions) and external distractions (noise in the surroundings in which we listen) can create barriers to effective listening. The fact that it is perceived to be a passive rather than an active task makes listening and accurately interpreting information a challenge. Effective listening is *not* a passive task at all; the effective and sensitive listener works hard to stay on task and focus mindfully on a sender's message.

At the heart of this principle is developing sensitivity to others. By sensitivity we are not talking about the touchy-feely-emotional-what-I-hear-you-saying approach to interpersonal relationships. We are, however, suggesting that you develop an orientation or sensitivity to others when you listen and respond. When you are **other-oriented,** you consider the needs, motives, desires, and goals of your communication partners while still maintaining your own integrity. The choices you make in both forming the message and selecting when to share it should consider your partner's thoughts and feelings.

Most of us are egocentric—self-focused. We are born with an innate desire to meet our own needs. As we grow and mature, we develop a consciousness of more than our own needs. Scholars of evolution might argue that it is good that we are self-focused; looking out for number one is what perpetuates the human race.

Yet an *exclusive* focus on ourselves inhibits effective communication. Do you know anyone who is self-absorbed? Most of us find such a person tedious and uncomfortable to be around. People who are skilled communicators both listen and respond with sensitivity; they are other oriented.

Principle Five: Appropriately Adapt Messages to Others

It is not enough to be sensitive and to accurately understand others; you must use the information you gather to modify the messages you construct. It is important to **adapt** your response appropriately to your listener. When you adapt a message, you make choices about how best to formulate it and respond to someone to achieve your communication goals. Adapting to a listener does not mean that you tell a listener only what he or she wants to hear. That would be unethical. Adapting involves appropriately editing and shaping your responses so that others accurately understand your messages and so that you achieve your goal without coercing or using false information or other unethical methods. To adapt a message is to make choices about all aspects of message content and delivery.

Regardless of whether you are giving a presentation, talking with a friend, or participating in a small-group meeting, as an effective communicator you consider who the listeners are when deciding what to say and how best to say it. One of the elements of a message that you adapt when communicating with others is the structure or organization of what you say. Informal, interpersonal conversations typically do not follow a rigid, outlined structure. Our conversation freely bounces from one topic to another. Formal presentations delivered in North America, however, are usually ex-

Listen and Respond

Adapt

other-oriented
Being focused on the needs and concerns of others while maintaining one's personal integrity.

adapt
To adjust both what is communicated and how a message is communicated; to make choices about how best to formulate a message and respond to others to achieve your communication goals.

Diversity *and* Communication

Principles for a Lifetime: Principles for All Cultures?

We've suggested that our five principles for a lifetime constitute a framework for all human communication. Again, let's review the five principles:

Principle One: Be aware of your communication with yourself and others.

Principle Two: Effectively use and interpret verbal messages.

Principle Three: Effectively use and interpret nonverbal messages.

Principle Four: Listen and respond thoughtfully to others.

Principle Five: Appropriately adapt messages to others.

The question is, "How applicable are these five principles for a lifetime to communication in a variety of cultures?" Culture is the learned system of knowledge, behavior, attitudes, beliefs, values, and norms that is shared by a group of people. People who were born and raised in Asian countries, for example, have different cultural expectations than do people who were born and raised in North America. But do these five communication principles apply to *all* people everywhere, despite cultural differences and a wide variety of cultural traditions and backgrounds in the world? Is it true that all people should be aware of their communication, use and interpret verbal and nonverbal messages, listen and respond thoughtfully, and appropriately adapt their messages to others?

We're not suggesting that all cultures use and interpret verbal or nonverbal messages the same way (principles two and three)—there are obvious differences from one culture to another in language and use of nonverbal cues. But we are suggesting that in all cultures, the use and interpretation of verbal and nonverbal messages is important in determining whether communication is effective. We are also not saying that people from all cultures adapt messages in the same way (principle five). There are clear cultural differences in the way people choose to adapt messages to others. But do people in all cul-

tures adapt messages to others in some way, even though the interpretation of the adapted message varies from culture to culture? We suggest that these five fundamental principles may provide a common framework for talking about communication in a variety of cultures. Do you agree or disagree with this statement?

In your communication class there are undoubtedly people from a variety of cultural backgrounds. Perhaps some of your classmates grew up in countries other than your own. Respond to the following questions, and then compare your answers with those of your fellow students.

1. How applicable are the five communication principles to your cultural experience?
2. Do any of the communication principles *not* apply in your culture?
3. Can you think of another fundamental communication principle that is not included in our list of five? If so, what is it?
4. Do you agree that these communication principles apply to all people?

---

pected to have a more explicit structure—an introduction, a body, and a conclusion. The major ideas of a formal presentation are expected to be clearly identified. North American audiences also seem to prefer a presentation that could be easily outlined. Other cultures, such as those in the Middle East, expect a greater use of stories, examples, and illustrations, rather than a clearly structured, outlined presentation. Knowing your audience's expectations can help you adapt your message so that it will be listened to and understood.

You also adapt the general style or formality of your message to the receiver. If you are speaking to your lifelong best friend, your style is less formal than if you are speaking to the president of your university. The language you use and jokes you tell when around your best chums will undoubtedly be different than your language and humor when you are attending a meeting with your boss or with faculty members from your school. Our point is that effective communicators not only listen and respond with sensitivity, they use the information they gather to shape the message and delivery of their responses to others. In Chapter 6 we will discuss this principle in greater detail by discussing the diverse nature of potential listeners and how to adapt to them. Adapting to differences in culture and gender, for example, may mean the difference between a message that is well received and one that creates hostility.

COMMUNICATING WITH OTHERS: THREE SITUATIONS

The five communication principles that we unveiled in this chapter operate whenever people communicate, regardless of the number of people present or the content of their messages. The three classic situations to which communication researchers apply these principles are interpersonal communication, group communication, and presentational communication.

Each of the next five chapters is devoted to one of the five principles we've identified and relates these principles to the three most typical unmediated communication situations you will experience. By *unmediated,* we mean those communication encounters that do not involve some kind of *medium* such as the telephone, the Internet, TV, fax, or another type of technology; any communication that involves such technology is *mediated communication.* Most of the research conclusions about interpersonal, group, and presentational situations are based on communication that takes place live and in person. So we'll spend most of our discussion focusing on how communication is expressed and interpreted when people are face to face. There is a growing collection of research findings, however, that is helping us understand how the Internet and other technological tools are affecting our communication. When appropriate, we'll offer some ideas and suggestions for interacting with others via mediated settings.

We now turn our attention to introducing these three contexts of communication: interpersonal, group, and presentational communication.

Interpersonal Communication

Interpersonal communication is a special form of human communication that occurs when we interact simultaneously with another person and attempt to mutually influence each other, usually for the purpose of managing relationships. At the heart of this definition is the role of communication in developing unique relationships with other people.[42]

For many years communication scholars considered any two-person interaction interpersonal communication. Today interpersonal communication is defined not by the number of people who communicate but by the quality of communication that occurs when we express and interpret verbal and nonverbal messages. Interpersonal communication occurs not just when we interact with someone, but when we treat the other person as a one-of-a kind human being.

Impersonal communication occurs when we treat people as objects, or when we respond to their roles rather than to who they are as unique people. Based on this definition, asking a server for a glass of water at a restaurant is impersonal rather than interpersonal communication. If you strike up a conversation with the server—say you discover it's her birthday, or you discover that you both know the same people—your conversation moves from impersonal to interpersonal. We're not suggesting that impersonal communication is unimportant or necessarily inferior or bad. Competent communicators are able to interact with others in a variety of situations.

Another attribute of interpersonal communication is that the communication is simultaneous. Both people are communicating at the same time, and there is mutual influence—both persons are

interpersonal communication
Communication that occurs simultaneously between two people who attempt to mutually influence each other, usually for the purpose of managing relationships.

impersonal communication
Communication that treats people as objects, or that responds only to their roles, rather than to who they are as unique people.

We engage in interpersonal communication when we interact with another person.

reacting or involved in the process. Interpersonal communication is not a one-sided monologue; it's a dialogue in the sense that all communicators are influenced and meaning is created simultaneously.[43] Interpersonal communication reflects the characteristics of the transactional model of communication that we discussed earlier.

A final attribute, and among the most important, is that interpersonal communication is the fundamental means we use to manage our relationships. A relationship is an ongoing connection we make with others through interpersonal communication. To relate to someone is to give and take, listen and respond, act and react. When we talk about a good or positive relationship with someone, we often mean that we are "together" or "in sync." In an effective relationship, the individuals involved feel that their verbal and nonverbal messages are understood and that there is a relational harmony based on a common understanding between the communicators. We will apply the five principles of human communication to interpersonal communication in Chapters 7 and 8.

Group Communication

Each of us belongs to a gang of some type; it's just that some gangs are more socially acceptable than others. Comparisons between a rambunctious street gang and the local PTA may seem a stretch. But even though the street gang and the PTA have radically different objectives, both share similarities of function and form that make them a **group:** a collection of people who have common goals, who feel they belong to the group, and who influence each other.

Human beings are social, collaborative creatures. We do most of our work and play in groups. And today's globe-shrinking technology makes it possible for people to be linked with others in virtual groups even when they are in different physical locations. One focus of this book is the communication that occurs in groups—how we make sense out of our participation in groups and share that sense with others. We define **small group communication** as the verbal and nonverbal message transactions that occur among from three to about fifteen people who share a common goal, who feel a sense of belonging to the group, and who exert influence on each other.[44]

A group must have at least three people; two people are usually referred to as a **dyad.** What is the upper limit on the number of people for meaningful group discussion? Some scholars say fifteen, others say more.[45] The bigger the group, the less influence each person has on the group and the greater the chance that subgroups or splinter factions will emerge.

Our definition of group communication includes the notion that in order to be considered a group, people need a common goal—something that members all would agree is the reason for the group's existence. Group members also have a sense of belonging to the group. A collection of travelers waiting for the subway may have a common goal of catching the train, but they probably don't see themselves as belonging to a group with a single goal of going to the same place. Members of a small group need to have a sense of identity with the group; they should sense that it is their group.

Here's another attribute of a small group: Group members exert influence on one another. Each person potentially influences the actions and responses of others. Even if a group member sits like a lump and says nothing, this nonverbal behavior exerts an influence. Each group member, by virtue of being a member of the group, has the potential to exert leadership on the group. To lead is to influence.

What's the difference between a group and a team? Although some people use the two terms interchangeably, we see a distinction. A **team** is a coordinated group of individuals intentionally organized to work together to achieve a specific, common goal. To us, a team is more highly structured and organized than a group. Team members have clearly defined roles, duties, and responsibilities. Think of a sports team. Team members have assigned roles and well-thought-out assignments. Team members don't just show up and mill around and do what comes their way. They are focused. Teams also have clearly defined rules and explicit expectations for team operations. Their goals

group
A collection of people who have a common goal, feel a sense of belonging to the group, and influence each other.

small group communication
The transactive process of creating meaning among from three to fifteen people who share a common purpose, feel a sense of belonging to the group, and exert influence on one another.

dyad
A two-person interaction.

team
A coordinated group of people intentionally organized to work together to achieve a common goal.

are well defined and measurable. And they coordinate their work efforts as they collaborate to achieve their well-articulated goals. In Chapters 9 and 10, we will discuss more thoroughly the five communication principles for a lifetime as they apply to groups and teams.

Presentational Communication

For many people, speaking in public is a major source of anxiety. **Presentational communication** occurs when a speaker addresses a gathering of people to inform, persuade, or entertain. In this book we will focus on applying the principles of communication when informing and persuading listeners.

Of the three contexts in which the principles we present in this book are applied, this context has the distinction of being the one that has been formally studied the longest. In 333 BC, Aristotle wrote his famous *Rhetoric*, the first fully developed treatment of the study of speech to convince an audience. He defined **rhetoric** as the process of discovering the available means of persuasion in a given situation. In essence, persuasion is the process of using symbols to persuade others. Today many communication departments have several courses that focus exclusively on how to persuade others, design and deliver both informative and persuasive messages, and evaluate the messages of others. Although we have certainly advanced in our understanding of informing and persuading others in the past two millennia, much of what Aristotle taught has withstood the tests of both time and scholarly research.

Our focus in Chapters 11 through 15 is on basic strategies for designing and delivering a speech to others. As with interpersonal and group communication, we will discuss presentational communication through the perspective of the five principles that anchor our study. Effective presentational speakers are aware of their communication and how they interact with their audience. They also effectively use, interpret, and understand verbal and nonverbal messages; listen and respond to their audience; and adapt their message to their listeners.

There is a wealth of information on and strategies for each of these three communication contexts. Most communication departments offer separate courses on these three areas. Our challenge is to present fundamental principles that illuminate all applications of human communication. Being aware of how you interact with others, monitoring your verbal and nonverbal messages, listening and responding thoughtfully, and adapting your messages to others will serve you well whether you are talking with a friend, participating in a meeting, or giving a speech.

Are interpersonal, group, and presentational communication the only contexts in which communication takes place? The answer is no—communication takes place in a variety of situations. One of the most prominent forms of communication in our lives involves the media. As we noted earlier, **mediated communication** is any communication that is expressed via some channel other than those that are used when we communicate in person. Some physical medium, such as a wire, a cable, a phone line, a telephone, a TV set, a computer, or some other technology, carries the messages between sender and receiver. The channel of communication is not only physical but also electronic, in the form of the signal coming into your TV set, your phone, or your computer. **Mass communication** occurs when a mediated message is sent to many people at the same time. A TV or radio broadcast is an example of mass communication. As we noted earlier in this chapter, our focus in this book is on unmediated communication. This is not meant to suggest that mass communication is not important, only that it is beyond the scope of this book. At some colleges and universities, mass communication is a focus of study in a separate department; at other colleges and universities, the study of mass communication is included in the same department that studies all human communication.

In the chapters ahead we will analyze the five principles of communication for a lifetime as they apply to the three typical unmediated communication situations—interpersonal, group, and presentational communication. Our primary goal is to help

presentational communication
Communication that occurs when a speaker addresses a gathering of people in order to inform, persuade, or entertain them.

rhetoric
The process of using symbols to influence or persuade others.

mediated communication
Any communication that is carried out using some channel other than those used in face-to-face communication.

mass communication
Communication accomplished through a mediated message that is sent to many people at the same time.

you better understand your communication and improve your ability to communicate with others for the rest of your life.

PRINCIPLES FOR A LIFETIME: Enhancing Your Skills

Aware

Principle One: Be aware of your communication with yourself and others.
- Be aware of your intrapersonal communication.
- Be conscious of how your own "self-talk" has an impact on your communication with others and your overall communication behavior.

Verbal

Principle Two: Effectively use and interpret verbal messages.
- Use clear and precise words to explain ideas and concepts to others.
- Make a concerted effort to accurately interpret the words of others.

Nonverbal

Principle Three: Effectively use and interpret nonverbal messages.
- Use nonverbal, unspoken cues to express feelings and emotions to others or to modify the explicit verbal message you are communicating to others.
- Make a conscious effort to accurately decode the nonverbal messages of others.

Listen and Respond

Principle Four: Listen and respond thoughtfully to others.
- Be other-oriented by taking special care to listen to both the verbal and the nonverbal messages of others.
- Be deliberate in how you provide feedback to those to whom you are listening.

Adapt

Principle Five: Appropriately adapt messages to others.
- Use your listening and nonverbal communication skills to help you appropriately adjust both your message and how you communicate it to others.
- Make ethical choices about how to best formulate a message and respond to others to achieve your communication goals.

SUMMARY

Communication is essential for life. At its most basic level, communication is the process of acting on information. Human communication is the process of making sense out of the world and sharing that sense with others by creating meaning through verbal and nonverbal messages. It is important to learn about communication, because being a skilled communicator can help you obtain a good job and enhance the quality of your relationships, as well as improve your physical and emotional health. Early models viewed human communication as a simple message-transfer process. Later models evolved to view communication as interaction and then as simultaneous transaction. Key components of communication include source, receiver, message, channel, noise, context, and feedback.

Communication has five characteristics: It is inescapable; it is irreversible; it is complicated; it emphasizes content and relationships; and it is governed by rules.

Five principles are fundamental to good communication. First, be aware of your communication with yourself and others. Being mindful of your communication is important to help you improve your communication. Second, effectively use and interpret verbal messages. Words are powerful and influence our thoughts, our actions, and our relationships with others. Third, effectively use and interpret nonverbal messages. Unspoken cues provide important information about our emotions, feelings, and attitudes. Fourth, listen and respond thoughtfully to others. Being able to interpret accurately the messages of others enhances comprehension and relational empathy. Fifth, appropriately adapt messages to others. It is important to adapt messages to others to enhance both understanding and empathy.

These five principles are applicable to the most common communication contexts: interpersonal, group, and presentational communication. Interpersonal communication is a special form of communication that occurs when two people interact simultaneously and mutually influence each other, usually for the purpose of managing relationships. Small-group communication is interaction among a small group of people who share a common purpose or goal, who feel a sense of belonging to the group, and who exert influence on the others in the group. Presentational communication occurs when a speaker addresses an audience for the purpose of informing, persuading, or entertaining.

Discussion and Review

1. Define the term *communication.* Compare and contrast this definition with the text's definition of *human communication.*
2. Why is it important to study communication?
3. Compare and contrast communication as action, interaction, and transaction.
4. What are characteristics of communication?
5. Identify the five fundamental principles of communication.
6. Discuss how the five principles of communication apply to interpersonal, group, and presentational communication contexts.

Putting Principles into Practice

1. Working alone or with a team of your classmates, develop one or more original models of communication. Include all of the elements that describe how communication works. You could develop a model for each of the three communication situations that we presented in this chapter (interpersonal, group, presentational speaking). Your model could be a drawing or you could use objects (like tinker toys or other building toys) to illustrate the communication process. Explain your model to the class.
2. In this chapter we noted that communication is complicated. There are really six "people" involved in a conversation that seemingly involves just two people. Choose a partner and try to verbalize your impressions about the six people involved in your exchanges with that person.
3. To get better acquainted with other members of a small group, try this ice-breaker activity. Tell three things about yourself, one of which is not true. Other group members should guess which one of the three things you have disclosed is false. The purpose of this activity is not to teach you how to lie or be unethical, but to assess the power and sometimes inaccuracy of the impressions we make on others. After all group members have made their guesses, provide the correct information. Discuss how you form first impressions and the role these impressions play in your communication with others.
4. In a small group, take turns introducing yourself to other class members. Consider the following ideas as ways to tell other classmates about yourself.
   - What does your name mean to you?
   - Describe what you do best and what you wish you did better.
   - Draw or symbolize your "lifeline." Show the high points and low points of your life, perhaps using simple drawings or symbols to illustrate your life hopes, joys, concerns, and goals.
   - If you could be someone other than yourself, who would you be? Why?

   After you have all introduced yourselves, discuss the interaction you've had according to the characteristics of communication included in the chapter. For example, how was your discussion guided by rules?

CHAPTER Two

A person who buries his head in the sand offers an engaging target.

Mabel A. Keenan

Marc Chagall, "The Painter." 1976. ©2005 Artists Rights Society (ARS), New York/ADAGP, Paris. ©Scala/Art Resource/NY.

Self-Awareness and Communication

CHAPTER OUTLINE

Self-Awareness: How Well Do You Know Yourself?

Self-Concept: Who Are You?

Self-Esteem: What Is Your Value?

Communication and the Enhancement of Self-Esteem

The Perception Process

Communication and the Enhancement of Perceptual Accuracy

Summary

CHAPTER OBJECTIVES

After studying this chapter, you should be able to:

1. Discuss the importance of self-awareness in the process of improving one's communication skills.

2. Define attitudes, beliefs, and values as they relate to self-concept development.

3. Name and briefly describe the three types of selves, according to James's research.

4. Describe the four factors that affect the development of self-concept.

5. Describe Stewart's four characteristics of identity.

6. Explain the difference between self-concept, self-image, self-esteem, and self-worth.

7. Describe how gender, social comparisons, self-expectations, and self-fulfilling prophecies affect one's self-esteem.

8. Provide examples of positive self-talk, visualization, and reframing that demonstrate the connection between these techniques and the enhancement of self-esteem.

9. Define perception and explain its three stages.

10. Discuss three ways to enhance your perceptual accuracy.

Do you have your own Web site? Many of you have designed a personal Web page as part of a class project or simply because you wanted a way to communicate who you are to people across the globe. Did you include a photo of yourself on the site? What information about you would someone who visited your site learn?

If you do not have your own Web page, you've probably had other opportunities to communicate who you are, perhaps by writing a self-exploratory essay as part of your college application process. Some of you have no doubt placed personal ads in your local or campus newspaper. What did you choose to focus on as you described yourself—physical attributes? personality characteristics? intellectual abilities? What information did you leave out, either because you're not proud of those aspects of yourself, you didn't think anyone would be interested, or you were concerned about privacy?

Still others of you have likely visited the Web site of an Internet dating service, such as eharmony.com, which asks you a battery of questions about yourself. Your responses are analyzed across multiple personality dimensions and your profile can be matched with compatible potential partners who also use the service.[1]

Activities such as designing a personal Web site, writing an essay about yourself, crafting a personal ad, or responding to dating service questions rely on a central, important element: awareness. Stephen Covey, author of the best-selling book *The Seven Habits of Highly Effective People*, describes self-awareness as that which "allows us to stand apart and examine even the way we 'see' ourselves—our self-paradigm, the most fundamental paradigm of effectiveness. It affects not only our attitudes and behaviors, but also how we see other people."[2]

Figure 2.1 presents the model introduced in Chapter 1—our "communication principles for a lifetime" model. You will no doubt become quite familiar with this model and its five principles as you read this book. As we said in Chapter 1, these integrative principles provide the foundation for effective communication in various contexts that you encounter throughout your life. In this chapter we explore the first principle: *Be aware of your communication with yourself and others.* Developing self-awareness involves being conscious not only of the present moment, but also of who you are (your self-concept), your value in this life (your self-esteem), and your perception of yourself and others.

FIGURE 2.1
Communication Principles for a Lifetime

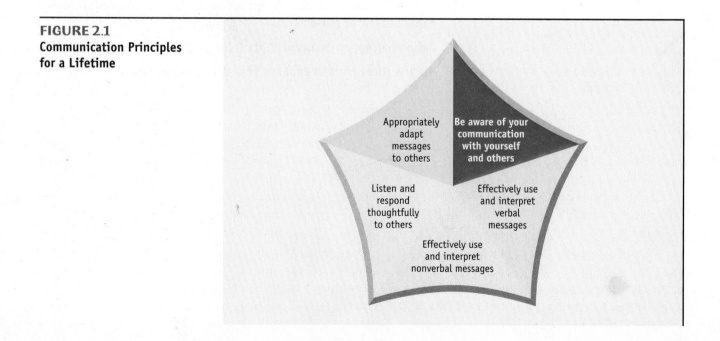

Appropriately adapt messages to others

Be aware of your communication with yourself and others

Listen and respond thoughtfully to others

Effectively use and interpret verbal messages

Effectively use and interpret nonverbal messages

SELF-AWARENESS: HOW WELL DO YOU KNOW YOURSELF?

Have you ever been standing in a line at the grocery store checkout and felt something brush past your legs? You look down and realize that a small child has crossed your path, no doubt on the way to the candy display. The child has no real awareness of what has occurred—that she or he has inadvertently touched a stranger while attempting to satisfy a goal. But you, as an adult, are aware. Moments of self-awareness arrive at different times for different people, and self-awareness is a never-ending process. You don't reach a point where you've "maxed out" your self-awareness. This fascinating process of understanding your own existence continues throughout life.

Social psychologists have categorized self-awareness into three types or dimensions.[3] The first is **subjective self-awareness,** an ability that humans and animals have to differentiate themselves from their social and physical environment. We see ourselves as being different and apart from the physical world and from other beings in it. A second category is termed **objective self-awareness,** which humans and only a few animals (primates) possess. This involves the ability to be the object of one's own attention, to be aware of one's state of mind, to realize that one is thinking and remembering. The final awareness state is termed **symbolic self-awareness,** a unique human ability to develop a representation of oneself and communicate that representation to others through language. This last form of awareness holds the most interest for those of us who study communication.

One framework, attributed to Abraham Maslow, helps explain the process of becoming self-aware; it has also been used to explain the attainment of communication skill. The framework suggests that people operate at one of four levels:

1. *Unconscious incompetence:* We are unaware of our own incompetence. We don't know what we don't know.
2. *Conscious incompetence:* At this level, we become aware or conscious that we are not competent; we know what we don't know.
3. *Conscious competence:* We are aware that we know or can do something, but it has not yet become an integrated skill or habit.
4. *Unconscious competence:* At this level, skills become second nature. You know or can do something but don't have to concentrate to be able to act on that knowledge or draw on that skill.

To better understand how this framework operates, let's use conversation skills as an example. Suppose Janie is a poor communicator but doesn't realize it, so she is at level 1 when it comes to interacting with other people. Either Janie hasn't thought about developing interaction skills or she actually believes herself to be a good conversationalist. Then Janie starts becoming more self-aware and realizes that her style of talking with people isn't winning her any friends. She's unsure about how to fix this problem, but she is conscious that she has some deficits in this area (level 2). She sets out to improve her communication skills by taking a class, purposefully working on how she talks with people and soliciting honest feedback from people with whom she interacts. Janie develops an improved interaction style and is now at the level of conscious competence. Once these skills are fully integrated into Janie's behavior with people, so she doesn't have to strive to communicate effectively, she will have reached level 4, unconscious competence. Almost any skill can be described in terms of these four levels. It is also possible to be at one level with one skill and another level with another skill. For example, you may be skilled at meeting new people but less skilled at managing conflict.

subjective self-awareness
An ability to differentiate the self from the social and physical environment.

objective self-awareness
An ability to be the object of one's own attention, to be aware of state of mind, and to realize that one is thinking and remembering.

symbolic self-awareness
A unique human ability to develop and communicate a representation of oneself to others.

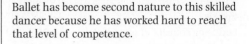
Ballet has become second nature to this skilled dancer because he has worked hard to reach that level of competence.

Aware

People can experience moments of heightened self-awareness and significant personal growth. Taking a communication course like the one you're enrolled in can spark such a moment. In this course, you will be challenged to think long and hard about your answers to the question "Who am I?" You'll be encouraged to survey what you believe about yourself and to think about the role such aspects as your gender, race or ethnicity, nationality, sexual orientation, and social class play in your view of self. You'll be challenged to consider how you communicate with others, how you are shaped and affected by those with whom you interact, and how you can use your powers of communication. But the key beginning point is awareness. Before attempting to communicate who you are to others, you must first be aware of yourself.

SELF-CONCEPT: WHO ARE YOU?

If someone were to say to you, "Who are you?" how would you respond? You might start with basic demographic information like your age and where you're from; perhaps you would describe yourself in relation to groups and organizations to which you belong. Or you might talk about yourself according to various roles you assume, like "I'm a student at State" or "I'm so-and-so's daughter (or son)." Whatever answer you give will be incomplete, because you can't really convey the totality of who you are to others. But it's an interesting place to begin, considering just how you would answer the "Who am I" question.

Psychologist Karen Horney defines **self** as "that central inner force, common to all human beings and yet unique in each which is the deep source of growth."[4] Your "Who am I" responses are also part of your **self-concept**—your identity, your subjective description of who you think you are, how you see *you as a person*.[5] Some people use the term *self-image* synonymously with self-concept, but we want to avoid confusion over these terms. We subscribe to a more narrow meaning for the term self-image, in that **self-image** is your view of yourself *in a particular situation*.[6] That view changes from situation to situation. For example, you may be extroverted in chemistry class but not at a party where you don't know too many people. You may become very nervous when giving a presentation but are quite comfortable communicating with people one on one. You have several self-images, because they change as the situation changes. These different self-images are part of the larger component we call self-concept. The self-concept is the way we *consistently* describe ourselves to others; it is deeply rooted and slow to change.

Self-Concept Components

Who you are is also reflected in the attitudes, beliefs, and values that you hold. An **attitude** is a learned predisposition to respond to a person, object, or idea in a favorable or unfavorable way. Attitudes reflect what you like and what you don't like. If you like sports, spaghetti, and history, you hold positive attitudes toward these things. You were not born with a fondness for sports; you learned to like them just as some people learn to enjoy the taste of exotic foods.

Beliefs are the way in which you structure your understanding of reality—what is true and what is false. Most of your beliefs are based on previous experience. You trust that the sun will rise in the morning and that you will get burned if you put your hand on a hot stove.

Values are enduring concepts of good and bad, right and wrong. Your values can be difficult to identify because they are so central to who you are. But knowing what you value in your life is part of this principle of self-awareness that we focus on in this chapter. When you go to the supermarket, you may spend a few minutes deciding on whether to buy chocolate or vanilla ice cream, but you probably do not spend much time deciding whether you will steal the ice cream or pay for it, because you value honesty over dis-

self
The sum of who a person is; a person's central inner force.

self-concept
A person's subjective description of who he or she is.

self-image
A person's view of herself or himself in a particular situation or circumstance.

attitude
Learned predisposition to respond to a person, object, or idea in a favorable or unfavorable way.

belief
The way in which you structure your understanding of reality—what is true and what is false.

value
Enduring concept of good and bad, right and wrong.

RECAP

Self-Concept Components

Component	Definition	Dimensions	Example
Attitude	Learned predisposition to respond favorably or unfavorably toward something	Likes–Dislikes	You like ice cream, scented candles, and tennis.
Belief	The way in which we structure reality	True–False	You believe your parents love you.
Value	Enduring concept of right and wrong	Good–Bad	You value honesty and truth.

honesty. Other values may reflect your sense of loyalty, patriotism, justice and fairness, and love and caring for others. Our values are instilled in us by our earliest connections with others; for almost all of us, our parents are the first influences on our development of values. Of the three elements, attitudes are the most superficial and likely to change; values are more at the core of a person and least likely to change. We consider attitudes, beliefs, and values again in our discussion of persuasion in Chapter 15.

One or Many Selves?

Shakespeare's famous line "To thine own self be true" suggests that you have a single self to which you can be true. But do you have just one self? Or is there a more "real you" buried somewhere within? "I'm just not myself this morning," sighs Sandy, as she drags herself out the front door to head for her office. If she is not herself, then *who is she?* Most scholars conclude that we have a core set of behaviors, attitudes, beliefs, and values that constitute our self—the sum total of who we are. But our *concept* of self can and does change, depending on circumstances and influences.

Perhaps the most enduring and widely accepted framework for describing who you are was developed by the philosopher William James. He identified three components of the self: the material self, the social self, and the spiritual self.[7]

The Material Self   Perhaps you've heard the statement, "You are what you eat." The material self goes a step further by suggesting, "You are what you have." The **material self** is a total of all of the tangible things you own: your body, your possessions, your home.

One element of the material self receives considerable attention in our culture: the body. Do you like the way you look? Most of us would like to change something about our appearance. Research has determined that in the United States, women experience more negative feelings about their bodies than men and experience significant self-esteem loss as a result.[8] Many women hold images of very thin women, such as supermodels, as ideals and develop dissatisfaction with their own bodies in comparison. Women's dissatisfaction with their bodies has markedly increased over the past 25 years.[9] However, research also shows that men are not immune to body dissatisfaction, in that they compare their own bodies with ideal male bodies displayed in the media and are concerned about what others want and expect them to look like.[10] When there is a discrepancy between our desired material self and our self-concept, we may respond to eliminate the discrepancy. We may try to lose weight, get a nose job, or acquire more hair. The multibillion-dollar diet industry is just one of many that profit from our collective desire to change our appearance.

We also attempt to keep up with the proverbial Joneses by wanting more expensive clothes, cars, and homes. By extension, what we own becomes who we are. The bigger,

material self
The element of the self reflected in all the tangible things you own.

Technology *and* Communication

Exploring Self-Concept through Computer-Mediated Communication

*T*echnology, particularly through the advances of computers and the Internet, allows us to explore our self-concepts in ways not possible to previous generations. Perhaps long-distance pen pals experienced something similar, in that they could choose which aspects of themselves to highlight in letters to someone they would never meet. But the ease with which the Internet enables us to experiment with expressions of our self-concepts to others online makes this a fascinating area of study.

One person who has conducted extensive research into online communication is Annette Markham, author of *Life Online: Researching Real Experience in Virtual Space*. Markham examines how online users communicate their sense of self in CMC (shorthand for computer-mediated communication) versus RL (real life).[11] In one online interview, Markham asked a user to compare his CMC and RL selves. His response was that he was "more confident online, because I'm a better editor than writer/speaker. I do well when I can backspace." Markham agreed with the user regarding the luxury of being able to edit one's online communication, saying that she liked the backspace key for its "ability to correct everything you say and therefore are." Markham recounts one particularly interesting

exchange with a user named Sherie, who felt much more confident and expressive online. Sherie explained:

> i choose to exist as myself in language online. i don't try to come up with other personae, so it feels more like being me than i sometimes feel offline. offline one often finds oneself in certain social roles that one must maintain; student, teacher, family member, etc. . . . i don't like my appearance all that much, and so i don't like myself in flesh all that much. i think myself in language is more communicative of who i am. eloquence makes me beautiful online.

Who is to say which is more real for an avid computer user—the online self or the offline self? As we delve more and more into what computers can do for us, and what they do *to* us, we will no doubt continue to question the real versus virtual self. Perhaps these selves aren't distinct; perhaps the online persona is merely an extension or facet of the real person. Should it be cause for concern when people feel positive self-esteem only when they are online? Or should we be glad that people have an outlet that allows them to feel good about themselves?

better, more "high-tech," and more luxurious our possessions, we may subconsciously conclude, the better *we* are.

The Social Self   Your **social self** is that part of you that interacts with others. William James believed that you have as many social selves as you have people who recognize you and that you change who you are depending on the friend, family member, colleague, or acquaintance with whom you are interacting. For example, when you talk to your best friend, you are willing to "let your hair down" and reveal more thoughts and feelings than you might in a conversation with your communication professor, your parents, or your boss. Each relationship that you have with another person is unique because you bring to it a unique social self. This means that you are multifaceted, not false with people, because you have different selves in relation to different people.

social self
Your concept of self as developed through your personal, social interactions with others.

RECAP

William James's Dimensions of Self

Dimension	Definition	Examples
Material Self	The physical elements that reflect who you are	The self you reveal through your body, clothes, car, home
Social Self	A variety of selves that change in situations and roles, reflected in your interactions with others	Your informal self interacting with friends; your formal self interacting with your professors
Spiritual Self	Introspections about values, morals, and beliefs	Belief or disbelief in God; regard for life in all its forms

The self-concept we develop through communication with our family stays with us throughout our life.

The Spiritual Self   Your **spiritual self** consists of all your internal thoughts and introspections about your values and moral standards. It is not dependent on what you own or with whom you talk; it is the essence of who you *think* you are and of your *feelings* about yourself. It is a mixture of your spiritual beliefs and your sense of who you are in relationship to other forces in the universe. It is your attempt to understand your inner essence, whether you view that essence as consciousness, spirit, or soul. Your spiritual self is the part of you that attempts to answer the question, "Why am I here?"

How the Self-Concept Develops

Some psychologists and sociologists have advanced theories that suggest we learn who we are through four basic means: (1) our communication with other individuals, (2) our association with groups, (3) roles we assume, and (4) our self-labels.

Communication with Others   A valued colleague of ours often says, when he teaches communication courses, that every time you lose a relationship you lose an opportunity to see yourself. What he means is that we don't come to know and understand ourselves in a vacuum. We learn who we are by communicating with others, receiving their feedback, making sense out of it, and internalizing or rejecting all or part of it, such that we are altered by the experience. For example, let's say you like to think of yourself as a real comedian. Now think about it for a moment: How would you know you were funny if it were not for others laughing at humorous things you say or do? Sure, you can crack yourself up, but the real test of whether you're funny or not is how others react to you.

In 1902, scholar Charles Horton Cooley first advanced the notion that we form our self-concepts by seeing ourselves in a figurative looking glass: We learn who we are by interacting with others, much as we look into a mirror and see our reflection.[12] Like Cooley, George Herbert Mead, author of *Mind, Self, and Society,* also believed that our sense of who we are is a consequence of our relationships with others.[13] So when we form new relationships and sustain the old ones, we gain opportunities to know ourselves better.

Interpersonal communication scholar John Stewart describes four characteristics of the self or one's identity.[14] First, identities are multidimensional and changing. Human beings are complex. Some of a person's aspects are stable, such as his or her ge-

spiritual self
Your concept of self, based on your thoughts and introspections about your values and moral standards.

Ethics and Communication

Cyber Selves

One of the values most people hold dear is honesty—a critical dimension in successful relationships. From interpersonal communication texts to self-help advice columns to *The Oprah Winfrey Show,* all stress the importance of honesty in conveying who you are to others. But are there any grey areas when it comes to honesty in an Internet interaction?

Whether you're in a chat room or e-mailing someone you met in cyberspace, the potential for identity exploration is very real. You can become anyone you want to be through cyber-communication, altering your sex, age, race, looks, nationality, and occupation as you describe them to others in order to explore alternate identities. People you communicate with on the Net can alter their identities too, so you never really know who you're talking to unless you move on to another context, like a face-to-face encounter.

In Chapter 1 we suggested three essential attributes of competent communication, the third of which was "The message should be ethical." The question is, Is it ethical to alter your identity in cyberspace—to purposefully communicate a false impression of yourself to another person over the Internet? What if the receiver of your communication believes that you are representing yourself truthfully? Is the exercise of altering your identity, of trying a different self on for size, and communicating a false sense to another person a breach of ethics? Is it wrong, or is it in a grey area in which it isn't a breach of ethics as long as no one gets hurt?

netic profile or ethnicity, but most aspects of the self are constructed and therefore fluid, meaning that identity changes because of circumstances and, primarily, our interactions and relationships with others.

Second, identity involves responsiveness to others. We do not form our sense of self in a vacuum. We come to know ourselves and construct our identities through communication with others. A third characteristic is that identities develop in both past and present relationships. Who you are today is greatly a function of your family background and relationships. Those early messages you received, nicknames you were given, and the ways family members related to you significantly influenced your view of self. While family relationships often remain important in our lives, these primary relationships may be replaced or de-emphasized, as present relationships with friends, romantic partners, classmates, and coworkers shape the self-concept and help to construct identity.

Finally, Stewart suggests that identities can be avowed and ascribed. An **avowed identity** is one you personally assign to yourself and act out, such as student, athlete, friend, and so forth. An **ascribed identity** is assigned to you by others, and you may or may not agree with the assignment. For example, a classmate may deem you an "overachiever," but you think your hard work and dedication to your studies make you a good student—an achiever, but not necessarily an over-achiever. Avowed and ascribed identities shift and are negotiated through our interactions with others.

Association with Groups   I'm a native New Yorker. I'm a soccer player. I'm a rabbi. I'm a real estate agent. I'm a member of the Young Democrats. Each of these self-descriptive statements answers the "Who am I" question by citing identification with a group or organization. Our awareness of who we are is often linked to who we associate with. How many of these kinds of group-associated terms could you use to describe yourself? Religious groups, political groups, ethnic groups, social groups, study groups, and occupational and professional groups play important roles in shaping your self-concept. Some of these groups we are born into; others we choose on our own. Either way, group associations are significant parts of our identities.

As you no doubt are aware, peer pressure is a powerful force in shaping attitudes and behavior, and adolescents are particularly susceptible to it. But adolescents are not alone in allowing the attitudes, beliefs, and values of others to shape their expectations

avowed identity
An identity you assign to yourself and act out.

ascribed identity
An identity assigned to you by others.

and behaviors. Most adults, to varying degrees, ask themselves, "What will the neighbors think? What will my family think?" when they are making choices.

Assumed Roles   A large part of most people's answers to the "Who am I" question reflects roles they assume in their lives. Mother, aunt, brother, uncle, manager, salesperson, teacher, spouse, and student are labels that imply certain expectations for behavior, and they are important in shaping self-concept.

Gender asserts a powerful influence on the self-concept from birth on. As soon as they know the sex of their child, many parents begin associating their children with a gender group by adhering to cultural rules. They give children sex-stereotypical toys, such as catcher's mitts, train sets, or guns for boys, and dolls, tea sets, and "dress-up" kits for girls. These cultural conventions and expectations play a major role in shaping our self-concept and our behavior.[15] Research indicates that up until the age of three, children are not acutely aware of sex roles. Between the ages of three and five, however, behaviors reflecting masculine and feminine roles begin to emerge (as encouraged by parents), and they are usually solidified between the ages of five and seven.[16] Research shows that by the time we reach adulthood, our self-concepts are quite distinguishable by gender, with men describing themselves more in terms of giftedness, power, and invulnerability; and women viewing themselves in terms of likability and morality.[17]

Self-Labels   Although our self-concept is deeply affected by others, we are not blank slates for them to write on. The labels we use to describe our own attitudes, beliefs, values, and actions also play a role in shaping our self-concept. Where do our labels come from? We interpret what we experience; we are self-reflexive. **Self-reflexiveness** is the human ability to think about what we're doing while we're doing it. We talk to ourselves about ourselves. We are both participants and observers in all that we do. This dual role encourages us to use labels to describe who we are.

When you were younger, perhaps you dreamed of becoming a rocker or a movie star. People along the way may have told you that you were a great musician or a terrific actor, but as you matured, you probably began observing yourself more critically. You struck out with a couple of bands; you didn't get the starring role in a local stage production. So you self-reflexively decided that you were not, deep down, a rocker or an actor, even though others may have labeled you as "talented." Sometimes, through this self-observation, we may experience a period of depression or disillusionment because who we thought we were does not pan out, and we confront the need to change. However, we may also discover strengths that encourage us to assume new labels.

self-reflexiveness
The human ability to think about what you are doing while you are doing it.

RECAP

How the Self-Concept Develops

Communication with Others	The self-concept develops as we communicate with others, receive their feedback, make sense out of it, and internalize or reject all or part of it.
Association with Groups	We develop our self-concept partly because of and through our identification with groups or organizations.
Assumed Roles	The self-concept is affected by roles we assume, such as son or daughter, employee, parent, spouse, student.
Self-Labels	The terms we use to describe our attitudes, beliefs, values, and actions play a role in shaping the self-concept.

SELF-ESTEEM: WHAT IS YOUR VALUE?

It may sound crass to consider a person's *value*, but we do this every day. Our assessment of our value as persons is termed **self-esteem.** Closely related to your self-concept, or your *description* of who you are, is your self-esteem, your *evaluation* of who you are. The term **self-worth** is often used interchangeably with self-esteem. As Gloria Steinem describes it, in her book *Revolution from Within: A Book of Self-Esteem,* "It's a feeling of 'clicking in' when that self is recognized, valued, discovered, *esteemed*—as if we literally plug into an inner energy that is ours alone, yet connects us to everything else."[18]

While the self-concept pertains to one's enduring identity, self-esteem pertains more to one's current state of mind or view of self. Self-esteem can fluctuate because of relatively minor events, such as getting a lower grade on a paper than one expected, or major upheavals, such as the break-up of an important relationship. Self-esteem can rise or fall within the course of a day; sometimes just a look from someone (or someone's failure to notice you) can send you into a tailspin and make you feel your value as a person is diminished. Or a certain level of self-esteem can last for a while—you may have a series of months or even years that you look back on and think, "Yeah; I felt pretty lousy about myself in those days. Glad that period is over." Researchers have identified four factors that provide clues about the fluctuating nature of self-esteem.

Gender

In Chapter 6 we provide a more extensive discussion of the role of sex and gender in the communication process. Research reveals that sex and gender have an impact on one's self-esteem. Before exploring that impact, let's first clarify our use of the terms *sex* and *gender,* because many people use them interchangeably, and that can lead to confusion.

One meaning for the term **sex** is the biological/physiological characteristics that make a person male or female. In another usage, *sex* can refer to sexual activity. The term used most often in this book is *gender.* In its most specific sense, gender refers to psychological and emotional characteristics of individuals that cause them to be masculine, feminine, or androgynous (having a combination of both feminine and masculine traits). Defined broadly, **gender** is a cultural construction that contains psychological characteristics but also includes your sex (being female or male), your attitudes about appropriate roles and behavior for the sexes in society, and your sexual orientation (to whom you are sexually attracted).[19] Because the term *gender* is more broad and all-inclusive, it's our preferred term in this book.

Research that has primarily focused on the development of self-esteem in childhood and adolescence docu-

---

self-esteem (self-worth)
Your assessment of your worth or value as reflected in your perception of such things as your skills, abilities, talents, and appearance.

sex
The biological and physiological characteristics that make a person female or male.

gender
A cultural construction that includes one's biological sex, psychological characteristics (femininity, masculinity, androgyny), attitudes about the sexes, and sexual orientation.

On the Web

Self-esteem is such a pervasive and important topic that there is even a national association devoted to its study. The National Association for Self-Esteem (NASE) is an organization whose purpose is, as described on its Web site, "to fully integrate self-esteem into the fabric of American society so that every individual, no matter what their age or background, experiences personal worth and happiness." The Web site for NASE offers links to books, tapes, and CDs, as well as seminars, conferences, and educational programs on topics associated with self-esteem, such as parenting strategies that help foster positive self-esteem in children. Check out the Web site at
www.self-esteem-nase.org

Supportive relationships with friends can help young girls overcome feelings of low self-esteem.

ments ways that boys' self-esteem develops differently from girls'. In a patriarchal (or male-dominated) culture, such as that of the United States, women and girls suffer loss of self-esteem to a much greater degree than men and boys.[20] A survey of 3,000 schoolchildren, conducted by the American Association of University Women, showed that self-esteem decreases between elementary grades and high school, but this decrease is significantly more pronounced in girls.[21] Myra and David Sadker, authors of the book *Failing at Fairness: How America's Schools Cheat Girls*, explain how boys experience a "self-esteem slide," while girls' self-esteem loss is a "free fall."[22]

The difference in self-esteem levels seems to pertain to such factors as boys feeling better able to do things than girls. A related factor is the reinforcement boys receive from participating in athletics, which helps them cope with changes in their bodies better than girls. But this trend has begun to change, as we witness rising participation in and appreciation for women's athletics.[23] In the summer of 1999, over 90,000 people—the largest audience to ever attend a women's sporting event—jammed a California stadium to see the U.S. women's soccer team defeat the team from China in the finals of the women's World Cup. The event drew over 4 million television spectators worldwide.[24] More professional teams for women—as well as college, university, and school teams—are being established and gaining momentum, as we continue to recognize the impact of athletic accomplishment on people's self-esteem.

Social Comparisons

One way we become more aware of ourselves and derive our sense of self-worth is by measuring ourselves against others, a process called **social comparison**.[25] I'm good at playing basketball (because I'm part of a winning team); I can't cook (because others cook better than I do); I'm good at meeting people (whereas most people seem to be uncomfortable interacting with new people); I'm not handy (but my dad can fix anything). Each of these statements implies a judgment about how well or badly you can perform certain tasks, with implied references to how well others perform the same tasks. A belief that you cannot fix a leaky faucet or cook like a chef may not in itself lower your self-esteem. But if there are *several* things you can't do or *many* important tasks that you cannot seem to master, these shortcomings may begin to color your overall sense of worth. If it seems like you're a "jack of all trades, master of none" and everyone else is a "master," your self-esteem may suffer as a result.

social comparison
Process of comparing oneself to others to measure one's worth in relationship to others who are similar.

Diversity and Communication

Self-Esteem and Ethnicity

Studies have shown that sex and gender affect self-esteem, but what other factors influence people's levels of self-esteem? Might people's ethnic or racial identity affect the way they value themselves? Research shows a positive correlation between self-esteem level and attachment to racial or ethnic groups.[26] More simply put, the more people feel committed to and positive about their ethnic group, the higher their levels of self-esteem tend to be. People who have negative attitudes about their ethnicity, who are unclear about their identification with a particular racial or ethnic group, or who are uncommitted to their racial or ethnic group tend to have lower levels of self-esteem. Additionally, people's views of their own ethnic group have more of an impact on self-esteem than other people's views, meaning that the way you identify with and view your own ethnicity has more effect on your self-esteem than the way another person views your ethnic group. All of these findings were less pronounced for persons who self-identified as white, which supports other studies showing that Caucasians often do not view "whiteness" as a racial or ethnic identity.

One powerful social comparison that contributes to self-esteem loss in girls and women is fueled by images of physical attractiveness in the media. Granted, it's easy to blame the media for society's ills as well as individual people's problems. But mediated messages are so pervasive, accessible, and influential that studies are determining a link between exposure to ads, films, TV, and Internet sources and diminished self-esteem among females. Mass media create and reinforce for consumers notions of what is considered physically attractive, and achieving that media-driven standard is next to impossible for most people.

So pervasive is the drive for physical beauty in U.S. culture that popular (and, some argue, disturbing) television programming capitalizes on this drive and on viewers' insecurities. *The Swan* and *Extreme Makeover* are but two examples of prime-time television shows that have aired in recent years, in which contestants or selected "ugly ducklings" are put through extreme physical transformations in very short time spans. These transformations often include painful nose jobs, chin implants, breast enlargements, liposuction, laser skin treatments, and rigorous short-term body-sculpting regimens. The climax of these shows occurs when contestants' "new and improved" faces and bodies are revealed to family and friends or to panels of judges who award prizes.[27]

One line of research has found that females of a wide range of ages—from preadolescents through college students—compare their own physical attractiveness to that of models in ads. When they perceive that they don't measure up, they often experience the "model trap." This trap is a continual cycle of viewing physically "perfect" models, hating them, then growing to like them, love them, followed by efforts to emulate them, failing in those efforts, resenting them again, and repeating the cycle.[28]

While this form of mediated social comparison has had a greater effect on females' than on males' self-esteem, advertisers have begun to target male consumers, too—so social comparisons to male models, and resulting self-esteem loss among males, are on the rise. In an analysis of *Men's Health* magazine, author Michelle Cottle explores increasing media attention being paid to male desires for physical beauty and effects on self-esteem. She explains, "With page after page of bulging biceps and Gillette jaws, robust hairlines and silken skin, *Men's Health* is peddling a standard of male beauty as unforgiving and unrealistic as the female version sold by those dewy-eyed pre-teen waifs draped across the covers of *Glamour* and *Elle*."[29]

It can be self-defeating to take social comparisons too far, to cause your self-esteem to suffer because you compare yourself unfairly or unrealistically to others. The wiser approach is to compare yourself to your friends and neighbors, people you know and who are similar to you in many ways, rather than to people who are obviously not like you. Expecting to be as wealthy as Microsoft Chair Bill Gates is unrealistic for most of us, so it's unwise to compare your income to his. You might, however, compare how much you make at your job with the incomes of others who have similar positions or abilities comparable to yours. A healthy sense of self-worth is derived in part from the conclusions we draw from realistic, fair comparisons.

Self-Expectations

Another factor that affects your self-esteem is an estimation of how well you accomplish your goals. **Self-expectations** are goals we set for ourselves, such as losing weight, developing a "buff" body, making better grades, being appointed or elected to an important office in an organization, graduating by a certain time, and acquiring wealth by a certain age. Self-esteem is affected when you evaluate how well you measure up to your own expectations. For instance, if you expect to receive all A's this semester and you don't achieve that, it's likely that your self-esteem will be affected negatively. You may have to readjust your goals and expectations, or just become more determined to achieve the straight-A goal next semester.

Some people place enormous expectations on themselves, probably because their parents had enormous expectations for them when they were growing up. We wish people who are stressed out all the time could give themselves a break, because they place such unrealistic, high demands on themselves. The popular achievement gurus will tell you that setting high goals is a good thing, that you will not accomplish much if you set easily attainable goals. But we are suspicious of that advice; we see too many people whose self-esteem is low because they place such pressure and unrealistic demands on themselves. When they can't live up to those demands, they feel guilty and begin to see themselves as failures. A downward trend involving expectation, failure, guilt, and low self-esteem is hard to reverse.

Self-Fulfilling Prophecy

A concept related to the creation of self-expectations is the **self-fulfilling prophecy,** the idea that what you believe about yourself often comes true because you expect it to come true. If you think you'll fail a math quiz because you have labeled yourself inept at math, then you must overcome not only your math deficiency but also your low expectations of yourself. If you hold the self-perception that you're pretty good at conversation, then you're likely to act on that assumption when you approach a conversation with someone. Your conversations, true to form, go well, thus reinforcing your belief in yourself as a good conversationalist.

Your level of self-esteem also affects the kinds of prophecies you make about yourself and colors your interpretation of events.[30] Persons with high self-esteem tend to anticipate or predict successes for themselves; they are then reinforced when they experience those successes. Conversely, persons with low self-esteem tend to interpret their successes as flukes; they attribute an achievement to luck rather than to their own efforts. Successes can enhance your self-esteem, but if you are in a downward spiral of low self-esteem, you may not recognize your own achievements to let them have a positive effect on your self-esteem.

self-expectations
Goals you set for yourself; how you believe you ought to behave and what you ought to accomplish.

self-fulfilling prophecy
The notion that predictions about one's future are likely to come true because one believes that they will come true.

RECAP

Factors Affecting Self-Esteem

Sex Differences	In male-dominated cultures, females suffer self-esteem loss to a much greater degree than men and boys, primarily as a result of males' feeling better able to do things than females.
Social Comparisons	Judgments about how well or poorly you can perform certain tasks compared to others can be self-defeating and can cause self-esteem to suffer.
Self-Expectations	Your estimation of how well you perform in comparison to your own goals or self-expectations has a profound impact on self-esteem.
Self-Fulfilling Prophecies	What you believe about yourself often comes true because you expect it to come true.

COMMUNICATION AND THE ENHANCEMENT OF SELF-ESTEEM

We know the damage low self-esteem can do to a person—it can limit her or his ability to develop and maintain satisfying relationships, to experience career successes and advancement, and to create a generally happy and contented life. But in recent years, teachers, psychologists, self-help gurus, clergy members, social workers, and even politicians have suggested that many of our societal problems stem from our collective feelings of low self-esteem. Our feelings of low self-worth may contribute to our choosing the wrong partners; becoming addicted to drugs, alcohol, sex, or gambling; experiencing problems with eating and other vital activities; and opting, in too many cases, for death over life. So we owe it to society, as well as ourselves, to develop and work to maintain a healthy sense of self-esteem, as an integral part of the process of becoming more self-aware.

While no simple list of tricks can easily transform low self-esteem into feelings of being valued and appreciated, you can improve how you think about yourself. One thing is clear from research about self-esteem: Communication is essential in the process of building and maintaining self-esteem.[31]

Engage in Positive Self-Talk

Intrapersonal communication refers to how you take in information or stimuli in your environment and make sense out of it.[32] It also involves communication within yourself—**self-talk,** or what some scholars term "inner speech."[33] Your self-concept and level of self-esteem influence the way you talk to yourself about your abilities and skills. The reverse is also true, in that your inner dialogue has an impact on both your self-concept and your level of self-esteem. One of your authors recalls a snow-skiing experience. After several unsuccessful tries to manage an archaic ski-lift contraption (not your simple chair lift), she was determined to reach the top of the slope (just so she could fall down it). She remembers actively talking to herself throughout the climb to the top, willing herself not to fall off the lift, and feeling exhilarated upon achieving even this small piece of the process. The "You can do this" self-talk helped her keep focused on the task at hand and provided positive reinforcement of her self-concept.

Although becoming your own cheerleader may not enable you to climb metaphorical mountains quite so easily, there is evidence that self-talk, both positive and negative, is related to the building and maintaining of one's self-concept.[34] Realistic, positive

intrapersonal communication
How you take in stimuli in the environment or information and make sense out of it; also, thoughts and ideas that you say to yourself.

self-talk
Inner speech; communication with the self.

self-talk can have a reassuring effect on your level of self-worth and therefore your interactions with others. Conversely, repeating negative messages about your lack of skill and ability can keep you from trying and achieving.

Positive self-talk is important in all forms of communication. When you communicate with someone, you probably also carry on an inner dialogue as you process what the other person is saying and doing and how you want to respond. In group meetings, self-talk enables group members to process the interaction. If the communication is excited or even heated, positive self-talk can motivate you to engage in the interaction, possibly offering disagreement with members' ideas. Another example of a situation that calls for positive self-talk is one that is challenging to most people—the presentational speaking context. Comedian Jerry Seinfeld commented a few years back that the number-one fear among Americans was of public speaking; people were more afraid of it than of death (which was number six). He joked that people would rather be in the coffin at a funeral than have to deliver the eulogy, or speech of tribute to the deceased.

Most speakers experience feelings that range from mild activation (feeling "jazzed" or "up" for the event) to debilitating, blinding fear. But don't worry—there are only a very few people at the upper end of the anxiety scale. When you make a presentation, you definitely need positive self-talk. You can create a negative self-fulfilling prophecy by telling yourself, "I can't do this; I won't be able to get through it. This speech is going to be lousy, and I'm going to fall flat on my face. My topic is lame; the audience will be bored and think I'm pathetic." Over years of teaching presentational speaking, we know that some students tell themselves just those kinds of negative messages.

But others have learned the power of getting "psyched" for presentations, just as an athlete would get psyched for a game or a performer for a show. These people harness the power of positive self-talk to get themselves "pumped" for a good outcome. When they hear negative messages creeping into their heads and creating self-doubt, they quash those messages before they have a chance to take hold. In any situation— from a mild challenge to the most pressure-filled circumstance you can envision—if you hear yourself start to say in your head, "I'm not sure I can do this" or "This isn't going to go well," stop right there and rephrase those statements. There's no need to completely turn the statement around ("This will be easy; a piece of cake") because you might not believe it. But simply tone down the negativity and say, "I can get through this; I'll be just fine. I CAN do this; I'll survive." While positive self-talk is not a substitute for preparation and effort, it can keep you on track by helping you focus and, ultimately, achieve your goal.

Visualize

Visualization—imagining oneself behaving in a certain way—takes the notion of self-talk one step further. Besides just telling yourself that you can achieve your goal, you can actually try to "see" yourself conversing effectively with others, performing well on a project, or exhibiting some other desirable behavior. Because the United States is such a visual culture, most of us have no trouble visualizing elaborate scenarios in our heads.

Research suggests that an apprehensive public speaker can manage her or his fears by visualizing positive results.[35] In fact, visualization reduces anxiety as well as negative self-talk or the number of debilitating thoughts that enter a speaker's consciousness.[36] If you are one of the many people who fears making presentations, try visualizing yourself walking to the front of the room, taking out your well-prepared notes, delivering a well-rehearsed and interesting presentation, and returning to your seat to the sound of applause from your audience. This visualization of positive results enhances confidence and speaking skill. The same technique can be used to boost your sense of self-worth about other tasks or skills. If you're nervous about a date, for example, visualize each step of the date (as realistically as you can). Think through what you might talk about on the date and how the night will progress. This mental re-

visualization
Technique of imagining that you are performing a particular task in a certain way; a method of enhancing self-esteem.

hearsal will help reduce your anxiety. In addition, visualizing yourself interacting or performing well can help you change long-standing feelings of inadequacy.

Reframe

The process of redefining events and experiences, of looking at something from a different point of view, is termed **reframing**. When a movie director gets different "takes" or shots of the same scene, she or he is striving to get the best work possible. The director alters small details, like camera angles or actor movements, to get yet another look or vision for a scene. Just like that movie director, you can reframe your "take" on events or circumstances that cause you to lose self-esteem.

Here's an example: If you get a report from your supervisor that says you should improve one area of your performance, instead of engaging in self-talk that says you're terrible at your job, reframe the event within a larger context. Tell yourself that one negative comment does not mean you are completely a bad employee.

Of course, you shouldn't leave negative experiences unexamined, because you can learn and profit from your mistakes. But it is important to remember that our worth as human beings is not contingent on a single *anything*—a single grade, a single failed relationship, a single response from a prospective employer, or a single play in a football game. Looking at the big picture—at the effect this one event will have on your whole life, on society, on history—places negative experiences we all have in realistic contexts.

Develop Honest Relationships

The suggestion that you develop honest relationships may sound like the latest advice from Dr. Phil, but it is actually harder to accomplish than it sounds. Think about it: How many people are in your life who really give you the straight scoop about yourself? How many people are so solid in their relationship with you that they can tell you the things that are the hardest to hear, things that no one else would dare tell you? Most of us can count the number of those people on one hand. That doesn't mean we aren't honest with the many friends and acquaintances we have in our lives, but most of us really trust only a select few enough to deal with the tough stuff.

Having at least one other person who will give you honest feedback and help you objectively reflect on your virtues and vices can be extremely beneficial in fostering healthy, positive self-esteem. As we noted earlier, other people play a major role in shaping our self-concept and self-esteem. You don't want to find yourself at a point where you're oblivious to the feedback of others. That kind of attitude can make you unrealistic and rigid, unable to adjust to life's changing circumstances. Most people who reject or overlook significant others' feedback end up isolated and with low self-esteem.

Surround Yourself with Positive People

Related to the development of honest relationships is a suggestion about the people you choose to associate with the most in your life. If you want to improve your self-esteem and to develop a more positive outlook, it's better to surround yourself with people who tend to have higher levels of self-esteem than with people who will bring you down. Granted, sometimes you don't have a choice; you get assigned a roommate in college, you end up with an instructor's choice of lab or study partner, and you rarely get to choose the people you work with. So we are not suggesting that you disassociate yourself from people who have low self-esteem, because that's unrealistic. Plus, we all suffer from bouts of low self-esteem at some time or another. People with low self-esteem need to be around uplifting people—those whose positive self-regard will rub off on them. What we mean is that it is hard enough to actively work on your self-esteem without constantly being around people with negative attitudes. Engaging in "pity parties" can lead to wallowing in poor self-esteem, which makes it doubly hard to alter that

reframing
Process of redefining events and experiences from a different point of view.

downward course. If you don't have a choice and must be around someone with low self-esteem, you can try to immunize yourself from his or her negativity—possibly by attempting to change a negative subject of conversation into a positive one.

On the Web

Some people are outgoing, others are shy. Extroverted, introverted—it takes all kinds. But shy people often struggle with self-esteem issues because it seems as though everyone around them can carry on conversations or give presentations with no problem. It's hard when you feel you have a lot to say but not the means or the confidence to say it. You probably won't be surprised to find that there are several Web sites devoted to just these kinds of problems. Two sites we visited offer particularly helpful insight into the problems of shyness and lack of self-confidence: **www.mapfornonprofits.org** and **www.managementhelp.org/prsn_wll/prsn_wll**

As an example, we know an elderly woman, Hazel, who was in good enough health to be able to help the Meals on Wheels organization deliver food to shut-ins in her town. Hazel often talked about how sour many of the people on her route were, how their attitudes had "gone south" because of poor health, limited options, and fading hope. She felt that her main purpose wasn't to deliver a hot meal but to extend the gift of her positive outlook. She often told us about how many complaints she heard in the course of one day, but she was determined to stay optimistic and to offer hope to those she visited. One time Hazel described what she viewed as a personal triumph. The most sour person on her route—a woman with very low self-esteem and a cranky disposition, one who never did anything but gripe to Hazel when she visited—began to "thaw." One day when Hazel delivered her meal, the woman actually greeted her at the front door and seemed genuinely glad to see Hazel. She complained less often as she slowly began to enjoy the warm glow of Hazel's sunny disposition and empathic responses. Hazel felt that the woman's self-esteem had begun to improve, that her outlook on life had begun to change.

So this is what we mean by surrounding yourself with positive people whenever you feel a loss of self-esteem. Misery may love company, but misery gets old quickly and can degenerate into permanent low self-esteem, sometimes without your realizing it's happening.

Lose Your Baggage

Not making the team. Getting passed over for a key promotion at work. Seeing a long-term relationship end. Feeling like a failure. We've all had experiences that we would like to undo or get a second chance at, so that we could do it differently or so that we would *be* different. We all carry around experiential or psychological "baggage," but the key question is, How much space does that baggage take up within your self-concept? To phrase this another way: How negatively is your self-esteem affected by your baggage?

Individuals with low self-esteem tend to lock on to events and experiences that happened years ago and tenaciously refuse to let go of or move past them. Looking back at what we can't change only reinforces a sense of helplessness. Constantly replaying negative experiences only serves to make our sense of self-worth more difficult to repair. As Stephen Covey explains, with regard to his Highly Effective Habit #2, "Begin with the End in Mind," self-awareness leads us to an exploration of our values. The way we are living, our "script" as Covey terms it, may not be in harmony with our values, but we have the power to change. As Covey puts it, "I can live out of my imagination instead of my memory. I can tie myself to my limitless potential instead of my limiting past. I can become my own first creator."[37]

If you were overweight as a child, you may have a difficult time accepting that who you are today is not determined by pounds you carried years ago. A traumatic or defining experience in the past has a serious impact on your self-concept; it will probably always remain a part of you. But it doesn't have to affect your current level of self-esteem. Becoming aware of changes that have occurred in your life can assist you in developing a more realistic assessment of your value. It's important to take mental inventory of experiences in your past and then decide to let go of and move past those experiences that cause your present-day self-esteem to suffer.

RECAP

Strategies for Enhancing Self-Esteem

Engage in Positive Self-Talk	If you want positive results, talk positively to yourself. If you are self-critical and negative, you may set yourself up for failure. Rephrase doubts and negative thoughts into positive, uplifting encouragement.
Visualize	In anticipation of a significant event, picture how you want the event to go, as a mental rehearsal. If you feel anxious or nervous, visualize success instead of failure.
Reframe	Try to look at experiences and events, especially those that can cause you to lose self-esteem, from a different point of view. Keep the larger picture in mind, rather than focusing on one isolated, negative incident.
Develop Honest Relationships	Cultivate friends in whom you can confide and who will give you honest feedback for improving your skills and abilities. Accept that feedback in the spirit of enhancing your self-esteem and making yourself a wiser, better person.
Surround Yourself with Positive People	Associating with persons with high self-esteem can help you enhance your own self-esteem and develop a more positive outlook.
Lose Your Baggage	Dump your psychological and experiential baggage from the past: work to move beyond the negatives of your past, so that you focus on the present and relieve your self-esteem of the burden of things you cannot change.

THE PERCEPTION PROCESS

This chapter focuses on the principle of awareness—developing greater understanding and skill by becoming more cognizant of yourself, others, and communication. In the first part of this chapter, we discussed self-concept (how we perceive ourselves) and self-esteem (how we value ourselves). We continue now by exploring how we perceive ourselves and our communication with others, as well as the many ways in which we perceive other people and their communication. But just what is perception?

On the most basic level, **perception** is the arousal of any of our senses. A sound travels through the air, vibrates in the eardrum, activates the nerves, and sends a signal to the brain. A similar sequence of events takes place when we see, smell, feel, or taste something. So perception begins with the process of attending to stimuli in the en-

perception
The arousal of any of your senses.

vironment. The process of perception also includes structuring and making sense out of information provided by the senses. You come out of a building and see wet pavement and puddles of water, hear thunder, smell a fresh odor in the air, and feel a few drops of water on your head. You integrate all those bits of information and conclude that it is raining and has been for a while.

Perceiving people, however, goes beyond the simple processing of sensory information. We try to decide what people are like, making judgments about their personalities, and we give meaning to their actions by drawing inferences from what we observe.[38] When you meet someone new, you notice certain basic attributes, like the person's sex, general aspects of physical appearance, the sound of her or his voice, whether or not he or she smiles, uses a friendly tone of voice, has an accent, and so forth. You also attend to specific details that the person communicates, verbally and nonverbally. Once you've chosen these stimuli to pay attention to, you then categorize the information into some sort of structure that works for you. Finally, you attempt to make sense out of your structured perceptions; you assign meaning to what you have perceived. Let's examine each of these three stages in the perception process.

Stage One: Attention and Selection

You are watching a group of parents at a playground with their children. The kids are playing, running around, laughing, and squealing, as children will do. You view the activity, hear the noise, feel the heat of the day on your skin, and perhaps smell hot dogs cooking on a grill. They smell so good you can almost taste them. After a moment, one of the parents who was sitting and chatting with other parents jumps up and runs over to comfort his or her child who has fallen down and is crying. You were watching the action but didn't see the particular incident and didn't register the child's cry amidst all the noise. But the child's parent did. How did this happen?

The ability of parents to discern their own child's voice from a chorus of voices is one of the mysteries of human nature, but it also exemplifies the first stage of perception. Our human senses simply cannot process all of the stimuli that are available at any given moment, so we select which sensations make it through to the level of awareness and ignore or filter out the rest. The activities of **attention** and **selection** constitute the first stage of the perception process. Have you ever listened to music in the dark, so you could eliminate visual sensations and focus only on what you were hearing? Have you ever watched TV with the sound turned off, just so you could enjoy the visual images without the "static" of sound? This is a particularly helpful strategy during televised sporting events, when the announcers continue talking over every bit of the action. (We believe this to be the original motivation for the development of the remote control's mute button.) What we're doing in these instances is selecting what we will and will not attend to.

Here's another example: Imagine a parent in a grocery store, pushing a cart with a small child sitting in it. The child wants something, so she or he says, "Mommy, I want this." When there's no reaction from the mother, the child repeats the statement, "Mommy, I want this." If there's still no response, the child will likely say the statement over and over again, increasing the volume and stressing different words each time, as in "Mommy, I WANT this." What's amazing to the casual observer is the way the parent can tune out the child's request. Sometimes, the child will repeat the phrase so many times that you want to intervene and say, "Hey, your kid's talking to you; get that thing for him (her)." But the parent has heard the child's voice many times before, so she or he finds it easy to choose not to attend to that particular stimulus.

This selectivity can also cause us to fail to perceive information that is important.[39] Jack and Jill are having an argument; Jack is so absorbed in making his points that he fails to see that Jill is crying. By selecting certain stimuli, we sometimes miss other clues that might be important, that might help us better understand what is happening and how to respond.

attention
The act of perceiving stimuli in your environment.

selection
The act of choosing specific stimuli in your environment to focus on.

Stage Two: Organization

After we select stimuli to attend to and process, we start to convert the information into convenient, understandable, and efficient patterns that allow us to make sense of what we have observed. This activity, termed **organization,** makes it easier for us to process complex information because it allows us to impose the familiar onto the unfamiliar, and because we can easily store and recall simple patterns.

Look at the three items in Figure 2.2. What does each of them mean to you? If you are like most people, you will perceive item A as a horseshoe, item B as the word *communication,* and item C as a circle. Strictly speaking, none of those perceptions is correct. For item A, you see a pattern of dots that you label a horseshoe because a horseshoe is a concept you know and to which you attach various meanings. The item really isn't a horseshoe; it could be an inverted U. It's actually a set of dots. But rather than processing a set of dots, it's much easier to organize the dots in a way that refers to something familiar. For similar reasons, we organize patterns of stars in the sky into various constellations with shapes, like the Big and Little Dippers.

In Figure 2.2, items B and C reveal our inclination to superimpose structure and consistency on what we observe. This tendency leads us to create a familiar word from the meaningless assemblage of letters in item B and to label the figure in item C a circle, even though a circle is a continuous line without any gaps. The process of filling in missing information is called **closure,** and it applies to our perceptions of people as well. When we have an incomplete picture of another human being, we impose a pattern or structure, classify the person on the basis of the information we do have, and fill in the gaps.

Perhaps you've sat in an airport or busy shopping mall watching people and tried to guess what they did for a living, what their personalities were like, or what their backgrounds were. Maybe you saw people you guessed were wealthy, hotheads, teachers, losers, athletes, loners, or surfer dudes. As you looked at people's clothing and saw how they walked or behaved, you made inferences about them. You superimposed some structure by using a general label and filling in the gaps in your information. This activity can get you into trouble, of course, but we'll save that discussion until the end of the chapter, when we focus on the problem of stereotyping.

Stage Three: Interpretation

Once we have organized stimuli, we are ready to assign meaning, a process termed **interpretation.** We attach meaning to all that we observe. In some cases, the meanings are fairly standardized, as they are for language, for example. But others are much more personalized. If you shake someone's hand and it feels like a wet, cold fish, what is your reaction and interpretation? If you notice someone you don't know staring at you from across a room, what thoughts go through your head? If a toddler is crying in a room full of people and a woman comes over and picks the child up, what do you assume about the woman? These examples all illustrate how we impose meaning on what we observe to complete the perceptual process.

organization
Converting information into convenient, understandable, and efficient patterns that allow us to make sense of what we have observed.

closure
Perceptual process of filling in missing information.

interpretation
Attaching meaning to what is attended to, selected, and organized.

FIGURE 2.2
What Do You See?

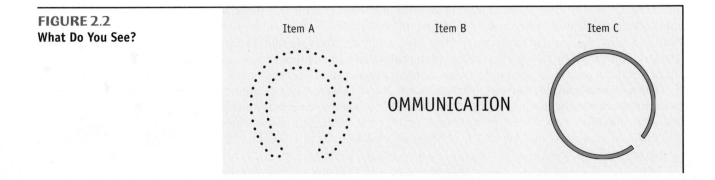

Item A   Item B   Item C

OMMUNICATION

Of course, our interpretations can be inaccurate or off-base; we may perceive a situation one way, when in fact something entirely different is occurring. For example, the final scene in the movie *Swingers* is hilarious because it illustrates the faulty nature of human interpretation. Two of the "swinging" male characters are sitting in a booth at a diner. One of them thinks that a woman several booths away is making eyes at him. She appears to be making flirtatious facial expressions and mouthing something which he interprets as a come-on. He's just about to make his move when he realizes that the woman is looking across her table at a baby in a portable carrier, positioned in the opposite side of the booth, and she's cooing and making faces at the child.

RECAP

The Perception Process

Term	Explanation	Examples
Perception	The arousal of any of our senses.	Tasting spicy food; hearing the sound of laughter; smelling smoke.
Attention and Selection	The first stage in the perception process, in which we perceive stimuli and choose which ones to focus awareness on.	Watching TV in your room while hearing giggling and laughter, and ignoring the TV show in order to eavesdrop on the giggler.
Organization	The second stage in the perception process, in which we structure stimuli into convenient and efficient patterns.	Realizing that the laughter is coming from your younger sister, who's on the phone.
Interpretation	The final stage in the perception process, in which we assign meaning to what we have perceived.	Deciding that your sister is talking on the phone to her boyfriend, because she only laughs like that when she talks to him.

COMMUNICATION AND THE ENHANCEMENT OF PERCEPTUAL ACCURACY

Our perceptions of others affect the way we communicate, just as others' perceptions of us affect the way they communicate with us. We continually modify the topics, language, and manner in which we communicate according to perceptions—ours and theirs.

Patrick sees Maria at a party and thinks she is attractive; Maria is nicely dressed and seems to be enjoying herself, laughing occasionally at a story someone is telling. Patrick thinks, "This might be someone I want to get to know," so he works his way over to join the conversation of Maria and the group she's sitting with. Maria notices Patrick coming over, because she checked him out too. However, not too long after joining the group, Patrick attempts to tell a humorous story, hoping to get a positive reaction from

*"Of course I care about how you imagined I thought
you perceived I wanted you to feel."*

Maria. Instead, he gets a cold stare from her, as though she didn't understand or appreciate his attempt at humor. Maria walks away from the conversation thinking that Patrick is rude, while Patrick decides that Maria is not as attractive as he first thought. In this example, the man and woman both formed perceptions based on minimal information. They then experienced each other in the form of a brief conversation, and that bit of communication significantly altered their original perceptions. This process happens often in daily life.

The goal in the perception process is to form the most accurate perceptions you can, because then you have better, more reliable information on which to act. So what can you do to improve your ability to form accurate perceptions? We offer three suggestions.

Increase Your Awareness

We've made this topic—awareness—our first of five communication principles for a lifetime, and we've done so for a reason. As we discuss in the next two chapters, developing your skills in perceiving and then decoding others' verbal and nonverbal communication is critical as you strengthen existing relationships and establish new ones.

Exercise your senses, especially your sense of hearing. Work at really listening to people—fully listening, without interrupting them to put in your two cents' worth. Try to be more verbally and nonverbally aware, meaning monitor how you communicate with others and how people respond to you. If you don't like the responses you're getting from people, it may be time for a change in *your* behavior, not theirs. You also want to monitor the verbal and nonverbal cues others exhibit. Pay attention to contextual cues, such as where an interaction is taking place, the time of day, the perceived moods of those interacting, and any physical or psychological barriers that impede the communication exchange. Learn from your mistakes, rather than repeat them.

The last thing anyone wants to be is a "communication clod," the kind of person who never notices things unless they're on fire. Communication clods seem to be in

Do you make any assumptions about these people based on their outfits and behavior? Should you?

their own worlds, rarely acknowledging that others exist, rarely pausing to perceive what's going on in the world around them. We suspect that all of us have known people like this. And we are all capable of clodlike behavior from time to time, but you just don't want "communication clod" to be what comes to mind when people think of you.

Avoid Stereotypes

"She's a snob." "He's a nerd." "They're a bunch of dumb jocks." All of these statements reflect **stereotypes**, or generalizations we apply to persons because we perceive them to have attributes common to a particular group.[40] Social psychologist Douglas Kenrick and his colleagues suggest that "Stereotyping is a cognitively inexpensive way of understanding others: By presuming that people are like other members of their groups, we avoid the effortful process of learning about them as individuals."[41]

What comes to mind when you hear the term *redneck?* (Maybe you think of the comedian Jeff Foxworthy, who has a repertoire of "you might be a redneck" jokes.) Do you associate with the term such qualities as being backward, ultra-conservative, or out of touch with what's happening in the world? If you perceive someone to have these qualities and you consider that person a redneck, then you have just invoked a stereotype.

First, let's examine the positive or functional aspects of stereotypes. They emerge from our human nature to simplify and categorize stimuli in our environment, which we described as components of the perception process. Further, they serve as a baseline of information. If you know nothing else about a person other than she or he is a "northerner," for instance, then you can think about commonly held characteristics of other persons you've met from the northern part of the United States and go from there. But obviously, there's a serious downside.

Have you ever taken a class and, from day one, felt that the teacher pegged you a certain way? The teacher perceived you to be a slacker or uninterested in the course topic, on the negative side, or a straight-A student or future Ph.D., on the positive side.

stereotype
Generalization applied to persons perceived to have attributes common to a particular group.

On the Web

The bottom line is that no one likes to be treated as a stereotype because it's limiting and impersonal. You can also feel pressure to try to live up to a stereotype, such as "All Asian students are exceptionally bright." Stereotypes are often degrading, as in age-old references to dumb blondes, bad women drivers, and dirty old men. Many of the worst stereotypes are related to gender, race/ethnicity, age, and physical appearance.

Scholars have been studying stereotypes for a couple of decades; some of this research explores the ways we try to inhibit stereotypical thoughts before they have a chance to affect our behavior.[42] For example, if you grew up hearing family members invoke stereotypes about different racial groups, you may decide as an adult that you will not follow suit—that inflicting racial stereotypes is inappropriate. However, because it's part of your upbringing and ingrained in you, your first thoughts may be stereotypical when you encounter someone from a racial group other than your own. You have to assert mental control to suppress the stereotypical thoughts. But researchers have found that this suppression actually has the opposite effect than desired, in that stereotypical thoughts are highly likely to reappear subsequently with even stronger intensity, what the researchers term a "rebound effect."[43] So it may be better never to let stereotypes form into expectations, rather than trying to rid ourselves of harmful stereotypical thinking after the fact.

In Chapter 3, we explore language that reveals stereotypical thoughts. In Chapter 6, when we discuss the skill of adapting communication to our listeners, we revisit the topic of stereotypes. For now, just remember that there's nothing inherently wrong with a stereotype, as a baseline of information. But the rigid way we enforce a stereotype, the expectations we form based on the stereotype, and our ensuing communication toward the stereotyped person are problematic.

Check Your Perceptions

You can check the accuracy of your perceptions and attributions indirectly and directly, so that you increase your ability to perceive things and people and respond to them effectively. **Indirect perception checking** involves an intensification of your own perceptual powers. You seek additional information to either confirm or refute your interpretations of someone's behavior. If you suspect that your romantic partner wants to end your relationship, for instance, you are likely to look for cues in his or her tone of voice, eye contact, and body movements to confirm your suspicion. You will probably also listen more intently and pay attention to the language your partner chooses to use. The information you gain is "checked" against your original perceptions.

Direct perception checking involves asking straight out whether your interpretations of a perception are correct. You can accomplish this in two ways: asking people directly for their interpretations of their own actions or asking other observers for their "take" on a situation (going to a third or outside party). Asking people directly is often more difficult than asking a third party for an interpretation. For one thing, we don't like to admit uncertainty or suspicions to others; we might not trust that they will respond honestly. And if our interpretations are wrong, we might suffer embarrassment or anger. But asking someone to confirm a perception shows that you are committed to understanding his or her behavior. If your friend's voice sounds weary and her posture is sagging, you may assume that she is depressed or upset. If you ask, "I get the feeling from your tone of voice and the way you're acting that you are kind of down and depressed; what's wrong?" your friend can then either provide another interpretation: "I'm just tired; I had a busy week"; or expand on your interpretation: "Yeah, things haven't been going very well. . . ." Your observa-

indirect perception checking
Using your own perceptual abilities to seek additional information to confirm or refute your interpretations of someone's behavior.

direct perception checking
Asking someone else whether your interpretations of what you perceive are correct.

tion might also be a revelation: "Really? I didn't realize I was acting that way. I guess I am a little down."

We have found over our years as professors that perception checking with our colleagues, as well as with family members and trusted friends, is an invaluable tool, particularly when emotions are involved. It can be very helpful to discuss situations with other people, to get their input as to what happened, why it happened, how they would feel about it if it happened to them, and what you might do about it. This is especially advisable in work settings, when the wisdom of someone else's perceptions can save you professional embarrassment or prevent you from losing your job because of an emotional or rash reaction. So we highly advocate seeking out the wise counsel of trusted colleagues. The "Can I run something by you?" strategy gives you a broader perspective and a basis of comparison.

PRINCIPLES FOR A LIFETIME: Enhancing Your Skills

Aware

Principle One: Be aware of your communication with yourself and others.

- Becoming aware of yourself, as you develop your self-concept, involves communicating with others, associating with groups with whom you identify, assuming social roles, and selecting self-labels that describe who you are.
- Inventory yourself for any negative self-fulfilling prophecies that can be detrimental to your self-esteem.
- Engage in positive intrapersonal communication, or self-talk, because a heightened awareness of how you talk to yourself can help you enhance self-esteem.
- Develop your perceptual abilities by becoming more aware of yourself and others.

SUMMARY

This chapter is devoted to the first communication principle for a lifetime: *Be aware of your communication with yourself and others.* Self-awareness is a process that continues throughout life, as we perceive and come to understand our own existence in the social world. The way we view ourselves is termed self-concept, which includes our attitudes, beliefs, and values. William James viewed the self as containing three components: The material self includes our bodies and those tangible possessions that give us identity. The social self is the part that engages in interaction with others. The spiritual self consists of thoughts and assumptions about values, moral standards, and beliefs about forces that influence our lives.

The self-concept develops through our interactions with other people and the groups with which we associate. The roles we assume are important in our view of self; they provide labels for who we are.

Self-concept, or who you think you are, and self-esteem, your evaluation of your self-worth, affect how you interact with others. Your gender has an effect on your self-esteem. When you compare yourself to others, especially others who are different from you, your self-esteem can be affected either positively or negatively. Your view of your own worth is also affected by those expectations or goals you set for yourself and how close you come to achieving them. You may set a goal for yourself that ends up creating a self-fulfilling prophecy. You may believe something about yourself and act in a way that reinforces that belief, and the cycle continues.

It is difficult to alter your self-esteem, but various techniques can prove helpful: engaging in positive self-talk, visualizing success instead of failure, avoiding inappropriate comparisons with others, reframing events and relationships from a different perspective, developing honest relationships with others, surrounding yourself with uplifting people, and letting go of the past by losing old baggage.

This chapter also pointed out that perception is the process of taking in stimuli through our senses, and it involves three components: attention and selection, organization, and interpretation. Our perceptions of others affect how we communicate, and how others perceive us affects how they communicate with us. If you want to increase your powers of perception, so that you develop greater sensitivity and awareness, you first need to pay greater attention to things and people around you. Observe with more detail over time, so that you take in more data. Second, when you're in the organizing stage of perception, avoid imposing stereotypes on people or trying to fit them into rigid categories, such that you expect certain behavior and exert pressure on individuals to behave as expected. Finally, conduct indirect and direct perception checks to determine the accuracy of your "take" on people and situations.

Discussion and Review

1. Why is self-awareness critical to the development of communication skill? How can you tell a self-aware communicator from those who are not self-aware?

2. What makes up the material self? The social self? The spiritual self?

3. What is the difference between your self-concept and your self-image? Between your self-concept and your self-esteem?

4. Do you believe that your gender and your self-esteem are related? Why or why not?

5. Have you known or do you know someone who has experienced a self-fulfilling prophecy? How did this affect your or the person's communication and general behavior?

6. If you lost some self-esteem because of an event, circumstance, or person's actions, which of the techniques in this chapter would help you regain your self-esteem?

7. Imagine that you're attending a sporting event. Describe how the three stages of perception affect the way you process the action.

8. Think of occasions when you've directly checked your perceptions with others. Did the perception checks change your perspective?

Putting Principles into Practice

1. On a sheet of paper write down major things you know to be true of yourself. For example, you might start with your values and write down, "I am an honest person." Include positive and negative attributes that you're aware of in your personality. After you've generated as many items as possible, review the list and see if it encapsulates your self-concept.

2. Have you ever needed the power of positive self-talk and visualization to get you through a particular experience? (For example, probably everyone has had a nerve-racking first date experience.) What kind of self-talk is helpful in such a situation? How can visualization help increase your self-confidence in a high-pressure situation such as a first date?

3. With a small group of classmates, venture outside the building where your class meets and conduct a perceptual experiment. Watch people passing by on their way to classes or as they leave campus. Decide as a group to focus on certain individuals and then discuss your differing perceptions of them. How do you each perceive the physical appearance of people you see? What clues do their nonverbal behaviors give about their personalities? Do you invoke any stereotypes as you discuss different people?

4. Generate statements that reveal common stereotypes about people in the following groups. Try to generate stereotypes that reflect positive as well as negative perceptions. We provide a couple of examples, just to get you started. Then focus on the damage that stereotypes can do to someone's self-esteem. Also, think about how your communication with someone from each group might be affected by stereotypes.

Group	Positive Stereotype	Negative Stereotype
elderly	Old people are wise.	Old people can't fend for themselves.
women	Women are naturally more loving and nurturing than men.	Women are terrible drivers.

Group	Positive Stereotype	Negative Stereotype
men		
blondes		
overweight people		
people of Irish descent		
athletes		
southerners		
politicians		
environmentalists		
tax accountants		
librarians		
professors		

The difference between the right word and the almost right word is the difference between lightning and the lightning bug.

Mark Twain

Adolf Fenyes, "Brother and Sister." National Gallery, Budapest/ET Archive, London/©SuperStock.

Understanding Verbal Messages

CHAPTER OUTLINE

Why Focus on Language?

The Nature of Language

The Power of Words

Confronting Bias in Language

Using Words to Establish
   Supportive Relationships

Summary

CHAPTER OBJECTIVES

After studying this chapter, you should be able to:

1. Describe the relationship between words (symbols) and meaning.

2. Explain the difference between denotative and connotative meanings people develop for words.

3. Explain the difference between concrete and abstract meanings of words.

4. Define culture-bound words and context-bound words.

5. Identify four primary ways in which words have power.

6. Describe the major ways in which biased language reveals attitudes about race, ethnicity, nationality, and religion.

7. Provide examples of language that reflects bias related to gender and sexual orientation.

8. Explain how biased language reveals attitudes about age, class, and ability.

9. Explain the difference between supportive and defensive ways to relate to others.

"yo will u plz help me? i can't make my dude get that i like him"
"i want 2 b yur friend bc yur funny"

If you understand the two sentences above, you probably do a lot of online chatting (instant messaging) or e-mailing, so you're familiar with and comfortable using a form of shorthand that makes computer-mediated communication faster. These adaptations of the English language are becoming more popular in everyday communication; for example, successful pop star Avril Lavigne titled one of her hit songs "Sk8rboi." However, parents and teachers alike have become concerned about the effects of such language shortcuts on students' writing ability and communication skills in general. Not only are words shortened, often by the omission of vowels, but numbers are substituted for letters, grammar rules are ignored, and standard punctuation and capitalization all but disappear. Some college professors of English composition courses have found it necessary to "un-teach Internet-speak," because students transfer online language shorthand to their written work.[1] A persistent use of slang may be fine when instant messaging with friends, but when it becomes such a habit that it slips into other written or oral communication—especially at inappropriate moments (like calling a potential boss at a job interview "dude")— then you've got a problem. When it comes to different uses of language, the key is to be able to develop "code-switching" abilities, meaning that you use more standard or formal language when appropriate (as in college papers, professional resumés, and job interviews) and relegate the shortcuts and "slanguage" to informal online chats, e-mail, and conversations with friends who translate.[2]

Before diving into our discussion of language, let's review for a moment. Figure 3.1 depicts our five core principles of communication. In Chapter 2, where we discussed the first of our five principles for a lifetime, we explored ways to become more aware of yourself and your perceptions of things and people with whom you come into contact. An important step in this process of coming to know and understand yourself better is an honest, insightful examination of how you talk. How do you come across when meeting someone new? When talking with your best friends? What kind of communicator do your closest friends and family members think you are? How would they describe the way you talk?

Consider this: What you say is who you are. That may sound like a strong statement, but it is true that the words you use reveal who you are. Granted, you commu-

FIGURE 3.1
Communication Principles for a Lifetime

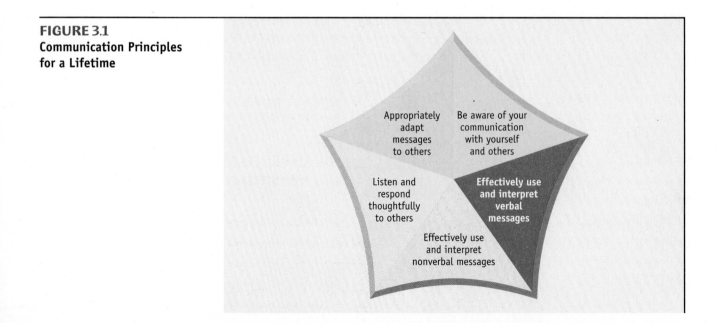

The late Barbara Jordan, former Congresswoman from Texas, recognized that language can be a powerful tool to help us exert influence and enhance our relationships.

nicate with more than your words. Your background, culture, values, experiences, and the way you express yourself nonverbally reveal who you are as well. But as we explore the power of words, we challenge you to think about the incredible tool you have at your disposal: verbal communication. Take an inventory of your use of language as you read this chapter. Do you use language that accurately and effectively represents to other people who you are? Do some areas need improvement? Because of the tremendous potential of verbal communication—its power to reveal the self, to make and break relationships and careers, and to shape cultures—we've chosen to make this one of our five key principles for a lifetime.

WHY FOCUS ON LANGUAGE?

On occasion, we do stop to consider the effects of our language on others—usually when we're attempting to persuade or we've said something that has injured or angered someone else. We've all been in situations that made us wish we could get a conversational second chance or a "take two." But it's important to keep in mind that every time we speak, every time we use language, we are revealing our thoughts, our very selves to others—no matter how inane, superficial, or emotion-laden the conversation.

One of our main messages in this chapter is this: *Words are powerful.* They affect your emotions, thoughts, actions, and relationships. They affect how you are perceived by others. In fact, recent interviews with employers revealed their concern about college graduates' lack of language skills, attributed to growing up in a culture that is more a visual one, which stresses nonverbal cues, than an oral one, which stresses language.[3] Their concern is that students' verbal skills, including both speaking and writing, are underdeveloped. This is clearly a negative trend, in light of other research that has determined that one's ability to use words to effectively participate in conversation with others is a key component in judgments about one's competence as a communicator. In this study, people who talked less in conversation were perceived by others as

On the Web

being less interpersonally skilled, compared to people who comfortably and actively engaged in conversation.[4] If you better understand the nature and power of language, if you attend to your use of language and work to use words with forethought and skill, you can exert great influence and enhance your relationships.

Our second main theme in this chapter is this: *You choose language.* You do not use language involuntarily, in the way that your knee might jerk when rapped with a doctor's mallet as an involuntary reflex to a stimulus. You choose the language you use—even if you make that choice in the split second it takes your brain to select a symbol (word) to communicate your thought or impulse. At times we go into "default mode," choosing language we've chosen before. We are prone to patterns in our language because, as humans, we prefer regularity. We also choose particular words because we like them, they've worked well for us in the past, or we grew up with those words and have used them for many years. But pattern and history can breed too much comfort, preventing you from asking yourself, "Is this the best way to say this? Should I say this another way?" You have an incredible wealth of words from which to choose, and the power to make choices that allow you to communicate who you are to others in the most effective way possible.

Our goal in this chapter is to help you improve your ability to choose and use words effectively, as well as to interpret the verbal communication of others. To accomplish that goal we explore the nature of language, the power of words, and ways to expose subtle and not-so-subtle bias in language—bias that can inhibit your ability to present yourself to others in a manner you desire. Finally, we examine the role of verbal communication in establishing supportive relationships.

THE NATURE OF LANGUAGE

A **language** is a system of symbols (words or vocabulary) structured by grammar (rules and standards) and syntax (patterns in the arrangement of words) common to a community of people. Australian communication scholar Dale Spender explains that language is "our means of ordering, classifying, and manipulating the world. It is through language that we become members of a human community, that the world becomes comprehensive and meaningful, that we bring into existence the world in which we live."[5] That last phrase is particularly important, because it suggests that the very words we use help create our world.

One supposition about language relates to this notion of creating existence. Two language researchers, Edward Sapir and Benjamin Lee Whorf, developed what has come to be known as the Sapir–Whorf Hypothesis.[6] This hypothesis suggests that human language and thought are so interrelated that thought is actually rooted in and controlled by language. One implication of the supposition is that you cannot conceive of something for which you have no word. As a fascinating illustration of what we mean by this, take the case of a speech therapist visiting an Indian tribe. When he noticed that very few Indians in the tribe stuttered, he also discovered that their language had no word for stuttering. He concluded that few people in the tribe had this affliction because it never entered their minds as a possibility.[7]

Words dictate and limit the nature of our reality. To extend the theory further, one could argue that the quality of one's language reflects the quality of one's thought. More simply, your verbal communication reveals how you think and what you think about. This is only one explanation for how language and thought operate in human beings, but it is a provocative notion to consider that language has such a powerful influence on our everyday thinking processes.

language
System of symbols (words or vocabulary) structured by rules (grammar) and patterns (syntax) common to a community of people.

Diversity and Communication

Words across the Country

Cultural diversity emerges because of the existence of co-cultures, or groups within a larger culture. The United States is a huge country, with many different co-cultures. Persons with disabilities, the elderly, Asian Americans, and gays and lesbians are examples of co-cultural groups within the larger United States culture. Another form of diversity that is less often researched and discussed results from regional differences. *Bypassing*, or differences in meanings or usages of certain words among persons from various regions of the country, is quite interesting to explore.

For example, one college student from Texas lived across the hall in a campus dormitory from a woman from Kansas. One night when the communal bathroom facilities stopped working,

the Texan told the Kansan, "Don't go down the hall right now—the commodes are stopped up." Later, the Kansan came by the Texan's room and said, "Why didn't you tell me the toilets weren't working?" They finally realized that the Kansan's meaning for the word *commode* was a small table built low to the ground; the Texan would never have used the term *toilet*. So the miscommunication had to do with a simple difference in meaning of one word.

Because we are such a mobile society now, you will no doubt encounter language differences as you move about the country or as you meet people from other areas who have moved to where you live. It's important to be aware of the potential for language differences right here in our own country, even if English is most Americans' first language.

People Use Words as Symbols

As we noted in Chapter 1, words are **symbols** that represent something else. Just as a flag is a symbol of a country, words are symbols that trigger thoughts, concepts, or feelings. For instance, what comes to mind when you see or hear the word *poverty?* The word may conjure up in your mind's eye a homeless person begging for change on the street corner or televised images of starving children in third-world countries. Or perhaps you envisioned your own lighter-than-you'd-like wallet.

People Attach Meanings to Words

Now imagine that you use the word *poverty* in a conversation, in an effort to convey to the other person the concept or image in your mind. You know what you're thinking when you say the word; the challenge is for the other person to understand your thoughts behind your choice of word. In communication terms, this is the process of creating **meaning.** The meaning of a word is a person's interpretation of that symbol—it is how the person makes sense of the symbol. Meanings don't reside in the words themselves but in the ways in which communicators use the words. You attach a meaning to the word *poverty*, the symbol you choose in conversation; your listener creates meaning for the word when he or she attempts to interpret what you've said. Words aren't the culprits in communication problems; the meanings people create for words lead to successful or problematic communication.

Sometimes the speaker's and the receiver's meanings do not correspond because the same words mean different things to different people; the term for this communication problem is **bypassing.** For example, have you ever found yourself at odds with someone because you had a different sense of what it meant to arrive "early" or "late" to an event? For some, getting there "early" means arriving at least a half an hour before the event begins; for some, "early" means right on time. Being "late" can mean different things to different people as well. Some heated arguments can be boiled down to a simple difference in meaning.

People Create Denotative and Connotative Meanings for Words

As we have said, language is a vehicle through which we share with others our sense of the world and who we are. Through language we convert our experience into sym-

symbol
A word, sound, gesture, or visual image that represents a thought, concept, object, or experience.

meaning
A person's interpretation of a symbol.

bypassing
A communication problem that arises when the same words mean different things to different people.

Frank and Ernest

bols and then use the symbols to share that experience. But as you learned in Chapter 1, the process of symbol sharing through language is not just a simple process of uttering a word and having its meaning clearly understood by another. Messages convey both content and feelings. So people create meanings for language on two levels: the denotative and the connotative.

The **denotative meaning** of a word conveys content. Denotation is the restrictive or literal meaning of a word. For example, one dictionary defines *apartment* as "a room or suite of rooms used as a residence."[8] This definition is a literal, or denotative, definition of the word *apartment;* it describes what the word means in U.S. culture.

By contrast, the **connotative meaning** of a word conveys feelings; people create personal and subjective meanings for words. Using the example above, to you, the word *apartment* might mean a comfortable place to relax at the end of the day or a setting in which to entertain friends. To others, though, the word *apartment* might engender feelings of guilt (if the apartment hasn't been cleaned in a while) or feelings of dread (if apartment rent is draining the wallet or relationships with roommates leave something to be desired). Clearly, the connotative level of language is more individual. While the denotative or objective meaning of the word *apartment* can be found in any dictionary, your subjective response to the word is probably not contained there.

People Convey Concrete and Abstract Meanings through Words

Meanings for words can be placed along a continuum from concrete to abstract. A word's meaning is **concrete** if we can experience what the word refers to (the referent) with one of our senses; if we can see it, touch it, smell it, taste it, or hear it, then it's concrete. If we cannot do these things with the referent, then the word's meaning is **abstract.** In general, the more concrete the language, the easier it is for others to understand. The more abstract a word, the more difficult it is to understand or agree on a meaning. For example, the word *patriotism* is abstract because we cannot hear or taste patriotism. But a word that suggests a demonstration of patriotism, such as voting, is more concrete, because we can physically perform the act of voting. It's wise to minimize the use of abstract words when you're trying to clarify a message. Concrete terms help make a message more clear.

Meanings Are Culture Bound

Culture is a learned system of knowledge, behavior, attitudes, beliefs, values, rules, and norms that is shared by a group of people and shaped from one generation to the next.[9] The meaning of a word, just like the meaning of any symbol, can change from culture to culture. To a European, for example, a *Yankee* is someone from the United States; to a player on the Boston Red Sox, a *Yankee* is an opponent; and to an American from the South, a *Yankee* is someone from the North. A few years ago, General Motors sold a car called a *Nova.* In English, *nova* means "bright star" and in Latin, *nova* means "new"— both appropriate connotations for a car. In Spanish, however, the spoken

---

denotative meaning
Restrictive, or literal, meaning of a word.

connotative meaning
Personal and subjective meaning of a word.

concrete meaning
Meaning that refers to something that can be perceived with one of the senses.

abstract meaning
Meaning that refers to something that cannot be perceived or experienced with one of the senses.

culture
A learned system of knowledge, behavior, attitudes, beliefs, values, rules, and norms that is shared by a group of people and shaped from one generation to the next.

word *nova* sounds like the words *no va,* which translates, "It does not go." As you can imagine, this name was not a great sales tool for the Spanish-speaking market.

Meanings Are Context Bound

A lot of people quoted in the media can be heard to say later, when questioned or interviewed, "My comments were taken out of context." We now have a term for a short statement that summarizes the essence of a longer message—the "soundbite." When you lift only a small piece of the greater text of what people have said, you take their words out of context. This practice can confuse and misrepresent a speaker's original message. Your English or communication teacher has undoubtedly cautioned you that taking something out of context changes its meaning. The meanings people attach to symbols are affected by situations. The statement, "That car is really bad," could mean that the car is a piece of junk or, in contemporary slang, a really great car. We need to know the context in order to decipher a communicator's specific meaning.

RECAP

The Nature of Language

- People use words as *symbols:* Symbols represent something else.
- People create *meanings* for words: Meaning is a person's interpretation of a symbol.
- Words have both *denotative* and *connotative* meanings: The denotative meaning is a restrictive, or literal, meaning; the connotation is a personal and subjective meaning.
- People convey *concrete* and *abstract* meanings through words: A word's meaning is concrete if we can experience what the word refers to with one of our senses; if not, then the meaning is abstract.
- Meanings are *culture bound:* The meaning of a word can change from culture to culture.
- Meanings are *context bound:* The situation or context for communication aids people as they attach meanings to symbols.

THE POWER OF WORDS

No doubt we've all heard the old schoolyard chant, "Sticks and stones may break my bones, but words can never hurt me." We don't know who first came up with that statement, but we imagine it to be someone who never experienced the sting of name-calling, the harmful effects of being labeled a "slow reader" or the legacy of an unfortunate family nickname. Words *do* hurt. They have the power to evoke a wide range of emotions in listeners. But words can also heal and inspire and transform the human spirit. Let's explore a few of the powerful attributes of words.

The Power to Create and Label Experience

How many diseases or medical conditions can you think of that are named after the person who discovered the condition? Some that come to mind include Alzheimer's, Parkinson's, and Tourette Syndrome. While you might not want your name associated with a disease, the point is that the name for a phenomenon labels the experience, thus

Studies show that people who describe their world in optimistic terms during their youth often enjoy good health in later life.

making it more real. It also etches it into history. As the English language continues to evolve, so does the need to name and describe new phenomena. For example, the term *sexual harassment* did not emerge until the 1970s; it was generated by feminists who wanted a term to correspond to a very real behavior many people experienced in the workplace.[10] Words give us tools to create and understand our world by naming and labeling what we experience.

Words also give us symbolic vehicles to communicate our creations and discoveries to others. As another example, when you label something "good" or "bad," you use language to create your own vision of how you experience the world. If you tell a friend that the movie you saw last night was vulgar and obscene, you not only provide your friend with a film critique, you also communicate your sense of what is appropriate and inappropriate.

One theorist believes that you also create your moods and emotional states with the words you use to label your feelings.[11] If you get fired from a job, you might say that you feel angry and helpless or liberated and relieved. The first response might lead to depression and the second to happiness. One fascinating study conducted over a 35-year period found that people who described the world in pessimistic terms when they were younger were in poorer health during middle age than those who had been optimistic.[12] Your words and corresponding outlook have the power to affect your mental, emotional, and physical health.

The Power to Affect Thoughts and Actions

A line from a Shakespearean tragedy reads, "That which we call a rose by any other name would smell as sweet." Would it really? If the name for this fragrant flower were

Technology *and* Communication

Minding Your Manners, Even on the Net

If you have access to a computer, it's highly likely that you have used e-mail. It has become the communication channel of choice for many people, but there are some important differences between e-mail and other forms of communication.

In a column for the *Houston Chronicle,* Jim Barlow discusses e-mail etiquette that goes beyond the basic rules—like using all caps means you're shouting or being emphatic.[13] He stresses that, just as with other more personal forms of communication, we should take the time to think before we hit the reply button in response to an e-mail message. Because of the impersonality of e-mail, many people communicate electronically in ways they wouldn't dare in person. A couple of Barlow's suggestions relate to appropriate language; the first is to remember your manners:

I've noticed over the years that people are often incredibly rude in e-mail. Ask yourself, would you say that in person? If the answer is no, then why are you sending it via e-mail? Over the years when I've gotten a nasty e-mail, I've sometimes called the person and pleasantly asked if he or she realized just how insulting that message sounded after it was read aloud. A couple of times my correspondent said indeed, that was why it was sent. But for the most part, there was simply an embarrassed silence.

Barlow also discusses bandwidth, meaning the number of cues in a form of communication that help listeners discern meaning. Face-to-face conversation has the greatest bandwidth; e-mail has the least. Barlow contends that the greater the bandwidth, the better the understanding. So he suggests that complicated subjects are best discussed in person, with a full range of verbal and nonverbal cues. Telephone communication is the next-best medium for discussing complicated topics, and e-mail has the greatest potential for misunderstanding.

Because of the ease and dazzle of technology, we sometimes forget to select the channel of communication that will best serve our purposes. E-mail may be a highly expedient means of communicating, but it may not be the best of all possible choices.

"aardvark," would it still be the flower of people in love? Can you imagine getting a delivery of a dozen long-stemmed red aardvarks?

Some of you who are reading this text may be old enough to remember a weight-loss product called Ayds. Ayds were small, brown, chewy squares that helped reduce one's appetite (or so the manufacturers claimed). You can guess why this product disappeared in the 1980s; if it is still on the market, it has certainly been renamed. Given what we now know about the threat of the deadly disease AIDS, who today would willingly ingest a product with a same-sounding name? Advertisers have long known that the way a product is labeled greatly affects the likelihood that consumers will buy it. So words affect the way we think about things and react to them.

Words not only have the power to affect how we think about and respond to something, they also affect policy and procedures. Consider the story about a young FBI agent who was put in charge of the supply department. In an effort to save money, he reduced the size of memo paper. One of the smaller sheets ended up on Director J. Edgar Hoover's desk. Hoover didn't like the small size and wrote on the narrow margin of the paper, "Watch the borders." For the next six weeks, it was extremely difficult to enter the United States from Canada or Mexico.

The Power to Shape and Reflect Culture

If an impartial investigator from another culture were to study a transcript of all of your spoken utterances last week, what would she or he learn about you and the culture in which you live? If you frequently used words like *CD* and *rollerblades*, the investigator would know that these things are important to you. But he or she might not know what you mean if these things are not also part of her or his culture.

You have grown up within a culture; you've learned the language of that culture. And the way you use the language, the words and meanings you choose as well as the way you interpret others' communication, has the effect of shaping your culture. For example, author Devorah Lieberman recounts a story of one of her students who was a professional translator of Japanese and English.[14] On one occasion when this student was translating for an American speaker to a Japanese audience, the speaker began with "humorous" anecdotes about his experiences in Japan. The translator's version of these anecdotes was, "The speaker is telling phrases that are considered funny in English but not in Japanese. I will tell you when he is finished so that you can laugh."

Co-cultures (cultural groups within a larger culture) also develop unique languages of their own as a way of forging connections and enhancing solidarity. For example, some gays and lesbians have reclaimed the once derogatory term *queer* and altered its meaning so that it's now a term of pride. Perhaps you have seen or heard of the cable television show *Queer as Folk*. Gang languages and symbols are also means of establishing an identity unique from other groups. This principle can even extend to just two people in a romantic relationship who develop nicknames or other forms of language as secret codes. They don't dare use that language in the company of others; the privacy of the language and their shared experiences create a sort of microculture—a culture of two.

The Power to Make and Break Relationships

Probably all of us have had the experience of saying something foolish, ridiculous, or embarrassing to another person. It seems that one of life's cruel ironies is the potential for human beings to say things they later regret. But if you've ever said something so inappropriate that it cost you a relationship—either one that didn't get off the ground or one that ended because of what you said—then you know firsthand the power of words to make and break relationships. For example, people in love sometimes overstate things when they get emotional. That's understandable. But it's wise to try to avoid word barriers, such as **polarization**—the tendency to describe things in extremes or opposites without any middle ground. You might hear one romantic partner say to the

polarization
The tendency to describe things in extremes, as though no middle ground exists.

other, "You either love me or you don't." These kinds of pronouncements can make people feel controlled, as though there are only two options and no compromise position. President George W. Bush was both praised and criticized for stating in his post–September 11, 2001, speech to Congress, "You're either with us or you're with the terrorists."

RECAP

The Power of Words

Words . . .

- *Create and Label Experience:* New experiences may lead to new words. For example, a personal connection that forms over the Internet can be called a "cybership"— a combination of the terms "cyberspace" and "relationship."
- *Affect Thoughts and Actions:* Words influence how we think. For instance, product names are critical to audience response and sales success. The critically acclaimed film *The Shawshank Redemption* was a box office failure, which some attributed to the film's obtuse title.
- *Shape and Reflect Culture:* Cultures change; language both creates and reflects the changing nature of culture.
- *Make and Break Relationships:* Verbal communication creates opportunities for us to know and be known by others. It is a primary tool for establishing relationships and deepening them; it can also be the reason a relationship ends.

CONFRONTING BIAS IN LANGUAGE

We don't want to sound like the "language police"— that is, we don't want to dictate to you how you ought to talk. But we have found that oftentimes insensitive or stereotypical language usage arises out of ignorance or a lack of education. Even well-meaning, educated people can communicate bias through the language they choose to use. Words that reflect bias toward members of other cultures or groups can create barriers for listeners. In addition, such language ignores the fact that the world is constantly changing.

Also, this is not a lesson in how to be "P.C." The term *political correctness* with regard to language is an unfortunate contemporary label for something communication instructors have taught for decades—the use of language that doesn't exclude or

---

Ethics *and* **Communication**

Ebonics or "Standard" English?

*I*n the late 1990s, a controversy arose over the teaching of and tolerance for ebonics in schools. *Ebonics* is a word coined to refer to what used to be referred to as "Black English," meaning different pronunciations of existing words and the development of slang among members of African American communities. Some argued that ebonics went against "standards" of "correct" pronunciation and use of English; they felt it should neither be taught in

public schools nor tolerated as a proper way of speaking. Proponents of ebonics, like the Reverend Jesse Jackson, pointed to the use of such language as an indicator of cultural pride and an expression of individuality. What is your view of ebonics? Do you believe that a "standard" form of English should be taught and used in schools and in society in general? If so, whose "standard" should be *the* standard?

offend listeners. In the following pages, we explore a few categories of language that illustrate the constant evolution of verbal communication and represent areas in which we can all heighten our sensitivity.

Biased Language: Race, Ethnicity, Nationality, and Religion

Think about whether you have ever said or overheard someone say the following:

> "I got a great deal on a car; the sticker price was a lot higher, but I jewed the dealer way down."
> "You can't have that back, you Indian giver!"
> "She's a real Bible banger."
> "He doesn't have a Chinaman's chance to make the team."
> "That divorce settlement gypped me out of what's rightfully mine!"

That last statement tends to puzzle people more than the others. It includes the term *gypped,* which is derived from the word for the nomadic cultural group known throughout the world as gypsies. The stereotype relates to being suckered or cheated out of what one is due.

What would your impression be of a person who made one of these statements? The language used in each of these examples demonstrates an insensitivity

THE FAR SIDE® BY GARY LARSON

The Far Side® by Gary Larson © 1983 FarWorks, Inc. All Rights Reserved. The Far Side® and the Larson® signature are registered trademarks of FarWorks, Inc. Used with permission.

© 1983 FarWorks, Inc. All Rights Reserved/Dist. by Creators Syndicate

to members of other cultures and groups. Such language reflects a word barrier known as **allness,** which occurs when words reflect unqualified, often untrue generalizations that deny individual differences or variations. It's important to continue to educate yourself and monitor your speech so that you are not, even unconsciously, using phrases that depict a group of people in a negative, stereotypical fashion.

Is Supreme Court Justice Clarence Thomas black or African American? Is someone of Mexican or Spanish descent Mexican American, Hispanic, Latina, or Chicano? Given the power of words, the terms we use to refer to ethnic groups directly reflect perceptions of culture and identity. If you use the wrong word, you may be labeled politically incorrect or worse, a bigot.

In the mid 1990s, the U.S. Bureau of Labor Statistics surveyed 60,000 households, asking people what ethnic labels they preferred. More than 44% of those then referred to as black by the government preferred the term *black*, while 28% preferred *African American*. Twelve percent preferred *Afro-American*, and a little over 9% had no preference. In another ethnic category, *Hispanic* was the choice of 58% of those currently labeled Hispanics, rather than such terms as *Latino* or *of Spanish origin*. The survey also reported that the label *American Indians* was the term of choice for slightly less than half of the respondents, while 37% preferred *Native American*. Most of those currently designated as white preferred that term, although 16% liked the term *Caucasian* and a very small percentage liked the term *European American*.[15]

A sensitive communicator keeps abreast of linguistic changes and adopts the designations currently preferred by members of various ethnic groups. Sometimes students ask why this continued flexibility is so important—and the question arises out of both a resistance to change and a general wish that language (and other things in life) were simpler. Consider this: What if you really liked your first name but didn't like a nickname or a shortened version of it? And what if someone you worked with never got your name right, if she or he constantly used that more familiar or "playful" version of

allness
A word barrier created through the use of language that reflects unqualified, often untrue generalizations that deny individual differences or variations.

On the Web

Here's an interesting Web site to check out: **www.yforum.com**

This is the site for the National Forum on People's Differences, described as a no-holds-barred question-and-answer opportunity. Users can ask questions—either as postings or in a real-time chat format—that would be impolite or too embarrassing to ask in a face-to-face or telephone format. Examples of questions that have been posted on the site include: "What do retired people do all day?" "Is it disrespectful for a straight person to go to a gay bar?" "Why do Muslim women cover their hair?" "Is it considered offensive if a white person calls a black person 'black'?" It's interesting to observe the kinds of freedom the relative anonymity of the Internet provides.[16]

your name? You'd probably get irritated and try to correct the person. The principle is the same with ethnic and cultural designations. It's wise to allow members of a certain group to designate their own terms, then attempt to learn and become comfortable using those terms so that you reflect sensitivity as a communicator. Don't be afraid to ask directly, but sensitively, what term or terms are appropriate. A few years ago, a reader wrote to an African American columnist for the *Miami Herald,* asking for the appropriate term to use when referring to black people. Leonard Pitts addressed the dilemma in his column, explaining that part of the problem stems from his view that "race is not a scientific reality, but a social and cultural one." He advocated the evolution of vocabulary, no matter "how unwieldy, how imprecise, or how much of a PC pain in the backside." Pitts wrote of a saner world, in which such language obstacles would not be obstacles at all, because racial and ethnic differences would be minimized and thus would not command so much attention; the only term one would need to know to refer to another person would be the person's name.[17] Expressing a similar sentiment, celebrity Whoopi Goldberg was asked by an interviewer whether she preferred to be called black or African American. Her reply was, "Just call me Whoopi—that's what I prefer."

Biased Language: Gender and Sexual Orientation

Language that reveals bias in favor of one sex and against another, termed **sexist** or **exclusive language,** is more prevalent than you'd think. Decades of effort, spurred by the women's liberation movement in the 1960s, have raised the consciousness of American culture regarding exclusive language. But many people still do not alter their language to reflect and include both sexes. In addition, insensitivity or intolerance toward persons who are gay, lesbian, or bisexual is often reflected in what is termed **heterosexist** or **homophobic language.** A person who uses heterosexist language speaks from an assumption that the world is heterosexual, as if romantic and sexual attraction to those of the same sex or to both sexes is simply not possible. Homophobic language more overtly denigrates persons of nonheterosexual orientations and usually arises out of a fear of being labeled gay or lesbian. We briefly consider sexist and heterosexist forms of biased language below.

sexist (exclusive) language
Language that reveals bias in favor of one sex and against another.

heterosexist language
Language that reveals an assumption that the world is heterosexual, as if homosexuality or bisexuality did not exist.

homophobic language
Language that overtly denigrates persons of nonheterosexual orientations, usually arising out of a fear of being labeled gay or lesbian.

generic language
General terms that stand for all persons or things within a given category.

Language and the Sexes   Even though women now constitute over 50% of the U.S. population, to listen to the language of some people, you'd think it was still a man's world. Sexist language can reflect stereotypical attitudes or describe roles in exclusively male or female terms. Research indicates that exclusive language usage does the following: (1) maintains sex-biased perceptions, (2) shapes people's attitudes about careers that are appropriate for one sex but not the other, (3) causes some women to believe that certain jobs and roles aren't attainable, and (4) contributes to the belief that men deserve more status in society than women do.[18] Even dictionaries fall into patterns of describing women and men with discriminatory language.[19] Included in the *Oxford English Dictionary* definition for *woman* were (1) an adult female being, (2) female servant, (3) a lady-love or mistress, and (4) a wife. Men were described in more positive and distinguished terms: (1) a human being, (2) the human creation regarded abstractly, (3) an adult male endowed with many qualities, and (4) a person of importance of position.

The most common form of sexism in language is the use of a masculine term as though it were **generic** or a term to describe all people. There are two primary ways that masculine-as-generic language typically appears in written and oral communication: in pronoun usage and man-linked terminology.

Consistent evidence from research on sexist language shows that people—particularly in U.S. culture—simply do not tend to think in neuter. We think in male or female, which is another example of the polarization aspect of language discussed earlier. We don't tend to think of living entities as *it*, and we rarely use that pronoun to refer to them. When most people read or hear the word *he*, they think masculine, not some image of a sexless person.[20] Using generic masculine language, in essence, turns all persons into male persons.

Sexist language can be so deeply embedded in some persons' experience that it is used habitually, without much thought. For example, a student was giving a speech on how to project a winning, confident style on a job interview. The student said, "When you greet the boss for the first time, be sure to look him straight in the eye, give him a firm hand-shake, and let him know you're interested in the job." This language would be perfectly acceptable if the speaker were only describing a specific situation in which the job candidate was to meet a male boss. But his exclusive language choice only allowed for the possibility of a male boss, not a female boss, unless he meant the term *he* to stand for all persons—male and female bosses, in this case. What if the speaker had used only female pronouns, as in "look her straight in the eye, give her a firm hand-shake, and let her know you're interested in the job"? No doubt the exclusive female language would have drawn undue attention and perhaps distracted listeners. It is common for male terms to be used to refer to all persons, but less common for female language to serve as generic.

We don't know what you were taught in high school or in other college classes about generic language. Nevertheless, publishing standards today require the use of nonsexist language, which allows no masculine terms to stand for all persons. You'll notice that we use inclusive language in this text—because it reflects our value system and because our publisher requires it.

The solution to the problem of sexist language is not to replace all *he*s with *she*s, which would be an equally sexist practice. The point is to use terms that include both sexes so that your language reflects the contemporary world. If you want to refer to one person—any person of either sex—the most clear, grammatical, nonsexist way to do that is to use either *she or he, he/she,* or *s/he.*[21] Other options include (1) omitting a pronoun altogether, either by rewording a message or by substituting an article (*a, an,* or *the*) for the pronoun; (2) using *you* or variations of the indefinite pronoun *one*; or (3) using the plural pronoun *they.*[22]

Some college campuses are taking the pronoun issue even a step further. The Student Government at Smith College, a private women's college, recently voted to change the language of their Constitution. References to *she* and *her* were replaced by *the stu-*

The gender-neutral term *firefighter* describes both of these people, whereas the sexist term *fireman* excludes the person on the right.

dent, in an effort to show sensitivity to students who identified themselves as transgender.[23] Transgender individuals do not view themselves in terms of standard cultural constructions of male or female, masculine or feminine. They contend that they have transcended societal confines of sex and gender, so standard references to *she, he, him,* and *her* do not apply to transgender people and could cause them to feel excluded. If you think the changes to the Smith College Student Government Constitution are really "out there," realize that several other colleges and universities are currently considering such linguistic innovations for their campus documents.

As with pronouns, research shows that masculine mental images arise when the term *man* is used, again rendering women invisible and reinforcing the male-as-standard problem.[24] Words such as Congress*man*, police*man*, and *man*kind ignore the fact that women are part of the workforce and the human race. Contrast these with *member of Congress* (or *senator* or *representative*), *police officer,* and *humankind,* which are gender neutral and allow for the inclusion of both men and women. Some progress in this area has been made to reflect changed attitudes toward women in the professional arena. Compare some terms used in the past to describe workers to terms we now use (see Table 3.1).

A related issue concerns the generally accepted use of the phrase *you guys* as a generic reference. This language is not generic, since it includes the male term *guys,* but it is one of the most widely used, by both women and men, and unintentionally exclusive terms in everyday English. About using *you guys* to refer to a group of women, renowned author Alice Walker states, "I see in its use some women's obsequious need to be accepted, at any cost, even at the cost of erasing their own femaleness, and that of other women. Isn't it at least ironic that after so many years of struggle for women's liberation, women should end up calling themselves this?"[25]

Consciously remembering to use nonsexist, inclusive language brings several benefits.[26] First, inclusive language reflects inclusive attitudes. Your attitudes are reflected in your speech and your speech affects your attitudes. Monitoring your verbal communication for sexist remarks can help you monitor any sexist attitudes or assumptions you may hold. Second, using gender-inclusive language helps you become more other oriented, which will have a positive impact on your relationships. Consciously ridding your language of sexist remarks reflects your sensitivity to others. Third, inclusive language makes your speech more contemporary and unambiguous. If you use *he,* for example, how is a listener to know if you are referring to a male person or any person in general? And finally, inclusive language strengthens your style and demonstrates sensitivity that can empower others. By eliminating sexist bias from your speech, you affirm the value of all individuals with whom you interact.

Language and Sexual Orientation   We realize that sexual orientation is one of the more difficult topics to discuss, mainly because people tend to hold strong opinions

TABLE 3.1	
Terms from the Past	*Terms Used Today*
stewardess	flight attendant
chairman	chair
fireman	firefighter
salesman	salesperson or clerk
mailman	mail carrier
female doctor or lady doctor	physician or doctor
girls at work or girl Friday	women at the office
Miss/Mrs.	Ms.
mankind	people, humans, or humankind

about it. But no matter your views about sexuality, it is vital to use sensitive, appropriate communication with whomever you encounter.

Just as you have learned to avoid racially charged terms that degrade and draw attention to someone's ethnicity, it's important to learn to avoid language that denigrates a person's sexual orientation and draws undue attention to this element of cultural diversity. One of your authors was quite taken aback a few years ago when she received a paper from a first-year student in which the derogatory term *fag* frequently appeared. You've no doubt heard this term, probably bantered about in high school, but its use can be a signal of homophobia—the fear of being labeled or viewed as gay or lesbian. Heterosexist language is more subtle; it often emerges through omission, meaning what is *not* said, rather than commission, or what *is* said. For example, have you ever heard an instructor in one of your classes give a dating example using two persons of the same sex? Most examples about relationships that you read or hear about in courses such as interpersonal communication or introduction to psychology reflect heterosexual romantic relationships. As another example, how often do you hear or use the term *partner* instead of *husband* or *wife?* The first term, *partner*, is inclusive of all forms of couples, while the latter terms, at least in most states, refer only to heterosexual marriage. These tendencies can communicate a heterosexist bias and suggest that other sexual orientations are inappropriate or nonexistent.

Biased Language: Age, Class, and Ability

"Just turn the car, grandpa!" Ever heard a driver say this in irritation, or said it yourself? Ever call an elderly person a "geezer" or an "old-timer"? Just as some people contend that Americans are hung up on gender and racial diversity, many believe that Americans are hung up on age. We live in a culture that glorifies youth and tends to put its elders "out to pasture." Age discrimination is a very real problem in the workforce—so much so that laws have been enacted to guard against someone's being denied professional opportunities because of age. Likewise, some older people may hold stereotypes of young people and may speak to them as though their youth exempted them from intelligence or responsible action. We recommend that you inventory your language for any terms that either show disrespect for elders or are patronizing or condescending to younger persons.

Another factor that influences language that has received research attention of late is socioeconomic class. Class distinctions typically are revealed in derogatory references to "blue-collar workers," "manual laborers," or "welfare recipients." Another class slur is the term "white trash." In the late 1990s, when Paula Jones filed a sexual harassment lawsuit against then-President Bill Clinton, she was called "white trash" and "trailer trash" as she was ridiculed in the press and in living rooms across the country. Avoid references that reveal a condescending or disrespectful attitude toward someone's education (or lack of it) and socioeconomic status.

Finally, an area of bias in language that most people became conscious of by the turn of the twenty-first century relates to ability. Some years ago, Helen Keller was described as "deaf, dumb, and blind." Nowadays, the appropriate term for her inability to communicate vocally would be *mute.* Be careful that your language doesn't make fun of or draw attention to someone's physical, mental, or learning disability, such as calling someone a "cripple," "retard," or "slow reader." Research has found that when people with disabilities were called demeaning names, they were perceived as less trustworthy, competent, persuasive, and sociable than when they were described in positive terms.[27] The researchers warn against using derogatory language that is offensive to persons with disabilities. Also, scholars who research communication and disability recommend that you use the reference "persons with disabilities" rather than "disabled persons." The former language usage makes the person primary and the disability secondary; the emphasis is on a person, who just happens to have some form of disability. The latter usage emphasizes the disability over the human-ness of the person.[28]

RECAP

Confronting Bias in Language

Inventory your language for subtle and not-so-subtle indications of bias in several areas:

- *Race, Ethnicity, and Nationality:* Avoid language that denigrates members of a racial or ethnic group; be careful not to overemphasize race or ethnicity or "mark" a person by using adjectives referring to national origin, as in "that Oriental student in my class."
- *Religion:* Watch stereotypical language pertaining to religious affiliation, such as derogatory references to Jews, Muslims, or fundamentalist Christians, for example.
- *Gender:* Include both sexes in your language, especially in your use of pronouns; avoid masculine generic pronouns and male-linked terms that exclude women.
- *Sexual Orientation:* Be alert to the potential for heterosexism in your language—the assumption that everyone is heterosexual or that heterosexuality is the only possible orientation. Eliminate homophobic language that degrades and stereotypes gays, lesbians, bisexuals, and transgender individuals.
- *Age:* Avoid calling too much attention to a person's age in your verbal communication. Be especially vigilant not to label or stereotype the elderly or to condescend to or glorify youth.
- *Class:* Monitor references to socioeconomic differences, such as distinctions between blue-collar and white-collar workers.
- *Ability:* Avoid verbal communication that draws attention to a person's physical, mental, or learning ability.

USING WORDS TO ESTABLISH SUPPORTIVE RELATIONSHIPS

As we said early on in this chapter, one reason verbal communication is important is because it has an impact on other people. Language is our primary tool for communicating who we are to others—for knowing them and being known by them. Relationships of all sorts bring life's greatest satisfactions, so the motivation for assessing and improving our verbal communication with others is obvious.

In our introductory communication classes, we often discuss **trigger words**—those forms of language that arouse certain emotions in us. One student, Travis, was immediately able to identify a word his wife used during arguments that really sparked his frustration and anger more than anything else. When Travis would make a point that would frustrate his wife —one for which she had no comeback—she would look at him, toss her hand in the air, and say, "Whatever." Perhaps this word triggers you too, because it punctuates a conversation; it acts as a dismissal of the other person and her or his point. Do you know what words trigger your emotions? These words or phrases can incite positive as well as negative feelings, but they acutely illustrate the power of words in the context of relationships. Certain uses of language can make us feel accepted and appreciated, or disrespected and hostile.

For over four decades, communication scholar Jack Gibb's research has been used as a framework for both describing and prescribing verbal behaviors that contribute to feelings of either supportiveness or defensiveness.[29] Gibb spent several years listening to and observing groups of individuals in meetings and conversations, noting that

trigger word
A form of language that arouses strong emotions in listeners.

some exchanges seemed to create a supportive climate whereas others created a defensive one. Words and actions, he concluded, are tools we use to let someone know whether we support them or not. Thus Gibb defined **supportive communication** as communication that uses language to create a climate of trust, caring, and acceptance. The language used in **defensive communication,** in contrast, creates a climate of hostility and mistrust. When someone gets defensive, communication is seriously impeded. Think about times when your words made someone defensive and how hard you had to work (if you attempted it at all) to get the person to let the defenses down. In this section, we suggest ways to use verbal communication to create a supportive climate rather than an antagonistic one.

Describe Your Own Feelings Rather Than Evaluate Others

Most of us don't like to be judged or evaluated; not only do we fear negative responses from others, we fear the potential that we will become defensive and say things we'll later regret. Criticizing and name-calling obviously can create relational problems, but so can our attempts to diagnose others' problems or weaknesses. As Winston Churchill declared, "I am always ready to learn, although I do not always like being taught."

One way to avoid evaluating others is to attempt to decrease your use of an accusatory *you.* Statements such as, "You always say you'll call but you never do" or "You need to pick up the dirty clothes in your room" attack a person's sense of self-worth and usually result in a defensive reaction. Instead, use the word *I* to describe your own feelings and thoughts about a situation or event: "I find it hard to believe you when you say you'll call" or "I don't enjoy the extra work of picking up your dirty clothes." When you describe your own feelings instead of berating the receiver of the message, you take ownership of the problem. This approach leads to greater openness and trust because your listener is less likely to feel rejected or as if you are trying to control him or her.

Related to this point about description versus evaluation is the suggestion that you separate behaviors from persons in order to create a supportive climate. We probably all know people whose behaviors seem self-destructive, and we all do things from time to time that aren't in our own best interest. Maybe in reaction to getting dumped in a relationship that means a great deal to you, you call that person's answering machine 20 times, just to hear the voice recording. Maybe you indulge in self-defeating behavior like drinking too much, overeating (or the opposite, starving yourself), or driving around late at night with the music blasting, feeling sorry for yourself. In these critical moments, do people respond to you or to your behavior? A supportive response focuses on the behavior, not the person. A supportive response sounds something like this: "Here's what I see you doing; I'm still your friend and I care about you, but this behavior isn't healthy. How can I help you?" Responses that engender defensiveness might sound something like "You're really out of control," "You've become someone I don't recognize," and "Stop acting like this or I won't be able to be around you or be your friend." The supportive response doesn't characterize the person as the embodiment of his or her destructive behavior; it focuses only on the behavior, because that's what's happening at the moment. In religious circles, the advice goes: "Hate the sin, love the sinner."

Solve Problems Rather Than Control Others

When you were younger, your parents gave you rules to keep you safe. Even though you may have resented their control, you needed to know that the stovetop was hot, when not to cross the street, and how dangerous it is to stick your finger in a light socket. Now that you are an adult, when people treat you like a child, it often means they are trying to control your behavior, to take away your options.

Most of us don't like to be controlled. Someone who presumes to tell us what's good for us instead of helping us puzzle through issues and problems to arrive at our own solutions or higher understanding is likely to engender defensiveness. In truth, we have

supportive communication
Language that creates a climate of trust, caring, and acceptance.

defensive communication
Language that creates a climate of hostility and mistrust.

Empathy, the ability to understand and experience the feelings of another, is a building block of a supportive relationship.

little or no control over others. Open-ended questions, such as "What seems to be the problem?" or "How can we deal with this issue?" create a more supportive climate than critical comments, such as "Here's where you are wrong" and "You know what your problem is?" or commands such as "Don't do that!"

Be Genuine Rather Than Manipulative

To be genuine means honestly being yourself rather than attempting to be someone you are not. It also means taking a sincere interest in others, considering the uniqueness of each individual and situation, and avoiding generalizations or strategies that focus on your own needs and desires. A manipulative person has hidden agendas and her or his own concerns and interests most at heart. A genuine person has the other person's interests at heart and uses language to facilitate an open and honest discussion of issues and problems.

Empathize Rather Than Remain Detached from Others

Empathy, one of the hallmarks of supportive relationships, is the ability to understand and actually feel or approximate the feelings of others and then to predict the emotional responses they will have to different situations.[30] You work to put yourself in the other person's shoes, to experience as closely as you can what she or he is experiencing. The opposite of empathy is neutrality. To be neutral is to be indifferent or apathetic toward others. (Even when you express anger or irritation toward another, you are investing some energy in the relationship.) A statement that epitomizes this concept of neutrality is "I don't love you or hate you; I just *don't* you."

Remaining detached from someone when empathy is obviously called for can generate great defensiveness and damage a relationship. Here's an example: You're upset about an argument you just had with someone you're dating, so you seek the support and listening ear of a good friend. But that friend is in "party mode" or such a good mood that he or she chooses not to concentrate and listen to what's going on with you. Rather than engage in your situation, your friend remains detached and blows off your concerns. In situations like this, most of us become defensive and frustrated, and the quality of our friendship may suffer. Empathy takes work, but it is a building block of a supportive relationship.

Be Flexible Rather Than Rigid toward Others

Some people are just *always* right, aren't they? (These people spend a lot of time alone, too.) Most people don't like someone who always seems certain that she or he is right. A "you're wrong, I'm right" attitude creates a defensive climate. This does not mean that you should have no opinions and go through life passively agreeing to everything. And it doesn't mean that there isn't a clear-cut right and wrong in a given situation. But instead of making rigid pronouncements, at times you may want to qualify your language by using phrases such as "I may be wrong, but it seems to me . . ." or "Here's something you might want to consider." Conditional language gives your opinions a softer edge that allows room for others to express a point of view; it opens the door for alternatives. Declarations tend to shut the door. Again, there are times when equivocation is not an appropriate or advisable way to communicate. But in those cases when you want to induce supportiveness and reduce the potential for defensiveness, conditional, flexible language works best.

empathy
The ability to understand and feel what another person is feeling.

Present Yourself as Equal Rather Than Superior

You can antagonize others by letting them know that you view yourself as better or brighter than they are. You may be gifted and extraordinarily intelligent, but it's not necessary to announce or publicize it. And although some people have the responsibility and authority to manage others, "pulling rank" does not usually produce a supportive climate. With phrases such as "Let's work on this together" or "We each have a valid perspective," you can avoid erecting walls of resentment and defensiveness. "We" language can be preferable to "you" language; it builds a sense of camaraderie and shared experience, and by using it you avoid setting yourself apart from listeners.

Also, avoid using "high-falutin'" (or unnecessarily complicated) words just to impress others or to project some image. Sometimes referred to as "bafflegab," this kind of language can come in the form of words, phrases, or verbal shorthand that no one understands but you. Persons with particular expertise may use abbreviated terms or acronyms (words derived from the first letters of several words in a phrase). The military is notorious for its use of language that doesn't easily translate outside of military circles. "Be sure to complete the Fit Reps on those Non-Coms ASAP before returning to the BOQ." Translation: "Be sure to complete the Fitness Reports on those Non-Commissioned Officers as soon as possible before returning to the Bachelor Officers' Quarters." If both speaker and listener are military personnel, then such a sentence may be a perfectly acceptable way to communicate. The problem comes when you use lingo no one understands, perhaps to create drama, exclude someone from the conversation, or posture yourself. It's better to use informal language appropriate to the situation and your listeners than to attempt to talk over the heads of everyone in the room.

You can also create defensiveness by using language that is too simplistic for your listeners. Granted, when you communicate with someone from another culture or even from another U.S. cultural group, you may need to alter your message to get your meaning across. But this means that your verbal communication should be explicit, not condescending. For example, some people use oversimplified words when communicating with elderly persons. It's inappropriate to assume that aging diminishes one's capacity to understand. Try to use language to present yourself on equal ground with your listeners and establish a supportive, open climate for communication.

Avoid Gunny-Sacking

In one of his hit songs, Garth Brooks sings, "We buried the hatchet; we left the handle sticking out." Brooks makes mild reference here to a process known as gunny-sacking, which can be like a handle sticking out within easy reach; when grasped, it serves to remind you of a past conflict or wound. Gunny-sacking involves dredging up someone's past mistakes or problems and linking them to a current situation. The language comes from the imagery of reaching down into a bag (a gunny sack) to pull out something from the past. For example, suppose your best male friend has just been dumped by his "one true love," but you—being the good friend that you are—remind him that the last three women he dated were also his "one true love," at least at the time. Your friend wants empathy, but you respond by highlighting his tendency to turn "Miss Right" into "Miss Right Now." Such an approach will likely make him feel criticized and engender defensive reactions in him. This kind of scenario rarely deepens a relationship.

However, in some situations, it may be wise to point out a pattern of destructive behavior that you observe in someone, especially if the person is someone you value highly and with whom you want to maintain a healthy, supportive relationship. Occasionally, people repeat behaviors that are not to their benefit, but they are unaware that a pattern is being established. A caring friend, romantic partner, or family member might use the supportive communication techniques described in this chapter to describe past instances and reveal the pattern to the person. Once the negative patterns are revealed and explored, he or she may work to overcome them so that the destructive behavior isn't repeated.

RECAP

Using Words to Create a Supportive Climate

- Describe your own feelings instead of evaluating the points of view or behavior of others.
- Keep the focus on problem solving, not control of others.
- Be genuine rather than manipulative in your approach.
- Show that you understand others' points of view instead of ignoring their feelings.
- Use conditional language and demonstrate flexibility rather than rigidity in your communication with others.
- Present yourself as an equal rather than as a superior. Make it clear that you do not have all the answers; avoid acting like a know-it-all. Don't attempt to talk over the heads of listeners or condescend to them, because either approach can breed defensiveness.
- Avoid gunny-sacking, or reminding someone of past mistakes or issues, unless you believe the person remains blind to his or her destructive patterns.

PRINCIPLES FOR A LIFETIME: Enhancing Your Skills

Verbal

Principle Two: Effectively use and interpret verbal messages.

- Realize that communication problems may not have to do with the words used, but with the meanings that people attach to the words.
- Recognize the difference between denotative and connotative language.
- Use concrete terms whenever appropriate, because abstract language is harder to understand than concrete language.
- Understand that meanings of words are affected by the culture within which the language is used.
- Pay attention to the words communicators choose to use and attempt to interpret those words in the spirit and context in which they were intended.
- Avoid biased language when speaking about race, ethnicity, nationality, religion, gender, sexual orientation, age, class, and ability.
- Use words to engender supportiveness, rather than defensiveness.

SUMMARY

In this chapter, we explored the importance of effective verbal communication with others. The words we choose have great power to communicate who we are and to influence the relationships we establish. People use words as symbols for thoughts, and they create meanings for those symbols. We interpret their meanings in terms of the culture and context to which they belong. Communication is complex because people develop both denotative (literal) meanings and connotative (subjective) meanings for words and because meanings range from concrete to abstract.

The power of words stems from their ability to create images and to help us label and understand our experience. Words influence our thoughts and actions, as they both shape culture and are shaped by culture. Language also has the power to make and break relationships.

Biased language that is insensitive and exclusive of others creates noise that interferes with the meaning of a message; it also can create the impression that the user of such language is biased and can impede the development of satisfying relationships. The most common forms of biased language relate to race, ethnicity, nationality, religion, gender, sexual orientation, age, class, and ability.

The words you use can enhance or detract from the quality of relationships you establish with others. In contrast to defensive communication, supportive communication is descriptive rather than evaluative, problem oriented rather than control oriented, genuine rather than contrived or manipulative, empathic rather than neutral, flexible rather than rigid, equal rather than superior, and focused on current behaviors, not on past mistakes.

Discussion and Review

1. Why should we focus on language?
2. Explain the nature of words as symbols to which people attach meanings. How can meanings vary?
3. Describe what is meant by denotative and connotative meanings for words.
4. Describe what is meant by concrete and abstract meanings for words.
5. What does it mean to say that language is culture bound and context bound? How does one's culture shape language? How does one's language shape culture?
6. Identify four ways that words have power.
7. Provide some examples of biased language related to race, ethnicity, nationality, and religion. Then generate unbiased terms as alternatives.
8. Provide some examples of biased language related to gender, sexual orientation, age, class, and ability. Then generate unbiased terms as alternatives.
9. What is the role of verbal communication in the establishment of supportive relationships? Identify some ways that one can create a supportive communication climate with others.

Putting Principles into Practice

1. Below we review the differences between denotative and connotative meanings of words and provide examples.

Level	Definition	Examples
Denotative	Literal, restrictive definition of a word	Teacher: the person primarily responsible for providing your education
Connotative	Personal, subjective reaction to a word	Teacher: the warm, supportive person who fostered a climate in which you could learn OR the cold taskmaster who drilled lessons into you and made you feel inferior

For each of the following terms, provide a denotative, or dictionary-type, definition; then generate connotative meanings of your own.

work	commitment
parent	professionalism
love	loyalty

2. We know that words have the power to influence our thoughts and actions. In a small group, have each member reveal a nickname given by either a family member or friends. Discuss whether group members attribute positive or negative meanings to the nicknames and whether each person's development was affected by his or her nickname.

3. This activity illustrates how people reveal their biases through their use of language. Generate a list of stereotypical language that is often associated with each of the words below. For example, for the word *Democrat*, you might think of positive and negative terms like "liberal," "tax and spend," "big government," "dove," and "populist."

conservatives	the military
foreigners	churchgoers
homeless persons	politicians

4. With a group of classmates, generate and write down a list of trigger words—terms that set off emotional reactions. Consider words that evoke positive emotions, such as happiness and surprise. Then explore words that prompt anger, fear, sadness, and disgust. Discuss how certain words came to trigger your emotions; look for common experiences among group members.

5. In this chapter you've learned that the words you use can enhance or detract from the quality of relationships you establish with others. Conduct role plays with classmates to demonstrate ways to establish supportive communication climates with others: (1) being descriptive rather than evaluative, (2) being problem oriented rather than control oriented, (3) communicating in a genuine rather than a contrived or manipulative manner, (4) showing empathy rather than neutrality, (5) being flexible rather than rigid, (6) representing yourself as equal rather than superior to others and (7) concentrating on the present, rather than gunny-sacking and dredging up the past. First act out the wrong way to behave or an example of ineffective communication that leads to defensiveness. Then repeat the role play, using the same or different players, altering the conversation so that a supportive climate is established.

We respond to gestures with an extreme alertness and, one might say, in accordance with an elaborate and secret code that is written nowhere, known by none, and understood by all.

Edward Sapir

Edouard Vuillard, "Girls Walking," © 2005 Artists Rights Society (ARS), New York/ADAGP, Paris. Erich Lessing/Art Resource, NY.

Understanding Nonverbal Messages

CHAPTER OUTLINE

Why Focus on Nonverbal
Communication?

The Nature of Nonverbal
Communication

Codes of Nonverbal
Communication

How to Interpret Nonverbal Cues
More Accurately

Summary

CHAPTER OBJECTIVES

After studying this chapter, you should be able to:

1. Provide four reasons for studying nonverbal communication.

2. Describe the five ways in which nonverbal communication functions with verbal communication.

3. Discuss six elements that reveal the nature of nonverbal communication.

4. Be able to identify and explain the seven groupings of nonverbal communication codes.

5. Summarize major research findings regarding codes of nonverbal communication.

6. Explain Mehrabian's three-part framework for interpreting nonverbal cues.

"Don't give me that confused look—you know what I'm talking about."
"I knew that was you at my door; I know your knock."
"Hey, is this really you? You sound just like your sister on the phone."
"If I tied your hands together, I bet you couldn't talk."
"Back off from me; I need my space."

What do these statements have in common? They all have to do with a form of human communication that occurs without words—what we term *nonverbal communication*. **Nonverbal communication** is communication other than written or spoken language that creates meaning for someone. The one exception to this definition is that to hearing persons, sign language appears to be nonverbal communication. However, to persons who are deaf, sign language is verbal communication, with certain movements, signs, and facial expressions conveying words, phrases, and emphasis.

We know you're becoming familiar with our five-sided model of communication principles for a lifetime, but let's do a quick recap (see Figure 4.1). In Chapter 2 we explored ways to become more aware of yourself and your perceptions of things and people with whom you come into contact. An important step in this process of coming to know and understand yourself better is an honest, insightful examination of how you talk. In Chapter 3 we challenged you to consider the power of words, to take inventory of your use of language, and to think about ways to improve your verbal communication so that you extend yourself to others and respond to them in an appropriate, effective manner. Now we get to what most people consider an even greater challenge—understanding and evaluating your nonverbal communication and improving your ability to interpret the nonverbal behavior of others. Nonverbal communication is of great importance; a person who can read others' nonverbal communication with sensitivity and skill makes a memorable impression on other people. Because of the power of nonverbal communication to complement verbal communication, to further reveal the self—particularly in those situations when talking is inappropriate, impossible, or inadequate—and to affect how you connect with others as you initiate and build relationships, we've chosen to make this the third of our five key principles for a lifetime.

We have two primary goals in this chapter. The first is to help you become more aware of your own nonverbal behavior—to help you understand how and why you behave as you do. Because much nonverbal communication behavior is subconscious,

nonverbal communication
Communication other than written or spoken language that creates meaning for someone.

FIGURE 4.1
Communication Principles for a Lifetime

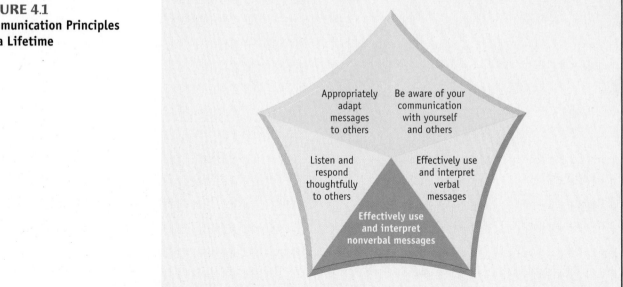

most people have limited awareness or understanding of it. Once you become more aware of this important form of communication, you will increase your ability to use nonverbal skills to interact more effectively with others. The second goal is to enhance your nonverbal receiving skills, or your ability to more accurately detect and interpret the nonverbal communication of others.

WHY FOCUS ON NONVERBAL COMMUNICATION?

Have you ever watched someone interact with someone else and thought, "That person just doesn't have a clue"? We've all seen or met people who appear not to pick up on the communication clues of others. For example, have you ever tried to end a conversation because you were late or needed to be somewhere else, and the person you were talking to just wouldn't let you out of the conversation? The person didn't seem to notice you looking at your watch, angling your body away, taking a few steps back, and making minimal vocal responses to what was being said. Now, we all have times when we can't "catch a clue," even if we consider ourselves to be fairly sensitive, perceptive people. Certain people, places, moods, or topics of conversation may impede our ability to give and receive nonverbal communication effectively. But we don't want to be clueless. We want to be able to exhibit effective nonverbal communication and to read and interpret the clues others give us more sensitively and accurately.

However, there's something very important to keep in mind as we proceed: No one can become a perfect interpreter of the nonverbal communication of others. It's unwise and inappropriate to assume that you can become an infallible judge of others' nonverbal cues, because human beings are unique, complicated, and ever-changing creatures. Although we encourage you to deepen your understanding of nonverbal communication, sharpen your powers of observation, and develop greater skill in interpreting the meanings behind others' nonverbal actions, we also suggest that you remain keenly aware of the idiosyncratic and complex nature of nonverbal communication. We hope that you catch more clues as a result of studying this topic, but avoid making the mistake of believing that your interpretations of nonverbal messages are always correct. To begin to explore this topic, let's look at four reasons for studying nonverbal communication.

Nonverbal Messages Communicate Feelings and Attitudes

What do you look like when you're happy and excited about something? When you're mad? When you're really worried about something? When you're surprised or disappointed? Videotapes or pictures of yourself in different moods can be quite revealing, because your face, body, and voice communicate volumes about what's going on inside of you.

Nonverbal communication is a primary tool for conveying our feelings and attitudes and for detecting the emotional states of others. In the study of nonverbal communication, Albert Mehrabian is an expert. He concluded from his research that the most significant source of emotional information is the face, which can channel as much as 55% of our meaning. Vocal cues such as volume, pitch, and intensity convey another 38% of our emotional meaning. In all, we communicate approximately 93% of the emotional meaning of

Which communicates the emotions more effectively: body movements; the volume, pitch, and intensity of the voice; or the meaning of the actual words spoken?

Technology *and* Communication

Conveying Emotions Online

*W*ithout the usual nonverbal mechanisms that allow us to reveal our emotions to others in face-to-face communication, how do we let others at a distance know what we're feeling? E-mail has all but replaced the fine art of letter writing, but people who used to or still write letters typically insert parenthetical phrases or symbols to convey the nonverbal message behind the verbal. The most common one is the happy face, or "smiley," which, when typed, is made by combining a colon, dash, and right parenthesis mark, as in :-).

If you use e-mail, perhaps you've learned a few other nonverbal methods for communicating emotion. One is to put certain words in all caps, a technique known as "shouting," which typically reveals emphasis, frustration, or even anger. You may have also seen the clever use of punctuation and other keyboard symbols to form a visual image. These sideways im-

ages, termed "emoticons," are forms of nonverbal communication that help convey the meaning or emotion behind a message. Here are some emoticons located from various sources.[1]

:-(	Depressed or upset by a remark
:-l	Indifferent
:-|	Straight face
:-o	Surprise
;-)	Winking at a suggestive or flirtatious remark
:-/	Skeptical
:-P	Sticking your tongue out
:-D	Laughing
:-@	Screaming
8-)	Wearing sunglasses
::-)	Wearing regular glasses
(-:	Left-handed

our messages nonverbally; as little as 7% of the emotional meaning is communicated through explicit verbal channels.[2] Although these percentages do not apply to every communication situation, Mehrabian's research illustrates the potential power of nonverbal cues to communicate emotion and attitude.

Nonverbal Messages Are More Believable Than Verbal Ones

"Hey—are you mad or something?" asks Jonas.
(Big sigh.) "Oh, no. I'm not mad," responds Danita (in a subdued tone of voice and without making eye contact).
"You sure? Because you're acting funny, like you're ticked off." (One more try and then Jonas will likely give up.)
"I SAID I'M NOT MAD, OKAY? WILL YOU LEAVE IT ALONE PLEASE?"

Despite Danita's claim to the contrary, the real story is—she's mad. "Actions speak louder than words." This cliché became a cliché because nonverbal communication is more believable than verbal communication. Verbal communication is a conscious activity; it involves the translation of thoughts and impulses into symbols. Some nonverbal communication is conscious, but a great deal of it is generated subconsciously as we act and react to stimuli in our environment. It's easier to control your words than to control a quiver in your voice when you're angry, the heat and flush in your face when you talk to someone you're attracted to, or shaky knees when you're nervous.

When a person's verbal and nonverbal communication contradict, as in Danita's case, which should an astute observer believe? The nonverbal actions carry the truer message most of the time. When we can't catch a clue, it's most likely because we're wrapped up in ourselves or because we attend more to a person's verbal messages than to her or his nonverbal messages.

Nonverbal Messages Are Critical to Successful Relationships

One researcher suggests that as much as 65% of the way we convey meaning in our messages is through nonverbal channels.[3] Of course, the meaning others interpret from your behavior may not be the one you intended. But we begin making judgments about people just a fraction of a second after meeting them, based on nonverbal information. You may decide whether a date is going to be pleasant or dull during the first 30 seconds of meeting your date, before your date has had time to utter more than "Hello."[4]

As another example, consider the handshake—a simple ritualistic greeting between two people, used in many cultures. Have you ever considered the power of a handshake to communicate? If you get a weak, half-handed, limp handshake from someone, what are you likely to conclude about that person? Research has focused on judgments we make about someone's personality based on a simple greeting ritual. William Chaplin and his colleagues determined characteristics of handshakes that contribute to what they term a handshake index.[5] These researchers examined such attributes as strength, vigor, completeness of grip, and duration. The high index or most positive handshake was strong (but not so strong as to cut off the blood supply), vigorous (meaning it conveyed an appropriate amount of energy), adequate in duration

(not too brief or too long), and complete in its grip (meaning that the people gripped each others' hands fully, with palms touching). Next the researchers studied subjects' judgments of persons with a high handshake index versus those with a low handshake index. These researchers found that the higher a person's handshake index, the more extroverted, open to experience, and less shy that person was believed to be. In addition to these traits, women with high handshake indexes were also perceived to be highly agreeable, in comparison to women with weak or poor handshakes. Subjects in the study also formed more favorable first impressions of those persons with high handshake indexes than those with low indexes. Thus, even a simple symbolic, culturally rooted gesture can have a definite and long-lasting impact on how others perceive you.

Nonverbal cues are important not only in the early stages of relationships, but also as we maintain, deepen, and sometimes terminate those relationships. In fact, the more intimate the relationship, the more we use and understand the nonverbal cues of our partners. Long-married couples spend less time verbalizing their feelings and emotions to each other than they did when they were first dating; each learns to interpret the other's subtle nonverbal cues. If a spouse is silent during dinner, the other spouse may deduce that the day was a tough one and decide to give the person a lot of space. In fact, all of us are more likely to use nonverbal cues to convey negative messages than to announce our explicit dislike of something or someone.[6] We also use nonverbal cues to signal changes in the level of satisfaction with a relationship. When we want to cool things off, we may start using a less vibrant tone of voice and cut back on eye contact and physical contact with our partner.

Functions of Nonverbal Messages

Nonverbal messages can serve multiple functions. First, nonverbal cues can *substitute* for verbal messages. An extended thumb signals that a hitchhiker would like a ride, a water skier wants more speed, or a pilot is ready for takeoff. When someone asks,

"Where's the elevator?" we can point instead of voicing a response. In these instances, we substitute nonverbal cues for verbal messages.

Nonverbal cues delivered simultaneously with verbal messages *complement*, clarify, or extend the meaning of the verbal, conveying more information and allowing for a more accurate interpretation. When someone waves, makes eye contact, and says "hello," the gesture and eye contact serve as nonverbal complements to the verbal greeting. Complementary cues also help color our expressed emotions and attitudes. The length of a hug while you tell your daughter you're proud of her provides additional information about the intensity of your pride. A long, heavy sigh may reveal how tired or bored you are.

Sometimes, however, our nonverbal cues *contradict* rather than complement our verbal cues. Remember Danita, who said she wasn't mad even though she was acting and sounding mad? In an instance like this, the nonverbal cues contradict the verbal ones. The nonverbal message is almost always the one we should believe.

We also use nonverbal cues to *repeat* our words. "I'm new on campus; where's the Center for the Arts?" asks a student. "Go to the right of that two-story, red brick building, and it's just on the other side" says a security guard, who then points to the building. The guard's pointing gesture repeats the verbal instruction and clarifies the message.

We also use nonverbal cues to *regulate* our participation in conversation. In most informal meetings, it's not appropriate or necessary to signal your desire to speak by raising your hand. Yet somehow you're able to signal to others when you'd like to speak and when you'd rather not. You use eye contact, raised eyebrows, an open mouth, an audible intake of breath, a change in posture or seating position, or a single raised index finger to signal that you would like to make a point. If your colleagues don't see these signals, especially the eye contact, they may assume you're not interested in engaging in conversation.[7]

Finally, we use nonverbal behavior to *accent* or reinforce a verbal message. "We simply must do something about this problem," bellows the mayor, "or else we will all bear the blame." When the mayor says the word *must*, she pounds the podium and increases her volume for emphasis. When she says "all bear the blame," she uses a circling gesture with her arms to convey a shared responsibility among those in the room. These vocalizations and gestures serve to accent or add intensity to the verbal message.

RECAP

Why Focus on Nonverbal Communication?

- Nonverbal communication is our primary means of communicating feelings and attitudes toward others.
- Nonverbal messages are usually more believable than verbal messages.
- Nonverbal communication is critical in the initiation, development, and termination of relationships.
- Nonverbal messages can substitute for, complement, contradict, repeat, regulate, and accent verbal messages.

THE NATURE OF NONVERBAL COMMUNICATION

While the benefits of studying and improving one's facility with nonverbal communication are clear, deciphering unspoken messages is a tricky activity. Dictionaries help us interpret words, but no handy reference book exists to help decode nonverbal cues.

Below are some of the challenges inherent in the interpretation of nonverbal communication.

The Culture-Bound Nature of Nonverbal Communication

Some evidence suggests that humans from every culture smile when they are happy and frown when they are unhappy.[8] They also all tend to raise or flash their eyebrows when meeting or greeting others, and young children in many cultures wave to signal they want their parents, raise their arms to be picked up, and suck their thumbs for comfort.[9] This evidence suggests that there is some underlying commonality in human emotion. Yet each culture tends to develop unique rules for displaying and interpreting the expression of emotion.

It's important to realize that nonverbal behavior is culture bound. No common cross-cultural dictionary of nonverbal meaning exists. You will make critical errors in communicating nonverbally, as well as in attempting to interpret the nonverbal behavior of others, if you don't situate nonverbal actions within a cultural context. As intercultural communication scholars Richard Porter

Most nonverbal communication is culture bound. But one of the most universal nonverbal cues among human beings is the smile.

and Larry Samovar explain, one culture's friendly or polite action may be another culture's obscene gesture.[10] For example, during his second inaugural parade, President George W. Bush displayed the two-finger, "hook 'em horns" gesture to salute members of the University of Texas marching band as they passed by his stand. According to the Associated Press, a Norwegian newspaper expressed outrage over the gesture, since it is considered an insult or a sign of the devil in Norse culture. In sign language used by and for deaf persons, the gesture translates into "bull_____." In Mediterranean countries, the gesture implies that a man is the victim of an unfaithful wife. In Russia, it is considered a symbol for newly rich, arrogant, and poorly educated Russians; in many European countries it serves to ward off the "evil eye"; and in some African nations, it's used to put a hex or curse on another person.[11] Concerns about potential international gaffes led Southern Methodist University to publish a pocket-size guide for its students studying abroad. Tips include sticking out your tongue as a way of saying hello in Tibet; making certain to take your hands out of your pockets when talking with someone in Belgium; and avoiding touching someone's head in Indonesia, where such an action would be considered a serious insult.[12]

The Rule-Governed Nature of Nonverbal Communication

You operate according to many rules in your nonverbal communication. You may be unaware that you function according to these rules, but when your rules are violated, you definitely know it. For example, have you ever been in a conversation with someone who seemed as though he or she couldn't talk to you without touching you? Maybe it's just a series of simple touches on the forearm or shoulder, but it's not what you expect in casual conversation. For some reason, the other person's rule about appropriate touch is likely to be different from yours. Or perhaps you've been annoyed when people talk at the movie theater, as if they were sitting at home in their own living rooms instead of out in public. Maybe you have a rule that says people lower their voices and whisper at movie theaters, if they must talk at all; other people may not conform to that same rule.

One of the most prolific nonverbal communication researchers is Judee Burgoon, who developed a fascinating model for how nonverbal communication functions, termed the **expectancy violations model**.[13] The model suggests that we develop

expectancy violations model
A model that suggests that we develop rules or expectations for appropriate nonverbal behavior and react when those expectations are violated.

expectations for appropriate nonverbal behavior in ourselves and others, based on our cultural backgrounds, personal experiences, and knowledge of those with whom we interact. When those expectations (or rules) are violated, we experience heightened arousal (we become more interested or engaged in what's happening), and the nature of our interpersonal relationship with the other person becomes a critical factor as we attempt to interpret and respond to the situation. Because the expectancy violations model was first developed with regard to personal space, let's consider an example that deals with this form of nonverbal communication.

One *Seinfeld* episode depicted a person nicknamed the "close talker," because he got too close for most people's comfort when he talked to them. Most people within a given culture adhere to a widely agreed-on rule or expectation as to appropriate conversational distances. But there are those people who don't seem to catch the cultural clue—those who get too close to our face in casual conversation. Burgoon's model says that we register such a nonverbal violation and react in order to adjust to the circumstances. If the violating person is what Burgoon terms a "rewarding" communicator, meaning that the person has high credibility, status, and attractiveness (physically or in personality), we may view the behavior as less of a rule violation and simply adjust our expectations. We may even reciprocate the behavior. However, if the violator is not a rewarding communicator, we will use reactive nonverbal behaviors in an effort to compensate for or correct the situation. So if an attractive, credible, and high-status person stands too close to you while talking, you may adapt to the situation and not think negatively of the person. If the person has less attractiveness, credibility, and status, you may back away from the person or move to the side so as to increase the conversational distance, break eye contact, and so forth.

Our tendency in a rules violation situation is to attempt to adapt or correct the violation by nonverbal means before resorting to verbal communication. You're more likely to back away from a "close talker" than to say to her or him, "Please back up; you're violating my personal space." We all violate nonverbal rules from time to time; it is at those moments when we become acutely aware that rules or expectations of appropriateness have a powerful influence on nonverbal communication.

The Ambiguous Nature of Nonverbal Communication

Most words are given meaning by people within a culture who speak the same language. But the exact meaning of a nonverbal message is known only to the person displaying it; the person may not intend for the behavior to have any meaning at all. Some people have difficulty expressing their emotions nonverbally. They may have frozen facial expressions or monotone voices. They may be teasing you, but their deadpan expressions lead you to believe that their negative comments are heartfelt. Often it's a challenge to draw meaningful conclusions about other people's behavior, even if we know them quite well. One strategy that helps us interpret others' nonverbal cues is called **perception checking**, a strategy we mentioned in Chapter 2 in our discussion of self-awareness. Observe in detail the nonverbal cues, make your own interpretation, and then do one of two things (or both): (1) Ask the people you're observing how they feel or what's going on and (2) run your interpretation by another observer, to get a second opinion or more input before you draw a conclusion. Remember our earlier warning about not assuming that your interpretation is necessarily the right one; perception checking can enhance the likelihood of your interpretation's being more accurate.

The Continuous Nature of Nonverbal Communication

perception checking
Skill of asking other observers or the person being observed whether your interpretation of his or her nonverbal behavior is accurate.

Words are discrete entities; they have a beginning and an end. You can point to the first word in this sentence and underline the last one. Our nonverbal behaviors are not as easily dissected. Like the sweep of a second hand on a watch, nonverbal behaviors are continuous. Because gestures, facial expressions, and eye contact can flow from one situation to the next with seamless ease, interpreting nonverbal cues is challenging.

The Nonlinguistic Nature of Nonverbal Communication

Even though some writers in the 1960s and 70s tried to make readers think otherwise, there is no "language of the body." Julius Fast, author of the 1970 book *Body Language*, believed that nonverbal communication was a language with pattern and grammar, just like verbal communication.[14] He suggested that if you were savvy and observant enough, you could quickly and easily interpret certain nonverbal behaviors to mean certain things—in any case, at any time. For example, Fast contended that if a woman sat cross-legged and pumped her foot up and down while talking to a man, that was a clear-cut sign of her romantic interest in him. If someone didn't make eye contact, she or he was automatically dishonest and untrustworthy. If people crossed their arms in front of them, that indicated hostility.

The problem with this approach is that it didn't take into account the complexities of individual, contextual, and cultural differences. Pumping the foot might be an indication of nervousness, not attraction. Some people are shy; others come from a culture in which making direct eye contact is considered rude. It's important to remember that nonverbal communication doesn't conform to the patterns of a language.

The Multichanneled Nature of Nonverbal Communication

Have you ever tried to watch two or more TV programs at once? Some television sets let you see as many as eight programs simultaneously so that you can keep up with three ball games, two soap operas, the latest news, and your favorite sitcom. Like programs on a multichannel TV, nonverbal cues register on our senses from a variety of sources simultaneously. Just as you can really pay close attention to only one program at a time on your multichannel television, you actually attend to only one nonverbal cue at a time, although you can switch your attention very rapidly. Before you try to interpret the meaning of a single nonverbal behavior, look for clusters of corroborating nonverbal cues, in conjunction with verbal behavior, to get the most complete picture possible.

RECAP

The Nature of Nonverbal Communication

- *Nonverbal Communication Is Culture Bound:* Nonverbal behaviors vary widely across cultural and co-cultural groups. Interpret nonverbal cues within a cultural context.
- *Nonverbal Communication Is Rule Governed:* We develop rules or expectations for appropriate nonverbal behavior in ourselves and others.
- *Nonverbal Communication Is Ambiguous:* Nonverbal behavior is difficult to interpret accurately because the meanings for different actions vary from person to person.
- *Nonverbal Communication Is Continuous:* Unlike the stop-start nature of verbal communication, nonverbal messages flow from one situation to the next.
- *Nonverbal Communication Is Nonlinguistic:* Nonverbal communication does not have the regularities of vocabulary, grammar, and pattern that language has.
- *Nonverbal Communication Is Multichanneled:* Nonverbal cues register on our senses from a variety of sources simultaneously, but we can actually attend to only one nonverbal cue at a time.

CODES OF NONVERBAL COMMUNICATION

Because human nonverbal behavior is so diverse and vast, the need arises for classifications. Many individuals have long been fascinated with nonverbal communication, but those who have made perhaps the greatest contributions to our understanding are Paul Ekman and Wallace Friesen, sometimes referred to as the "great classifiers" of nonverbal behavior.[15] The primary categories or codes of nonverbal information researchers have studied include appearance; body movement, gestures, and posture; eye contact; facial expressions; touch; vocalics; and use of the physical environment, space, and territory. Although we concentrate on these codes as they are exhibited in mainstream Western culture, recognize that these behaviors are evidenced differently in other cultures. We introduce and explain each code, then provide a few research findings to illustrate how we can apply knowledge of nonverbal communication to further our understanding of human behavior.

Appearance

Many cultures around the world place a high value on appearance—body size and shape, skin color and texture, hairstyle, and clothing. We realize that we're writing from an American perspective, but it seems as though Americans place an undue emphasis on looks. For example, our views of and preferences for government leaders, especially presidents, are affected by their height.[16] College students give higher evaluation scores to professors whom they deem physically attractive.[17] We put such pressure on ourselves and others to be physically attractive that our self-esteem may decline when we realize we cannot match up with some perceived "ideal."[18] Americans elevate onto a pedestal persons who are perceived to be highly physically attractive, whether or not they actually deserve this kind of accolade. We also attach all sorts of desirable qualities to highly attractive people. Research shows that we tend to think physically attractive people are more credible, happy, popular, socially skilled, prosperous, employable, persuasive, honest, poised, strong, kind, outgoing, and sexually warm.[19]

Clothing functions primarily to keep us warm and within society's bounds of decency. Another important function is to convey a sense of one's culture. Clothing such as baseball caps, baggy pants, and distinctive T-shirts, as well as other appearance aspects, termed **artifacts** (jewelry, tattoos, piercings, makeup, cologne, eyeglasses, and so on), are displays of culture. This is particularly detectable when you travel abroad or entertain foreign visitors in your home country. The brightly colored gowns and matching headpieces worn by some African women, the beautiful saris (draped dresses) many Indian women wear, and veils over the faces of Muslim women are but a few examples of how clothing reveals one's culture.

Although we don't believe that "clothes make the man," clothing and artifacts do affect how we feel about ourselves and how we are perceived by others.[20] Studies have attempted to identify a "power" look. Advertisers are constantly giving us prescriptions for ways to be attractive and stylish, but the fact is that there is no formula for dressing for success.[21] Styles and expectations about appearances change. We have only to look at the clothing norms of the 1950s, 60s, or 70s to note how they are different from those of today. Other interesting applications of what we know about appearance include the development of "casual Friday" in the corporate world, the connection between black uniforms and aggression in sports, and the growing trend in public schools to require school uniforms.[22]

artifact
Clothing or another element of appearance (e.g., jewelry, tattoos, piercings, makeup, cologne).

Body Movement, Gestures, and Posture

Have you ever traveled in a country where you couldn't speak the language? Or have you tried to have a conversation locally with a person who didn't speak English or who was deaf and didn't read lips? What do you do in these situations? Chances are, you risk looking extremely foolish by using overexaggerated gestures or slowly and deliberately shouting words the listener cannot understand. These responses are nonverbal attempts to compensate for a lack of verbal understanding. Even when we do speak the same language as others, we often use gestures to help us make our point.

Kinesics is a general term for human movements, gestures, and posture. Technically, movements of the face and eyes are included in this category, but because one's face and eyes can produce such a wealth of information, we discuss them as separate codes. Researchers have long recognized that our kinesics provide valuable information to others. Have you ever seen someone and said "I just really like the way he carries himself"? We know that a person can't literally carry himself or herself, but what we refer to in this description is a person's posture, stance, and walk. Posture is greatly affected by self-esteem and emotional state, such that when you're feeling upbeat and good about yourself, you're likely to carry yourself more upright and possibly exhibit a "spring in your step." Conversely, if you're having a bad day, your posture might be more slumped over or stooped, because some days it's just hard to hold your head and shoulders up.

Gestures are also a subset of kinesics and, as we've said earlier in this chapter, they are culture bound, context bound, and rule governed. Nancy Armstrong and Melissa Wagner are the authors of a book entitled *Field Guide to Gestures,* in which they describe and interpret a wide variety of gestures, particularly as used in U.S. culture.[23] They

When your clothing functions as an *artifact* rather than simply a way to cover your body, it conveys some sense of your culture.

organize gestures into such categories as Arrival and Departure, Approval and Disapproval, Mating, and Offensive and Profane. Among the gestures in the Arrival and Departure category are the Bow, the Blown Kiss, the Fist-Chest Pound, and the Live Long and Prosper gesture (which needs no interpretation for *Star Trek* fans).

Various scholars and researchers have proposed models for analyzing and coding kinesics, just as we do for spoken or written language.[24] In one of their most comprehensive contributions to nonverbal research, Ekman and Friesen classified movement and gestures according to their function. They identified five kinesic categories: emblems, illustrators, affect displays, regulators, and adaptors.[25]

Emblems   Nonverbal cues that have specific, widely understood meanings in a given culture and may actually substitute for a word or phrase are called **emblems**. When you're busy typing a report that is due tomorrow and your roommate barges in to talk about weekend plans, you turn from your computer and hold up an open palm to indicate your desire for uninterrupted quiet. A librarian who wants people to stop talking in the stacks puts an index finger up to pursed lips. But remember that emblems emerge or are negotiated within cultures. Something as seemingly universal as a pointing gesture can be used in a culturally specific way to mean something different than you expect.

Illustrators   We frequently accompany a verbal message with nonverbal **illustrators** that either contradict, accent, or complement the message.[26] Yawning while proclaiming that you're not tired is an example of a nonverbal illustrator that contradicts the verbal message. Slamming a book closed while announcing, "I don't want to read this any more" is a nonverbal accent to a verbal message. Frequent complementary illus-

kinesics
Human movement, gesture, and posture.

emblem
A nonverbal cue that has a specific, generally understood meaning in a given culture and may substitute for a word or phrase.

illustrator
A nonverbal behavior that accompanies a verbal message and either complements, contradicts, or accents it.

trators are used when one person gives another directions to a location. You probably even use them when you talk on the phone, although probably not as many as you use in face-to-face conversation.[27]

Affect Displays   Nonverbal cues that communicate emotion are called **affect displays**. As early as 1872, when Charles Darwin systematically studied the expression of emotion in both humans and animals, scientists realized that nonverbal cues are the primary ways humans communicate emotion.[28] Facial expressions, posture, and gestures reveal our emotions.[29] Your face tends to express which *kind* of emotion you are feeling, while your body reveals the intensity or how *much* of the emotion you are feeling. If you're happy, for example, your face may telegraph your joy to others. The movement of your hands, the openness of your posture, and the speed with which you move tell others just how happy you are. Likewise, if you're depressed, your face reveals your sadness or dejection, unless you're very practiced at masking your emotions. Your slumped shoulders and lowered head indicate the intensity of your despair.

Regulators   **Regulators** control the interaction or flow of communication between people. When we're eager to respond to a message, we're likely to make eye contact, raise our eyebrows, open our mouth, take in a breath, and lean forward slightly. When we do not want to be part of the conversation, we do the opposite: We tend to avert our eyes, close our mouth, cross our arms, and lean back in our seats or away from the verbal action.

Adaptors   As teachers, we find it interesting to watch a group of students take an exam. Students who are nervous about the exam or who have general test anxiety exhibit their nervousness in many different ways. They shift frequently in their seats, tap their pencils or pens on the desktop (often unconsciously), or run their hands through their hair over and over again. Then there's the thigh shaker. Some students can make their legs quiver up and down at a high speed, and they don't usually realize they're doing it. All of these behaviors are examples of **adaptors**—nonverbal behaviors that help us to satisfy a personal need or adapt to the immediate situation.

What are some of the more interesting applications of the research on kinesics? Consider flirting. Even if you're married or in some other form of committed relationship, you probably find it interesting to think about how people flirt or show attraction and interest in one another. Research has explored verbal and nonverbal indications of attraction.[30] One study found 52 gestures and nonverbal behaviors that women use to signal their interest in men. Among the top nonverbal flirting cues were smiling, surveying a crowded room with the eyes, and moving closer to the object of one's affection.[31] However, other studies have found that men tend to view flirting as more sexual than women do, and men often misinterpret women's friendly behaviors as signs of sexual attraction and interest.[32] One study found that the likelihood for this kind of misinterpretation greatly increased as alcohol consumption increased.[33]

Another body of research along these lines has examined **quasi-courtship behavior**, those nonverbal actions we consciously and unconsciously exhibit when we are attracted to someone.[34] The first stage of quasi-courtship behavior is *courtship readiness*. When we are attracted to someone, we may alter our normal pattern of eye contact, suck in our stomach, tense our muscles, and stand up straight. The second stage includes *preening* behaviors, which include combing our hair, applying makeup, straightening our tie, pulling up our socks, and double-checking our appearance in the mirror. Research shows that women tend to preen more than men.[35] In stage three, we demonstrate *positional cues*, using our posture and body orientation to make sure we are seen and noticed by another person, as well as to position ourselves to prevent invasion by a third party. We intensify these cues in the fourth stage, termed *appeals to invitation*, using close proximity, exposed skin, open body positions, and direct eye contact to signal our availability and interest.

affect display
A nonverbal behavior that communicates emotions.

regulator
A nonverbal behavior that helps to control the interaction or level of communication between people.

adaptor
A nonverbal behavior that helps satisfy a personal need and helps a person adapt or respond to the immediate situation.

quasi-courtship behavior
Nonverbal behaviors exhibited both consciously and unconsciously when we are attracted to someone.

Ethics and *Communication*

Lie Detectors

*W*e have good information now as to how most people behave when they are being untruthful. Unless we have ice in our veins, most of us register some kind of higher activation in our bodies when we attempt to deceive, such as increased heart rate and elevated skin temperature. Lie detector machines track just such physiological changes as indications of deception. Other instruments track patterns in the voice, such as vocal emphasis and rising intonation. Research has shown that most people's voices have a tendency to get higher in pitch when they try to deceive. What lie detector professionals look for is a change in a person's normal behavior, any change from the baseline that is typically taken at the beginning of a lie detector session. Do you think that modern lie detectors are sophisticated enough that the results of lie detector tests should be allowed as evidence in court trials? Is it unethical to "wire up" a suspect in

order to track bodily and vocal changes that might indicate deception? Do you believe that someone can actually "beat" a lie detector?

RECAP

Categories of Movements and Gestures

Category	Definition	Example
Emblems	Behaviors that have specific, generally understood meanings	A hitchhiker's raised thumb
Illustrators	Cues that accompany verbal messages and provide meaning	A speaker pounding on the podium to emphasize a point
Affect Displays	Expressions of emotion	Hugging to express love
Regulators	Cues that control and manage the flow of communication	Making eye contact when you wish to speak
Adaptors	Behaviors that help you adjust to your environment	Chewing your fingernails, indicating nervousness

Eye Contact

Do you agree that the eyes are the "windows to the soul"? What can people tell about you by looking into your eyes? Are you comfortable making eye contact with most people or only with people you know well? Eye contact is extremely important in U.S. culture, as well as in many other cultures around the world. Americans, in particular, make all kinds of judgments about others—particularly about their trustworthiness and sincerity—on the basis of whether they make or avoid eye contact. It's an interesting exercise to inventory your own eye behavior, thinking about when you're apt to look at someone and when you're apt to avert your gaze.

You are most likely to look at a conversational partner when you are physically distant from her or him, are discussing impersonal topics, have nothing else to look at, are interested in your partner's reactions, are romantically interested in your partner, wish to dominate or influence your partner, come from a culture that emphasizes visual contact in interaction, are an extrovert, are listening rather than talking, or are female.

On the Web

Are you a "people watcher"? Most of us who study communication become more avid people watchers, particularly in the realm of nonverbal communication, because human beings are truly fascinating creatures. The human face is capable of producing an enormous number of expressions, most of which arise through a combination of movements of various areas of the face. The more aware you become of your own capacity for facial expression, the better able you will be to convey your emotions and thoughts to others. In addition, the more perceptive and sensitive a receiver and interpreter of others' facial expressions you become, the better a communicator you will become as you listen, respond, and adapt to other people.

To help you develop these skills, we direct your attention to a Web site entirely devoted to the study of the human face: www.face-and-emotion.com/dataface/.

On this site, scholars who study the face for its communicative abilities explore its permanent and transient features and offer research citations and information about people who study this topic.

You are less likely to look at your partner when you are physically close; are discussing intimate topics; have other objects, people, or backgrounds to look at; are not interested in your partner's reactions; are talking rather than listening; are not interested in or dislike your partner; come from a culture that does not value visual contact during interaction; are an introvert; are embarrassed, ashamed, sorrowful, sad, submissive, or trying to hide something; or are male.[36]

Research shows that eye contact plays a significant role in judgments of a public speaker's credibility.[37] In the first televised presidential debate, John F. Kennedy appeared comfortable and confident as he made eye contact with television cameras. It seemed as though he was making eye contact directly with the American public. In contrast, Richard Nixon darted his eyes nervously from side to side at times and generally made less eye contact with the camera and the viewing audience. This created a perception that Nixon was shifty, untrustworthy, and lacking credibility. American presentational speaking teachers emphasize eye contact as a key nonverbal element of speech delivery.

Studies on eye behavior continue to contribute to our understanding of deception and how people behave when they lie or mislead others.[38] Eye behaviors most often associated with deception include rapid blinking, diminished eye contact, and rapid eye movement. One fascinating study examined videotaped footage of the Senate Confirmation Hearings in which now-Supreme Court Justice Clarence Thomas and Anita Hill offered strikingly different accounts of events in their professional relationship, with Hill claiming that Thomas had sexually harassed her.[39] The researchers concluded, from evaluating a range of deception cues (including eye behavior), that Thomas exhibited a pattern of deception in his testimony to the Senate committee, while Hill did not.

Facial Expressions

Whether or not you like actor/comedian Jim Carrey, you've got to admit that the guy's face seems made of rubber. He seems to be able to display a broader range of emotions and reactions on his face than the average person, even if many of these facial contortions are more exaggerated than those the average person would use. Ekman and Friesen suggest that the human face is capable of producing 250,000 different facial expressions.[40] Jim Carrey can probably make all of them.

The face is the exhibit gallery for our emotional displays. Suppose you buy a new expensive gadget and show it to your romantic partner or a friend. Or as an interviewer reads your resumé you sit in silence across the desk. In both of these situations, you scan the other person's face, eagerly awaiting some reaction. To interpret someone's facial expressions accurately, you need to focus on what the other person may be thinking or feeling. It helps if you know the person well, can see her or his whole face, have plenty of time to observe, and understand the situation that prompted the reaction.[41]

How accurately do we interpret emotions expressed on the face? Researchers who have attempted to measure subjects' skill in identifying the emotional expressions of others have found it a tricky business.[42] According to Ekman and Friesen, the human face universally exhibits six primary emotions: happiness, sadness, surprise, fear, anger, and disgust or contempt. But these researchers note that, even though our faces provide a great deal of information about emotions, we quickly learn to control our facial expressions.[43] One fascinating study examined children's facial expressions when they received either wonderful, new toys or broken, disappointing toys.[44] When they received the disappointing toys, the children showed a flash of disappointment on their

faces, but then very quickly they masked their disappointment and changed their facial expressions to reveal a more positive, socially appropriate reaction. Even very young children learn to control the way an emotion registers on their face. Another study found that abused children, sensitive to violence at home, are hypersensitive to anger in facial expressions. They are more likely to interpret sad or fearful facial expressions as angry.[45]

As adults, we come to realize that there are times when it is inappropriate and unwise to reveal our emotions fully, such as crying in front of superiors when we've been passed over for promotion or becoming visibly angry when a project doesn't come our way. But there are times when this learned masking of emotion—the development of a "poker face"—can endanger your relationships. Consider aloof, distant parents who can't separate themselves from their work to enjoy the company of their own children, or romantic partners who complain that they can't tell how their partners feel about them because emotional displays have been squelched. The best approach is a balance of control and spontaneity. You want to stay real and human, to be able to reveal to others what you feel, but there are times when doing so can be inappropriate or damaging.

Touch

Touch is the most powerful form of nonverbal communication; it is also the most misunderstood and carries the potential for the most problems if ill used. Consider some moments involving accidental touch. Standing elbow to elbow in an elevator or sitting next to a large individual in a crowded airplane, you may find yourself in physical contact with total strangers. As you stiffen your body and avert your eyes, a baffling sense of shame and discomfort floods over you. Why do we react this way to accidental touching? Normally, we touch to express intimacy. When intimacy is not our intended message, we instinctively react to modify the impression our touch has created.

Countless studies on touch, termed **haptics** in research, have shown that intimate human contact is vital to our personal development and well-being.[46] Infants and children need physical contact to confirm that they are valued and loved. Advocates of breast-feeding argue that this form of intimate touching strengthens the bond between mother and child.[47]

Think about your role models and the lessons you learned about touch while growing up. If you grew up in a two-parent family, did your parents display affection in front of the children? If not, you may have grown up believing that affectionate touching should not be done in front of others. As an adult, you may be uncomfortable with public displays of affection. If you grew up with parents or family members who were affectionate with each other and their children, then, as an adult, your **touch ethic**— what you consider appropriate touching—is influenced by that experience. We don't mean to insinuate that a touch ethic that accepts public affection is somehow more psychologically healthy than one that relegates touching to private moments. But what if you date or partner with someone whose experiences while growing up led to a very

haptics
The study of human touch.

touch ethic
A person's own guidelines or standards as to appropriate and inappropriate touch.

different touch ethic than yours? You may be headed for some conflict, but hopefully some compromise as well.

The amount of touch we need, initiate, tolerate, and receive depends on many factors. As we've indicated, the amount and kind of touching you receive in your family is the biggest influence. Your cultural background has a significant effect as well. Certain cultures are high-contact—meaning that touching is quite commonplace—such as some European and Middle Eastern cultures in which men kiss each other on the cheek as a greeting. Other cultures are low-contact, like some Asian cultures in which demonstrations of affection are rare and considered inappropriate.[48]

Research on haptics has explored such topics as the role of touch in receiving sexual consent and how touch may be involved in behavior deemed sexually harassing.[49] Other research continues to focus on gender differences and touch. For years, studies showed that women touched members of both sexes more often and received more touches than men, leading to the conclusion that touch was more appropriate behavior for females than for males. Recent studies suggest that sex differences in the frequency of touch have diminished, but men and women still tend to differ in the meanings they assign to touch.[50]

The Voice

"We have nothing to fear but fear itself."
"Ask not what your country can do for you—ask what you can do for your country."
"I have a dream . . . I have a dream today."
"I am not a crook."
"Mr. Gorbachev, tear down this wall."

If you read these statements and recognize them as having been made by American leaders, you are likely to read them using the same pauses and changes in pitch, volume, and emphasis as did the famous person. John F. Kennedy greatly emphasized the word *not*, as in "Ask NOT what your country . . . ." Martin Luther King Jr., used rising pitch and increased volume as he uttered the word *dream* over and over again in his speech. These leaders learned to use the tremendous capacity and versatility of the voice to create memorable moments, even if those moments occurred in unpleasant circumstances.

Like your face, your voice is a major vehicle for communicating your thoughts and emotions. The pitch, rate, and volume at which you speak, and your use of silence— elements termed **paralanguage** or **vocalics**—all provide important clues. Imagine that your spouse, romantic partner, or best friend modeled a new outfit, asking you what you think. If you really hated the person's new outfit, would you say enthusiastically, "That looks GREAT!"—which could either be an untruth designed to prevent hurt feelings or an expression of sarcasm? Or would you say, "That looks nice" in a halfhearted way? Or would you go into some long, careful explanation of why you thought the outfit was okay, but just not your favorite thing? Your ability to convey these different reactions is accomplished by the human voice.

The voice reveals our thoughts, emotions, and the nature of our relationships with others, but it also provides information about our self-confidence and knowledge, and influences how we are perceived by others.[51] Most of us would conclude, as has research, that a speaker who mumbles, speaks very slowly and softly, continually mispronounces words, and uses "uh" and "um" is less credible and persuasive than one who speaks clearly, rapidly, fluently, and with appropriate volume.[52]

In addition to providing information about thoughts, emotions, self-confidence, and knowledge, vocal cues serve a regulatory function in conversation, signaling when we want to talk and when we don't.[53] When we're finished talking, we tend to lower the volume and pitch of our final words. When we want to talk, we may start by interjecting sounds such as "I . . . I . . . I . . ." or "Ah . . . Um . . ." to interrupt the speaker and grab the verbal ball. We also may use more cues like "Sure," "I understand," "Uh-huh," or

paralanguage (vocalics)
Nonverbal aspects of voice (e.g., pitch, rate, volume, use of silence).

Diversity and Communication

Cultural Meanings of Silence

*I*n his essay "Cultural Uses and Interpretations of Silence," communication scholar Charles Braithwaite explores the functions of silence "beyond one's own speech community" in an effort to discover cross-cultural generalizations.[54] He examined descriptions of the use of silence within many cultural groups and found two common themes:

1. When people don't know each other very well or circumstances between them create a degree of uncertainty, silence may increase, but it is seen as expected and appropriate. This tendency emerged within cultural groups as diverse as some Indian tribes, Japanese Americans in Hawaii, Japanese, and Americans in rural Appalachia.

2. Recognized status differences are associated with silence. When a difference in power level or status is detected, lower status persons are expected to be silent and monitor when it is appropriate to engage in conversation. This tendency was particularly distinct within parent–child relationships, evidenced in such diverse peoples as the Anang of Southwestern Nigeria, the Wolof of Senegal, some urban African American women, the residents of the LaHave Islands (off the coast of Nova Scotia), some Indian tribes, and some American blue-collar workers.

"Okay" to signal that we understand another's message and now we want to talk or end the conversation. These vocalizations, termed **back-channel cues**, are particularly useful in telephone conversations when no other nonverbal cues can help signal that we would like to get off the phone.

Sometimes it's not what we say or even how we say it that communicates our feelings. Pausing and being silent communicate volumes.[55] You may be at a loss for words or need time to think about what you want to contribute to a conversation, so pausing or being silent may be better than fumbling about for the right way to express yourself. When someone tells a lie, he or she may need a few moments to think up what to say. Nonverbal researchers have studied **response latency**, or how long it takes someone to formulate a response to a statement or question in conversation, to better understand vocal cues that may indicate deception.[56] You may be silent because you want to distance yourself from those around you or indicate that you don't want to engage in conversation. Silence can be a sign of respect, but it can also be an indication of anger (as when you give someone "the silent treatment") or discomfort (as in "an awkward silence"). At other times you may feel so comfortable with someone that words aren't necessary; psychologist Sidney Baker calls these moments "positive silence."[57]

Physical Environment, Space, and Territory

Close your eyes and picture your bedroom as it is right now—whether it's a dorm room that you share with someone, the room you've lived in for many years in your parents' house, or a bedroom shared with a spouse or partner. Try to get a clear, detailed mental image of how that room looks right now. Then think about this: If one of your professors were to walk into your bedroom right now, what would she or he think about you? What impressions about you would he or she form, given the physical setup of that room? Does the room reveal your need for privacy? Are there hints as to who owns the space, meaning do you have any territorial clues in the room? Is the closet door in that room open or closed?

These questions all have to do with your interaction with the physical environment and the space around you. You may be unused to looking at the environment as a form of nonverbal communication, but the mini-world you create for yourself reveals a good deal about you. Also, your preferred amount of space, the level of ownership you attach to that space, and your behavior as you delineate and protect that space are fascinating nonverbal elements that researchers continue to study.

back-channel cue
A vocal cue that signals when we want to talk and when we don't.

response latency
The amount of time it takes someone to formulate a response to a statement or question in conversation.

The Physical Environment   What's so great about a corner office with wall-to-wall windows? It's one of many indications in U.S. culture of high status. In a working world increasingly structured into cubicles, an employee's desk location serves as a symbol of importance.[58] As one scholar put it, "People cannot be understood outside of their environmental context."[59] In Chapter 3 we discussed several principles governing the use of verbal language, one being that language is context bound—people derive the meaning of words in context. Likewise, nonverbal actions are only meaningfully interpreted when context is taken into account.[60] The environment is important to the study of nonverbal behavior in two ways: (1) The choices you make about the environment in which you live and operate reveal a good deal about who you are, and (2) your nonverbal behavior is altered by the various environments in which you communicate.

First, the physical environments in which we function can be seen as extensions of our personalities. You may not be able to manipulate all elements of your environment, like the physical limitations of room size, but to whatever extent you are allowed, you will make your "signature" on your physical environs. Humans like to structure and adorn the settings in which they work, study, and reside to make them unique and personal. Rarely will you find an office, even a cubicle, that contains absolutely no personal artifacts.

Second, your behavior and perceptions are altered because of the physical environments in which you find yourself.[61] Your body may be more rigid, gestures more restrained, clothing more formal, and speech limited and whispered when you're in a church. (Obviously, this depends on the church.) In contrast, at a concert by a favorite musician, you move freely, wear comfortable clothing, and scream and applaud wildly.

The knowledge that humans react according to their interface with a physical environment has been put to some interesting uses. For example, designers of fast-food restaurants often use vibrant colors, uncomfortable seating, and brightly lit eating areas to discourage patrons from lingering. The point in the fast-food business is high volume, which means high turnover. So these environments are constructed so that you will be attracted to come in, eat, and leave quickly to make room for another customer. In contrast, some restaurants offer an intimate and warm environment, one that makes customers want to linger and enjoy a long meal (with a pricey tab).[62]

Space   Imagine that you are sitting alone at a long, rectangular table in your campus library. As you sit dutifully with your head in a textbook, you are startled when a complete stranger sits directly across from you at the table. Since there are several empty chairs at the other end of the table, you may feel uncomfortable that this unknown individual has invaded *your* area.

Every culture has well-established ways of regulating spatial relations. Normally, we don't think much about the rules or norms we follow regarding space until those rules are violated. Violations can be alarming, possibly even threatening. How physically close we are willing to get to others relates to how well we know them, to considerations of power and status, and to our cultural background.

One of the pioneers in helping us understand personal space was Edward T. Hall. In his study of **proxemics**, the distances that people allow between themselves and objects or other people, Hall identified four spatial zones that we unconsciously define for ourselves, as shown in Figure 4.2.[63] Two people who are between 0 and 1½ feet apart are occupying an *intimate space*, in which the most personal communication occurs. This space is open only to those with whom we are well acquainted, unless we're forced to stand in an elevator or some other crowded space.

The second zone, ranging from 1½ to 4 feet from another person, is called *personal space*. Most of our conversations with family and friends occur in this zone. If someone we don't know well enters this space on purpose, we may feel uncomfortable. Zone three, *social space*, ranges from 4 to 12 feet from another person. Most formal group interactions, as well as many of our professional relationships, take place in this zone. *Public space*, the fourth zone, begins at 12 feet from another person. Interpersonal com-

proxemics
Study of how close or far away from people and objects we position ourselves.

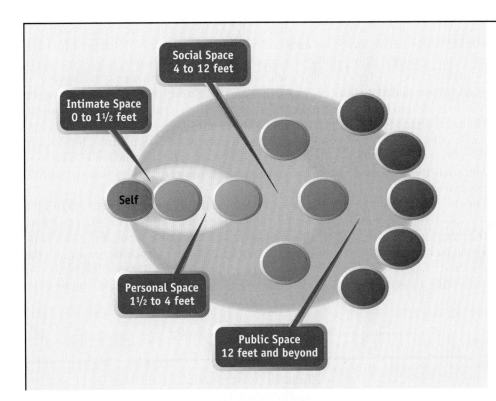

FIGURE 4.2
Edwin T. Hall's Four Zones of
Space

munication does not usually occur in this zone; many presentational speakers position themselves at least 12 feet away from their audiences.

The specific space that you and others choose depends on several variables, most specifically your cultural background. But the more you like people, the closer you will stand to them. Higher-status and larger persons are afforded more space than lower-status and smaller persons.[64] We also tend to stand closer to others in a large room than we do in a small room. In general, women tend to stand closer to others than men do.[65]

RECAP

Edward T. Hall's Classification of Spatial Zones

Category	Definition	Distance between Individuals
Zone One	Intimate Space	0–1½ feet
Zone Two	Personal Space	1½–4 feet
Zone Three	Social Space	4–12 feet
Zone Four	Public Space	12 feet and beyond

Territory   The study of how people use space and objects to communicate occupancy or ownership of space is termed **territoriality**.[66] You assumed ownership of that table in the library and the right to determine who sat with you. You may have reacted negatively not only because your sense of personal space was invaded, but also because the intrusive stranger broke a cultural rule governing territoriality.

You announce your ownership of space with **territorial markers**—things and actions that signify an area has been claimed. When you arrive at class, for example, you may put your book bag on a chair while you get up and sharpen a pencil or run across the hall to the "facilities." That book bag signifies temporary ownership of your seat. If you returned to find that someone had moved your stuff and was sitting in your

territoriality
Study of how humans use space and objects to communicate occupancy or ownership of space.

territorial marker
A thing or action that signifies an area has been claimed.

seat, you would probably become indignant. The most common form of territorial marker is a lock. We lock our doors and windows, cars, offices, briefcases, luggage, televisions (using V-chips), and computers so as to keep out intruders.

We also use markers to indicate where our space stops and someone else's starts. "Good fences make good neighbors," wrote the poet Robert Frost. When someone sits too close, we may try to erect a physical barrier, such as a stack of books or a napkin holder, or we might use our body as a shield by turning away. If we can't erect a physical barrier, we may erect a symbolic barrier to convey ownership, through the use of such things as partitions, objects, lighting, or elevation.[67] If an intruder doesn't get the hint that "this land is our land," we may ultimately resort to words to announce that the space is occupied.

One interesting line of research explores verbal and nonverbal behaviors in the workplace that contribute to a "hostile climate" of sexual harassment.[68] In relation to the environment, space, and territoriality, a workplace might contain art (posters, flyers on bulletin boards) that depicts sexual images, a boss might come too far into the personal space of an employee, or a coworker might commit a territorial breach by "snooping" in someone's office for evidence of personal relationships, like photos.

RECAP

Codes of Nonverbal Communication

Appearance	Influences perceptions of credibility and attractiveness
Body Movement, Gestures, and Posture	Communicate information, status, warmth, credibility, interest in others, attitudes, and liking
Eye Contact	Conveys trustworthiness, sincerity, honesty, and interest
Facial Expressions	Reveal thoughts and express emotions and attitudes
Touch	Communicates intimacy, affection, and rejection
Voice	Communicates emotion and clarifies the meaning of messages through pitch, rate, and volume
Environment	Communicates information about the person who functions in that environment; provides context that alters behavior
Space	Provides information about status, power, and intimacy
Territory	Provides cues as to use, ownership, and occupancy of space

HOW TO INTERPRET NONVERBAL CUES MORE ACCURATELY

How do we make sense out of all of the nonverbal cues we receive from others? Time and patience improve your receiving ability. If you earnestly want to accurately interpret and sensitively respond to someone's nonverbal communication, you must be willing to spend time and effort to develop this skill. You have already learned a good deal about nonverbal communication from reading this chapter, studying this topic in class, and living as many years as you have lived. But enhancing your interpretive skills requires, first, an awareness of the importance of nonverbal elements in the communication process. Many people make interpretive mistakes because they overemphasize

What nonverbal cues tell you that these three men are friends who genuinely like each other? Are there any cues that contradict that impression?

the words people say. Verbal communication is important, but remember that the greater portion of someone's total message is conveyed nonverbally. A second requirement is the willingness and emotional maturity to make your own behavior secondary to that of someone else. In other words, if you're so wrapped up in yourself that you can only think about and deal with how *you're* feeling, what *you're* thinking, and what *you* want at a given moment, you can't possibly hope to take in others' nonverbal cues, interpret them accurately, and respond appropriately. As we discussed in Chapter 2, an awareness of oneself as a communicator expands with each interaction with another person.

It's also important to remember to take into account the cultural backgrounds of those with whom you communicate. Be careful not to automatically attach your own cultural frame of reference when you decipher nonverbal cues. As we've stated, the context within which nonverbal cues are communicated plays an important role. It's wise to be aware of your surroundings and other situational factors when interpreting the meaning of nonverbal actions. Be prepared to fail. We all struggle to make sense out of others' actions; no one has this skill down pat. Use your interpretive failures to learn lessons you can apply to the next encounter.

Beyond these suggestions, we recommend that you keep in mind a three-part framework developed by Albert Mehrabian to help you improve your nonverbal interpretive skills. Mehrabian found that we synthesize and interpret nonverbal cues along three primary dimensions: immediacy, arousal, and dominance.[69]

Immediacy

Why do we like some people and dislike others? Sometimes we can't put a finger on the precise reason. Mehrabian contends that **immediacy**—nonverbal behavior that communicates liking and engenders feelings of pleasure—is a probable explanation. The principle underlying immediacy is simple: We like and respond positively to people who tend to display immediacy cues and avoid or respond negatively to those who don't. Among the immediacy cues that show liking and interest are the following:[70]

- Proximity: Close, forward lean
- Body orientation: Face-to-face or side-by-side position
- Eye contact: Eye contact and mutual eye contact
- Facial expression: Smiling
- Gestures: Head nods, movement

immediacy
Feelings of liking, pleasure, and closeness communicated by such nonverbal cues as eye contact, forward lean, touch, and open body orientation.

- Posture: Open and relaxed, arms oriented toward others
- Touch: Culture- and context-appropriate touch
- Voice: Higher pitch, upward pitch

So how do you apply this information to help you improve your nonverbal receiving skills? Let's say that you go to a party and become attracted to someone there. You're introduced to the person and engage in a get-to-know-you kind of conversation. Your best bet is to attend to the person's nonverbal cues to determine if the person likes you. Although you can't know for sure that someone's nonverbal behavior translates into liking, immediacy cues can provide some information. Watch for a direct body orientation, as opposed to turning away from you and orienting toward the rest of the room. Watch for eye contact, smiling and other pleasant facial expressions, a rising intonation in the voice, and a forward lean toward you, rather than a backward lean, which can signal disinterest.

Arousal

When the term **arousal** is used in nonverbal research, it doesn't necessarily mean sexual arousal. According to nonverbal scholar Peter Andersen, the term relates to "the degree to which a person is stimulated or activated."[71] Arousal prepares the body for action, with such physiological indications as increased heart rate, blood pressure, and brain temperature. Arousal, in this sense, can occur when you drive fast or experience athletic exhilaration. Externally, the face, voice, and movement are primary indicators of arousal. If you detect arousal cues in someone, such as increased eye contact, closer conversational distances, increased touch, animated vocalics, more direct body orientation, and more smiling and active facial expressions, you can conclude with some degree of certainty that the other person is responsive to and interested in you or what you have to say. If the person acts passive or bored, as evidenced by few (or no) arousal cues, you can safely conclude that he or she is uninterested.

The next time you're at a party, become a people-watcher for a moment. Check out which people look interested in the persons they're talking to and which ones look bored or like they'd rather be somewhere else, anywhere else. You can tell how people feel about each other—not with absolute accuracy, but with a high degree of certainty—just by looking for things like body orientation (whether they are facing each other directly or not), synchronized movement (meaning that when one shifts in position, the other shifts, as in a rhythmic response), smiling, laughter, and other arousal cues.[72]

Dominance

The third dimension of Mehrabian's framework communicates the balance of power in a relationship. **Dominance** cues communicate status, position, and importance. When interacting with a person of lower status, a higher-status person tends to have a relaxed body posture, less direct body orientation to the lower-status person, a downward head tilt, and less smiling, head nodding, and facial animation.[73] When you talk to professors, they may lean back in the chair, put their feet on the desk, and fold their hands behind their head during the conversation. But unless your professors are colleagues or friends, you will maintain a relatively formal posture during your interaction in their offices.

The use of space is another dominance cue. High-status individuals usually have more space around them; they have bigger offices and more "barriers" (human and nonhuman) protecting them. A receptionist in an office is usually easily accessible, but to reach the CEO of the company you probably have to navigate through several corridors and past several secretaries and administrative assistants who are "guarding" the door.

arousal
Feelings of interest and excitement communicated by such nonverbal cues as vocal expression, facial expressions, and gestures.

dominance
Feelings of power, status, and control communicated by such nonverbal cues as relaxed posture, greater personal space, and protected personal space.

Other power cues are communicated by clothing, furniture, and locations. You may wear jeans and a T-shirt to class; the president of the university probably wears a business suit. You study at a table in the library; the college dean has a large private desk. Your dorm may be surrounded by other dorms; the president's residence may be a large house surrounded by a lush, landscaped garden in a prestigious neighborhood. You struggle to find a parking place within a half-a-globe of your classroom buildings; high-ranking campus administrators usually have reserved parking spots (sometimes with their names on them).

When you attempt to interpret someone's nonverbal communication, realize that there is a good deal of room for error. Humans are complex, and they don't always send clear signals. But the more you learn about nonverbal communication, the more you become aware of your own communication and the communication of others, the greater your chances of accurately perceiving and interpreting someone's nonverbal message.

RECAP

Dimensions for Interpreting Nonverbal Behavior

Dimension	Definition	Nonverbal Cues
Immediacy	Cues that communicate liking and pleasure	Eye contact, touch, forward lean, direct body orientation, physical closeness, smiling
Arousal	Cues that communicate active interest and emotional involvement	Eye contact, varied vocal cues, touch, animated facial expressions, direct body orientation, movement, physical closeness
Dominance	Cues that communicate status	Larger and protected space, eye contact, initiated touch, relaxed posture, status symbols

PRINCIPLES FOR A LIFETIME: Enhancing Your Skills

Nonverbal

Principle Three: Effectively use and interpret nonverbal messages.

- Realize the importance of physical appearance and attractiveness in U.S. culture.
- Use culturally appropriate body movement, including posture and gestures, to convey messages.
- Work on making appropriate eye contact with others, given that eye contact is the key nonverbal behavior linked with credibility and trustworthiness.
- Become more aware of your facial expressions and the facial expressions of others, since this nonverbal channel is a primary one for conveying emotions.
- Use touch appropriately, given the cultural context within which you communicate.
- Become more aware of the potential you have for vocal expression and of how others use their vocal capacities to communicate emotions and ideas.
- Survey yourself to become aware of your own rules regarding space and territoriality, so that you may better understand and enact proxemic nonverbal behaviors in your interactions with others.
- Recognize that body movement, eye contact, facial expressions, touch, vocal behaviors, and use of space and territory can all communicate liking, interest, and dominance.

SUMMARY

Successful communicators effectively use and interpret nonverbal messages. Nonverbal communication is central to our ability to function competently in relationships, because we convey our feelings and attitudes and detect the emotional states of others primarily through nonverbal channels. In most cases when verbal and nonverbal messages contradict, we should believe the nonverbal because it tends to carry the truer meaning of the message. (Again, leave open the option that you may be wrong.) Nonverbal cues are important not only in the early stages of relationships, but also as we maintain and deepen and sometimes terminate those relationships. Nonverbal messages function with verbal messages, in that they can substitute for, complement, contradict, repeat, regulate, and accent our words.

Accurately interpreting nonverbal cues is a challenge because of the nature of nonverbal communication. First, nonverbal communication is culture bound, meaning that we must account for the cultural context within which behavior occurs before making an interpretation of that behavior. Second, nonverbal communication is rule governed, in that we form rules or expectations as to appropriate behavior. Third, nonverbal communication is ambiguous; the exact meanings of nonverbal messages are truly known only to the person displaying them. Fourth, nonverbal communication is continuous; it flows in a steady stream without a definite starting and stopping point. Fifth, unlike verbal communication, nonverbal communication is not a language with a set pattern and rules of usage. Its nonlinguistic nature makes for more complicated interpretation. Finally, nonverbal communication is multichanneled, meaning that cues register on our senses from a variety of sources simultaneously.

Nonverbal cues have been categorized into separate codes. Personal appearance is a powerful communicator, especially in U.S. culture, where people make all sorts of judgments based on someone's looks. Kinesics, which include body movement, posture, and gestures, communicate both content and relational information when we use them as emblems, illustrators, affect displays, regulators, and adaptors. Eye contact is an important code for conveying liking and regulating interaction. Facial expressions and vocal cues provide a wealth of information about our thoughts, emotions, and attitudes. Touch is the most powerful nonverbal cue; it communicates the level of intimacy in a relationship, as well as liking and status. Finally, the way we react to and manipulate environments, as well as our use of space and territory, communicate a variety of messages related to power and status.

It is a challenge to assess our own nonverbal communication and to read and interpret others' nonverbal messages, but a general framework of three dimensions developed by Mehrabian can assist us in the process. Immediacy cues provide information about liking; arousal cues tip others off as to our interest and level of engagement with them; and position, power, and status are often communicated through dominance cues. Humans are complex, so the interpretation of nonverbal cues is never simple. However, the more we learn about this form of behavior and become aware of our own and others' nonverbal communication, the more sensitively and effectively we will interact with others.

Discussion and Review

1. Why focus on nonverbal messages? Why are nonverbal cues important?
2. Identify six elements that describe the nature of nonverbal communication. Then think about people who seem to be "clueless," meaning that they do not readily attend to or accurately interpret others' nonverbal behavior. What makes some people savvy readers of nonverbal cues while others remain clueless?
3. How is nonverbal communication affected by culture? Provide examples of ways that a lack of cultural understanding can cause problems.
4. Why do you think that people in the United States place such importance on appearance and attractiveness? Is this emphasis helpful, harmful, or a bit of both?

5. Explain how eye contact, facial expressions, and various vocal cues reveal our thoughts, emotions, and attitudes.

6. What is your "touch ethic"? What experiences growing up contributed to your standards for appropriate and inappropriate touch?

7. How you manipulate the environments within your control and use space and territory reveal a great deal about you. What would someone learn about you if she or he observed you in your home environment? What kind of interpretations would the observer make from watching you use and control space?

8. Explain Mehrabian's three-part system for interpreting nonverbal cues more accurately.

Putting Principles into Practice

1. Take a field trip with some classmates to a fast-food restaurant. Assign some members the task of observing nonverbal cues in the environment, noting colors, furniture and other fixtures, lighting, and temperature. Others should take note of the employees' appearance, paying special attention to clothing and signs of status and individuality. Finally, have some members watch for gestures that act as emblems, such as signals indicating how many burgers a customer wants. Coworkers often develop nonverbal "shorthand" that facilitates efficient communication; note any such behaviors.

2. Generate examples of how nonverbal behaviors in the categories of kinesics, facial expressions, eye contact, and proxemics are affected by deception. For example, how is eye contact affected? Do the best liars avert their gaze, or do they learn to lie while looking right in someone's eyes?

3. Generate examples of body movements that reveal the following six emotions. Then generate alternative meanings for the movement. For example, we've said that crossed arms might reveal either anger or that someone is closed off or not open to discussing something. We've provided an example.

Emotion	Body Movements	Alternative Meanings
Embarrassment	Covering the face with one's hands	Could also indicate deception
Happiness		
Anger		
Surprise		
Fear		
Disgust		
Sadness		

4. We've explored the nonverbal codes of space and territory, and you should now have a better understanding of the range of human reactions to space invasions. Read each of these situations, decide if a proxemic or territorial violation has occurred, and then generate two tactics you would use in response to each situation. Try not to think of things a person *might* do, but of what you actually would do in the situation.

   a. You are at a bar or club, sitting alone, possibly waiting to order or for a friend to join you. A stranger sits down beside you and starts a conversation.

   b. You are a business executive. You enter your office after lunch and find your secretary sitting at your desk.

   c. You are taking racquetball lessons and it is your turn on the glass (observable) court. A group of people gather to watch your lesson.

   d. You are interviewing for a part-time job. The interviewer moves from behind the desk toward you and touches you on the knee.

   e. You want to wear your favorite sweater but can't find it. You discover it wadded up in the bottom of the laundry hamper, reeking of smoke, and you realize that your roommate or a family member wore it without your permission.

5. Conduct a series of role plays that illustrate Mehrabian's system for interpreting nonverbal behavior. Have someone in your group play the role of a student who is sitting in a small auditorium waiting for a lecture to begin. Another person should play the role of a student who arrives for the lecture at the last moment. This second student must shuffle past already seated students to the last empty seat in the auditorium, next to the first student. Role play the nonverbal cues the two students would use with each other that would communicate immediacy, arousal, and dominance, and explain how such cues might be interpreted.

Listening, not imitation, may be the sincerest form of flattery.

Joyce Brothers

Phoebe Beasley, "Training Ground #2," © Omni-Photo Communications, Inc.

Read Chapter 5

Nov 5th, Exam #2 (takehome) Due: Nov 7th)

Listening and Responding

CHAPTER OUTLINE

How We Listen

Listening Styles

Adapting to Your Listening Style

Listening Barriers

Improving Your Listening Skills

Responding Skills

Responding with Empathy

Summary

CHAPTER OBJECTIVES

After studying this chapter, you should be able to:

1. Explain the principle of listening and responding thoughtfully to others.

2. Identify the elements of the listening process.

3. Identify and describe barriers that keep people from listening well.

4. Describe four listening styles

5. Identify and use strategies that can improve your listening skills.

6. Identify and use appropriate responding skills.

It shows up on every list of what effective communicators do: They listen. You spend more time listening to others than doing almost anything else you do. Americans spend up to 90% of a typical day communicating with people, and they spend 45% of that communication time listening to others.[1] As shown in Figure 5.1, if you're typical, you spend the *least* amount of your communication time writing, yet you receive more training in writing than in any other communication skill. One of the hallmarks of an effective leader is being a good listener.[2] To be sensitive is to be aware of others and to be concerned about others. Increasing your skill in listening to others is one of the most productive ways to increase your communication sensitivity.

Most people have not had formal training in listening or responding. In this chapter we focus on the principle of increasing your sensitivity to others by listening. Becoming sensitive to others includes more than just understanding and interpreting their words, thoughts, and ideas—sensitivity also involves understanding the emotions underlying the words and unspoken messages of others.

As shown in our now familiar model of the communication principles for a lifetime in Figure 5.2, effective communicators do more than absorb a message; they provide an appropriate response to the speaker. We'll address both listening and responding to others in this chapter.

Listening and responding to others is an important principle of communication, not only because you spend more time listening than in any other communication activity, but also because of its importance in establishing and maintaining relationships with others. In interpersonal communication situations, the essence of being a good conversationalist is being a good listener. Rather than focusing only on what to say, a person skilled in the art of conversation listens and picks up on interests and themes of others.

Being a good listener is also an essential skill when communicating with others in small groups. Whether you are the appointed or emerging leader of a group or a group or team member, your ability to listen and connect to others will affect your value to other group members. Group members afflicted with bafflegab, those who verbally dominate group meetings, are not usually held in high esteem. Groups need people who can listen and connect conversational threads that often become tangled or dropped in group dialogue.

It may be less clear how being an effective listener can enhance a presentational speaker's ability to connect with an audience. Effective speakers, however, are those who can relate to their listeners; good speakers know how to establish a relationship

FIGURE 5.1
What You Do with Your Communication Time

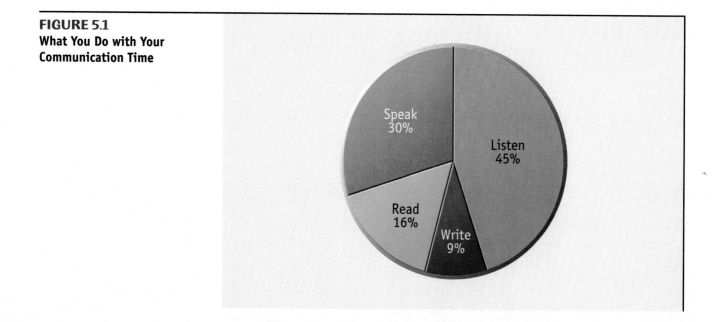

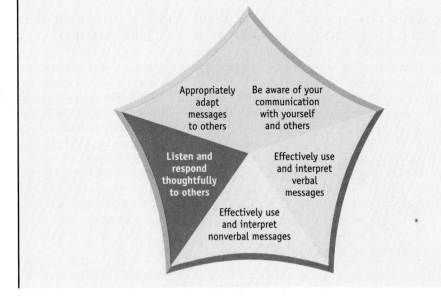

FIGURE 5.2
**Communication Principles
for a Lifetime**

with the audience by listening to audience members one-on-one before a talk or lecture. Good speakers are also audience-centered. They consider the needs of their listeners first. They understand what will hold listeners' attention.

HOW WE LISTEN

Do you know someone who is interpersonally inert? Interpersonally inert people are those who just don't "get it." You can drop hints that it's late and you'd rather they head home instead of playing another hand of cards, but they don't pick up on your verbal and nonverbal cues. They may *hear* you, but they certainly aren't listening; they are not making sense out of your symbols. **Hearing** is the physiological process of decoding sounds. You hear when the sound waves reach your eardrum and cause the middle ear bones (the hammer, anvil, and stirrup) to vibrate. Eventually, the sound vibrations are translated into electrical impulses that reach your brain. In order to listen to something, you must first select that sound from competing sounds. **Listening**, defined succinctly, is the process we use to make sense out of what we hear; it is a complex process of receiving, constructing meaning from, and responding to verbal and nonverbal messages.[3] Listening involves five activities: (1) selecting, (2) attending, (3) understanding, (4) remembering, and—to confirm that listening has occurred—(5) responding.

Understanding these five elements in the listening process can help you diagnose where you sometimes get off track when listening. Having a framework to better describe the listening process can help you figure out how to get back on track and increase your listening skill.

Selecting

To **select** a sound is to focus on one sound as you sort through the myriad of noises competing for your attention. Even now, as you are reading this book, there are probably countless sounds within earshot. Stop reading for a moment. What sounds surround you? Do you hear music? Is a TV on? Maybe there is the tick of a clock, a whir of a computer, or a whoosh of a furnace or an air conditioner. To listen—to be sensitive to another person—you must first select the sound or nonverbal behavior that symbolizes

hearing
The physiological process of decoding sounds.

listening
A complex process of receiving, constructing meaning from, and responding to verbal and nonverbal messages, which involves five steps: selecting, attending, understanding, remembering, and responding.

select
To sort through various sounds competing for your attention.

"I'm sorry, dear. I wasn't listening. Could you repeat what you've said since we've been married?'

meaning. The interpersonally inert person does not pick up on the clues because he or she is oblivious to the information.

Attending

To **attend** is to maintain a sustained focus on a particular message. When you change channels on your TV, you first select the channel and then you attend to the program you've selected. Attention can be brief. You may attend to the program or commercial for a moment and then move on or return to other thoughts or other sounds. Just as you tune in to TV programs that reflect your taste in information while you channel surf, you attend to messages of others that satisfy your needs or whims.

What holds our attention? Typically, conflict, new ideas, humor, or something we can see or that is concrete holds our attention more easily than abstract ideas that don't relate to us. If you're having difficulty sustaining attention to a message, it may be because what you're listening to does not immediately seem to relate to you. So you may need to work a bit harder, either to concentrate on the message or to consider ways in which the message is relevant or important to you.

Understanding

It's been estimated that we hear over one billion words each year, but we understand a mere fraction of that number. To **understand** is to assign meaning to messages—to interpret a message by making sense out of what you hear. You can select and attend to sounds and nonverbal cues but not interpret what you see and hear. Hearing and seeing are physiological processes. Understanding occurs when you relate what you hear and see to your experiences or knowledge. Perhaps you have heard the Montessori

attend
To focus on a particular message.

understand
To assign meaning to messages.

Once we *select* the sounds we want to listen to, we need to *attend* to, or focus on, those sounds, for communication to take place.

school philosophy: I hear, I forget; I see, I remember; I experience, I understand. It is when we can relate our experiences to what we hear and see that we achieve understanding.

Remembering

Remembering information is considered part of the listening process because it's the primary way we determine whether a message was understood. To **remember** is to recall information. Some scholars speculate that you store every detail you have ever heard or witnessed; your mind operates like a computer's hard drive, recording each life experience. But you cannot retrieve or remember all of the bits of information. Sometimes, even though you were present, you have no recollection of what occurred in a particular situation. You can't consciously remember everything; your eye is not a camera; your ear is not a microphone; your mind is not a hard drive.

The first communication principle we presented in this book is to become self-aware. When we are not self-aware of our actions, thoughts, or what we are perceiving—when we are mindless—our ability to remember what occurs plummets. We increase our ability to remember what we hear by being not only physically present, but mentally present.

Our brains have both short-term and long-term memory storage. Short-term memory is where you store almost all the information you hear. You look up a phone number in the telephone book, mumble the number to yourself, then dial the number, only to discover that the line is busy. Three minutes later you have to look up the number again because it did not get stored in your long-term memory. Our short-term storage area is limited. Just as airports have only a relatively few short-term parking spaces, but lots of spaces for long-term parking, our brains can accommodate a few things of fleeting significance, but not vast amounts of information. Most of us forget hundreds of bits of insignificant information that pass though our cortical centers each day.

You tend to remember what is important to you, or something you try to remember or have practiced to remember (like the information in this book for your next communication test). You tend to remember dramatic information (such as where you were when you heard about the September 11, 2001, terrorist attacks) or vital information (such as your phone number or your mother's birthday).

Responding

As you learned in Chapter 1, communication is a transactive process—not a one-way, linear one. Communication involves responding to others as well as simply articulating messages. You **respond** to people to let them know you understand their message. Your lack of response may signal that you didn't understand the message. Your predominant response is often unspoken; direct eye contact and head nods let your partner know you're tuned in. An unmoving, glassy-eyed, frozen stupor may tell your communication partner that you are physically present, yet mentally a thousand miles away. As you'll discover in the next section, most people have a certain style of listening and responding to others.

LISTENING STYLES

Although we've described the typical elements in the listening process, not everyone has the same style or approach to listening. Your **listening style** is your preferred way of making sense out of the messages you hear and see. Some people, for example, prefer to listen to brief chunks of information. Others seem more interested in focusing on the feelings and emotions expressed.

remember
To recall information that has been communicated.

respond
To confirm your understanding of a message.

listening style
A person's preferred way of making sense out of messages.

What's your listening style? Knowing your style can help you adapt and adjust your listening style when listening to others. Listening researchers Kitty Watson, Larry Barker, and James Weaver have found that people tend to listen using one or more of four listening styles: people-oriented, action-oriented, content-oriented, or time-oriented.[4]

People-Oriented Listeners

People-oriented listeners tend to prefer listening to people's emotions and feelings. They are quite interested in hearing personal information from others. A people-oriented listener searches for common interests and seeks to empathize with the feelings of others—she or he connects emotionally with the sentiments and passions others express. There is some evidence that people-oriented listeners are less apprehensive when communicating with others in small groups and interpersonal situations.[5]

Action-Oriented Listeners

Action-oriented listeners like information to be well organized, brief, and free of errors. While listening to a rambling story, the action-oriented listener may think, "Get to the point" or "Why should I be listening to this?" Action-oriented listeners want to do something with the information they hear; they want it to serve a purpose or function, and they become impatient with information that doesn't seem to have a "bottom line."

Action-oriented listeners tend to be a bit more skeptical and critical than are people-oriented listeners of the information they hear. Researchers call this skepticism **second-guessing**—questioning the assumptions underlying a message.[6] It's called second-guessing because the listeners don't always assume that what they hear is accurate or relevant; they make a second guess about the accuracy of the information they are listening to. Accuracy of information is especially important to action-oriented listeners, because if they are going to use the information in some way, the information should be valid.

Content-Oriented Listeners

Content-oriented listeners are more comfortable listening to detailed, complex information than are those with other listening styles. A content-oriented listener is likely to perceive a message presented without details, facts, and evidence as less important and valuable than a message that includes rich content. Content-oriented listeners, like action-oriented listeners, are likely to second-guess the information they hear.[7] They are constantly checking messages for accuracy, because accurate, detailed information is highly valued. Content-oriented listeners are skilled at listening to arguments and debates, because they prefer to listen to messages with a significant amount of information in them. They are less patient listening to stories, anecdotes, and illustrations that don't convey much information.

Time-Oriented Listeners

Time-oriented listeners like brief, short messages. They have much to do and don't want to waste time listening to lengthy talk. A time-oriented listener is likely to look at his or her watch and be conscious of how long it is taking to listen to a message. Whereas the content-oriented listener prefers to hear messages that are chock-full of details, the time-oriented listener would rather hear brief "sound bites" that quickly get to the point. Time-oriented listeners are typically busy people; they gauge their success by what they can accomplish, so they are more sensitive to the length of messages than are people with the other three listening styles.

people-oriented listeners
Those who prefer to focus on the emotions and feelings communicated by others verbally and nonverbally.

action-oriented listeners
Those who prefer that the messages communicated by others contain information that is functional, well organized, brief, and accurate.

second-guessing
Questioning the assumptions underlying a message.

content-oriented listeners
Those who prefer that messages communicated by others contain complex and detailed information.

time-oriented listeners
Those who prefer that messages communicated by others be brief.

ADAPTING TO YOUR LISTENING STYLE

How does knowing that most people have preferences for particular types of messages benefit you? There are at least two reasons to give some thought to your listening style and the listening styles of others. First, knowing your own listening style can help you adapt and adjust your listening style to fit the listening situation. If, for example, you are a people-oriented listener and you're listening to a message that has little information about people but lots of technical details, be aware that you will have to work harder to stay tuned in to the message.

Second, it can be useful to be aware of the listening style of others so that you can communicate messages that others are more likely to listen to. If you know your spouse is a content-oriented listener, then communicate a message that is rich in information; that's what your spouse prefers. Tell the content-oriented listener, "Here are three things I have to tell you." Then say those three things. The content preview tells your content-oriented listener that you are about to convey three pieces of information. Content-oriented listeners like to know that the message about to be presented contains useful information. Of course, it may be difficult to determine someone's listening style, especially someone you don't know very well. But it is both easier and worth the time to consider the listening styles of people you *do* know well (such as your family members, your coworkers, your boss). Knowing your listening style and the listening styles of others can help you adapt your communication to enhance the accuracy of your own listening and the appropriateness of information you communicate to others.

Diversity and Communication

East and West Listening Styles

*N*orth American communication very often centers on the sender. Much emphasis is placed on how senders can formulate better messages, improve credibility, polish their delivery skills, and so forth. In contrast, the emphasis in East Asia has always been on listening and interpretation.

Communication researcher C. Y. Cheng has identified *infinite interpretation* as one of the main principles of Chinese communication.[8] The principle presumes that the emphasis is on the receiver and listening rather than on the sender and speaking. According to T. S. Lebra, "anticipatory communication" is common in Japan: Instead of the speaker's having to tell or ask explicitly for what he or she wants, others guess and accommodate his or her needs, sparing him or her the embarrassment that could arise if the verbally expressed request could not be met.[9] In such cases, the burden of communication falls not on the message sender but on the message receiver. A person who "hears one and understands ten" is regarded as an intelligent communicator. To catch on quickly and to adjust oneself to another's position before his or her position is clearly revealed is regarded as an important communication skill.

One thing that puzzles some foreign students from East Asia is why they are constantly being asked what they want when they are visiting in American homes. In their own countries, the host or hostess is supposed to know what is needed and to act accordingly. The difference, of course, is that in North America it is important to provide individual freedom of choice; in East Asia, it is important to practice anticipatory communication and to accommodate the speaker.

With the emphasis on indirect communication, the receiver's sensitivity and ability to capture the under-the-surface meaning and to understand implicit meaning becomes critical. In North America an effort has been made to improve the effectiveness of message senders through such formal training as debate and public speaking, whereas in East Asia, the effort has been on improving the receiver's sensitivity. One achieves the greatest sensitivity when one empties the mind of preconceptions and makes it as clear as a mirror.[10]

Recently, there has been increased interest in listening in the United States. Both communication scholars and practitioners recognize that listening is necessary not only for the instrumental aspect of communication (comprehension) but, more importantly, for the affective aspect (granting the speaker the satisfaction of being listened to).[11]

RECAP

Listening Styles

People-oriented listening style	Listeners prefer to attend to feelings and emotions and to search for common areas of interest when listening to others.
Action-oriented listening style	Listeners prefer to focus on information that is organized and accurate; they want a speaker to get to the point and emphasize what action should be taken with the information they hear.
Content-oriented listening style	Listeners prefer to hear complex, detailed information and expect facts and evidence to support key ideas.
Time-oriented listening style	Listeners prefer brief messages that are presented efficiently without digressions; they are busy listeners and don't want to spend a lot of time listening to long-winded stories and anecdotes.

LISTENING BARRIERS

Although we spend almost half of our communication time listening, some say we don't use that time well. One day after hearing something, most people remember only about half of what was said. It gets worse. Two days later, our listening comprehension drops by another 50%. The result: Two days after hearing a lecture or speech, most of us remember about 25% of what we hear.

Our listening deteriorates not only when we listen to speeches or lectures, but when we interact interpersonally. Even in the most intimate relationships (or perhaps we should say *especially* in the most intimate relationships), we tune out what others are saying. One study reported that we sometimes pay more attention to strangers than to our close friends or spouses. Married couples tend to interrupt each other more often than nonmarried couples and are usually less polite to each other than are strangers involved in a simple decision-making task.[12]

What keeps us from listening well? The most critical elements are (1) self barriers—personal habits that work against listening well; (2) information-processing barriers—the way we mentally manage information; and (3) context barriers—the surroundings in which we listen.

Self Barriers

"We have met the enemy and he is us" is the oft-quoted line from the comic strip *Pogo*. Evidence suggests we are our own worst enemy when it comes to listening to others—whether it's listening to enjoy, learn, evaluate, or empathize. We mentally comment on the words we hear and the behavior we observe. Our internal thoughts are like a play-by-play sports commentator describing the action of a sports contest. If our internal narration is focused on the message, then it may be useful. But we often attend to our own internal dialogues and diatribes instead of to others' messages; when we do that, our listening effectiveness plummets.

Self-Focus   That personal play-by-play commentary we may be carrying on in our minds is typically about us. "How long will I have to be here for this lecture?" "Wonder what's for dinner tonight?" "I've got to get that report finished." "She's still talking—will we be out of here in ten minutes?" "Do I have a school meeting tonight or is that tomorrow night?" Focusing on an internal message often keeps us from selecting and attending to the other person's message. If there is a competition between listening to what someone else may be droning on about and focusing on our own needs and agenda, our personal needs often come out on top. Another symptom of self-focus is our tendency to think about what we are going to say while we look like we are listening to someone else.

What can you do to regain your listening focus if you are focused on yourself rather than on the other person's message? Consider these suggestions:

- *Become aware of the problem.* Become consciously competent. Note when you find yourself drifting off, thinking about your agenda, rather than concentrating on the speaker.
- *Concentrate.* After you become aware that your internal self-focused messages are distracting you from listening well, intensify your efforts to stay on task. If your internal "announcer" is telling you that the message is boring, useless, or stupid, make sure you don't mindlessly tune the message out. Yes, some messages are boring, useless, and stupid. But the habit of quickly dismissing ideas and messages without making an effort to stay focused on them will keep you from being nominated for the Listening Hall of Fame.
- *Be active rather than passive.* The key to concentration is finding ways to be involved in the communication process. Taking notes when appropriate and providing nonverbal and even sometimes verbal feedback to the speaker can help keep your focus on the speaker rather than on you. If you don't understand something the speaker says, ask for clarification. Don't just sit there and "take it"; if you find your concentration waning, you'll more than likely "leave it."

Some people find that yoga or quiet meditation can help them control the internal barriers that prevent them from listening effectively.

Emotional Noise   Emotions are powerful. Your current body posture, facial expression, and even your blood pressure are affected by your emotional state. What we see and hear affects our emotions. **Emotional noise** occurs when our emotional arousal interferes with communication effectiveness. Certain words or phrases can arouse emotions very quickly; and, of course, the same word may arouse different emotions in different people. You respond emotionally because of your cultural background, religious convictions, or political philosophy. Words that reflect negatively on your nationality, ethnic origin, or religion can trigger strong emotional reactions. Cursing and obscene language may also reduce your listening efficiency. If you grew up in a home in which R-rated language was never used, then four-letter words may distract you.

Sometimes it's not just a word but a concept or idea that causes an emotional eruption. Third-trimester abortion and public school prayer, for example, are topics guaranteed to get radio talk show hosts' audiences involved in lively discussion. Whether you love him or hate him, TV talk show host Jerry Springer is a master at pushing emotional hot buttons for his talk show guests; and when emotions become heated, thoughtful listening is rare.

The emotional state of the speaker may also affect your ability to understand and evaluate what you hear. One researcher found that if you are listening to someone

emotional noise
A form of communication noise caused by emotional arousal.

Mother Teresa understood the value of open listening without prejudging a person.

who is emotionally distraught, you will be more likely to focus on his or her emotions than on the content of the message.[13] Another researcher advises that when you are communicating with someone who is emotionally excited, you should remain calm and focused, and try simply to communicate your interest in the other person.[14]

What are other strategies to keep your emotions from getting the best of you? It's not always easy, but research suggests there are ways of not letting your emotions run amok. Daniel Goleman offers several research-based strategies in his best-selling book *Emotional Intelligence*.[15] To be emotionally intelligent is to have the ability to understand, manage, and appropriately express emotions. For example, one simple yet powerful strategy to manage emotions when you find you may be ready to lose it is to take a deep breath. Yes, just breathe. Taking a deep, slow breath is a way of regaining control by calming down. It helps make you more conscious of your anger or frustration, much like the old technique of counting to ten.

Another strategy for managing emotions is to use the power of self-talk, a concept we discussed in Chapter 2. Tell yourself you won't get angry. Early detection of the emotions bubbling inside you can help you assess and then manage emotions before your nonrational, emotional impulses take control. As we've noted, it's not inappropriate to experience emotions; however, unchecked, intense emotional outbursts do not enhance your ability to listen, comprehend, or empathize with others.

Sometimes, of course, expressing your frustration is appropriate. We're not suggesting you go through life unrealistically serene or that you avoid experiencing emotions. Only the dead never become emotional. We do suggest that you become aware of the effect that emotions have on your listening ability; this is a constructive first step to avoid being ruled by unchecked emotions. The principle of self-awareness gives you *choice* and control. Your listening challenge is to avoid emotional sidetracks and keep your attention focused on the message. When emotionally charged words or actions kick your internal dialogue into high gear, make an effort to quiet it down and steer back to the subject at hand. Becoming consciously aware of our emotions and then talking to ourselves about our feelings is a way of not letting emotions get out of hand.

Criticism   We usually associate the word "criticism" with negative judgments and attitudes. Although critiquing a message can provide positive as well as negative insights, most of us don't like to be criticized. Mother Teresa once said, "If you judge people, you have no time to love them."[16] Being inappropriately critical of the speaker may distract us from focusing on the message.

A person's appearance and speech characteristics can affect your ability to listen to him or her. Many a speaker's droning monotone, lack of eye contact, and distracting mannerisms have contributed to his or her ideas not being well received—even if the ideas are potentially life-changing for the listener. The goal of a sensitive communicator is to be conscious of when the delivery or other distracting features of the message or messenger are interfering with the ability simply to listen. In fact, now that you are studying principles of communication, you may find that this problem looms even larger, because you now pay more attention to nonverbal cues.

It would be unrealistic to suggest that you refrain from criticizing speakers and their messages. It is realistic, however, to monitor your internal critiques of speakers to make sure you are aware of your biases. Good listeners say to themselves, "While this speaker may be distracting, I am simply not going to let appearance or mannerisms keep my attention from the message." For example, Stephen Hawking is a prize-winning physicist at Cambridge University in England; because of a disability, he is able to speak only with the aid of computer-synthesized sounds. He is unquestionably brilliant. If you let his speaking delivery overpower you, you'd miss his marvelous message. Avoid using your mental energy to criticize a speaker unnecessarily; the longer your mental critique, the less you'll remember.

Information-Processing Barriers

In addition to self barriers that contribute to our loss of focus on messages, sometimes the way in which we use the information that comes to our eyes, minds, and hearts creates listening problems. The way in which we process the information we hear may keep us from being good listeners. Four information-processing listening barriers are (1) our information-processing rate, (2) information overload, (3) receiver apprehension, and (4) shifting attention.

Processing Rate   One of the barriers to listening that has long been documented is the difference between our ability to process information and the rate at which information comes to us. The barrier boils down to this: You can think faster than people speak. Most people speak 125 words per minute, give or take a few words. You have the tremendous ability, however, to process four to ten times that amount of information. Some people can listen to 600 to 800 words a minute and still make sense out of what the speaker is saying; another estimate puts the processing rate up to 1200 words per minute. Yet another estimate claims that we think not just in words but also in images and sounds: We can process 2000 bits of information a minute for short periods of time. This difference between average speaking rate and your capacity to make sense out of words as they register in your cortical centers can cause trouble. You have extra time on your hands to tune in to your own thoughts, rather than focus on the speaker.[17]

You can use your information-processing rate to your advantage if you use the extra time to summarize mentally what a speaker is saying. By periodically sprinkling in mental summaries during a conversation, you can dramatically increase your listening ability and make the speech-rate/thought-rate difference work to your advantage.

Information Overload   Information abounds. We are constantly bombarded with sights and sound bites, and experts suggest that the amount of information competing for our attention is going to increase in the future. Incoming messages and information on computers, fax machines, e-mail, mobile phones, beepers, and other devices can interrupt conversations and distract us from listening to others.

The amount of information coming at us on any given day also wears us out. The one word to describe many a poor listener is "weary." We spend 45% of our communication time listening, and the pace at which the information zips toward us exhausts us. The billion words that we hear contribute to our fatigue.

Again we recommend self-awareness. Be on the alert for drifting attention due to information overload. And when the encroaching information dulls your attentiveness, either take a break or consider conducting some *communication triage* (determining what's urgent and what's not urgent) so you can focus on the information that is most important.

Receiver Apprehension   Just as some people are fearful of presenting a speech or speaking up during a meeting, research suggests that some people are fearful of receiving information. **Receiver apprehension** is fear of misunderstanding or misinterpreting the messages spoken by others or of not being able to adjust psychologically to messages expressed by others.[18] Some people may just be fearful of receiving new information and being able to understand it. Or it may just be a characteristic or pattern in the way some people respond psychologically to information; they may not be able to make sense out of some of what they hear, which causes them to be anxious or fearful

receiver apprehension
Fear of misunderstanding or misinterpreting the messages spoken by others, or of not being able to adjust psychologically to messages expressed by others.

of listening to others.[19] If you are fearful of receiving information, you'll remember less information.

What are the implications for you of research on receiver apprehension? If you know that you are fearful of listening to new information, you'll have to work harder to understand the information presented. Using a tape recorder to record a lecture may help you feel more comfortable and less anxious about trying to remember every point. Becoming actively involved in the listening experience by taking notes or mentally repeating information to yourself may also help.

Shifting Attention   Can you multitask? Some people can easily do two things at once; some people can't. Emerging research evidence suggests that men are more likely to have difficulty attending to multiple messages: When they are focused on a message, they may have more difficulty than women in carrying on a conversation with another person.[20] Men have a tendency to lock on to a message, while women seem more adept at shifting between two or more simultaneous messages. When many men watch a TV program, they seem lost in thought—oblivious to other voices around them. Women, on the other hand, are more likely to be carrying on a conversation with one person and also focusing on a message they may hear nearby. No, this difference doesn't mean that women are more likely to eavesdrop intentionally but that some women have greater potential to listen to two things at once. What are the implications? It may be especially important for women to stop and focus on the messages of others, rather than on either internal or external competing messages. And men may need to be sensitive to others who may want to speak to them, rather than becoming fixated on their own internal message or on a single external message such as a program on TV.

Context Barriers

In addition to listening barriers related to how you process information and self barriers that occur when your emotions and thoughts crowd out a message, listening barriers can arise from the communication context or situation. Specifically, time, place, and outside noise can distract you from selecting, attending, understanding, remembering, and responding to messages.

Barriers of Time and Place   The time of day can interfere with your listening acuity. Are you a morning person or an evening person? Morning people are cheerfully and chirpily at their mental peak before lunch. Evening people prefer to tackle major projects after dark; they are at their worst when they arise in the morning. Use the skill development activity on page 131 to plot your ideal work time, the period when you are at your sharpest.

If you know you are sharper in the morning, whenever possible schedule your key listening times then. Evening listeners should try to shift heavy listening to the evening hours. Of course, that's not always practical. If you can't change the time of listening, you can increase your awareness of when you will need to listen with greater concentration.

Don't assume that because you are ready to talk, the other person is ready to listen. If your message is particularly sensitive or important, you may want to ask your listening partner, "Is this a good time to talk?" Even if he or she says yes, look for eye contact and a responsive facial expression to make sure the positive response is genuine.

External Noise   **Noise** is anything that interferes with your ability to listen to a message. Although you may think of noise as sounds you hear, noise can be processed by any one of your five senses. Not just sounds but also sights, the feeling of something touching you, even tastes and smells can affect your listening ability.

For most people, the best listening environment is one that offers as few distractions as possible. When you want to talk to someone, pick a quiet time and place, especially if you know you will be discussing a potentially difficult topic. Even in your own

noise
Anything that interferes with your ability to listen to a message.

home it may be a challenge to find a quiet time to talk. (Perhaps a good title for a text on listening would be *How to Turn Off the TV.*) Listening takes all the powers of concentration that you can muster. A good listener seeks a quiet time and place to maximize listening comprehension. Closing a door or window, turning off the television or radio, asking noisy or offensive talkers to converse more quietly or not at all, or simply moving to a less distracting location are steps that you may need to pursue to manage the noise barrier.

RECAP

Managing Listening Barriers

Listening Barriers	What to Do
Self Barriers	
Self-Focus	• Consciously become aware of the self-focus and shift attention back to the speaker. • Concentrate: Find ways of becoming actively involved in the message, such as taking meaningful notes.
Emotional Noise	• Act calm to remain calm. • Use self-talk to stay focused on the message. • Take a deep breath if you start to lose control.
Criticism	• Focus on the message, not on the messenger.
Information-Processing Barriers	
Processing Rate	• Use the difference between speech rate and thought rate to mentally summarize the message.
Information Overload	• Realize when you or your partner is tired or distracted and not ready to listen. • Assess what is urgent and not urgent when listening.
Receiver Apprehension	• If you are fearful or anxious about listening to new information, use a backup strategy, such as recording the message, to help you capture the message; review the tape later. Seek ways to become actively involved when listening, such as taking notes or making mental summaries of the information you hear.
Shifting Attention	• Men are more likely to focus on a single message; women typically shift their attention between two or more messages. If you know you have a tendency to shift your attention between two or more messages, make a conscious effort to remain focused on one message.
Context Barriers	
Barriers of Time and Place	• Note when your best and worst listening times are; if possible, reschedule difficult listening situations for when you're at your best.
External Noise	• When possible, modify the listening environment by eliminating distracting noise.

IMPROVING YOUR LISTENING SKILLS

At the heart of listening is developing sensitivity to focus on the messages of others, rather than on your own thoughts. Improving your listening involves a set of skills that can increase your sensitivity toward others. At first glance, these skills may look deceptively simple—as simple as the advice given to most elementary students about crossing the street: (1) stop, (2) look, and (3) listen. Despite the appearance of simplicity, these three words summarize decades of research and insight about how to avoid being labeled "interpersonally inert." Let's consider each separately.

Stop: Turn Off Competing Messages

Many of the barriers to improved listening skill arise because we focus on ourselves and our own messages, rather than focusing on others. As we noted earlier, while you are "listening," you may also be "talking" to yourself—providing a commentary about the messages you hear. These internal, self-generated messages may distract you from giving your undivided attention to what others are saying. In order to select and attend to the messages of others, we need to become aware of our internal dialogue and stop our own running commentary about issues and ideas that are self-focused rather than other-focused.[21]

Members of some religious groups take a vow to be silent and not talk to anyone else. They literally stop talking. Does this make them better listeners? One research team wanted to know the impact of various types of listening training, including being silent for 12 hours.[22] One group heard a lecture about how to be better listeners—probably like the lectures you hear in this course; the group then took a test to assess their overall listening skill. A second group promised not to talk to anyone for 12 hours—they literally gave others the "silent treatment." Then they, too, took a test to assess their listening ability. A third group both heard a listening lecture and were silent for 12 hours; then also took the listening test. The results: There were no differences in listening test scores among the groups—all groups seemed to listen equally well, according to test results. But those who kept silent for 12 hours reported that they thought they were more attentive to others, more conscious of being good listeners. The researchers concluded that literally stopping to listen more and talk less can increase awareness of listening. Their research supports the maxim that "You have been given two ears and one mouth so that you will listen more and talk less." We're not suggesting you not talk, but we are suggesting that you increase your awareness of how your own thoughts and talk can interfere with being a good listener. Stop—do your best to eliminate mental messages that keep you from listening well.

Try a process called social decentering. **Social decentering** involves stepping away from your own thoughts and attempting to experience the thoughts of another. In essence, you're asking yourself this question: "If I were the other person, what

social decentering
Stepping away from your own thoughts and attempting to experience the thoughts of another.

would I be thinking?" To decenter is to practice the first principle of communication—self-awareness—and to be aware that your own thoughts are keeping you from focusing on another's message, so that you can focus on the other person.[23] Of course, we are not suggesting that your own ideas and internal dialogue should be forever repressed; that would be both impossible and inappropriate. We are suggesting, however, that to connect to another, you must place the focus on the other person rather than on yourself.

To decenter requires conscious effort. Decentering is a mental or cognitive process that involves trying to guess what someone else may be thinking. In attempting to decenter, consider this question, "If I were my communication partner, what would I be thinking?"

The essence of the "stop" step is to become aware (our first communication principle for a lifetime that we discussed in Chapter 2) of whether you are listening or not listening to someone. You are either on task (focusing on another) or off task (oblivious to another and focusing on your own thoughts and emotions). The goal, of course, is to be on task—listening to others.

Look: Listen with Your Eyes

As you learned in Chapter 4, nonverbal messages are powerful, especially in communicating feelings, attitudes, and emotions.[24] A person's facial expression, presence or lack of eye contact, posture, and use of gestures speak volumes, even when no word is uttered. When words are spoken, the added meaning that comes from vocal cues provides yet another dimension to the emotion and nature of the relationship.

Sensitive listeners are aware of nonverbal as well as verbal messages; they listen with their eyes as well as their ears. A person's body movement and posture, for example, communicate the intensity of his or her feelings, while facial expression and vocal cues provide clues as to the specific emotion being expressed. A competent listener notices these cues, and an incompetent listener attempts to decode a message based only on what is said rather than "listening between the lines." When there is a contradiction between the verbal and nonverbal message, we will almost always believe the unspoken message; nonverbal cues are more difficult to fake.

Besides looking at someone to discern his or her emotions and relational cues, it is important to establish eye contact, which signals that you are focusing your attention on your partner. Even though mutual eye contact typically lasts only one to seven seconds, when we carry on an interpersonal conversation, it is important to establish and reestablish eye contact to signal that you are on task and listening. We usually have more eye contact with someone when we are listening than when talking.[25] Looking over your partner's head, peeking at your watch, or gazing into space will likely tell him or her you're not tuned in. Even though there are cultural variations in the advice to establish eye contact (for example, some children in African American homes have been taught to avoid eye contact with high-status people), generally, for most North Americans, eye contact signals that the communication channel is open and the communication is welcome.

In addition to eye contact, other nonverbal cues signal whether you are on task and responsive to the messages of others. If you look like you are listening, you will be more likely to listen. Remaining focused, not fidgeting with your hands and feet, and even leaning forward slightly are other nonverbal cues that communicate to someone that you are listening. Appropriate head nods and verbal responses also signal that you are attending to your partner's message.[26]

Listen: Understand Both Details and Major Ideas

How do you improve your listening skill? Now that you've stopped your own internal dialogue and looked for nonverbal cues, it's time to listen. Here are six additional strategies for improving your listening skill.

Diversity *and* Communication

Who Are Better Listeners, Men or Women?

There is evidence that men and women can be equally good listeners, but research suggests that they sometimes (although not always) have different approaches to listening. The following chart summarizes research conclusions about how men and women listen.[27]

	Women	Men
Differences in attending to information	• Tend to search for the relation- ships among separate pieces of information • Tend to identify individual facts and other iso- lated pieces of information	• Tend to look for a new structure or organiza- tional pattern when listening • Tend to listen for the "big picture" and seek the major points being communicated
Differences in listening goals	• More likely to listen to new information to gain new under- standing and new insights • Tend to use information to develop rela- tionships with their listening partners	• More likely to listen to new information to solve a problem • Tend to listen to reach a conclu- sion; are less concerned about relationship cues and more concerned about using the infor- mation gained
Differences in attending to nonverbal cues	• Tend to empha- size meaning communicated through nonver- bal cues • Typically have more eye con- tact with the other person when listening	• Tend to empha- size the mean- ing of the words and information exchanged • Typically have less eye contact with the other person when listening

So what does all this information mean? How is knowing differences in the way men and women listen useful to us? Although not all men and women fit into these categories of listening behavior, we think there are several good reasons to be mindful of gender-based differences in listening.[28] First, it's useful to be aware of different tendencies in listening so that we can be less critical and more accepting of others, should differences in communication arise. Conflicts may arise simply because you and your listening partner are focusing on different parts of the message expressed.

Second, by being aware of whether you fit the general profile of male or female listener, you can determine whether you need to adapt your listening style. If, for example, you know you have a tendency to be less interested in relational information and that you listen to get to the "bottom line" or solve a problem, being aware that your listening partner is not as focused on those objectives when listening can be helpful.

Third, the best listener may be one who is the most flexi- ble and doesn't always default to his or her typical pattern or preferred listening approach, but rather combines listening approaches.[29] Make an effort to listen for both individual facts and the overall ideas. Listening for both relational and emo- tional meaning as well as for explicit content can also en- hance listening skill. Be more aware of the way you tend to listen to others, and expand your listening repertoire to in- crease your ability to be other-oriented.

Finally, although we've noted differences in the way men and women listen, we end our discussion of men's and women's listening styles by repeating our caution: Don't assume that all men or all women have typical male or female listening styles. Listening expert Stephanie Sarget suggests that studies of listening style differences between men and women may simply be measuring listening stereotypes.[30] Because it's often assumed that men and women listen differ- ently, researchers may be documenting listening stereotypes or self-expectations. What may be occurring is a self-fulfilling prophecy—men and women assume they *are* listening the way they think they *should* listen.[31] But although there are some discernible patterns in male and female listening styles, the differences may not be as consistently pronounced as was once thought. Our conclusion: Differences in the way men and women listen may indeed exist, but these differences are only a few of a host of factors that may explain why men and women sometimes have difficulty reaching a common under- standing.

Identify Your Listening Goal   You listen to other people for a variety of reasons. Knowing your listening goal can increase your self-awareness of the listening process and increase your skill. If you're listening to Aunt Deonna talk about her recent trip to Northern Minnesota for her annual bear hunt, you need not worry about taking extensive notes and trying to remember all of the details of her expedition. But when your sociology professor tells a story to illustrate a sociological theory, you should be more attuned to the point he is making; his theory may be on a test. There are also times when you need to be on your guard to evaluate the message of a politician or salesperson. There are four primary listening goals: to enjoy, to learn, to evaluate, and to empathize.

One of the pleasures of developing good listening skills is the ability to listen for pure enjoyment.

- *Listening to Enjoy:* Sometimes we listen just because it's fun. You might listen to music, watch TV, go to a movie, or visit with a friend. Because you know you won't be tested on Jay Leno's *Tonight Show* monologue, you can relax and just enjoy his humor; you don't have to worry about passing a test to remember each punch line.
- *Listening to Learn:* Nothing snaps a class to attention more quickly than a professor's proclamation that "This next point will be covered on the test." Another key reason we listen is to learn. But you don't have to be a college student to listen to learn. Phone calls and conversations with family and friends contain information that we want to remember. In interpersonal situations, you listen for such everyday information as who will pick up the kids after school and what to buy at the grocery store for tonight's dinner. If you are aware that your listening goal is to learn and remember information, you can increase your powers of concentration and pay more attention to understanding and remembering the message.
- *Listening to Evaluate:* When you listen to evaluate, you try to determine whether the information you hear is valid, reliable, believable, or useful. One problem you may have when you listen to evaluate is that you may become so preoccupied with your criticism that you may not completely understand the message. Often the very process of evaluating and making judgments and decisions about information interferes with the capacity to understand and recall. To compensate for this tendency, first make sure that you understand what a person is saying before making a judgment about the value of the information. When listening to evaluate, you use critical-listening skills such as separating facts from inferences, identifying fallacies in reasoning, and analyzing evidence. We discuss these important skills throughout this book.
- *Listening to Empathize:* The word *empathy*, which we introduced in Chapter 3 and will discuss in more detail later in this chapter, comes from a Greek word for "passion" and the German word *Einfühlung*, meaning "to feel with." To empathize with someone is to try to feel what he or she is feeling, rather than just to think about or acknowledge the feelings. In effect, you act as a sounding board for the other person. Empathic listening serves an important therapeutic function. Just having an empathic listener may help someone out. No, we are not empowering you to be a therapist, but we are suggesting that simply listening and feeling with someone can help your communication partner sort things out. Empathic listeners don't judge or offer advice. They listen because being listened to is soothing and can often restore a person's perspective. Being aware that your listening goal is to empathize, rather than to remember or to evaluate what you are listening to, is the first step to being a skilled empathic listener.

If you were listening to someone give you directions to Centennial Hall, one of the oldest buildings on campus, you would listen differently than if your sister were telling you about her fears that her marriage was on the rocks. In the case of your sister, your job is to listen patiently and provide emotional support. In trying to get to Centennial

Hall, you would be focusing on the specific details and making either mental or written notes.

Mentally Summarize the Details of the Message   This suggestion may seem to contradict the suggestion to avoid focusing *only* on facts, but it is important to have a grasp of the details your partner presents. Yet to listen is to do more than focus on facts. Studies suggest that poor listeners are more likely to focus on *only* facts and data, rather than the overall point of the message.[32] To listen is to connect the details of the message with the major points. You can process words more quickly than a person speaks, so you can use the extra time to your advantage by periodically summarizing the names, dates, and facts embedded in the message. If the speaker is disorganized and rambling, use your tremendous mental ability to reorganize the speaker's information into categories, or try to place events in chronological order. If you miss the details, you will likely miss the main point.

Link Message Details with the Major Idea of the Message   Facts and data make the most sense when we can use them to support an idea or point. Mentally weave your summaries of the details into a focused major point or series of major ideas. So as you summarize, link the facts you have organized in your mind with key ideas and principles. Use facts to enhance your critical thinking as you analyze, synthesize, evaluate, and finally summarize the key points or ideas your partner makes.

Practice by Listening to Difficult or Challenging Material   You learn any skill with practice. Listening experts suggest that our listening skills deteriorate if we listen only to easy and entertaining material. Make an effort to listen to news or documentary programs. As you listen to material in a lecture that may seem chock full of content, make a conscious effort to stay focused, concentrate, and summarize facts and major ideas.

Work to Overcome Listening Barriers   If you can avoid the listening barriers we presented earlier, you will be well on your way to improving your listening skill. Make it a deliberate goal not to be self-focused, let emotional noise distract you, or criticize a message before you've understood it. Watch out for information overload. And, when possible, take steps to minimize external noise and provide an environment more conducive to listening.

Listen Actively   Our suggestion that you listen actively is a distillation of the other recommendations we've offered. Active listeners are engaged listeners who listen with both their minds, and their hearts. They are engaged physically and mentally in the listening process.[33] They are aware of what they are doing; they stop thinking about things that might take them off the track.[34] They also have good eye contact with the speaker and communicate their interest with an intent facial expression and slight forward lean. By contrast, passive listeners are not involved listeners; they are detached and may fake attention with a frozen, nonexpressive facial expression. One listening research team noted that a passive listener receives information by being talked to rather than as an equal partner in the speaking-listening exchange.[35]

This same team described active listeners as people who

- Give full attention to others.
- Focus on what is being said.
- Expend considerable energy participating in the listening process.
- Have an alert posture.
- Maintain much direct eye contact.

It seems the best listeners are mentally alert, physically focused on the other person, and actively involved in seeking understanding. In short, they stop, they look, and they listen.

RECAP

How to Listen Well

What to Do	How to Do It
Identify your listening goal.	Decide whether you are listening to enjoy, to learn, to evaluate, or to empathize. Your listening goal should determine the strategies you use to achieve it.
Mentally summarize the details of the message.	Every few minutes, take time to create your own mental recap of the key information presented. In just a few seconds, you can summarize much information.
Link message details with the major ideas of the message.	Consciously relate the bits of information you hear to the key points the speaker is developing, rather than focusing only on facts and details or only on major points.
Practice by listening to difficult or challenging material.	Periodically make an effort to listen to material that is complex and richer in detail and information than you typically listen to; while listening to this more complex material, make a conscious effort to stop, look, and listen.
Work to overcome listening barriers.	Identify the key obstacles that keep you from listening at peak effectiveness (self barrier, information-processing barrier, or context barrier); make conscious efforts to overcome their underlying causes.
Listen actively.	Be engaged in the listening process by maintaining good eye contact with the speaker and an alert posture (slight forward lean; sitting up rather than slouching).

RESPONDING SKILLS

To respond is to provide feedback to another about his or her behavior or communication. Your response can be verbal or nonverbal, intentional or unintentional.

Your thoughtful response serves several purposes. First, it tells a speaker how well you have understood his or her message. Second, your response lets a speaker know how the message affects you. It indicates whether you agree or disagree. Third, it pro-

Boyd likes to bring empathy to the task at hand.

vides feedback about statements or assumptions that you find vague, confusing, or wrong. It helps an individual keep the communication on target and purposeful. Finally, your response signals to the speaker that you are still "with" him or her—that you are still ready to receive messages. To respond appropriately and effectively, consider the following strategies.

Be Descriptive

"I see that from a different point of view" sounds better than "You're wrong, I'm right." Effective feedback describes rather than evaluates what you hear. Although one listening goal is to evaluate and make critical judgments of messages, evaluate once you're sure you understand the speaker. We're not suggesting it's easy to listen from a nonevaluative perspective, or that you should refrain from ever evaluating messages and providing praise or negative comments. Remember: Feedback that first acts like a mirror to help the speaker understand what he or she has said is more useful than a barrage of critical comments. Describing your own reactions to what your partner has said rather than pronouncing a quick judgment on his or her message is also more likely to keep communication flowing. If your partner thinks your prime purpose in listening is to take pot-shots at the message or the messenger, the communication climate will cool quickly.

Be Timely

Feedback is usually most effective at the earliest opportunity after the behavior or message is presented, especially if the purpose is to teach. Waiting to provide a response after much time has elapsed invites confusion.

Now let us contradict our advice. Sometimes, especially if a person is already sensitive and upset about something, delaying feedback can be wise. Use your critical-thinking skills to analyze when feedback will do the most good. Rather than automatically offering immediate correction, use the just-in-time (JIT) approach. Provide feedback just before the person might make another mistake, just in time for the feedback to have the most benefit.

Be Brief

Less information can be more. Cutting down on the amount of your feedback can highlight the importance of what you do share. Don't overwhelm your listener with details that obscure the key point of your feedback. Brief is usually best.

Be Useful

Perhaps you've heard this advice: "Never try to teach a pig to sing. It wastes your time, it doesn't sound pretty, and it annoys the pig." When you provide feedback to someone, be certain that it is useful and relevant. Ask yourself, "If I were this person, how would I respond to this information? Is it information I can act on?" Immersing your partner in information that is irrelevant or that may be damaging to the relationship may make you feel better but may not enhance the quality of your relationship or improve understanding.

RESPONDING WITH EMPATHY

Empathy, as we noted earlier in the chapter, is the process of feeling what another person is feeling. To empathize is more than just to acknowledge that another person feels a particular emotion—being empathic is making an effort to feel the emotion yourself. Responding with empathy is especially important if you are listening to provide support and encouragement to someone. Being empathic is not a single skill but several related skills that help you predict how others will respond.[36]

Central to being empathic is being emotionally intelligent. As we noted earlier in this chapter, emotional intelligence is the ability to understand and express emotion, interpret emotions in yourself and others, and regulate or manage emotions.[37] Daniel Goleman suggests that people who are emotionally intelligent—sensitive to others, empathic, and other oriented—have better relationships with others. Goleman summarizes the importance of emotions in developing empathy by quoting Antoine De Saint-Exupery: "It is with the heart that one sees rightly; what is essential is invisible to the eye."[38]

At the heart of empathic listening is the ability not only to know when to speak but also to know when to be silent. Henri Nouwen eloquently expressed both the challenge and the rewards of empathic listening:

> To listen is very hard, because it asks of us so much interior stability that we no longer need to prove ourselves by speeches, arguments, statements, or declarations. True listeners no longer have an inner need to make their presence known. They are free to receive, to welcome, to accept.
>
> Listening is much more than allowing another to talk while waiting for a chance to respond. Listening is paying full attention to others and welcoming them into our very beings. The beauty of listening is that those who are listened to start feeling accepted, start taking their words more seriously and discovering their true selves. Listening is a form of spiritual hospitality by which you invite strangers to become friends, to get to know their inner selves more fully, and even to dare to be silent with you.[39]

Some people are simply better at being empathic than others. Just as you inherit physical qualities from your parents, there is also evidence that you inherit communication traits as well.[40] This does not mean that if you are not naturally empathic, you can never develop empathic skills; it does mean you may have to work a bit harder to enhance these skills. To assess your empathic skill, take the "Test Your Empathy Ability" quiz at the end of this chapter.

Here are four strategies to help you respond empathically when you listen.

Understand Your Partner's Feelings

If your goal is to empathize, or "feel with," your partner, you might begin by imagining how you would feel under the same circumstances. If your roommate comes home from a hassle-filled day at work or school, try to imagine what you might be thinking or feeling if you had had a stressful day. If a friend calls to tell you his mother died, consider how you would feel if the situation were reversed. Even if you've not yet experienced the loss of your mother, you can identify with what it would be like to suffer such a loss. Of course, your reaction to life events is unlikely to be exactly like someone else's response. Empathy is not telepathically trying to become your communication partner.[41] But you do attempt to decenter—to consider what someone may be thinking—by first projecting how you might feel and then asking appropriate questions and offering paraphrases to confirm the accuracy of your assumptions. Considering how others might feel has been called the Platinum Rule—even more valuable than the Golden Rule ("Do unto others as you would have others do unto you"). The Platinum Rule invites you to treat others as *they* would like to be treated—not just as *you* would like to be treated.

Ask Appropriate Questions

As you listen for information and attempt to understand how another person is feeling, you may need to ask questions to help clarify your conclusions. Most of your questions will serve one of four purposes: (1) to obtain additional information ("How long have you been living in Buckner?"); (2) to check how the person feels ("Are you frustrated be-

Ethics and Communication

Honest Listening

*I*s it ethical to just pretend to listen to someone? Imagine this situation: You've had a stress-filled day. As you come in your front door and sink down into your favorite chair, all you want to do is relax. Perhaps you'll just fix a little dinner, watch TV, and unwind. Then the phone rings. It's your good friend, and she too has had a difficult, stressful day and needs a listener. Since you're on the phone, you could probably get away with just adding a few "uh-huhs" and "mm-hmms" and your friend would think you were listening to everything she is saying. While appearing to listen you could even read your e-mail and do other daily tasks, and your friend would never know it. Your friend is not likely to take offense at your inattentiveness because she'll not be aware that you're just going through the motions of listening. Consider these questions: Is it ethical to fake paying attention to someone? By faking your attention you are not harming your friend. In fact, the case could be made that you're helping her out by giving her an audience.

Should you be honest and disclose that you're tired and would rather listen when you can be more attentive? How might your friend react to your honesty? How would you respond empathically to her reaction?

cause you didn't get your project finished?"); (3) to ask for clarification ("What do you mean when you say you wanted to telecommute?"); or (4) to verify that you have reached an accurate conclusion about your partner's intent or feeling ("So are you saying you'd rather work at home than at the office?").

Another way to sort out details and get to the emotional heart of a dialogue is to ask questions to help you (and your partner) identify the sequence of events. "What happened first?" and "Then what did he do?" can help both you and your partner clarify a confusing event.

Your ability to ask appropriate questions will demonstrate your supportiveness of your partner and signal that you are interested in what he or she is sharing. Of course, if you are trying to understand another's feelings, you can just ask how he or she is feeling in a straightforward way—don't ask questions just for the sake of asking questions. Also, monitor how you ask your questions. Your own verbal and nonverbal responses will contribute to the emotional climate of your interaction.

Paraphrase Message Content

After you have listened and asked questions, check whether your interpretations are accurate by paraphrasing the content you have heard. **Paraphrasing** is restating in your own words what you think a person is saying. Paraphrasing is different from repeating something exactly as it was spoken; that would be parroting, not paraphrasing. Your paraphrase can summarize the essential events, uncover a detail that was quickly glossed over, or highlight a key point. Typical lead-ins to a paraphrase include statements such as

> "So here is what seems to have happened . . ."
> "Here's what I understand you to mean . . ."
> "So the point you seem to be making is . . ."
> "You seem to be saying . . ."
> "Are you saying . . ."

paraphrasing
Checking the accuracy of your understanding by restating your partner's message in your own words.

Here's an example of a conversation punctuated by appropriate paraphrases to enhance the message receiver's understanding:

Technology *and* Communication

Can Computers Listen Empathically?

*I*s it possible for a computer to listen and respond sensitively to others? Although there is software that permits you to speak words that your personal computer will then print, computers do not yet have the sophistication to listen and respond with the same sensitivity as people. But computer programmers are working on it. Stanford University professors Clifford Nass and Byron Reeves have been working since 1986 to devise software that will enable PCs to interact with people in human ways.[42] They have summarized research regarding how people respond to other people and have been trying to translate these research conclusions into strategies that can be used by a computer to interact with others in real-time dialogues. Professors Nass and Reeves have identified four major personality types—

dominant, submissive, friendly, and unfriendly—and have programmed computers to respond to the computer user. The researchers are trying to match more than personality. As Professor Nass explains, "Personality is one aspect. Gender, politeness, cooperation, and even humor are other factors. We decide what the agent [computer user] is going to do, then develop a backstory—each character's likes and life history. This guides the scripting, voice type, animation, and interaction style."[43] The researchers are also working on integrating computer-generated speech into the program. Although computers may not yet listen with the sensitivity and empathy of your best friend, researchers are working on software that can emulate human interaction and responses. So for now, realize that the opportunity to listen to others is something that can't be delegated to a virtual friend.

Alice: I'm swamped. My boss asked me to take on two extra projects this week. And I already have the Henrikson merger and the Affolter project. I promised I'd arrange to have the lawnmower fixed and pay the bills, but I don't see how I can take the dog to the vet, pick up the kids after school, *and* get Keshia to the orthodontist at 7 A.M. I'm up to my neck in work.

Matt: It sounds like you're feeling overwhelmed with responsibilities. Would you like me to take care of the stuff around the house so you can focus on office assignments?

Alice: Well, some of them, yes. Could you take on a couple of things I said I'd do?

Matt: Okay. I'll take care of the kids and run the errands.

We are not suggesting that you paraphrase when it's not needed or appropriate, only when you need to confirm your understanding of a murky message or to help the speaker sort out a jumbled or confusing situation. When a listener paraphrases the content and feelings of a speaker's message, the speaker is not only more likely to know that the message is understood but also more likely to trust and value the listener.

Paraphrase Emotions

The bottom line in empathic responding is to make certain that you understand your communication partner's emotional state.

"So you feel . . ."
"So now you feel . . ."
"Emotionally, you are feeling . . ."

These are typical lead-in phrases when paraphrasing feelings.

We have discussed empathic responses and the active listening process using a tidy, step-by-step textbook approach. Realize that in practice, the process won't be so neat and tidy. You may have to back up and clarify content, ask more questions, and rethink how you would feel before you summarize how your partner feels. Or you may be able to summarize feelings without asking questions or summarizing the content of the message. A sensitive communicator

On the Web

Several Web sites provide a wealth of information about how to improve your listening skills. There are also many Internet resources to bolster your responding and paraphrasing skills. The following Web addresses give you tips, tools, and techniques to help you listen and respond better:

http://conflict911.com/resources/Communication/Listening/
is a site from Project911.com that provides resources and assistance in improving communication and listening skills.

www.listen.org
is the Web site of the International Listening Association. It offers a panoply of resources, quotations, and information about improving listening skills.

http://web.cba.neu.edu/~ewertheim/interper/commun.htm#top
provides numerous practical tips and techniques to enhance listening and responding skills.

tries not to let his or her technique show. Overusing paraphrasing skills can slow down a conversation and make the other person uncomfortable or irritated. But if used with wisdom, paraphrasing can help both you and your partner clarify message accuracy.

Reflecting on the content or feeling through paraphrasing can be especially useful in the following situations:

Before you take an important action
Before you argue or criticize
When your partner has strong feelings
When your partner just wants to talk
When your partner is speaking "in code"—using unclear jargon or unclear abbreviations
When your partner wants to understand your feelings and thoughts
When you are talking to yourself (you can question and check your own emotional temperature)
When you encounter new ideas[44]

When you ask questions and paraphrase content and feelings, keep the following additional guidelines in mind:

Use your own words—don't just repeat exactly what the other person says.
Don't add to the information presented when paraphrasing.
Be brief.
Be specific.
Be accurate.

Don't use paraphrasing skills if you aren't able to be open and accepting; if you try to color your paraphrased comments to achieve your own agenda, you aren't being ethical.

Don't be discouraged if your initial attempts to use these skills seem awkward and uncomfortable. Any new set of skills takes time to learn and use well. The instructions and samples you have seen here should serve as a guide, rather than as hard-and-fast prescriptions to follow every time. Being an empathic listener can be rewarding in both your personal and your professional lives.[45] And here's some encouraging news about listening and responding skills: These skills can be improved. People who have received listening training show overall improvement in their ability to listen to others.[46] Reading this chapter, listening to your instructor give you tips to enhance your skills, and participating in skill-building activities is well worth your time.

The poem below, "Listen," by an unknown author, summarizes the essential ideas of how to listen and respond with empathy.

Listen
When I ask you to listen to me and you start giving advice, you have not done what I asked.
When I ask you to listen to me and you begin to tell me why I shouldn't feel that way, you are trampling on my feelings.
When I ask you to listen to me and you feel you have to do something to solve my problems, you have failed me, strange as that may seem.
Listen! All I asked was that you listen. Not talk or do—just hear me.
Advice is cheap: 50 cents will get you both Dear Abby and Billy Graham in the same newspaper.
And I can do for myself; I'm not helpless. Maybe discouraged and faltering, but not helpless.
When you do something for me that I can and need to do for myself, you contribute to my fear and weakness.
But when you accept as a simple fact that I do feel what I feel, no matter how irrational, then I quit trying to convince you and can get about the business of understanding what's behind this irrational feeling.

And when that's clear, the answers are obvious and I don't need advice.
Irrational feelings make sense when we understand what's behind them.
Perhaps that's why prayer works, sometimes, for some people, because God is mute, and
    doesn't give advice or try to fix things,
God just listens and lets you work it out for yourself.
So, please listen and just hear me, and, if you want to talk, wait a minute for your turn;
    and I'll listen to you.

—Anonymous

RECAP

How to Respond with Empathy

Strategy	Action
Understand Your Partner's Feelings	Ask yourself how you would feel if you had experienced a similar situation or recall how you *did* feel under similar circumstances. Or recall how your *partner* felt under similar circumstances.
Ask Questions	Seek additional information to better understand your partner's message.
Reflect Content by Paraphrasing	Summarize for your partner the essence of the information, as you understand it.
Reflect Feelings by Paraphrasing	When appropriate, try to summarize what you think your partner may be feeling.

PRINCIPLES FOR A LIFETIME: Enhancing Your Skills

Listen and Respond

Principle Four: Listen and respond thoughtfully to others.

- Stop: Work to turn off competing mental messages that distract your listening focus.
- To overcome self barriers to listening effectively, consciously become aware of your drifting attention. Then, to get back in sync, use self-talk skills and emotion management skills (such as deep breathing) to remain calm and focused on the message, not the messenger.
- To overcome information-processing listening barriers, make mental summaries of the message you hear, recognize when you are tired and not at your listening best, take effective notes, and remain focused.
- To overcome context listening barriers, become aware of your best and worst times of the day for listening; consciously intensify your concentration if you know you're not at your listening best, and assertively take action, such as closing a door or a window, to reduce external noise when listening.
- Look: Listen with your eyes to discern nonverbal information that provides important information about emotions, attitudes, and relationship cues.
- Listen: Work to link facts and details with major ideas you hear.
- Respond: Use effective responding skills by providing feedback that is descriptive, timely, brief, and useful while remaining an active listener.
- Be empathic: Try to imagine how you would feel in a situation like the one your communication partner is in. To confirm your interpretation of his or her message, ask appropriate clarifying questions, then paraphrase both the content and the emotions expressed.
- Paraphrase by briefly summarizing the message in your own words while trying to accurately capture the essence of what your listening partner said; don't add to the information presented when paraphrasing.

SUMMARY

An important principle of communication is to listen and respond thoughtfully to others. Listening is the process of receiving, constructing meaning from, and responding to verbal and nonverbal messages. It includes the processes of selecting, attending, understanding, remembering, and responding to others.

Each person develops a preferred listening style. The four listening styles are people-oriented, action-oriented, content-oriented, and time-oriented. Knowing your listening style can help you adapt your listening approach for maximum listening effectiveness.

Most people struggle with the skill of listening. Barriers to effective listening include focusing on our personal agenda, being distracted by emotional noise, criticizing the speaker, daydreaming, shifting attention, and being distracted by information overload and external noise.

To become a better listener, consider three simple steps: Stop, look, and listen. To stop means to be mindful of the message and avoid focusing on your own distracting inner "talk," which may keep you from focusing on the messages of others. To look is to listen with your eyes—to focus on nonverbal information that provides a wealth of cues about emotional meaning. To listen involves the skill of capturing the details of a message while also connecting those details to a major idea.

The other half of listening is responding to others accurately and appropriately. To respond thoughtfully means to stop and consider the needs of the other person. Check the accuracy of your listening skill by reflecting your understanding of what your partner has said. Responding skills are especially important if your listening goal is to empathize with and support others. Responding skills include understanding the feelings of others, asking appropriate questions, and paraphrasing the message's content and the speaker's feelings. Responding effectively does not mean being a parrot and repeating a message exactly as it was spoken. Paraphrasing means summarizing the gist of the message. The most effective responses to others are carefully timed, provide usable information, avoid cluttering details, and are descriptive rather than evaluative.

Discussion and Review

1. What is the difference between listening and hearing?
2. What are some of the key barriers that keep people from listening effectively?
3. What are similarities and differences between listening to gain information, to evaluate, to enjoy, and to empathize?
4. Identify and describe the four listening styles.
5. List the essential skills to improve your listening, and discuss strategies that will help you improve your listening skills.
6. What are suggestions for improving your ability to empathize with others?
7. What are suggestions for effectively paraphrasing or reflecting messages back to others?
8. How can you respond appropriately and thoughtfully to others?

Putting Principles into Practice

1. Test Your Empathy Ability

   Take this short test to assess your empathy. Respond to each statement about how you typically communicate with others by indicating the degree to which the statement is true. Use a 5-point scale: 1 = Always false; 2 = Usually false; 3 = Sometimes false and sometimes true; 4 = Usually true; 5 = Always true.

   _____ 1. I try to understand others' experiences from their perspectives.

   _____ 2. I follow the Golden Rule ("Do unto others as you would have them do unto you") when communicating with others.

   _____ 3. I can "tune in" to emotions others are experiencing when we communicate.

_____ 4. When trying to understand how others feel, I imagine how I would feel in their situation.

_____ 5. I am able to tell what others are feeling without being told.

_____ 6. Others experience the same feelings I do in any given situation.

_____ 7. When others are having problems, I can imagine how they feel.

_____ 8. I find it hard to understand the emotions others experience.

_____ 9. I try to see others as they want me to.

_____ 10. I never seem to know what others are thinking when we communicate.

To determine your score, first reverse the responses for the even-numbered items (if you wrote 1, make it 5; if you wrote 2, make it 4; if you wrote 3, leave it as 3; if you wrote 4, make it 2; if you wrote 5, make it 1). Next add the numbers given to the ten statements. Scores range from 10 to 50. The higher your score, the more you are able to empathize.

Source: William Gudykunst, *Bridging Differences,* 2e (Thousand Oaks, CA: Sage Publications, 1998). Reprinted by permission of Sage Publications, Inc.

2. Assessing Receiver Apprehension

Take the following test to assess your level of receiver apprehension. Respond to each of the statements by indicating how much it describes you, using a 5-point scale: 5 = Strongly agree; 4 = Agree; 3 = Uncertain or sometimes; 2 = Disagree; 1 = Strongly disagree.

_____ 1. When I am listening, I feel nervous about missing information.

_____ 2. I worry about being able to keep up with the material presented in lecture classes.

_____ 3. Sometimes I miss information in class because I am writing notes.

_____ 4. I feel tense and anxious when listening to important information.

_____ 5. I am concerned that I won't be able to remember information I've heard in lectures or discussions.

_____ 6. Although I try to concentrate, my thoughts sometimes become confused when I'm listening.

_____ 7. I worry that my listening skill isn't very good.

_____ 8. I regularly can't remember things that I have just been told.

_____ 9. I feel anxious and nervous when I am listening in class.

_____ 10. I prefer reading class material rather than listening to it, so I don't have to be stressed about catching all the information the first time.

Scores range from 50 to 10. The higher your score, the more you're likely to experience some anxiety when you listen to others and the harder you'll have to work at developing strategies to improve your listening comprehension.

Source: L. Wheeless, "An Investigation of Receiver Apprehension and Social Context Dimensions of Communication Apprehension," *The Speech Teacher* 24 (1975): 261–268. Taylor & Francis Ltd. <http://www.tandf.co.uk/journals>

3. On pages 112–117 we noted several barriers to listening. Rank order these barriers, with 1 being the most problematic for you. After you have identified your top three or four barriers, identify at least one specific strategy for overcoming each barrier.

4. Charting Your Listening Cycle

Are you a morning person or an evening person? Use the chart shown below to plot your listening energy cycle. Draw a line starting at 6:00 A.M., showing the highs and lows of your potential listening effectiveness. For example, if you are usually still asleep at 6:00 A.M., your line will be at 0 and start upward when you awake. If you are a morning person, your line will peak in the morning. Or perhaps your line will indicate that you listen best in the evening.

After you have charted your typical daily listening cycle, compare listening cycles with your classmates. Identify listening strategies that can help you capitalize on your listening "up" periods. Also, based on information you learned from this chapter and your own experiences, identify ways to enhance your listening when you traditionally have low listening energy.

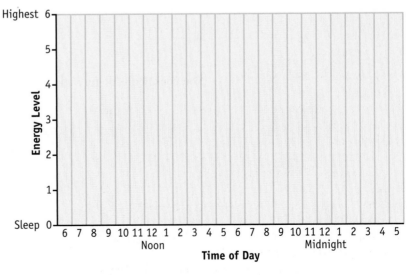

5. The following items relate to your listening style. Circle the response to each statement. Please be candid.

Listening Styles Inventory[47]

Item	Almost Always	Often	Sometimes	Seldom	Almost Never
1. I want to listen to what others have to say when they are talking.	5	4	3	2	1
2. I do not listen at my capacity when others are talking.	1	2	3	4	5
3. By listening, I can guess a speaker's intent or purpose without being told.	5	4	3	2	1
4. I have a purpose for listening when others are talking.	5	4	3	2	1
5. I keep control of my biases and attitudes when listening to others speak so that these factors won't affect my interpretation of the message.	5	4	3	2	1
6. I analyze my listening errors so as not to make them again.	5	4	3	2	1
7. I listen to the complete message before making judgments about what the speaker has said.	5	4	3	2	1
8. I cannot tell when a speaker's biases or attitudes are affecting his or her message.	1	2	3	4	5
9. I ask questions when I don't fully understand a speaker's message.	5	4	3	2	1
10. I am aware of whether a speaker's meaning for words and concepts is the same as mine.	5	4	3	2	1

_____ + _____ + _____ + _____ + _____ +

Grand total =

Now consult the Interpretation Scale on the facing page.

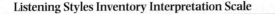

Listening Styles Inventory Interpretation Scale

Place an X on the part of the scale below that corresponds to your grand total score. Your listening style is described below.

Active

The active listener gives full attention to listening when others are talking and focuses on what is being said. This person expends a lot of energy participating in the speaking-listening exchange, which is usually evidenced by an alert posture or stance and much direct eye contact.

Involved

The involved listener gives most of his or her attention to the speaker's words and intentions. This person reflects on the message to a degree and participates in the speaking-listening exchange. The involved listener practices some direct eye contact and may have alert posture or stance, although this may be intermittent.

Passive

The passive listener receives information as though being talked to rather than as an equal partner in the speaking-listening exchange. While the passive listener assumes that the responsibility for the success of the communication is the speaker's, he or she is usually attentive, although attention may be faked at times. The passive listener seldom expends any noticeable energy in receiving and interpreting messages.

Detached

The detached listener withdraws from the speaking-listening exchange and becomes the object of the speaker's message rather than its receiver. The detached listener is usually inattentive, disinterested, and may be restless, bored, or easily distracted. This person's noticeable lack of enthusiasm may be marked by slumped or very relaxed posture and avoidance of direct eye contact.

Note: (1) The listening inventory gives you a general idea of your preferred listening style, based on how you view yourself. The scores indicating styles are approximations and should be regarded as such. (2) You may change your listening style, depending on the given situation or your interests, intentions, or objectives.

CHAPTER Six

Christian Pierre, "Share the World." © SuperStock, Inc.

There are no ordinary people.

C. S. Lewis

Adapting to Others:
Bridging Culture and Gender Differences

CHAPTER OUTLINE

Ethically Adapt Your
  Communication to Others

Culture and Communication

Gender and Communication

Barriers to Bridging Differences
  and Adapting to Others

Adapting to Others Who Are
  Different from You

Summary

CHAPTER OBJECTIVES

After studying this chapter, you should be able to:

1. Define culture.

2. Describe, compare, and contrast high-context and low-context cultures.

3. Describe four cultural values.

4. Identify differences and similarities between male and female communication patterns.

5. Describe the importance of gender within the larger context of culture.

6. Understand how gender relates to content and relational approaches to communication.

7. Illustrate five barriers that inhibit communication between individuals.

8. Describe six strategies that will help bridge differences between people and help them adapt to differences.

s C.S. Lewis observed, there are no ordinary people—which implies that each of us is unique. And the not-so-startling fact that people *are* different from one another provides the context for discussion of our final communication principle: *Effective communicators appropriately adapt their messages to others.* We introduce this principle last because often people learn how to adapt only after they have learned the other communication principles. Figure 6.1 presents our now-familiar model, which includes this final principle of appropriately adapting to others. Being able to adapt to others suggests that you already have a sense of who you are and a consciousness of the presence of others—self-awareness and other-awareness, the components of the first principle we presented. We learn to use verbal and nonverbal messages as infants, though it may take several years to develop sophistication in using language and nonverbal symbols. Hearing and listening also develop early in our lives. Studies in developmental communication suggest that the ability to appropriately adapt our behavior to others evolves after we have become aware that there is a "me," after we have learned to use verbal and nonverbal symbols to communicate, and after we have developed an ability to hear and listen to others. To adapt to others requires a relatively sophisticated understanding of the communication process.

One of life's unprofound principles with profound implications for human communication is this: *We each have different backgrounds and experiences.*[1] As you learned in Chapter 2, we each see, hear, and experience the world differently. To some degree, we are each estranged from others.

In a world of ever-increasing tensions and conflict arising from differences in culture, religious beliefs, and political ideologies, being able to understand and appropriately adapt to others is of vital importance. When differences are heightened by attitudes of superiority and beliefs about being divinely ordained to dominate others, violence is the typical result.

The greater our differences in background, experience, religion, and culture, the more difficult it is for us to interpret verbal and nonverbal symbols and to listen accurately to the messages of others, and the more challenging it is to adapt messages to others. When we meet someone for the first time, we often try to determine whether we have people, places, or backgrounds in common. It is usually easier to develop a relationship with someone who is similar to us rather than dissimilar.

The goal of this chapter is to identify culture and gender differences that may inhibit communication with others and to suggest adaptive strategies that can improve

FIGURE 6.1
Communication Principles for a Lifetime

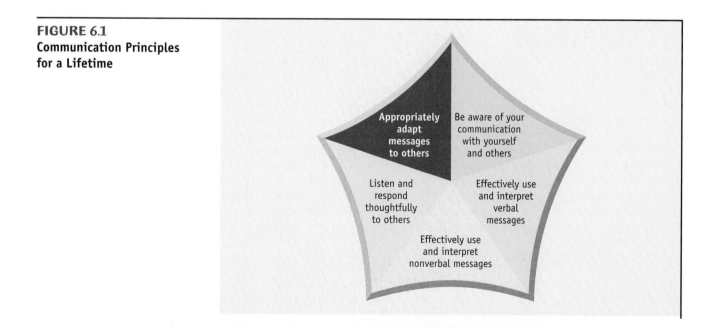

the quality and effectiveness of our communication with others. Throughout the first five chapters, we have noted in our discussions (and in the Diversity and Communication boxed feature) that culture and gender differences affect our communication with others. In this chapter we examine in more detail the influence of these differences on our lives and suggest some communication strategies for bridging these differences in our relationships with others.

As we focus on culture and gender differences and how to adapt to them, we will discuss the nature of culture and gender, identify barriers that stem from culture and gender differences, and suggest strategies that can help you better understand, appreciate, and adapt to people who are not just like you. Our premise: In order to live comfortably in the twenty-first century, we must learn ways to appreciate and understand culture and gender differences, rather than ignore them, suffer because of them, or wish they would disappear. But simply understanding that there are differences is not enough to improve communication; it is important to learn how to use effective communication skills to adapt to those differences.

Even though the focus of this chapter is on culture and gender differences, realize that these are only two of many differences that can divide people. Differences in age (sometimes called the generation gap), socioeconomic status, sexual orientation, and even in height, weight, or clothing choices have created tension between people in the past and probably will in the future. The principle of adapting to others is applicable to virtually all communication situations. The ideas and strategies for bridging differences in culture or gender that we suggest at the end of this chapter apply to other differences that create conflict and tension. The challenge is not to let our differences create a chasm so large that we can't find ways to ethically adapt our communication to create shared meaning.

ETHICALLY ADAPT YOUR COMMUNICATION TO OTHERS

The key principle of adapting to others that we propose in this chapter does not mean that you only do or say what others expect or that your primary goal in life is always to please others. You have a responsibility to ethically adapt your messages to others. To be ethical is to be truthful and honest while also observing the rights of others. Ethical communication is communication that is responsible, honest, and fair, that enhances human dignity, and that maintains listener options rather than coerces or forces someone to behave against his or her will. When we encourage you to adapt your messages to others, we are not recommending that you become a spineless jellyfish and say things only to make others happy. It would be unethical to abandon your own ethical principles and only communicate to please others. Such placating behavior is neither wise nor effective; it would also violate the principles of ethical communication.

Effective communicators are *appropriate* communicators—they are sensitive to others' needs while also communicating to enhance the probability that the message expressed will be the message interpreted. To be an appropriate communicator is to express your ideas in ways that fit the time, place, and situation.

Adapting your communication to others also does not mean that you manipulate a conversation so that only *you* can accomplish your goals. Ideally both (or all) parties' goals are met. We do not advocate a form of adapted communication that is false or manipulative. Whether you are in an interpersonal interaction, a group, or a presentational speaking situation, adapting your message to others makes common sense. Even so, being sensitive to others and wisely adapting behaviors to others are often not so common.

CULTURE AND COMMUNICATION

Overheard from a student before class:

> I've had it with all this cultural diversity and gender stuff. It seems like every textbook in every class is obsessed with it. My music appreciation class is trying to force the music of other cultures down my throat. What's wrong with Bach, Beethoven, and Brahms? In English lit, all we're reading is stuff by people from different countries. And it seems my history prof talks only about obscure people I've never heard of before. I'm tired of all this politically correct nonsense. I mean, we're all Americans, aren't we? We're not going off to live in Africa, China, or India. Why don't they just teach us what we need to know and cut all this diversity garbage?

Have you heard this kind of sentiment expressed before? Perhaps you've encountered this kind of "diversity backlash" among some of your classmates, or you may harbor this attitude yourself. It may seem unsettling to some that school curricula and textbooks are focusing on issues of culture and gender differences. But these changes are not motivated by an irrational desire to be politically correct. They are taking place because the United States is changing. The Diversity and Communication feature documents how diverse the United States is now and will increasingly become in the future. There is evidence that the trend toward greater diversity will continue.[2] With this growing diversity comes a heightened awareness that learning about culture and gender differences can affect every aspect of our lives in positive ways. You may not plan to travel the world, but the world is traveling to you. Your employers, teachers, religious leaders, best friends, or romantic partners may have grown up with cultural traditions different from your own. School textbooks and courses are *reflecting* the change, not *initiating* it.

One statistician notes that if the world were a village of 1000 people, the village would have 590 Asians, 123 Africans, 96 Europeans, 84 Latin Americans, 55 mem-

Diversity and Communication

Diversity Almanac

1. Two-thirds of the immigrants on this planet come to the United States.[3]

2. According to 2000 U.S. Census data, there are more than 35 million people of Hispanic origin in the United States—a 58% gain of 13 million people since 1990.[4]

3. It is estimated that more than 40 million U.S. residents learned something other than English as their first language, including 18 million people for whom Spanish is a first language.[5]

4. Almost one-third of U.S. residents under the age of 35 are members of minority groups, compared with one-fifth of those age 35 or older. According to U.S. Census Bureau population projections, by the year 2025, nearly half of all young adults in this country will come from minority groups.[6]

5. If the current trend continues, by the year 2050 the proportion of the U.S. population of non-Hispanic whites will decrease to 53%, down from a current 72%. Asians will increase to 16%, up from 4.5%; Hispanics will more than double their numbers, to over 25%, up from just

over 11.5%; and African Americans will increase their proportion slightly from the current 12%.[7]

6. It is estimated that between 2000 and 2010, Vermont's Asian population will grow by 80%, Arizona's will increase by 52%, and Delaware's will grow by 56%.[8]

7. Between 1995 and 2005, the combined population of African Americans, Native Americans, Asians, Pacific Islanders, and Hispanics grew 13 times faster than the non-Hispanic white population.[9]

8. One out of every eight U.S. residents speaks a language other than English at home, and one-third of children in urban U.S. public schools speak a first language other than English.[10]

9. For the first time since the 1850s, when California was seized from Mexico, a majority of the babies born in California in 2004 were Hispanic.[11]

10. Non-Hispanic whites constitute a minority of the population in Texas, New Mexico, and California.[12]

11. Sixty percent of the residents of Miami, Florida, are foreign-born.[13]

bers of the former Soviet Union, and 53 North Americans.[14] Clearly, a global economy and the ease with which technology permits us to communicate with others around the world increase the likelihood that you will establish relationships with people who are different from you and who have cultural traditions different from your own. You need not travel abroad to encounter cultural differences; the world is here.

Journalist Thomas Friedman argues that **globalization,** the integration of economics and technology that is contributing to a worldwide, interconnected business environment, is changing the way we work and relate to people around the world.[15] The world is now "flat" rather than round, suggests Friedman, because if you have a computer connected to the Internet or a cell phone, you can connect with anyone else in the world who also has those technologies. Saying that the world is flat is a metaphor Friedman uses to describe the interconnectedness of people throughout the world. Globalization results in a more competitive, level playing field because individuals have increased access to others with whom they can form entrepreneurial partnerships. Hence, globalization increases the probability that you will communicate with someone today who has a cultural background different from your own.

Friedman notes that during what he calls "Globalization 1.0," the period between Columbus's 1492 voyage and approximately 1800, *countries* were involved in globalization. "Globalization 2.0" was between 1800 and 2000, when *companies* were the globalization leaders. Today, to use Friedman's scheme, we are in "Globalization 3.0," and *individuals* are making contact with other individuals.[16] For example, when you call someone to get technical assistance with your computer or advice on fixing your TV, you are more likely to talk to someone who is in India rather than Indiana. Our point is not to debate the advantages or disadvantages of globalization, but only to suggest that one implication of a "flat" world is that you will increasingly communicate with people who have cultural backgrounds different from your own.

Defining Culture

Culture is a learned system of knowledge, behavior, attitudes, beliefs, values, and norms that is shared by a group of people and shaped from one generation to the next.[17] Communication and culture, says anthropologist Edward T. Hall, are inseparable—you can't talk about one without the other.[18] There is ample evidence that documents the influence of culture on how we work and live.[19] In the broadest sense, culture includes how people think, what they do, and how they use things to sustain their lives. Researcher Geert Hofstede says culture is the "mental software" that helps us understand our world.[20] Like the software and operating system in a computer, our culture provides the framework within which we interpret the data and information that enter our life.

Cultures are not static; they change as new information and new technologies modify them. We no longer believe that bathing is unhealthy or that we should use leeches as the primary medical procedure to make us healthy. Through research, we

globalization
The integration of economics and technology that is contributing to a worldwide, interconnected business environment.

culture
A learned system of knowledge, behavior, attitudes, beliefs, values, and norms that is shared by a group of people and shaped from one generation to the next.

Technology *and* Communication

Adapting to Cultural Differences When Communicating Electronically

*I*t is increasingly likely that you communicate with people who are far away from where you work and live. It's not unusual to have e-mail conversations with people from around the globe. Nor are conference calls or video conferences among people thousands of miles apart rare or surprising. The world is indeed small when it comes to communicating with people from around the globe.

A team of communication researchers points out that when we communicate via e-mail or phone, it takes a bit longer to interpret information about relationships, because often there are fewer nonverbal cues available.[21] In the case of e-mail, we can't see or hear the person we're exchanging messages with. With a telephone call, we can hear a person, but we miss facial expressions and body posture information. Even during a video conference, we're not able to see all of a person's body posture or watch everyone participating 100 percent of the time. The potential for misunderstanding, already present because of cultural differences, a key focus of this chapter, is compounded by the lack of nonverbal information that usually provides vital information about the nature of the relationship we have with others.

When nonverbal messages are diminished because we're not communicating with people face to face, it's important to seek other sources of information about the nature of the relationship with them. Specifically, what should we do?

- First, you may need to be more direct when responding or expressing how you feel; you may need to describe your emotional responses in writing.
- Second, you may need to ask more questions to clarify meanings.
- Third, it may be necessary to do more paraphrasing to confirm that you understand what others are saying.
- Finally, you simply may need to be more patient with others; relationships may take longer to develop because of the diminished nonverbal cues.

---

co-culture
A culture that exists within a larger cultural context (e.g., gay and lesbian cultures, Amish culture).

intercultural communication
Communication between people who have different cultural traditions.

culture shock
Feeling of stress and anxiety a person may experience when encountering a culture different from his or her own.

worldview
Perception shared by a culture or group of people about key beliefs and issues, such as death, God, and the meaning of life, which influences interaction with others; the lens through which people in a given culture perceive the world around them.

have replaced both of these cultural assumptions with the values of personal hygiene and modern, sophisticated methods of medical care.

Some groups of individuals can best be described as a **co-culture**—a cultural group within a larger culture. Examples of co-cultures in the United States include the Amish and some communities in Appalachia. A person's gender places her or him in one of the co-cultures that researchers have used to analyze and investigate the influence of communication on our relationships with others. We discuss the impact of gender on our communication in more detail later in the chapter. Gays and lesbians constitute another example of an important co-culture in our society.

Intercultural communication occurs when individuals or groups from different cultures communicate. The transactional process of listening and responding to people from different cultural backgrounds can be challenging. As we stressed earlier, the greater the different in culture between two people, the greater the potential for misunderstanding and mistrust. That's why it is important to understand the nature of culture and how cultural differences influence our communication with others. Such understanding helps us develop strategies to make connections and adapt to others with different "mental software."

When you encounter a culture that has little in common with your own, you may experience **culture shock,** a sense of confusion, anxiety, stress, and loss.[22] If you are visiting or actually living in the new culture, your uncertainty and stress may take time to subside as you learn the values and message systems that characterize the culture. If you are trying to communicate with someone from a background quite different from yours—even on your home turf—it is important to consider the role of culture as you interact.

Our culture and life experiences determine our **worldview**—the general cultural perspective that determines how we perceive and respond to what happens to us. A culture's worldview, according to intercultural communication scholar Carley Dodd, encompasses "how the culture perceives the role of various forces in explaining why events occur as they do in a social setting."[23] These beliefs shape our thoughts, language, and actions. Your worldview permeates all aspects of how you interact with society; it's like a lens through which you observe the world. If, as we noted in Chapter 1, communication is how we make sense out of the world and share that sense with others, our worldview is one of the primary filters that influence how we make sense out of the world. Two frameworks for describing how culture influences our worldview include cultural context and cultural values.

Cultural Contexts

The **cultural context** of any communication consists of the nonverbal cues that surround and give added meaning to the message. In this sense, *all* nonverbal cues are part of a cultural context. Some cultures give more weight to the surrounding nonverbal context than to the explicit verbal message when interpreting the overall meaning of a message. Other cultures place less emphasis on the nonverbal context and greater emphasis on what someone says.

For example, when you interview for a job, you may be scanning the face of your interviewer and looking for nonverbal messages to provide cues about the impression you are making on the interviewer. These contextual cues (in this case, the nonverbal messages) give meaning to help you interpret the message of your interviewer. Edward T. Hall helped us understand the importance of cultural context when he categorized cultures as either high- or low-context.[24]

Members of high-context cultures are skilled in using nonverbal cues to communicate. Members of low-context cultures rely more on actual words to send and receive messages.

High-Context Cultures   In **high-context cultures,** nonverbal cues are extremely important in interpreting messages. Communicators rely heavily on the context of more subtle information such as facial expression, vocal cues, and even silence in interpreting messages; hence, the term *high-context cultures,* to indicate the emphasis placed on the context. Asian, Arab, and Southern European peoples are more likely to draw on the context for message interpretation.

Low-Context Cultures   People in **low-context cultures** rely more explicitly on language and the meaning of words and use fewer contextual cues to send and interpret information. Individuals from low-context cultures, such as North Americans, Germans, and Scandinavians, may perceive people from high-context cultures as less attractive, knowledgeable, and trustworthy, because they violate unspoken low-context cultural rules of conduct and communication. Individuals from low-context cultures often are less skilled in interpreting unspoken contextual messages.[25] Figure 6.2 describes differences in communication style between high-context and low-context cultures.

Cultural Values

Ancient Egyptians worshiped cats. The Druids of England believed they could tap into spiritual powers in the shadow of the mysterious rock circle of Stonehenge at the summer solstice. Some would say contemporary Americans place a high value on accumulating material possessions and making pilgrimages to sports arenas on weekends. By paying attention to what a culture values, we can learn important clues about how to respond to communication messages, establish relationships, and avoid making embarrassing errors when interacting with people from a given culture. Identifying what a given group of people values or appreciates can give us insight into the behavior of an

cultural context
Additional information about a message that is communicated through nonverbal and environmental cues rather than through language.

high-context culture
Culture in which people derive much information from nonverbal and environmental cues and less information from the words of a message.

low-context culture
Culture in which people derive much information from the words of a message and less information from nonverbal and environmental cues.

individual raised within that culture. Although there are considerable differences among the world's **cultural values**—clearly, not all cultures value the same things— Geert Hofstede has identified four categories for measuring values that are important in almost every culture.[26] Even though his data were collected more than 30 years ago and only sampled employees (predominantly males) who worked at IBM—a large international company with branch offices in many countries—his research remains one of the most comprehensive studies to help us understand how to describe what people from a culture may value.

According to Hofstede's research, every culture establishes values relating to (1) individualism versus collectivism, (2) distribution of power (either centralized or shared), (3) avoidance of uncertainty versus tolerance for uncertainty, and (4) masculine or feminine cultural perspectives. An overview of Hofstede's research conclusions for several countries is included in Table 6.1. These generalizations are based on several surveys that he developed and administered to over 100,000 people. We'll consider each of these four categories of values in more detail.

Individualistic and Collectivistic Cultural Values   Which of the following two sayings best characterizes your culture: "All for one and one for all" or "I did it my way"? If you chose the first one, your culture is more likely to value group or team collaboration—it is what researchers call a **collectivistic culture.** Collectivistic cultures champion what people do together and reward group achievement. In contrast the "I did it my way" phrase emphasizes the importance of the individual over the group. A culture that celebrates individual achievement and in which individual recognition is important is an **individualistic culture.** The United States—with its Academy Awards; its reality TV shows in which contestants vie for the title of "American Idol" or try to be the lone "Survivor"; its countless sports contests; its community awards to firefighters for dedicated service, to winners of spelling bees, to chefs for their barbecue recipes—perhaps epitomizes the individualistic culture.

Some researchers believe that the values of individualism and collectivism are the most important values of any culture—they determine the essential nature of every other facet of how people behave.[27] Other researchers, however, caution that cultures are complex and that it is dangerous to label an entire culture as "individualistic" or

cultural values
Whatever a given group of people values or appreciates.

collectivistic culture
A culture that places a high value on collaboration, teamwork, and group achievement.

individualistic culture
A culture that values individual achievement and personal accomplishments.

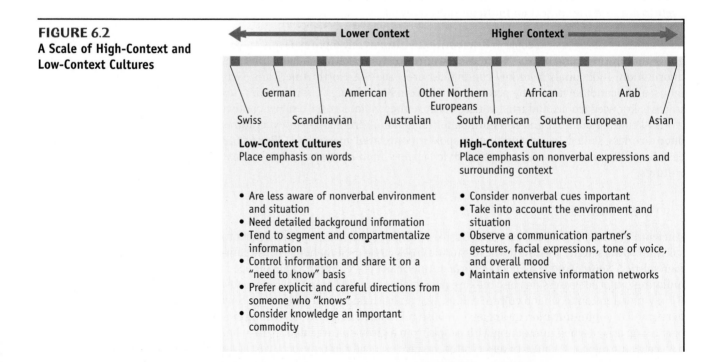

FIGURE 6.2
A Scale of High-Context and Low-Context Cultures

Lower Context   Higher Context

German   American   Other Northern Europeans   African   Arab

Swiss   Scandinavian   Australian   South American   Southern European   Asian

Low-Context Cultures
Place emphasis on words

- Are less aware of nonverbal environment and situation
- Need detailed background information
- Tend to segment and compartmentalize information
- Control information and share it on a "need to know" basis
- Prefer explicit and careful directions from someone who "knows"
- Consider knowledge an important commodity

High-Context Cultures
Place emphasis on nonverbal expressions and surrounding context

- Consider nonverbal cues important
- Take into account the environment and situation
- Observe a communication partner's gestures, facial expressions, tone of voice, and overall mood
- Maintain extensive information networks

TABLE 6.1
Countries That Illustrate Four Categories of Cultural Values

Cultural Value	Countries That Scored Higher on This Cultural Value	Countries That Scored Lower on This Cultural Value
Individualism: People with higher individualism scores generally value individual accomplishment rather than collective or collaborative achievement.	United States, Australia, Great Britain, Canada, Netherlands, New Zealand, Italy, Belgium, Denmark, Sweden, France	Guatemala, Ecuador, Panama, Venezuela, Colombia, Indonesia, Pakistan, Costa Rica, Peru, Taiwan, South Korea
Power Distribution: People with higher power distribution scores generally value greater power differences between people; they are generally more accepting of fewer people having authority and power than are those with lower scores on this cultural dimension.	Malaysia, Guatemala, Panama, Philippines, Mexico, Venezuela, Arab countries, Ecuador, Indonesia, India	Austria, Israel, Denmark, New Zealand, Ireland, Sweden, Norway, Finland, Switzerland, Great Britain
Uncertainty Avoidance: People with higher uncertainty avoidance scores generally prefer to avoid uncertainty; they like to know what will happen next. People with lower scores are more comfortable with uncertainty.	Greece, Portugal, Guatemala, Uruguay, Belgium, Japan, Peru, France	Singapore, Jamaica, Denmark, Sweden, Hong Kong, Ireland, Great Britain, Malaysia, India, Philippines, United States
Masculinity: People with higher masculinity scores value high achievement, men in more assertive roles, and more clearly differentiated sex roles than people with lower scores on this cultural dimension.	Japan, Australia, Venezuela, Italy, Switzerland, Mexico, Ireland, Jamaica, Great Britain	Sweden, Norway, Netherlands, Denmark, Costa Rica, Finland, Chile, Portugal, Thailand

Source: Adapted from Geert Hofstede, *Cultures and Organizations: Software of the Mind* (London: McGraw-Hill, 1991). © Geert Hofstede.

"collectivistic."[28] We agree—obviously, not everyone in a given culture fits a single label. But in trying to understand the role of culture and its impact on human communication, we believe that Hofstede's concept of cultural values, with special emphasis on individualism and collectivism, helps explain and predict how people may send and interpret communication.[29] Using Hofstede's four cultural values to describe a given culture or geographic region is a bit like flying over a country at 35,000 feet; at that height you can't see the details and note nuances of difference, but you can gain a broad overview of the cultural landscape.

Traditionally, North Americans place a high value on individual achievements. People from Asian cultures are more likely to value collective or group achievement. Hofstede summed up the American value system this way:

> Chief among the virtues claimed . . . is self-realization. Each person is viewed as having a unique set of talents and potentials. The translation of these potentials into actuality is considered the highest purpose to which one can devote one's life.[30]

In a collectivistic culture, conversely, people strive to accomplish goals for the benefit of the group rather than the individual. Here's a description of the Kenyan culture's emphasis on group or team collaboration:

> . . . nobody is an isolated individual. Rather, his [or her] uniqueness is a secondary fact. . . . In this new system, group activities are dominant, responsibility is shared and accountability is collective. . . . Because of the emphasis on collectivity, harmony and cooperation among the group tend to be emphasized more than individual function and responsibility.[31]

Members of a *collectivistic* culture may find team sports to be more satisfying than individual sports.

Individualistic cultures tend to be more loosely knit socially; individuals feel responsibility for taking care of themselves and their immediate families.[32] Individuals in collectivistic cultures expect more loyalty and support from others and demonstrate more loyalty to the community. Because collectivistic cultures place more value on "we" than on "I," teamwork approaches usually succeed better in their workplaces. U.S. businesses have tried to adopt some of Japan's successful team strategies for achieving high productivity. However, while teamwork training has been successful, U.S. workers still need constantly to be reminded to collaborate and work collectively.

Decentralized and Centralized Approaches to Power and Cultural Values

Some cultures are more comfortable with a broad distribution of power. People from such cultures prefer a decentralized approach to power. Leadership is not vested in just one person. Decisions in a culture that values decentralized power distribution are more likely to be made by consensus rather than by decree. Research suggests that people from Australia, Israel, Denmark, New Zealand, and Ireland typically prefer minimized power differences between others; they strive for more equal distribution of authority and control.[33]

Cultures that place a high value on centralized power are more comfortable with a more structured form of government, as well as managerial styles that feature clear lines of authority. Hierarchical bureaucracies are common, and the general assumption is that some people will have more power, control, and influence than others. Research by Hofstede suggests that people from Malaysia, Guatemala, Panama, and the Philippines are all high on the centralized power scale.[34]

Uncertainty and Certainty and Cultural Values

"Why don't they tell me what's going on?" exclaims an exasperated student. "I don't know what my grades are. I don't know what my SAT score is. I'm in a complete fog." Many people like to know "what's going on." They like to avoid uncertainty and to have a general sense of what's going to happen. Too much uncertainty makes them uncomfortable.

Some people tolerate more ambiguity and uncertainty than others. Cultures in which people need certainty to feel secure are more likely to develop and enforce rigid rules for behavior and establish more elaborate codes of conduct. People from cultures with a greater tolerance for uncertainty have more relaxed, informal expectations for others. "It will sort itself out" and "Go with the flow" are phrases that characterize their attitudes.[35] As shown in Table 6.1, people from Greece, Portugal, and Guatemala generally do not like uncertainty, while people from Singapore, Jamaica, and Denmark are more comfortable not knowing what will happen next.

Again, we remind you that although there is evidence for the existence of the general cultural value of uncertainty avoidance, not all people in a given culture or country find this cultural value equally important. There is considerable variation within a culture as to how people respond to uncertainty.

Masculine and Feminine Cultural Values Some cultures emphasize traditional male values—such as getting things done and being more assertive; other cultures place greater emphasis on traditional female values—building relationships and seeking peace and harmony with others. People from **masculine cultures** also tend to value more traditional roles for men and women. These values are not only about biological differences; they are general approaches to interacting with other people. People (both men and women) from masculine cultures value achievement, heroism, material wealth, and making things happen. Men and women from **feminine cultures** tend to value such things as caring for the less fortunate, being sensitive toward others, and enhancing the overall quality of life.[36] Later in this chapter, we will discuss how gender contributes to the development of a culture, but for now it is enough to realize that whole cultures can be typified by whether they identify with or emphasize masculine or feminine values.

Having said all of the above, we caution you to avoid making sweeping generalizations about every person in any cultural group. Just as there are differences between and among cultures, there are differences within a cultural group. For centuries, most countries have had masculine cultures. Men and their conquests are featured in history books and all aspects of society more than women. But today's cultural anthropologists see some shift in these values. There is some movement toward the middle, with greater equality between masculine and feminine roles.

On the Web

You need not travel to a foreign destination to experience another culture; opportunities to experience cultural differences may be as close as talking with your roommate, an instructor, or a good friend. To learn more about the role of culture in communication, check out one of the following Web sites, which offer more information about intercultural communication.

www.awesomelibrary.org/ is the Web address of Awesome Library. Once you're at this site, type in the words "intercultural communication" in the Search box to access information and resources about intercultural communication skills and principles.

www.takingitglobal.org/home.html is the site for Taking It Global. It provides resources that focus on student travel, including cultural tips and ideas to facilitate better understanding between people from different cultures.

RECAP

Cultural Values

Individualistic vs. Collectivistic	• Individualistic cultures value individual accomplishments and achievement.
	• Collectivistic cultures value group and team collaboration.
Decentralized vs. Centralized Power	• Centralized power cultures value having power in the hands of a smaller number of people.
	• Decentralized power cultures favor more equality and a more even distribution of power in government and organizations.
Uncertainty vs. Certainty	• Cultures that value certainty do not like ambiguity and value feeling secure.
	• Cultures with a greater tolerance for uncertainty are comfortable with ambiguity and less information.
Masculine vs. Feminine	• Masculine cultures value achievement, assertiveness, heroism, material wealth, and more traditional sex roles.
	• Feminine cultures value relationships, caring for the less fortunate, overall quality of life, and less traditional distinctions between sex roles.

masculine culture
A culture that values achievement, assertiveness, heroism, material wealth, and traditional male and female roles.

feminine culture
A culture that values being sensitive toward others and fostering harmonious personal relationships with others.

GENDER AND COMMUNICATION

Perhaps the most obvious form of human diversity is gender—the division of human beings into female and male. As we pointed out in Chapter 2, a person's sex is determined by biology; gender is the culturally constructed and psychologically based perception of one's self as feminine, masculine, or **androgynous** (having both feminine and masculine traits). One's gender is learned and is socially reinforced by others, as well as by one's life experience and genetics. Some scholars prefer to study gender as a subset of culture (a co-culture), as a form of cultural diversity on the level of such other aspects as race, ethnicity, and religion. We view gender as one of many basic elements of culture; but because it so pervades our everyday existence, we choose to treat gender more fully in this chapter as we continue our focus on adapting to others.

At one time or another, you have probably thought, "Why doesn't she (or he) act like persons of *my* sex?" Have you ever heard yourself or someone else say, "You men are all alike," or "If women would just be more reasonable, like men are, life would be simpler"? You may also have heard (or said) "Vive la difference"—a French expression that celebrates the fact that men and women are different. Why celebrate? Because that difference makes us fascinating and mysterious, and it keeps the world from being awfully dull. Whatever your view of the relationship between the sexes, your day-to-day interaction with members of both sexes is a fact of life (unless you're a hermit). Women and men work, live, and play together, so it's important to explore the effects of gender on communication in order to improve our ability to relate to one another.

In fact, the likelihood that all of us will come into more frequent contact with members of both sexes is increasing, because Americans are working longer hours. Recent statistics reveal that we spent 10% more time on the job at the turn of the twenty-first century than in the 1960s.[37] Projections suggest that women will soon account for 63% of all employees.[38]

The Importance of Gender in Culture

In the predominant culture of the United States, someone's gender is an important thing to know. Think about it: What's the first question a new parent is asked? "Ten fingers and ten toes?" "Hairy or bald-headed?" "Blue eyes or brown?" No—usually the first question asked is, "Is it a boy or girl?" We place a great deal of importance on a person's sex in this culture, as do all cultures around the world. Some critics contend that we're too concerned with gender, with emphasizing differences between women and men and conditioning young boys to be masculine and girls to be feminine. Some men and women in our culture are chastised or ostracized because they don't conform to society's expectations for their sex.

Fascinating research reveals that sex-based expectations and conditioning start practically from birth. Adults, beginning with parents, talk to and respond to girls and boys differently.[39] Female babies are held more gingerly; as they become toddlers, they receive more attention from parents when they fall and are kept in closer proximity than male children. Boys are encouraged to rough and tumble, to "shake it off" when they fall, and to explore greater distances than girls. Girls are often allowed to reveal their emotions more readily than boys, while many boys may be taught to control or hide their emotions. When carried into adulthood, these early gender-based lessons may cause serious harm to our bodies, professional advancement, and relationships. For example, women who want to succeed in their careers often learn the hard way that revealing their emotions isn't considered professional. Many men find that years of suppressing emotion can lead to health problems and estrangement from family members.

An important question to consider is this: Just how different are you and members of your sex from members of the opposite sex? Do you think that women are from one planet and men another? Do you think that men constitute one cultural group and women another? Or do you think the media and other moneymaking enterprises oversell sex differences in an effort to create conflict and drama to generate high ratings and profits?

androgynous
Exhibiting both masculine and feminine characteristics.

John Gray, author of the book *Men Are from Mars, Women Are from Venus,* would have us believe that the sexes are so different that we actually approach life from two distinct "planets" or spheres of perspective.[40] Although several of Gray's conclusions have been challenged by communication scholars because they are not supported by research, there are some research-documented differences in the ways men and women communicate.[41] Deborah Tannen, author of several books on the behavior of the sexes, views men and women as distinctly different cultural groups.[42] She suggests that female–male communication is cross-cultural communication, with all the challenges inherent in exchanging messages with persons of very different backgrounds and value systems. Perhaps these viewpoints are a bit extreme, and the sexes are actually more alike than different.

There are, however, some interesting differences based on research—not popular opinion or media hype—that are worthy of mention. We will discuss some of these in the next section. After reading that discussion, here's what we suggest you do:

- First, work to understand the differences we discuss.
- Second, make an insightful examination of your own behavior in light of the differences discussed and then determine how you conform to and differ from the description of members of your sex.
- Third, be a gender researcher yourself. Make a note of differences as well as similarities between you and members of the opposite sex. Be careful not to ascribe differences in communication only to gender, but also consider a host of other reasons such as age, personality, or culture.
- Finally, make a conscious effort to adapt your behavior appropriately. We don't mean that you have to always communicate as you think members of your sex would or should communicate, but be mindful of how you interact with others to enhance the quality of your relationships with them.

Why Women and Men Communicate Versus *How*

In an earlier section of this chapter, we explored ways in which whole cultures are typified by their emphasis on masculine or feminine values. Some of the values associated with masculinity include being assertive and getting things done. Classic sociological research has termed such qualities an **instrumental orientation,** a term that implies action and a "me against the world" view of self.[43] Feminine cultural values emphasize connecting with others and fostering harmonious relationships, what has been termed an **expressive orientation.**

Translating these orientations into actual communication behavior is revealing. Research using multiple methods and originating in various disciplines consistently shows that differences in men's and women's communication have more to do with *why* we communicate than *how*. Men tend to talk to accomplish something or complete a task. Women often use conversation to establish and maintain relationships.

instrumental orientation
A masculine approach that involves assertiveness and action, in a "me against the world" view of self and reality.

expressive orientation
A feminine approach that emphasizes connecting with others and fostering harmonious relationships and community.

NON SEQUITUR © 2002 Wiley Miller. Dist. by Universal Press Syndicate. Reprinted with permission. All rights reserved.

In Chapter 1, we discussed some basic characteristics of communication, the first being that communication is inescapable. We expanded on that characteristic by describing how every message has a content dimension and a relational dimension. The **content dimension** is what is said, or the verbal message. The **relational dimension** involves how the verbal message is said, including tone of voice, facial expressions, and other nonverbal behaviors. The content dimension is the *what*, the relational dimension is the *how*; the latter aspect tells you how to interpret the former. You also receive clues from the relational dimension about the state of the relationship between the two communicators. How are these characteristics of communication affected by gender?

Research reveals that men tend to approach communication from a content orientation, meaning that they view the purpose of communication as primarily information exchange. You talk when you have something to say. This is also consistent with the tendency for men to base their relationships, especially their male friendships, on sharing activities rather than talking. Women, research suggests, tend to use communication for the purpose of relating or connecting to others, of extending themselves to other persons to know them and be known by them. What you talk about is less important than the fact that you're talking, because talking implies relationship. There is a short way of summarizing this difference: *Men often communicate to report; women often communicate to establish rapport.*[44] So the point of difference isn't in the way the sexes actually communicate but in the motivations or reasons for communicating. The *how* may not be that different; the *why* may be very different.[45] Our instrumental and expressive orientations to the world translate into our communication behavior.

So here's one reason why adaptation is a premium skill. Can you see that by understanding both approaches to communication—content and relational (or instrumental and expressive)—and by developing the ability to accomplish both, you broaden what you can do? Just because you're female doesn't mean that you have to take an expressive approach to every interaction; just because you're male doesn't mean that conversations are always about information exchange. In a conversation with a member of the opposite sex, try to assess the person's communication motivation. Analyze what the other person must view as the purpose for the conversation, and adjust your response accordingly. Sometimes it's wise simply to ask the person what he or she wants.

content dimension
The *what* of a communication message; the verbal message.

relational dimension
The nonverbal elements of a message, such as tone of voice and facial expressions, that convey *how* the message should be interpreted and provide clues about the state of the relationship between the communicators.

RECAP

Gender-Based Approaches to Communication

Masculine Approach	Feminine Approach
• More instrumental: Often characterized by assertiveness and getting things done	• More expressive: Often characterized by an emphasis on connecting with others and fostering harmonious relationships
• Usually more emphasis on the content of messages	• Usually more emphasis on the relational elements of messages
• Focuses more on the information being exchanged (the *what*) rather than on relational elements (the *how*) in the message	• Focuses more on the quality of the relationship between communicators than on information exchanged
• Attends more to verbal than nonverbal messages	• Attends more to nonverbal elements, *how* something is said rather than *what* is said

BARRIERS TO BRIDGING DIFFERENCES AND ADAPTING TO OTHERS

Now that we've paid attention to how people are different from one another, let's identify barriers that increase the differences that exist between people. Differences, whether culture or gender based, often breed misunderstanding. And misunderstanding can lead to feelings of distrust, suspicion, and even hostility. The phrase "battle of the sexes" suggests that men and women perceive and respond to the world differently, which may result in disagreement and evolve into literal battles. Among the most common reasons for a woman to end up in an emergency room in the United States today is bodily harm inflicted by a male whom she knows.[46]

The front pages of newspapers continue to chronicle the prevalence of terrorism, war, and conflict around the globe, which are due, in part, to different cultural perspectives. Our hopes for harmony in our own country erode when we learn of hate crimes committed against members of co-cultural groups within the larger U.S. culture. Our hopes for peace and prosperity among all of the world's peoples are often dashed when we read of violent clashes between people of different religions, races, sexual orientations, and ethnicities.

Is it possible to develop effective relationships with people who are different from ourselves? The answer is, "Of course." Although almost every relationship experiences some degree of conflict, most of the world's people do not witness annihilating destruction each day. Bridging culture and gender differences is possible.

The first step to bridging differences between people is to identify what hinders effective communication. Sometimes communication falters because of different meanings created by different languages or interpretations of nonverbal messages. And sometimes communication is not effective because of our inability to stop focusing exclusively on our own goals; we fail to consider the needs of our communication partners. To develop effective strategies to adapt to others who are different from ourselves, we'll examine some of the barriers that often separate us from one another.

Assuming Superiority

We shook our heads in absolute horror and disbelief as we watched TV images of the twin towers of the World Trade Center crumbling in a shroud of smoke and ash and the Pentagon erupting in flames. These indelible images of September 11, 2001, are seared in our consciousness. Collectively we asked "Why?" There are no easy answers. Part of the answer, however, may lie in the belief of self-righteous superiority held by those who seek to destroy cultural and religious traditions that are different from their own. Of course, terrorism and violence are not new; historical records document that differences, especially religious differences, have for centuries created conditions that have resulted in unspeakable human atrocities. One of the most powerful barriers to adapting to others is the belief that one's own culture or gender is better than that of others.

Ethnocentrism is the attitude that our own cultural approaches are superior to those of other cultures.[47] Extreme ethnocentrism is the opposite of being other oriented. When fans from two rival high schools at a Friday-night football game scream, "We're number one!" they are hardly establishing quality communication. Competition is, of course, expected in sports; but when the mindset of unquestioned superiority is created through cultural or religious identification, the resulting mistrust and suspicion are breeding grounds for conflict. Ethnocentrism and cultural snobbery create a barrier that inhibits rather than enhances communication.

It would probably be impossible to avoid feeling most comfortable with our own culture and people who are like us. In fact, some degree of ethnocentrism can play a useful role in perpetuating our own cultural traditions; we form communities and groups based on common traditions, beliefs, and values. A problem occurs, however, if we become so extremely biased in favor of our own cultural traditions that we fail to recognize that people from other cultural traditions are just as comfortable with their approach to life as we are to ours. And when we mindlessly attack someone else's cultural traditions (which may be a prelude to physical aggression), we begin to erect communication barriers.

"My dad is smarter than your dad." "Boys are smarter than girls." "U.S. workers are more industrious than workers in other countries." What may start out as a child's chant may evolve into a cultural consciousness that leads to perceptions of cultural and gender superiority. Cultural anthropologists caution against assuming that one culture is superior to another; as we just noted, this creates a barrier. If you have ever talked with someone with an overinflated ego, you know what a hindrance such a self-promoting attitude can be to communication. If a group or nation harbors that sense of unchallenged superiority and feeling of ordained righteousness, it will be difficult to establish quality communication relationships with that group.

A person who assumes superiority may also assume greater power and control over others. Conflicts are often about power—who has it and who wants more of it. Differences in power, therefore, are breeding grounds for mistrust and conflict. The nineteenth-century British scholar Lord Acton said that absolute power corrupts absolutely; although this may not always be the case, an ethnocentric mindset that assumes superiority may add to the perception of assumed power over others. Although it's true that there are cultural differences in attitudes toward power (whether power is centralized or decentralized), world history documents that those who are consistently pushed and pulled and pummeled eventually revolt and seek greater equity of power.

Assuming Similarity

ethnocentrism
The belief that one's own cultural traditions and assumptions are superior to those of others.

Just as it is inaccurate to assume that all members of the opposite sex or all people who belong to other social groups or classes are worlds apart from you, it is also wrong to assume that others will act and think just like you. Even if they appear to be like you, all people do not behave the same way.[48] Anthropologists Clyde Kluckhohn and Henry Murray suggested that every person is, in some respects (1) like all other people, (2) like some other people, and (3) like no other people.⁴⁹ Our challenge when meeting others is to sort out how we are alike and how we are unique. Focusing on superficial factors such as appearance, clothing, and even a person's occupation can lead to false impressions. Instead, we must take time to explore the person's background and cultural values before we can determine what we really have in common.

On meeting a new acquaintance, we usually explore what we may have in common. "Do you know so and so?" "Oh, you're from Missouri. Do you know Mamie Smith from Buckner?" The search for similarities helps us develop a common framework for communication. But even when we find a few similarities, it's a mistake to make too many assumptions about our new friend's attitudes and perceptions. Because of our human tendency to develop categories and use words to label our experiences, we may lump people into a common category and assume similarity where no similarity exists. Each of us perceives the world through our own frame of reference. As one ancient Greek sage put it, "Every tale can be told in a different way." We not only see the world differently, we express those differences in the way we talk, think, and interact with others. If we fail to be mindful that each of us is unique, we may take communication shortcuts, use unfamiliar words, and assume our communication will be more effective than it is.

Assuming Differences

Although it may seem contradictory to say so, given what we just noted about assuming similarities, another barrier that may keep you from bridging differences between yourself and someone else is to automatically assume that the other person will be different from you. It can be just as detrimental to communication to assume someone is essentially different from you as it is to assume someone is just like you. The fact is, human beings *do* share common experiences and characteristics despite their differences. So we suggest that while you don't want to assume everyone is just like you, it's also detrimental to communication to assume you have nothing in common with others.

Cultural anthropologists have spent considerable effort to identify cultural differences among people. The gist of this entire chapter is that people are different—in culture, gender, and a host of other factors such as personality, age, sexual orientation, and innate talents. Yet if we don't seek to connect with those factors that make us all members of the human family, we may miss opportunities for bridging the real differences that exist.

The point of noting that humans have similarities as well as differences is not to diminish the role of culture as a key element that influences communication, but to recognize that despite cultural differences we are all members of the human family. The words *communication* and *common* resemble one another. We communicate effectively and appropriately when we can connect to others based on discovering what we hold in common. Identifying common cultural issues and similarities can also help you establish common ground with your audience.

How are we all alike? Cultural anthropologist Donald Brown has compiled a list of hundreds of "surface" universals of behavior.⁵⁰ According to Brown, people in all cultures

- have beliefs about death
- have a childhood fear of strangers
- have a division of labor by sex
- experience certain emotions and feelings, such as envy, pain, jealousy, shame, and pride
- use facial expressions to express emotions

Because the communication process may be difficult between members of different cultures, both parties need to work to understand each other.

- have rules for etiquette
- experience empathy
- value some degree of collaboration or cooperation
- experience conflict and seek to manage or mediate conflict

Of course, not all cultures have the same beliefs about death or the same way of dividing labor according to sex, but all cultures address these issues. Communication researcher David Kale believes that another universal value is the dignity and worth of other people. Thus, he suggests that all people can identify with the struggle to enhance their own dignity and worth, although different cultures express that in different ways.[51] Another common value that Kale notes is world peace. Intercultural communication scholars Larry Samovar and Richard Porter assert that there are other common elements that cultures share.[52] They note that people from all cultures seek physical pleasure as well as emotional and psychological pleasure and seek to avoid personal harm. It's true that each culture and each person decides what is pleasurable or painful; nonetheless, argue Samovar and Porter, all people operate within this pleasure-pain continuum.

Another advocate for common human values was the Oxford and Cambridge professor and widely read author C. S. Lewis. In his book *The Abolition of Man*, Lewis argued for the existence of universal, natural laws, which he called the Tao, that serve as benchmarks for all human values.[53] Lewis identified such common values as do not murder; be honest; hold parents, elders, and ancestors with special honor; be compassionate to those who are less fortunate; keep your promises; honor the basic human rights of others.

Educators have long debated whether there are common human values and whether they can be taught. There are over 50 consulting organizations in the United States that develop "character education" programs for primary and secondary schools.[54] One district adopted a curriculum to teach "touchstone character skills" that include caring, courage, fairness, honesty, integrity, perseverance, respect, responsibility, self-discipline, and trustworthiness.[55]

What are the practical implications of trying to identify common human values or characteristics? If you find yourself disagreeing with another person about a particular issue, identifying a larger common value such as the value of peace and prosperity or the importance of family can help you find common ground so that the other person will at least listen to your ideas. It's useful, we believe, not just to categorize our differences but also to explore how human beings are similar to one another. Discovering how we are alike can provide a starting point for human understanding. Yes, we are all different; but we share things in common as well. Communication effectiveness is diminished when we assume we're all different from one another in every aspect, just as communication is hindered if we assume we're all alike. We're more complicated than that.

Stereotyping and Prejudice

Closely related to ethnocentrism and feelings of cultural and gender superiority is the barrier of making a rigid judgment against a class or type of people.

All Russians like vodka.
All men like to watch wrestling.
All Asians are good at math.
All women like to go shopping.

stereotype
To place a person or group of persons into an inflexible, all-encompassing category.

These statements are stereotypes. They are all inaccurate. To **stereotype** someone is to place him or her in an inflexible, all-encompassing category. The term *stereotype* started out as a printing term to describe a process in which the typesetter uses the same type to print text again and again. When we stereotype, we "print" the same

Ethics and Communication

Stereotyping Others

We've pointed out that being prejudiced toward others, as well as stereotyping people into predetermined, rigid categories (especially because of racial, ethnic, or cultural backgrounds) can hinder effective communication. Reaching conclusions about someone before you get to know him or her can result in a dishonest relationship. Most people are taught not to be prejudiced toward others. Yet might stereotypes sometimes serve a useful purpose, especially when a quick decision is needed and you have only partial information?

Imagine, for example, that you are driving your car late at night and have a flat tire in a neighborhood that's known to have a high crime rate. While wondering what to do, you see two people who have observed your plight and are moving toward you. Do you hop out of your car and seek their help? Or do you lock your doors and be thankful that you have your cell phone to call for assistance? Are there times when prejudging a situation and reaching stereotypical conclusions about others may make common sense? Could a case be made that the ability to create and respond stereotypically may be useful in times of stress when quick thinking is needed? We never know all of the facts about a situation, and we sometimes (maybe even often) have to respond with only the partial information we have at hand. Some might argue that we sometimes need to make stereotypical, snap judgments. Malcolm Gladwell, author of *Blink: The Power of Thinking Without Thinking,* describes how people often make quick, snap decisions and argues that sometimes these "thin-sliced," momentary decisions can be quite accurate.[56] Of course, sometimes snap judgments can be way off base. What do you think? Is it ever appropriate to hold stereotypical views of others and to make judgments about them without knowing all of the facts? When do stereotypical evaluations hinder communication? When is it preferable not to make stereotypical decisions?

judgment over and over again, failing to consider the uniqueness of individuals, groups, or events. Such a "hardening of the categories" becomes a barrier to effective communication and inhibits our ability to adapt to others.

A related barrier, **prejudice,** is a judgment based on the assumption that we already know all of the information we need to know about a person. To prejudge someone as inept, inferior, or incompetent based on that person's ethnicity, race, sexual orientation, gender, or some other factor is a corrosive practice that can raise significant barriers to effective communication. Some prejudices are widespread. Although there are more females than males in the world, one study found that even when a male and a female held the same type of job, the male's job was considered more prestigious than the female's.[57] Even though it is illegal in the United States to discriminate because of a person's gender, race, or age in offering employment or promotions, women and members of minority groups may still be discriminated against. In the workplace, stereotyping and prejudice are still formidable barriers to communicating effectively with others.

Mark Twain once said, "It is discouraging to try and penetrate a mind such as yours. You ought to get out and dance on it. That would take some of the rigidity out of it." Learning how to break rigid stereotypes and overcome prejudice is an important part of the process of learning how to adapt to others.

Different Communication Codes

When Janice and Ron were on their vacation in Miami, Florida, they visited a market on Calle Ocho, in the heart of Little Havana—a district populated by many Cuban immigrants. When they tried to purchase some fruit, it was a frustrating experience for Janice and Ron as well as the market salesclerk; Janice and Ron spoke no Spanish, and the clerk knew no English. It is not uncommon today, when you travel within the United States, to encounter people who do not speak your language. Obviously, this kind of difference poses a formidable communication challenge. Even when you do speak the same language as another, he or she may come from a place where the words and gestures have different meanings. Your ability to communicate will depend on whether you can understand each other's verbal and nonverbal cues.

prejudice
A judgment of someone based on an assumption that you already know relevant facts or background information about the person.

RECAP

Barriers to Bridging Differences and Adapting to Others

Assuming Superiority	Becoming ethnocentric—assuming that one's own culture and cultural traditions are superior to those of others
Assuming Similarity	Assuming that other people respond to situations as we respond; failing to acknowledge and consider differences in culture and background
Assuming Differences	Assuming that other people are always different from ourselves; failing to explore common values and experiences that can serve as bridges to better understanding
Stereotyping and Prejudice	Rigidly categorizing others and prejudging others based on limited information
Different Communication Codes	Differences in language and the interpretation of nonverbal cues that lead to misunderstanding

ADAPTING TO OTHERS WHO ARE DIFFERENT FROM YOU

It is not enough simply to identify some of the common barriers that highlight our differences. Although becoming "consciously competent" about what may keep us from adapting and connecting with others is important, there are also some strategies that can help in our quest to adapt to others. Eleanor Roosevelt once said, "We have to face the fact that either we, all of us, are going to die together or we are going to live together, and if we are to live together we have to talk."[58] In essence, she was saying that we need effective communication skills to overcome our differences. It is not enough just to point to the barriers we have identified and say, "Don't do that." Identifying the causes of misunderstanding is a good first step, but most people need more concrete advice with specific strategies to help them overcome these barriers.

To become competent at any task you need three things: knowledge, motivation, and skill. To help you become competent in appropriately adapting to others, we suggest that you use two strategies to help you increase your knowledge about others: seek information about a culture and ask questions and listen to the responses. To maintain your motivation to adapt when communicating with others who are different from you, we encourage you to be patient and to strive to tolerate ambiguity and uncertainty; in addition, being mindfully aware of the differences between you and others can help you adapt. Finally, the key skills for communicating with people who are different from you including becoming other oriented and then appropriately adapting your communication to others.

Seek Information

Philosopher André Gide said, "Understanding is the beginning of approving." Prejudice often is the result of ignorance. Learning about another person's values, beliefs, and culture can help you understand his or her messages and their meaning. As you speak to a person from another culture, think of yourself as a detective, watching for implied, often unspoken messages that provide information about the values, norms, roles, and rules of that person's culture.

You can also prepare yourself by studying other cultures. If you are going to another country, start by reading a travel guide or another general overview of the culture. You may then want to learn more detailed information by studying the history, art, or geography of the culture. The Internet offers a wealth of information about the cultures and traditions of others. In addition to reading books and magazines and using cyber sources, talk to people from other cultures. If you are trying to communicate with someone closer to home who is from a different background, you can learn about the music, food, and other aspects of the culture. Given the inextricable link between language and culture, the more skilled you become at speaking another language, the better you will understand the traditions and customs of the culture where it is spoken.

As we discussed at the beginning of the chapter, the broad concept of culture also includes the notion of a co-culture, a cultural group within a larger culture. Learning how men and women, members of separate co-cultures, communicate differently can help improve your communication with members of the opposite sex.

As you read about other cultures or co-cultures, it is important not to develop rigid categories or stereotypes for the way others may talk or behave. Proclaiming, "Oh, you're just saying that because you're a woman," or "You men are always saying things like that," can increase rather than decrease communication barriers. In this chapter and throughout this book, we will identify research-based gender differences in the way men and women communicate to improve your understanding of and communication with members of the opposite sex. But, as noted earlier, we don't recommend that you treat men and women as completely separate species from different planets and automatically assume you will be misunderstood. Such a stereotypical judgment does not enhance communication—it hinders it.

Ask Questions and Listen

When you talk with people who are different from you, you may feel some discomfort and uncertainty. This is normal. We are more comfortable talking with people we know and who are like us. Communication, through the give-and-take process of listening, talking, and asking questions, helps to reduce the uncertainty present in any relationship. When you meet people for the first time, you are typically not certain about their likes and dislikes, including whether they like or dislike you. When you communicate with a person from another culture or co-culture, the uncertainty level escalates. As you begin to talk, you exchange information that helps you develop greater understanding. If you continue to ask questions, eventually you will feel less anxiety and uncertainty. You will be more able to predict how the person will behave. When you meet a person who is different from you, ask thoughtful questions, then pause to listen. This

is a simple technique for gathering information and also for confirming the accuracy of your expectations and assumptions.

Just asking questions and sharing information about yourself is not sufficient to remove communication barriers and bridge differences in culture and background, but it is a good beginning. The skills of stopping (focusing on the message of the other person), looking (observing nonverbal cues), and listening (noting both details and major ideas) that we presented in the last chapter will serve you well in enhancing communication with people from cultural traditions different from your own.

Tolerate Ambiguity

Many people become uncomfortable with uncertainty and ambiguity—especially if they are from a low-context culture such as those in North America. As we discussed earlier in the chapter, people from low-context cultures prefer a more direct approach to getting information. North Americans, for example, often say things like "Tell it to me straight," "Don't beat around the bush," or "Just tell me what you want."

Communicating with someone from a culture that does not value such directness produces uncertainty. It may take time and several exchanges to clarify a message. If you are from a cultural tradition that values certainty, and you are uncomfortable with uncertainty, you may have to acknowledge the cultural difference. Be patient and work at tolerating more ambiguity. Don't be in a hurry to have all of the details nailed down. Remind yourself that the other person does not have the same attitudes about knowing the future or appreciating details.

Develop Mindfulness

To be **mindful** is to be aware of how you communicate with others. A mindful communicator puts into practice the first communication principle we presented in this book: *Be aware of your communication with yourself and others.* To be a mindful communicator, you should constantly remind yourself that other people are not like you. Also, you should be aware that other people do not use different communication strategies to offend or to be rude, they just have different culturally based strategies of interacting with others. Intercultural communication scholar William Gudykunst suggests that being mindful is one of the best ways to approach any new cultural encounter.[59] Mindfulness is a conscious state of mind, a realization of what is happening to you at a given moment. If you are not mindful, you are oblivious to the world around you. You are on mental cruise control.

How can you cultivate the skill of being mindful? You can become more mindful through **self-talk,** something we discussed earlier in the book. Self-talk consists of messages you tell yourself to help you manage your discomfort, emotions, or negative thoughts about situations. When Ron and Janice tried to purchase the fruit in the Cuban market in Miami, they could have become offended and muttered, "Doesn't anyone speak English around here?" Instead, Janice reminded Ron "You know, it's not surprising that only Spanish is spoken here. Yes, it would be more comfortable for us if the clerk spoke our language. But we have to realize that there is no intent to offend us." Janice was being mindful of the cultural differences; by acknowledging the differences rather than emotionally and mindlessly becoming offended, she was able to maintain her composure and communicate in a manner appropriate to the circumstances.

Become Other-Oriented

Scholars of evolution might argue that it is our tendency to look out for number one that ensures the continuation of the human race. But if we focus exclusively on ourselves, it is very unlikely that we will be effective communicators. As we noted earlier, assuming superiority is a major barrier to communicating with others. Most of us are

mindful
Aware of what you are doing and how you are communicating with others.

self-talk
Inner speech; communication with the self; the process of mentally verbalizing messages that help a person become more aware or mindful of how he or she is processing information and reacting to life situations.

egocentric—focused on ourselves.[60] Our first inclination is to focus on meeting our own needs before addressing the needs of others.[61]

In this chapter we have emphasized the principle of adapting to others. If we fail to adapt our message to listeners, especially listeners who are different from us (and isn't everyone different from you?), it is less likely that we will achieve our communication goal. As we noted earlier, adapting messages to others doesn't mean that we tell others only what they want to hear. That would be unethical, manipulative, and ineffective. Nor does being considerate of others mean we abandon all concern for our own interests. **Other-oriented communication** is communication that takes into account the needs, motives, desires, and goals of our communication partners while still maintaining our own integrity. The choices we make in forming messages and selecting the time and place to deliver them should consider the thoughts and feelings of others.

Becoming other-oriented is not a single skill but a family of skills anchored in a willingness to try to understand others' thoughts and feelings. Research in emotional intelligence documents that focusing on the needs and interests of others is essential to adapting communication messages to others.[62]

How do you become other-oriented? We suggest a two-stage process, using skills discussed previously. The first stage, which we previewed in Chapter 5, is called social decentering—consciously *thinking* about another's thoughts and feelings. The second stage is developing empathy, a set of skills we also discussed in the last chapter. To empathize is to respond *emotionally* to another's feelings and actions. We'll discuss each of these two stages in more detail.

Social Decentering

Social decentering is a *cognitive process* through which we take into consideration another person's thoughts, values, background, and perspectives. It is seeing the world from the other person's point of view. To socially decenter is not to be a mind reader but to use past experiences and our ability to interpret the clues of others to understand what others may be thinking or how they may be perceiving issues or situations. According to Mark Redmond, a scholar who has extensively studied the process of social decentering, there are three ways to socially decenter.[63]

First, develop an understanding of the other person, based on how you have responded when something similar has happened to you in the past.[64] You know what it's like when you've been late for a meeting or an important appointment. When someone you know says he or she feels frazzled because he or she was late for a major meeting, you can think about what would be going through your mind if the same thing happened to you.

A second way to socially decenter is to base your understanding of what another person might be thinking on your knowledge of how that person has responded in the past. In communicating with someone who is different from you, the more direct experience you have interacting with that person, the better able you usually are to make predictions about how that person will react and respond. Suppose, for example, you have never seen one particular friend of yours be late for a meeting; you know how generally punctual your friend is. You therefore can guess that your friend would be quite frustrated by being late for a meeting.

A third way we socially decenter is to use our understanding of how most people, in general, respond to situations. If your roommate is from France, you probably have some general sense of the cultural differences between you and your French friend. You may harbor some general theories or assumptions about other French people. The trick, however, is to avoid rigid stereotypes or prejudices that confine or limit your perceptions. The more you can learn about others' cultural or gender perspectives, the more accurate you can become in socially decentering. It is important, however, not to develop inaccurate, inflexible stereotypes and labels for others or to base your perceptions of others only on generalizations.

egocentric
Focused on oneself and one's importance.

other-oriented communication
Communication that focuses on the needs and concerns of others while maintaining one's personal integrity, achieved through the processes of socially decentering and being empathic.

social decentering
Cognitive process in which we take into account another person's thoughts, values, background, and perspectives.

The first step in developing the ability to empathize is to stop focusing on your own messages and begin focusing on the messages of others.

Developing Empathy   Socially decentering involves attempting to understand what another person may be thinking. Developing **empathy,** a second strategy for becoming other-oriented, is feeling the *emotional* reaction that the other person may be experiencing. When we feel empathy, we feel what another person feels.

As we discussed in the last chapter, you develop the ability to empathize by being sensitive to your own feelings and assessing how you feel during certain situations and then projecting those feelings onto others.[65] To develop empathy, we suggested that you first *stop* focusing on only your own messages and thoughts and focus instead on the messages of others. We also recommended that you *look* for information about the emotional meaning of messages by focusing on nonverbal cues. Then *listen* by concentrating on what someone is telling you. In addition, *imagine* how you would feel if you were in your partner's position. Then *ask* appropriate questions, if you need to, to gain additional information. Finally, *paraphrase* your communication partner's message content and feelings and monitor his or her reactions to what you communicate.

Some emotional reactions are almost universal and cut across cultural boundaries. The ravages of war, famine, and natural disasters such as floods or earthquakes evoke universal emotions. As you see pictures on the news of people who have experienced tragedies, you empathize with them. If you've seen the now classic movie *E. T. the Extra Terrestrial,* you may remember that Elliott, the young boy who discovers E. T., experiences an emotional bond with the alien. Elliott feels what E. T. feels. Such extreme empathic bonding may only happen in the movies. It would be unusual, if not impossible, for us to develop such empathy in our everyday relationships with others. Yet it is possible to develop emotional connections to others, and some people are more skilled and sensitive than others in developing emotional, empathic bonds.

Empathy is different from sympathy. When you offer **sympathy,** you tell others that you are sorry that they feel what they are feeling. When you sympathize, you acknowledge someone's feelings. When you empathize, however, you experience an emotional reaction that is similar to the other person's; as much as possible, you strive to feel what he or she feels.

The late author and theologian Henri J. M. Nouwen suggested that empathy lies at the heart of enhancing the quality of our relationships with others. As Nouwen phrased it, in order to bridge our differences we need to "cross the road for one another":

We become neighbors when we are willing to cross the road for one another. There is so much separation and segregation: between black people and white people, between

empathy
An emotional reaction that is similar to the reaction being experienced by another person.

sympathy
Acknowledgment that someone is feeling a certain emotion, often grief; compassion.

gay people and straight people, between young people and old people, between sick people and healthy people, between prisoners and free people, between Jews and Gentiles, Muslims and Christians, Protestants and Catholics, Greek Catholics and Latin Catholics.

There is a lot of road crossing to do. We are all very busy in our own circles. We have our own people to go to and our own affairs to take care of. But if we could cross the road once in a while and pay attention to what is happening on the other side, we might indeed become neighbors.[66]

RECAP

How to Become Other-Oriented

Socially Decenter	View the world from another person's point of view.
	• Develop an understanding of someone, based on your own past experiences.
	• Consider what someone may be thinking, based on your previous association with the person.
	• Consider how most people respond to the situation at hand.
Develop Empathy	Consider what another person may be feeling.
	• Stop: Avoid focusing only on your own ideas or emotions.
	• Look: Determine the emotional meaning of messages by observing nonverbal messages.
	• Listen: Focus on what the other person says.
	• Imagine: Consider how you would feel in a similar situation.
	• Paraphrase: Summarize your understanding of the other person's thoughts and feelings.

Adapt to Others

Adapting to others gets to the bottom line of this chapter. After you have thought about how you may be different from others, considered culture and gender differences, and even identified potential barriers to communication, you reach this question: So now what do you *do?* What you do is appropriately adapt. To **adapt** is to adjust your behavior in response to the other person or persons you are communicating with. You don't just keep communicating in the same way you always did. You make an effort to change how you communicate, to enhance the quality of communication.

We adapt messages to others to enhance their understanding of the message, to help us achieve the goal or intended effect of our communication, to ensure that we are ethical in our communication with others, and to establish and develop satisfying relationships. To enhance understanding, you may need to slow your rate of speech or talk faster than you normally do. You may need to use more examples or speak in a very structured, organized way. To ensure that you achieve your communication objectives, you may need to draw on statistics and other forms of evidence to prove your point. Or your communication partner may not be impressed with statistics but might be quite

adapt
To adjust behavior in response to someone else.

moved by a story that poignantly illustrates your point. We also adapt messages to be ethical. Ethical communication gives your communication partner choices, rather than forcing or coercing him or her to do what you demand. Telling the truth, not withholding information, and identifying options are ways to adapt your message to be an ethical communicator. Finally, we adapt our communication to generate more positive feelings or regard for others, so as to enhance our relationships and improve our quality of life.

Can the skills and principles we have suggested here make a difference in your ability to communicate with others? The answer is a resounding "yes." Communication researcher Lori Carell found that students who had been exposed to lessons in empathy as part of their study of interpersonal and intercultural communication improved their ability to empathize with others.[67] There is evidence that if you master these principles and skills, you will be rewarded with greater ability to communicate with others who are different from you—which means everyone.

It is not possible to prescribe how to adapt to others in all situations. We can suggest that you draw on the other four communication principles for a lifetime that we have presented in this book. You will be more effective in adapting to others if you are aware of your own cultural traditions and gender-related behavior and how they are different from those of other people. Being able to use and interpret verbal and nonverbal symbols appropriately and effectively will also increase your ability to adapt and respond to others. The essential skills of listening and responding to others are key competencies in being able to adapt to others—to be other oriented. To interpret spoken information accurately (as well as "listening" with your eyes to unspoken messages) is a linchpin of competence in adapting to others.

Adapting your messages to others does not mean you have to abandon your own ethical principles or personal positions. It would be unethical to change your opinions and point of view just to avoid conflict and keep the peace—like a politician who only tells his or her audience what they want to hear. It was President Harry Truman who said, "I wonder how far Moses would have gone if he'd taken a poll in Egypt?"[68] A spineless, wishy-washy approach to communication does not enhance the quality of your relationships with others. But you can be sensitive and mindful of how your comments may be received by others.

RECAP

Adapting to Others

Develop Knowledge

Seek Information	Learn about a culture's worldview.
Ask Questions and Listen	Reduce uncertainty by asking for clarification and listening to the answer.

Develop Motivation

Tolerate Ambiguity	Take your time and expect some uncertainty.
Develop Mindfulness	Be consciously aware of cultural differences, rather than ignoring the differences.

Develop Skill

Become Other-Oriented	Put yourself in the other person's mental and emotional frame of mind; socially decenter and develop empathy
Adapt to Others	Listen and respond appropriately.

PRINCIPLES FOR A LIFETIME: Enhancing Your Skills

Principle Five: Appropriately adapt messages to others.

- It's important to learn to ethically adapt messages to others to enhance understanding, because we're all different for a variety of reasons (culture, age, background, experience, sexual preference, attitudes, beliefs, values).
- Appropriately adapt messages to others based on whether an individual is from a high-context culture (in which an emphasis is placed on nonverbal messages and the surroundings) or a low-context culture (in which an emphasis is placed on words and explicitly communicated messages).
- Appropriately adapt messages to others based on the cultural value of individualism versus collectivism, preference for certainty versus tolerance of uncertainty, tendency to emphasize masculine versus feminine values, and preference for centralized or decentralized power.
- Appropriately adapt messages based on gender differences in communication by doing the following four things: (1) seek to understand differences between genders, (2) consider your own preferences, needs, and communication goals, (3) avoid assuming that differences between people are solely the result of gender, (4) consider both your needs and goals and those of the other person.
- Avoid being ethnocentric—always assuming that your cultural traditions and approaches are superior to other cultural traditions.
- Don't assume everyone does things the same way you do or holds the same attitudes, beliefs, or values that you hold.
- Don't assume that because someone is from another culture or geographic area, you don't have anything in common with the person; seek to establish common ground.
- Avoid making rigid, inflexible stereotypes and prejudgments of others based on limited information.
- Seek to bridge differences between yourself and others who speak a different language or have different interpretations for nonverbal expressions; learn the language of others.
- Bridge cultural differences by learning as much as you can about another culture.
- Listen and ask questions to enhance your understanding of others.
- Be patient and tolerate some ambiguity and uncertainty when you communicate with people who are different from you.
- Being mindful, or aware that differences will exist, can help you better tolerate differences.
- Develop your skills at being other-oriented: Focus on the needs and concerns of others while maintaining your personal integrity.
- Socially decenter: Think about how your communication partner would respond to information and situations; take into account people's thoughts, values, background, and perspectives.
- Empathize: Try to imagine how you would feel if you were in the other person's position.

Adapt

SUMMARY

Human differences result in the potential for misunderstanding and miscommunication. Differences in culture and gender contribute to the challenge of communicating with others. The relevant communication principle is: *Effective communicators appropriately adapt their messages to others.* One concept that makes a difference when we communicate with others is taking into consideration cultural perspective or worldview. Culture is a system of knowledge that is shared by a group of people. Our worldview is the overarching set of expectations that helps us explain why events occur as they do and gives us a perspective for explaining what happens to us and others. Intercultural communication occurs when individuals or groups from different cultures communicate.

Culture and communication are clearly linked because of the powerful role culture plays in influencing our values. Cultural values reflect how individuals regard masculine perspectives (such as achieving results and being productive) and feminine perspectives (such as consideration for relationships), their tolerance of uncertainty or preference for certainty, their preference for centralized or decentralized power structures, and the value they place on individual or collective accomplishment.

Two gender-related cultural values are the instrumental, or masculine, orientation, which involves assertiveness and action; and the expressive, or feminine, orientation, which emphasizes connection and the development of harmonious relationships and community. These orientations translate into communication behavior that differs depending on one's sex. Women tend to attend to the relational dimension of communication; that is, they focus on *how* something is said more than on *what*. Their purpose in communication typically is to establish and develop relationships and connections with others. In contrast, men tend to approach communication from a content perspective, meaning that they view communication as functioning primarily for information exchange. The principle of adaptation is quite useful in bridging gender differences in communication style. People can and should break out of sex-specific behavior to choose the best approach to communicating in a given situation.

Several barriers inhibit effective communication. When one culture or gender assumes superiority, communication problems often occur. Ethnocentrism is the belief that one's own cultural traditions and assumptions are superior to those of others. Sexism is the attitude that one sex is superior to the other. It is not productive when individuals or groups from different backgrounds or cultures assume that others behave with similar responses. But it is also important not to automatically assume that other people are different from you. We stereotype by placing a group or person into an inflexible, all-encompassing category. A related barrier is prejudice. When we prejudge someone before we know all the facts about him or her, we also create a potential communication problem. Stereotyping and prejudice can keep us from acknowledging others as unique individuals and therefore can hamper effective, open, honest communication. Differences in language codes and the way we interpret nonverbal messages interfere with effective communication.

Strategies for adapting to others include developing knowledge, motivation, and skill to bridge differences of culture and gender. To enhance understanding, actively seek information about others who are different from you, ask questions, and listen to the responses. Motivational strategies include being tolerant of ambiguity and uncertainty and being more conscious or mindful when interacting with others who are different from you. Finally, to develop skills in adapting to others, become other oriented by socially decentering and emotionally empathizing with others. Then appropriately respond by adapting your messages to others; consider their thoughts and feelings.

Discussion and Review

1. What is intercultural communication?
2. Describe the differences between high-context and low-context cultures.
3. What are the characteristics of masculine and feminine cultural values?
4. What are the differences between cultures that value certainty and those that have a greater tolerance for uncertainty?
5. How are decentralized and centralized cultural perspectives different?

6. What are the characteristics of and differences between individualistic and collectivistic cultures?
7. How important is a person's gender in U.S. culture?
8. What are the primary differences between the sexes in terms of listening behavior?
9. How can one adapt communication to bridge gender differences?
10. Identify and describe some barriers that hinder intercultural communication.
11. What communication strategies will help you bridge differences in communication and achieve the goal of adapting to others?

Putting Principles into Practice

1. Describe your perceptions of your cultural values, based on the discussion of cultural values beginning on page 141 in this chapter. Using a scale from 1 to 10, rate yourself in terms of the value of a masculine (1) versus a feminine (10) perspective; individual (1) versus group (10) achievement; tolerance of uncertainty (1) versus need for certainty (10); and preference for decentralized (1) versus centralized (10) power. Provide an example of your reaction to an interpersonal communication encounter to illustrate each of these values. Share your answers with your classmates.

2. Role play with someone of the opposite sex a first conversation or a conflict or disagreement between dating partners. First, enact the roles from the perspective of your own sex—in other words, both you and your partner play the roles of people of your own sex. Then enact the conversation again, but with the roles reversed. Note any differences that emerge in how the conversation plays out. Do you detect any stereotypical behaviors that emerge when you swap roles? Do you think an activity like this helps you better understand members of the opposite sex and their communication patterns?

3. This chapter presented five specific strategies or skills to help bridge differences in background and culture. Rank order these skills and strategies in terms of what you need to improve in your interactions with people from different backgrounds. Give a rank of 1 to the skill or strategy that you most need to develop, a rank of 2 to the next area you feel you need to work on, and so on. Rank yourself on all five strategies.

   _____ Seek information about the culture
   _____ Listen and ask questions of others
   _____ Tolerate ambiguity
   _____ Be mindful
   _____ Be other oriented

   Write a journal entry about how you will develop skill in the areas in which you most need improvement. How will you put what you have learned in this chapter into practice?

4. With a group, go on an intercultural scavenger hunt. Your instructor will give you a time limit. Scavenge your campus or classroom area to identify influences of as many different cultures as you can find. For example, you could make note of ethnic foods offered in the dining hall; or you could identify clothing, music, or architecture that is influenced by certain cultures.

5. In a small group, identify examples from your own experiences of each barrier to effective intercultural communication discussed in the text. Use one of the examples as the basis for a skit to perform for the rest of the class. See if the class can identify which intercultural barrier your group is depicting. Also, suggest how the skills and principles discussed in the chapter might have improved the communication in the situation you role-played.

6. Try an exercise that will help clarify the different reasons men and women communicate. Ask the following questions of both men and women and then see if you note any major differences.

   a. What is the general purpose or function of communication?

   b. Which of the following statements best summarizes your preferred approach to communication?

      (1) It's better to get to the point when asking for information or making a request of someone.

      (2) It's better to take some time to talk about the background of a situation rather than quickly trying to get to "the bottom line" of what you're saying.

   c. What bothers you the most when you talk to someone of the opposite sex?

   d. What general impressions do you have about the way men and women listen to each other?

   Compare the answers you collect with those collected by your classmates. Do you note any general trends or differences and similarities in light of the research conclusions we've summarized in this chapter?

CHAPTER Seven

Diana Ong, "Sisy," © Diana Ong/SuperStock, Inc.

The best of life is conversation, and the greatest success is confidence, or perfect understanding between sincere people.

Ralph Waldo Emerson

Understanding Interpersonal Communication

CHAPTER OUTLINE

What Is Interpersonal
   Communication?

Initiating Relationships

Maintaining Relationships

Summary

CHAPTER OBJECTIVES

After studying this chapter, you should be able to:

1. Define interpersonal communication and discuss its three unique attributes.

2. Distinguish interpersonal communication from impersonal communication.

3. Explain the difference between relationships of circumstance and relationships of choice.

4. Define interpersonal attraction and distinguish short-term initial attraction from long-term maintenance attraction.

5. Discuss three human needs that relate to complementarity in interpersonal relationships.

6. Provide examples of verbal and nonverbal ways we reveal our attraction to others.

7. Explain uncertainty reduction and describe three strategies of information seeking to reduce uncertainty.

8. Explain what is meant by the "art and skill" of asking great questions.

9. Describe some common verbal and nonverbal behavioral indicators of a self-absorbed communicator style.

10. Explain how one should give and receive a compliment.

11. Define self-disclosure and explain its role in relationship maintenance.

12. Discuss what is meant by reciprocity, appropriateness, and risk in self-disclosure.

13. Clarify ways in which self-disclosure and intimacy are affected by gender.

14. Identify and explain two models of self-disclosure pertaining to relationship maintenance.

15. Discuss how emotional expression, as a form of self-disclosure, affects relationship maintenance.

"Hi. I'm _____. Nice to meet you." This simple statement can strike fear in the heart of even the most outgoing individual. Yet we know that meeting and getting to know people, as well as becoming known, are some of the most rewarding experiences in this life. If we cannot break out of our comfort zones to communicate with others, we won't survive. As we said in Chapter 1, communication is inescapable. We communicate—intentionally and unintentionally, verbally and nonverbally—to accomplish things great and small throughout our lifetimes. And the most common, everyday kind of communication we accomplish comes in the form of simple conversations with loved ones, friends, coworkers, acquaintances, and even strangers as we go about our daily routines.

Think about your best childhood friend for a moment. Perhaps you're still in touch with that person; maybe that person is still your closest friend. But can you remember the very first time you talked to that person? Maybe something the person did contributed to your first impression. It's fun to try to remember and reflect on first conversations as we grow with others and progress in our relationships. If you're dating someone you've dated for a while or if you are married, think back to your very first conversation with your partner. Was it awkward? Was your first date so uncomfortable that you thought you'd never go out with that person again? Or was the conversation so engaging that you couldn't wait to see her or him again?

These elements are part of what we call interpersonal communication, the form of communication we experience most often in our lives. Interpersonal communication involves all five of our principles for a lifetime (see Figure 7.1). *In the remaining chapters of the book, you will see a small version of the communication principles model in the margin to highlight our reference to one or more of the communication principles that we discuss.*

Effective interpersonal communication begins with an *awareness* of oneself. As you interact with people in your life, you make mental notes of what works well and not so well. You learn from these experiences and develop a personal style of communication. We continue this process by reassessing and reshaping our communication styles throughout our lives, with the goal of becoming better communicators. The second and third principles involve the *effective use of verbal and nonverbal messages.* We experiment with verbal and nonverbal communication as we interact with people, form relationships, develop those relationships, and, in some cases, let go of those relationships. A major element that enhances relationships is the ability to *listen carefully and respond sensitively* to others, our Principle Four. Finally, few interpersonal relationships last without *adaptation.* We live in an extremely diverse world. It's imperative to learn to adapt our communication to others—to their cultural backgrounds and values, per-

Aware
Verbal
Nonverbal
Listen and Respond
Adapt

FIGURE 7.1
Communication Principles for a Lifetime

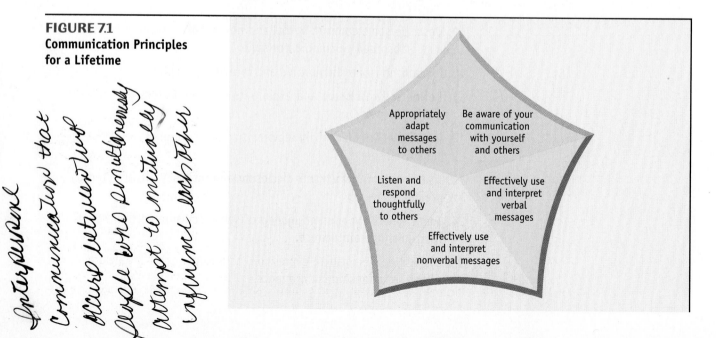

Appropriately adapt messages to others

Be aware of your communication with yourself and others

Listen and respond thoughtfully to others

Effectively use and interpret verbal messages

Effectively use and interpret nonverbal messages

sonalities, communication styles, needs, and goals—so that we form satisfying relationships that help us enjoy our lives to the fullest.

In this chapter we examine interpersonal communication, distinguish it from other forms of human communication, and explore how interpersonal communication establishes and facilitates our relationships. As you work through this material, keep in mind those individuals who mean the most to you right now. Consider your communication with these valued people, assessing areas that are working well and areas that might need some attention. The more you personalize this information, the more you will gain from it.

WHAT IS INTERPERSONAL COMMUNICATION?

Early in a relationship, it's important to concentrate on listening to your partner's responses to your questions, so you can offer an appropriate follow-up response.

In Chapter 1 we looked at three contexts in which communication most commonly occurs: interpersonal communication, group communication, and presentational communication contexts. In this chapter we explore the interpersonal context in more depth. To review the definition provided in Chapter 1, **interpersonal communication** is a special form of human communication that occurs when two people interact simultaneously and attempt to mutually influence each other, usually for the purpose of managing relationships.

Traditionally, interpersonal communication research has focused primarily on the face-to-face (FtF) encounter, as we have attempted to better understand how people use conversation and nonverbal cues to initiate and maintain relationships. However, given the immense popularity and general accessibility of the Internet, researchers are also studying interpersonal communication that occurs through this unique medium.[1] As our global society becomes more interconnected and we find we are able to "meet" all kinds of people worldwide through computer channels, it's important to examine how interpersonal communication functions online. So, as we proceed through the various topics related to interpersonal communication, we explore how online communication is similar to and different from FtF interpersonal communication. As you read, think about your own relationships, both FtF and online, and consider how interpersonal communication facilitates each one. To begin, we consider three unique attributes that help us better understand the nature of interpersonal communication.

Interpersonal Communication Involves Quality

Imagine you're on a date and having dinner at a restaurant. The communication you have with your date is different from the communication you have with the person who waits on your table. (At least we certainly hope so; if not, you're probably having a lousy date!) Most likely, it is the quality of communication that differs.

Interpersonal communication occurs not just when we interact with someone, but when we treat the other as a unique human being. Conversely, **impersonal communication** occurs when we treat people as objects or respond to their roles rather than to who they are as unique people.

In fact, aspiring doctors are now required by the National Board of Medical Examiners to pass a daylong test of "bedside manner," revealing their ability to establish rapport with patients, ask clear questions, and listen effectively to answers. Until medical students pass the bedside manner test, they are not allowed to practice medicine. So they must learn to treat patients as people, using interpersonal communication skills, rather than as objects who warrant only impersonal communication.[2]

interpersonal communication
Communication that occurs between two people who simultaneously attempt to mutually influence each other, usually for the purpose of managing relationships.

impersonal communication
Communication that treats people as objects or that only responds to their roles rather than to who they are as unique people.

Eric & Bill

"Harrison, it's time we had a
face-to-face conversation — also known as
wireless communication."

We engage in a good deal of impersonal communication each day. We may pass people on the sidewalk and say hello, whether or not we know them. The first few days of a semester are always interesting because of the presence of so many people new to the campus, so we may find ourselves giving directions to various campus buildings. Giving directions or instructions is a common yet important form of impersonal communication. Many people's jobs involve a great deal of impersonal communication. In the online context, an e-mail message to a friend is an example of interpersonal communication. Posting a message on an electronic bulletin board would be impersonal communication, since it is likely you would not even know the receivers of your posting.

Interpersonal Communication Involves Mutual Influence

Interpersonal communication also involves attempts at mutual influence. This means that both partners are affected by the interaction. We do not mean to imply that interpersonal communication exclusively involves persuasion—changing someone's mind or swaying someone's opinion. We simply mean that people who interact affect each other. For example, during dinner, you ask your date where he or she grew up, and you assume that your date hears you. If so, you've both been affected by the question—there's something you want to know and information your date can provide. But what if your date doesn't hear you? In this case, interpersonal communication has not really occurred between you and your date because there is no mutual interaction; only you have been affected by your attempt at communication.

Every interpersonal communication interaction influences us. Sometimes it changes our lives dramatically, sometimes in small ways. Long-lasting interpersonal relationships are sustained not by one person giving and another taking, but by mutually satisfying communication.

Interpersonal Communication Helps Manage Relationships

Relationships are ongoing connections we make with others through interpersonal communication. For some people, the term *relationship* signals something serious and usually romantic. But we use the term *relationship* in a much broader sense in this text. You probably have a wide variety of relationships that include family members, coworkers, classmates, friends, and romantic interests. You may have some relationships that form and are maintained solely online. Many relationships involve a combination of FtF and online interaction.

We initiate and form relationships by communicating with those whom we find attractive in some way. We seek to increase our interactions with people we would like to know better, and we interpersonally communicate to maintain those relationships. We also use interpersonal communication to end relationships that we have decided are no longer viable.

Relationships form for different reasons. **Relationships of circumstance** form situationally—simply because our lives overlap with others' lives in some way or because a situation brings us into contact. Relationships with family members, teachers, classmates, and coworkers typically fall into this category. In contrast, relationships that we seek out and intentionally develop are termed **relationships of choice**. These relationships typically include those with friends, lovers, and spouses or relational partners (such as gay and lesbian partners in committed relationships). These categories of relationships are not mutually exclusive. Relationships of circumstance can change

relationship
An ongoing connection made with another person.

relationship of circumstance
A relationship that forms situationally, simply because one life overlaps with another in some way.

relationship of choice
A relationship that is sought out and intentionally developed.

into relationships of choice: Your sister or brother can turn out to be your best friend. Conversely, you may be extremely close to a certain family member, but over time that relationship becomes more distant and evolves into more of a relationship of circumstance than one of choice. Probably most of your relationships that involve online communication are relationships of choice. An online relationship of circumstance might be formed between members of a group, such as students enrolled in a class or employees of a company with several corporate locations, who interact through a listserv to discuss course topics or current projects.

We communicate differently in these two types of relationships because the stakes are different. Generally, relationships of choice are more important to us and central to our sense of well-being than relationships of circumstance. Also, we tend to be more intimate in relationships of choice, choosing to reveal more sensitive things about ourselves only with our closest friends or lovers. And with less intimate acquaintances or family members who have known us for some time we might "get away with" some behaviors that would be intolerable or a source of conflict within a relationship of choice.

RECAP

What Is Interpersonal Communication?

- Interpersonal communication involves **quality:** The quality of communication within interpersonal relationships is superior to communication that occurs impersonally.
- Interpersonal communication involves **mutual influence:** Both people in the relationship are affected by the interaction.
- Interpersonal communication helps **manage relationships:** Communication facilitates the initiation, maintenance, and, in some cases, termination of interpersonal relationships.

[handwritten margin note: 3 quality mutual influence manage relationship]

INITIATING RELATIONSHIPS

Some people make relationships look so easy; they just seem to meet people and make positive impressions effortlessly. For others, meeting and getting to know people is a huge challenge. We'll let you in on a little secret: Initiating relationships really isn't all that easy for anyone. Let's begin our discussion of relationship initiation by exploring the nature of attraction—what draws us into a conversation in the first place.

Interpersonal Attraction: Why We Like Whom We Like

What does it mean to say that you are attracted to another person? Most of the time we tend to think of physical or sexual attraction. But there are many forms of attraction besides physical and sexual, including intellectual, spiritual, and personality attraction. **Attraction**, in general, is a motivational state that causes someone to think, feel, and behave in a positive manner toward another person.[3] More specifically, **interpersonal attraction** is the degree to which you desire to form and possibly maintain an interpersonal relationship with another person. Remember that interpersonal relationships imply some form of ongoing connection, so we're not talking here about those instances when you can't breathe because an incredibly attractive person walks by. Whenever we feel a positive regard for another person or when we like someone, we can say that we feel attracted to that person regardless of the sex of the person or our sexual

attraction
A motivational state that causes someone to think, feel, and behave in a positive manner toward another person.

interpersonal attraction
The degree to which one desires to form or maintain an interpersonal relationship with another person.

People use various forms of communication to convey their attractiveness to others and to form new relationships.

orientation. However, the intensity of that attraction varies from relationship to relationship.

Interpersonal attraction occurs in both the early stages and the later stages of relational development. **Short-term initial attraction** is the degree to which you sense a potential for developing an interpersonal relationship. For instance, you might find one of your classmates physically attractive but never move to introduce yourself. Or you might interact with someone in a chat room and then decide that the person's comments attract you enough to begin private online exchanges. The information you gather in your first interaction with someone can generate a short-term initial attraction for a relationship, which you may or may not pursue, depending on the circumstances.

Long-term maintenance attraction, on the other hand, is the type that sustains relationships like best friendships or marriages. It refers to a level of liking or positive feeling that motivates you to maintain or escalate a relationship. Short-term attraction gives way to long-term attraction as a relationship progresses. Rarely do you maintain a long-term intimate relationship, such as marriage, solely on the basis of what you initially found attractive.[4] You usually need something more as you develop an interpersonal attraction and deepen a relationship. Several factors come into play when you decide to act on your attraction and establish a relationship.

short-term initial attraction

A degree of potential for developing an interpersonal relationship with someone.

long-term maintenance attraction

A level of liking or positive feeling that motivates one to maintain or escalate a relationship.

similarity

Having like characteristics, values, attitudes, interests, or personality traits with another person.

Similarity   Let's discuss the idea that "opposites attract." Opposites certainly do attract, and differences between people can be interesting. They can also form the basis for a good friendship or coworker relationship—after all, we learn a great deal from people who are unlike us. But we like to add another phrase onto the "opposites attract" cliché: "Opposites attract, but dramatic opposites seldom last." People who are opposites or significantly different in dispositions and preferences may intrigue each other and teach each other something, but they don't typically maintain a long-term relationship.

In general, you are attracted to people with whom you have **similarity**—those whose personality, values, upbringing, experiences, attitudes, and interests are similar to yours.[5] You may also be attracted more to persons who are similar to you in age, intelligence, and life goals. One of the most beneficial aspects of online communication is the unique structure of the Internet, which allows people with similar interests to find one another easily and form online relationships.[6] For example, new parents can find comfort in online chat rooms devoted to discussions of common experiences and predicaments in raising children. Interesting studies on dating partners and college roommates found that for both the partners and the roommates, similarity in the emotional dimensions of the relationship (such as comfort, ego support, conflict management, sincerity, and warmth) were more important than other dimensions of attraction and led to greater enjoyment of the relationship.[7]

Ethics and Communication

The Harmless Crush?

Some years ago we came across a newspaper article that discussed flirtations or minor obsessions people have with one another, more familiarly known as "crushes."[8] One view suggests that crushes come in three sizes, "small, medium, and totally-ruin-your-life." However, many people extol the virtues of crushes, contending that

"Crushes are great because they're harmless and limited in scope. They're little ego boosts. Even if you're already in a happy relationship, it's always nice to have someone paying attention to you." What ethical issues, if any, arise when someone who is in a monogamous romantic relationship feels physical and sexual attraction for someone other than his or her partner?

In the initial stages of a relationship, we try to emphasize positive information about ourselves to create a positive and attractive image. We reveal those aspects of ourselves that we believe we have in common with the other person, and the other person does the same.[9] Think about your initial interactions with strangers, whether online or face to face; typically, you spend the first few minutes trying to find topics of mutual interest. You discover that the person is from a place near your hometown, has the same taste in music or sports, has the same attitude about school, and on and on. But the depth of this information is limited. You are likely to save your revelations about important attitudes and issues for later, as your relationship progresses. Attitude similarity is more likely to be a source of long-term maintenance attraction than of short-term initial attraction.

Aware

Physical and Sexual Attraction   Volumes have been written about the role that physical and sexual attraction play in the formation of relationships.[10] While these forms of attraction are often lumped together or viewed as the same thing, they actually are different. In FtF situations, the degree to which we find another person's physical self appealing represents our **physical attraction** to that person. That appeal might be based on height, size, skin tone and texture, clothing, hairstyle, makeup, vocal qualities, gestures, and so forth. By this definition, even if you are heterosexual, you can still be attracted to a person of your own sex because you admire her or his physical attributes.

Nonverbal

Is physical attraction a factor in establishing online relationships? Research reveals that many online communicators find the *lack* of emphasis on physical appearance and attractiveness in online relationships to be one of the most positive features of this approach to relationship development.[11] One set of researchers described the Internet as "a world where what you write, not how you look or sound, is who you are."[12]

Sexual attraction has been defined as "the desire to engage in sexual activity with someone," a desire that "typically is accompanied by feelings of sexual arousal in the presence of the person."[13] You may be physically attracted to someone but not sexually attracted, as we stated before. But can you be sexually attracted but not physically attracted? We're not sure about the answer to that one because it may be a uniquely individual judgment. You may find another person's online communication sexually arousing, even if you've never seen the person in the flesh. Suffice it to say that these two forms of attraction usually operate in tandem, even though they represent different kinds of appeal.

physical attraction
The degree to which one finds another person's physical self appealing.

sexual attraction
A desire to have sexual contact with a certain person.

The adage "Beauty is in the eye of the beholder" is particularly true with regard to physical and sexual attraction. Each culture teaches and perpetuates its own definition

---

Diversity and Communication

What Attracts You?

Social psychologist Alan Feingold attempted to discover whether heterosexual women and men vary in terms of how much importance they place on physical appearance in the decision to date someone.[14] Looking for trends, Feingold reviewed a large number of studies on the subject and discovered that, indeed, men and women look for different things when deciding to initiate and develop heterosexual romantic relationships. Approximately 50 studies determined that men value physical attractiveness most in a potential partner, while women value personality, intelligence, kindness, sensitivity, and a sense of humor more than looks.

This information doesn't mean that heterosexuals are doomed because women and men look for and value very different attributes in each other. The sexes don't have to resent one another, claiming that men are superficial because they're drawn to looks while women are picky because they have "laundry lists" of qualifications for men. The information can be empowering, in that members of both sexes can understand and anticipate what attracts the other. Granted, there are exceptions; not everyone adheres to these sex-based findings on attraction. But in your experience, do men tend to emphasize a woman's looks over other aspects of her character? Do women prioritize psychological elements over physical ones in their interests in men?

On the Web

How do people who are looking for romantic relationships meet other people? While singles bars and personal ads in newspapers are still around, people are turning increasingly to the Web to meet others. If you're interested in virtual dating, here are a few sites to try. (But be careful: Some services charge fees just to access the site and get started.)

www.eHarmony.com
www.Match.com
www.Matchmaker.com
www.eCrush.com

Here's some sound advice about Internet dating services.[15]

1. Browse the dating services to find one that will best suit you. Sites often focus on people with particular interests and profiles.
2. Do a free trial, if the site offers one, to see if you like the process before becoming a paying member.
3. Once you choose to invest time and money in a particular site, be as honest as possible in completing your profile. Don't describe yourself as you'd like to *think* you are; answer as you *really* are.
4. Provide a recent, realistic, yet flattering picture of yourself, even if you feel insecure doing so. You will receive more replies than if you choose not to include a picture (which can set off alarm bells in some people).
5. Don't be discouraged by responses you receive; it's typical to receive some rude or inappropriate messages from people whose motives are questionable.
6. If you do make a connection with someone and begin to exchange e-mail messages, pay attention to what is communicated, as well as what is *not* communicated.
7. If you decide to meet face to face with someone you've been e-mailing, be careful. Meet in a public place and have your own transportation so you can make a safe departure if need be. Make sure someone knows what you're doing, where you're going, and when you're meeting the person.
8. Once you meet, if you don't feel a romantic connection, don't be shy about telling the person you're really not interested. Be assertive and firm, but not rude, in expressing your desire not to pursue things further. No one likes to be strung along.

matching hypothesis
A tendency to seek out individuals who represent the same level of physical attractiveness as oneself.

proximity
The likelihood of being attracted to people who are physically close rather than to those who are farther away.

of the physical ideal. In the United States, for instance, advertisements and TV programs promote a slender ideal for both females and males. This ideal contributes to the American obsession with losing weight and getting fit.[16] However, in some cultures, and at various times throughout U.S. history, physical attractiveness was synonymous with bulkiness.

Our perceptions about others' physical attractiveness reduce relationship possibilities. In general, while we may be attracted to a range of persons, we tend to seek out individuals who represent the same level of physical attractiveness we do.[17] In nonverbal communication research, this is termed the **matching hypothesis**.[18] Perhaps you perceive yourself to be average looking, not model-beautiful but not unattractive either. You may be physically or sexually attracted to extremely good-looking people; but if you are average-looking, you are more likely to seek someone who is also average-looking to date, and even marry or become partners with. Look around the next time you're in a public place, like an airport or a mall, and notice the couples—people who obviously look like they are together. Most couples will match each other in terms of physical attractiveness.

Proximity   The principle of **proximity** in interpersonal relationships refers to the fact that we are more likely to be attracted to people who are nearer to us physically and geographically than to those who are farther away.[19] In your classes, you are more likely to form relationships with classmates sitting on either side of you than with someone seated at the opposite end of the room. Physical proximity increases communication opportunities, and opportunities to interact are likely to increase our attraction to those with whom we communicate. People involved in long-distance romantic relationships—those initiated through FtF encounters, but that evolve into long-distance, geographically separated relationships—understand the principle of proximity first-hand. They typically use multiple channels of communication to maintain their relationship, and the lack of proximity and accessibility to each other, over time, can become problematic.[20]

Social psychologist Sharon Brehm explains, "To meet people is not necessarily to love them, but to love them we must first meet them."[21] Of course, nowadays to "meet" someone need not refer to meeting someone physically. How many times have you heard someone say "I met someone on the Internet"? They didn't actually meet in the physical sense, but that meeting is just as real (sometimes more real) and valuable to those involved as FtF meetings. One line of research contends that proximity affects online relationships differently than it does FtF relationships.[22] The global presence and general accessibility of the Internet as a facilitator of interpersonal communication means that people can establish relationships even though they are geographically separated; without the Internet, they most likely would never "meet." But the instantaneous and pervasive nature of online communication bridges the physical distance, creating a virtual closeness that FtF relationships may not achieve. Thus the impact of proximity—a long-standing predictor of relationship development and success—is minimized in an online relationship.

Complementarity   While we tend to like people with whom we have much in common, most of us wouldn't find it very exciting to spend the rest of our lives with someone who had identical attitudes, needs, and interests. We may tend to be attracted to someone similar to us in important things like human values, but for other things we may be more interested in someone with whom we share **complementarity** of qualities and needs.[23] For example, if you are highly disorganized by nature (and that's fine by you), you might be attracted to someone who is very organized because you appreciate that person's sense of structure.

Social psychologist Will Schutz identified three interpersonal needs that motivate us to form and maintain relationships with others: inclusion, control, and affection.[24] **Inclusion** is the need to include others in our activities or to be included in theirs. **Control** is the need to make decisions and take responsibility or the level of willingness to accept others' decision making. **Affection** is the need to be loved and accepted by others or the willingness to give love and acceptance to others. Most people are attracted to those whose interpersonal needs complement their own.

If you have a high need to control and make decisions and a general disrespect or mistrust of others' decision making, you will be more compatible with someone whose need for control is minimal—a person who wants others to make decisions for her or him. Many committed couples reflect this pattern regarding finances. The person who is better at keeping track of bills and balancing the checkbook pairs with someone who is good at maintaining a budget, to create a strong personal finance team. If you have high affection needs, you are likely to be less attracted to someone who is distant or aloof and who does not show affection. If you resent it when someone you are dating spends time away from you with his or her friends, you are likely to be less attracted to that person over time because you may have different, noncomplementary inclusion needs. In essence, we can view pairs of individuals as teams in which each person's needs complement those of the other person in some way. In reality, there are no perfect matches, only degrees of compatibility.

RECAP

Elements of Interpersonal Attraction

Short-Term Initial Attraction	This form of attraction involves a judgment that there is potential for an interpersonal relationship to develop with someone.
Long-Term Maintenance Attraction	This form of attraction is deeper and more long-lasting than short-term initial attraction and involves positive feelings that cause us to choose to maintain and escalate relationships.
Similarity	Attraction increases if our characteristics, values, attitudes, interests, and personality traits are similar to those of another person.
Physical Attraction	Attraction to another person's physical self.
Sexual Attraction	The desire to have sexual contact with a certain person.
Proximity	We are more likely to be interpersonally attracted to people who are physically close to us.
Complementarity	We may be attracted to someone whose abilities, interests, and needs differ from but balance or round out our own.

complementarity
The tendency to be attracted to persons with abilities, interests, and needs that differ from one's own, but that balance or round out one's own.

inclusion
The need to involve others in one's activities or to be involved in the activities of others.

control
The need to make decisions and take responsibility; the level of willingness to accept others' decision making.

affection
The need to be loved and accepted by others; the willingness to give love and acceptance to others.

Communicating Our Attraction

Nonverbal

In general, the more we are attracted to someone, the more we attempt to communicate with him or her. So the amount of interaction we have with someone indicates the level of attraction in the relationship.

When we are attracted to people, we use both indirect and direct strategies to communicate our liking, through nonverbal and verbal cues. Nonverbal cues are typically indirect and are often referred to as **immediacy**.[25] Immediacy behaviors work to reduce the physical and psychological distance between people. For example, with people we are attracted to, we may sit closer, increase our eye contact and use of touch, lean forward, keep an open body orientation, use more vocal variety or animation, and smile more often than we normally do. Research also shows that individuals are more likely to preen in the presence of an attractive other.[26] For example, people may alter their posture to accentuate certain body parts, straighten or adjust their clothing, and fidget with their hair when interacting with someone they find attractive.

Most often we communicate our attraction nonverbally. But how do we let our online partners know that we're attracted to them? If the nonverbal cues that primarily communicate attraction in face-to-face encounters aren't available in online interaction, how do we communicate our interest?

Verbal
Listen and Respond

One study asked almost 6000 people how they flirt in person as well as in online encounters.[27] The majority of people in the study reported that flirting was accomplished in relatively the same way, whether the exchange was face to face or online. They described how they translate physical actions into online text. For example, body movements such as laughing in response to someone's humor are represented by an acronym, such as LOL (for "laugh out loud"), placed in the text of a message or in response to one. Eye behaviors associated with flirting, such as a wink, are communicated through the use of emoticons (symbols formed with combinations of keystrokes to represent an expression or substitute for an action). Survey respondents explained that other indications of attraction, such as closer proxemics and touch, had to be accomplished through descriptions in the text of messages, such as saying "I wish I could reach out and give you a hug right now."

On occasion, in both FtF and online contexts, we may communicate attraction verbally by using informal and personal language, addressing the person by her or his first name and often referring to "you and I" and "we." We ask questions to show interest, probe for details when our partner shares information, listen responsively, and refer to information shared in past interactions, in an attempt to build a history with the person. All of these behaviors demonstrate that we value what the other person is saying.

Getting That First Conversation Going

In some ways, online interpersonal relationships have an advantage over FtF relationships, in that they develop out of conversation, meaning that an online conversation is probably what launched the relationship in the first place. In an FtF situation, the process of noticing someone interesting, realizing you're interested (either physically, sexually, or interpersonally), finding a way to meet the person (either by introducing yourself or through a third-party introduction), and starting up the first conversation—all of these things can be nerve-racking. But these steps don't happen the same way in online interactions. Researchers have described online relationships as occurring in an "inverted developmental sequence."[28] Initial interactions are critical, in that they make or break future online exchanges. Through repeated virtual contact, online topics of discussion often become very personal, and intimacy often develops at a more rapid pace than typically happens in FtF relationships. If rapport develops, it may lead to telephone conversations or FtF meetings.[29]

In FtF settings, once you realize you're attracted to someone (and that realization usually happens very quickly), what do you do next? That's a question that we've all no

immediacy
Nonverbal cues such as eye contact, forward lean, touch, and open body orientation that communicate feelings of liking, pleasure, and closeness.

doubt asked ourselves at times, when we feel that awkwardness about wanting to find a way to meet someone we find attractive and get to know her or him. We have some practical suggestions for how you approach those first conversations, so that you feel confident and keep your self-esteem intact, while communicating effectively to impress the other person positively.

Reducing Uncertainty Even though most of us like surprises from time to time, human beings are much more comfortable with certainty than with uncertainty. We prefer the known to the unknown, the predictable to the chaotic. Both FtF and online relationships involve uncertainty. One communication research team developed **uncertainty-reduction theory**, an explanation of how we use information as we endeavor to reduce our uncertainty, especially as it relates to communicating with persons we don't know (or know well). Communication researchers Charles Berger, Richard Calabrese, and James Bradac contend that this driving motivation among humans to reduce our uncertainty prompts us to communicate.[30] We typically respond to uncertainty in three ways—using passive, active, and/or interactive strategies.

To illustrate these strategies, let's consider an example. You're at a social gathering with some friends; a lot of people are there, some you know, some you don't. You spot an attractive person across the room and decide that you would like to know more about him or her. What's the first thing you would likely do in this situation? Charge right over to the person and introduce yourself? Maybe some of us would, but most of us respond less actively at first to an uncertain situation like this. The first thing most of us would do would be to scope out the situation—see who the "object of our affections" is talking with, watch to see if he or she seems to be with anyone at the party, and

As online relationships grow more intimate, the partners' expectations for more emotional expression increase.

uncertainty-reduction theory
A driving human motivation to increase predictability by reducing the unknown in one's circumstances.

Technology *and* Communication

Gender and Online Communication

Do women and men communicate differently online? One study of online behavior found that men met more people online than women, and a greater percentage of men (77%) reported lying to their online relational partners than did women (46%).[31] Most of the lies were about age and physical appearance. While most of the participants described their online relationships as casual or friendly, more women than men reported forming intimate or romantic relationships online.

Another study examined how online relationships develop out of postings to Internet newsgroups.[32] Sampling approximately 700 newsgroups devoted to different topics, researchers surveyed online participants regarding their expressions of "real" versus "virtual" selves, the type of relationship formed from postings, the depth of the relationships formed, and actions taken online (e.g., sending e-mail messages) and in person (e.g., meeting face to face, having an affair). While men and women e-mailed, exchanged pictures, engaged in instant messaging, wrote traditional letters, and met in person with

equal frequency as their relationships developed, some differences emerged that mirror research results for FtF relationships. Women characterized their online relationships as being more intimate than men did. Women were more likely to express emotions and to self-disclose more and about more intimate topics than men in this study.

While gender differences are being detected in research, other scholars contend that the "online gender gap" is narrowing. As one team of researchers suggest, "conversing on the Internet may permit the user to step outside of constricting gender roles of communication and may allow males and females to communicate as equally robust and unfettered."[33] The view that more men use the Internet than women but that women are more likely than men to use the Internet to meet members of the opposite sex may be more myth than reality. As the Internet continues to become a more accessible, affordable, and acceptable forum for making new friends and exploring romantic connections, more men and women will no doubt experience the pros and cons of online relationships.

Aware

Verbal

passive strategy
A noncommunicative strategy of reducing uncertainty by observing others and situations.

active strategy
A communicative strategy of reducing uncertainty by getting information from a third party.

interactive strategy
A strategy of communicating directly to the source who has the greatest potential to reduce one's uncertainty.

casually observe how the person communicates to get some sense of her or his personality. These are all **passive strategies**; we seek more information in order to reduce our uncertainty. Passive uncertainty reduction is related to the first of the communication principles for a lifetime that we have discussed in this text—becoming more aware of yourself, your circumstances, and others.

After you've observed the person at the party, if you need more information before deciding what to do next, you might employ an **active strategy**. This approach involves perception checking, or getting information from a third party, such as asking your friends if they know the person, if he or she is dating anyone exclusively, what their opinions are about the situation or the person, and so forth. Finding out what your friends think of the person at the party increases your information and helps you decide how to behave.

The final approach is termed an **interactive strategy**, going directly to the source who has the greatest potential to reduce your uncertainty. In our example, an interactive strategy would involve actually going over to the person and starting a conversation or joining one in progress. In some situations, enough uncertainty can be reduced through passive and active strategies; there may be no cause for an interactive strategy. At the party, you may learn enough about the person you saw across the room by watching and talking to others about her or him that you decide against initiating a conversation.

Uncertainty reduction strategies aren't necessarily used in any particular order; you might bypass passive and active strategies and decide that the best way to cope with a situation is to get the information "straight from the horse's mouth." Interactive strategies are frequently used in online relationships, because starting up an online conversation or exchanging e-mails with someone tends to evoke less uncertainty than FtF first conversations. Online exchanges usually happen in private, with less potential for embarrassment than in FtF situations, when such factors as physical appearance and nervousness are in play.

But one element can inject uncertainty into the online situation: the potential for deception. Since you stare at a computer monitor rather than into someone's eyes when you "meet" online, you really don't know who you're talking to. Research has shown people's tendencies to give false information or to omit pertinent facts in their online communication.[34] Subjects in studies reported lying about age, weight, details of physical appearance, marital status, and even their sex, meaning that some gender-bending experimentation certainly occurs. The uncertainty caused by the relative ease of online deception makes many a computer user gun shy about getting involved with people through the Internet.

RECAP

Strategies for Uncertainty Reduction

Strategy	Definition	Example
Passive	Observing and gathering useful information without interacting with anyone	While attending your first staff meeting at a new job, you observe colleagues and listen to their interaction, noting verbal and nonverbal behaviors in an attempt to "get the lay of the land."
Active	Getting opinions and information from third parties	As a form of perception checking, you ask colleagues their views on other coworkers. You compare their perceptions with your own observations.
Interactive	Getting opinions and information from those parties most directly involved	You ask the boss directly for her or his opinion and for information about the company and your job.

What Do You Say First?   In some contexts, the first words you exchange with someone may be fairly scripted or expected, such as in a job interview, in which introductions and ritualistic greetings typically take up the first few minutes. (See Appendix A for helpful information on communicating in interviews.) But what about situations in which there are no prescribed, explicit rules or expectations for behavior? Social situations, where you are meeting new people who may become friends or potential dating partners, create a level of anxiety for all of us—even the most confident person, who swears that he or she has absolutely no problem meeting new people.

Some interesting research has been conducted on just this kind of challenge. One study found that over 90% of college students surveyed agreed that it was just as acceptable for a woman to initiate a first conversation with a man as the reverse.[35] Students also believed that cute or flippant opening lines were less effective than an honest, direct approach. A book from the 1970s, entitled *How to Pick Up Girls!* provides some laughs today in its suggestions for opening lines men could use to start conversations with women.[36] Here are a couple of memorable ones: "You're Miss Ohio, aren't you? I saw your picture in the paper yesterday." "Here, let me carry that for you. I wouldn't want you to strain that lovely body of yours." "Haven't I seen you here before?" (and the all-time favorite from the 70s) "What's your sign?" We don't recommend the use of standard lines in opening conversations because that approach ignores the particular situation and the unique qualities of each person you will meet. Our fifth principle for a lifetime suggests that effective communicators adapt their messages to their listeners, so using the same type of communication in each new encounter is ill-advised. You should do some thinking about how you come across—and how you *want* to come across—when meeting new people.

Adapt

One of the best strategies, whether in an FtF or an online situation, is to find something you perceive you might have in common with the person. In person, we all give off a certain amount of "free" information that others can easily observe. If someone is wearing a T-shirt from a place you recognize or have visited, or carrying a book from a course you've taken or are taking, you can use that information as a starting point for conversation. If your online conversation springs from exchanges in a chat room, you have the commonality of the chat room to rely on to get the communication flowing.

The Art and Skill of Asking Great Questions   When students ask us, as they frequently do, "What makes someone a good conversationalist?" a variety of things come to mind. All five of our principles for a lifetime could be reflected in our answer. But perhaps the most important element is the ability to ask a great question of another person. Research from the 1970s through the present shows that asking questions to generate conversation tends to be more of a woman's behavior than a man's.[37] However, men and women alike need to develop this skill so that communication in initial encounters isn't necessarily one person's responsibility and so that we don't perpetuate sex-role stereotypes. The ability to ask great questions doesn't just magically appear—it takes time, maturity, and experience with a variety of people and relationships to develop fully.

Adapt

Your conversational partners are likely to be impressed if you are able to show genuine interest and concern for them by learning to form great questions. What do we mean by "asking great questions"? We don't mean tossing rapid-fire, superficial questions at someone, as though you were in the first five minutes of a job interview. You don't want someone to think that you're gathering data for the census. Asking a great question means, first, tailoring the question to the person as much as possible. Use what you've observed and learned from other sources to formulate your questions. Online, it's typical to ask basic information just to break the ice, but the use of too many "yes/no" questions or questions requiring one-word responses doesn't advance the conversation. Avoid questions that might be too personal or probing in the early stages of developing FtF and online relationships.

Listen and Respond

A second, very critical skill to develop is to really listen to the person's answers to your questions. Then pose a follow-up question—one that is based on the person's response to your question. You can offer your opinion on something, but opinions work best when followed up with "Do you agree?" or "That's what I think, but what do you think?" Great conversationalists are great because they listen and then form responses that show they're listening—responses that are designed to draw other people out and let them shine.

Too many people think the best way to be conversationally impressive is by talking glibly, smoothly, confidently, and virtually nonstop *about themselves.* In an online context, when one person's messages are constantly five times as long as the other's and the content rambles on and on about the person, it's a definite turnoff. Terms for this behavior include **conversational narcissism** and a **self-absorbed communicator style**.[38] For some people, this approach to communication is an outgrowth of a personality trait—a belief in oneself as the center of the universe. Other times it is a state, not a trait, meaning a temporary style of interacting rather than a more pervasive characteristic of a person. We can all be self-absorbed from time to time, but if the self-absorbed communication continues, if it moves from a temporary state into a more permanent trait, or style of a person, then the likelihood that the person will be positively perceived seriously declines.

Aware

You probably know what self-absorption sounds like and looks like in another communicator. Some verbal indications include the number of times a person uses the pronoun *I* instead of *you* or *we*. Narcissistic communicators converse mostly about themselves and typically provide more detail in their narratives than necessary (because they enjoy the sound of their own voices or the clicking of the keys on their keyboard).[39] They talk more in statements than questions and constantly try to top someone's story or to draw the topic of conversation toward themselves, as in "Oh, you think *you're* tired, let me tell you about the kind of day *I* had." No one's day is as bad, no one's opinion as valuable nor information as correct as the self-absorbed communicator's. The person may also feign empathy in a conversation: "Oh, I know exactly how you feel." This usually leads to "The same thing happened to me," followed by a long story that takes attention away from the original communicator. Another indication of self-absorption is evidenced in people who talk ad nauseam on topics about which they have some particular knowledge or expertise but that bore the socks off of listeners. Many times these types of communicators are driven by

conversational narcissism
A communication style emerging from the view that one is the center of the universe.

self-absorbed communicator style
A dominating communication style in which one focuses attention on oneself.

insecurity and uncertainty, rather than a belief that they truly are the center of the universe.

In FtF encounters, nonverbally self-absorbed communicators use vocal cues (such as increasing volume) and dominant body postures to hold their turns at talk and stave off interruptions from others. They may even physically block another person from attempting to leave the conversation and are generally insensitive to others' nonverbal cues. Online, self-absorbed chatters attempt to dominate the contributions of other chatters, make their postings more frequent and lengthier, and control the topic of conversation. People with self-absorbed personalities soon find themselves with few FtF or online friends, because few of us can tolerate such an out-of-balance relationship.

So, in sum, the best conversationalists aren't great talkers, they're great listeners and responders (as we've articulated in Principle Four). In other words, it's not what *you* say, but how you respond to what *others* say that makes you a good conversationalist.

Nonverbal

Listen and Respond

The Art and Skill of Giving and Receiving Compliments   Sometimes it seems as though people don't comment about one another unless it's to criticize. That's unfortunate, because positive reinforcement and support from others is central to our self-esteem. So let's discuss the lost art of the compliment. First, think about yourself: Are you a person who compliments others? If so, what do you tend to compliment people for—their appearance, hard work, scholarly achievement, athletic prowess? If you are a person who tends not to compliment others, why is that the case? Do you believe you'll be sticking your nose into others' business if you comment, even positively, about their behavior? Or are you somewhat oblivious to others, meaning that you tend not to notice what others do or how they look?

British linguistic scholar Janet Holmes calls compliments "social lubricants."[40] She explains that the most common purpose of a compliment is to make someone feel good by offering praise and encouragement, but an important byproduct is a sense of increased goodwill and solidarity between the complimenter and the receiver of the compliment. Research shows that compliments between romantic partners are viewed as a form of intimate talk, and that the sharing of positive feelings is linked to how satisfied partners are with the relationship.[41] In heterosexual relationships, women tend to be more aware of the presence and absence of compliments from their partners, although men and women equally believe that compliments are important in a relationship.

Giving compliments is a tricky business, because some attempts at flattery can be taken in ways other than you intend. For example, many female professionals tire of receiving workplace compliments on their appearance while their male coworkers are more often complimented on their work-related achievements. Some compliments are too personal and can make people feel uncomfortable. A pattern of personal compliments may be grounds for a claim of sexual harassment. But these are extreme examples. We encourage you to think about complimenting as a communication skill and a strategy particularly useful in first conversations, whether online or face to face. You don't want to come across as a phony or a predator, but a well-thought-out compliment can open the door to further conversation.

Verbal

It's also important to know how to receive a compliment graciously—not by agreeing with the complimenter (and sounding cocky) or by disagreeing or attempting to talk the person out of his or her compliment, as in "This old outfit? I've had it for years—I just threw it on today." The best response is a simple "thank you" that acknowledges that something nice was said about you.

Listen and Respond

MAINTAINING RELATIONSHIPS

Many forms of interpersonal communication are necessary to maintain successful, satisfying relationships. In this section, we explore a few of the most central forms, which represent some of the most heavily researched topics in the communication discipline.

On a first date, we reveal less information about ourselves than we do after a more intimate relationship develops.

Verbal

Listen and Respond

self-disclosure
Voluntarily providing information to others that they would not learn if one did not tell them.

reciprocity
The sharing of information about oneself with another person, with the expectation that the other person will share information that is similar in risk or depth.

appropriateness
An aspect of self-disclosure related to the propriety of revealing certain information to another person.

Self-Disclosure: Revealing Yourself to Others

Imagine that you're on a first date. (If you have been married for quite a while, this will take some work, but try it anyway.) Things are going fairly well. You find that you like the other person, and you become more comfortable as the evening progresses. But while you're engaged in conversation, your date manages to turn the topic of discussion to sex. The person starts describing sexual details about his or her last date or romantic partner—information that is just too intimate and private for a first date or, by some people's standards, for *any* date. Have you ever been in a situation where your date told you "TMI" (too much information)? How did you feel about the person after that experience? Did the inappropriate disclosure stop the relationship from getting off the ground?

Self-disclosure, originally researched by psychologist Sidney Jourard, occurs when we voluntarily provide information to others that they would not learn if we did not tell them.[42] People can learn our approximate age, height, and weight by just observing us. But they can't learn our exact age, height, or weight unless we disclose it. Disclosing personal information not only provides a basis for another person to understand us better, it conveys our level of trust in and acceptance of the other person.

Reciprocity in Self-Disclosure   One thing we expect when we self-disclose is **reciprocity**, meaning that when we share information about ourselves with other persons, we expect them to share information that is similar in risk or depth about themselves. If you introduce yourself to someone and give your name, you expect that person to respond by telling you his or her name. If you reveal to someone online where you're from, you expect similar information to be revealed in the person's response. This cultural rule allows us to use disclosure as a strategy for gaining information and reducing uncertainty.

If the other person doesn't reciprocate, however, you might feel embarrassed or resentful. Sharing information about yourself gives others a certain amount of power over you. If the other person reciprocates and discloses similar information, it helps maintain an equal balance of power. But if one person shares information and the other doesn't, the resulting imbalance may cause discomfort. Over time, unreciprocated self-disclosure may cause someone to end a relationship.

Relationship experts John Harvey and Ann Weber describe relationship maintenance as "minding the close relationship," which they define as "thought and behavior patterns that interact to create stability and feelings of closeness in a relationship."[43] In a "well-minded" relationship, partners facilitate self-disclosure by questioning one another about feelings and behaviors, utilizing effective listener responses (such as head nods, eye contact, and vocalizations like "uh-huh" when face to face or emoticons online), accurately repeating or paraphrasing their partner's disclosure, and remembering their partner's opinions and preferences.

Appropriateness in Self-Disclosure   **Appropriateness** is another key variable related to self-disclosure. Certain kinds of information are inappropriate to disclose at an early stage of relational development but appropriate at a later stage. However, people vary a good deal on this dimension. It's sometimes hard to gauge what is appropriate to talk about and what is not while you're in the process of getting to know someone. Sometimes unwanted disclosures emerge because one person misjudges the nature of the relationship, assuming or wanting a greater level of intimacy than his or her partner assumes or wants.

Be sensitive to your partner when you choose what and when to disclose. Consider how the other person will react to the information. Although you may not think of some information as intimate, the other person may. Conversely, when your partner reveals information, try to determine whether it is highly personal to her or him. You could upset the other person if you fail to treat the information appropriately.

Adapt

Assessing the Risks of Self-Disclosure   Self-disclosure can be extremely rewarding because of its potential to deepen a relationship and enhance trust, but it is not without its risks.[44] For example, even in a society that seems to be becoming more accepting of homosexuality and bisexuality, "coming out of the closet" as a form of self-disclosure is still a very risky prospect. Relationships with family members and friends can be hurt at the revelation, and the potential for rejection of and hostility toward the discloser is very real.[45] When we disclose, we make ourselves vulnerable and forfeit control of information. We might hurt or insult the other person by saying things she or he finds offensive, signal an unintended level of intimacy, or damage the relationship with ill-timed and inappropriate disclosures. Typically, in relationships we seek a balance between the potential risks and rewards of disclosing personal information.

What is high self-disclosing for one person may be low self-disclosing for another. In judging what, when, and how much to disclose, it's important to realize that different people have different standards or expectations. For example, some individuals are quite comfortable talking about their personal problems with relative strangers, whereas others prefer such discussions only in the most intimate relationships, if at all.

Online and FtF relationships typically include periods of frequent self-disclosure early in the development process.[46] However, while the *level* of intimacy (or risk) in the information increases over time, the *amount* of disclosure tends to decrease as the relationship becomes more intimate. As a relationship proceeds, we share a good deal of low-risk information fairly rapidly, move on to share higher-risk information, and then, finally, to share our most intimate disclosures. The more intimate the relationship becomes, the more intimate the information that is disclosed. Holding back from sharing intimate information may signal a reluctance to develop a relationship.

Verbal

Self-Disclosure, Intimacy, and Gender   Interpersonal communication research is extensive on the topic of self-disclosure and the development of intimacy in a relationship. But just what is intimacy? Experts use such terms as *bonding*, *closeness*, and *emotional connection* when referring to the sharing of personal, private information and experiences over time.[47] We especially like the definition developed by couples therapist Jeffrey Fine: "To be intimate is to be totally transparent, emotionally naked in front of another who is equally transparent. You want to see into the other's heart. What people should mean when they say *intimacy* is in-to-me-see."[48]

The conventional wisdom, borne out by early studies, contends that relationships cannot fully develop into intimacy unless both partners share (ideally, with equal frequency and depth) information about themselves.[49] Without self-disclosure, we form only superficial relationships. However, research on gender and self-disclosure calls the conventional wisdom and prior findings into question.[50]

Consider for a moment men's friendships with other men. Think about golfing buddies, a group of guys who gather over lunch a few times a week to

On the Web

Does self-disclosure, as a tool for enhancing intimacy in relationships, operate the same way in cyberspace as it does face to face? Apparently, according to research on Internet usage, people are telling other people all kinds of things about themselves over the Net. Revealing personal information about oneself isn't as threatening to many people when accomplished through machines to someone in another location, rather than in face-to-face encounters. What's your view of self-disclosure and relationship development in cyberspace? Have you shared personal information with an online partner, or has someone shared personal information with you? If you haven't, but you're daring enough to try, here are a couple of sites to check out:

www.love.com   This site, created by America Online, contains close to 200,000 personal ads. Chat rooms at this site serve as meeting places and arenas for exploring relationships. If you are a member of AOL, you also have access to their site Love@AOL.[51]

luvcoach@aol.com   Robert Bruce Starr is known as the "Luvcoach" at America Online. He opens his chat room, called "Relationship Coaching," a few times a week and gives relationship advice to computer users. Users also chat with each other about a wide variety of relational issues.[52]

Verbal

shoot some hoops, or men who enjoy one another's company over a few beers. Do these relationships tend to be based on an intimate sharing of personal information? Or are they based on shared experiences, on doing things together or having interests in common? Now think about how women's friendships form, in general. Do they form more through shared activities or through communication? It's not a stereotype: Women's friendships with other women *are* more often developed through interpersonal communication, particularly self-disclosure, than through common experiences.[53]

So, if men's friendships tend to form on the basis of shared activities, are they any less meaningful than relationships that develop through communication? Research has attempted to discover what constitutes intimacy for men, how men's friendships form, and what makes them meaningful.[54] Most men describe their friendships with other men as forming quite differently than their friendships with women, but being just as satisfying and important.[55] Men's friendships more often develop by doing, while relationships with female friends involve more talking. Men who experience the terror of battle together form powerful bonds, developed from shared experience rather than shared personal information down in the trenches. To suggest that only superficial relationships can be accomplished by doing, while deep ones must be accomplished by communicating, is to measure relational intimacy with a feminine yardstick.[56]

RECAP

Self-Disclosure

. . . is providing someone with information about yourself that she or he couldn't learn about you unless you revealed it.

. . . should be reciprocal, meaning that the person you reveal something to should respond with information about himself or herself that is similar in depth. The frequency with which partners self-disclose should be reciprocal as well.

. . . should be appropriate, meaning that it can be a mistake to reveal information that is too personal too soon in the development of a relationship.

. . . involves some risk, because knowledge is power. By revealing information to another person, you give that person a degree of power over you.

. . . is highly rewarding, in that it is a building block of relational intimacy.

Two Models of Self-Disclosure

Research has explored the way in which self-disclosure works to move a relationship toward intimacy. Here, we examine two of the more prominent models that illustrate the process by which this happens.

The Social Penetration Model   A pair of researchers, Irwin Altman and Dalmas Taylor, developed a model of **social penetration** that illustrates how much and what kind of information we reveal in various stages of a relationship.[57] According to their theory, interpersonal communication in relationships moves gradually from the superficial to the more intimate. Two aspects of this communication increase: the breadth of the information (the variety of topics discussed) and the depth (the personal significance of what is discussed).

Their model is a configuration of rings, or concentric circles (see Figure 7.2). The outermost circle represents breadth, or all the potential information about yourself that you could disclose to someone—information about athletic activities, spirituality, family, school, recreational preferences, political attitudes and values, and fears. Then

social penetration
A model of self-disclosure that asserts that both the breadth and the depth of information shared with another person increase as the relationship develops.

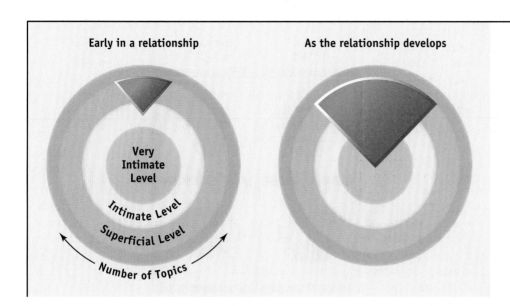

FIGURE 7.2
Altman and Taylor's Concentric Circles and Wedge of Social Penetration

there are a series of inner circles, which represent the depth of information you could reveal about yourself. The innermost circle represents your most personal information.

As an online or FtF relational partner interacts with you, that interaction can be seen as a wedge that is at first narrow (few topics are discussed) and shallow (topics are fairly superficial). People who have just started dating might talk about commonalities (like being students at the same college), hobbies, interests, and favorite activities. As the relationship progresses, the wedge becomes broader (as more topics are discussed) and deeper (as more personal topics are discussed). After several dates or conversations about hobbies and interests, topics might turn more to values, like the importance of family and friendships or attitudes about politics or social issues. Self-disclosure causes your layers to be penetrated, as you penetrate the layers of the other person.

Each of your relationships exhibits a certain degree of social penetration, or the extent to which the other person has entered your concentric circles. Some relationships, such as those with professors, distant family members, and acquaintances, may reflect a narrow, shallow wedge. The relationship does not involve a great deal of personal disclosure. A few relationships represent almost complete social penetration, the kind you achieve in an intimate, well-developed relationship, in which a large amount of indepth self-disclosure has occurred. But many contend that no one can ever completely know another person; there may be no such thing as complete social penetration. This model is a helpful way to assess your relationships, in terms of who you allow or encourage to get close to you and why. It may also help you diagram the level of intimacy you have in online and FtF relationships with others, as you attempt to penetrate their layers.

The Johari Window   The **Johari Window** in Figure 7.3 is another model of how self-disclosure varies from relationship to relationship. It reflects various stages of relational development, degrees of self-awareness, and others' perceptions of us. Its name comes from the first names of the two men who developed it (Joe Luft and Harry Ingham) and from its windowlike appearance.[58] The square window, like the circles in the social penetration model, represents your self. This self encompasses everything about you, including things you don't see or realize. A vertical line divides the square into what you have come to know about yourself and what you don't yet know about yourself. A horizontal line divides the square into what another person knows about you and doesn't know about you. The intersection of these lines creates a four-paned window.

The *Open* quadrant represents that part of yourself that you know and have revealed to the other person. As a relationship becomes more intimate, the Open quad-

Aware

Johari Window
A model that explains how self-disclosure varies from relationship to relationship; the model reflects various stages of relational development, degrees of self-awareness, and others' perceptions.

FIGURE 7.3
Johari Window

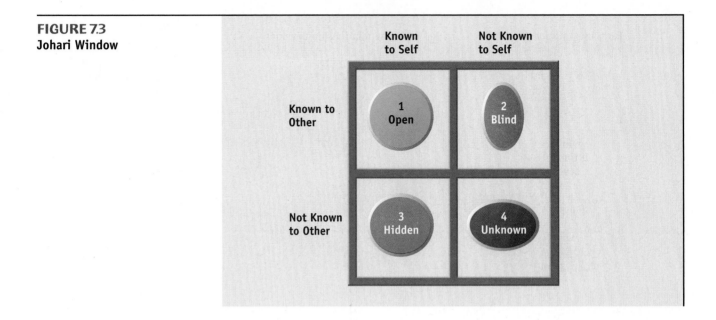

rant grows larger. The *Hidden* quadrant is information you know about yourself but have not shared with the other person. This quadrant is fairly large initially; but, as you self-disclose, it shrinks, and the Open quadrant grows. The information in the *Unknown* quadrant is that part of yourself that you have yet to discover or realize. As you learn and self-disclose more, or as others learn more about you, this quadrant becomes smaller. Individuals who are not very introspective and do not have a very well-developed sense of self will have larger Unknown areas than those who have made a concerted effort to come to know themselves.

Sometimes our friends observe things about us that we don't realize or perceive about ourselves. This kind of unintentional self-disclosure is represented by the *Blind* quadrant. This quadrant includes real aspects of ourselves that we fail to recognize. The Blind quadrant is usually small when someone doesn't know us very well; it grows larger as that person observes more information that is in our Unknown quadrant. However, as the relationship becomes more intimate, the other person is more likely to reveal his or her perceptions of us, so the Unknown and the Blind quadrants shrink as the information becomes known and accessible to us. As you can see, then, intimate relationships play an important role in the growth of self-knowledge.

Expressing Emotions

Expressing emotions is another powerful way we reveal ourselves to others and deepen our relationships. Such expression comes more easily to some people than others, but it is a skill that can be improved in both your online and your FtF relationships.[59] However, there are cultural barriers to achieving this skill, in that many cultures designate particular emotions as appropriate for only some people to display in certain situations.[60] If you placed emotional expression on a continuum according to cultural groups, with one end being an open approach to emotional display and the other end being the suppression of emotional display, U.S. culture would fall somewhere in the middle. Some cultural groups (such as Latin cultures) are comfortable with and accepting of emotional display, while other groups (such as Asian cultures) value emotional inhibition more than people in the United States.[61] People from countries where the norm is emotional inhibition often think that Americans "wear their hearts on their sleeves," while people from some other cultures view Americans as being "pent up" emotionally.

Some researchers believe that many men are drawn to sports because the sporting event allows them emotional release that might be considered inappropriate in other contexts.

Nonverbal

Families teach children very specific rules about the appropriateness of emotional display. One fascinating nonverbal communication study found that, at very young ages, children learn to mask disappointment in order to be socially appropriate.[62] We also perpetuate gender distinctions regarding emotions.[63] Many American men are taught to contain their emotions for fear that emotional expression may make them appear weak. Acquiring a "poker face" is a goal. Men are allowed to show anger and jealousy (short of physical violence), but it is frowned on for men to reveal sadness, fear, or great joy—unless they reveal it in a sporting context. (Some believe that this is one reason so many men are drawn to sports; the sporting context allows them emotional release that would most likely be considered inappropriate or "unmanly" in other contexts.) In fact, the male tendency to suppress emotion is so pronounced, it led Sidney Jourard (who first studied self-disclosure) to entitle one of his book chapters, "The Lethal Aspects of the Male Role."[64] Jourard found that men who had difficulty expressing their feelings had high levels of stress-related disease. Research suggests that if and when men do disclose their feelings to someone, most seek women as listeners because they report feeling safer expressing emotions to women than to other men.[65]

Women in American culture, in most settings, are allowed the emotional display of crying that can be prompted by sadness, fear, or joy. (Exceptions include some professional settings, where "keeping one's cards close to the vest" is valued and displaying emotion is deemed inappropriate.) But many women receive negative reactions when they display anger. The view persists that an angry woman is "out of control" or "hormonal," while an angry man is behaving more in line with societal expectations for members of his sex. While these trends and expectations have changed somewhat with recent generations, there is still a significant tendency for men (and many women as well) to believe that emotional expression of any kind is more appropriate in women than men.[66]

Many of us are reluctant or embarrassed to talk about our feelings or show our emotions, yet expressing feelings is a primary way we develop and deepen our relationships. We share feelings with our partners in two primary ways. First, we disclose

Verbal

more indirectly information about our past and current emotional states and experiences, such as sadness about the death of a family member or fear about what we will do after we graduate. This form of disclosure is more common in a growing relationship. The second way is the direct expression of emotions such as expressing attraction, love, or disappointment toward our partners. This form typically emerges later in the development of a relationship.[67]

As relationships become more intimate, we have a greater expectation that our partner will disclose emotions openly. The amount of risk associated with such emotional disclosure varies from person to person. Most of us are comfortable sharing positive emotions such as happiness and joy but are more reserved about sharing negative emotions such as fear or disappointment. In a study of 46 committed, romantic couples, subjects reported that the number-one problem in their relationship was an inability to talk about negative feelings.[68] For example, partners often made the following types of observations: "When she gets upset, she stops talking"; "He never lets me know when he's upset with something he doesn't like"; and "He just silently pouts." We generally want to know how our partners in intimate relationships are feeling, even if those feelings are negative.[69]

PRINCIPLES FOR A LIFETIME: Enhancing Your Skills

Aware

Principle One: Be aware of your communication with yourself and others.

- Attraction emerges in several different forms; it's important to discover what traits in other persons are attractive to you.
- Early in an online or FtF relationship, be aware of aspects of your personality that you want to emphasize to another person in order to create a positive and attractive image.
- One strategy to reduce uncertainty in interpersonal contexts is to be aware of your surroundings and situation as you passively observe others' interactions.
- The Johari Window is a model that can help you become more aware of your relationships and your interpersonal communication.

Verbal

Principle Two: Effectively use and interpret verbal messages.

- In initial interactions, honest, direct approaches are preferable to "canned" opening lines.
- When initiating online or FtF relationships, use questions that will engage and draw out another person.
- You may verbally reveal your liking for another person by using informal, personal, and inclusive language.
- You may verbally reveal your liking for another person by asking questions, probing for further information, and directly expressing your feelings.
- An active strategy to reduce uncertainty in interpersonal contexts is to ask third parties for their perceptions and knowledge.
- An interactive information-seeking strategy involves direct communication with the source who has the greatest potential for reducing your uncertainty.
- Asking great questions in a conversation draws a person out and helps a communicator avoid creating a perception of being self-absorbed.
- Practice giving sincere compliments generously and receiving others' compliments graciously.
- One of the key variables in relationship development is self-disclosure.
- As relationships grow more intimate, the expectation for deeper, more personal self-disclosure increases.
- Women's relationships tend to rely more on verbal communication, especially self-disclosure, while men's relationships with other men more often develop out of shared activities or common experiences.
- As online and FtF relationships grow more intimate, the expectation for more emotional expression increases.

Nonverbal

Principle Three: Effectively use and interpret nonverbal messages.

- Physical attraction is the degree to which you find another person's physical self appealing, while sexual attraction is the desire to have sexual contact with a certain person.
- In an FtF relationship, you may nonverbally reveal your liking for another person through the display of immediacy cues.
- In an online relationship, acronyms and emoticons help convey interest.
- Certain nonverbal behaviors, such as increasing the volume of your voice to keep someone from interrupting you or posting multiple, lengthy messages in a chat rooom, can signal a self-absorbed style of interpersonal communication.
- As children, we learn early on to mask some emotions (disappointment, for example) so as to behave "appropriately."

Listen and Respond

Principle Four: Listen and respond thoughtfully to others.

- Early in online and FtF relationships, it's important to concentrate on and listen to your partner's responses to your questions, so you can offer an appropriate follow-up response.
- You may verbally reveal your attraction and liking for other people by listening, asking questions to elicit more detail, and then responding appropriately and sensitively to the added information.
- The best conversationalists aren't great talkers, they're great listeners and responders.
- The formulation of great questions in conversation requires listening carefully and responding appropriately to someone's communication.
- It's important to attend carefully to someone's self-disclosure, because it comes with an expectation of reciprocity, meaning that a receiver is expected to self-disclose in response to a sender's self-disclosure.

Adapt

Principle Five: Appropriately adapt messages to others.

- Adapt to others' communication, especially in first conversations, by attending to what is said and following up with great questions.
- A self-absorbed style of communication involves very little adaptation to others.
- Adapt your self-disclosure to the other person and the context, so that your revelations are appropriate.

SUMMARY

In this chapter we explored the important topic of interpersonal communication—the form of communication that we use most frequently in our lives. Effective interpersonal communication is intricately related to one's ability to enact the five communication principles for a lifetime. We first defined interpersonal communication as a special form of human communication that occurs when we interact with another person and attempt to mutually influence each other, usually for the purpose of managing online or FtF relationships. We then differentiated interpersonal communication from impersonal communication and relationships of circumstance from relationships of choice.

We all know that relationships are important, but just how do they begin? In this chapter we explored the concept of attraction in its various forms, distinguishing interpersonal attraction as the form that causes us to forge ongoing connections with others. Four primary factors play a role in interpersonal attraction, including how similar we perceive ourselves to be to our relational partners, how physically and/or sexually attracted we are to them, our proximity to them, and whether our personality traits, values, and needs are complementary to theirs. We explored ways that we verbally and nonverbally communicate our attraction to others, as we attempt to form friendships, relationship with coworkers, romances, and committed partnerships.

Once you acknowledge that you are attracted to another person and desire a relationship with her or him, how do you use communication to get that relationship off the ground? Whether our relationships form online or in person, most of us face a degree of uncertainty when meeting new people. We attempt to reduce that uncertainty by seeking information in passive, active, and/or interactive ways. We then must call on our best communication skills to get to know the other person. Rather than communicating about ourselves in a self-absorbed or narcissistic fashion, it is better to learn to ask questions of the other person that will draw him or her out and get a conversation going. Learning to give and receive compliments graciously and sincerely is a skill we can all benefit from, because the compliment is a unique form of interpersonal communication that can have a profoundly positive effect on a relationship.

One of the most important forms of interpersonal communication that facilitates our online and FtF relationships is self-disclosure, defined as revealing something about ourselves to another person that she or he would not otherwise know if we did not reveal it. The rate and depth of self-disclosure vary as a relationship progresses, but we expect self-disclosure to be reciprocal. This means that if we share something about ourselves, we expect our partners to respond in kind, both in frequency and depth of information. Self-disclosure is also expected to be appropriate to the level of intimacy of the relationship. And self-disclosing involves a degree of risk.

One way to develop intimacy in a relationship is to disclose personal information, but research has determined that self-disclosure is not the only road to intimacy. Gender affects how one develops relationships, in that men may develop close friendships with other men more through shared activities than through shared information. Women, on the other hand, are more likely to deepen relationships by disclosing information than by sharing an experience. We discussed two models of self-disclosure: the social penetration model, which focuses on how one's personal layers are revealed to others; and the Johari Window, which illustrates self-awareness and relational partners' perceptions of us. Another form of disclosure is the expression of emotions to relational partners. The degree to which we feel safe discussing or displaying our emotions to others is a measure of intimacy in a relationship.

Discussion and Review

1. Why is interpersonal communication important in our lives?
2. What three components make up the definition of interpersonal communication?
3. Discuss three forms of attraction explained in this chapter. Then explore ways in which we verbally and nonverbally communicate our attraction for others.
4. What are the three basic interpersonal needs, according to Will Schutz, whose research we reviewed in this chapter? How does the concept of complementarity in a relationship relate to these three needs?
5. Discuss uncertainty-reduction theory in the context of online and FtF interpersonal relationships. What three information-seeking strategies do we typically use to reduce our uncertainty?
6. We've all met people who were self-absorbed or who exhibited self-absorbed communication styles. Explain, first, what is meant by self-absorption in interpersonal communication; then provide some examples that illustrate this style.
7. What is a "great" question? Provide examples of great questions that could be used to initiate conversations and relationships with others.
8. What is self-disclosure and how does it function to develop intimacy in a relationship?
9. What does the social penetration model teach us about relationship development?
10. Explain how the Johari Window reveals our view of self, as well as others' views of us. In what ways could the Johari Window be helpful in the assessment of our relationships?

Putting Principles into Practice

1. Using a model of concentric circles, map out your interpersonal relationships. Put your name in the core circle, then write the names of those persons closest to you on the circle closest to the core, continuing outward and noting the names of those with whom you have personal relationships according to intimacy. Note whether these are FtF or online relationships, or a combination of the two.

Once you have completed your model, think about how your communication differs with people on the innermost circles versus those on the outermost circles. What kind of communication is required to move someone from an outer circle to an inner one; in other words, how do you communicate in order to increase closeness or intimacy with someone? Do you ever sense a need to "lighten up" with someone on an inner ring, possibly moving them to an outer ring? How do you use interpersonal communication to accomplish this?

2. Think about someone to whom you are now or once were extremely attracted. Assess that attraction by considering these questions: How similar were you to that person, in terms of temperament, values, personality, and interests? Was your attraction to that person physical? Sexual? Intellectual? Psychological (meaning an attraction to his or her personality)? Spiritual? A combination of some of these? What kind of proximity did you have to the person? Did you have ready access to him or her? If not, what kind of effect did that have on your attraction? How complementary were your abilities and needs?

3. With a group of classmates, generate lists of the worst opening lines you can think of for getting a first conversation off the ground. Then discuss the use of canned opening lines as a strategy for initiating conversation. Should these types of lines be used? If someone uses a standard line to start a conversation, what happens to the ability to adapt one's communication to one's listeners?

4. Because we think that learning to ask great questions is so important, we want to provide you an opportunity to practice this art and skill. For each of the situations and snippets of conversations below, generate effective follow-up questions that would deepen and extend the conversation. We've provided a complete example to get you started.

a. *Sample Situation and Conversation:* The situation is a first conversation between two classmates who have never met; they are seated in the classroom before class begins.

   Bob: Hi; my name's Bob, what's yours?

   Sue: Hi; I'm Sue.

   Bob: I've never taken a philosophy course before, have you? What do you think this course will be like?

   Sue: Well, I've never taken a philosophy course either, but I expect there will be lots of reading. And I've heard that the professor's tests are pretty tough.

   Bob: Oh great; is it too late to drop?! When you say the tests are tough, tough in what way? Do you mean they cover lots of material, the prof's a hard grader, or what?

b. *Situation:* At a fraternity/sorority mixer, a woman and a man are introduced to each other for the first time by other members of their organizations.

c. *Situation:* After a staff meeting, two new coworkers who will be working on the same important project introduce themselves to each other.

5. As a class, develop a list of categories of information for self-disclosure. For example, categories could include academic achievement, religion, family background, cultural heritage, romantic experiences, and sexuality. Then have each class member write down (privately) something that pertains to each category that the person *would* and *would not* feel comfortable disclosing to another person. For example, under the category of family background, an item that might be disclosed could be that one's parents were divorced; an item that might not be disclosed could be that one suffered emotional or physical abuse in one's family. This activity will help you clarify your own "rules" about self-disclosing personal information.

CHAPTER Eight

Pal Szinyel Merse, "Picnic in May," © SuperStock, Inc.

*Relationship is a pervading and changing mystery . . . brutal or
lovely, the mystery waits for people wherever they go,
whatever extreme they run to.*

Eudora Welty

Enhancing Relationships

CHAPTER OUTLINE

The Importance of Friendship

The Importance of Family

The Importance of Colleagues

Stages of Relationship
  Development

Managing Interpersonal Conflict

Summary

CHAPTER OBJECTIVES

After studying this chapter, you should be able to:

1. Explain how the five communication principles for a lifetime apply to interpersonal communication among friends, family members, and coworkers.

2. Identify the interpersonal communication skills that are most critical for effectiveness in the workplace.

3. Identify and describe the five stages of relational escalation.

4. Identify and describe the five stages of relational de-escalation.

5. Define interpersonal conflict and distinguish between constructive and destructive conflict.

6. Discuss power dynamics in complementary, symmetrical, and parallel interpersonal relationships.

7. Explain the difference between assertive and aggressive communication.

8. Explain the key characteristics of nonconfrontational, confrontational, and cooperative styles of conflict management.

9. Discuss the major ways to manage emotions, information, goals, and problems in conflict situations.

What makes you happy in this life? Think a bit before answering that question. What really gives you enjoyment? Staring at a computer screen? Working on a project for your job? Reading a great book? Playing a video game? Being by yourself, writing in your journal? Taking a long walk? Let us venture a guess: While any one of these things might bring some level of pleasure into your life, none of them could be considered *the* thing in life that gives you the most enjoyment. Probably most of us would answer that question with some response that involves other people or, perhaps, only one other person. Our family members, friends, and coworkers are very important to us.

To some degree, we all come from dysfunctional families—there is no such thing as a perfect, or "functional," family. As Tolstoy said, "Happy families are all alike; every unhappy family is unhappy in its own way." But no matter how imperfect our families are, no matter how crazy our siblings used to make us (or still make us), or how far apart we feel we may have grown from family members, almost all of us would agree that family relationships are extremely important. Likewise, when people talk about their jobs and what they like best about where they work, most often they talk about the people they work with. So, disregarding the few true hermits out there, most of us are "people who need people." It may sound corny, but we all know that our relationships with other people are what bring us joy.

In Chapter 7 we examined some fundamental aspects of interpersonal communication that facilitate online and face-to-face relationships. We discussed attraction and those first conversations that can launch relationships or stop them dead in their tracks. In this chapter we move forward to discuss interpersonal communication as it occurs in ongoing relationships. Where appropriate, we describe how interpersonal communication functions to maintain and, in some situations, terminate online relationships, but our primary focus in this chapter is the good old-fashioned, face-to-face relationship. We attempt to answer the question, Once a relationship has been initiated, how does it progress?

First, let's reconsider our five communication principles for a lifetime as they pertain to certain relationships. Most of our examples in this chapter and the previous one tend to focus on romantic relationships, so we want to explore in some detail how communication principles apply to three other types of relationships most people experience: friendships, family relationships, and relationships with colleagues.

Aware
Verbal
Nonverbal
Listen and Respond
Adapt

THE IMPORTANCE OF FRIENDSHIP

One of the best definitions of a friend, attributed to Aristotle, is "a soul that resides in two bodies." A friend is someone we like and who likes us. We trust our friends and share good and bad times with them. We enjoy being with them, so we try to make time for that purpose. We expect a certain level of self-sacrifice from our friends. For example, you know you've got a good friend when that person gives up something (like a hot date) just to help you through a tough time.

Researchers have examined some differences among friendships at four stages in life: childhood, adolescence, adulthood, and old age.[1] When we start to talk (around the age of two), we begin to play and interact with others and perceive playmates as those who can help meet our needs. Our first friendships are typically superficial, self-centered, and fleeting, because they are based on momentary sharing of activities.[2] As we grow, we develop more of a give-and-take in friendships. During adolescence we move away from relationships with parents and toward greater intimacy with our peers. At this point in our development, peer relationships are the most important social influence on our behavior. Adolescents are likely to join groups, such as a sports or debate team, or, unfortunately, less socially desirable groups bent on violence and destruction of property.

Adult friendships are among our most valued relationships, even though they may be few in number. Research has found that, on average, adults have ten to twenty casual friends, four to six close friends, and only one to two best friends.[3] Rather than progressing through a series of stages in which intimacy deepens, which is typical of romantic relationships, friendships often alternate between periods of development and deterioration.[4]

As Americans continue to spend more hours at work each year, we often find that our closest friends are also our coworkers.[5] We share common interests, concerns, and schedules with coworkers, so it's natural for colleagues to fulfill each others' social needs as well. No doubt some of you reading this text are working a job, taking classes that demand significant blocks of time, and juggling all of this with a home and family life. Given all this activity, you may find that friendships get less of your attention. Unless we make maintaining friendships a priority, we may find ourselves becoming too busy to "work them in" and, sadly, losing them over time.

A new term has emerged for what we suspect is a long-standing phenomenon: "friends with benefits." Sexual liaisons between persons who are supposed to be "just friends" have been popularized through such television shows as *Sex and the City*, *Jake in Progress*, and a *Seinfeld* episode entitled "The Deal." Such media exposure

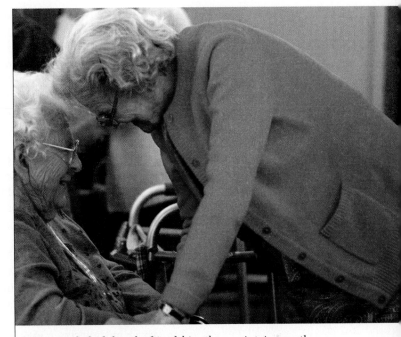

Many people find that the friendships they maintain over the years are among their most valuable.

has spurred research into this unique form of relationship. Communication scholars Mikayla Hughes, Kelly Morrison, and Kelli Jean Asada define the "friends with benefits" relationship (FWBR) as one that emerges from a pre-existing friendship but that evolves to include sexual activity. The sexual contact does not change the friendship into a romantic relationship or imply a commitment; in fact, the people involved in an FWBR do not want anything more from their partners than what they have. These researchers explain that "these types of relationships are distinct in that they combine both the benefits of friendship with the benefits of a sexual relationship, yet avoid the responsibilities and commitment that romantic sexual relationships typically entail."[6]

The FWBR differs from a "hookup"—a casual one-night sexual encounter that has also been observed among college student populations—in that it is more long-lasting and stable because it builds on a pre-existing friendship.[7] Hughes and her colleagues discovered that FWBRs are relatively common on college campuses today, that participants in such relationships perceive them as important, and that the relationships function effectively, provided both participants adhere to the following rules.

1. FWBR participants must maintain their original friendship, meaning that sexual activity doesn't change the friendship and the participants continue to do things together that they typically did as friends.
2. Emotions don't become involved, or the FWBR will be at risk.
3. The FWBR is maintained in secret, even if, for some people, this means that their romantic/sexual partners don't know about the FWBR.
4. The relationship may be renegotiated, with either participant opting out at any time.[8]

We don't know your views about this kind of relationship, whether your moral or religious views preclude your acceptance of the FWBR as a viable relational form, or whether you've had or currently have this type of relationship in your life, but it is an interesting type of relationship that communication researchers have begun to study.

Friendships are extremely important in old age.[9] During retirement, when many individuals have more time for socializing, friendships become increasingly critical. Older adults tend to rely on enduring friendships and to maintain a small, highly valued network of friends.

Communication Principles for a Lifetime: Enhancing Friendships

Noted author and motivational speaker Dale Carnegie suggested, "You can make more friends in two months by becoming interested in other people than you can in two years by trying to get other people interested in you."[10] Attraction is what draws you to potential friends, just as various forms of attraction draw you to potential dates or romantic partners. So how do you reveal your interpersonal attraction to someone so as to form a friendship?

Aware

Like many other things, friendship development begins with an awareness of yourself—Principle One. Knowing your own interests, likes, and dislikes is a first step if you are trying to expand your circle of friends. If, for example, you consider yourself a spiritual person, then you're more likely to make new friends with those kinds of people at a church gathering or in a yoga and meditation class than in some other setting.

Verbal Nonverbal

We need communication to initiate, develop, deepen, and maintain friendships. Principles Two and Three, which involve the effective use of verbal and nonverbal communication, are essential in friendship. Our verbal communication tends to become more frequent and to deepen as friendships develop. We also use immediacy cues to establish friendships—behaviors that reveal our liking of other people, such as leaning forward, moving closer, making eye contact, smiling, and nodding in response to others.

Listen and Respond

Listening and responding are important communication skills in friendship. Most of us don't stay friends with people who don't seem to listen to us, or who listen but respond inappropriately. With friends, it's important to be aware of what they *say* as well as what they *do,* as we attempt to read what's going on with them and determine the best response. That may be an empathic response that allows your friend to vent or emote while you merely attempt to feel what your friend is feeling. Your best response on other occasions may be to offer advice and counsel. Probably no other communication skill develops a friendship more than the ability to listen and respond appropriately.

Adapt

Finally, we learn to adapt to our friends or they probably don't stay our friends for very long (Principle Five). This means that we extend different parts of ourselves and communicate differently with various friends. You may enjoy your dancing buddies because you can let a creative, wilder side of yourself show with them, while you communicate more seriously as you study with a group of classmates who have become your friends.

THE IMPORTANCE OF FAMILY

Of all the relationships we experience in our lifetimes, none are more complicated than family relationships. Family members have the power to shape our self-concepts and affect self-esteem more than other people. Granted, at some point we can choose to stop or lessen the effect family members can have on our lives. But for most of us, those early messages we received as children, primarily from our parents and secondarily from our siblings, still remain in our psyches and affect who we are today.

To say that family life has changed is an understatement. Family units are dramatically different than they were when the predominant profile was a two-parent, father-as-bread-winner, mother-as-homemaker arrangement.[11] In the 1980s, the New York Supreme Court provided a very broad definition of a family, stating that "The best description of a family is a continuing relationship of love and care, and an assumption of responsibility for some other person."[12] Estimates for the first part of the new century suggest that the most common profile of American family is the step-family, or blended family.[13]

DILBERT: © Scott Adams/Dist. by United Feature Syndicate, Inc.

Communication Principles for a Lifetime: Enhancing Family Relationships

Growing up in families, we begin to discover who we are and how we should communicate with others. If you were raised by the rule of "children should be seen and not heard," then you got clear messages about when it was appropriate to speak out and when to be silent. If you witnessed a good deal of conflict in your family, you no doubt have been affected by that experience. You may have turned out to be someone who avoids conflict at all costs, but research suggests that it is more likely that you will engage in the same form of conflict you witnessed or participated in as you grew up.[14] In addition, research shows that family interaction patterns affect people's views of their own communication abilities.[15] People who grow up in a *pluralistic* family environment—one that is highly conversational and that encourages children to develop and express opinions about the world without fear of rejection or negative consequences from their parents—tend to perceive themselves as being skilled communicators in their friendships and romantic relationships. Those who grow up in families that encourage conformity and that do not expose children to other ways of thinking or controversial views of the world tend to believe less in their own abilities to communicate effectively in relationships, particularly when it comes to self-disclosing to others.

Our earliest lessons about verbal and nonverbal communication come from our families. Virginia Satir has conducted extensive research on family communication.[16] She suggests that in healthy families, "the members' sense of self-worth is high; communication is direct, clear, specific, and honest; rules are flexible, humane, and subject to change; and the family's links to society are open and hopeful." In such families, Satir notes, people listen actively; they look *at* one another, not *through* one another or at the floor; they treat children as people; they touch one another affectionately regardless of age; and they openly discuss disappointments, fears, hurts, angers, and criticism, as well as joys and achievements. The degree to which parents and children can reveal what they are thinking and feeling is a measure of family cohesiveness. Another aspect Satir highlights corresponds to our Principle Four, that of listening and responding. Healthy family relationships are built on foundations of trust, which involves listening to one another and responding helpfully. Many conflicts arise because family members don't listen well to one another and respond based on that faulty listening.

Finally, family relationships involve a good deal of adaptation, particularly when, as adults, we visit our parents. Here's an example: A colleague of ours describes the tension he feels when he visits his parents on certain holidays. His father was born in 1920, so he has very different experiences and values than his 40-something son. During key moments (like over Thanksgiving dinner), when the father begins to talk in stereotypes (usually derogatory) about certain racial or ethnic groups, the son cringes. He must decide whether to engage his dad and risk ruining the occasion for his mother (which he has done at times) or squelch his own views, which could be seen as an act of cowardice and a tacit acceptance of racism. Most of the time now he says he "keeps the peace," adapting his communication for the higher goal of avoiding conflict and keeping the family holiday pleasant.

Aware

Verbal Nonverbal

Listen and Respond

Adapt

The best managers listen carefully and then respond effectively.

THE IMPORTANCE OF COLLEAGUES

For many of us, our work is our livelihood, our most time-consuming activity. In fact, many Americans are working longer hours—10% more time on the job in the twenty-first century than 30 years ago.[17] Many things make a job worthwhile and rewarding, but most working people say that relationships with people they work with make the most difference between job satisfaction and dissatisfaction.

What are the most important skills people need to be successful on the job? Year after year, the number-one skill employers look for in new hires is the ability to communicate effectively with others.[18] You land your job through a face-to-face interview (in most cases). You keep your job based on your ability to do the work and get along with coworkers and bosses, which usually involves a large amount of interpersonal interaction.

Communication Principles for a Lifetime: Enhancing Workplace Relationships

Getting accustomed to a new job takes a while. There are the rudimentary things to discover and adjust to, such as finding out where to park or which subway or bus route to take, learning the procedures that make an organization function, and observing general office protocol. Then there are the more important things, like learning how to do your job well, ascertaining the chain of command, and discovering which colleagues have the potential to develop into friends.

When most of us enter a new situation, such as a new job, we experience uncertainty. We discussed in Chapter 7 how the motivation to reduce uncertainty causes us to seek information. On the job, our uncertainty will most likely be reduced by those who hired us, those who are assigned to train or orient us to the new situation, and coworkers who are at our same level within the organization. We are most likely to use passive strategies first, meaning that we observe our surroundings and how people interact on the job, as a way of becoming more aware so that we will know how to behave appropriately (Principle One). Perception checking with colleagues also increases awareness. For example, after attending your first staff meeting, you might want to ask a few colleagues whether the gathering was typical of the kind of staff meetings the organization holds.

As we begin to interact with persons of varying status in the organization, we draw on our most effective verbal and nonverbal communication skills so that we make positive impressions on others (Principles Two and Three). The higher you go in an organization, the more your job involves communicating with others. In one research project, scholar Harvey Mintzberg observed chief executive officers for five weeks. He found that managers spend almost 80% of their day communicating orally with others.[19] In most organizations, working is communication; communicating is working.

One skill that makes for an effective worker—any worker, in any organization—is the ability to listen and respond effectively to colleagues (Principle Four). The best managers of other people are the best listeners. They listen patiently, fully, and nonjudgmentally. They also exercise caution before responding, so that they will respond appropriately.

Finally, our Principle Five about adaptation is critical to successful coworker relationships. You cannot hope to be successful on the job if you communicate the same

Aware

Verbal
Nonverbal

Listen and Respond

way to your boss as you do to your peers on the job, your subordinates, and others in your life—including long-term friends, intimates, and family members. This may seem obvious, but we find that people sometimes experience isolation on the job because they cannot get along with coworkers. Or they've trusted coworkers too much and revealed personal information, only to have that information used against them later. Some people don't realize that they can't talk at work about everything they talk about at home. They don't adapt to the situation, and it often costs them their jobs.

Adapt

STAGES OF RELATIONSHIP DEVELOPMENT

Researchers have determined that relationships develop in discernible stages, although they differ in their use of terms and the number of stages.[20] While the research on relational stages is most often applied to dating or romantic relationships, the information can also apply to other types of relationships.

Verbal
Nonverbal

Understanding these stages is important. First, interpersonal communication is affected by the stage of the relationship. For instance, individuals in an advanced stage discuss topics and display nonverbal behaviors that rarely appear in the early stages of a relationship. Second, interpersonal communication facilitates movement between the various stages. Relationships change and are continually renegotiated by those involved. Interpersonal communication moves a relationship forward as we progress from being acquaintances, to friends, to lovers, and, possibly, to marital or committed partners. Ideally, communication should move a relationship back from partners to friends as well, although regressing a relationship is difficult to accomplish. Research indicates that after a breakup, couples who continue to have something of value to offer to each other, such as status or information, are likely to maintain a friendship. But former romantic couples who experience barriers to friendship, such as negative reactions by friends and family or the development of a new romantic relationship, are unlikely to be able to become friends.[21]

It's helpful to think of relational stages as floors in a high rise (see Figure 8.1). The bottom floor represents a first meeting; the penthouse is intimacy. Relational development is an elevator that stops at every floor. As you ascend, you might get off the elevator and wander around for a while before going to the next floor. Each time you get on, you don't know how many floors up the elevator will take you or how long you will

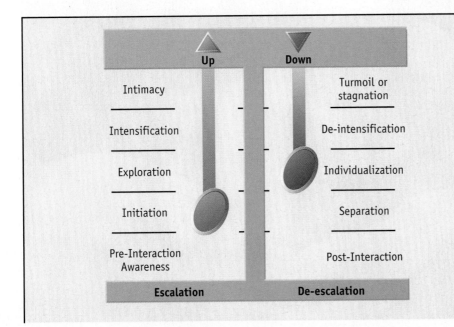

FIGURE 8.1
Relationship Stages

Source: From Steven A. Beebe, Susan J. Beebe, and Mark V. Redmond, *Interpersonal Communication: Relating to Others.* Published by Allyn & Bacon, Boston, MA. Copyright © 2002 by Pearson Education. Reprinted by permission of the publisher.

pre-interaction awareness stage
Stage of becoming aware of one's attraction to another person and observing that person but not actually interacting.

initiation stage
The first contact with a person with whom one desires a relationship; usually characterized by asking and answering questions.

exploration stage
Stage that involves more in-depth interactions.

Aware

Verbal
Nonverbal
Listen and Respond

stay at any given floor. In fact, sometimes you never get back on the elevator, electing instead to stay at a particular stage of relational development. This may represent stability or stagnation. Stability is not the same as stagnation; it may simply mean that a relationship has reached a comfortable point for both partners. But notice that we say *both* partners; if one partner feels the relationship has stabilized at an appropriate stage, but the other partner feels the relationship has stagnated, dissatisfaction and conflict are often the result.

If you fall head over heels in love, you might want to escalate quickly from floor to floor toward intimacy, possibly even skipping some floors. The process of de-escalating a relationship does not occur in every relationship, but if it does, it may be a slow or quick descent through various floors. The best approach to relationship development is to share this elevator with your partner, so that the two of you make decisions about how high you will ride the elevator, how long to stay at each floor, and whether to take the elevator back down. Often partners do not share decisions about movement within the relationship. Sometimes one of the partners rides the elevator alone. Let's explore in more depth this process of escalating and de-escalating relationships.

Relational Escalation

As depicted in Figure 8.1, the first level of relational development is termed the **pre-interaction awareness stage**. In this stage, you might observe a person or even talk with others about that person without having any direct interaction. You might not move beyond the pre-interaction awareness stage if your impressions of the person aren't favorable or the circumstances aren't right.

If you are attracted to the other person and the circumstances are right, you might proceed to the **initiation stage**. First conversations typically involve each person responding to the other's questions as they try to determine what they have in common. Try to ask engaging questions and then listen carefully to the answers. The answers suggest follow-up questions that can draw the person out and make you both more comfortable. Your nonverbal behavior should also indicate your interest.

If you decide to go to the **exploration stage**, you will begin to share more in-depth information. You will probably have minimal physical contact and you may limit the amount of time you spend together because you are building a relationship. But it's

At the intensification stage, a couple's relationship becomes the central focus of their lives.

important to realize that some relationships move through stages very quickly. For example, we probably all know people whose relationships were extremely physical, and perhaps sexual, from the very start. Are those relationships doomed because they didn't follow set or prescribed paths for development? No; some relationships may just proceed through stages faster than others. However, relationships that are extremely physical or sexual may burn out quickly because they lack the emotional foundation necessary to survive.

If you proceed to the **intensification stage**, you will start to depend on each other for self-confirmation, meaning that your partner's opinion of or feelings about you weigh more heavily than those of others. Partners tend to spend more time together, increase the variety of activities they share, adopt more intimate physical distance and contact, and personalize their language. The frequency and level of shared personal information increases and deepens, and the couple may decide to label their connection.

The top level of relationship escalation is the **intimacy stage**. Partners who are in this stage provide primary confirmation of each other's self-concept, meaning that your partner knows how you view yourself and accepts that view. Communication is highly personalized and synchronized. Partners talk about anything and everything, and a commitment to maintaining the relationship might even be formalized and socially recognized, such as with a decision to marry. The partners share an understanding of each other's language and nonverbal cues and have a great deal of physical contact. They use fewer words to communicate effectively because they understand each other without words. Reaching this stage takes time—time to build trust, share personal information, observe each other in various situations, and create an emotional bond and commitment.

RECAP

Relational Escalation

Stage	Explanation
Pre-Interaction Awareness	You become aware of your attraction to someone and begin to observe that person.
Intiation	You initiate contact with the person with whom you want a relationship.
Exploration	Interactions deepen as questions and answers elicit more information from partners.
Intensification	Partners begin to depend on each other for confirmation of their self-concepts. They spend more time together, engage in more intimate touch, and personalize their language.
Intimacy	Partners provide primary confirmation of each other's self-concept. Verbally, language is highly personalized; nonverbal behaviors are synchronized.

Relational De-Escalation

Sometimes relationships begin to unravel; this can happen for a variety of reasons. Some unravel to the point of termination. But as you may already know, ending a relationship is not as simple as going down the same way you came up; it is not a mere reversal of the escalation process.[22]

Communication scholar Mark Knapp provides a model for how relationships come apart.[23] When an intimate relationship is not going well, it usually enters a stage of either turmoil or stagnation. The **turmoil stage** involves an increase in conflict, as one

intensification stage
Stage in which partners begin to depend on each other for self-confirmation; characterized by more shared activities, more time spent together, more intimate physical distance and contact, and personalized language.

intimacy stage
Stage in which partners provide primary confirmation of each other's self-concept; characterized by highly personalized and synchronized verbal and nonverbal communication.

turmoil stage
Stage characterized by increased conflict, less mutual acceptance, a tense communication climate, and an unclear relationship definition.

Ethics *and* Communication

Making Breaking Up Easier to Do?

Students in an interpersonal communication class were discussing online relationships, when one said a surprising thing: "I got a break-up notice over the Internet once. I couldn't believe it; this girl actually had the nerve to break up with me through an e-mail message. We never ever discussed it face-to-face or over the phone." No one in the class had heard of a "Dear John" message being conveyed online.

Breakups are tough, but what is a person's ethical obligation when she or he wishes to terminate a relationship? The Internet allows for a certain level of impersonality, but is sending an e-mail an appropriate way to "dump" someone? Would you want someone to break up with you in such a "high-tech" way?

stagnation
A stage in which a relationship loses its vitality, partners begin to take each other for granted, and communication and physical contact decline.

de-intensification stage
Stage involving significantly decreased interaction, increased distance, and decreased dependence on one's partner for self-confirmation.

individualization stage
Stage in which partners define their lives more as individuals and less as a couple.

separation stage
Stage in which individuals make an intentional decision to minimize or eliminate further interpersonal interaction.

post-interaction stage
The bottom, or final, level in relational de-escalation, which represents the lasting effects of a relationship on the self.

or both partners find more faults in the other. The definition of the relationship seems to lose its clarity, and mutual acceptance declines. The communication climate is tense; interactions are difficult and forced. **Stagnation** occurs when the relationship loses its vitality and the partners become complacent, taking each other for granted. Communication and physical contact between the partners decrease; they spend less time together but don't necessarily engage in conflict. Partners in a stagnating relationship tend to go through the motions of an intimate relationship without the commitment or the joy; they simply follow their established relational routines. But a stagnating relationship can be salvaged. A relationship can remain in turmoil or stagnate for a long time, but the individuals can repair, redefine, or revitalize the relationship and return to intimacy.

If the turmoil or stagnation continues, however, the individuals will likely experience the **de-intensification stage**. This involves significantly decreased interaction; increased physical, emotional, and psychological distance; and decreased dependence on the other for self-confirmation. The partners might discuss the definition of their relationship, question its future, and assess each other's level of dissatisfaction. The relationship can be repaired and the individuals can move once again toward intensification and intimacy, but it's more difficult to accomplish at this point.

After de-intensification, the **individualization stage** occurs. Partners tend to define their lives more as individuals and less as a couple or unit. Neither views the other as a partner or significant other any more. Interactions are limited, and the perspective changes from "we" and "us" to "you" and "me." Both partners tend to turn to others for confirmation of their self-concepts; physical intimacy is at an all-time low, if not nonexistent; and nonverbal distance is easily detected.

In the **separation stage**, individuals make an intentional decision to minimize or eliminate further interpersonal interaction. If they share custody of children, attend mutual family gatherings, or work at the same place, the nature of their interactions changes. They divide property, resources, and friends. Early interactions in this stage are often tense and difficult, especially if the relationship has been intimate.

Although interaction may cease, the effect of a relationship is not over. Relationships—even failed ones—are powerful experiences in our lives. The final level in relational de-escalation is termed the **post-interaction stage**. This level represents the lasting effects the relationship has on the self, and therefore on other interactions and relationships. Relationship scholar Steve Duck explains that in this final stage of terminating relationships, we engage in "grave-dressing"—we create a public statement for people who ask why we broke up or why we're no longer friends with someone. It also means that we come to grips with losing the relationship.[24] Sometimes our sense of self gets battered during the final stages of a relationship; we have to work hard to regain a healthy sense of self.

Prepare yourself for some news, if you haven't already heard this: In February 2004, just before Valentine's Day, Barbie and Ken officially broke up. Having met on the set of a television commercial in 1961, the two had been inseparable ever since . . . until now. A spokesperson for Mattel said that Barbie and Ken felt it was "time to spend some quality time apart"; however, the two say that they will remain friends. Apparently even dolls can experience the heartbreak of termination of a relationship.[25]

Research over several decades has shed light on how people prefer to end relationships, as well as how they prefer someone to end a relationship with them.[26] In most relationships, the breakup is unilateral (done by one party) rather than bilateral (agreed to by both parties). Studies show that most people use and prefer indirect breakup strategies, such as avoidance, requests for "distance" or "space" in the relationship, a general fading away rather than an abrupt or definite breakup, and the staging of a conflict that leads to blaming and relationship termination. Direct breakup strategies, typically accomplished face-to-face, are probably the most interpersonally communicative but not the most preferred by most people in relationships. Being told we're being dumped just isn't something too many of us prefer to experience. If you're really

Technology *and* Communication

Cheating in Cyberspace

Research reveals that the primary use for the home computer is relationship maintenance, mainly in the form of e-mailing to keep in touch with family members and friends.[27] Another, less mainstream, use of the personal computer is to establish "liaisons" outside one's primary relationship.

Typically, these liaisons don't begin as sexual relationships. They may begin through common interests, such as those you may share with someone who posts frequently in a chat room, for example; after a while you decide to begin exchanging comments with only that person in a private chat room. Since these exchanges are anonymous (chatters most often use pseudonyms), a private exchange between two chatters seems harmless, but this form of cyber-relationship can escalate and take on another level of intimacy and meaning.

We've probably all heard of cybersex—sexual activity that occurs online, but without any physical contact between participants—but you may not have thought about the damage cybersex can do to a monogamous, committed relationship. Most people have negative reactions to marital infidelity, whether they themselves have experienced it or know someone who has; even those who haven't experienced it say that they would respond negatively to a partner's infidelity if it were to happen.[28] But few people in committed, monogamous relationships think much about cyber-infidelity—until it happens to them. Is online cheating really *cheating* in the traditional sense? No physical contact has taken place; the sexual activity is accomplished through verbal exchanges within virtual reality—so how real is virtual reality? Should cyber-infidelity affect a committed relationship as much as in-person infidelity, or is it somehow different?

Putting a positive spin on this situation, some research suggests that people who form sexual liaisons online are able to explore their sexuality with little concern that friends, coworkers, and spouses will discover their activities.[29] People may feel sexually hindered in their face-to-face relationships, so in a

sense, the Internet becomes the arena in which their "true" sexual selves find expression. They may come to understand themselves better sexually because they feel under less pressure, and the benefits of such discovery can carry over into their face-to-face relationships. Some are drawn to the Internet for sexual gratification if their in-person relationships are in turmoil or decline and their opportunities for sexual expression and gratification are limited. In addition, since online sexual exchanges don't occur in person, the eroticism is based on other factors, such as emotional intimacy and verbal expressiveness, rather than on physical attractiveness. Concerns about STDs or unwanted pregnancies disappear. A final benefit cited in research relates to the fact that if a virtual sexual liaison goes awry, participants don't suffer such consequences as in-person retribution or confrontation, since online exchanges, for the most part, remain anonymous, with true identities withheld.

One study asked participants about their online sexual activity, including what initially motivated them to engage in cybersex, why they continued to engage in it, the role it played in their lives, and the effects it had on them.[30] Interestingly enough, 41% of subjects revealed that they did not believe that online sexual activity constituted cheating on a partner under any circumstances. Fourteen percent believed it to be cheating if a person engaged in cybersex repeatedly with the same person. Smaller percentages of participants believed that online sex was cheating only if interactive video cameras were used or if the online sex led to phone sex. Thirty-three percent of subjects believed that online sex was cheating and that it was just as much an act of infidelity as in-person sex with someone other than one's partner.

What's your view of cybersex? Should someone who is in a monogamous, committed, face-to-face relationship be seeking sexual liaisons over the Internet? Does online sexual activity constitute a breach of faith with one's partner, or is it merely an exercise in "sexploration" that has no bearing on one's primary relationship?

sheepish about breaking up with someone and you have some money to burn, a payment of $50 to the Web site breakupservice.com will buy you the services of someone who will call or write a letter and break up your relationship for you. An employee of the service will even pick up any possessions you've left in the care of your ex and make sure they get returned to you. The service's employees report a significant increase in business just after major holidays.

What typifies each of the different relational stages of escalation and de-escalation is the communication—verbal and nonverbal—that is present or absent. Interpersonal communication facilitates movement through the stages of escalation; the lack of communication moves people through the stages of de-escalation.

RECAP

Relational De-Escalation

Stage	Explanation
Turmoil	Partners take each other for granted and have more conflict. They exhibit less mutual acceptance, their communication climate is tense, and their relationship definition is unclear.
Stagnation	Relationship loses its vitality, partners begin to take each other for granted, and communication and physical contact decline.
De-Intensification	Partners significantly decrease their interaction and their dependence on each other for self-confirmation; they increase their physical distance.
Individualization	Partners define their lives more as individuals and less as a couple.
Separation	Partners make an intentional decision to minimize or eliminate further interpersonal interaction.
Post-Interaction	This is the bottom or final level in relational de-escalation; it represents the lasting effects of a relationship on the individuals.

MANAGING INTERPERSONAL CONFLICT

A World of Conflict

We live in a world full of conflict. You can hardly watch the news on television, listen to a radio talk show, or read a newspaper headline without being confronted with another story of conflict. Whether it's the Middle East, a political coup in a country in Africa, or a disturbance generated by extremist groups right here at home, conflict on a global scale seems inevitable. While conflicts throughout the world have always existed, the events of September 11, 2001, launched the United States into a series of intense conflicts across the globe. How can we understand conflict on such a scale? What can we learn about conflict that might help mediate its destructive effect across the world? An understanding of conflict and the development of effective communication skills to manage conflict begins one-on-one, in our day-to-day relationships. Conflict is rooted in interpersonal communication.

Do you know the three most important words a person can say to someone? The answer isn't "I love you"; the answer is "I was wrong." These words are actually better to hear than "I'm sorry," because saying you're sorry could mean that you're sorry you're having a disagreement or you're sorry you got caught doing something that caused the conflict, or it could be just something to say in an attempt to end the conflict. It's quite hard for most of us to admit that we were at fault, but it's very meaningful in a conflict situation when someone admits that she or he was wrong.

Interpersonal conflict is a struggle that occurs when two people cannot agree on a way to meet their needs. When needs are incompatible, if there are too few resources to satisfy them, or if individuals opt to compete rather than to cooperate to satisfy them, then conflict occurs. The intensity of a conflict usually relates to the intensity of the unmet needs. The bedrock of all conflict is differences—different goals, experiences, expectations, and so forth.

Humans are generally need driven and goal oriented, so it's not surprising that most conflict is goal driven. You want something; your partner wants something else. If your partner interferes with your achievement of your goal, there may be a conflict. Suppose you are trying to find a place to park in an overcrowded lot on campus. Just as you find an empty spot, another student zips into "your" space. Your blood boils and you get out of your car fighting mad. Or suppose you have had a difficult day at work or school (or both). All you want to do is hunker down with a bowl of popcorn and watch a game (*any* game). But your roommate announces that some mutual friends are coming over for dinner. "That's not what *I* feel like doing tonight. Why didn't you ask *me* before you invited them?" you shout. In both instances, your goals collide head-on with someone else's, and you feel as if you have lost control of the situation.

How Conflict Functions in Relationships

Conflict is a normal, inevitable element within relationships. The more important the relationship, the greater the potential for conflict, because we aren't as likely to voice disagreement with people who don't matter very much to us. Psychologist Phillip Mc-Graw (better known as Dr. Phil) contends that there is a third inevitability in life beyond death and taxes—conflict (or as he terms it, verbal fighting with the one you love).[31] McGraw describes three "fundamental truths" about fighting: (1) Fighting is unquestionably painful; (2) fighting is an unavoidable part of every relationship; and (3) there are right and wrong ways to fight— you just have to learn to conduct disagreements in ways that enhance your relationship.

It's surprising (and disconcerting) when people in relationships say, "We just get along so well; we belong together because we've never even had a fight." While we don't advocate staging or picking a fight with a partner as an experiment, we do believe that it is worrisome to commit to a person when you don't know how she or he handles conflict. If your partner or close friend is a "screamer" and you prefer to walk away from a conflict in silent protest, your relationship is headed for very rough waters. People's responses to conflict must be known quantities if a relationship is to be successful.

Conflict Can Be Constructive or Destructive   To construct something is to build or make something new. Characterized by cooperation in dealing with differences, **constructive conflict** can help identify which elements of a relationship need to change or be improved, so that new patterns are established. Here's an example:

Mike: You know, I'm getting tired of always going to your mother's on Sundays. It's like we're in a rut or something. Just one weekend, I'd like to have a Sunday with no schedule or agenda.

Claire: Mike, I thought you liked going over there, because my mom's such a good cook and you and dad are working on that project together. Plus, it's one of the few times I get to spend time with my folks.

Mike: Well, I do like going over there, but not every weekend.

Claire: I didn't realize that you were starting to resent it or feel like you were getting into a rut. Let's talk more about this, and figure something out.

interpersonal conflict
A struggle that occurs when two people cannot agree on a way to meet their needs.

constructive conflict
Conflict characterized by cooperation in dealing with differences; helps build new insights and patterns in a relationship.

Diversity *and* Communication

Conflict and Culture

*I*nterpersonal conflict is difficult to manage, but cross-cultural conflict can be even more overwhelming. Some people are trained in negotiation and mediation techniques, so that they can facilitate peaceful relations between nations and peoples. But what if you're not planning on becoming an international negotiator? What if you simply want to know a few things to keep you from being tossed in jail in a foreign country?

Intercultural communication scholar Stella Ting-Toomey has written extensively on this subject and produced some insightful information that can help you anticipate and avoid intercultural conflict.[32] Persons from individualistic cultures, such as the United States, emphasize the importance of the individual over the group. Those in collectivistic cultures, such as the Japanese, emphasize group rather than individual achievement. These differing values contribute to intercultural conflict.

So what should members of individualistic cultures (such as Americans) know when interacting with members of collectivistic cultures? Note the seven assumptions about conflict that individualistic cultures hold; compare this list with the seven assumptions about conflict that collectivistic cultures hold. Then assess the differences.

Not only do members of different cultural groups have different views of conflict, they have vastly different ways of dealing with or managing conflict. It's wise to do some research on the country you will be visiting or moving to, so that you understand how basic cultural values differ from those of your home country.

Individualistic Cultures	Collectivistic Cultures
1. The purpose of conflict is to air out major differences and problems.	1. Conflict is damaging to self-respect and relational harmony; it should be avoided as much as possible.
2. Conflict can be either functional or dysfunctional.	2. For the most part, conflict is dysfunctional.
3. Repressed, unconfronted problems can lead to dysfunctional conflict.	3. Conflict signals a lack of self-discipline and emotional immaturity.
4. Functional conflict provides an opportunity for solving problems.	4. Conflict provides a testing ground for skillful negotiation and "face-saving."
5. Substantive and relational issues in conflict should be handled separately.	5. Substantive and relational issues are always intertwined.
6. Conflict should be handled directly and openly.	6. Conflict should be handled discreetly and subtly.
7. Effective conflict management should be a problem-solving activity with a win-win outcome.	7. Effective conflict management should be a face-saving negotiation game with a win-win outcome.

Adapt

destructive conflict
Conflict characterized by a lack of cooperation in dealing with differences; dismantles relationships without restoring them.

Note that Claire recognizes the need for further dialogue about Mike's complaint. She transforms the issue of disagreement into a topic for discussion and relational adjustment. If Mike hadn't expressed his dissatisfaction, the issue might have taken on larger proportions. He might have expressed his feelings of being in a rut in a cruder, more hurtful way on the next drive over to the parents' house, for example. Many times these expressions contain more venom than we intend or actually feel. A well-managed disagreement that includes expressing one's own needs or revising goals can lead couples or friends first to examine and then revitalize their relationship. Constructive conflict enables both people to view a disagreement from different perspectives, even if the information shared seems negative at first.

A rapidly spiraling **destructive conflict** can do as much damage as a tornado churning through a trailer park. A conflict may start over a seemingly small issue, but it increases in intensity as other issues and differences are brought into the discussion.

Such destructive escalation blocks off options for managing differences and makes a win–win solution more elusive. The hallmark of destructive conflict is a lack of flexibility in responding to others.[33] Combatants view their differences from a win–lose perspective, rather than looking for solutions that allow each individual to gain. This form of conflict dismantles relationships without restoring them. If both individuals are dissatisfied with the outcome of the conflict, then it has been more destructive than constructive.

In their book on interpersonal conflict, William Wilmot and Joyce Hocker discuss six hallmarks of constructive conflict, which involve analysis, adaptation, and effective interpersonal communication.[34]

1. *People change.* In relationships, people are involved with each other. In conflict, people must work hard to stay involved with each other, because an interaction that escalates into conflict can pull people apart. Flexibility and a willingness to change are key. Wilmot and Hocker explain that "rigid, insistent communication defeats the purpose of constructive conflict."

2. *People interact with an intent to learn instead of an intent to protect themselves.* You can learn a great deal about yourself, your partner, and your relationship if you approach conflict as a learning experience—one that will take your relationship forward instead of allowing it to stagnate or regress. Protecting yourself against conflict doesn't help a relationship grow.

3. *People do not stay stuck in conflict when the conflict is constructive.* A destructive conflict, or series of conflicts, can make you feel stuck in one place within a relationship. Wilmot and Hocker point out that constructive conflict doesn't define who people are in a relationship; conflict is a dynamic process that emerges, plays out, and recedes.

4. *Constructive conflict enhances self-esteem in the participants.* You probably don't associate conflict with enhanced self-esteem, because most of us think of conflict as negative and destructive. However, constructive conflict brings energy and productivity to a relationship and provides a more honest, complete picture of oneself.

5. *Constructive conflicts are characterized by a relationship focus instead of a purely individualistic focus.* If parties in a conflict focus on the relationship instead of themselves, then the conflict will more likely be constructive than destructive. Participants should emphasize the "we" over the "I," so that conflict is seen as an experience that builds the relationship. If individual winning is more important than the relationship winning, then conflict will erode the relationship.

6. *Constructive conflict is primarily cooperative.* Conflict built on competition, power struggles, and self-interest will destroy a relationship. Conversely, a cooperative, win–win approach to conflict will open the door for greater growth in a relationship.

Conflict Involves Power   One of the most significant elements within interpersonal relationships is power. We might not realize it, but distributing power between partners requires a lot of subtle negotiation. Without this negotiation, conflict can become rampant. Furthermore, our ability to manage power successfully is a major factor in relational development. Power has been defined in a variety of ways, but for our purposes, **interpersonal power** means the ability to influence another in the direction we desire—to get another person to do what we want.[35] It also involves our ability to resist others' influences on us.[36] Perhaps it is easier to think of it in terms of who has more *control* in a relationship, rather than to use the term *power.*

All interactions, including conflicts, involve some level of power or control. If you ask a friend to go to a movie with you, you attempt to influence him or her. If the answer is no, your friend is mustering resistance and demonstrating power over you. If you don't like the negative response, you might attempt to assert control once more, perhaps by offering to buy your friend's ticket or to drive.

Listen and Respond

Aware

Verbal

interpersonal power
The ability to influence another in the direction one desires; getting another person to do what one wants.

Romantic relationships can be typified by power dynamics.[37] In what is termed a **complementary relationship**, one partner willingly and continuously cedes power to the other. For example, a couple may feel completely comfortable with only one partner planning most of the activities, controlling the purse strings, and making decisions for the future of the relationship. Some partners prefer this arrangement because conflict doesn't arise over who wants control. However, the out-of-power partner may come to resent this status over time.

Symmetrical relationships are characterized by similar degrees of control on the part of each person. Both partners compete in order to dominate the other and assert control, or both relinquish control to the other to avoid making decisions or committing to something. In the first case, partners may argue over which television program to watch. In the second case, partners don't express preferences but engage in endless exchanges of "I don't know; whatever you want." The negotiation process can be time-consuming, fatiguing, and ineffective when quick decisions are needed.

In a **parallel relationship**, power continually shifts from one partner to the other, depending on the nature of the interaction or situation. One partner may take control because he or she is more experienced or equipped to handle a particular circumstance. This doesn't mean that one partner is constantly in an out-of-power position; rather, partners alternate being in control according to their strengths and weaknesses. For instance, if one partner is in charge of keeping the finances straight, she or he will have more power in budgetary decisions. If the other partner is a better cook, he or she probably will exert more power over decisions about diet and menus. This form of give and take works extremely well in intimate relationships, but partners need to agree on (and integrate into their self-concepts) who is really better suited to take control in certain situations. For example, when traveling by car, men and women often argue over directions to locations. (This may be a stereotype, but it's a stereotype many people experience.) Perhaps the man in the relationship believes that it is manly to be able to navigate, to know where one is going, and not to need to ask directions. However, when the couple ends up lost, they may find that the woman may actually be more adept at map-reading and navigating than the man. She may also be more comfortable stopping and asking for directions.

RECAP

Relationship Types Based on Power Dynamics

Relationship Type	Symbols	Explanation
Complementary	↑ ↓	One up, one down; one partner is almost always in power; the other is almost always out of power.
Symmetrical	↑ ↑ ↓ ↓	Both up or both down; partners either compete for power and control or relinquish power.
Parallel	→ ←	Give and take; power alternates between partners, depending on who is better equipped or more adept in certain situations.

complementary relationship
A relationship in which one partner willingly and continuously cedes power to the other.

symmetrical relationship
A relationship characterized by similar control behaviors in partners; partners compete to dominate each other or both relinquish control to the other to avoid making decisions.

parallel relationship
A relationship in which power shifts from one partner to the other.

Conflict May Involve Assertive or Aggressive Communication   Sometimes our emotions cause us to communicate aggressively, when assertive communication would be preferable. You may tend to think of assertive and aggressive communication as being the same thing, but they are actually quite different. The best way to distinguish

Verbal

between the two is this: **Assertive communication** takes the listener's feelings and rights into account; **aggressive communication** does not. Let's say that you experience a mix-up with a close friend over when and where you are supposed to meet. You get your signals crossed and don't end up going out together. When next you see your friend, you have the choice of responding to the frustration over the situation in a passive, assertive, or aggressive manner. You could be passive, say nothing about the mix-up, and simply "go along to get along." While this may sound like an unrealistic response, some people choose not to communicate even when they have been wronged. They are afraid of or unwilling to engage in any form of confrontation, no matter how benign or superficial, with strangers and intimates alike. A passive approach tends merely to internalize frustration, which may build into a destructive rage that at some point is bound to erupt.

Another option is to blow up at your friend. This is an aggressive, self-oriented approach because it does not take into account the rights of the recipient of such communication. Unfortunately, this is the tactic of choice for some people, especially if they have a great deal of anxiety and feel justified taking out their frustrations on others. An aggressive approach rarely achieves one's objectives.

Verbal aggression, also termed verbal abuse, has received much research attention in recent years, in an attempt to better understand the kind of threatening communication tactics persons in conflict occasionally resort to. Communication scholar Dominic Infante and various colleagues launched an interesting body of work on this topic, suggesting that verbal aggression is a form of communication violence because it attacks the heart of a person's being, her or his self-concept.[38] Conflicts that degenerate into verbal aggression can be characterized by insults ("You wouldn't say that if you had half a brain"), ridicule ("You're just too selfish to understand"), merciless teasing with an angry edge to it, character assassination ("You're low class"), and profanity.[39] Typically, the verbally aggressive person claims that the other person is the source or cause of the problem. Rather than focusing on the problem or the issues at hand, the verbally aggressive person shifts the focus to more personal issues.

We can more easily fend off verbal aggression from those who don't matter much to us, but we can be deeply wounded, and the relationship can be permanently damaged, by verbal aggression from someone important to us, whom we care about.[40] Unfortunately, verbally aggressive tactics are used widely in conflicts, according to research. One study surveyed dating partners and found that more than 70% reported using or experiencing some form of verbal aggression in their relational conflicts.[41] When the verbally aggressive tactics were used only occasionally—as lapses into "bad" behavior—partners were able to weather the aggression without much damage to the relationship. However, when the verbal aggression was more frequent, it signalled a relationship in trouble. Another study of verbal aggression among 5000 American college-age couples found that women and men are equally capable of producing verbally aggressive communication when in conflict.[42]

Infante and his associates have developed a measure that determines one's propensity for verbal aggression. However, one interesting finding from his research is that many persons who are deemed "highly verbally aggressive," as determined by the scale, don't characterize their behavior as such. Many believe their verbally aggressive comments in conflict situations to be humorous or benign kidding, not personal attacks that damage their relationships.[43] Research has also determined a connection between verbal aggression and physical aggression or abuse.[44]

Probably all of us, at some time or another, have been in a conflict situation with someone we cared about and we let a big, nasty, old "toad" fly out of our mouths. We probably felt terrible about it—maybe at the moment it flew out, or perhaps later, after we had time to reflect on the damage we'd done. As the research suggests, while it's not advisable or constructive for the relationship, occasional verbal aggression is likely to occur within a meaningful relationship. If you can remember some things you've said to someone that you wish you could take back, then you've had a moment of verbal aggression. But if you find that in a relationship with a romantic partner,

assertive communication
Communication that takes a listener's feelings and rights into account.

aggressive communication
Self-serving communication that does not take a listener's feelings and rights into account.

The best communicators haved learned to solve conflict through the use of assertive rather than aggressive communication.

close friend, family member, or even a coworker, verbally aggressive communication typifies your approach to conflict, then you definitely will want to spend some time thinking about why you tend to behave in an abusive manner. What is it about you—not the other person—that causes your communication to spiral downward and morph into a personal attack?

Clearly, an assertive approach is best—for ourselves and for the people we interact with. It's important to assert yourself and express your perception of a problem to the person who can best correct or clear it up rather than blowing off steam to an innocent bystander or third party. Communicating assertively means that you explain your concerns or cause for disagreement in a direct and firm manner, staying in control of your emotions but not allowing yourself to be bullied or discounted as you take the receiver's rights into account.

An assertive response to the timing mix-up with your friend might be something like this: "Hey, Joe, we were supposed to meet at five o'clock last night at the bowling alley, but you never showed up. What happened?" In this statement, you express your perception of the situation, but ask the person for his or her perception, rather than aggressively saying something in an angry tone that would make the other person defensive, such as, "Why did you leave me hanging when we made definite plans?" If the person offers a lame excuse for not showing up, another assertive follow-up comment might be as follows: "Well, whatever happened, I just want you to know that I don't like being stood up; it's no big deal, but I just hope this doesn't happen again." If you communicate in this manner, you're far more likely to reach a positive resolution to any conflicts than if you behave passively or aggressively, violating the receiver's right to be treated humanely.[45]

Styles of Managing Conflict

Scholars in the communication discipline like to talk about conflict in terms of *management*, meaning that interpersonal communication can help people work through and handle conflict so that something positive results. What's your approach to managing interpersonal conflict: fight or flight? Do you tackle conflict head-on or seek ways to remove yourself from it? Most of us don't have a single way of dealing with disagreements, but we do have a tendency to manage conflict following patterns we learned early in life and have used before.[46] The pattern we choose depends on several factors, including our personality, the individuals with whom we are in conflict, and the time and place of the confrontation.

Researchers have attempted to identify styles of conflict management. One widely accepted approach organizes conflict styles into three types: (1) nonconfrontational; (2) confrontational or controlling; and (3) cooperative (also known as a *solution orientation*).[47]

Aware

Nonconfrontational Style   One approach to managing conflict is to back off, either avoiding the conflict or giving in to the other person. Placating, distracting, computing, withdrawing, and giving in are responses that typify a **nonconfrontational style**.

A *placating* response is an attempt to please; placaters are uncomfortable with negative emotions and may adopt this approach because they fear rejection if they rock the boat. Typically, they seek approval and try to avoid threats to their sense of self-worth. Placaters never seem to get angry, are so controlled that they seem unresponsive to the intensity of the situation, quickly agree with others to avoid conflict, and try to avoid confrontation at all costs.

Another nonconfrontational style is called *distracting*. Distracters attempt to change the subject or make a joke to avoid conflict or stress, rather than face issues di-

nonconfrontational style
A conflict management style that involves backing off, avoiding conflict, or giving in to the other person.

rectly. They hope that eventually the problem will just go away if it can be put off long enough.

A third nonconfrontational style is called *computing.* Computers remove themselves from conflict by remaining aloof and cool. They avoid emotional involvement and refuse to be provoked or ruffled, even under intense pressure. This detachment allows them to avoid expressing genuine feelings about issues and ideas. Instead, they respond to emotional issues with impersonal words and phrases, such as "One would tend to become angry when one's car is dented, wouldn't one?" The computing style is characterized by low empathy and minimal involvement with the issues at hand.

Withdrawing from conflict, either physically or psychologically, is another nonconfrontational approach. "I don't want to talk about it," "It's not my problem," or the one-word "Whatever" are typical responses from someone who uses this style.

"Well, if it doesn't matter who's right and who's wrong, why don't I be right and you be wrong?"

Finally, some people consistently *give in* when faced with conflict. They are so uncomfortable that they surrender before the conflict escalates. Skip hates romantic movies. Yet when his girlfriend wants to rent *Must Love Dogs,* Skip agrees, just to avoid a conflict. A nonconfrontational or avoidant style often leads to a perpetuating conflict cycle that has a chilling or silencing effect on a relationship.[48] In addition, research shows that when conflict arises during problem-solving discussions, people who exhibit a nonconfrontational style of responding to the conflict are perceived as incompetent.[49]

Confrontational Style   Each of us has some need to control others, but some people always want to dominate and make sure that their objectives are achieved. In managing conflict, people with a **confrontational style** have a win–lose philosophy. They want to win at the expense of the other person, to claim victory over their opponents, and to control others. They focus on themselves and usually ignore the needs of others. Confronters often resort to blaming or seeking a scapegoat, rather than assuming responsibility for a conflict. "I didn't do it," "Don't look at me," and "It's not my fault" are typical responses. If this strategy doesn't work, confronters may try hostile name-calling, personal attacks, or threats.

Cooperative Style   Those who have a **cooperative style** of conflict management view conflict as a set of problems to be solved, rather than a competition in which one person wins and another loses. They work to foster a win–win climate by using the following techniques:[50]

- *Separate the people from the problem.* Leave personal grievances out of the discussion. Describe problems without making judgmental statements about personalities.
- *Focus on shared interests.* Emphasize common interests, values, and goals by asking such questions as "What do we both want?" "What do we both value?" "Where do we already agree?"
- *Generate many options to solve the problem.* Use brainstorming and other techniques to generate alternative solutions.
- *Base decisions on objective criteria.* Try to establish standards for an acceptable solution to a problem. These standards may involve cost, timing, and other factors.

confrontational style
A win–lose approach to conflict management in which one person wants control and to win at the expense of the other.

cooperative style
A conflict management style that views conflict as a set of problems to be solved, rather than a competition in which one person wins and another loses.

RECAP

Conflict Management Styles

Nonconfrontational	A person avoids conflict by placating (agreeing), distracting, computing (becoming emotionally detached), withdrawing from conflict, or giving in to another person.
Confrontational	A person wants to manipulate others by blaming and making threats; sets up win–lose framework.
Cooperative	A person seeks mutually agreeable resolutions to manage differences; works within a win–win framework. • Separates people from problems • Focuses on shared interests • Generates many options to solve problems • Bases decisions on objective criteria

Conflict Management Skills

As we saw in the previous section, nonconfrontational and confrontational styles of conflict management do not solve problems effectively, nor do they foster healthy long-term relationships. The skills we review here are those we touched on in our discussion of the cooperative style.[51]

Managing conflict, especially emotionally charged conflict, is not easy. Even with a fully developed set of skills, you should not expect to melt tensions and resolve disagreements instantaneously. The following skills can, however, help you generate options that promote understanding and provide a framework for cooperation.

Manage Emotions   For weeks you have been working on a group project for an important class; your group has a firm deadline that the professor imposed. You submitted your portion of the project to your fellow group members two weeks ago. Today you check in with the group for a progress report and discover that very little has been done. The project is not much further along than when you completed your portion two weeks ago. Your grade is on the line; you feel angry and frustrated. How should you respond? You may be tempted to march into the next group meeting and scream at your classmates. You might consider going to the professor and complaining about what has happened. Our best advice is this: Try to avoid taking action when you are in such an emotional state. You may regret what you say and you will probably escalate the conflict, making the situation worse.

Often the first sign that we are in a conflict situation is a combined feeling of anger, frustration, and fear that sweeps over us. Emotions that are aroused in us during conflict situations are understandable and to be expected. As psychotherapist Jeffrey Rubin explains, "Your feelings are your reality," meaning that the feelings conflict generates are real and should not be ignored.[52] In actuality, anger is not the predominant emotion generated by conflict. Many of us are unprepared for the aching, lonely, sad, and forlorn feelings that can emerge in conflict.[53] As tall an order as it is, it's important to try to understand the other person's feelings and to take the emotion of the situation seriously.

Expressing our feelings in an emotional outburst may make us feel better for the moment, but it also may exacerbate the situation and close the door to negotiation. Until we can tone down (not eliminate) and channel our emotions, we'll find it difficult to use appropriate communication skills to resolve conflict. Here are some specific strategies that you can draw on when an intense emotional response to conflict clouds your judgment and decision-making skills.[54]

- *Select a mutually acceptable time and place to discuss a conflict.* If you're upset or tired, you're at risk for an emotion-charged confrontation. If you ambush someone with an angry attack, you can't expect her or him to be in a productive frame of mind. Give yourself time to cool off before you try to resolve a conflict. In the case of the group project, you could call a meeting for later in the week. By that time, you could gain control of your feelings and think things through. Of course, sometimes issues need to be discussed on the spot; you may not have the luxury of waiting. But whenever it's practical, make sure your conflict partner is ready to receive you and your message and that you are prepared to present the message in a nonthreatening way.
- *Plan your message.* If you approach someone to discuss a disagreement, take care to organize your message, even if that means organizing ideas on paper. Identify your goal and determine what outcome you would like; don't barge in unprepared and dump your emotions on the other person. You might also consider sounding things out with a trusted friend or colleague first, to check your perceptions and to help clarify the issues in the conflict.
- *Monitor nonverbal messages.* Your nonverbal communication plays a key role in establishing an emotional climate. Monitor nonverbal messages—your own and those of others—to help defuse an emotionally charged situation. Speak calmly, use direct eye contact, and maintain a calm facial expression and body position to signal that you wish to collaborate rather than control. Try also to place yourself on the same level as other people involved in the conflict. Standing while others sit, for example, can serve as a power cue and an impediment to resolving conflict.
- *Avoid personal attacks, name-calling, profanity, and emotional overstatement.* Threats and derogatory language can turn a small conflict into an all-out war. When people feel attacked, they usually respond by becoming defensive in an effort to protect themselves. It's also important to avoid exaggerating your emotions. If you say you are irritated or annoyed rather than furious, you can still communicate your feelings, but you will take the sting out of your description. Avoid the bad habit of gunny-sacking—dredging up old problems and issues from the past (like pulling them out of an old bag or gunny sack) to use against your partner. Gunny-sacking usually succeeds only in increasing tension, escalating emotions, and reducing listening effectiveness. It's more helpful to keep everyone's focus on the issues at hand, not on old hurts from the past.
- *Use self-talk.* Back to the problem of the group project: At the next meeting, what if a member lashes out at you, suggesting that you're a big part of the problem? Instead of lashing back at that person, the best advice would be to pause, take a slow, deep breath, and say to yourself, "I could get really mad, but that won't make things better. I'll respond calmly and coolly, so we keep the problem in proportion." You may think that talking to yourself is an eccentricity, but nothing could be further from the truth. Thoughts are directly linked to feelings; the messages we tell ourselves play a major role in how we feel and respond to others.[55]

Verbal

Nonverbal

Aware

Manage Information   Because uncertainty, misinformation, and misunderstanding are often byproducts of conflict and disagreement, skills that promote mutual understanding are important components of cooperative conflict management. The following skills can help you reduce uncertainty and enhance the quality of communication during conflict.

Verbal

Listen and Respond

Aware

Aware

- *Clearly describe the conflict-producing events.* Instead of blurting out complaints in random order, try to deliver a brief, well-organized presentation. Public speaking teachers recommend that, for certain speech topics, you describe events in chronological order. The same technique works well when describing a conflict. In our example of the group project situation, you could offer your perspective on what created the conflict, sequencing the events and describing them dispassionately so that your fellow group members end up sharing your understanding of the problem.

- *"Own" your statements by using descriptive "I" language.* In Chapter 3, we described the use of "I" language instead of "you" language in order to create a supportive climate. The same applies in conflict. "I feel upset when it seems like little is getting done and we're running the risk of not making our deadline." This is an example of an "I" statement that you could say to your group members. The statement describes your feelings as your own and keeps the issue manageable. Saying "You guys aren't pulling your weight and you're gonna blow our deadline" has an accusatory sting that will likely make members defensive, escalating the conflict. Also notice that, in the second statement, you don't take any responsibility for the problem but suggest that it belongs to several other people. This "ganging-up" approach almost always heightens people's defensiveness.

- *Use effective listening skills.* Managing information is a two-way process. Whether you are describing a conflict situation to someone or that individual is bringing a conflict to your attention, good listening skills are invaluable. Give your full attention to the speaker and make a conscious point of tuning out your internal messages. Sometimes the best thing to do after describing the conflict-producing events is simply to wait for a response. If you don't stop talking and give the other person a chance to respond, he or she will feel frustrated, the emotional pitch will go up a notch, and it will become more difficult to reach an understanding. Finally, not only should you focus on the facts or details, you should also analyze them so you can understand the major points the speaker makes. As Stephen Covey suggests in his book *The Seven Habits of Highly Effective People,* it is wise to "seek to understand rather than to be understood."[56]

- *Check your understanding of what others say and do.* Checking perceptions is vital when emotions run high. If you are genuinely unsure about facts, issues, or major ideas addressed during a conflict, ask questions to help you sort through them instead of barreling ahead with solutions. Then summarize your understanding of the information; don't parrot the speaker's words or paraphrase every statement, but check key points to ensure that you comprehend the message. Your response and that of your conflict partner will confirm that you understand each other.

Manage Goals   As we have seen, conflict is goal driven. Both individuals involved in an interpersonal conflict want something. And, for some reason—competitiveness, scarce resources, or lack of understanding—the goals appear to be in conflict. To manage conflict, it is important to seek an accurate understanding of these goals and to identify where they overlap. Here are a couple of techniques to help you accomplish just that.

- *Identify your goal and your partner's goal.* After you describe, listen, and respond, your next task should be to identify what you would like to have happen. What is your goal? Most goal statements can be phrased in terms of wants or desires. Continuing with the group project example, you express to your fellow group members your goal of turning the project in on time. Next, it's useful to identify the goals of other people involved in the conflict. Use effective describing, listening, and responding skills to determine what each conflict partner wants. Obviously, if goals are kept hidden, it will be difficult to resolve the conflict.

- *Identify where your goals and your partner's goals overlap.* Authorities on conflict negotiation stress the importance of focusing on shared interests when seeking to manage differences.[57] Armed with an understanding of what you want and what your partner wants, you can then determine whether the goals overlap. Suppose that after you explain your goal about the project deadline, another group member states that her or his goal is to make the project the best it possibly can be. These goals may be compatible, so you've identified a commonality that can help unify the group, rather than keep it splintered. But what if that goal of making the project the best means that your group will have to ask the professor for an extension on the deadline? Now you may have competing goals. But at least you've identified a central part of the problem. Framing the problem as "how can we achieve our mutual goal" rather than arguing over differences of opinion moves the discussion to a more productive level.

Listen and Respond

Adapt

Manage the Problem   If you can view conflicts as problems to be solved rather than battles to be won or lost, you will better manage the issues that confront you in your relationships with others. Of course, not all conflicts can be easily managed and resolved. But using a rational, logical approach to conflict management is more effective than emotionally flinging accusations and opinions at someone. Structuring a disagreement as a problem to solve helps manage emotions that often erupt; a problem-solving orientation to conflict also helps keep the conversation focused on issues rather than personalities. Once conflict becomes personal, people become defensive and emotions flare.

In the chapters ahead we suggest that the groups and teams that function most effectively use a structured approach to solving problems; ideas shouldn't just tumble over one another. A logical, organized approach usually works best when trying to solve vexing problems.

The problem-solving process is one you may have used in managing problems that have come your way. The approach is relatively simple: Define the problem, analyze the problem, generate possible solutions, evaluate the pros and cons of the solutions under consideration, and then select the solution that is agreeable to all concerned. The best solution is one that meets the goals of the persons involved in the conflict. As you apply the problem-solving approach to managing conflict, consider the following suggestions:

- *Resist developing solutions to manage the conflict until you and the other person fully understand the precise nature of the problem as well as each other's goals.* When there is a problem to be solved, we typically want to head directly for solutions. Resist that temptation. Before blurting out solutions, realize that you're more likely to reach agreement on the solution to a problem if you each understand the specific issues that trigger the problem.
- *The more possible solutions you identify and consider, the greater the likelihood that the conflict will be managed successfully.* If you're just batting around one or two solutions, you're limiting your options in managing the conflict. Rather than making the conflict a tug of war with only two ends of the rope pulling against each other, consider multiple creative strategies for achieving what you both want. Many people find it helps to make a written list of many possible ways to achieve each other's goals. The more options you discuss, the more likely it is that the two of you will find common ground.
- *Systematically discuss the pros and the cons of the possible solutions together.* After you have a list of possible solutions, honestly identify advantages and disadvantages of each solution. How do you know which is the best solution? If you discussed the

goals that each of you seek to achieve, you are well on your way to developing a vision of the future that can help you sort out the advantages and disadvantages of the potential solutions you're considering. Determine which solution, or combination of solutions, best achieves the goals you and your feuding partner are trying to accomplish.

We emphasize again that there are no sure-fire techniques that will manage or resolve the interpersonal conflicts that will inevitably occur even in the best of relationships. In reality, you don't simply manage your emotions and then march easily on to coolly communicate your ideas, followed by neatly sorting out goals and then rationally solving the problem that created the conflict. Conflict management is messier than this step-by-step process suggests. You may, for example, first try to manage your emotions, then communicate your ideas and feelings, only to find you need to go back and again manage your emotions. You are more than likely to bounce forward and backward from one step to another.

Our suggestions for managing emotions, information, goals, and the problem will not eliminate conflict from your life. Turning conflicts into problems to solve and seeking mutually agreeable solutions may, however, provide the necessary structure to help you manage conflict constructively.

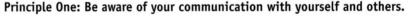

PRINCIPLES FOR A LIFETIME: Enhancing Your Skills

Aware

Principle One: Be aware of your communication with yourself and others.
- Know your own interests, likes, and dislikes as you expand your circle of friends.
- Awareness and an understanding of self begin in your family as you grow up.
- Perception checking with colleagues increases your awareness of yourself and your workplace.
- The first stage of relational escalation, the pre-interaction awareness stage, begins with an awareness of the self and the other person to whom you are attracted.
- Even after relationships terminate, they still have an effect on our self-concept; be aware of the effect of relationships (even failed ones) on your view of yourself.
- It's important to know your conflict management style, especially if your style is different from that of other people involved in the conflict.
- Self-talk is appropriate in conflict, because it can help you manage your emotions and think clearly.
- Check your perceptions of a conflict with trusted others.
- Be aware of your own goals, as well as the goals of others, in conflict situations.

Principle Two: Effectively use and interpret verbal messages.
- Language patterns we learn as children in our families stay with us into adulthood.
- Persons in advanced stages of relationships tend to use verbal communication to discuss topics that typically are not discussed in early stages.
- Assertive communication takes the receiver's rights into account; aggressive communication does not.
- The management of the verbal expression of your emotions in conflict situations is an important skill.
- Plan your message carefully in a conflict situation.
- Avoid personal attacks, name-calling, profanity, and emotional overstatements in conflict situations.
- Use "I" language instead of "you" language in a conflict, so as to lessen defensiveness.

Verbal

Nonverbal

Principle Three: Effectively use and interpret nonverbal messages.

- Nonverbal immediacy behaviors, such as eye contact and forward body lean, are important in the maintenance of friendships, family relationships, and workplace relationships.
- Persons in advanced stages of relationships tend to display nonverbal behaviors that typically are not in evidence in early stages.
- Nonverbal skills are important in your first conversations with people, as you attempt to establish and escalate relationships.
- Nonverbal immediacy cues diminish when a relationship is in de-escalation.
- Monitor and adapt your nonverbal behaviors in conflict situations.
- Monitor the nonverbal behaviors of other persons involved in your disagreement.

Listen and Respond

Principle Four: Listen and respond thoughtfully to others.

- Listening is important in friendships, family relationships, and workplace relationships.
- Listening and responding appropriately are key skills potential employers value.
- Destructive conflict is characterized by a lack of listening.
- Conflict often escalates because the parties don't listen to one another; continue to listen, even if you feel yourself becoming emotional in the conflict.

Adapt

Principle Five: Appropriately adapt messages to others.

- It's important to learn to adapt our communication in friendships, family relationships, and workplace relationships.
- In conflict situations, partners often have to adapt to one another and admit that they were wrong. Destructive conflict often involves a reluctance to adapt to the other person and see the problem from her or his point of view.
- Be flexible and adapt to other cultures' approaches to conflict; don't assume that your home culture's approach to conflict management is applicable in conflicts with members of other cultural groups.
- After checking your perceptions of a conflict with trusted others, adapt your communication accordingly.
- One way to adapt in a conflict is to look for overlaps between your goals and the goals of your conflict partner.

SUMMARY

In this chapter we focused on interpersonal communication that enhances relationships and discussed three types of relationships that have tremendous impact on our lives: friendships, family relationships, and workplace relationships. We reviewed the five communication principles for a lifetime in light of each of these three forms of important relationships.

Most relationships develop in stages that are characterized by the type and presence (or absence) of interpersonal communication. Once relationships are initiated, they begin to escalate if the partners want the relationship to develop and become more intimate. Relationships also de-escalate as they move away from intimacy.

Conflict is a significant element within interpersonal relationships. The chapter distinguished between constructive and destructive conflict in relationships and explored six building blocks of constructive conflict. Power and control create patterns that can lead to harmony or strife in relationships. We also contrasted assertive communication (which takes receivers' rights into account) with aggressive communication (which ignores the rights of receivers). We examined three conflict management styles—nonconfrontational, confrontational, and cooperative—and discussed the forms of communication that characterize these styles. In a final section on conflict management skills, we suggested that you view conflicts as manageable events rather than as personal battles. We also offered suggestions for effective ways to manage emotions, information, goals, and problems, so that the resolution of conflict can actually make your relationships stronger.

Discussion and Review

1. How does interpersonal communication facilitate the development of friendships? family relationships? workplace relationships?
2. What are the five stages of relational escalation? Do relationships necessarily have to go through each of the stages in order? What are the five stages of relational de-escalation? How do you prefer a relationship to end?
3. Define interpersonal conflict; provide examples of constructive and destructive conflicts.
4. A common issue faced by couples concerns shared activities, meaning who decides what the couple will and will not do together. How would a couple who have a complementary relationship (in terms of power) approach this issue? a symmetrical relationship? a parallel relationship?
5. What is the difference between assertive communication and aggressive communication? Provide an example of an aggressive response to someone's communication; then demonstrate how an assertive response would be preferable in the example.
6. What characterizes nonconfrontational, confrontational, and cooperative styles of conflict management?

Putting Principles into Practice

1. Think about your best friend, your closest family member, and a colleague (or classmate) with whom you feel close. Put the names of these three individuals across the top of a sheet of paper, forming columns down the page. Next, indicate in each column which forms of communication are most critical to the maintenance of each of these relationships. Finally, look for skills that appear in more than one column.

2. Work with a small group of classmates. Have each person think of a relationship—a friendship or romance—that has undergone the process of relational escalation and de-escalation. Discuss these processes and listen for commonalities in classmates' experiences. How did the quality of people's interpersonal communication move the relationship through the stages?

3. Sometimes it's hard to discern the difference between assertive and aggressive communication. To gain some practice, consider the following situations. For each one, first generate aggressive and inappropriate communication. Then rethink the situation and generate an assertive form of communication that would be more effective. We've provided an example to get you started.

Situation: You are expecting a raise at work but find out that another coworker, who has less time on the job than you, received a raise and you did not.

Aggressive Communication: You interrupt a staff meeting that your boss is holding, storm about the room and demand an explanation of why you did not receive the expected raise.

Assertive Communication: You make an appointment with your boss for a meeting outside the office. At the meeting, you calmly ask the boss to assess your value to the company, leading up to the question of why you did not receive the expected raise.

Situation: Two people have been in a monogamous dating relationship for several months, when one partner finds out that the other person has cheated.

Situation: A student receives a disappointing grade on a paper. After reading the papers of a few fellow classmates and finding that lesser quality papers received higher grades, the student decides to confront the teacher about the grade.

4. Generate an example of a common source of conflict for romantic couples. Then brainstorm ways that persons with nonconfrontational, confrontational, and cooperative styles of conflict management might approach the situation.

CHAPTER Nine

Patricia Ossa, "Citizens," © SuperStock, Inc.

The best way to have a good idea is to have a lot of ideas.

Linus Pauling

Understanding Group and Team Performance

CHAPTER OUTLINE

Groups and Teams Defined

Understanding Types of Groups and Teams

Understanding Group and Team Dynamics

Understanding Phases of Group and Team Development

Summary

CHAPTER OBJECTIVES

After studying this chapter, you should be able to:

1. Define and note similarities and differences between a group and a team.

2. Identify and describe types of small groups.

3. Identify and appropriately perform task and social roles in groups and teams.

4. Avoid performing individual roles in a group.

5. Describe group rules and norms.

6. Define and differentiate between status and power.

7. List strategies to enhance group cohesiveness.

8. Recognize group and team interaction patterns.

9. Identify the four stages of group development.

Do you like working with others in groups? Although you may be one of those people who relish working on team projects and going to meetings, many people don't like collaborating with others. Here are some typical sentiments people sometimes have about working in groups:

> To be effective, a committee should be made up of three persons. But to get anything done, one member should be sick and another absent.
>
> A committee is a group of people who individually can do nothing and who collectively decide nothing can be done.
>
> A group task force is a collection of the unfit chosen from the unwilling by the incompetent to do the unnecessary.

Whether you are one of those people who like group work or one who finds it frustrating and a waste of time, the evidence suggests that groups are here to stay. Human beings collaborate. We are raised in groups, educated in groups, worship in groups, entertained in groups, and work in groups. Today's technology makes it easier for us to collaborate in teams, even when we're not meeting face to face. There is evidence that most of you reading this book will spend about one-third of your time on the job working in groups or teams and attending meetings or preparing for meetings.[1] And if you aspire to upper-management leadership positions, you'll spend up to two-thirds of your time in meetings.[2] Your work will be based on that kindergarten skill called "getting along with others."

To help you with the inevitable group and team projects that will come your way, this chapter offers descriptions of how groups and teams work. In the next chapter, we'll offer specific strategies for improving group and team performance. As we examine concepts and strategies of group skills and theories, we'll remind you how the core of group communication research can be discussed in terms of the five principles we've used to frame our presentation of human communication:

Aware
Verbal
Nonverbal
Listen and Respond
Adapt

1. *Be aware of your communication with yourself and others.* Your awareness of your own behavior and the behavior of other group members is often the first step in understanding why you and other group members behave as you do and adjusting your behavior for improved group performance.
2. *Effectively use and interpret verbal messages.* The verbal messages you and other group members use are pivotal in shaping the roles you assume and how the group accomplishes its work.
3. *Effectively use and interpret nonverbal messages.* The social climate of a group is influenced by the way group members behave nonverbally; eye contact, tone of voice, facial expression, and the use of space and time influence what it feels like to be in a group.
4. *Listen and respond thoughtfully to others.* The quintessential skill of listening and responding to others is vital for an effectively functioning group; how group members interact (or don't interact) is directly shaped by group members' skill in listening and responding to what others say and do.[3]
5. *Appropriately adapt messages to others.* The ability to modify messages and adjust to the behavior of others is especially important when communicating with three or more people in a small group.

GROUPS AND TEAMS DEFINED

What makes a group a group? Is a collection of people waiting for an elevator a group? How about students assigned to a class project—do they meet the technical definition of a group? And what about the term *team*? Teams are often viewed as a management innovation that can improve both productivity and morale. Is there a difference between a group and a team? By exploring these questions, you can better understand

Many important workplace decisions are made within small groups of coworkers.

what groups and teams do and develop strategies for improving group and team performance.

Communicating in Small Groups

A **small group** consists of three to fifteen people who share a common purpose, who feel a sense of belonging to the group, and who exert influence on one another.[4] Let's look at this definition more closely.

A Group Consists of a Small Number of People   How many people does it take to be a group? We suggest at least three people. Two people do not usually exhibit the characteristics of group behavior that we will present later in this chapter, such as the formation of group member roles and norms. If a group becomes too large, it typically operates as a collection of sub-groups rather than as a single body. When more than fifteen people meet together, it is difficult for all members to participate; usually, when the group gets so big that it is impractical to give everyone a chance to talk, a few people monopolize the discussion. Large groups need formal rules, such as parliamentary procedure, to provide structure that will help the group stay focused on the task at hand.

A Group Has a Common Purpose   In order to be a group, people need to be united by a common goal or purpose. They must all seek the same thing. A collection of people waiting for an elevator may all want to go somewhere, but they probably haven't organized their efforts so they are going the same place. If you are assigned to a class project by an instructor, your classmates do have a common goal—to complete the project and earn a good grade. This class-project group would meet our definition of a group.

Group Members Feel a Sense of Belonging   In order to be a group, the members must realize that they are part of the group. Again, people waiting for the elevator doors to open probably do not feel an obligation to others around them. Group members develop a sense of identity with their group. They know that they are in the group and who is not in the group.

Group Members Exert Influence on Others in the Group   When you are in a group, your presence and participation influence other people in the group. Group

small group
Three to fifteen people who share a common purpose, feel a sense of belonging to the group, and exert influence on one another.

On the Web

Teams are becoming an integral part of today's workforce. How to become an efficient, productive team is among the most popular training seminars presented to U.S. workers. The following site offers additional information about the nature and function of teams and links to other sites that provide interesting information about the power of teamwork:
www.workteams.unt.edu

members are interdependent; what one group member says or does affects other group members. Your comments and even your silence help shape what the group does next. Your nonverbal messages have a powerful effect on personal relationships. Each member of a group potentially has some influence on others. Even silence, facial expressions, and eye contact (or lack of it) affect what the group does.

Small group communication is the transactive process of creating meaning among three to fifteen people who share a common purpose, who feel a sense of belonging to the group, and who exert influence on each other. Communicating in small groups is sometimes a challenge because of the potential for misunderstanding. But don't assume that working in a group will inevitably be a frustrating experience. People accomplish much when working together. It was anthropologist Margaret Mead who said, "Never doubt that a small group of concerned citizens can change the world. Indeed, it's the only thing that ever has." In this chapter and the next chapter, we'll provide concepts and strategies to enhance the quality of your collaborations with others.

Communicating in Teams

Most of us have participated on a sports team at some time. The goal of a sports team is usually to win the game or competition. A work team has some of the same characteristics as a sports team.[5] Instead of winning the game, the goal may be to get the contract, build the best mousetrap, or achieve some other objective. A **team** is a coordinated group of people organized to work together to achieve a specific, common goal.[6]

Often the terms *team* and *group* are used interchangeably. Is there a difference? Yes. Given the increased importance teams have in the workforce today, it's important to know precisely how groups and teams are different from each other. Although both groups and teams are made up of a small number of people who work to achieve a goal, teams are often structured deliberately to achieve the goal. Also, teams spend a great deal of time coordinating their efforts to accomplish the goal.[7] Every team is a group, but not every group is highly organized or coordinated enough to meet the definition of a team. Let's consider several specific characteristics of teams.

Teams Develop Clearly Defined Responsibilities for Team Members   On a sports team, most team members have specifically assigned duties, such as shortstop, pitcher, quarterback, or fullback. On a work team, team members' duties and roles are usually explicitly spelled out. Team members may perform more than one function or role, but they nonetheless have well-defined duties.[8]

Teams Have Clearly Defined Rules for Team Operation   Team members develop explicit rules for how the work should be done. A rule is a followable prescription for acceptable behavior.[9] Just as there are written rules in the game of Monopoly, there are usually explicit rules for how a team will function. For example, a team may establish a rule that a member who will be absent from a meeting must tell another team member beforehand. Team members know what the rules are and know how those rules affect the team.

Teams Develop Clear Goals   A third way to characterize a team is to look at the importance and specificity of the team goal.[10] A team goal is usually stated in such a way that the goal can be measured: to win the game, to sell more cornflakes than the competition, or to get to the North Pole before anyone else, for example.

Teams Develop a Way of Coordinating Their Efforts   Team members spend time discussing how to accomplish the goals of the team. Their work is coordinated to avoid

small group communication
The transactive process of creating meaning among three to fifteen people who share a common purpose, feel a sense of belonging to the group, and exert influence on each other.

team
A coordinated group of people organized to work together to achieve a specific common goal.

duplication of effort. A sports team spends considerable time practicing how to work together. Watching a sports team at work is like watching a choreographed dance. Team members have developed a system of working together rather than at cross-purposes. Just as a football team develops a list of the plays to get the ball down the field, a work team develops collaborative strategies to achieve its goal.

Although we have differentiated between groups and teams, don't get the idea that they are completely exclusive entities. Both groups and teams are made up of a small number of people striving to achieve a goal. Since every team is a small group, whenever we refer to a team, we are also suggesting that it's a group as well. Think of groups and teams as existing on a continuum; some deliberations will make the people seem more like a group, whereas other behavior—a more coordinated and structured process, with clear rules and explicit goals—will make the people appear to be a team.

Characteristics of Effective Team Members   Now that you understand what a team is, you may still wonder, "But what do effective team members do?" Several communication researchers have sought to answer that question by asking seasoned team members what they consider to be the characteristics of an excellent team. Here's what they found.[11]

1. *Experience.* Effective team members have "been there, done that." They have practical experience in collaborating with others. More experienced team members were better able to see the big picture; less experienced members tended to lack the technical background needed to be successful at their collaborative work.

2. *Problem-Solving Ability.* Team members who were effective were perceived as decisive. It wasn't just that they made quick decisions; they carefully analyzed information and issues while staying focused on the problem. Their ability to examine a problematic situation and select effective strategies for managing it set skilled team members apart from less skilled collaborators.

3. *Openness.* Have you ever worked in a team and found one or more members not willing to express ideas and opinions honestly, yet tactfully? Communication researchers Frank LaFasto and Carl Larson found that openness was an essential characteristic for team success. Effective team members were willing to discuss delicate and sensitive issues and topics in an appropriate way that didn't make people defensive. Team members who were more secretive and participated less were perceived as less important to team success.

4. *Supportiveness.* Supportive team members listened to others. They didn't just stand by and watch someone else work; they found out what needed to be done, then pitched in and did it. Nonsupportive team members tended to focus on their individual agendas, rather than being aware of the needs of the team as a whole.

5. *Action Oriented.* "Just do it!" That advertising slogan sold lots of tennis shoes for a sports equipment company. It's also a good motto for effective team members. Ineffective team members hung back and watched others do the work.

6. *Positive Personal Style.* There's the story about a boy who awoke on the morning of his birthday to find only a large pile of manure where he'd hoped to find birthday presents. But undaunted, he smiled and said, "With this much horse manure, there's got to be a pony here somewhere!" Effective team members were optimistic. Even in bad times, they found something to be positive about. Their encouraging, patient, enthusiastic, and friendly attitude contributed to their being well-liked by other team members. Here's how to be perceived as an ineffective team member: Argue with others frequently, be intolerant and impatient, and cultivate skills that will help you win the "pain-in-the-neck" award.

7. *Positive Overall Team Perceptions.* Effective teams and effective team members believed they were effective; they were optimistic that they had the skills and resources to accomplish their task.[12] Teams that were less effective thought they were less effective. Was the team effective because of a self-fulfilling prophecy (just expecting to be effective caused the team to act effectively)? Or did team members

Listen and Respond

think they were effective because they really were top notch? We're not quite sure what the precise cause-and-effect relationship is between self-perceptions of being effective and actually being effective. But it does appear that teams that have a positive, can-do attitude will perform better than those teams whose members have doubts, worries, and uncertainties about whether they will get the job done. The bottom line: Optimism enhances effectiveness.

RECAP

Comparing Groups and Teams

	Groups	Teams
Roles and Responsibilities	Individual responsibilities of group members may not always be explicitly defined.	Expectations, roles, and responsibilities of team members are clearly developed and discussed.
Rules	Rules are often not written down or formally developed; rules evolve, depending on the group's needs.	Rules and operating procedures are clearly identified to help the team work efficiently and effectively.
Goals	Group goals may be discussed in general terms.	Clearly spelled out goals are the focus of what the team does.
Methods	Group members may or may not decide to divide the work among group members.	Team members develop clear methods of collaborating and coordinating their efforts to achieve the team goal.

UNDERSTANDING TYPES OF GROUPS AND TEAMS

Groups and teams are formed for a variety of reasons. The type of group is determined by its purpose. The following group descriptions focus on the different goals or purposes of groups.

Primary Groups

A **primary group** exists to fulfill the basic human need for associations with others. One of the best examples of a primary group is your family. While some families may have a family business or have other goals, in most family discussions, one person does not whip out an agenda while the rest of the group follows a process to achieve a specific outcome. As in other primary groups, family communication is informal. People talk just because they are together.

Study Groups

As a college student, you probably don't need this type of group defined for you. A **study group** meets to learn new ideas. Learning theory suggests you are more likely

primary group
A group, such as a family, that exists to fulfill basic human needs.

study group
A group that exists to help group members learn new information and ideas.

Ethics and Communication

Ethically Achieving a Team Goal

Teams have a strong sense of purpose and a well-structured, clear, coordinated plan to achieve the goals of the team. Without a clear goal, teams falter. But sometimes you may be part of a team whose goal or means of achieving the goal you don't support. Suppose, for example, you are a valued and skilled member of a soccer team that has a "win at all costs" mentality. The team wants to win so badly that team members bend some of the rules to enhance their chance of winning: They knowingly allow someone to play who, because of poor grades, is not eligible. Team members let the person play because the person's skill will increase the team's chances of winning. You're the only person who seems concerned about the rule violation. What would you do? Would you continue to participate on the team and not let the other members of the team down, even though permitting an illegal player to participate violates your own ethical standards? Do the ends justify the means? Is winning more important than following the rules?

Here's another example: What if it's not a sports team but a work group? Assume you're a salesperson and part of a sales team; to get a raise in salary, everyone in the team has to meet the sales goal assigned to the team. One team member consistently lies to customers about the company's product to get a sale; that team member's sales success helps make the whole team look good in terms of sales, but look bad in terms of

ethics. What would you do? Would you keep quiet and enjoy the benefits of being part of a "successful" sales team? Or would you bring the unethical behavior of your team member to the attention of your supervisor, even though it would place your other team members in jeopardy for knowingly "going along to get along"? Are team goals more important than individual ethical standards?

to learn when you actively participate in the learning process. Students sometimes form study groups because they know that by participating in the give and take of a discussion, they'll be more likely to remember what is discussed. Teachers, too, often assign students to groups as a means of accomplishing what is called *collaborative learning*. Assigning students to small groups and inviting participation is a time-proven strategy to help students learn. Such groups are also training grounds for the groups and teams students will participate in during their careers.

Therapy Groups

Therapy is treatment designed to solve a personal concern or problem or to resolve an issue. A **therapy group** exists to provide treatment for the personal problems that group members may have. Weight Watchers, Alcoholics Anonymous, and Gamblers Anonymous are examples of therapy groups. People gain insight by being in a group with others who have similar needs. Also, the feedback people receive from the therapy group leader and other group members is an important part of the treatment. We learn about ourselves from the perceptions of others.

therapy group
A group that provides treatment for problems that group members may have.

Problem-Solving Groups

A **problem-solving group** exists to resolve an issue or overcome an unsatisfactory situation or obstacle and achieve a goal. Problem-solving groups are the most common type of groups in businesses and other organizations. In business, the problem a group

problem-solving group
A group that meets to seek a solution to a problem.

Technology *and* Communication

Does Virtual Group Communication Improve Decision Making?

The chances are increasing that you will work in a **virtual group or team**—a group or team that doesn't meet face to face but is instead connected via some electronic channel such as a telephone, the Internet, or a video conference. A growing body of research notes advantages and disadvantages of working in virtual groups and teams. Here are some key research conclusions about virtual group and team communication:[13]

- During computer-mediated meetings, ideas can be recorded quickly and accurately.
- Electronically mediated communication seems to work best for more structured, linear tasks.
- The increased speed of information transfer in a virtual communication context allows less time for reflection. Thus, technology may sometimes help us make mistakes faster.

Although there are some clear advantages of using virtual groups, such as the saving of travel time and the expense of meeting face to face, the use of technology does not inherently result in better solutions and decisions. Problems are solved and decisions are made by people. Technology may allow greater access to accurate information, help structure the process, and keep a group focused on essential facts, but decisions will continue to be made by people skilled in the art and science of making decisions and solving problems.

So what is the answer to our question? Does virtual group communication improve decision making? The answer is both "yes" and "no." Yes it can, because the technology can help track ideas, connect people from long distances who might not be able to participate in the decision-making process otherwise, and structure the conversation. But no, the use of technology does not replace the intellectual energy exerted by human beings. People, not machines, need to make sense out of the information, turn information into communication, and then develop creative options.

---

focuses on often is "How can we overcome an obstacle to make more money?" A problem-solving group or team in a hospital or health clinic will focus on ways to make people healthy. Most problems boil down to something you want more of or less of. The problem-solving group goal is often to figure out how to get more or less of something (time, money, help from others) in order to achieve the goal of the group or organization.

Focus Groups

virtual group or team
A group or team whose members are not together in the same physical location but who are typically connected via an electronic channel such as the Internet, a telephone, or a video conference.

focus group
A group that is asked to discuss a particular topic or issue so that others can better understand how the group members respond to the topics or issues presented to them.

social group
A group that exists to provide opportunities for group members to enjoy the company of others.

A **focus group** is a small group of people who are asked to discuss a particular topic or issue so that others can better understand how these group members respond to the topics or issues presented. One person usually acts as the moderator or facilitator and asks open-ended questions and then gives group members a chance to share their views on the issues at hand. Many advertising agencies will present a new advertising campaign to a focus group and then listen to the responses of the group members to assess the impact or effectiveness of the campaign. Before launching a new kind of potato chip, a snack company may use reactions from a focus group to guide them in marketing the new product. Politicians often use focus groups to determine the effectiveness of a political strategy or new policy. In some ways, a focus-group discussion is like a group interview. The purpose is to listen to group members' ideas about and responses to whatever is being discussed.

Social Groups

Some groups exist just for the joy of socializing with others. Such a group is a **social group**. Travel groups, dinner clubs, or music groups are often formed because group members enjoy the fellowship of interacting and meeting with others. They also like the activity that the group supports. In most cases, people could still do the activity (eat, travel, play music) without a group—but a group makes the experience more enjoyable.

A therapy group can be more effective than an individual therapy session for treating many personal problems.

UNDERSTANDING GROUP AND TEAM DYNAMICS

Groups and teams are dynamic; their structure changes. Those dynamic or changing factors that fuel the energy for groups to achieve goals include how group members interact with and relate to one another. The study of group dynamics includes a discussion of the roles, norms, status, power, and cohesiveness of groups. We'll examine each concept and note how it is related to the five principles of communication.

Roles

How you communicate with others in a group is a function of your role. Your **role** is the consistent way you communicate with others in a group. It is based on your expectations of yourself and the expectations others place on you. Do you often become a leader of a group, or are you more comfortable just blending in and taking directions from others? Or are you the one who makes sure the group gets the work done instead of just having a good time? And then there are those group members who seem especially gifted at smoothing conflict and disagreement. Or perhaps there is no typical pattern to what you do in a group; your role depends on the group and who else is in it.

There are three classic categories of group roles. **Task roles** are behaviors that help the group achieve its goal and accomplish its work; gathering and sharing research conclusions with the group, taking minutes of meetings, or writing ideas on a chalkboard are examples of task-role behaviors.

Social roles focus on behavior that manages relationships and affects the group climate; these roles help resolve conflict and enhance the flow of communication. Smoothing hurt feelings and helping the group celebrate its accomplishments are examples of social-role behavior.

Finally, **individual roles** focus attention on the individual rather than the group. These are roles that do *not* help the group; they emphasize individual accomplishments and issues rather than those of the entire group. Dominating group discussions to talk about personal issues or concerns, telling frequent jokes that routinely get the group off

role
The consistent way a person communicates with others in a small group.

task role
A role that helps a group achieve its goal and accomplish its work.

social role
A role that helps the group manage relationships and affects the group climate.

individual role
A role that focuses attention on the individual rather than on the group.

Aware
Verbal
Nonverbal
Listen and Respond
Adapt

track, and constantly complaining or whining about how one's individual needs aren't being met are examples of individual roles.

All five of the communication principles we've presented throughout the book are involved in influencing whether the role you assume from moment to moment in a group is primarily about the task, relationship maintenance, or individual concerns. Effective group members are aware of the roles they are assuming, rather than oblivious to how their communication affects the groups. The role behavior is communicated by the verbal and nonverbal messages expressed. Roles are not static. We adjust our behavior by listening and responding to other group members and then adapting our behavior accordingly.

Nearly 60 years ago, Kenneth Benne and Paul Sheats identified a list of group roles that remains a classic way of dividing up the group and individual roles that group and team members typically assume.[14] Table 9.1 presents a summary of these roles. As you review the list of roles and their descriptions, note whether you usually assume roles in the task, social, or individual category. Or perhaps you'll see yourself in a variety of roles in all three categories.

Adapt

As you look at the list of roles in Table 9.1, you may think, "Yes, that's what I usually do. That's the role I usually take." You can probably see roles that fit other group members. Most group members don't assume only one or two roles during group meetings. Most of us assume several roles when we interact in a group. A role is worked out jointly between us and the group, and the roles we assume change depending on which group we're in. Effective group members adapt their behavior to what is happening or needed in the group. In some groups, your expertise may give you the confidence to give information and share your opinions freely. In other groups, you may assume a role to maintain social harmony and peace.

What are the best or worst roles to assume? We don't recommend that you assume any individual role; by definition, these roles focus attention on an individual rather than the group. The group needs a balance of task and social roles, not attention drawn to an individual.

What is the proper balance between task and social concerns? Some experts recommend a 60:40 balance between task and social roles.[15] What is clear is that groups seem to operate most effectively when it's not all work and no play. Conversely, an out-of-balance group that focuses just on having a good time is not going to achieve its task goals. In general, more comments need to be about getting the work done than about having fun or managing the social climate, but don't neglect making sure that there are good working relationships among group members.

Aware
Adapt

The action steps for you: Monitor what roles are being assumed and not assumed in your group. Be aware of your communication. Then help meet a need. Adapt your behavior to the needs of the group. If your group seems unduly focused on the task and members are insensitive to the harmony of the group relationships, the group will not be as effective as it might be.

Rules

As we noted both in Chapter 1 and earlier in this chapter, rules are followable prescriptions that indicate what behavior is expected or preferred.[16] Rules also clearly specify what behavior is inappropriate. Leaders or members of groups and teams often develop rules that specify how people should behave. Think of rules as serving the same function as the U.S. Constitution or the laws of your state or community.

Teams, in particular, often develop team ground rules that help a team function more smoothly. **Team ground rules** are just another way of talking about the behaviors that are expected of group members. They are important to help manage uncertainty when working with others. Imagine playing on a sports team if there were no written rules; it would be chaos. Highly structured teams need rules to ensure that they are both efficient and effective. While most informal groups may not develop explicit, written rules, more formal teams may take time to develop such rules as the fol-

team ground rules
A way of talking about the behaviors that are expected of team members; team members work together to develop explicit rules of acceptable behavior.

TABLE 9.1
A Classification of Group Roles

Task Roles	Description	Example
Initiator/contributor	Offers new ideas or approaches to the group; suggests ways of getting the job done.	"How about developing an agenda to help us organize our work?"
Information seeker	Asks for additional clarification, facts, or other information that helps the group with the issues at hand.	"Can anyone tell me how many times the university has threatened to close the fraternities and sororities on campus because of the problem of underage drinking?"
Opinion seeker	Asks group members to share opinions or express a personal point of view.	"So, what do you all think of the new dress code the school board is proposing?"
Information giver	Provides facts, examples, statistics, or other evidence that relates to the task confronting the group.	"Within the past year, the Vice President for Student Affairs has given a special award to three fraternities and one sorority for developing a program to combat underage drinking."
Opinion giver	Offers opinions or beliefs about what the group is discussing.	"I think the new school dress code proposed for first graders is unworkable."
Elaborator	Provides comments or examples to extend or add to the comments of others.	"Tom, that's a good point. I had the same thing happen to me when my children were attending a private school in New York last year."
Coordinator	Clarifies and notes relationships among the ideas and suggestions that have been offered by others.	"Tyrone, your ideas sound a lot like Juanita's suggestion. Juanita, why don't you elaborate on your idea so Tyrone can decide whether he agrees or disagrees with you?"
Orienter	Summarizes what has occurred and seeks to keep the group focused on the task at hand.	"I think we're getting a bit off track here. Let's go back to the issue on the agenda."
Evaluator/critic	Assesses the evidence and conclusions that the group is considering.	"How recent are those statistics? I think there are newer figures for us to consider."
Procedural technician	Helps the group accomplish its goal by handling tasks such as distributing reports, writing ideas on a chalk board, or performing other tasks that help the group.	"I'll write your ideas on the board as you suggest them. After the meeting, I'll copy them and summarize them in an e-mail message to each of you."
Recorder	Makes a written record of the group's progress by writing down specific comments, facts, or the minutes of the meeting.	"I'll take the minutes of today's meeting."

Social Roles	Description	Example
Encourager	Offers praise and support, and confirms the value of other people and the ideas they contribute.	"You're doing a wonderful job."
Harmonizer	Manages conflict and mediates disputes among group members.	"Tynesha, you and Mandy seem to be agreeing more than you are disagreeing. Both of you want the same goal. Let's brainstorm some strategies that can help you both get what you want."
Compromiser	Resolves conflicts by trying to find an acceptable solution. Seeks new alternatives.	"Jane, you want us to meet at 7:00 PM and Sue, you'd like us to start at 8:00. What if we started at 7:30? Would that work?"

(continued)

TABLE 9.1
(continued)

Social Roles	Description	Example
Gatekeeper	Encourages people who talk too much to contribute less and invites those who are less talkative to participate.	"Tim, we've not heard what you think. What do you suggest we do?"
Follower	Goes along with the suggestions and ideas of other group members.	"I can support that option. You have summarized the issues about the same way I see them."
Emotion expresser	Verbalizes how the group may be feeling about a specific issue or suggestion.	"We seem to be frustrated that we are not making more progress."
Group observer	Summarizes the group's progress or lack of progress.	"We are making great progress on all of the issues except how much salary we should offer."
Tension reliever	Monitors stress within the group and offers suggestions for breaks, using humor or other appropriate strategies.	"Hey, what we need is a good laugh. Here's a joke I saw on the Internet today."

Individual Roles	Description	Example
Aggressor	Deflates or disconfirms the status of other group members or tries to take credit for the work of others.	"Lee, your idea is the pits. We all know that what I suggested two meetings ago is the only way to go."
Blocker	Is negative, stubborn, and disagreeable without an apparent reason.	"I just don't like it. I don't have to tell you why. I just don't like it."
Recognition seeker	Seeks the spotlight by dwelling on his or her personal accomplishments; seeks the praise of others.	"Don't you remember this was my idea? And say, did you see my picture in the paper? I won the grand prize at the science fair."
Self-confessor	Uses the group as a forum to disclose unnecessary personal feelings and personal problems unrelated to the group's task.	"Let me tell you how my parents are so unfair. They won't let me live off campus next year. My parents just don't understand me."
Joker	Wants to crack jokes, tell stories, and just have fun instead of focusing on the task or what the group needs.	"Hey, let's forget this project and go to the mall. Then I'll tell you the gossip about Professor Smith. What a kook!"
Dominator	Tries to take control of the group, talks too much, and uses flattery or aggression to push his or her ideas off on the group.	"Now, here's what we're going to do: Marcie, you will take notes today; Phil, you go get us some pizza; and Russ, I want you to just sit there in case I need you to run an errand."
Special-interest pleader	Seeks to get the group to support a pet project or personal agenda.	"My service club would like it if we would support the new downtown renovation project. I'll stand a good shot at group president if I can get you on board."
Help seeker	Seeks to evoke a sympathetic response from others; often expresses insecurity stemming from feelings of low self-worth.	"I don't know if I can participate in this project. I'm not very good with people. I just feel like I don't relate well to others or have many friends."

lowing: Everyone should attend all meetings; meetings will start on time; each team member should follow through on individual assignments. Making the rules explicit makes it easier to foster appropriate behavior and prevent inappropriate behavior.

Norms

While not all groups develop explicit rules, most groups and teams develop norms. **Norms** are general standards that determine what is appropriate and inappropriate behavior in a group. Is it normal for group members to raise their hands before speaking in your group? Is it okay to move around while the group is in session or to go get a cup of coffee while someone is talking? Norms reflect what's normal behavior in the group; they influence how group members are supposed to behave—such as the type of language that is acceptable, the casualness of the clothes they wear, or whether first names are used.

How do you know what the norms of any group are? Watch the group. Listen and observe any repeated verbal or nonverbal behavior patterns. Note, for example, consistencies in the way people talk or dress. Consider the following questions:

"The problem boils down to this — Harrison *woulda*, Reynolds *coulda* and Sorenson *shoulda*."

- What are group members' attitudes toward time (do meetings start and stop on time)?
- How do group members dress?
- Is it acceptable to use informal slang terms or to use obscenity?
- What kind of humor is acceptable?
- How does the group treat the leader?

Noting when someone breaks a norm can also help you spot a norm. If a member waltzes into a meeting 20 minutes late and several folks grimace and point to their watches, that's a sure sign that a norm has been violated. The severity of the punishment corresponds to the significance of the norm.[17] Mild punishment is usually unspoken—such as silent glances or frowning stares. More serious punishment might include a negative comment about the behavior in front of other group members or even expulsion from the group. You don't have to worry about whether your group will have norms or not; norms happen. You should, however, monitor the group norms to ensure that your behavior doesn't distract from the work of the group, or to note the possible development of an unproductive group norm (such as spending too much time socializing) that the group should talk about.

How do norms differ from rules? Rules are more explicit. Group and team rules are either written down or at least verbalized. Here's an example of a rule: If you have more than three absences in this course, you lose 10 points. Here's another: Any member of this team who does not pay his or her dues on time will pay an extra $5 in dues. Norms, on the other hand, are more general standards or expectations that are not as clearly spelled out. It may be a norm in your group that no one uses four-letter words; there's probably no written policy that prohibits expletives, and group members may never have said, "No one should ever use a curse word during our discussions." But even without such specific admonitions, group members don't use offensive or obscene words. Norms develop based on norms that you and other team members have experienced in other groups, as well as on behavior that occurs naturally as the groups interacts. If after a couple of meetings no one is telling off-color jokes or stories, then a norm has begun to gel.

Aware
Verbal
Nonverbal
Listen and Respond
Adapt

Verbal
Nonverbal

norms
Standards that determine what is appropriate and inappropriate behavior in a group.

Status

As she walks into the room, all eyes are fixed on her. Group members watch every move. As the chairperson, her influence is important. Without her support, no new is-

Based on what you can see in this photo, how many sources of power would you think the leader of this group exerts?

sues will come before the board. She has high status. **Status** refers to an individual's importance and prestige. Your status in a group influences whom you talk to, who talks to you, and even what you talk about. Your perceived importance affects both your verbal and your nonverbal messages. A person with high status typically

- Talks more than low-status members.
- Directs comments to other high-status group members.
- Has more influence on the decisions the group makes.
- Is listened to by group members.
- Addresses more comments to the entire group.[18]

Because high-status people enjoy more privileges, most people want to be in the "in group"—the group with status and influence. Being aware of status differences can help you predict who talks to whom. If you can discern status differences, you'll also be better able to predict the type of messages communicated.

But just because a person has status does not mean that his or her ideas are good. Don't let status difference influence your perceptions of the value of the ideas contributed. Some groups get into trouble because they automatically defer to the person with more status, without reviewing the validity of the ideas presented. Status influences group communication, but don't let status differences influence your critical thinking about the merit of the ideas presented. Conversely, don't dismiss ideas out-of-hand because the person who suggested them doesn't have status or prestige. Focus on the quality of the message, not just on the messenger.

Power

Status refers to perceived importance, while power refers to whether the status influences behavior. **Power** is the ability to influence others' behavior. Although status and power often go hand-in-hand, a group member can have status and still not be able to influence how others behave. People have power if they can affect what others do. Their power stems from the resources available to them to influence others. Who does and doesn't have power in a group influences how people relate to one another.

A power struggle often creates ripples of conflict and contention through a group. Power struggles also often focus attention on individual group members rather than on the group as a whole. People with less power tend to participate less in group discussion unless they're trying to gain power. A group that is not power balanced may have problems; the "power people" may dominate the discussion. In any group or team, when one or more members dominate the discussion, the group loses the contributions and insights of others. Research supports the conclusion that groups with equal power distribution usually have better quality outcomes.[19]

According to a classic discussion of how individuals become powerful, there are five power bases: legitimate, referent, expert, reward, and coercive power. These power bases explain why certain people have power and why others don't.[20]

Legitimate Power   You have **legitimate power** if someone elected or appointed you to a position of power. Your power source comes from holding a position of responsibility. The president of your university or college has the legitimate power to establish and implement school policy. U.S. senators, police officers, and parent/teacher association (PTA) presidents are other examples of people who have legitimate power. A group or team member who has been elected chair or president of the group is given legitimate power to influence how the group operates.

status
An individual's importance and prestige.

power
The ability to influence other people's behavior.

legitimate power
Power that stems from being elected or appointed to a position of authority.

Referent Power   You have **referent power** if people like you. Put simply, people we like have more power over us than people we do not like. If you are working on a committee with your best friend, your friend exerts power over you in the sense that you will tend to give more credence to what your friend recommends. Just the opposite occurs if you are working with someone you don't like; you will be more likely to ignore the advice that comes from someone you don't admire.

Expert Power   Knowledge is power. People who have **expert power** are perceived as informed or knowledgeable. They will have more influence in a group or team than people who are perceived as uninformed. Suppose you are working with a group to develop strategies to clean up the river that runs through your town. Your colleague who is majoring in aquatic biology will probably have more power than other, less knowledgeable group members.

Reward Power   People who can grant favors, money, or other rewards have more power than people who can't provide such rewards; those who can bestow rewards have **reward power**. People who have greater power to reward are typically sent more positive, supportive messages than people who don't have the ability to reward others. Someone has reward power if he or she can also take away a punishment or other unpleasant experience. But reward power is effective only if the person being rewarded finds the reward satisfying or useful. What is rewarding to one person may not be rewarding to another person.

Coercive Power   You have coercive power if you can punish others. **Coercive power** is the flip side of reward power. The ability to influence comes from the ability to make others uncomfortable. If someone can cut your salary, lower your grade, demote you, or force you to do unpleasant jobs, then that person has coercive power. The power results from the perception that the person with the power will actually use the power. If a person has the authority to punish, but group members don't perceive that the person will use this power, then there really is no coercive power.

Even though we have categorized power into five different types, don't get the idea that group members may exert just one type of power. In reality, group or team members often have more than one type of power. For example, because a group member may be the elected leader (legitimate power), he or she may also be able to offer more rewards (reward power) or punishments (coercive power).

RECAP

Types of Power

Legitimate Power	Power that results from being elected, appointed, or ordained to lead or make decisions for a group or a team.
Referent Power	Power that results from being popular and well liked.
Expert Power	Power that results from having information or being knowledgeable about issues or ideas.
Reward Power	Power that results from having the resources to bestow gifts, money, recognition, or other rewards that group members value.
Coercive Power	Power that results from having the ability to punish others.

referent power
Power that stems from being liked.

expert power
Power derived from having expertise and information.

reward power
Power that comes from the ability to provide rewards or favors.

coercive power
Power that stems from being able to punish others.

Cohesiveness

If you have ever read about the Three Musketeers or have seen a movie about them, you know that their motto was "One for all, and all for one." They were a cohesive group—they liked to be around one another. Group **cohesiveness** is the degree of attraction that members of a group feel toward one another and the group. In a highly cohesive group, the members feel a high degree of loyalty to one another; the goal of the group is also the goal of the individual. Cohesive group members listen to one another. Members of a cohesive group are also more likely to use words and phrases that have unique meaning to group members; they are also more likely to tell "inside jokes"—jokes that mean something only to the group members.[21]

Groups become cohesive because of a variety of forces that attract people to the group and to one another. Similarity of goals, feelings of genuine liking, and similarity of backgrounds and culture are variables that influence group cohesion. Cohesiveness also is more likely to occur when group members' needs are satisfied by participating in the group. In the case of the Three Musketeers, the desire to do good deeds and assist those in need provided the clear, elevating goal from which the Musketeers derived satisfaction. Think of a group you belong to in which there is a high degree of *esprit de corps* and cohesiveness. You will also probably find that you like both the group members and the overall goals and objectives that the group is trying to accomplish.

What makes groups and teams cohesive? Table 9.2 summarizes some strategies that enhance group cohesiveness and those that make a group less cohesive. The common element in cohesive groups is the manner in which group members communicate with one another. Cohesiveness is more likely to occur if group members have the opportunity to talk with one another freely about a goal all members have in common and if this interaction increases group members' affection and liking for each other.

Can a group be too cohesive? Yes. If group members are focused only on developing a positive, cohesive relationship to the exclusion of getting their work done, group productivity can suffer. There is a curvilinear relationship between cohesiveness and amount of work a group produces. This means that rather than a direct, linear relationship between cohesiveness and work output, after a group achieves a certain level of group cohesiveness, group productivity actually decreases. If you think about it, this makes perfect sense. If the group becomes obsessed primarily with having fun and enjoying one another's company, they will produce *less* work. Although usually cohesiveness is a good thing, a group can have too much of a good thing. Strive for group cohesiveness, but balance it with concern for accomplishing the group's task.

cohesiveness
The degree of attraction members feel toward one another and toward their group.

TABLE 9.2
Suggestions for Enhancing Group Cohesiveness[22]

Cohesive Groups	Uncohesive Groups
Talk about the group in terms of "we" rather than "I"; stress teamwork and collaboration.	Emphasize the individual contributions of group members; stress individual accomplishment.
Reinforce good attendance at group meetings.	Make little effort to encourage group members to attend every meeting.
Establish and maintain group traditions.	Make little effort to develop group traditions.
Set clear short-term and long-term goals.	Avoid setting goals or establishing deadlines.
Encourage everyone in the group to participate in the group task.	Allow only the most talkative or high-status members to participate in the group task.
Celebrate when the group accomplishes either a short-term or a long-term goal.	Discourage group celebration; make sure group meetings are all work and little or no fun.

Communication Interaction Patterns

When you participate in a group or a team meeting, do you notice that you frequently talk with some people but hardly speak to others? It is normal for most of us to develop preferences for whom we do and don't talk with. Group communication scholars have studied and classified the various distinct patterns that emerge when people talk to one another in groups. A **communication interaction pattern** is a pattern of who talks to whom. Some groups have an equal distribution of interaction among members, while others develop distinct patterns of interaction between two or more people.[23]

In most groups, we often speak to specific people in the group rather than to the group as a whole. We tend to speak to people who have more power and status. In addition, we talk to people we like more than people we don't like. There will also, however, be more communication directed toward someone in the group who holds an opinion different from that of the rest of the group. This person is called a **group deviate**. Other group members may spend considerable talk time trying to change his or her opinion.

A group in which everyone talks to everyone else is called an all-channel network. All channels are open and used, as you can see in the first model in Figure 9.1. There

Verbal

communication interaction pattern
A consistent pattern of who talks to whom.

group deviate
A group member who holds an opinion, attitude, or belief that is different from that of other group members.

FIGURE 9.1
Small Group Communication Networks

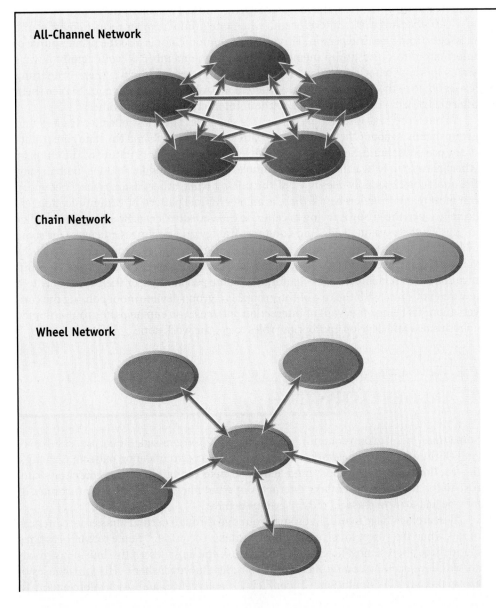

All-Channel Network

Chain Network

Wheel Network

is considerable interaction, and no cliques or small subgroups emerge. A **clique** is a smaller group of people within a group who form a common bond among themselves. Perhaps in your social, service, or religious groups you have special friends whom you seek out and who seek you out when you attend meetings. During meetings you probably sit together, share private jokes and stories, and talk about other members. Although there is nothing wrong with having special friends and colleagues, cliques can become detrimental to a group or team if they foster rivalries within the group or if they inhibit the flow of communication with others. Groups should avoid subgroups or cliques that can develop divisive power plays that foster conflict. You don't want cliques or groups to ratchet up the emotional tension as the group seeks to deliberate rationally. How do you avoid being in a clique? Become aware that you are in a subgroup that could be detrimental to the larger group.

The chain network in Figure 9.1 illustrates a form of group communication in which people convey a message to one person at a time rather than communicating with all group members at once. In organizations, it is typical to find a hierarchical chain communication pattern. Here's an example: The president of the company sends a message to the vice president, who talks to the director. The director then talks to the manager, who eventually gives the message to the other employees. As you might suspect, passing a message through many different ears and minds often results in misunderstanding by the time the message reaches the last person in the chain.

The wheel network pattern occurs when one group member receives most of the messages from a central person. This pivotal communicator is also the prime source of information to other group members. Perhaps one member of your family always seems to know what's going on. The wheel pattern emerges when there is a strong leader or when the group members do individual tasks and need someone to keep them informed of what others are doing, without interacting with those others.

What's the best interaction pattern? It depends. The most effective leaders and group members adapt their interaction pattern to fit the task and the time constraints of the project at hand. Sometimes, the efficiency and structured nature of the chain or wheel pattern may be called for. For example, during the huddle before a football play, the quarterback usually does most of the talking while others listen (wheel network). But most teams function best if there is an all-channel pattern of communication, especially when the group is trying to generate new, creative ideas. Breaking into smaller groups can be a useful divide-and-conquer strategy and enhances efficiency for some tasks. If the group is not too large, the all-channel pattern serves most groups well. As you participate in or lead group meetings, be aware of the general pattern of communication. Are all members participating? Do some people whisper their ideas only to a few and not share with the rest of the group? Is a group deviate monopolizing the conversation? By being observant of interaction patterns, you can help the group enhance cohesiveness and develop appropriate roles to get the work done.

UNDERSTANDING PHASES OF GROUP AND TEAM DEVELOPMENT

Sometimes, small group communication can be a disorganized, messy process—especially if the all-channel network is the predominant communication pattern. Although the free flow of ideas is a good thing, it may seem as though there is no order or structure to the way group members interact. But what may look like chaotic talk may, in fact, be just a normal aspect of how groups behave.

Researchers have found that some groups go through certain phases or sequences of talk when they meet to solve a problem or make a decision.[24] Some researchers have found three phases; most have found four. One of the most descriptive four-phase models was developed by communication researcher Aubrey Fisher.[25] His four phases of group talk are (1) orientation, (2) conflict, (3) emergence, and (4) reinforcement. To

Aware

Adapt

Verbal

clique
A smaller, cohesive group within a group.

understand the sequence of these four phases can be like having a group map. By listening to what people are saying, you can identify where the group is. We will describe these phases so that you can identify them when they occur in your group.

Orientation

As you might suspect, when people first get together in a group, they enter the **orientation phase**, in which they adjust to at least two things: who's in the group (group process) and what they will be doing (group task).

When you join a group for the first time, you have high uncertainty about how the group will be organized, who's in charge, and exactly how things will work. Research on the orientation phase suggests that your earliest communication is directed at orienting yourself to others, as well as to the group's task. Another name for what happens during this first phase is **primary tension**. This is the tension that results from the uncertainty and discomfort people experience when they meet for the first time.[26] Just as you may have some tension and anxiety when you give a speech, some tension and anxiety occur in a group when group members are trying to figure out who is supposed to do what, who's in charge, and why they are there. Some group members who don't like uncertainty at all and are eager to start sorting things out will suggest an agenda: "Hello, my name is Steve. Let's each introduce ourselves." Other group members are quite content to sit quietly in the background and let others take the lead. As people begin to become acquainted and group members start talking about the purpose of the meeting, typical groups experience the second phase—conflict.

Conflict

As we've pointed out, people are different—and nowhere is that more evident than in a group discussion after the group gets down to business. As group members become more comfortable and oriented toward the task and one another, they start asserting opinions about what the group should be doing and who should be doing it. They have tested the water in the first phase and are now ready to jump in. This second phase, which is characterized by increased disagreement, is known as the **conflict phase**, and the conflict that arises in the phase is sometimes called **secondary tension**. This tension or conflict occurs when there may be a struggle for leadership or when group members disagree with each other.

Conflict is not always bad—it occurs when people are honest about sharing their opinions. If there is no conflict, it usually means people aren't honest about how they really feel. As journalist Walter Lippman once said, "When we all think alike, then no one is thinking." The conflict phase is necessary for solving problems and maintaining group relationships. When ideas aren't challenged and tested, groups are more likely to make unwise decisions. Also, honest yet tactful expressions of personal disagreement are more likely to foster genuine cohesiveness than phony relationships. So conflict and disagreement are not necessarily bad, especially if the disagreement is about issues, rather than personalities or relationships. Conflict that results in attacking people rather than ideas is not productive. We are not suggesting that you celebrate when you have conflict, only that you take some comfort in knowing that conflict is an expected part of group deliberations. The amount and intensity of the conflict varies, depending on how important the issues are to the group. The more important the issues are to group members, the more likely it is that conflict will emerge with greater intensity.

Research suggests that when intense conflict arises in your group, especially conflict that results in heightened emotions and tension because of cultural differences, it may be best to "cool it."[27] Taking time to back off, rather than continuing to hash out issues verbally, may be helpful in managing the tension. Regardless of the issue or trigger for the conflict, when emotions are aroused, rational discussion is hard to achieve. Especially if the group you're in includes people from a variety of cultural backgrounds, letting the group "breathe" rather than continuing to hammer out meaning with more talk may be best. We're not suggesting that all conflict should be managed

orientation phase
The first phase of group interaction, in which members become adjusted to one another and to the group's task.

primary tension
Anxiety and discomfort that occurs when a group first meets.

conflict phase
The second phase of group interaction, in which group members experience some degree of disagreement about social and task issues.

secondary tension
Conflict that occurs over group norms, roles, leadership, and differences among member opinions; it develops after the members of the group have become acquainted with one another.

During the conflict phase of group development, tensions may emerge if there is a struggle for leadership.

by avoiding it; we are suggesting that when emotions become aroused it's difficult to make headway on the issues with words that may fan the flames of the conflict.

Emergence

You know you are in the **emergence phase** when the group begins to solidify a common point of view. Decisions emerge; conflict is reduced. Though conflict is still evident in this third phase, what sets the emergence phase apart from the conflict phase is the way in which group members manage conflict. Norms, roles, and leadership patterns that have been established in the group now help the group get work accomplished. In the emergence phase, the group settles on norms and moves closer toward agreement. The group begins to get a clearer glimpse of how issues will be resolved and what the group outcome will be.

Not all of what emerges may be productive. The group could decide that the conflict is so intense that the best decision is to disband the group. Or an individual could decide to leave the group.

Reinforcement

Group members become more unified in the **reinforcement phase**. During the orientation, conflict, and emergence phases, group members struggle through getting acquainted, developing cohesiveness, competing for status and prominence, and puzzling over action the group could take. The group eventually emerges from those struggles and develops a new sense of direction. This accomplishment results in a more positive feeling about the group. The group more clearly develops a sense of "we." In fact, one of the ways you can identify the reinforcement phase is when group members use more collective pronouns *(we, us, our)* than personal pronouns *(I, me, my)* to talk about the group.

emergence phase
The third phase of group interaction, in which conflict or disagreement is managed, decisions are made, and group problems begin to be solved or managed.

reinforcement phase
The fourth phase of group interaction, in which group members express positive feelings toward each other and toward the group.

RECAP

A Map of Group Phases

Phase One: Orientation	• What are we doing here?
	• What is our goal?
	• Who are these people?
	• What is my role?
Phase Two: Conflict	• Who put him/her in charge?
	• I see the goal differently.
	• I have different ideas.
	• I have different strategies.
Phase Three: Emergence	• Something happens.
	• Decisions are made.
	• Issues are managed.
	• The group moves forward.
Phase Four: Reinforcement	• The group is aware it is making progress.
	• Members seek to justify their actions.
	• Members reward others.
	• The team celebrates its success or rationalizes its failure.

The Process Nature of Group Phases

Even though we have identified four distinct phases that groups can experience, don't get the idea that all groups neatly progress through these phases in exactly the same way. They don't.[28] Some researchers have found that only about one-third of all groups experience these distinct stages.[29] Other studies have difficulty identifying four phases and find just one or two. Even if you have trouble identifying these phases in your group, you will probably see some elements of these four phases during your group meetings.

On the Web

For a collection of resources and strategies to help you work with others in small groups and teams, check out the Allyn & Bacon Web site: www.abacon.com/commstudies/groups/group.html. This site provides tips to help you investigate key small group communication concepts. You can also participate in an interactive activity or take a quick quiz to test your knowledge of groups and teams.

Some groups may simply get stuck in one of the phases. For example, have you ever participated in a group that could never quite figure out what it was supposed to do? It was stuck in the orientation phase.

Some groups remain in the conflict phase for long periods of time, perhaps bouncing between orientation and conflict. The group either seems torn by personal conflict between group members, or it just can't reach agreement or make a decision.

Eventually something will emerge from the group (phase three), even if it is not a wise decision or quality solution. The group may decide, for example, to disband and never meet again because the group is so dysfunctional. Although not the original objective of the group, something emerged—the group members quit.

Reinforcement is likely to occur because we like to make sense out of what happens to us. Even if the group disbands, we are likely to celebrate its demise or reinforce the decision to disband. Because of our culture's emphasis on efficiency and productivity, many groups quickly gloss over the reinforcement aspects of group celebration. Wise

Diversity and Communication

The Impact of Individualism and Collectivism on Groups and Teams

As you recall from Chapter 6, individualism is the cultural tendency to focus on individual achievement. Most North Americans value individual accomplishment over group or team achievement. In general, people from the dominant cultural groups in the United States, Great Britain, and Australia savor and celebrate individual accomplishment. Collectivism emphasizes group or team accomplishment rather than individual achievement. Research suggests that the collectivist mind-set is prevalent in Asian countries, Latin America, and some parts of Eastern Europe.[30]

These two perspectives have important implications for group and team collaboration. People who hold individualistic cultural values may find it more difficult to work collaboratively than people from collectivistic cultures. The following summary compares individualistic assumptions with collectivistic assumptions about working in groups and teams.[31] These differences can sometimes explain why groups and teams have difficulty accomplishing their tasks. If you're from a culture that places a high value on individual achievement, you may find it challenging to work collaboratively with others.

Individualistic Assumptions	Collectivistic Assumptions
The best decisions are made by individuals.	The most effective decisions are made by teams.
Planning should be done by leaders.	Planning is best done by the entire group.
Individuals should be rewarded.	Groups or teams should be rewarded.
Individuals should work primarily for themselves.	Individuals should work primarily for the team.
Healthy competition among group and team members is more important than teamwork.	Teamwork is more important than competition.
Meetings are for sharing information with others.	Meetings are for making group or team decisions.
To get something accomplished, you should work with individual people.	To get something accomplished, you should work with the entire group or team.
The prime objective of meetings is to advance your own ideas.	The prime objective of meetings is to reach consensus or agreement.
Group or team meetings are often a waste of time.	Group or team meetings are the best way to achieve a quality goal.

group leaders and participants make sure that accomplishments are celebrated and both group and individual efforts are recognized. The cohesiveness and positive feelings that result from such celebrations will be helpful as the group prepares for its next task.

PRINCIPLES FOR A LIFETIME: Enhancing Your Skills

Aware

Principle One: Be aware of your communication with yourself and others.
- Be knowledgeable of the definitions of and differences between groups and teams.
- Be aware of your role and the roles of others in groups and teams.
- Be aware of how you and your group develop and maintain group norms.
- Be mindful of how your power and the power of others influence group interaction.
- Be aware of the forces that affect group and team cohesiveness.
- Be aware of and sensitive to the stages of orientation, conflict, emergence, and reinforcement that influence group interaction.

Verbal

Principle Two: Effectively use and interpret verbal messages.
- Be verbally supportive of other team members so as to foster a collective sense of team spirit.
- Verbally help clarify team goals; clear, elevating goals are the hallmark of an effective team.
- Express positive, but realistic optimism when working with others in groups and teams; groups and teams with a positive outlook are more effective than those with a pessimistic perspective.
- Verbally help to clarify individual member roles and your own roles.
- Help the group or team set clear ground rules and clarify norms that may be ambiguous.
- Set short-term as well as long-term goals to help enhance cohesiveness.
- Talk about your group or team in terms of "we" rather than "I."

Nonverbal

Principle Three: Effectively use and interpret nonverbal messages.
- Watch for nonverbal cues to help you understand group and team norms.
- Observe group and team members' use of space, touch, and eye contact to pick up clues about status and power.
- Be supportive of other group members nonverbally as well as verbally; reinforce statements with positive facial expressions, eye contact, and head nods to indicate agreement when appropriate.
- Use supportive nonverbal messages to help groups and teams manage both primary tension (early tension that occurs when a group first meets) and secondary tension (conflict that may emerge about leadership, norms, rules, and roles) that typically is present in many groups.

Listen and Respond

Principle Four: Listen and respond thoughtfully to others.
- Being a good listener is one of the most important ways to help a group; listening skills help you identify your role and the role of others.
- Listen to others to help identify group and team norms and rules.
- Listen attentively to other group members to help foster a climate of cohesiveness.

Adapt

Principle Five: Appropriately adapt messages to others.
- Be sensitive to the needs of your group so that you can adapt your messages to help the group achieve its goal.
- Adapt to the group by paying attention to roles, norms, rules, and status differences.
- Effective group members adapt to help the group become oriented to the task, manage conflict, facilitate emergent decisions, and reinforce group behavior.
- Effective group members appropriately adapt to cultural differences within the group.

SUMMARY

Groups and teams are an ever-present aspect of our lives. Small group communication is the transactive process of creating meaning among a small number of people (three to fifteen people) who share a common purpose, who feel a sense of belonging to the group, and who exert influence on one another. Groups and teams are similar in that they are collections of a small number of people who meet to achieve a goal. A team can be differentiated from a group in that it is more highly organized, and the members' collaborative efforts are more coordinated to achieve the team goal. Groups exist for a variety of reasons. Some primary groups, such as families, exist to meet basic human needs; other types of groups include study groups, therapy groups, focus groups, problem-solving groups, and social groups.

Groups and teams are dynamic. This means that a variety of factors influence the ever-changing nature of what occurs when you interact with others in groups and teams. The role you assume in a group, the consistent way you communicate with others, influences your behavior and the behavior of others. There are three primary types of roles in small groups and teams: task roles—those that help the group do its work; social roles—those that help the group members relate to one another; and individual roles—roles that inappropriately divert the group's focus onto individual concerns rather than group concerns. Other factors that affect the dynamic nature of groups and teams include norms (standards of what is normal or expected), rules (explicit statements about appropriate and inappropriate behavior), status (a person's importance or prestige), power (the ability to influence others), cohesiveness (the degree of loyalty and attraction the group members feel toward one another), and interaction patterns (the consistent communication networks that emerge based on who talks to whom).

Group communication may sometimes seem chaotic, but researchers have noted that many (though not all) groups experience predictable phases. During the orientation phase, group members get acquainted with both the task and one another. The second phase, conflict, occurs when group members recognize that they have differing ideas and opinions about both the group's task and procedures for accomplishing the task. The third phase, emergence, is evident when the group begins to make decisions and starts completing the task. The reinforcement phase occurs when the group has accomplished its task and takes some time to recognize and confirm the group's actions; the reinforcement phase may be brief, especially in groups that don't take time to celebrate their success or attend to the social dynamics of the group.

Group members and leaders need to be sensitive to differences in cultural expectations that may affect groups and teams and adapt accordingly. In the next chapter we identify practical strategies to help you make decisions and solve problems as a group member, lead a group, or organize a meeting. Throughout our discussion, we will continue to interweave the five foundation principles that are fundamental to communicating with others, including in groups and teams.

Discussion and Review

1. Define small group communication and team communication. What are the differences and the similarities between the two?
2. Describe and provide examples of task, social, and individual group roles.
3. Identify and describe group norms.
4. Differentiate between the concepts of *status* and *power*.
5. What are the five bases of power discussed in this chapter?
6. What are strategies for enhancing group cohesiveness?
7. Describe the wheel, chain, and all-channel communication patterns. What are the implications of these patterns for group productivity?
8. What are the stages of group development discussed in this chapter?
9. Identify cultural differences that can affect people's approaches to working in groups and teams.

Putting Principles into Practice

1. "Ice-Breaker" Activities: The following activities are designed to help you "break the ice" at initial group or team meetings.

   a. If you were in a gift shop, what gift would you buy for each member of the group? Discuss why you would buy the gift.

   b. If you could invite a famous person to join your group, whom would you invite and why?

   c. Make a drawing of your "lifeline." Use symbols and pictures to illustrate the high and low points in your life; not only show your past, but also make some predictions about your future.

   d. Tell three things about yourself, one of which is false. Group members should guess which of the things you've disclosed about yourself is false. After the group has guessed, reveal what is true and not true about you.

   After you have completed one or more of these ice breakers, consider the following questions:

   • How did your group experience the orientation phase? Did these activities help the group become oriented to one another?

   • What norms emerged as group members participated in these activities?

   • Can you identify the role or roles you assumed (task, social, individual) and the roles of other group members?

   • What interaction patterns were evident in your group?

2. Agree–Disagree Statements: Read each of the following statements once. Take four or five minutes to do this. Then, in small groups, try to reach consensus about each statement (everyone either agreeing or disagreeing with the statement). Try especially to find reasons for differences of opinions. If your group cannot reach consensus, you may change the wording in any statement enough to promote unanimity. Mark A on the line preceding a statement if you agree, D if you disagree.[32]

   1. _____ Despite its flaws, a meeting is the best way to get work done in an organization.

   2. _____ There are often occasions when an individual who is a part of a working team should do what he or she thinks is right, regardless of what the group has decided to do.

   3. _____ Sometimes it is necessary to change people in the direction you yourself think is right, even if they object.

   4. _____ It is sometimes necessary to ignore the feelings of others in order to reach a group decision.

   5. _____ When the leader is doing his or her best, one should not openly criticize or find fault with his or her conduct.

   6. _____ In most team conflicts, someone must win and someone must lose. That's the way conflict is.

   7. _____ Much time is wasted in talk when everybody in the group has to be considered before making a decision.

   8. _____ Almost any job that can be done by a committee can be done better by having one individual responsible for the job.

   9. _____ Body language and nonverbal messages are more important than verbal messages when communicating with others in team meetings.

   10. _____ If people spend enough time together, they will find something to disagree about and will eventually become upset with one another.

   11. _____ Most hidden agendas are probably best kept hidden to ensure a positive social climate and manage conflict.

   12. _____ If you disagree with someone in a group, it is usually better to keep quiet than to get the group off-track with your personal difference of opinion.

   13. _____ When a team can't reach a decision, members should abide by the decision of the group leader if the leader is qualified and competent.

   14. _____ Some people produce more conflict and tension than others. These people should be restricted from decision-making meetings.

3. Losing Your Job[33]

   Assume that you are your family's breadwinner and that you have a take-home income of $43,200. You hear through the grapevine at work that because of organizational restructuring, everyone in your department will be laid off within four months. It is probable that you will be without your monthly salary check in the very near future. You do have skills that could lead to income from consulting. You have $3000 in a savings account and a $5000 stock portfolio, but you also have $1500 charged to your credit cards. Because of the nature of your job, you pay the IRS quarterly rather than in monthly payroll deductions. You have the following monthly budget:

30-year fixed mortgage	$1000
Food	$600
Bank-financed car payment	$300
Clothing and personal items	$400
Miscellaneous	$500
College savings fund	$200
Pension fund	$300
Medical bills	$300

   You are sure you will get a good job recommendation from your boss, yet it may take you four to six months to find work at a comparable salary. With other members of a small group, rank the following strategies from the most to the least important actions you should take to prepare for the impending loss of your income.

a. Change your mortgage from a 30-year to a 15-year term.

b. Reevaluate your budget to allow a dramatic increase in your savings plan.

c. Transfer your car bank loan to a home equity loan.

d. Pay off charge cards.

e. Borrow more money from the bank.

f. Charge most of your food and living expenses to your credit card to help you save.

g. Quit adding money to your pension plan now.

h. Switch investments from stocks into a money market fund.

i. Skip your next IRS payment.

j. Make more efforts to buy things such as clothes and food when they are on sale.

k. Start your own consulting practice.

l. Use this opportunity to go back to school to get retrained for a higher-paying job.

Following the group discussion, consider one or more of the following questions:

- Did your group go through the phases of orientation, conflict, emergence, or reinforcement? Or did the group go through only one or two of these phases? Did the group get bogged down in one of the phases?
- What was the predominant pattern of communication? Did members use the all-channel, chain, or wheel pattern? Were there any group deviates who influenced the communication pattern?
- What roles did group members assume? Were the roles appropriate for the group's task?
- What norms developed? Were the norms useful or unproductive?

4. Norms are standards for acceptable behavior. Even though there are certain cultural standards of appropriate and inappropriate behavior, acceptable conduct may vary from group to group. Several group member behaviors are listed below. Indicate how appropriate or inappropriate each behavior is as a group norm, using the following scale:

5 = Definitely appropriate as a norm
4 = Probably appropriate as a norm
3 = Uncertain whether appropriate as a norm
2 = Probably inappropriate as a norm
1 = Definitely inappropriate as a norm

1. Did not talk or participate in group discussion.

2. Talked about fight he/she had with roommate.

3. Disagreed with another group member.

4. Challenged the evidence used by another group member.

5. Interrupted two other group members who were talking.

6. Was often absent.

7. Asked for additional information to help clarify the purpose of the meeting.

8. Told other group members about a great movie that he/she saw last weekend.

9. Used obscene language and shouted at another group member.

10. Wore dressy clothes (dress shirt and tie for men or fashionable tailored dress for women).

11. Told group members that he/she did not have to abide by the decision of the group.

12. Told another group member that he/she was being rude and disruptive.

13. Brought information gained through an Internet search to support a decision the group was making.

14. Frequently got up and walked around the room while other group members were talking.

15. Brought food to the group meeting but did not offer to share it with other group members.

16. Was usually 15 minutes late to group meetings.

Compare your responses with those of other group members to see if you agree about what would be appropriate group norms.[34]

Ben Shahn, "Four Piece Orchestra," 1944. © Copyright VAGA, NY. Fundacion Coleccion Thyssen-Bornemisza, Madrid, Spain.
© Estate of Ben Shahn/Licensed by VAGA, New York, NY. Scala/Art Resource. NY.

Never doubt that a small group of concerned citizens can change the world; it's the only thing that ever has.

Margaret Mead

Enhancing Group and Team Performance

CHAPTER OUTLINE

What Effective Group Members Do

When Not to Work in Groups and Teams

Structuring Group and Team Problem Solving

Enhancing Group and Team Leadership

Enhancing Group and Team Meetings

Summary

CHAPTER OBJECTIVES

After studying this chapter, you should be able to:

1. Identify five functions that effective group members perform.

2. List and describe the five steps of group problem solving (reflective thinking).

3. Compare and contrast the trait, functional, styles, situational, and transformational approaches to understanding leadership.

4. Develop and use an agenda to ensure that meetings have appropriate structure.

5. Use strategies to maintain appropriate discussion and dialogue to ensure that meetings include appropriate interaction.

What's so great about groups? Why does every organization, from the U.S. Congress to the local Parent Teacher Association, use groups, teams, and committees to get something done? The simple fact is that groups work. Collaborating with others produces clear benefits that just don't happen when you give a task to an individual. Research clearly supports the following conclusions:

- Groups and teams come up with more creative solutions to problems than a person working alone.
- Working with others in groups improves group members' comprehension of the ideas presented.
- Group and team members are more satisfied with the group's conclusions and recommendations if they participated in the discussion.
- Groups have access to more information when they tap into the experience of group members.[1]

All of these advantages sound wonderful. But these benefits of collaboration don't just occur automatically when people work in groups and teams. Sometimes there are significant disadvantages to working collaboratively.

- Overly talkative or insensitive, overbearing people may speak too much; the advantage of working collaboratively is lost when one or more people dominate the conversation.
- Group members sometimes feel pressure to conform to what other groups members are doing and saying; it can be difficult to stick up for your own ideas when everyone else sees issues differently.
- Some group members just sit back and wait for others to do the work; it may be easy for some people to loaf and not do their share of the work. If not enough people carry part of the load, then the advantages of working together as a group don't materialize.
- Working in groups and teams takes more time than working individually; it takes time to talk and listen.[2]

This chapter is designed to help you achieve the advantages of working in groups and minimize the disadvantages of working collaboratively. We can't claim that if you follow all of the strategies we suggest, your life will be free of unpleasant and unproductive group experiences. We do believe that group members who both understand how groups work (see Chapter 9) and know principles and strategies for enhancing the quality of group work are much more likely to avoid the pitfalls and reap the benefits of working in groups. Working in groups will usually involve more time than working by yourself, but the benefit of improved quality of decision can far outweigh the disadvantage of investing more time.

WHAT EFFECTIVE GROUP MEMBERS DO

Aware
Verbal
Nonverbal
Listen and Respond
Adapt

"I hate groups," mutters an exasperated group member who has just finished a two-hour meeting in which nothing was accomplished. "Not me," chirps another group member. "Meetings and team projects are fun. I like the energy and productivity that occurs when we work together." What is it the second group member knows that the first one doesn't? As we noted at the start of the last chapter, working in groups can be frustrating, but it doesn't have to be if you and other group members learn some fundamental ways to perform effectively as group members.

Underpinning all of the suggestions we offer in this chapter are the same five communication principles for a lifetime that we introduced in Chapter 1 and have been discussing throughout the book. Effective group members are aware of what they are doing. They effectively use verbal and nonverbal messages, listen and respond, and then appropriately adapt their messages to others.

Identify and Implement Key Functions to Achieve Results

Effective group and team members help to ensure that key functions or communication behaviors that enhance the overall quality of the group are put into practice. Researchers have found that when these critical functions are not performed, the group is less effective. This **functional approach** to group communication describes the kinds of behaviors or functions that lead to better quality solutions and decisions in group deliberations.[3]

Researchers have spent several years trying to identify the key functions of high-performing groups and teams so that you can make sure you do them in your group. The primary means by which researchers have identified these functions is by comparing the way group members in high-performing groups talk with the way group members in low-performing groups talk.

The essence of these functions involves group members being vigilant thinkers.[4] **Vigilant thinkers** pay attention to the *process* of how problems are solved. A vigilant thinker assesses, evaluates, and tests ideas; he or she effectively uses verbal messages and listens to what others are saying. Communication researcher Randy Hirokawa and his colleagues identified four essential questions that vigilant-thinking group members should consider:

1. What goal does the group want to achieve?
2. Does something in the present situation need to be changed in order to achieve the goal?
3. What options does the group have that will help achieve the goal?
4. What are the positive and negative implications of the options?[5]

Even though these questions are usually discussed in the order listed, some productive, vigilant-thinking groups don't always follow this sequence.[6] What is clear, however, is that if one or more of these critical questions is not discussed, the group is less effective in solving problems and making wise decisions. These questions lead to the achievement of the following six critical functions that effective groups need to consider.

Identify a Clear, Elevating Goal

What are we trying to do? Note that the first question that a vigilant-thinking group asks relates to the group's goal. Articulating a clear and elevating goal is one of the early functions that group members should make sure to accomplish in their group. According to one research team, the goal should not only be clear, but also *elevating,* or exciting to the group.[7] The group needs to know that it is pursuing a goal that is significant; the group goal needs to be something more exciting and important than anything an individual could achieve on his or her own. A professional baseball team during spring training camp may hang up signs in the locker room that say "World Series Champs!" A professional football team may see itself as a Super Bowl contender at the beginning of summer training camp. Groups, too, need to identify a clear, exciting, yet realistic goal that drives all aspects of what the group does. Without a goal and a results-driven structure to achieve the goal, group performance sputters.[8]

Some tasks, like creating a smooth concrete floor, cannot be completed without the cooperation of all the group members involved in the task.

Verbal

functional approach
An approach to group problem solving that assumes that to achieve a group goal, group members should perform certain communication functions.

vigilant thinker
A group member who pays attention to the process of how problems are solved, is sensitive to the need to make changes, identifies the goal of the group, identifies options the group has, and evaluates the positive and negative implications of the options.

Develop a Results-Driven Structure

A group with a **results-driven structure** is organized around the action steps that it needs to take to achieve its goal.[9] At any given moment during group discussion, the group is either on task or off task in working to achieve the group goal. Perhaps you've been part of a group or team that was quite busy but didn't seem to accomplish much; that kind of activity reflects a non-results–driven structure. A group that structures itself for results makes sure that the work is clearly linked to the desired outcome.

A group or team may have a clear goal, such as winning the Super Bowl, getting an A on a group assignment, or selling more widgets than other groups in the company—but just having a clear, elevating goal doesn't mean that the group will achieve what it wants to achieve. The old saying, "If wishes were horses, then beggars would ride" comes to mind. Just wishing something to happen won't make it happen. Results-driven action has to follow goal setting. The action that must be taken should be focused on the group goal; the group should be driven by results. If you want to win the Super Bowl, you have to invest time in becoming physically fit and working on executing successful football plays. If you want to get an A on the assignment, you need to be doing those things that the instructor wants you do to, rather than socializing and just having fun. To be results-driven means that you "keep your eye on the prize" and then develop a group or team structure to achieve the prize.

Gather and Use Information Effectively

Computer programmers are familiar with the acronym GIGO. "Garbage in, garbage out." If you develop a computer program using bad information or a bad program command (garbage), you're likely to come out with low-quality output (more garbage). Information is the fuel that makes a group function well. High-performing groups and teams don't just rely on the unsupported opinions of group members; group members should conduct research and find relevant information to accomplish the goal. Effectively functioning groups ask, "Does something need to be changed?" They gather information and analyze the situation to answer that question.

If a group or team's purpose is to solve a problem, it gathers information to help analyze the problem. To analyze an issue, an effective group should do at least three things:

1. Gather the information the group members need.
2. Share the information with group and team members.
3. Draw accurate conclusions from the information.

Group members who don't gather and use information effectively are more likely to make bad decisions. Having too little evidence—or no evidence at all—is one of the reasons groups sometimes fail to analyze their current situation correctly.[10] Even if group members do have plenty of evidence, it may be bad evidence or they may not have tested the evidence to see whether it is true, accurate, or relevant.

Develop Options

Another hallmark of an effectively functioning group is that group members generate many ideas and potential solutions *after* gathering information and analyzing a situation. Effective groups don't just settle on one or two ideas and then move on. They list multiple creative approaches.

Sometimes groups get stuck and ideas just don't flow. Rather than continuing to hammer away at the problem, the group may want to take a break from the difficult issues or knotty problems. Perhaps you've had a great idea come to you when you were taking a walk or driving. Taking a break gives your mind a chance to thrash through some of the issues and generate a breakthrough solution. The principle of self-awareness operates here: As a group member, you have a responsibility to become aware of the group's ability to generate high-quality ideas. Be sensitive to the group's need to take a fresh look at the problem or issue.

Aware

results-driven structure
A structure that causes a group to focus its efforts on the actions it needs to take to achieve its goals.

For meetings to be effective, group members must use good verbal and nonverbal communication skills and must listen and respond thoughtfully.

Evaluate Ideas

High-performing groups know a good idea when they see it. They are able to evaluate evidence, opinions, assumptions, and solutions to separate good ideas from bad ones. Low-performing groups are less discriminating. A group that is too eager to make a decision just so it can get a job done and that does not critically evaluate ideas usually comes up with lower-quality decisions.

An effectively functioning group examines the advantages and disadvantages of an idea, issue, or opinion.[11] When the group is zeroing in on a particular course of action, the effective group has at least one member who suggests, "Let's consider the positive and negative consequences of this decision." Research suggests that it's especially important to talk about the negative consequences of a specific proposal.[12] Some groups use a chalkboard or flip chart and make a written list of the pros and the cons. Groups that do this are more likely to come up with a better decision than groups that don't systematically evaluate the good and bad aspects of a potential solution or decision.

Develop Sensitivity toward Others

Most of the functions we've described so far focus on getting work done effectively and efficiently; but group success is about more than just focusing on the task. In effectively functioning groups, members also listen and are sensitive to one another's needs. Group members are aware of how the comments they make might be perceived by other members. Effectively functioning group members also make comments that confirm the value of others' contributions and nonverbally show that they are genuinely interested in what others are saying. Fostering a climate of fairness and supportiveness is essential to developing a well-functioning team.[13]

Effective group members balance concern for the task with concern for the feelings of others. Being solely task-oriented is not beneficial to the functioning of a group. Group members also listen to what each group member has to say—even members who may hold a minority opinion. One of the benefits of working in a group is that you can hear a variety of ideas. If opinions of others are quickly squelched because they are not what most other groups think or believe, the group loses the power of many different points of view.

Being sensitive to others also involves effectively interpreting nonverbal messages. The group climate is influenced by the positive support expressed through eye contact, responsive facial expressions, and a positive tone of voice.

Verbal
Nonverbal
Listen and Respond

Nonverbal

RECAP

What Effective Group and Team Members Do

Group Function	Description of Function
Identify and Implement Key Functions to Achieve Results	Help the group • Identify the goal • Identify what needs to be changed • Identify options • Identify positive and negative implications of the options
Identify a Clear, Elevating Goal	Ensure the group has developed a clear, elevating, or important goal that anchors the purpose of group discussion.
Develop a Results-Driven Structure	Make sure the group stays on task and is doing those things that will help it achieve its goal.
Gather and Use Information Effectively	Conducting research and using accurate information is an important element in the deliberation of any group or team.
Develop Options	Effective groups expand the number of alternatives or options before choosing a course of action.
Evaluate Ideas	Effective groups or teams examine the pros or cons of an option before implementing the strategy.
Develop Sensitivity toward Others	Group members do more than focus on the task, they express sensitivity to the needs and concerns of group members by using appropriate verbal and nonverbal messages, listening, responding, and adapting messages to others.

WHEN NOT TO WORK IN GROUPS AND TEAMS

Because we've listed the advantages of working in groups, and because we've laid out the specific behaviors of effective group members, you may think that two (or more) heads are *always* better than one. But are there clear instances when it is best not to work collaboratively? Yes, there are some situations in which it may be better to have an individual work on a problem or tackle a project rather than assigning a group or team to the task. Here are four situations when it is better to work individually rather than collectively.[14]

1. *When you have very limited time.* One of the key disadvantages to working in groups and teams is that it takes more time than working individually. If a very quick decision is needed, it may be better to ask one person than to ask for group decision. It's true that groups and teams often make better decisions than a single individual, but you have to balance the need for a quick decision against the need for a thorough discussion. In times of extreme crisis or emergency, it may be best to have a leader ready to provide some initial direction.

2. *When an expert already has the answer.* Creating a group to gather information when an expert already knows the answer wastes time. If you want to know what tomorrow's weather will be, ask a meteorologist. Don't collaboratively puzzle through questions that can be readily answered by someone who already has the answer.

3. *When the information is quickly available from research sources.* If you want a bit of data, a specific date, or more information about something, it may be better to do individual research rather than to commission a group, team, or task force to get the answers. Some groups find it's useful for individual members to gather information and then meet with the rest of the group to analyze and discuss the information. But if you just need information and need it fast, head to the library or click your mouse.

Verbal

4. *When conflict and tension in a group are unmanageable.* Don't avoid group and team conversations just because they may arouse conflict and disagreement. In fact, it's quite normal for groups to experience conflict. An absence of conflict can be a sign of an ineffective group. But if the conflict is so entrenched that group members just can't listen and thoughtfully respond, it may be better to take a break from group deliberations. What may be needed is a more structured conversation, such as mediation or negotiation with a trained facilitator to help sort things out. Or, as is the case with our legal system, an impartial judge may be needed to help make a decision. Don't give up on a group or team just because there is conflict, but if the conflict is so pervasive that no progress is likely, seek other ways of moving forward rather than having the group engage in more contentious talk.

STRUCTURING GROUP AND TEAM PROBLEM SOLVING

"Just tell me what to do. What I want to know is, what techniques will help me solve the problem? Make it simple." We usually want simple techniques or steps that will help us achieve our goal. The truth is, however, that there are no magic techniques that will enable a group or team always to come up with the right solution to a problem.

The functional approach to group problem solving that we just discussed is based on the assumption that high-performing groups and teams perform certain functions or communication behaviors that ineffective groups and teams don't enact. We now turn our attention to a more structured, prescriptive approach to solving problems. You will note some obvious similarities between the two approaches. But the more prescriptive approach to group problem solving we present now offers a sequence of steps and techniques to help your group stay on task and remain productive while still being sensitive to group members. Just as a prescription from your doctor is a specific dose of medicine that is given to help solve a specific ailment, a prescriptive approach to problem solving is based on the assumption that there are specific things you can do to enhance the communication health of the group.

Communication researcher Arthur Van Gundy suggests that problems can be classified on a continuum from *structured* to *unstructured*.[15] A structured problem is one to which there is a single best correct solution. A math problem is structured in the sense that there is one right answer. When group members are highly uncertain about how to solve a problem, have little information about how to proceed, and are confused, they are facing an unstructured problem. Problems such as how to "save" Social Security, how to solve the parking problem on campus, or how to increase teachers' salaries without raising taxes are examples of unstructured problems; there is more than one way to tackle each one. The more uncertainty there is (or the less structured the problem), the greater the need for a structured approach to help the group manage their uncertainty. Leaders who give the group structure by setting goals, keeping track of the time, and suggesting procedures enhance the group's perceived effectiveness.

More than 70 methods or sequences of prescriptive steps and techniques have been identified for structuring problem solving in groups and teams.[16] Several researchers have sought to identify the sequence that works best. Their conclusion? *No single prescriptive method or series of steps works best in every situation. But having some structured sequence of steps or questions works better than having no structure.*[17]

Structure is the way a group or team discussion is organized to follow a prescribed agenda. Because of the number of people working together to solve a problem, groups need structure to avoid hopping from topic to topic. According to one researcher, groups that engage in free-ranging discussion without an agenda change topics about once a minute.[18]

Can a group have too much structure? Yes. If you've been to a meeting or group discussion that seemed more like a seminar than an interactive discussion, then there

structure
The way a group or team discussion is organized, focusing on the group's agenda and the task that needs to be achieved.

FIGURE 10.1
Groups Need a Balance of Structure and Interaction

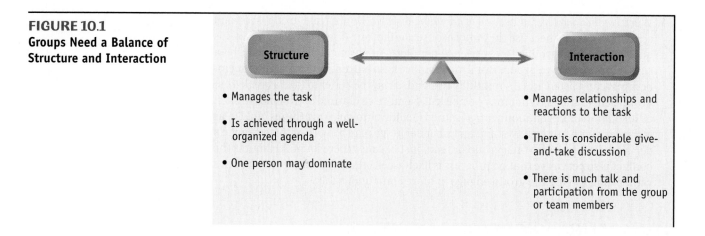

was too much structure. If a meeting is so controlled that one or two people do most of the talking, you're not at a meeting, you're at a speech. The goal is to balance the amount of structure with group interaction.

Interaction includes give-and-take discussion and the responsiveness group members have to the comments of others. In an interactive group, there are fewer long utterances; more people are contributing; more people are taking turns to talk. In a highly structured meeting, there is more control over who talks, about what, and for how long; overly structured meetings include less interaction. As suggested in Figure 10.1, the key is to find the right balance between structure and interaction. When there is too much interaction, the group experiences the chaos of unbridled talk that may not be focused; group and team members may need help in structuring or focusing on one idea at a time, rather than bouncing from topic to topic. When there is too much structure, however, the group loses the freedom to listen and respond with sensitivity to what others are saying.

In the pages that follow, we present a set of steps that can help you develop a sequence of things group members should be talking about. These five steps are inspired by educator and philosopher John Dewey, who in 1910 wrote a book called *How We Think*.[19] His book described how individuals go about the problem-solving process; in essence, he described the scientific method of defining and analyzing a problem, identifying solutions, picking a solution, and putting the solution into practice that scientists still use to solve problems. He called this process **reflective thinking.** We present these steps here, not as a one-size-fits-all prescription that you should always follow, but as a way of structuring the problem-solving process to manage uncertainty and also to ensure that the key functions we talked about earlier are accomplished during your discussion. In addition to describing each step of the reflective thinking process, we present several techniques to help you structure discussion.

Verbal

Step 1: Identify and Define the Problem

"What's your problem?" Groups work best when they have identified a clear, elevating goal that unites their problem-solving effort. To reach a clear statement of the problem, consider asking the following questions:

- What is the specific problem that concerns us?
- What do we want more of, or less of?
- What terms, concepts, or ideas do we need to define in order to understand the problem?
- Who is harmed by the problem?
- When do the harmful effects of the problem occur?

Most group experts recommend that an effective way to give your problem-solving task appropriate structure is to phrase your problem in the form of a policy question. A

interaction
The give-and-take discussion and responsiveness to all group members that occurs during group discussion.

reflective thinking
A problem-solving process based on the scientific method.

Who?	
What?	
When?	
Where?	
Why?	
How ?	

FIGURE 10.2
Journalist's Six Questions

policy question is phrased so that the group will recommend some action (policy) to eliminate, reduce, or manage the problem. Policy questions begin with the words "What should be done about . . . " or "What could be done to improve . . . "

Here are some examples:

- What should be done to lower the cost of tuition at our university?
- What could be done to decrease property taxes in our state?
- What should be done to make health care more affordable for all U.S. citizens?

One specific technique for structuring the discussion so as to identify a problem is to use the Journalist's Six Questions method.[20] Most news reporters are taught to include the answers to six questions when writing a news report: Who? What? When? Where? Why? and How? Using a chart like the one in Figure 10.2, the group poses these six questions about the problem the group has identified and then writes a response to each question. This method can help further define and limit the problem and can also help the group move to the next step in the process—analyzing the problem. Whatever method or technique a group uses, it is essential that group members know precisely what problem they are trying to solve.

Step 2: Analyze the Problem

To analyze something is to break it down into smaller pieces; to analyze a problem is to consider the causes, effects, symptoms, history, and other information that will inform the group about how to best solve the problem. Many groups want to "cut to the chase" quickly and start spinning out solutions, without taking the time to analyze the problem thoroughly. Resist this temptation. Analyzing a problem well is an important prerequisite to finding an effective solution. When analyzing a problem, group members will need to spend time in the library or on the Internet to gather information and determine how experts view the problem. Essential questions that can help you analyze problems include the following:

- How long has the problem been in existence?
- How widespread is the problem?
- What are the causes of the problem?
- What are the effects of the problem?
- What are the symptoms of the problem?
- Who is harmed by the problem?
- What methods already exist for managing the problem?
- What are the limitations of existing methods?
- What obstacles keep the group from achieving the goal?

In addition to considering these questions, group members should develop criteria for an acceptable solution. **Criteria** are standards for an acceptable solution to a problem. Identifying clear criteria can help you spot a good solution when you see one. Sample criteria for solutions include the following:

- The solution should be inexpensive, not to exceed 5% of our budget.
- The solution should be implemented by a certain date.

Verbal

criteria
Standards for an acceptable solution.

FIGURE 10.3
Force Field Analysis

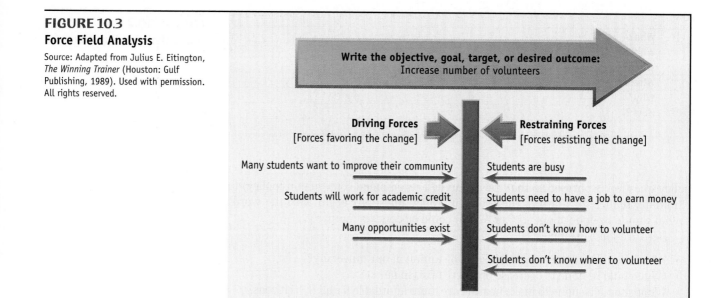

Write the objective, goal, target, or desired outcome:
Increase number of volunteers

Driving Forces
[Forces favoring the change]

Restraining Forces
[Forces resisting the change]

Driving Forces	Restraining Forces
Many students want to improve their community	Students are busy
Students will work for academic credit	Students need to have a job to earn money
Many opportunities exist	Students don't know how to volunteer
	Students don't know where to volunteer

Verbal

force field analysis technique
A method of analyzing a problem or issue by identifying forces that increase the likelihood that the desired goal will occur (driving forces) and forces that decrease the probability that the goal will occur (restraining forces).

creativity
The generation, application, combination, and extension of new ideas.

- The solution should be agreed on by all group members.
- The solution should be agreed on by all persons affected by our recommendations.

Don't rely on your memory when you verbalize criteria. Write down on a chalkboard or flip chart the list of criteria your group has identified and include the list in the minutes or notes that summarize the meeting.

After you have gathered information and developed criteria, your group may need to develop a systematic way of analyzing the information you've gathered. One technique that can help structure the analysis of your problem and also help your team identify criteria is the **force field analysis technique**.[21] This technique works best when your group has identified a clear goal and needs to assess what is happening now that would increase the probability that the goal will be achieved.

Here's how to conduct a force field analysis. After identifying a goal, the group lists all of the driving forces currently at work that would help achieve the goal. Then the group does just the opposite: It identifies the restraining forces that are keeping the group from achieving the goal. When complete, the analysis can help the group see what needs to be increased (the forces that currently favor achieving the goal) and what needs to be decreased (the forces working against the goal). Figure 10.3 shows an example of a force field analysis conducted by a group that wanted to increase the number of students who volunteer for community projects; the goal is written on the top. On the left side of the diagram is a list of all of the factors that the group identified as increasing the chances of achieving the goal—getting more students to volunteer. On the right side is a list of the restraining forces, or forces that keep the group from achieving the goal. The task of the group in developing solutions is now clear: Increase the driving forces and decrease the restraining forces.

One final observation: Be careful not to spend so much time overanalyzing data that you forget the purpose of the group—to solve the problem. Beware of "the killer inch" problem. This occurs when group members agree on the major points but are distracted by minor details; they've traveled a long way to reach their goal, but get distracted in the last inch of the journey. Avoid analysis paralysis.

Step 3: Generate Creative Solutions

Now that you've identified a specific problem, analyzed its causes and history, and established clear criteria for solutions, you're ready to generate creative options to solve the problem. **Creativity** is the generation, application, combination, and extension of

new ideas. Researchers have found that your entire group is more likely to be creative if individual group members are creative; it's important not to rely on others to be creative, but to develop your own creative skill. It's simply not true that only a few gifted and talented people are creative; creative ideas can come from anyone. Author Malcolm Gladwell believes that our powers of intuition and creativity harbor the greatest potential for generating the breakthrough ideas that can change the world.[22] Your group is more likely to be creative if you do the following things:[23]

- Make sure everyone knows the precise nature of the problem.
- Review and summarize the analysis of the problem.
- Promote a climate of freedom: Let people experiment and play with ideas.
- Don't judge and evaluate the ideas of others prematurely.
- Listen to minority points of view; you never know who may have the next great insight.
- Provide enough time for creativity to occur: don't rush the creative process.

Brainstorming is the classic technique to identify possible solutions to a problem. This technique was developed by an advertising executive over 40 years ago to encourage a group to be creative.[24] You've probably used this technique before. Many groups, however, don't use the technique effectively.

The key to making brainstorming work—to generating many creative ideas—is to *separate the generation of ideas from the evaluation of ideas.* This means group members are supposed to feel free to offer ideas without fear of criticism, snickering, or being made to feel foolish. Reality, however, may be quite different. When group members start suggesting ideas, there may be either verbal or, more likely, nonverbal evaluation of ideas. People may laugh at the more offbeat suggestions; or, when someone announces a suggestion, others may frown, sneer, or voice an editorial comment. Another subtle form of evaluation occurs when some group ideas are praised and some are not. Group members whose ideas are not praised may feel that their ideas are considered stupid. Clearly, when ideas are evaluated, brainstorming doesn't work well; members may be reluctant to share ideas. This is especially true of group members who are shy or uncomfortable talking in a group; these people, however, may have great ideas that are worth sharing. The key to making brainstorming work is to separate the generation of ideas from the evaluation of ideas.

One solution to this problem is to have a period of **silent brainstorming** before members share their ideas verbally. Another name for silent brainstorming is the **nominal group technique.**[25] For a few moments, people work individually—for that period of time, they are a group in name only (hence the name *nominal group technique*). After group members have brainstormed individually, they share their ideas with the group.

The same rules of brainstorming apply to silent brainstorming:

- Set aside judgments and criticism when people offer ideas.
- Think of as many ideas as possible; volume is important.
- Piggyback off of someone else's idea.

Verbal
Nonverbal

brainstorming
A technique for generating many possible solutions to a problem by withholding evaluation while group members suggest ideas; ideas are evaluated after suggestions have been offered.

silent brainstorming (nominal group technique)
A method of generating creative ideas; group members brainstorm individually and write down their ideas before meeting together to share them.

Technology *and* Communication

E-Brainstorming

Computer technology makes it possible to brainstorm electronically. Electronic brainstorming (e-brainstorming) is a technique that helps a team or group to generate many creative ideas. The ideas generated by the electronically linked group are displayed onscreen so that all group members can see and piggyback off those ideas. The screen can be an individual computer screen or one large screen that is visible to all team members; electronic brainstorming can occur when all group members are in the same room or computer lab or when they are at computers in various places such as at home or in different offices.

Is e-brainstorming effective? Research suggests it is.[26] One of the chief virtues of electronic brainstorming is that more ideas are likely to be generated.[27] E-brainstorming groups come up with more ideas than do groups that meet face to face. Some researchers surmise that electronic brainstorming results in more ideas because the ideas are generated anonymously; group members don't have to worry about being criticized for suggesting a wacky or wild idea.[28] They're less likely to be criticized because group members don't know whether they are critiquing an idea that was suggested by the boss or by the newest member of the organization. When brainstorming, it is desirable to have many ideas, even the wild and wacky ones that can be tamed down later.

One of the disadvantages to electronic brainstorming is that it requires the appropriate software and a networked computer system. But when the goal is to generate lots of ideas, electronic brainstorming is an effective method.

- Try to identify one or more zany or wild ideas—this triggers creativity and may lead to a less zany but workable idea.
- Record the ideas on a flip chart or chalkboard when people share them. It's usually best to go around the group one at a time to have group members share what they have written down.
- Evaluate the ideas *after* all of the group members have finished sharing.

Verbal

You may ask group members to do some individual brainstorming before they come to the group meeting. For example, you could say, "Each group member should bring five or ten suggestions for solving our problem." Or you could just invite group members to brainstorm ideas silently for a few minutes and then get into small groups to share and piggyback off of ideas. If everyone has e-mail access, ask group members to do some private brainstorming and e-mail their responses to either the group leader

"All those in favor say 'Aye.'"
"Aye."   "Aye."   "Aye."
"Aye."   "Aye."

or other group members. Another creative way to generate ideas is to have group members first write each idea or suggestion on a Post-It Note®.[29] Once the ideas are on the Post-It Notes®, group members can stick them to the wall and then arrange them in groups. Seeing other group members' ideas may trigger additional creative ideas from the group. The goal is to separate generating or listing ideas from critiquing the ideas. When those two parts of brainstorming get mixed together, fewer ideas flow because of group members' fear of being criticized.

RECAP

Brainstorming Steps

1. Select a problem that needs to be solved.
2. Discuss the history, causes, and background of the problem. Make sure the group knows precisely what options are needed.
3. Tell the group to develop a creative mindset:
   - Put aside judgments and evaluations.
   - Stress quantity of ideas.
   - Avoid criticizing ideas, including your own.
   - Try to come up with one or more wild ideas—stretch your imagination; it's easier to modify wild ideas.
   - Piggyback off someone else's ideas.
4. Start brainstorming. Give the group a time limit.
5. To reduce the possibility that people will evaluate ideas, consider using a period of silent brainstorming before having people verbalize their ideas.
6. Write all of the ideas on the board or flip chart.
7. Keep reminding the group not to evaluate the ideas of others when first expressed.
8. Evaluate the ideas after all ideas have been presented.

Step 4: Select the Best Solution

The next step is to evaluate the ideas your group has identified and pick the best solution. The group now takes the long list of ideas generated and determines which ones best meet the criteria you identified when you analyzed the problem. You also determine which solutions best achieve the clear, elevating goal you identified. This means it's really important that you have both a clear goal and specific criteria—without them, it will be difficult to recognize a good solution when you see it.

It is usually easier for groups to expand alternatives (brainstorm) than it is to narrow alternatives. The methods used by groups to whittle a long list down to a manageable number for more serious debate include these five:

1. *Decision by expert.* Let someone who has high credibility narrow the list.
2. *Rank.* Tell group members to rank their top five choices from 1 to 5.
3. *Rate.* Ask group members to evaluate each solution on a scale from 1 to 5; the solutions rated best get the most serious discussion.
4. *Majority vote.* Group members simply vote for the ideas they like.
5. *Consensus.* Group members seek a solution that all group or team members can accept.

Consensus occurs when there is enough support so that group members will abide by the decision. Consensus doesn't mean everyone agrees enthusiastically and completely with what the group has decided—but at least group members won't stand

consensus
Agreement among all members of a group or team to support an idea, proposal, or solution.

in the way of what the group has decided. Reaching a consensus decision has the advantage that all group members can verbalize support for the decision. But reaching consensus takes time.

Three primary strategies can help groups reach consensus:

1. *Be goal oriented.* Keep the outcomes in mind as you talk.[30] Because groups often bounce from topic to topic, it's important to keep the group oriented toward the goal. When you see the group starting to stray from its task, remind the group what the goals are. It also helps to write ideas and facts on a flip chart or chalkboard; this helps keep groups focused.
2. *Listen.* Work to clarify misunderstandings. When you do agree with something that is said, say so. Maintain eye contact with the speaker and give him or her your full attention.
3. *Promote honest dialogue and discussion.* True consensus is more likely to occur if many ideas are shared and group members don't just give in to avoid conflict.

Table 10.1 compares what effective group members do to achieve consensus with ineffective strategies for reaching agreement.

Be cautious if all group members agree too quickly. You may be experiencing groupthink instead of consensus. **Groupthink** occurs when group members seemingly agree but they primarily just want to avoid conflict. On the surface, it seems as though group members have reached consensus—but it's an illusion of agreement. Another way of describing groupthink is to call it faulty consensus; too little disagreement often reduces the quality of group decisions. If a group does not seriously examine the pros and cons of an idea, it's likely that the quality of the decision it makes will suffer because the group has not used its full power to analyze and evaluate ideas.

Verbal
Listen and Respond

groupthink
A faulty sense of agreement that occurs when members of a group fail to challenge an idea; a false consensus; conflict is minimized and group members do not express concerns or reservations about an idea or proposal.

TABLE 10.1
Suggestions for Reaching Group and Team Consensus

Effective Group Members	Ineffective Group Members
Keep the Group Oriented toward Its Goal	
Remind the group what the goal is.	Go off on tangents and do not stay focused on the agenda.
Write facts and key ideas on a flip chart or chalkboard.	Fail to summarize or rely on oral summaries to keep group members focused on the goal.
Talk about the discussion process; ask questions that keep the group focused on the agenda.	Do little to help summarize or clarify group discussion.
Listen to the Ideas of Others	
Clarify misunderstandings.	Do not clarify misunderstandings or check to see whether others understand their message.
Emphasize areas of agreement.	Ignore areas of agreement.
Maintain eye contact when listening to someone and remain focused on the speaker without interrupting.	Do not have eye contact with the speaker and do not focus attention on the speaker; interrupt the speaker.
Promote Honest Dialogue and Discussion	
Seek out differences of opinion.	Do not seek other opinions from group members.
Do not change their minds quickly to avoid conflict.	Quickly agree with other group members to avoid conflict.
Try to involve everyone in the discussion.	Permit one person or just a few people to talk too much and dominate the conversation.

Source: Adapted from Steven A. Beebe and John T. Masterson, *Communicating in Small Groups: Principles and Practices* 8e (Boston: Allyn and Bacon, 2006).

Failure to test ideas and the resulting groupthink can have serious consequences. Wrong, dangerous, or stupid decisions can be the result. The following list identifies a few well-known disasters or problems in which groupthink was a key factor.

- In 1986 American viewers watched in horror as the *Challenger* space shuttle exploded on live TV. The tragedy resulted from both faulty engineering and groupthink: Some people knew the shuttle wouldn't fly in cold temperature, but because of pressure to stay on schedule, decided not to stop the launch.[31]
- In 1999 several students were killed in a traditional pre-football game bonfire at Texas A&M University in College Station, Texas. Some thought the bonfire construction unsafe before the accident occurred, but because of tradition, the bonfire continued to be built, and tragedy was the result.[32]
- The commission that investigated the terrorist attacks of September 11, 2001, concluded that groupthink was one of the contributing factors to the nation's not being prepared for the attacks.[33] The 9/11 commission believed there was pre-existing evidence of a terrorist threat, yet not enough action was taken to address the problem fully.
- In 2003 the *Columbia* space shuttle disintegrated on re-entry into the earth's atmosphere because of damage sustained during takeoff. Some thought there might be a problem but didn't speak up, so no corrective action was attempted.

The headlines are not the only places to look for examples of groupthink. If you think about it, you'll find plenty of examples in groups and teams you've worked with.

What causes groupthink? Sometimes it occurs because group members are not particularly interested in the topic or are tired and want to get on with other work. If a group has a highly revered leader, someone with high status whom all group members respect, the group is more likely to agree with the leader, rather than test and challenge the leader's ideas. Groupthink also occurs when group members feel they can do no wrong; they feel invincible. So rather than taking time to test and evaluate ideas, the group may quickly decide that their decision is a good one. Groupthink can also occur when (1) the group feels apathetic about its task; (2) group members don't expect to be successful; (3) one group member has very high credibility—group members tend

Ethics and Communication

Managing Conflict in Groups and Teams

Some people think of conflict as bad and detrimental to a group. Yet, in our discussion of groupthink—a false sense of agreement arrived at when people fail to challenge ideas and conclusions—we note that it's important for group members to challenge ideas. Being too uncritical and failing to raise reservations about group conclusions can breed a climate of groupthink. The question is, however, how do you know when to challenge ideas?

Moya knows that she doesn't like to disagree with other members of her project team. When working with this group, she consistently tries to find something positive or pleasant to say about others' comments. When she does disagree with an idea or suggestion of another group member, she usually doesn't voice her opinion. Is it ethical to remain silent because you want to maintain peace when you actually disagree with an idea suggested? When is it best to keep quiet rather than express disagreement that could escalate to more intense conflict? What are your personal criteria for expressing disagreement with others in a group or team? Specifically, when do you speak up, and when do you avoid creating a fuss?

to believe what he or she says; (4) one group member is very persuasive; and (5) group members don't usually challenge ideas—it's expected that group members will agree with one another.[34] Be on the lookout for these symptoms in your groups and teams.

Of course, as the saying goes, "Hindsight is 20/20." After the fact, it can be easy to spot an example of groupthink. The hard part is to be aware of groupthink when it occurs in your group. Knowing the causes and symptoms of groupthink can help you spot it if it occurs in your group and then put an end to it.

To overcome groupthink, consider the following strategies.[35]

Verbal

- Don't agree with someone just because he or she has high status; examine the ideas of others carefully, regardless of their position.
- Consider asking someone from outside the group to evaluate the group's decisions and decision-making process.
- Assign someone to be a devil's advocate—to look for disadvantages to a proposed idea.
- Ask group members to break into smaller teams or pairs to consider both the pros and the cons of a proposed solution.

An easy way to structure the discussion suggested in the last item above is to use a T-chart like the one in Figure 10.4. Simply write the possible solution at the top of the chart (on a flip chart, chalkboard, or transparency using an overhead projector) and then list both the pros and the cons. This technique will help you look at the positive and negative consequences of an action before you leap into a specific recommendation.

RECAP

Top Six Reasons Groups and Teams Sometimes Make Stupid Decisions

No Common Goal	Group does not begin with the end in mind—no collective vision.
Analysis Paralysis	Team members overanalyze unimportant details: talk is valued more than action.
Jumping to Solutions	People propose solutions before the facts are known.
Groupthink	Group and team members agree too quickly—ideas are not questioned or challenged.
Topic Hopping	There is a lack of agenda and structure; discussion is not focused on the goal.
Killer Inch	People agree on major points but argue over minor details.

Step 5: Take Action

Once you have identified your solution(s), your group needs to consider the question "Will it work?" You may want to do a pilot test (practice test) or ask a small group of people what they think of your idea before you "go public" with it. Bouncing your proposed solution off an expert and checking to see if the solution has been successful when others have adopted it can help you test the solution's effectiveness.

If your group not only has to identify a solution but also put it into action, your group will need structure to make sure that details don't fall through the cracks in getting the job done. Perhaps you know the people in the following story:

This is a story about four people: Everybody, Somebody, Anybody, and Nobody. There was an important job to be done and Everybody was asked to do it. Everybody was sure Somebody would do it. Anybody could have done it but Nobody did it. Somebody got

Pros	Cons

FIGURE 10.4
T-Chart

angry about that because it was Everybody's job. Everybody thought Anybody could do it but Nobody realized that Everybody wouldn't do it. It ended up that Everybody blamed Somebody when actually Nobody asked Anybody.

Make a written list of who should do what. Follow up at the next group meeting to see whether the assignments have been completed. Effective groups and teams develop an action plan and periodically review it to make sure Anybody asked Somebody.

RECAP

Reflective-Thinking Steps and Techniques

Steps	Techniques
1. Identify and define the problem.	• Phrase the problem as a policy question. • Use the Journalist's Six Questions (Who? What? When? Where? Why? How?) to help define the issues.
2. Analyze the problem.	• Use force field analysis to identify driving and restraining forces. • Develop clear criteria that clarify the issues and can help in evaluating solutions.
3. Generate creative solutions.	• Use brainstorming • Use silent brainstorming (nominal group technique) or electronic brainstorming.
4. Select the best solution.	• Narrow alternatives using ranking, rating, majority vote, or expert decision. • Reach consensus by being goal oriented, listening, and promoting honest dialogue.
5. Take action.	• Develop a clear action plan. • Make a written list of who should do what.

ENHANCING GROUP AND TEAM LEADERSHIP

Leadership is the ability to influence others through communication. Some view a leader as someone who delegates and directs the group. Others see a leader as someone who is primarily responsible for ensuring that whatever task is assigned or designed by the group is completed. Actually, most groups have many leaders—not just one person who influences others. In fact, each group or team member undoubtedly influences what the group does or does not achieve. Following are the prevailing approaches to analyzing the behavior of effective leaders.

Trait Approach

Are leaders born or made? The **trait approach to leadership** suggests that there are certain attributes or traits that make leaders. According to this approach, if you are born with these traits or if you cultivate leadership skills, then you will be a leader. Researchers have identified intelligence, confidence, social skills, general administrative skill, physical energy, and enthusiasm as some of the traits effective leaders possess.[36] Although many leaders do seem to have traits or special skills that can enhance their ability to influence others, just having these traits does not mean you will be an effective leader. Many of these attributes that researchers have found may be important, but they are not sufficient to make a leader effective. If you are looking for someone to be a leader, you may want to find someone who is intelligent, confident, and has good verbal skills. Another research study found support for two of the communication principles for a lifetime that we've presented in this book: Effective leaders are self aware and adapt to the people they lead and the context in which they lead.[37] But these traits alone will not ensure effective leadership behavior. Leadership is more complicated than that.

Functional Approach

Rather than identifying personality characteristics or other traits, the **functional approach to leadership** categorizes the essential leadership behaviors or functions that need to be performed to enhance the workings of a group. According to the functional approach, there are two broad leadership functions: (1) task functions and (2) process functions. These two functions should look familiar. They are similar to the types of group roles that we discussed in the last chapter.

Task functions include behaviors that help the group or team get the work done. Whether the leader is appointed or elected, one of the responsibilities of leaders is to ensure that the group completes the task it is tackling. The functional approach to leadership suggests that several people can share the leadership functions. These are some of the jobs that often need to be done:

- Helping to set the group's agenda
- Recording what the group does
- Determining when meetings begin and end
- Preparing and distributing handouts
- Initiating or proposing new ideas
- Seeking and giving information
- Suggesting options
- Elaborating on the ideas of others
- Evaluating ideas

In most groups, these key functions are assumed by many if not most group members. A group member who rarely helps with any of these tasks often earns the uncoveted title of "slacker."

---

leadership
The ability to influence the behavior of others through communication.

trait approach to leadership
Leadership approach that identifies specific qualities or characteristics of effective leaders.

functional approach to leadership
Leadership approach that identifies the key task and process roles that need to be performed in a group.

task function
Leadership behavior that helps a group accomplish its job.

Process functions are the second major function leaders assume in groups. Process leaders help maintain a harmonious group climate by encouraging amiable relationships in a group. They seek to maintain a friendly environment that also promotes honest, frank discussion. Process leaders are skilled at "people skills." They listen sensitively to others and are observant of nonverbal cues. They focus on managing relationships by adapting to the needs of individual members. Although a single person can perform these functions, just as with task leadership, more than likely, several people will help maintain the group's process. Specific process roles include the following:

- Energizing the team by encouraging team members to keep at it
- Mediating conflict
- Compromising or helping others to compromise
- Gatekeeping: monitoring discussion to ensure that some members don't talk too much and others too little

In most groups or teams, these process roles are not formally assigned. Although some of the task group functions may be explicitly assigned to others ("Daria, would you make copies of this report?"), process roles are assumed when needed; they emerge based on the needs of the group and the personality, skills, sensitivity, and past experiences of the group members who are present. It is unlikely that you will start a meeting by saying, "Okay, Janice, you're in charge of settling the arguments between Ken and Daryl. And Carl, you try to encourage Muriel and Russell to talk more." Effective leaders are on the lookout for opportunities to enhance the overall climate of the group; they try to catch people doing something right and then offer sincere praise and recognition.

Although Condoleezza Rice may have been born with many of the traits that make her an effective leader, she also has to work at maintaining communication skills that facilitate teamwork.

Styles Approach

The **styles approach to leadership** suggests that leaders operate in one of three primary styles: (1) authoritarian, (2) democratic, and (3) laissez-faire. The methods used to influence group members usually fall into one of these broad categories, outlined in Table 10.2.[38]

Authoritarian leaders influence by giving orders and controlling others. Dictators and military officers assume this leadership style. But you don't have to be in the military or living in a dictatorship to experience an authoritarian leadership style. Perhaps you've felt like mumbling, "Who put *her* in charge?" during a group meeting. Or maybe you have observed that some action needed to be taken and asked someone in the group to do what you thought was needed. As we discussed, groups need a certain amount of structure. The authoritarian leader assumes he or she knows the type and amount of structure the group needs and proceeds to tell others what to do. Authoritarian leaders may be self-aware and may use appropriate verbal and nonverbal messages, but they are not always known for listening and responding to others; they also may not be worried about adapting their messages to those whom they lead. They often speak and expect others to follow. Of the three primary leadership styles, the authoritarian leader is least effective over a long period of time.[39] Yet when a group or team experiences increasing stress, a decisive leader is perceived as more charismatic.[40] Group members don't like an authoritarian leader all of the time, but they may tolerate or even appreciate a bold, charismatic leader when there's a need for a quick, important decision.

The **democratic leader,** as you might guess from the name, consults with the group before issuing edicts. The democratic leader listens and adapts messages to others. This type of leader seeks to join in the process of influencing without bulldozing or shoving the group into action it may resent. Sometimes formal votes are taken in larger groups or assemblies; but in smaller groups, the leader or leaders gauge the reaction of

Nonverbal
Listen and Respond

process function
Leadership behavior that helps maintain a positive group climate.

styles approach to leadership
Leadership approach that identifies three methods of interacting when leading others: authoritarian or directive, democratic, and laissez-faire.

authoritarian leader
One who leads by directing, controlling, telling, and ordering others.

democratic leader
One who leads by developing a consensus among group members; a leader who asks for input and uses the input of others when leading and making decisions.

TABLE 10.2
Leadership Styles

Authoritarian	Democratic	Laissez-Faire
The leader makes all policy decisions.	The leader discusses all policy decisions with group members. The group makes decisions by consensus.	The leader gives minimal direction to discussions of policy decisions. Group members must initiate discussions about policy and procedures.
The leader determines what will happen one step at a time; future steps are unclear or uncertain.	The group discusses what steps need to be taken. Group members work together to develop both short-term and long-term action steps.	The leader may supply information about what steps to be taken, if asked. The leader does not volunteer information.
The leader tells people what to do.	The leader serves as a facilitator to develop a collaborative approach to accomplishing the group's work.	The leader does not participate in making work assignments.

the group through dialogue and nonverbal cues. The democratic leader leads by developing a consensus decision, rather than telling people what to do or think.

The **laissez-faire leader** takes a hands-off, laid-back approach to influencing. This type of leader shies away from actively influencing the group. He or she influences only when pushed to lead. Like the authoritarian leader, this type of leader often does not adapt to the needs of the group. This leadership approach is easiest to spot when an elected or appointed leader won't lead. Some laissez-faire leaders fear making a mistake. Others just want to be liked and don't want to ruffle anyone's feathers. But as the slogan goes, "Not to decide is to decide." The laissez-faire leader is influencing the group by his or her silence or inactivity. The team may have a problem to unravel, but the laissez-faire leader is reluctant to act.

Which leadership style works best? It depends. During times of crisis, the group needs a decisive leader who can help manage uncertainty and provide appropriate structure.[41] During a military battle, the commander doesn't ask for a democratic vote; someone needs to lead the group to take decisive action. If the group's task is to solve a problem or make a decision collaboratively, then the democratic leadership style is what the group needs. An authoritarian or dictatorial leader may squelch the free flow of ideas needed to analyze issues and identify a solution. And if a group's goal is primarily social or creative, a laissez-faire leader may be best. Rather than needing structure and agendas, when trying to come up with a creative idea, such a group may function best with no direct influence from a leader.

The effective leader adapts his or her style to fit the needs of the group and the task at hand. The principle of adapting to others gives rise to the situational approach to leadership. Remember, leadership in groups and teams is usually shared by several people. Even when someone has been appointed or elected to be "the leader," leadership roles are often assumed by several group members.

Situational Approach

The **situational approach to leadership** views leadership as an interactive process whereby such factors as culture, time limitations, group member personalities, and the work the group needs to do determine a particular style of leadership. Sometimes a group needs a strong, authoritarian leader to make decisions quickly so that the group can achieve its goal. Although a democratic leadership style is preferred by most groups, leaders sometimes need to be more assertive, especially in times of crisis or high uncertainty.

laissez-faire leader
One who fails to lead, or who leads or exerts influence only when asked or directed by the group.

situational approach to leadership
A view of leadership as an interactive process in which a leader gauges how to lead based on such factors as the quality of the relationship among group members, the power of the leader, the nature of the task, and the maturity of the group.

One of the most popular Situational Leadership models used to train managers in corporate settings was developed by Paul Hersey and Kenneth Blanchard.[42] Their model, shown in Figure 10.5, considers three key factors: (1) relationship behavior, (2) task behavior, and (3) the readiness of the group members. Relationship behavior involves whether group members like one another and work together easily. Task behavior includes whether the work is highly structured or not. Readiness is the group's overall "ability and willingness to accomplish a specific task."[43] The authors of the Situational Leadership model say that readiness is not a specific personality characteristic; rather, it's simply how ready someone is to complete the task before him or her. Group members are ready if they have two things: (1) the *ability* to do the work (they have knowledge, skill, and experience), and (2) the *willingness* to do the work (they have the confidence, commitment, and motivation to complete the task).

You'll notice that the graph in Figure 10.5 is divided into quadrants. Quadrant S1 represents a group that needs high structure: Group members need to be told what to do, because the task behavior is important (they need to act), their relationship skills are low, and they are insecure in their ability to do the work. The leader would do well to provide clear agendas and tell group members what to do. As relationship skill develops and trust evolves, the group's behavior moves into quadrant S2. The leader can ease up a bit and "sell," rather than "tell." Structure is needed, but the group is begin-

Adapt

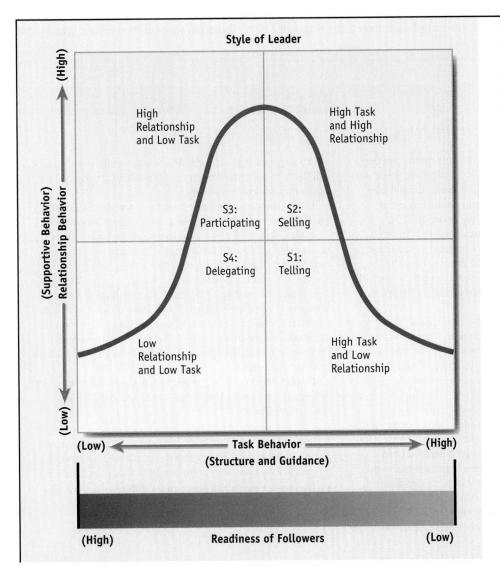

FIGURE 10.5
Situational Leadership® Model

Source: Paul Hersey et al. *Management of Organizational Behavior: Leading Human Resources*, 8th ed. © Copyrighted material. Adapted/reprinted with permission of Center for Leadership Studies, Escondido, CA 92025. All Rights Reserved.

ning to find its way without rigid direction. In quadrant S3, a more ready group with high relationship skills can participate in the process with even less structure; a participatory, democratic style will work best. If trust and relational comfort decline and the task is more unstructured the group has moved to quadrant S4. The leader can best help the group by delegating—giving assignments to specific people to get the job done.[44]

One simple rule of determining your leadership style is this: When the leader emerges naturally from the group or leads a one-time-only group, then the group will permit him or her to be more directive. If the group will be together for some time and the quality of group relations is important to the functioning of the group, a more participative, democratic leadership style is in order.[45]

Transformational Leadership

One of the newest leadership approaches to emerge is called the **transformational approach to leadership**.[46] The transformational leader influences the group or organization by *transforming* the group—giving it a new vision, energizing or realigning the culture, or giving the group a new structure. The leader leads by helping the group see all the possibilities within the group. The transformational leader also develops a relationship with those whom he or she leads. Author Peter Senge suggests three fundamental skills of transformational leadership: (1) Build a shared vision, (2) challenge existing ways of thinking, and (3) be a systems thinker—help a group or team see that everything is connected to everything else.[47] Emerging research results suggests that

transformational approach to leadership
A view of leadership that defines a leader as one who leads by shaping the vision of the group and by developing trust through quality interpersonal relationships with group members.

monochronic
Preferring to do one thing at a time, pay attention to deadlines and schedules, and use time efficiently.

polychronic
Preferring to do many things at once, place less emphasis on deadlines and schedules, and consider relationships to be more important than work and meeting deadlines.

Diversity and Communication

Differences in the Use of Time in Groups and Teams

Mark was frustrated. He was sure the meeting was supposed to start at 11:00 AM. But it was now 11:15 AM, and no one else was there. About 5 minutes later Gilbert arrived; Samantha showed up a few minutes after that. Then Joe arrived at about 11:30. "Where were you guys?" Mark asked, exasperated. "Oh, we thought you knew. When we say 11:00 AM in our organization, that means we'll actually start 20 or 30 minutes after that," said Joe. While Mark now had at least some insight, he was still frustrated and puzzled. Mark and his colleagues had different assumptions about time.

Have you ever worked with people who just never quite seemed to be punctual, didn't pay attention to deadlines, and took their own sweet time getting things done? Yet other people never miss a deadline and are always punctual. One cultural difference that makes a difference in how we communicate in groups and teams is the use of time.

Some people are **monochronic;** they like to do only one thing at a time, pay attention to deadlines and schedules, and make plans to use time efficiently. Others are **polychronic;** they do many things at a time, don't worry about deadlines and schedules, believe relationships are more important than work, change plans more frequently, and are less concerned about deadlines than are monochronic individuals.[48]

People from North America and Northern Europe tend to be more monochronic; deadlines and timelines are valued. Re-

search suggests that for North Americans, monitoring the clock and being aware of how much time there is to accomplish the work can enhance productivity.[49]

Latin Americans, Southern Europeans, and Middle Easterners are often more polychronic; deadlines and strict adherence to schedules are less important. Western cultures have a tendency to approach a discussion of problems in groups or teams in a more linear, step-by-step manner. Structuring, scheduling, and agendas are important. In Eastern cultures, such as China and Japan, problem-solving approaches often follow a less structured, more narrative approach.[50] One team of scholars found that North Americans tend to believe that only one thing can or should be done at a time.[51] People from Latin American cultures, in contrast, are more comfortable working on multiple tasks simultaneously.

If you find you're in a group whose members have different cultural approaches to time, what should you do? Consider these suggestions:

- Don't pounce on other team members and accuse them of being laggards (or slave drivers). Let them know some of your assumptions about how the work should be done.
- Take some time to talk about those differences. Conversation and compromise can accomplish a lot when cultural differences exist.

transformational leaders can contribute to enhanced team cohesiveness and can improve perceptions of team performance.[52] They achieve these benefits by linking with other groups and teams either inside or outside the organization; they help the group span boundaries and stay connected with issues and forces that influence the group.[53]

Articulating a collective vision is an important part of what a transformational leader does. An authoritarian leader would just tell the group, "Here's your vision; now get to work." The democratic leader would say, "What vision do you want?" The laissez-faire leader would do nothing about a vision unless asked to do something. The situational leader would say, "Let me see what type of group I'm leading and listen to group members, and then I'll share a vision." The transformational leader paints a picture of the future for the group by getting to know individual members in the group. Drawing on the approaches of both the democratic leader and the situational leader, the transformational leader leads by establishing quality interpersonal relationships with others. Transformational leaders provide inspiration, motivation, and intellectual stimulation for the group by being aware of individual needs. A wise leader will also consider the cultural backgrounds of those whom she or he leads. Research supports the important role of culture in influencing the style of leadership that seems to be best suited to a team.[54] A group with a collective cultural framework seems to appreciate more participative styles of leadership.

Aware
Listen and Respond

Transformational leadership is less a set of prescribed skills or techniques and more a general philosophy that says people can be trusted and can be motivated to achieve important goals if they have someone they can trust to help them see the possibilities. Transformational leaders like to think of themselves as coaches or mentors rather than leaders who dictate or even just facilitate interaction; they are sometimes viewed as "the guide on the side" rather than "the sage on the stage."

Can transformational leadership skills, or any leadership skills, be taught, the way you can teach someone to drive a car? Some suggest that experience is the best teacher.[55] You can learn how to communicate, listen, relate, and solve problems, but having an opportunity to practice these skills in real-life settings may be the best way to develop your leadership skills. Whether you learn leadership skills and principles from a book or from the "School of Life," the role of a good leader should be that of a servant, helping others accomplish a goal. This ancient description of a wise leader offers considerable insight into what makes a leader great:

The wicked leader the people despise.
The good leader the people revere.
Of the great leader the people say,
"We did it ourselves."

—Lao Tsu

ENHANCING GROUP AND TEAM MEETINGS

Humor columnist Dave Barry said, "If you had to identify, in one word, the reason why the human race has not achieved, and never will achieve, its full potential, that word would be meetings."[56] Meetings are an inescapable fact of life for most people and will undoubtedly be inescapable for you as well.

Aware
Verbal
Nonverbal
Listen and Respond
Adapt

Why does meeting participation inspire such a negative reaction—not only from Dave Barry, but from many people? Often, it's because meeting leaders and participants have not mastered the principles we've stressed as fundamental to communication success in any context. Meetings are more productive if participants are aware of their behaviors and the behavior of others. Using and interpreting verbal and nonverbal messages effectively is also vital for meeting effectiveness, as is listening and responding to messages with sensitivity. Because of the complexity and uncertainty that arise when people collaborate, being able to adapt message content and message struc-

The participants at this meeting likely have all three of the most common goals of meetings: giving information, discussing information and taking action.

ture is essential. We conclude this chapter by providing some tips for managing one of the most likely collaborative contexts you'll encounter—meetings.

What specific problems occur most frequently in meetings? Based on a survey of meeting participants, the most common meeting "sin" is getting off the subject.[57] The second biggest problem is not having clear goals or a meeting agenda. Meeting goers also reported that meetings were often too long, people weren't prepared, nothing really happened, meetings started late, and there were often no follow-up action plans.

Meetings need two essential things in order to be effective: *structure* and *interaction*. Sound familiar? As we noted earlier in the chapter, groups also need a balance of these two things.

Many of the meeting problems we've described stem from a lack of clear structure—no clear written agenda, no one helping to keep the group on track. You can also see that too many unstructured interactions lead to unfocused discussion. Consequently, nothing gets done. Being able to adapt to the need for structure and interaction is a fundamental principle of meeting management. The essential tool for giving a meeting structure is the agenda. To manage interaction, meeting participants need to be good facilitators of talk. We'll look more closely at how to provide these two essential needs.

Manage Meeting Structure

As we just noted, the essential weapon to combat disorganized, rambling meetings is a clear, well-developed agenda. An **agenda** is a list of the key issues, ideas, and information that will be discussed, in the order of discussion. How do you develop a well-crafted agenda? Consider these three steps.

agenda
The written plan for achieving the goals during a group meeting; typically includes items for discussion, action, and information.

Step One: Determine Your Meeting Goals   Every meeting seeks to accomplish something. (If you don't have something to accomplish, don't hold a meeting!) Most meetings have one or more of the following three goals: (1) giving information, (2) discussing information, and (3) taking action.

- *Giving information.* An information-giving meeting is like a briefing or a series of short speeches. If the only task is to share information, you may not really need a meeting at all—a written memo or an e-mail message will suffice. But if you want to share information with others face to face to emphasize its importance, then giving information is an appropriate primary meeting goal.
- *Discussing information.* An information-discussion meeting is one in which there is considerable interaction and give-and-take discussion. The key in this type of meeting is not to let it become a series of long-winded speeches. Also, if you're not careful, discussions digress off the topic. The meeting leader or meeting participants should be aware of the goals of the discussion so that the comments remain relevant.
- *Taking action.* A meeting may involve making a decision, solving a problem, or implementing a decision or solution. If the purpose of the meeting is to take action, it's helpful if group members know before they arrive for the meeting that they will be asked to take some action.

On the Web

When you lead a meeting, you need all the help you can get. An informative Web site called The Virtual Meeting Assistant provides a list of skills and strategies that adds to the discussion in this chapter about facilitating a meeting. Here's the Web address:

www.ku.edu/~coms/virtual_assistant/vma/vms.htm/

Another site offers information to help you conduct a meeting via the Internet. Here you'll find an introduction to software and other resources that will enhance your ability to conduct a virtual meeting:

www.learnthenet.com/english/html/30conf.htm/

Step Two: Identify What Needs to be Discussed to Achieve the Goal   After you have determined your goal(s), you need to determine how to structure the meeting to achieve the goal. What topics need to be covered to achieve the goal? What information do we need? What issues do we need to focus on? Brainstorm answers for these questions, but don't worry about the precise order of the items yet; focus on organizing the agenda after you know what you need to discuss.

Step Three: Organize the Agenda   Once you have identified your meeting goals (giving information, discussing information, taking action) and assessed what you need to talk about, take time to arrange the items in the most effective way to achieve your goals. There are several strategies for organizing effective meetings.[58]

- Organize the agenda around your meeting goals. If you're meeting to solve a problem you could use the five problem-solving steps as an agenda-setting guide: (1) identify and define the problem, (2) analyze the problem, (3) generate creative options, (4) select the best option, (5) take action. A single meeting may focus on only one or two of those steps; don't feel you have to cram all five problem-solving steps into every meeting.
- Use subheads of "Information Items," "Discussion Items," and "Action Items" as you construct your agenda to signal to group members the goal of the discussion, as shown in the sample meeting agenda.
- Consider putting your most important agenda item first, because usually what is introduced first takes the most time.
- There may be times when you will want to put your most challenging issue for discussion in the middle of the meeting; this gives the group a chance to get oriented at the beginning and ease out of the discussion at the end.[59]
- Consider making your first agenda item something that will immediately involve all meeting participants in active discussion. If you start with routine reports (a common practice), you establish a norm of passivity, and boredom is the usual result.
- If you are going to discuss a conflict-producing topic, you may want to put that agenda item after an issue on which you think the group will reach agreement;

groups may be more likely to reach agreement on a contentious issue if they have already reached agreement on another point.

- Start the meeting by asking meeting participants if they have any other agenda items to consider. That way you aren't as likely to be surprised by people who want to add something after you've planned the meeting agenda.
- After you've prepared your agenda, estimate how long you think the group will take to discuss each agenda item. Most groups take more time than you would expect to talk about issues and ideas.

A sample agenda is shown below. Note how the meeting has clear goals. Also note how many of the agenda items are phrased as questions. Questions give an agenda focus and help to manage discussion.

When your job is to lead the meeting, you have several specific tasks to perform, including the following:

1. Call the group together; find out when is the best time to meet (often a major problem for busy people).
2. Develop an agenda, using the steps already described.
3. Determine whether there is a **quorum**—the minimum number of persons who must be present at a meeting to conduct business.
4. Call the meeting to order.
5. Use a flip chart, chalkboard, or dry-erase board to summarize meeting progress; written notes of the meeting become the "group mind" and help keep the group structured.
6. Decide when to take a vote.
7. Prepare a final report or delegate to a group member the preparation of a report or minutes.

SAMPLE MEETING AGENDA

Meeting Goals:

1. Discuss new product proposal: evaluate the pros and cons
2. Decide whether to implement the personnel policy and mentor program
3. Receive updates from committees

    I. Discussion Items

       A. How should we revise today's agenda?

       B. Identify new problems: What new issues or problems have you identified?

       C. React to new product team proposal (distributed by e-mail): What are the pros and cons of the proposal?

    II. Action Items

       A. Should we approve the new personnel policy (distributed by e-mail)?

       B. Issue: Should we implement new mentor program? If so, what should the program policies be?

    III. Information Items

       A. New employee orientation report

       B. Planning committee report

       C. Finance committee report

       D. Announcements

quorum
The minimum number of persons who must be present at a meeting to conduct business.

RECAP

Making Meeting Agendas Useful

Potential Meeting Agenda Problem	Suggested Meeting Agenda Strategy
Meeting participants tend to spend more time on the first or second agenda item.	Make sure the early agenda items are something the group needs to spend time on.
Meeting participants want to talk, even if the meeting leader just wants them to listen.	Take advantage of the desire to participate by inviting input and discussion early in the meeting rather than trying to squelch discussion or interrupt group members.
Meeting participants aren't prepared. They haven't done their "homework."	Take a few minutes for silent reading. Let members get up to speed by reviewing information or quickly looking at key pieces of data.
Meeting participants won't stick to the agenda.	Continue to remind the group of the agenda and the overall goal of the meeting. Make sure to distribute a written agenda ahead of the meeting.
There is an agenda item that may produce conflict and disagreement.	Help the group develop a sense of success by putting one or more noncontroversial items on the agenda ahead of the item that may produce conflict. Build on the group's ability to reach agreement.

Manage Meeting Interaction

Interaction, as you recall, is the back-and-forth dialogue and discussion in which participants engage during meetings. Without interaction, meetings would be like a monologue, a speech, or a seminar, rather than a lively discussion. But too much unfocused interaction can result in a disorganized, chaotic discussion. To keep a meeting on track, meeting leaders and participants need facilitation skills. The most important facilitation skills include being a gatekeeper, using metadiscussion, monitoring discussion time, and structuring discussion techniques to keep discussion focused.

- *Use gatekeeping skills.* A gatekeeper helps to encourage less-talkative members to participate and tries to limit long-winded contributions by other group members. Gatekeepers need to be good listeners so that they can help manage the flow of conversation. Gatekeepers make such comments as, "Ashley, we haven't heard your ideas yet. Won't you share your thoughts with us?" Or, "Mike, thanks for sharing, but I'd like to hear what others have to say." Polite, tactful invitations to talk or limit talk usually work. You may need to speak privately with a chronic oververbalizer to let him or her know that you'd appreciate a more balanced discussion.
- *Use metadiscussion.* **Metadiscussion** literally means "discussion about discussion."[60] It's a comment about the discussion process rather than about the topic under consideration. Metadiscussional statements include, "I'm not following this conversation. What is our goal?" Or, "Can someone summarize what we've accomplished so far?" Or, "Peggy, I'm not sure I understand how your observa-

metadiscussion
Discussion about the discussion process; comments that help the group remain focused on the goals of the group or that point out how the group is doing its work.

Listen and Respond

Verbal

tion relates to our meeting goal." These comments contain information and advice about the communication *process*, rather than about the issues that are being discussed.

Metadiscussional phrases are helpful ways to keep the team or group focused on the task. Obviously, metadiscussional statements should not be phrased to personally attack others. Don't just blurt out, "You're off task" or "Oh, let's not talk about that anymore." Instead, use tactful ways of letting other group members know you'd like to return to the issues at hand. Use "I" messages rather than "You" messages to bring the group back on track. An **"I" message** begins with the word "I," such as "I am not sure where we are in our discussion" or "I am lost here." A **"you" message** is a way of phrasing a message that makes others feel defensive—for example, "You're not following the agenda" or "Your point doesn't make any sense." Another way to express these same ideas, but with less of a negative edge, is to use "I" messages such as "I'm not sure where we are on the agenda" or "I'm not sure I understand how your point relates to the issue we are discussing." Being able to carry on metadiscussion is an exceptionally powerful skill, because you can offer metadiscussional statements even if you are not the appointed leader.

- *Monitor time.* Being sensitive to the time the group is spending on an issue is yet another skill necessary to manage meeting interaction. Think of your agenda as a map, helping you plan where you want to go. Think of the clock as your gas gauge, telling you the amount of fuel you have to get where you want to go. In a meeting, keeping one eye on the clock and one eye on the agenda is analogous to focusing on the map and the gas gauge on a car trip. If you are running low on fuel (time), you will either need to get more gas (budget more time) or recognize that you will not get where you want to go. Begin each meeting by asking how long members can meet. If you face two or three crucial agenda items, and one-third of your group has to leave in an hour, you may need to reshuffle your agenda to make sure you can achieve your goals.

- *Use structure to manage interaction.* Another way to manage interaction is to use some of the prescriptive structures that we talked about earlier. For example, using silent brainstorming is a way to gain maximum participation from everyone. Yet another strategy is to ask people to come to the meeting with written responses to questions that you've posed in the agenda that group members received in advance of the meeting. This signals that you want people to prepare for the meeting rather than doing their "homework" at the meeting. An essential task of the meeting facilitator is to orchestrate meaningful interaction during the meeting so that all group or team members have opportunity to share. Another structured method of inviting involvement is to have group members first write individually and then share their ideas with the group. Having members write before speaking is like

"I" message
A message in which you state your perspective or point of view.

"you" message
A message that is likely to create defensiveness in others because it emphasizes how another person has created a problem, rather than describing the problem from one's own perspective ("I" message).

providing them with a script that can be effective in garnering contributions from *all* group members—not just the people who talk the most or who aren't shy about speaking up.

One of the best ways to ensure appropriate interaction as a meeting participant when you are not assigned the specific role of leader is to consider the following suggestions from Roger Mosvic and Robert Nelson in their book *We've Got to Start Meeting Like This!*.[61]

- Organize what you say. Don't ramble.
- Speak to the point. Make sure your contributions are relevant to the goal.
- Make one point at a time.
- Speak clearly and forcefully. Weak, timid suggestions mumbled to the group will probably not be listened to.
- Support your ideas with evidence. Don't just assert opinion without data or expert opinion backing you up.
- Listen. Listen. Listen. Connect your comments to those of others.

What are the best strategies to make yourself a valuable meeting leader or participant? The five communication principles for a lifetime that we've emphasized throughout the book will serve you well. In general, be aware of your own behavior and the behavior of others. Monitor your verbal and nonverbal messages to make sure you are making comments relevant to the task at hand, but also be sensitive to the needs of the people in your group. You develop that sensitivity by listening to others and thoughtfully responding. Ineffective meeting participants make little effort to link their comments to what others are saying. They also don't adapt to the messages of others. Effective communicators adapt what they say and do to help achieve the goals of the group.

Verbal

Listen and Respond

Aware
Verbal
Nonverbal
Listen and Respond
Adapt

RECAP

Strategies for Effective Meetings

How to Give a Meeting Structure	How to Ensure Managed Interaction
Prepare an effective agenda by • Determining your meeting goals • Identifying what needs to be discussed to achieve the goals • Organizing the agenda to achieve the goals	Keep discussion on track by • Using effective gatekeeping skills • Using metadiscussion to help the group focus on the goals • Helping the group be sensitive to elapsed time and time remaining for deliberation • Using strategies to manage interaction (for example, writing before speaking, nominal group technique, or silent brainstorming)

Structure ⟷ Interaction

PRINCIPLES FOR A LIFETIME: Enhancing Your Skills

Principle One: Be aware of your communication with yourself and others.
- Be sensitive to your group's need for appropriate structure to organize and focus the discussion or interaction and to encourage dialogue.
- Be aware of the appropriate leadership style to meet your group's needs.

Aware

Principle Two: Effectively use and interpret verbal messages.
- Use appropriate verbal messages to identify and define the problem, analyze the problem, generate creative solutions, select the best solution, and take action.
- Clearly describe the goal of the group.
- Evaluate the merits of ideas by verbalizing both the pros and the cons.
- Use verbal messages to express your need for information and your sensitivity to other group members' feelings.
- Use verbal messages to articulate a vision and motivate a team.
- Develop and use written agendas to give meetings structure.
- Manage the amount of interaction in a group by encouraging quiet members to participate and overly dominant members to let others express ideas.
- Use metadiscussion to keep a meeting on track.

Verbal

Principle Three: Effectively use and interpret nonverbal messages.
- Use appropriate nonverbal messages to establish and maintain a positive group climate.
- Do your best to avoid nonverbally expressing your evaluation of others' ideas when brainstorming.
- Communicate your sensitivity to other group members through your nonverbal behavior.
- Use eye contact and other nonverbal cues to regulate the flow of interaction in group and team meetings.

Nonverbal

Principle Four: Listen and respond thoughtfully to others.
- Listen to other group members to determine whether your group is accomplishing the appropriate group functions.
- Listen and respond to others to express your sensitivity to other's ideas and opinions.
- Listen and respond to others to provide appropriate leadership.
- Listen and respond to provide appropriate contributions to group meetings and problem-solving discussions.

Listen and Respond

Principle Five: Appropriately adapt messages to others.
- Adapt your comments to ensure that your group spends an appropriate amount of time on the five functions of effective groups.
- Adapt your leadership and group membership styles to achieve the goals of the group.
- Adapt your messages to help the group identify, define, and analyze the problem, create solutions, select the best solution, and take action.
- Adapt your messages to give group meetings appropriate structure and to foster interaction.

Adapt

SUMMARY

Specific strategies can help groups and teams operate at peak performance levels. Research has identified several essential functions that, when performed in a group, enhance the group performance. Effective group members describe the goal, analyze information, generate creative ideas, evaluate ideas, and are sensitive to group social and relationship concerns.

Groups also perform best if they have appropriate structure to make an often bumpy process smoother. Although group communication researchers have identified different steps, methods, and procedures, there is no single best series of steps that will ensure high performance. In his book *How We Think*, John Dewey described five problem-solving steps: (1) Identify and define the problem, (2) analyze the problem, (3) generate creative solutions, (4) select the best solution, and (5) take action.

High-performing groups have competent group leaders. Researchers have devised several approaches to analyzing leadership. The trait approach to leadership seeks to identify certain characteristics or traits that all leaders possess. Leadership is more complicated than finding leaders with just the right traits, however. The functional approach to leadership suggests that leaders need to be concerned with both task functions and group process functions. The functional leadership approach identifies specific roles that leaders should perform. A third approach to understanding leadership, the styles approach, identifies leaders as authoritarian, democratic, or laissez-faire. No one style seems to work all of the time. The situational leadership approach suggests that the best leadership style depends on a variety of factors, including the readiness of the group, the urgency of the problem, and the type of issue the group is discussing. Finally, transformational leadership is an approach that encourages leaders to help shape the vision and goals of the group by being in touch with followers. Groups can be transformed if the leaders help articulate a vision for the future that takes the group in new directions yet builds on the vision and goals of the group.

Groups need a balance of structure and interaction. Groups can gain appropriate structure if meeting planners develop and use an agenda to keep the discussion focused and on track. Meetings also need appropriate amounts of dialogue and discussion. Effective meeting participants monitor the amount of participation from other group or team members and serve as gatekeepers to ensure that ooververbalizers don't monopolize the discussion or quiet members don't feel intimidated.

Discussion and Review

1. What are the five essential functions that groups should perform?
2. What are the five steps to structure group problem solving?
3. What is the trait approach to leadership?
4. Describe the functional leadership approach.
5. What are the differences between authoritarian, democratic, and laissez-faire leadership styles?
6. Identify the assumption underlying the situational leadership approach.
7. What is the transformational leadership approach?
8. How can you provide appropriate structure for a group meeting?
9. What are strategies or techniques for ensuring appropriate interaction during group or team meetings?

Putting Principles into Practice

1. *Hurricane Preparedness Case*[62]

    Although you have idly watched local meteorologists track Hurricane Bruce's destructive course through the Caribbean for several days, you have not given any serious thought to the possibility that the storm might directly affect your coastal city. However, at about 7 o'clock this morning, the storm suddenly veered northward, putting it on course for a direct hit. Now the National Hurricane Center in Miami has posted a Hurricane Warning for your community. Forecasters are predicting landfall in approximately 9 to 12 hours. Having taken no advance precautions, you are stunned by the amount of work you have to do to secure your three-bedroom suburban home, which is about a half-mile from the beach. You have enough food in the house for

2 days. You also have one candle and a transistor radio with one weak battery. You have no other hurricane supplies, nor have you taken any hurricane precautions.

Your task is to rank the following items in terms of the importance for ensuring your survival and the safety of your property. Place number 1 by the first thing you should do, 2 by the second, and so on through number 13. Please work individually on this task.

_____ Fill your car's gas tank
_____ Trim your bushes and trees
_____ Fill your bathtub with water
_____ Construct hurricane shutters for your windows
_____ Buy enough food for a week
_____ Buy batteries and candles
_____ Bring in patio furniture from outside
_____ Buy dry ice
_____ Invite friends over for a hurricane party
_____ Drain your swimming pool
_____ Listen to TV and radio for further bulletins before doing anything
_____ Make sure you have an evacuation plan
_____ Stock up on charcoal and charcoal lighter for your barbecue grill

After you have made your individual decisions, work in a small group with others and try to reach consensus on a ranking of the items according to their importance.

2. *Stranded in the Desert Situation*[63]

You are a member of a geology club that is on a field trip to study unusual formations in the New Mexico desert. It is the last week in July. You have been driving over old trails, far from any road, in order to see out-of-the-way formations. At about 10:30 AM, your club's specially equipped minibus overturns, rolls into a 20-foot ravine, and burns. The driver and the club advisor are killed. The rest of you are relatively uninjured.

You know that the nearest ranch is approximately 45 miles east of where you are. There is no closer habitation. When your club does not report to its motel that evening, you will be missed. Several people know generally where you are but will not be able to pinpoint your whereabouts.

The area around you is rather rugged and dry. There is a shallow waterhole nearby, but the water is contaminated by worms, animal feces and urine, and several dead mice. Before you left, you heard on a weather report that the temperature would reach 108 degrees, making the surface temperature 128 degrees. All of you are dressed in lightweight summer clothing, and all have hats and sunglasses.

While escaping from the minibus, each group member salvaged a couple of items; there are 12 items in all. Your group's task is to rank these items according to their importance to your survival, starting with 1 for the most important and proceeding to 12 for the least important. You may assume that the number of club members is the same as the number of persons in your group and that the group has agreed to stick together.

_____ Magnetic compass
_____ A piece of heavy-duty, light-blue canvas, 20 square feet in size
_____ Book, *Plants of the Desert*
_____ Rearview mirror
_____ Large knife
_____ Flashlight
_____ One jacket per person
_____ One transparent, plastic ground cloth (6 feet by 4 feet) per person
_____ A .38-caliber loaded pistol
_____ One 2-quart plastic canteen of water per person
_____ An accurate map of the area
_____ A large box of kitchen matches

3. *Assessing Group and Team Problem-Solving Competencies*[64]

Use the evaluation form on pages 278–279 to assess the presence or absence of small group communication competencies in a group or team discussion. Competencies are specific behaviors that group and team members perform. This assessment form includes nine competencies organized into four general categories. Here's how to use the form:

a. Observe a group or team that is attempting to solve a problem. Write the names of the group members at the top of the form. (If the group includes more than five group members, photocopy the form so that each group member can be evaluated.)

b. When using the form, first decide whether each group member has performed each competency. Circle NO if the group member was not observed performing the competency. Circle YES if you did observe the group member performing the competency (e.g., defining the problem, analyzing the problem, identifying criteria, and so on).

c. For each competency for which you circled YES determine how effectively the competency was performed. Use a scale from 0–3:

0 = The group member performed this competency but did so inappropriately or inadequately. For example, the person observed tried to define the problem but did so poorly.

1 = Overall, the person's performance of this competency was adequate.

2 = Overall, the person's performance of this competency was good.

3 = Overall, the person's performance of this competency was excellent.

d. Total the score for each group member in each of the four categories.

The first category, *Problem-Oriented Competencies*, consists of items 1 and 2. These are behaviors that help the group or team define and analyze the problem. If a group member performed the competencies, his or her total number of points will range from 0 to 6. The higher the number of points, the better the individual performed this competency.

Solution-Oriented Competencies include items 3, 4, and 5; the total number of points for this category can range from 0 to 9. These competencies focus on how well the group or team member helped develop and evaluate a solution to the problem.

Discussion Management Competencies, competencies that helped the group or team remain focused or helped the group manage interaction, are items 6 and 7. The total points for this category can range from 0 to 6.

Relational Competencies are behaviors that focus on dealing with conflict and developing a positive, supportive group climate. Items 8 and 9 reflect this competency; points for this category can range from 0 to 6.

e. You can also assess the group's or team's overall ability to perform these competencies. The column marked "Group Assessment" can be used to record your overall impressions of how effectively the group or team behaved. Circle NO if no one in the group performed a particular competency. Circle YES if at least one person in the group or team performed this competency. Then evaluate how well the entire group performed this competency, using the scale already described.

Sometimes it is difficult to make so many judgments about group competencies by just viewing a group discussion once. Many people find that it's easier to videotape the group discussion so that you can observe it more than once.

Competent Group Communicator				
Problem-Solving Group Communication Competencies		Group Member		Group Member

Problem-Oriented Competencies

	Group Member			Group Member		
1. **Defined the problem** the group attempted to solve.	NO	YES 0 1 2 3		NO	YES 0 1 2 3	
2. **Analyzed the problem** the group attempted to solve. Used relevant information, data, or evidence, discussed the causes, obstacles, history, symptoms, or significance of the problem.	NO	YES 0 1 2 3		NO	YES 0 1 2 3	

Solution-Oriented Competencies

	Group Member			Group Member		
3. **Identified criteria** for an appropriate solution to the problem.	NO	YES 0 1 2 3		NO	YES 0 1 2 3	
4. **Generated solutions** or alternatives to the problem.	NO	YES 0 1 2 3		NO	YES 0 1 2 3	
5. **Evaluated solution(s):** Identified positive or negative consequences of the proposed solutions.	NO	YES 0 1 2 3		NO	YES 0 1 2 3	

Discussion Management Competencies

	Group Member			Group Member		
6. **Maintained task focus:** Helped the group stay on or return to the task, issue, or topic the group was discussing.	NO	YES 0 1 2 3		NO	YES 0 1 2 3	
7. **Managed group interaction:** Appropriately initiated and terminated discussion, contributed to the discussion, or invited others to contribute to the discussion. Didn't dominate or withdraw.	NO	YES 0 1 2 3		NO	YES 0 1 2 3	

Relational Competencies

	Group Member			Group Member		
8. **Managed conflict:** Appropriately and constructively helped the group stay focused on issues rather than personalities when conflict occurred.	NO	YES 0 1 2 3		NO	YES 0 1 2 3	
9. **Maintained climate:** Offered positive verbal comments or nonverbal expressions which helped maintain a positive group climate.	NO	YES 0 1 2 3		NO	YES 0 1 2 3	

Scoring	NO = Not observed	YES 0 = Overall inappropriate or inadequate performance of competency	1 = Overall adequate performance of competency

Problem-Oriented Competencies (0–6)
Solution-Oriented Competencies (0–9)
Discussion Management Competencies (0–6)
Relational Competencies (0–6)

Group Member	Group Member	Group Member	Group Assessment
NO YES	NO YES	NO YES	NO YES
0 1 2 3	0 1 2 3	0 1 2 3	0 1 2 3
NO YES	NO YES	NO YES	NO YES
0 1 2 3	0 1 2 3	0 1 2 3	0 1 2 3
NO YES	NO YES	NO YES	NO YES
0 1 2 3	0 1 2 3	0 1 2 3	0 1 2 3
NO YES	NO YES	NO YES	NO YES
0 1 2 3	0 1 2 3	0 1 2 3	0 1 2 3
NO YES	NO YES	NO YES	NO YES
0 1 2 3	0 1 2 3	0 1 2 3	0 1 2 3
NO YES	NO YES	NO YES	NO YES
0 1 2 3	0 1 2 3	0 1 2 3	0 1 2 3
NO YES	NO YES	NO YES	NO YES
0 1 2 3	0 1 2 3	0 1 2 3	0 1 2 3
NO YES	NO YES	NO YES	NO YES
0 1 2 3	0 1 2 3	0 1 2 3	0 1 2 3
NO YES	NO YES	NO YES	NO YES
0 1 2 3	0 1 2 3	0 1 2 3	0 1 2 3

2 = Overall good performance of competency

3 = Overall excellent performance of competency

Jacob Lawrence. "The Library," 1960. Tempera on fiberboard, 24" × 29 7/8". Artwork © 2005 The Jacob and Gwendolyn Lawrence Foundation, Seattle/Artists Rights Society (ARS), New York. Photo credit: Photograph courtesy of Gwendolyn Knight Lawrence/Art Resource, NY.

Freedom of speech is of no use to a man who has nothing to say.

Franklin D. Roosevelt

Developing Your Presentation

CHAPTER OUTLINE

An Overview of the Presentational
Speaking Process

Understanding Speaker Anxiety

Managing Speaker Anxiety

Selecting and Narrowing Your
Topic

Identifying Your Purpose

Developing Your Central Idea

Generating Main Ideas

Gathering Supporting Material

Summary

CHAPTER OBJECTIVES

After studying this chapter, you should be able to:

1. Explain the practical value of presentational speaking skills.

2. List the nine components of the audience-centered public speaking model.

3. Define speaker anxiety, explain what causes it, and offer at least three suggestions for managing it.

4. Suggest three questions and three strategies that can help a speaker discover a topic.

5. List the three general purposes for presentations.

6. Explain how to write an audience-centered specific-purpose statement.

7. List and explain four criteria for a central idea.

8. Explain how to generate main ideas from a central idea.

9. Describe three sources and five types of supporting material for a presentation, and offer guidelines for using each type effectively.

10. List six types of library resources.

A good friend of ours who has lived in Hong Kong for several years recently remarked that she found traveling back to the United States exhausting. Her reason? Not so much the long plane trip or the 13-hour time difference, but, as she explained, "When I begin to hear airport public announcements in English instead of Cantonese, I suddenly feel compelled to pay attention to every word. All that listening wears me out!"

Few of us can take for granted that others will listen to us merely because we are speaking their native language. However, when we study the presentational speaking process and learn its component skills and principles, we certainly increase the likelihood that others will listen to us out of genuine, compelling interest.

Far from being a rare talent possessed only by an inspired few, **public speaking**, or **presentational speaking**, is a teachable, learnable process—a process of developing, supporting, organizing, and presenting ideas orally. It is a process that has much in common with expository writing. Yet preparing an oral presentation and writing a paper are not exactly the same. For one thing, the language you use when you speak is less formal and more conversational than the language you use when you write. You are more likely to use shorter words, more first- and second-person pronouns (*I* and *you*), and shorter sentences when you speak than when you write. Second, while a writer can rely on parenthetical citations and Works Cited pages to document his or her sources, a speaker must document sources orally, within the text of the speech itself. And third, perhaps the most important way in which presentational speaking and writing differ is that speaking is more redundant than writing. What might seem unnecessary repetition in a paper is essential in a presentation. A person listening to a presentation does not have the luxury of rereading something he or she missed or did not understand the first time. Neither can the listener rely on paragraphing to indicate when a speaker is moving on to another point or idea. Instead, the listener must depend on the speaker to repeat important ideas and to provide oral organizational cues, such as transitions, previews, and summaries. Certainly you can apply to presentational speaking some of the skills and strategies you have learned as a writer. But you will also learn new and sometimes slightly different ones. As with the writing process, the more you practice, the easier and more "natural" the presentational speaking process will become.

public speaking (presentational speaking)
A teachable, learnable process of developing, supporting, organizing, and presenting ideas orally.

The 5th Wave   By Rich Tennant

Still not convinced that you want or need to learn presentational speaking? Perhaps you will feel more motivated if you consider that the skills you will develop as you study presentational speaking will be of practical use in the future. They will give you an edge in other college courses that require oral presentations. They may help you convince some current or future boss that you deserve a raise. And they may even land you a job. Ethernet inventor Bob Metcalf recently told a group of MIT students (who expected, no doubt, to hear technology-related advice) that "Communication is key" to their success.[1] Young entrepreneurs in technical fields need presentation skills, Metcalf pointed out, to "secure funding, win customers, recruit talented employees, and talk with the media."

The communication skills that Metcalf was talking about are grounded in the five communication principles for a lifetime and can be learned and practiced in the various stages of the presentational speaking process. Let's begin our discussion of presentational speaking with an overview of that process. Then—because even if you are fully convinced of the value of learning to speak in public, you may still feel nervous about delivering a presentation—we will explore why you feel that way and offer suggestions for managing your anxiety and developing confidence. In the final pages of this chapter, we will focus more closely on the first five stages of the public speaking process, which involve generating, exploring, and developing ideas for presentations.

AN OVERVIEW OF THE PRESENTATIONAL SPEAKING PROCESS

Chances are that you didn't complete a driver-education course before you got behind the wheel of a car for the first time. Similarly, you don't have to read an entire book on public speaking before you give your first presentation. An overview of the presentational speaking process can help you with your early assignments, even if you have to speak before you have a chance to read Chapters 12 through 15.

Figure 11.1 illustrates the presentational speaking process. Viewing the model as a clock, you find "Select and narrow topic" at 12 o'clock. From this stage, the process proceeds clockwise in the direction of the arrows, to "Deliver presentation." Each stage is one of the tasks of the public speaker:

1. Select and narrow topic.
2. Identify purpose.
3. Develop central idea.
4. Generate main ideas.
5. Gather supporting material.
6. Organize presentation.
7. Rehearse presentation.
8. Deliver presentation.

Note that a ninth component, "Consider the audience," appears at the center of the model. Double-headed arrows connect this center with every other stage, illustrat-

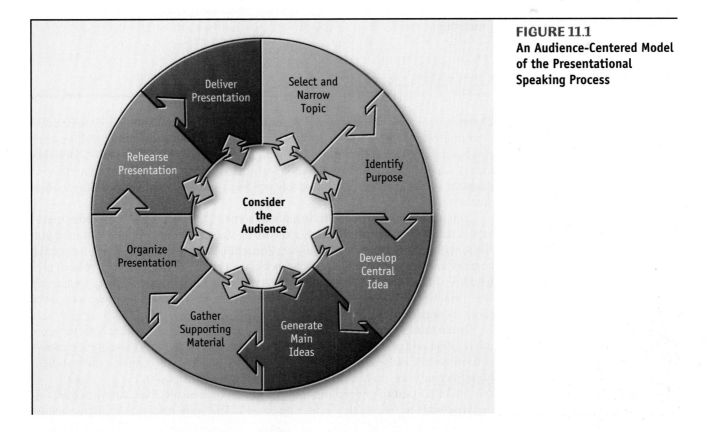

FIGURE 11.1
An Audience-Centered Model of the Presentational Speaking Process

Developing Your Presentation
STEP BY STEP

Consider Your Audience

A well-known Chinese proverb says that a journey of a thousand miles begins with a single step. Developing and delivering a presentation may seem like a daunting journey. But we believe that if you take it one step at a time and keep your focus on your audience, you'll be rewarded with a well-crafted and well-delivered message.

To help you see how the audience-centered presentation process unfolds step by step, we will explore each step of that process by showing how one student prepared and delivered a presentation. Ben Johnson, a student at the University of Nevada, Reno, participated in the 132nd annual contest of the Interstate Oratorical Association. His presentation, "Coricidin:

No Prescription Needed," is outlined in Chapter 12.[2] In the pages ahead, we will walk you through the process Ben used to develop his award-winning presentation.

Ben thought about his audience even before selecting his topic. Realizing that his listeners would include both students and faculty, he decided to look for a topic that was relevant to both groups. And he knew that he could discuss complex issues, using a fairly advanced vocabulary. The Developing Your Presentation Step by Step feature will provide a window through which you can watch Ben at work on each step of the presentational speaking process.

Adapt

ing that at any point, you may revise your ideas or strategies as you learn more about your audience. Your audience influences every decision you make.

Audience-centered presentational speakers are inherently sensitive to the diversity of their audiences. While guarding against generalizations that might be offensive, they acknowledge that cultural, ethnic, and other traditions affect the way people process messages. They apply the fundamental principle of appropriately adapting their messages to others. How? They might choose to use pictures to help them communicate. They might select topics and use illustrations with universal themes such as family and friendship. They might adjust the formality of their delivery and even their dress to whatever is expected by the majority of the audience members. The fundamental communication principle of adapting to the audience is the key to the success of any presentation.

UNDERSTANDING SPEAKER ANXIETY

The above overview of the stages of the public speaking process should help to increase your understanding of how to prepare for your first speaking assignment. However, if you still feel nervous at the prospect, you are definitely not alone. One study found that more than 80 percent of the population feel anxious when they speak to an audience.[3] Another survey discovered that people are more afraid of public speaking than of death![4]

You might be surprised at the names of some of the people who have admitted to experiencing **speaker anxiety**, also known as stage fright or communication apprehension. John F. Kennedy and Winston Churchill, among the greatest orators of the twentieth century, were anxious about speaking in public. Contemporary public figures who have talked about their speaker anxiety include Katie Couric, Conan O'Brien, Jay Leno, and Oprah Winfrey.[5] In fact, almost everyone feels at least some anxiety about speaking or performing in public. Why?

To answer this question and to manage your own anxiety, you need both accurate information and practical advice. Even if the prospect of giving a presentation makes you feel a sense of heightened excitement rather than fear, you can use these suggestions to make your excitement help you, rather than distract you.

It is important to understand that speaker anxiety results from your brain signaling your body to help with a challenging task. The body responds by increasing its

audience-centered presentational speaker
Someone who considers and adapts to the audience at every stage of the presentational speaking process.

speaker anxiety
Also known as stage fright; anxiety about speaking in public that is manifested in physiological symptoms such as rapid heartbeat, butterflies in the stomach, shaking knees and hands, quivering voice, and increased perspiration.

breathing rate and blood flow and by pumping more adrenaline, which in turn results in the all-too-familiar symptoms of a rapid heartbeat, butterflies in the stomach, shaking knees and hands, quivering voice, and increased perspiration.

Although these physical symptoms may annoy and worry you, remember that they indicate that your body is trying to help you with the task at hand. The same increased oxygen, blood flow, and adrenaline that cause the uncomfortable symptoms can actually be helpful. You may find that you speak with heightened enthusiasm. Your brain thinks faster and more clearly than you would have believed possible. Your state of increased physical readiness can help you speak better.

Keep in mind, too, that most speakers feel more nervous than they look. Although the antiperspirant advertising slogan "Never let 'em see you sweat" suggests that our increased perspiration, along with our shaking hands and knocking knees, is likely to be visible to our audience, rarely is this true. Communication researchers call this mistaken belief the **illusion of transparency** and have found that simply informing speakers that their nervousness is not as apparent as they think can improve the quality of their speeches.[6]

Speaker anxiety is a normal physiological reaction. It can actually help us in our speaking tasks. Its physical symptoms are seldom apparent to anyone else; rarely does it become so severe that it is actually debilitating. Still, it can be uncomfortable. Some practical tips can help you manage that discomfort and further build your confidence in your speaking ability.

Even performers like Barbra Streisand suffer from communication anxiety; we all need to take positive steps to control anxiety before a performance.

MANAGING SPEAKER ANXIETY

Perhaps you've read books or magazine articles that address the topic of speaker anxiety with such advice as "Look over the audience's heads, rather than at them," and "Imagine that your audience members are naked." Interesting though they may be, these techniques are not particularly helpful in reducing speaker anxiety. (After all, wouldn't you be pretty anxious if you had to talk to a group of naked people?) In addition, these strategies create new problems. Gazing at the back wall robs you of eye contact with your audience, an important source of information about how they are responding to your speech. And your audience can tell if you are looking over their heads instead of at them. Rather than pay attention to your speech, they may begin to glance surreptitiously over their shoulders to find out what in the world you're staring at.

If these techniques won't help, what will? Fortunately, several proven strategies exist for managing anxiety.

Know How to Develop a Presentation

Communication researchers have found that public speaking instruction decreases students' perception of their own speaker anxiety.[7] If you have read the first part of this chapter, then you have already taken this first step toward managing anxiety—learning about the public speaking process. Just knowing what you need to do to develop a presentation can boost your confidence in being able to do it.

Be Prepared

Being well prepared will also mean less anxiety. Being prepared includes selecting an appropriate topic, researching that topic thoroughly, and organizing your ideas logically. But perhaps most important, it also includes rehearsing your presentation.

illusion of transparency
The mistaken belief that the physical manifestations of a speaker's nervousness are apparent to an audience.

Research suggests that people who experience high speaker anxiety typically spend less time rehearsing than do those who report lower speaker anxiety.[8]

When you rehearse your presentation, imagine that you are giving it to the audience you will actually address. Stand up. If you cannot rehearse in the room where you will deliver the presentation, at least imagine that room. Practice rising from your seat, walking to the front of the room, and beginning your presentation. Speak aloud, rather than rehearsing silently. Thorough preparation that includes realistic rehearsal will increase your confidence when the time comes to deliver your presentation.

Focus on Your Audience

Adapt

The fundamental communication principle of being audience-centered is key to reducing speaker anxiety. As you are preparing your presentation, consider the needs, goals, and interests of your audience members. As you rehearse your presentation, visualize your audience and imagine how they may respond; practice adapting your presentation to the responses you imagine. The more you know about your audience and how they are likely to respond to your message, the more comfortable you will feel about delivering that message. And as you finally deliver your presentation, focus on connecting to your listeners. The more you concentrate on your audience, the less you can attend to your own nervousness.

Focus on Your Message

Verbal

Focusing on your message can also be a constructive anxiety-reducing strategy. Like focusing on your audience, it keeps you from thinking too much about how nervous you are. In the few minutes before you begin your presentation, think about what you are going to say. Mentally review your main ideas. Silently practice your opening lines and your conclusion. Once you are speaking, maintain your focus on your message and your audience, rather than on your fears. Communication researchers have found that most public speakers become progressively more comfortable as they speak, a phenomenon they term **habituation**.[9]

Give Yourself a Mental Pep Talk

Aware

habituation
The process of becoming more comfortable as you speak.

Even if you focus primarily on your audience and your message, you are bound to have some lingering thoughts about your performance. Rather than allowing yourself to dwell on how worried or afraid you are, make a conscious effort to think positively. Remind yourself that you have chosen a topic you know something about. Give yourself a mental pep talk before getting up to speak: "I know I can give this presentation. I have prepared and practiced, and I'm going to do a great job." This kind of positive thinking can help you manage your anxiety.

Use Deep-Breathing Techniques

Two of the physical symptoms of nervousness are shallow breathing and rapid heart rate. To counter these symptoms, take a few slow, deep breaths before you get up to speak. As you slowly inhale and exhale, try to relax your entire body. These simple strategies will increase your oxygen intake and slow your heart rate, making you feel calmer and more in control.

Take Advantage of Opportunities to Speak

As you gain public speaking experience, you will feel more in control of your nervousness. Past successes build confidence. This course will provide opportunities for frequent practice, which will increase your skill and confidence.

Seek Professional Help

For a few people, the above strategies may not be enough help. These people may still experience a level of speaker anxiety that they consider debilitating. If you feel that you may be such a person, ask your communication instructor where you might turn for additional help. Some college or university departments of communication maintain communication labs that teach students various additional strategies to help manage counter-productive anxiety.

One such strategy is **systematic desensitization**, which helps you learn to manage anxiety through a combination of general relaxation techniques and visualization of successful and calm preparation and delivery of a presentation.

Another proven strategy is **performance visualization**: viewing a videotape of a successful, effective speaker, becoming familiar enough with the videotaped presentation that you can imagine it, and eventually visualizing yourself as the speaker.[10] This process may offer one of the best long-term strategies for managing speaker anxiety. Studies suggest that student speakers who practice performance visualization view themselves as more positive, vivid, and in-control speakers both immediately after performance visualization and up to several months later.[11]

Additional services may be available through university counseling or other student support services. If you think that you might benefit from professional help, find out what is available and use it.

RECAP

Managing Speaker Anxiety

- Know how to develop a presentation.
- Be prepared.
- Focus on your audience.
- Focus on your message.
- Give yourself a mental pep talk.
- Use deep-breathing techniques.
- Take advantage of opportunities to speak.
- Seek professional help.

systematic desensitization
An anxiety management strategy that includes general relaxation techniques and visualization of success.

performance visualization
An anxiety management strategy that involves viewing a videotape of a successful presentation and imagining oneself delivering that presentation.

SELECTING AND NARROWING YOUR TOPIC

Sometimes a speaker is invited or assigned to speak on a certain topic and doesn't have to think about selecting one. At other times, however, a speaker is given some guidelines—such as time limits and perhaps the general purpose for the presentation—but otherwise allowed freedom to choose a topic. When this happens to you—as it almost

Your task of selecting a topic is made easier if you think about the needs of the audience who will be listening to your presentation.

Adapt

certainly will in your communication class—you may find your task made easier by exploring three questions: Who is the audience? What is the occasion? What are my interests and experiences?

Who Is the Audience?

As we have noted several times throughout this book, the principle of appropriately adapting messages to others is central to the communication process. In presentational speaking, that adaptation begins with topic selection. Who are the members of your audience? What interests and needs do they have in common? Why did they ask you to speak?

One professional speaker calls the answers to such questions "actionable intelligence"—information that you can use as you select your topic.[12] Your college classmates are likely to be interested in such topics as college loans and the job market. Older adults might be more interested in hearing a speaker address such topics as the cost of prescription drugs and investment tax credits. Thinking about your audience can often yield an appropriate topic.

What Is the Occasion?

You might also consider the occasion for which you are being asked to speak. A Veteran's Day address calls for such topics as patriotism and service to one's country. A university centennial address will focus on the successes of the institution's past and a vision for its future.

What Are My Interests and Experiences?

Self-awareness, another communication principle you already know, can also help you discover a topic. Exploring your own interests, attitudes, and experiences may suggest topics about which you know a great deal and feel passionately, and result in a presentation that you can deliver with energy and genuine enthusiasm. One speaker thinking about her own interests and experiences quickly produced the following list of possible topics:

> San Diego, California: city of cultural diversity
> Are world climates really changing?
> The reconstructed Globe Theatre
> Working at Six Flags
> What a sociologist does

Even after considering audience, occasion, and personal interests and experiences, you may still find yourself facing a speaking assignment for which you just cannot come up with a satisfactory topic. When that happens, you might try silent brainstorming, scanning Web directories and Web pages, or listening and reading for topic ideas.

Silent Brainstorming

silent brainstorming
A technique used to generate creative ideas.

Silent brainstorming, discussed in Chapter 10 as a technique used by small groups to generate creative ideas, is a useful strategy for generating possible topics for presentations. A silent brainstorming session of about 3 minutes yielded the following list of 11 potential topics:

Gargoyles
Gothic architecture
Notre Dame
French food
Disney's *The Hunchback of Notre Dame*
Collecting Disney movie celluloids
Grammy Award winning movie themes
Academy Award winning movies of the 1940s
The Motion Picture Academy's Lifetime Achievement
    Award
John Wayne
The California Gold Rush

On the Web

The Internet can be a useful source to help you search for an interesting speech topic. Remember, the best topic is one that relates to your audience, the occasion, and your own interests and background. Consider using a Web directory such as Yahoo! to help you find a topic that meets the three criteria we've noted. Here's the address:
www.yahoo.com

Another interesting source of speech ideas is current headlines. Here's a source that has links to many media outlets, including most major news networks:
www.totalnews.com

Having generated a list of topics, you can now go back to it and eliminate topics that don't have much promise or that you know you would never use. For example, you may not have any real interest in or reason for discussing the California Gold Rush. However, perhaps your film course has given you good background for discussing Academy Award winning movies of the 1940s or some other decade. Keep the topics you like in your class notebook. You can reconsider them for future assignments.

Scanning Web Directories and Web Pages

You know how addicting it can be to surf the Web—to follow various categories and links out of interest and curiosity. What may seem an idle pastime can actually be a good way to discover potential speech topics. For example, a recent random search on Yahoo! starting with the general category of Health yielded the following subcategories and possible topics, arranged from broad to narrow:

Diseases and conditions
Depression
Prevention of depression
Benefits of fish

An additional advantage of this strategy is that you now have both a broad topic and one or more potential sources for your presentation. An article found in the final subcategory discusses the role of Omega-3 fats, found in fish, as a critical component of nerve cells.

Listening and Reading for Topic Ideas

It is not unusual to see on television or read in a newspaper something that triggers an idea for a presentation. For example, the following list of quite varied topics was suggested by the headlines in a recent daily newspaper:

Corporate accounting scandals
Forest fires in the southwestern United States
Diagnosing breast cancer
U.S. government aid to foreign nationals
Political turmoil in South America

Listen and Respond

The nightly news is not the only media source of potential topics. You might also get topic ideas from television talk shows or from general interest or news magazines. Or you might get an idea from a book. Perhaps you have just read Daniel Goleman's *Working with Emotional Intelligence.* You might decide to give a speech on what emotional intelligence is and why it is important in the workplace.

You might also find a topic in material you have studied for a class. Perhaps you recently had an interesting discussion of minimum mandatory sentencing in your crim-

Developing Your Presentation
STEP BY STEP

Select and Narrow Your Topic

While lazily scanning the newspaper headlines one Sunday afternoon, Ben happens on one that catches his eye. He settles down to read the article, which discusses a relatively new form of drug abuse—the abuse of common over-the-counter cold medications. Ben is surprised. He had no idea that such medications could produce the kind of side effects that would lead to their abuse. As he finishes the article, another thought goes through his mind: Maybe the abuse of over-the-counter cold medicines would make a good topic for his upcoming persuasive presentation.

inology class. It might make a good topic for a presentation. And your instructor would probably be happy to suggest additional resources.

Even a topic that comes up in casual conversation with friends may make a good speech topic. Perhaps everyone in your dorm seems to be sniffling and coughing all at once. "It's sick-building syndrome," gasps one. Sick-building syndrome might be an interesting topic for a presentation.

The point is to keep your eyes and ears open. You never know when you might see or hear a potential topic. If you do, write it down. Nothing is so frustrating as to know you had a good idea for a topic but not to be able to remember what it was!

If you discover potential topics through brainstorming, surfing the Web, or listening or reading, you should still consider the communication principles of adapting to your audience and being aware of your own interests and experiences before you make your final topic selection. And you will also need to consider the time limits of the speaking assignment. Many good topics need to be narrowed before they are appropriate for a given assignment. Be realistic. Although many beginning speakers worry about how they will ever fill 3 minutes, in reality, more speakers run over their time limits than under.

One strategy for narrowing topics is to construct the kinds of categories and subcategories created by Web directories. Write your general topic at the top of a list, making each succeeding word or phrase more specific and narrow. For example, in order to narrow the topic "animals," write it down and then write an increasingly specific list of topics under it:

Aware
Adapt

> Animals
> Pets
> Reptiles
> Bearded dragons
> Caring for a bearded dragon

If you have 10 minutes for your presentation, you might decide that the last topic is too narrow. If so, just go back one step. In 10 minutes, you may be able to discuss characteristics and habits of bearded dragons, as well as how to care for them.

RECAP

Select and Narrow Your Topic

- Consider the audience, the occasion, and your interests and experiences
- Practice silent brainstorming
- Scan Web directories and Web pages
- Listen and read for topic ideas
- Narrow your topic by generating increasingly specific categories and subcategories

IDENTIFYING YOUR PURPOSE

Now that you have a topic in mind, you need to clarify your purpose for your presentation. If you are unclear about exactly what you hope to accomplish, you probably won't accomplish anything, except to ramble about your topic in some sort of vague way. A clear purpose, on the other hand, can help you select main ideas, an organizational strategy, and supporting material, and can even influence the way in which you deliver the presentation. You should determine both your general purpose and your specific purpose for every presentation that you give.

General Purpose

Your **general purpose** is the broad reason for giving your presentation: to inform, to persuade, or to entertain. When you inform, you teach. You define, describe, or explain a thing, person, place, concept, or process. You may use some humor in your presentation; you may encourage your audience to seek out further information about your topic. But your primary purpose for speaking is to give information.

If you are using information to try to change or reinforce your audience's ideas or convictions or to urge your audience to do something, your general purpose is persuasive. The insurance representative who tries to get you to buy life insurance, the candidate for state representative who asks for your vote, and the coordinator of Habitat for Humanity who urges your fraternity to get involved in building homes, all have persuasive general purposes. They may offer information about life expectancy, the voting record of an incumbent opponent, or the number of people in your community who cannot afford decent housing, but they use this information to convince you or to get you to do something. Their primary purpose is persuasive.

The speaker whose purpose is to entertain tries to get the members of his or her audience to smile, laugh, and generally enjoy themselves. For the audience members, learning something or being persuaded about something is secondary to having a good time. Most after-dinner speakers speak to entertain. So do most stand-up comedians and storytellers.

In your speech class, the general purpose for each assignment will probably be set by your instructor. Because the general purpose influences the way you develop and organize your presentation, as well as the way you deliver it, it is important that you be aware of your general purpose throughout the process of developing and delivering your presentation.

Aware

Verbal

Specific Purpose

Knowing whether you want to inform, persuade, or entertain clarifies your general purpose for speaking. You also need to determine your specific purpose. A **specific purpose** is a concise statement of what your listeners should be able to do by the time you finish your presentation. In other words, a specific purpose is an audience-centered behavioral goal for your presentation. You can begin a specific-purpose statement for any presentation with the words:

> At the end of my presentation, the audience will . . .

And then specify a behavior. For example, if you are giving an informative presentation on eating disorders, you might state,

> At the end of my presentation, the audience will be able to explain the causes and most successful treatments for anorexia and bulimia.

If your topic is Zen meditation and your general purpose is to persuade, you might say,

> At the end of my presentation, the audience will try Zen meditation.

Wording your specific purpose like the examples above will help you keep your audience foremost in your mind during the entire presentation preparation process.

Every subsequent decision you make while preparing and delivering your presentation should be guided by your specific purpose. As soon as you have formulated it, write it on a note card and keep it with you while you are working on your presentation. Think of it as a compass pointing true north—toward your audience. Refer to it often.

general purpose
The broad reason for giving a presentation: to inform, to persuade, or to entertain an audience.

specific purpose
A concise statement of what listeners should be able to do by the time the speaker finishes the presentation.

RECAP

Identify Your Purpose

General Purpose

- To inform   To define, describe, or explain a thing, person, place, concept, or process
- To persuade   To change or reinforce audience members' ideas or convictions, or to urge them to do something
- To entertain   To amuse an audience

Specific Purpose

- Specifies what you want audience members to be able to do by the end of your presentation
- Uses the words "At the end of my presentation, the audience will . . . "

Examples of General Purposes	Examples of Specific Purposes
To inform	At the end of my presentation, the audience will be able to list two benefits for adults of learning to play a musical instrument.
To persuade	At the end of my presentation, the audience will enroll in a music appreciation course.
To entertain	At the end of my presentation, the audience will be laughing at my misadventures as an adult cello student.

DEVELOPING YOUR CENTRAL IDEA

While your specific purpose indicates what you want your audience to know or do by the end of your presentation, your **central idea** makes a definitive point *about* your topic. It focuses on the content of the speech.

Professional speech coach Judith Humphrey explains the importance of a central idea:

> Ask yourself before writing a speech . . . "What's my point?" Be able to state that message in a single clear sentence. Everything else you say will support that single argument.[13]

Sometimes, as in the following example, wording the central idea can be as simple as copying the part of the specific purpose statement that specifies what the audience should be able to do.

TOPIC:	Foreign-language education
SPECIFIC PURPOSE:	At the end of my presentation, the audience will be able to explain two reasons foreign-language education should begin in the elementary grades.
CENTRAL IDEA:	Foreign-language education should begin in the elementary grades.

Even though they may seem similar, the specific purpose and central idea are used quite differently. The specific purpose guides you as you prepare your presentation; the central idea will guide the audience as they listen to the presentation. Although the specific purpose is never actually stated in the presentation itself, the central idea is,

central idea
A definitive point *about* a topic.

Developing Your Presentation
STEP BY STEP

Determine Your Purpose

Ben's assignment is to prepare and deliver a persuasive presentation, so he knows that his general purpose is to persuade. He will have to try to change or reinforce his audience's attitudes and beliefs about the abuse of common over-the-counter cold medications and perhaps also get his listeners to take some sort of action.

Ben also knows that his specific purpose should begin with the phrase "At the end of my presentation, the audience will . . . ." So he jots down,

> *At the end of my presentation, the audience will know about the cold medication Coricidin.*

As Ben thinks further about this draft specific purpose, he sees some problems with it. How can he determine what his audience "knows" at the end of his presentation? And just what

is it the audience should know about Coricidin? He edits his purpose statement to read,

> *At the end of my presentation, the audience will be able to discuss the current epidemic of abuse of the common cold medication Coricidin.*

This version is more specific, but perhaps more appropriate for an informative speech than a persuasive one. What does he want his audience to *do* about the problem? Maybe a better statement would be

> *At the end of my presentation, the audience will take steps to end the abuse of the cold medication Coricidin.*

Ben is pleased with this third version. It is a concise statement of what he wants his audience to do at the end of his speech. He is ready to move to the next step of the process.

---

usually at or near the end of the speaker's introduction. It provides the focus for the body of the presentation.

The most successful central ideas meet the following criteria: They are audience-centered; they reflect a single topic; they are complete declarative sentences; and they use direct, specific language. Let's consider each of these criteria in turn.

Adapt

Audience-Centered

If your specific purpose is audience-centered, your central idea probably will be, too. It should reflect a topic in which the audience has a reason to be interested and should provide some knowledge they do not already have or make some claim about the topic that they may not have previously considered. The second of the following central ideas is more appropriate to an audience of college students than the first.

> INAPPROPRIATE: Taking Advanced Placement classes in high school can help fulfill your general education requirements. *(Inappropriate because taking Advanced Placement classes is something college students either did or did not do in the past. They cannot make any decisions about them at this point.)*
>
> APPROPRIATE: Taking Web-based classes can help fulfill your general studies requirements. *(Appropriate because students are probably looking for various options for completing required courses. They can choose to take courses on the Web.)*

A Single Topic

A central idea should reflect a single topic. Trying to cover more than one topic, even if multiple topics are related, only muddles your presentation and confuses the audience.

> MULTIPLE TOPICS: Clubbing and running in marathons are two activities that appeal to many college students.
>
> SINGLE TOPIC: Clubbing appeals to many college students.

Effective speakers state their central idea during their introductory remarks to help their audience focus on the main points covered in the body of the speech.

Developing Your Presentation
STEP BY STEP

Develop Your Central Idea

Ben knows from reading Chapter 11 of *Communication: Principles for a Lifetime* that his central idea should be a complete declarative sentence that states a single audience-centered idea. He knows too that sometimes you can develop your central idea by copying the part of your specific purpose statement that specifies what the audience should do. So he writes,

> *We should take steps to end the abuse of the cold medication Coricidin.*

Verbal

A Complete Declarative Sentence

Your central idea should be more than just the word or phrase that is your topic—it should make a claim about your topic. Questions may help you come up with a central idea, but questions themselves are not good central ideas, because they don't make any kind of claim. A central idea should be a complete **declarative sentence**—not a topic and not a question.

TOPIC:	Study abroad
QUESTION:	Should students consider opportunities to study abroad?
CENTRAL IDEA:	Study abroad provides significant advantages for students in most fields of study.

Verbal

Direct, Specific Language

A good central idea should use direct, specific language, rather than qualifiers and vague generalities.

VAGUE:	Crop circles are not what they seem to be.
SPECIFIC:	Although they have been variously attributed to alien forces and unknown fungi, crop circles are really just a clever hoax.

RECAP

The Central Idea Should . . .

Be audience-centered
Reflect a single topic
Be a complete declarative sentence
Use direct, specific language

GENERATING MAIN IDEAS

declarative sentence
A complete sentence that makes a statement, as opposed to asking a question.

main ideas
Subdivisions of the central idea of a presentation, which provide detailed points of focus for developing the presentation.

If the central idea of a presentation is like the thesis statement of a paper, the **main ideas** of a presentation correspond to the paragraph topics of a paper. They support or subdivide the central idea and provide more detailed points of focus for developing the presentation.

Getting from the central idea to related but more specific main ideas can seem a challenging task, but actually you can use the central idea to generate main ideas. Here's how.

Write the central idea at the top of a sheet of paper or a word-processing document. Then ask yourself three questions:

1. Does the central idea have *logical divisions?*
2. Can I think of several *reasons* the central idea is true?
3. Can I support the central idea with a series of *steps* or a *chronological sequence?*

You should be able to answer yes to one of these questions and to write down the corresponding divisions, reasons, or steps. Let's apply this strategy to several examples.

Does the Central Idea Have *Logical Divisions?*

Suppose that your central idea is "Most accomplished guitarists play three types of guitars." The phrase "three types" is a flag that indicates that this central idea does indeed have logical divisions—those being, in this case, the three types of guitars. You list the three that come to mind:

1. Acoustic
2. Classical
3. Electric

You don't need to use Roman numerals or to worry particularly about the order in which you have listed the types of guitars. Right now you are simply trying to generate main ideas. They aren't set in concrete, either. You may revise them—and your central idea—several times before you actually deliver the presentation. For example, you may decide that you need to include steel guitars in your list. So you revise your central idea to read "four types of guitars" and add "steel" to your list.

Can You Think of Several *Reasons* the Central Idea Is True?

If your central idea is "Everyone should study a martial art," you may not be able to find readily apparent logical divisions. Simply discussing judo, karate, and taekwando would not necessarily support the argument that everyone should study one of them. However, the second question is more productive: You can think of a number of *reasons* everyone should study a martial art. You quickly generate this list:

1. Martial arts teach responsibility.
2. Martial arts teach self-control.
3. Martial arts teach a means of self-defense.

Unlike the list of types of guitars, this list is written in brief complete sentences. Whether words, phrases, or sentences, the purpose of your first list of main ideas is just to get the ideas in written form. You can and will revise them later.

Can You Support the Central Idea with a Series of *Steps* or a *Chronological Sequence?*

"The events of September 11, 2001, were the climax of a decade of deadly terrorist attacks against the United States." It seemed like a pretty good central idea when you came up with it. But now what do you do? It doesn't have any logical divisions. You couldn't really develop reasons that it is true. However, you could probably support this central idea with a chronological sequence or a history of the problem. You jot down the following list:

1. 1993—Bomb explodes in the underground parking garage of the World Trade Center, killing six people.
2. 1995—Car bomb in Riyadh, Saudi Arabia, kills seven people, five of them American military and civilian National Guard advisers.
3. 1996—Bomb aboard a fuel truck explodes outside a U.S. Air Force installation in Dhahran, Saudi Arabia, killing 19 U.S. military personnel.

Developing Your Presentation
STEP BY STEP

Determine Your Main Ideas

With his central idea in hand, Ben knows that he next needs to generate main ideas for his presentation. He asks three questions:

- Does the central idea have logical divisions?
- Can I think of several reasons the central idea is true?
- Can I support my central idea with a series of steps or a chronological sequence?

Ben's central idea does not seem to have logical divisions, but he can certainly provide reasons it is true. He jots down his central idea and writes *because* at the end of it:

We should take steps to end the abuse of the cold medication Coricidin because

And then he adds,

1. Coricidin abuse is rapidly becoming a significant problem.
2. Coricidin is widely available to teenagers.
3. Parents and teachers have only compounded the problem.

Ben thinks at first that these might make three good main ideas for his speech. Then he realizes that ideas 2 and 3 are really subdivisions of the same point—why Coricidin abuse is a growing trend. Additionally, glancing back at his purpose statement reminds him that he wants his audience to take steps to end Coricidin abuse. So he revises his original list of main ideas to read,

1. Coricidin abuse is rapidly becoming a significant problem.
2. Coricidin poses a problem because it is widely available to teenagers and because parents and teachers remain largely unaware of its abuse potential.
3. In addition to government and retailer regulation personal action is needed to solve the problem of Coricidin abuse.

Now Ben has main ideas that both support his central idea and fulfill his specific purpose.

4. 1998—Bombs destroy the U.S. embassies in Nairobi, Kenya, and Dar es Salaam, Tanzania. Three hundred and one people are killed, including 13 Americans.
5. 2000—Bomb damages the *USS Cole* in the port of Aden, Yemen, killing 17 American sailors.
6. 2001—Hijacked airliners crash into the World Trade Center in New York, the Pentagon in Washington, D.C., and a field in Pennsylvania, killing more than 3000.[14]

These six fatal terrorist attacks, arranged in chronological order, could become the main ideas of your speech.

How many main ideas should you have? Your topic and time limit will help you decide. A short presentation (3 to 5 minutes) might have only two main ideas. A longer one (8 to 10 minutes) might have four or five. If you find that you have more potential main ideas than you can use, decide which main ideas are likely to be most interesting, relevant, and perhaps persuasive to your audience. Or combine two or more closely related ideas.

GATHERING SUPPORTING MATERIAL

supporting material
Verbal or visual material that clarifies, amplifies, and provides evidence to support the main ideas of a presentation. Verbal support includes illustrations, explanations, descriptions, definitions, analogies, statistics, and opinions; visual support includes objects, charts, graphs, posters, maps, models, graphics, and other presentation aids.

By the time you have decided on your main ideas, you have a skeleton presentation. Your next task is to flesh out that skeleton with **supporting material**, both verbal and visual. Verbal supporting material includes illustrations, explanations, descriptions, definitions, analogies, statistics, and opinions—material that will clarify, amplify, and provide evidence to support your main ideas and your thesis. Visual supporting material includes objects, charts, graphs, posters, maps, models, and computer-generated graphics. You can also support your speech with audio aids such as music or sounds from a CD-ROM or DVD. The speaker who seeks out strong verbal and visual supporting material is adhering to the fundamental communication principles of effectively using verbal and nonverbal messages.

Sources of Supporting Material

Like a chef who needs to know where to buy high-quality fresh fruits and vegetables for gourmet recipes, you need to know where to turn for supporting material that will effectively develop your presentation and achieve your specific purpose. We will discuss three potential sources of supporting material: you and people you know, the Internet, and the library.

You and People You Know   You needn't look far for at least some of the supporting material for your presentation. If you were self-aware as you selected your topic, you may be your own source. You may have chosen a topic about your hobby—collecting CDs, raising cockatiels, or cooking. You may have chosen a topic with which you have had some personal experience, such as undergoing plastic surgery or negotiating a favorable apartment lease. Or you may have discovered your topic through listening to others. Your roommate may have confided in you about her mother's treatment for melanoma. Your political science professor may have delivered a fascinating lecture on the changes in Hong Kong after its 1998 return to China.

The point is that you don't necessarily need to consult the Internet or run to the library for every piece of supporting material for every topic on which you speak. For the presentations mentioned above, it would be logical to begin by considering your own personal experience in having plastic surgery or negotiating a favorable apartment lease or by interviewing your roommate or your political science professor. It is true that most well-researched presentations will include some objective material gathered from the Internet or from library resources. But don't overlook your own expertise and experience, or that of people you know. As an audience-centered speaker, realize, too, that personal knowledge or experience has the added advantage of heightening your credibility in the minds of your listeners. They will respect your authority if they realize that you have firsthand knowledge of the topic on which you are speaking.

The Internet   Only a few short years ago, the **Internet** was more of a research curiosity than a serious source of supporting material. Now it is the first place many of us turn when faced with a research task.

The most popular Internet information-delivery system is the **World Wide Web**. You have probably accessed material on the Web through a **directory** or **search engine** such as Yahoo!, Alta Vista, or another of the sites listed in Table 11.1.

You can use directories and search engines in two ways: by clicking on subject categories that are in turn broken down into ever-more-specific subcategories or by enter-

Aware
Listen and Respond

Internet
A vast collection of hundreds of thousands of computers accessible to millions of people all over the world.

World Wide Web
The most popular information delivery system of the Internet.

directory
An Internet site that offers the user ever-more-specific categories through which to search the World Wide Web.

search engine
An Internet site that works much like a traditional card catalog or index, allowing the user to perform a subject or keyword search of the World Wide Web.

Technology and *Communication*

A New Kind of Search Engine

For the past several years Google and Yahoo! have been the leading Internet search engines. However, vertical search engines, designed to select only certain types of information from the Internet, have been increasing in both number and popularity.

One such engine is Ziggs, which can help you find people with certain specific characteristics. For example, one person who has tested the search engine explains, "it might help you find a lawyer in Washington specializing in international trade, or an alumnus of Brandeis University who lives in Delaware."[15]

Another vertical search engine is Indeed.com, a search engine for job openings, which indexes more than 500 job Web sites (including Monster.com), newspaper-ad sites, and corporate sites. You can use Indeed.com to search for all jobs in a given location or at a given company, all jobs that require certain specific qualifications.

Whether vertical search engines will compete seriously with Google and Yahoo! remains to be seen. One reference librarian suggests that it is "more likely what we're seeing is a maturation of the industry that allows for both general purpose search engines and verticals to co-exist."[16]

TABLE 11.1	
Popular World Wide Web Directories and Search Engines*	
AltaVista	www.altavista.com AltaVista is both a directory and a keyword search engine.
Google	www.google.com In addition to providing both a directory and a keyword search engine, Google enables the user to conduct specific image searches.
Teoma	www.teoma.com A vertical search engine, Teoma both narrows and improves the relevance of a search by ranking sites based on the number of same-subject pages that reference them.
Yahoo!	www.yahoo.com Both a directory and a search engine, Yahoo! is one of the best for browsing a wide-ranging topical list of sites. Each topic branches to additional topical subcategories.

*If some of these or other URLs provided in this chapter change or become unavailable at a later date, you may be automatically forwarded to new sites. If not, you can search for the sites by name. And if you still can't find a site, chances are that several new and better ones have taken its place.

hit
A Web site or Web page discovered as a result of a search; also refers to any single access of a site or page.

Web site
A location on the World Wide Web that includes a number of related Web pages.

Web page
An individual file or screen that is part of a larger Web site.

advanced (Boolean) search
A Web search that ties words together so that a search engine can hunt for the resulting phrase.

ing key words or phrases into a designated space, clicking on a "Find" command, and then sorting through the **hits**, or resulting list of **Web sites** and **Web pages** that deal with the topic you entered.

The Web sites and Web pages you discover may include personal pages, books, periodicals, newspapers and wire services, reference material, and government documents. In addition, you may discover indexes and catalogs for accessing these various kinds of resources. You can even find sites designed to help you prepare and deliver your presentations. Although the sheer volume of material may be overwhelming for even the most experienced researchers, two strategies can help.

First, explore the **advanced** or **Boolean search** capabilities of your directory or search engine. Most offer directions on how to limit your search to those sites that are most relevant to what you are looking for. For a Boolean search, you enclose phrases in quotation marks or parentheses so that the search yields only those sites on which all the words of the phrase appear together, rather than sites that contain any one of the words. You can also insert the word *or* between two parenthetical phrases, directing your search to include documents in which either phrase appears. Or you can insert the word *and* between parenthetical phrases to indicate that you wish to see results that contain both phrases. These relatively simple strategies can help you narrow a list of hits from, in some cases, millions to a more workable number.

A second strategy for sorting through information you discover on the World Wide Web has to do with the principle of appropriately interpreting verbal and nonverbal messages. Specifically, you need to evaluate the sites you discover, according to a consistent standard. The following six criteria can serve as such a standard:[17]

1. *Accountability.* Find out what organization or individual is responsible for the Web site. A good place to start is to examine the domain, indicated by the last three letters of the site's URL. The following domains are used by the types of organizations indicated:[18]

.com or **.net**	commercial sites
.org	nonprofit groups
.edu	educational institutions
.gov	government agencies
.mil	military groups

You can also try entering the name of the organization, enclosed in quotation marks, in a search engine. If you cannot identify or verify the author or sponsor of a Web site, be extremely wary of the site. If no one is willing to be accountable for the information, you cannot be accountable to your audience for using it. Search elsewhere.

2. *Accuracy.* Sources of facts should be documented on a Web site just as they are in a print source. An additional advantage of the Web is that it can provide a **hyperlink** to any original source. Hyperlinks are usually colored and underlined words or images in the text. Clicking with your mouse on a hyperlink will take you directly to the linked site.

   Web sites should also be relatively free of errors in grammatical usage and mechanics. If a site contains such errors, it might also contain errors in content.

3. *Objectivity.* As noted above, you need to know who has posted the site. Consider the philosophies and possible biases of the organization or individual responsible for the site. Are those beliefs, interests, and biases likely to slant the information? The more objective the author, the more credible the facts and information.

4. *Date.* Many sites include information about when the site was posted and when it was last updated. In most cases, when you are concerned with factual data, the more recent, the better.

5. *Usability.* If you have spent much time exploring the Internet, you have probably at one time or another called up a site that contained such complex graphics that it took a long time to load or even caused your computer to crash. Frames, graphics, and multimedia resources can enhance a site, or they can simply complicate it. Consider the practical efficiency of the sites you explore.

6. *Sensitivity to diversity.* A diversity-sensitive Web site will be free of bias against either gender, against any ethnic, racial, or sexual-preference subgroup, and against people with disabilities.[19]

   Federal agencies are required by law to make their Web sites accessible to people with disabilities. For example, federal Web sites must be accessible in a mode that allows people with low vision to view them without relying on audio input.[20] Other requirements include making sure hyperlinks can be detected by color-blind users and providing audio and video clips with written captions for people with hearing disabilities.[21]

RECAP

Using the World Wide Web as a Source of Supporting Material

1. Use a directory or search engine to find relevant sites.
2. Expect to discover a wide variety of sites: personal pages, books, periodicals, newspapers and wire services, reference material, government documents, and indexes and catalogs.
3. Evaluate Web sites according to six criteria: accountability, accuracy, objectivity, date, usability, and sensitivity to diversity.

The Library   Despite the explosion of World Wide Web resources in recent years, the library remains a rich source of supporting material. Most libraries, from the largest research university library to the smallest village public library, house the following kinds of resources:

   Books
   Periodicals
   Full-text databases

hyperlink
A highlighted word or graphic on a Web page that takes a user who clicks on it directly to the site to which it refers.

Newspapers
Reference resources
Government documents
Special services

Books   The word *library* is almost synonymous with the word *book*. In spite of the predictions of some that electronic resources will someday make books obsolete, for now, books remain central to the holdings of most libraries.

A library's books are housed in the **stacks**, often several floors of shelves of books. Books are organized in the stacks according to **call number**, a reference number assigned to each book, which encodes the subject or topic, as well as the author. Most libraries use the **Library of Congress classification system** of call numbers.

A library's central catalog of all its books is called the **card catalog**. Today, most card catalogs are electronic ones. Banks of computer monitors in a central location in the library provide directions for looking up the books you need. Many college and university card catalogs these days are also accessible from remote locations, meaning that you can search them online and build preliminary bibliographies of books and call numbers before ever coming to the library building itself. Figure 11.2 illustrates a sample entry from a computerized card catalog.

You may be able to print out the card catalog records for the books you want. If you have to copy them from the screen, be sure to include the author's name, title of the book, publisher and date of publication, and the library's call number. Use a consistent format so that later you can easily interpret the information.

Books will be important sources as you prepare your presentations. They can provide in-depth coverage of topics, which is not possible in shorter publications. However, because most books are written 2 or 3 years before they are published, they are inherently outdated. If your presentation addresses a current topic, or if you want to use current examples, you will probably not find the information you need in books. You will turn instead to periodicals and newspapers, available both online and in hard copy.

Periodicals   The term **periodicals** refers both to magazines, such as *Time, People,* and *Sports Illustrated,* and to professional journals, such as *College English* and the *Quarterly Journal of Economics.* Both types of periodicals can be useful for presentations.

Periodical indexes are the equivalent of card catalogs in helping you locate information you need. A number of such indexes cover many topics and most of the

stacks
The collection of books in a library.

call number
The numerical code by which a book in a library is identified.

Library of Congress classification system
The most commonly used system of call numbers.

card catalog
A file of information about the books in a library; may be an index-card file or a computerized system.

periodical
A popular magazine or professional journal.

periodical index
A listing of bibliographical data for articles published in a group of magazines or journals during a given time period.

FIGURE 11.2
Entry from an Electronic Card Catalog

Title:	Ethics in the workplace : a systems perspective / William F. Roth.
Author:	Roth, William F.
Call Number:	HF5487 .R674 2005
Publisher:	Upper Saddle River, N.J. : Pearson Education, c2005.
Subject Heading(s):	Business ethics.
	0424L

Display Related Subjects

Description:	xiii, 140 p. ; 23 cm.
Notes:	Includes bibliographic references (p. 129-133) and index.
ISBN:	0131848151 (pbk.)
DBCN:	AFF-9865
Holdings:	**Item Holdings**

Ethics and Communication

The Question of Speechwriting

From at least the time of Franklin Delano Roosevelt, speechwriters have written many of the best speeches made by U.S. presidents, including George W. Bush's speech to Congress and the nation following the September 11 terrorist attacks. More recently, former *Wall Street Journal* editor William McGurn became Bush's chief speechwriter and helped to fashion Bush's 2005 State of the Union address. Is such use of speechwriters ethical? Is it ethical to credit presidents with memorable lines from speeches that were written for them by professionals?

thousands of periodicals published. Many periodical indexes are available on CD-ROM, and many can be accessed either from the library or from remote locations. In most periodical indexes, entries are indexed alphabetically according to both subject and author. Most people use them by searching for subjects or keywords, much as they would conduct a World Wide Web search. Some periodical indexes are **full-text databases**, meaning that you can access not only bibliographical information but the texts of the articles themselves.

Following are some frequently used periodical indexes and full-text databases:

- *The Reader's Guide to Periodical Literature* is the oldest periodical index and the one that many researchers first learn to use. It indexes popular magazines and a few trade and professional journals. Libraries can subscribe to the *Reader's Guide* either in hard copy or as an electronic database.
- *Info Trac* is a collection of indexes available through a single source. *Info Trac* includes the *Expanded Academic Index* and the *Business Index Backfile*.
- *The Public Affairs Information Service (P.A.I.S.) Bulletin*, available in both hard copy and electronic formats, indexes both periodicals and books in such fields as sociology, political science, and economics.
- *LEXIS/NEXIS* is an extensive full-text subscription database of periodicals, newspapers, and government documents. It is an excellent source of very current information.
- *Academic Search Premier* is billed as the world's largest multidisciplinary academic database. Updated daily, it provides full text of more than 4700 scholarly publications in virtually every academic field.

full-text database
An indexing system that provides not only bibliographic data but full texts of entries.

Developing Your Presentation
STEP BY STEP

Gather Supporting Material

With a draft of his specific purpose, central idea, and main ideas in hand, Ben begins to research Coricidin abuse. Fortunately, he had kept the newspaper article that gave him the idea for the topic, so he has one source already. Because this first source is a newspaper, Ben decides to check out other newspapers.

He goes online to his university library's Web site. There he accesses the database *Newspaper Source,* where he discovers another article entitled "Latest Trend in Drug Abuse: Youths Risk Death for Cough-Remedy High," in the December 29, 2003, issue of *USA Today. Newspaper Source* provides the full text of that article.

While Ben is online, he uses Google to search for additional information on his topic and discovers a site called *TheAntiDrug.com.* The National Youth Anti-Drug Media Campaign, an initiative of the White House Office of National Drug Control Policy, maintains the site. Ben decides it is another credible source.

Ben records in MLA format on note cards the essential bibliographical information for these and other sources he discovers. Then he begins to read carefully and take notes. As he does so, he copies verbatim material accurately and puts quotation marks around it.

Newspapers   You can find information that is only hours old by reading the latest edition of a daily newspaper. Newspapers also offer the most detailed coverage available of current events.

Newspapers today exist in three formats. The first is the traditional newsprint format. However, libraries usually keep only the most recent newspapers (probably less than a week old) in their racks because they take up so much storage space. Back issues are kept on microfilm, the second format. And in recent years, many newspapers, from major national newspapers to local and college newspapers, have also become available online.

As with books and periodicals, you need a subject index to help you find newspaper articles of potential value to your research. **Newspaper indexes** are published for a number of medium-to-large newspapers. Your library may subscribe to several of these. In addition, electronic indexes such as the *National Newspaper Index* reference multiple newspapers. *Newspaper Source* also provides full texts of selected articles from some 30 national and international newspapers and more than 200 regional U.S. newspapers. Keep in mind, too, that if you need information about a specific event and you know the day on which it occurred, you can locate a newspaper from that or the following day and probably find a relevant news story about the event.

Reference Resources   A library's **reference resources** include encyclopedias, dictionaries, directories, atlases, almanacs, yearbooks, books of quotations, and biographical dictionaries. As a speaker, you may at one time or another use most of these types of materials. Like periodicals, newspapers, and microfilm, reference resources are usually available only for in-house research and cannot be checked out.

Government Documents   Government agencies at all levels publish information on almost every conceivable subject, as well as keeping records of most official proceedings. Once a dauntingly complex collection of pamphlets, special reports, and texts of speeches and debates, **government documents** today are much more readily accessible through the World Wide Web.

The most important index of government documents has long been the *Monthly Catalog of U.S. Government Publications*, available online in recent years. At present, several government agencies are in the final stages of developing a more comprehensive online *National Bibliography of U.S. Government Publications*.[22]

Special Services   Interlibrary loan and reciprocal borrowing privileges are among the special services that can help you find resources not otherwise available through your own library or online.

Say you are reading an article and discover a reference to a book you would like to see. Your library does not own the book. You might be able to use **interlibrary loan** to locate the book at another library and have it sent to your library within a few days. Or, if your library has **reciprocal borrowing privileges** with another library, you may be able to go to that library yourself and locate the book.

Types of Supporting Material

If you have explored your own knowledge and insights and those of people you know, discovered material on the Internet, and examined a variety of library resources, you probably have a wealth of potential supporting material. Now you will need to decide what to use in your presentation. Keeping in mind your audience's knowledge, interests, and expectations will help you to determine where an illustration might stir their emotions, where an explanation might help them to understand a point, and where statistics might convince them of the significance of a problem. Let's discuss these and other types of supporting material and consider suggestions for using them effectively.

---

newspaper index
A listing of bibliographical data for articles published in a newspaper (or group of newspapers) during a given time period.

reference resources
Material housed in the reference section of a library; may include encyclopedias, dictionaries, directories, atlases, almanacs, yearbooks, books of quotations, and biographical dictionaries.

government documents
Material published by the government, including records of official proceedings, pamphlets and brochures, and statistical data.

interlibrary loan
A borrowing/lending arrangement between one library and another that allows patrons to have materials from another library sent to their own.

reciprocal borrowing privileges
A borrowing/lending arrangement among libraries that allows patrons of any one library to use the resources of the others on site.

Illustrations   **Illustrations** offer an example of or tell a story about an idea, issue, or problem a speaker is discussing. They can be as short as a word or phrase or as long as a well-developed paragraph. Sometimes speakers will offer a series of brief illustrations, as Illinois State Senator Barack Obama did in his address to the Democratic National Convention in July 2004:

Verbal

> . . . we have more work to do. More to do for the workers I met in Galesburg, Illinois, who are losing their union jobs at the Maytag plant that's moving to Mexico, and now are having to compete with their own children for jobs that pay seven bucks an hour. More to do for the father I met who was losing his job and choking back tears, wondering how he would pay $4,500 a month for the drugs his son needs without the health benefits he counted on. More to do for the young woman in East St. Louis, and thousands more like her, who has the grades, has the drive, has the will, but doesn't have the money to go to college.[23]

Other speakers may offer longer and more detailed illustrations:

> Toby Lee, six years old, was sitting in the bleachers at the Hutchinson Ice Arena, just outside Minneapolis, Minnesota. He got up and walked toward his mother to get money for the concession stand. To the horror of his parents, Toby slipped and fell through the 13-inch space between the seat and the footboard, dropped 8 feet and landed headfirst on the concrete floor. Still conscious, he was rushed to the hospital, where he later died of severe head injuries.[24]

Obama's illustrations and the story of Toby Lee are true examples. However, sometimes a speaker will use instead a **hypothetical illustration**—one that has not actually occurred. If you decide to use a hypothetical illustration, it is important to make clear to your audience that the scene you describe never really happened. Note how Matthew uses the word *imagine* to make clear to his audience that his illustration is hypothetical:

> Imagine an evening outing: You and your two children decide to have a fun night out. You look up to your rearview mirror to see a car slam into the back of your car—WHAM—killing your children. You survive the crash and so does the individual who rear-ended you.[25]

Whether you choose to use brief or extended illustrations, true or hypothetical ones, remember this principle: Everybody likes to hear a story. An illustration almost always ensures audience interest. In addition, communication researchers have found that listeners are less likely to generate counterarguments to a persuasive message supported by examples and personal narratives.[26]

The following suggestions should help you use illustrations effectively in your presentations.

- Be sure that your illustrations are directly relevant to the idea or point they are supposed to support.
- Choose illustrations that are typical, not exceptions.
- Make your illustrations vivid and specific.
- Use illustrations with which your listeners can identify.
- Remember that the most effective illustrations are often personal ones.

Verbal

Descriptions and Explanations   Probably the most commonly used forms of supporting material are descriptions and explanations. To describe is to provide detailed images that allow an audience to see, hear, smell, touch, or taste whatever you are describing. **Descriptions**—word pictures—can make people and scenes come alive for an audience, as does this description of an all-too-common encounter:

> You're walking down the main street when a loud thumping bass sound approaches you. To your annoyance, it is one of those hot rod drivers with all his car windows down, and from his tiny capsule, irritating, distorted sound waves of "Did It for the Nookie" hit your ears at 90 decibels.[27]

---

illustration
A story or anecdote that provides an example of an idea, issue, or problem the speaker is discussing.

hypothetical illustration
An example or story that has not actually occurred.

description
A word picture.

This speaker effectively uses an electronic presentation aid to complement his use of descriptions and explanations.

Verbal

Verbal

explanation
A statement that makes clear how something is done or why it exists in its present or past form.

definition
A statement of what something means.

classification
A type of definition that first places a term in the general class to which it belongs and then differentiates it from all other members of that class.

operational definition
A definition that shows how a term works or what it does.

An **explanation** of how something works or why a situation exists can help an audience understand conditions, events, or processes. In her presentation on "superbugs," Amanda explains how disease-resistant strains of bacteria develop:

> Bacteria are able to mutate when they are continually exposed to an antibiotic, rendering the antibiotic virtually useless against it. And the frequency with which antibiotics are prescribed today makes our pharmacies virtual classrooms for infections.[28]

Although descriptions and explanations are part of most presentations, they lack the inherent interest factor that illustrations have. The following suggestions may help you to keep audiences from yawning through your descriptions and explanations:

- Avoid too many descriptions and explanations.
- Keep your descriptions and explanations brief.
- Describe and explain in specific and concrete language.

Definitions   Speakers should offer **definitions** of all technical or little-known terms in their presentations. However, they do not need to define terms with which most or all audience members are likely to be familiar. If you determine that you should define a word or phrase for your audience, consider whether you can best define it by **classification**, the format of a standard dictionary definition, or by an **operational definition**, explaining how the word or phrase works or what it does. Joni uses both kinds of definition in this excerpt from her speech on the dangers of oral polio vaccination:

> Polio is a virus which attacks the tissue in the spinal cord and brain, causing inflammation. The effects of this inflammation range from fever and vomiting to bodily paralysis and damage to the nerve cells which control breathing and circulation.[29]

The first sentence defines *polio* by placing it in the general category in which it belongs (viruses) and then by differentiating it from other viruses. This is a definition by classification. The second sentence describes what polio does. This is an operational definition.

To use definitions effectively, consider the following suggestions:

- Use definitions only when necessary.
- Be certain that your definitions are understandable.

- Be sure that any definition you provide accurately reflects your use of the word or phrase throughout the presentation.

Analogies   An **analogy** demonstrates how unfamiliar ideas, things, and situations are similar to something the audience already understands. Speakers can use two types of analogies in their presentations. The first is a **literal analogy**, or comparison of two similar things. Kyle uses a literal analogy to compare the African slave trade to other historical travesties:

> The trans-Atlantic slave trade was one of the greatest tragedies in human history, rivaled by such horrible events as the Jewish Holocaust and the Spanish invasion of the Americas.[30]

The second type of analogy is a **figurative analogy**, a comparison of two seemingly dissimilar things that in fact share a significant common feature. In a recent speech to an environmental group, former Colorado Governor Richard Lamm drew on a figurative analogy that compared humanity's continuing long-term challenges to the flow of a river:

> ... River issues were the long-term flowing issues, which went on over generations if not centuries. The full sweep of history reveals some issues like the fight for religious freedom, the gradual, if glacial, emancipation of women, the search for freedom for self-government, the fight against authoritarian governance, etc. These issues can be observed in some form over the sweep of history.[31]

Two suggestions can help you use analogies more effectively in your presentations:

1. Be certain that the two things you compare in a literal analogy are very similar.
2. Make the similarity between the two things compared in a figurative analogy apparent to the audience.

Statistics   **Statistics**, or numerical data, can represent hundreds or thousands of illustrations, helping a speaker express the significance or magnitude of a situation. Statistics can also help a speaker express the relationship of a part to the whole. In this brief excerpt from a presentation on bogus airline parts, Jon uses both types of statistics:

> ... 26 million parts are installed on airplanes every year in the U.S., and the FAA estimates that at least 2% of these parts are counterfeits.[32]

Skilled speakers learn how to use statistics to their greatest advantage. For example, they try to make huge numbers more readily understandable and more dramatic to their audiences. Nicole emphasizes the vast amount of computer waste with a memorable image:

> ... outdated computer waste in America alone could fill the area of a football field piled one mile high.[33]

Or a speaker might present statistics about the world's growing population in these terms:

> In an average minute, 245 people are born and 107 die, for a net gain by the minute of 138 ... 8300 an hour, 200,000 per day, 6 million per month, and 72 million a year.[34]

In addition to simplifying and dramatizing your statistics, you can use statistics more effectively if you utilize the following three suggestions:

1. Round off large numbers.
2. Use visual aids to present your statistics.
3. Cite the sources of your statistics.

Opinions   The opinions of others can add authority, drama, and style to a presentation. A speaker can use three types of opinions: expert testimony, lay testimony, and literary quotations.

Verbal

Verbal

analogy
A comparison between two ideas, things, or situations, that demonstrates how something unfamiliar is similar to something the audience already understands.

literal analogy
A comparison between two similar things.

figurative analogy
A comparison between two seemingly dissimilar things that share some common feature on which the comparison depends.

statistics
Numerical data that summarize examples.

Verbal

Expert testimony is perhaps the most frequent type of opinion employed by speakers. If you lack authority on your topic, cite someone who can offer such expertise. In her speech on the college credit card crisis, Jeni realized that her audience might not believe that the misuse of credit cards by college students is a widespread problem. So Jeni quoted an expert:

> Ruth Suswein, executive director of the Bankcard Holders of America, told the . . . *Pittsburgh Post Gazette*, "I defy you to go on any college campus and find any student who doesn't know some other student who has messed up using credit cards."[35]

In the days and weeks that followed the September 11, 2001, terrorist attacks, countless eyewitnesses and people affected in various ways by the tragedy told their personal stories to reporters and news anchors. Audiences already aware of the magnitude of the tragedy—the number of lives lost and the damage inflicted—were perhaps even more moved by the stories of such individuals as Lisa Jefferson. Jefferson was the GTE customer care representative who stayed on the line for 15 minutes with Todd Beamer, a passenger on United Flight 93 that eventually crashed in Pennsylvania. Of course, few speakers will have eyewitnesses at hand when they speak. But they can quote firsthand witnesses of dramatic or traumatic events. Such **lay testimony** can stir an audience's emotions and provide the most memorable moments of a presentation.

Finally, speakers may wish to include **literary quotations** in their presentations. Newspaper publisher Mike Curtin quoted science fiction writer H. G. Wells in his speech on the importance of language education:

> H. G. Wells, the English writer who achieved fame with his publication of *The Time Machine* and *The War of the Worlds*, . . . wrote, "Civilization is a race between education and catastrophe."[36]

Whether you use expert testimony, lay testimony, or literary quotations, consider the following suggestions for using opinions effectively in your presentations:

- Be certain that any authority you cite is actually an expert on the subject you are discussing.
- Identify your sources.
- Cite unbiased authorities.
- Cite opinions that are representative of prevailing opinion. If you cite a dissenting viewpoint, identify it as such.
- Quote or paraphrase your sources accurately and note the context in which the remarks were originally made.
- Use literary quotations sparingly.

Acknowledgment of Supporting Material

Once you have supporting material in hand, you must decide whether it must be credited to a source. Some information is so widely known that you may not need to acknowledge a source. For example, you need not credit a source if you say that former FBI official Mark Felt has been identified as the long-anonymous Watergate informant "Deep Throat." This fact is general knowledge and is widely available in a variety of sources. However, if you decide to use any of the following, then you must give credit:

- Direct quotations, even if they are only brief phrases
- Opinions, assertions, or ideas of others, even if you paraphrase them rather than quote them verbatim
- Statistics
- Any nonoriginal visual materials, including graphs, tables, and pictures

expert testimony
The opinion of someone who is an acknowledged expert in the field under discussion.

lay testimony
The opinion of someone who experienced an event or situation firsthand.

literary quotation
A citation from a work of fiction or nonfiction, a poem, or another speech.

oral citation
The oral presentation of such information about a source as the author, title, and publication date.

To cite your source, you can integrate an **oral citation** into your presentation. For example, you might say,

> According to an article entitled "Wider Student Use Is Urged for New Meningitis Vaccine," published in the May 27, 2005, edition of *The New York Times*, the U.S. Centers for Disease Control and Prevention are now recommending "wider use of a new meningitis vaccine for adolescents and college freshmen," including routine vaccination for 11- and 12-year olds.[37]

As you select your illustrations, descriptions, explanations, definitions, analogies, statistics, and opinions, be guided not only by the suggestions provided in this chapter for each type of supporting material but also by the five communication principles for a lifetime. The best supporting material reflects self-awareness, taking advantage of your own knowledge and experience. Effective verbal supporting material is appropriately worded, concrete, and vivid enough that your audience can visualize what you are talking about. Effective visual supporting material enhances, rather than detracts from, your verbal message. Sensitivity to your audience will help you choose the verbal and visual supporting material that is most appropriately adapted to them. If a presentation is boring, it is probably because the speaker has not used the fundamental principles of communication as criteria for selecting supporting material.

Aware
Verbal
Nonverbal
Listen and Respond
Adapt

Diversity and Communication

Adapting to Diverse Audiences

One of the principles we've stressed throughout this book is the importance of adapting your message to others. Many, if not most, of the presentations you give will be to audiences that represent a mix of cultures and backgrounds rather than a single cultural tradition. Although you may not have immediate plans to deliver a presentation in Singapore, Moscow, Tokyo, or Warsaw, it will not be unusual for you to face audience members who come from one of these cities when you speak on campus or in your hometown.

People from the predominant culture in North America usually prefer a structured presentation that follows an outlined pattern; they also prefer an introduction that previews the ideas you'll present and a conclusion that crisply summarizes the essential points you've made. But a Russian or Eastern European audience would expect a less tightly structured presentation. When you're in doubt about listener preferences, we recommend being structured and organized. But realize that not all audience members may expect information to be presented as *you* prefer. One study found that members of some cultures prefer a more formal oratorical style of delivery than the conversational, extemporaneous style that is usually taught in American presentational speaking classes.[38] For example, Japanese speakers addressing a predominantly Japanese audience begin a presentation by making respectful references to their audience.

You may still be wondering, "So, what should I do when I speak to people who have a cultural background different from my own?" Here are some ideas that may help you.[39] First, con-

sider using a variety of different types of supporting materials. A mix of stories, examples, statistics, and other supporting illustrations can appeal to a wide range of audience backgrounds. Also consider the power of images over words. Use visual aids to illustrate your talk. Pictures and images can communicate universal messages—especially emotional ones. Telling a good story to illustrate your ideas is another effective strategy to appeal to a wide range of audience preferences. Most audiences value a good story with a point or moral that is relevant to the point you want to make. Our overarching suggestion: Be aware of who will be in your audience. If you're unsure of your listeners' speaking-style preferences, ask for tips and strategies from audience members or people you trust, before you design or deliver your presentation.

RECAP

Supporting Your Speech

Type of Supporting Material	Guidelines for Use
Illustrations	• Make illustrations directly relevant to the idea or point they support.
	• Choose illustrations that are typical.
	• Make illustrations vivid and specific.
	• Use illustrations with which your listeners can identify.
	• Remember that the most effective illustrations are often personal ones.
Descriptions and Explanations	• Avoid too many descriptions and explanations.
	• Keep descriptions and explanations brief.
	• Describe and explain in specific and concrete language.
Definitions	• Use definitions only when necessary.
	• Be certain that definitions are understandable.
	• Be sure that a definition accurately reflects your use of the word or phrase.
Analogies	• Be certain that the two things you compare in a literal analogy are very similar.
	• Make apparent to the audience the similarity between the two things compared in a figurative analogy.
Statistics	• Round off large numbers.
	• Use visual aids.
	• Cite your sources.
Opinions	• Be certain that any authority you cite is actually an expert on the subject you are discussing.
	• Identify your sources.
	• Cite unbiased authorities.
	• Cite representative opinions, or identify dissenting viewpoints as such.
	• Quote or paraphrase accurately and in context.
	• Use literary quotations sparingly.

PRINCIPLES FOR A LIFETIME: Enhancing Your Skills

Aware

Principle One: Be aware of your communication with yourself and others.

- Give yourself a pep talk before getting up to speak.
- Consider your own interests and experiences when searching for a topic.
- Remember that the most effective illustrations are often personal ones.

Principle Two: Effectively use and interpret verbal messages.

- Focus on your message to help manage speaker anxiety.
- Search for topics on the Web, in the media, and in books.
- Wording your specific purpose in terms of your audience will help you keep your focus on them.
- A central idea should reflect a single topic, be a complete declarative sentence, and use specific language.
- Consider the accountability, accuracy, objectivity, date, usability, and diversity sensitivity of verbal material you find on Web sites.
- Be sure that your illustrations are directly relevent to the idea or the point they are supposed to support.
- Make your illustrations vivid and specific.
- Avoid too many descriptions and explanations.
- Keep descriptions and explanations brief.
- Describe and explain in specific and concrete language.
- Make your definitions readily understandable, and be certain they accurately reflect how you use the word or phrase in the speech.
- Round off statistics to make them more readily understandable.
- Cite unbiased authorities.
- Cite opinions that are representative of prevailing opinion.
- Quote or paraphrase accurately and in context.
- Use literary quotations sparingly.
- Integrate oral citations of your sources into your presentation.

Verbal

Nonverbal

Principle Three: Effectively use and interpret nonverbal messages.

- Remember that the physical symptoms of speaker anxiety are rarely visible to an audience.
- Consider the accountability, accuracy, objectivity, date, usability, and diversity sensitivity of pictures and graphics you find on Web sites.
- Use visual aids to present statistics.

Principle Four: Listen and respond thoughtfully to others.

- Seek out information about your audience and how they are likely to respond to your message to increase your comfort with speaking in public.
- Listen for topic ideas in the course of casual conversation with friends.

Listen and Respond

Principle Five: Appropriately adapt messages to others.

- Revise your ideas or strategies at any point in the presentation-preparation process, as you seek out and learn more about your audience.
- Be audience-centered to reduce speaker anxiety.
- Be sensitive to and adapt to the diversity of your audience.
- Consider your audience's interests and expectations as you select the topic for your presentation.
- Keep in mind your audience's knowledge, interests, and expectations as you select supporting material for your presentation.
- Use illustrations with which your audience can identify. Consider making your audience members part of the scenario in a hypothetical illustration.
- Make the similarity between the two things compared in a figurative analogy apparent to your audience.

Adapt

SUMMARY

Public speaking is a teachable, learnable process of developing, supporting, organizing, and presenting ideas. Presentational speaking skills can help you in other college courses and in the workplace.

The stages of the public speaking process center around consideration of the audience, who influence every decision a speaker makes. A speaker's tasks include selecting and narrowing a topic, identifying a general and specific purpose for speaking, developing the central idea of the presentation, generating main ideas, gathering supporting material, organizing the presentation, and finally, rehearsing and delivering the presentation.

Nearly everyone feels some anxiety about speaking in public. Speaker anxiety triggers physiological responses that may be worrisome but are actually your body's attempt to help you. Focusing on your audience and message and giving yourself mental pep talks can help you manage speaker anxiety, as can knowing how to develop a presentation, being well prepared, and seeking out opportunities to speak. Professional help is available for those few who continue to suffer debilitating speaker anxiety.

As you begin to prepare your presentation, you will first have to select and narrow your topic, keeping in mind the audience, the occasion, and your own interests and experiences. You may find helpful such strategies as silent brainstorming, scanning Web directories and Web pages, and listening and reading for topic ideas. Once you have a topic, you need to identify both your general and your specific purpose. General purposes include to inform, to persuade, and to entertain. Specific purposes are determined by the general purpose, the topic, and the audience. You will also need to decide on the central idea for the presentation. You can use that central idea to help you generate your main ideas, which are usually logical divisions of the central idea, reasons the central idea is true, or a series of steps or a chronological sequence that develops the central idea.

Next, you will need to discover support for your main ideas. As a presentational speaker, you have at least three potential sources of supporting material: yourself and people you know, the Internet, and the library. Personal knowledge and experience increase the likelihood that the audience will find you a credible speaker. To supplement your own knowledge and experience, you might turn to the vast resources available on the Internet. And most likely, you will still use library resources—books, periodicals, newspapers, reference resources, government documents, and various special services—as sources of supporting material.

The types of supporting material you can use in a presentation include illustrations, descriptions, explanations, definitions, analogies, statistics, and opinions. Simple guidelines can help you use each of these types of supporting material effectively and cite your sources correctly.

Discussion and Review

1. Explain how presentational speaking skills can be of practical use, both while you are in college and afterward.
2. Sketch and label the stages of the audience-centered public speaking model.
3. Explain what causes the symptoms of speaker anxiety.
4. Offer at least three suggestions for managing speaker anxiety.
5. Suggest both criteria and strategies for discovering a good presentation topic.
6. What are the three general purposes for presentations?
7. With what phrase should an audience-centered, specific-purpose statement begin?
8. In what ways does a central idea differ from a specific purpose?
9. What are the characteristics of a good central idea?
10. List the three questions that you can apply to generate main ideas from a central idea.
11. Where might you find supporting material for a presentation?
12. List and explain the six criteria for evaluating Web sites.

13. What resources are available in most libraries?
14. What types of supporting material might you use in your presentations?

Putting Principles into Practice

1. Interview someone who regularly speaks in public as part of his or her job. Ask that person how he or she deals with speaker anxiety and what stages or steps he or she goes through in developing a speech.

2. Brainstorm a list of at least ten possible topics for an informative classroom presentation.

3. Write a specific-purpose statement for an informative presentation and a persuasive presentation on each of the following topics:

   Rap music
   Graduate school
   Primary elections
   Athletes as role models
   Credit cards

4. Generate at least three main ideas from each of the following central ideas. Apply the questions suggested in this chapter: Does the central idea have logical divisions? Can you think of several reasons the central idea is true? Can you support the central idea with a series of steps or a chronological sequence?

   Students who commute have at least three advantages over students who live on campus.
   Diplomatic relations between the United States and China have been strained over the last decade.
   Sleep deprivation is dangerous.
   Three specific strategies can help you deal with unsolicited telemarketers.
   Women should have annual mammograms.

5. Use a World Wide Web search engine to answer the following questions.[40] They're not as obvious as you think!

   a. How long did the Hundred Years War last?
   b. Which country makes Panama hats?
   c. From what animal do we get catgut?
   d. What is a camel's hair brush made of?
   e. The Canary Islands in the Pacific are named after what animal?
   f. What was King George VI's first name?
   g. What color is a purple finch?
   h. Where are Chinese gooseberries from?

6. Read a story in a newspaper or national news magazine. See how many different types of supporting material you can identify in the story.

7. The following passage comes from a book entitled *Abraham Lincoln, Public Speaker,* by Waldo W. Braden:

   > The Second Inaugural Address, sometimes called Lincoln's Sermon on the Mount, was a concise, tightly constructed composition that did not waste words on ceremonial niceties or superficial sentiment. The shortest Presidential inaugural address up to that time, it was only 700 words long, compared to 3700 words for the First, and required from 5 to 7 minutes to deliver.[41]

   Now determine which of the following statements should be credited to Braden if you were to use them in a presentation:

   • Lincoln's Second Inaugural is "sometimes called Lincoln's Sermon on the Mount."
   • Because he was elected and sworn in for two terms as President, Abraham Lincoln prepared and delivered two inaugural addresses.
   • Lincoln's Second Inaugural was 700 words and 5 to 7 minutes long.

CHAPTER Twelve

Don't agonize.
Organize.
Florynce R. Kennedy

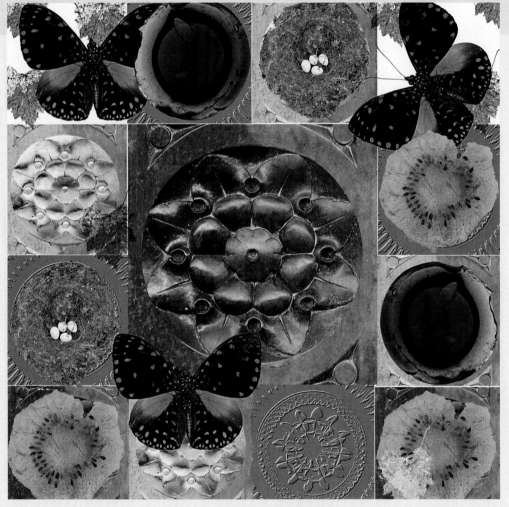

Jim Macbeth, "Mostly Round & Flat," © Jim Macbeth/Superstock, Inc.

Organizing and Outlining Your Presentation

CHAPTER OUTLINE

Organizing Your Main Ideas

Organizing Your Supporting Material

Organizing Your Presentation for the Ears of Others

Introducing and Concluding Your Presentation

Outlining Your Presentation

Summary

CHAPTER OBJECTIVES

After studying this chapter, you should be able to:

1. List and explain five strategies for organizing main ideas in a presentation.

2. Define the principles of primacy, recency, and complexity and explain how each can be applied to organizing main ideas.

3. List and explain five strategies for organizing supporting material in a presentation.

4. Explain three ways to organize a presentation for the ears of others.

5. List and explain the five functions of a presentation introduction.

6. Suggest at least five strategies for getting an audience's attention in a presentation introduction.

7. List and explain the four functions of a presentation conclusion.

8. Define a preparation outline and explain how a speaker would use one.

9. Outline a presentation according to standard outline format.

10. Define a delivery outline and explain how a speaker would use one.

D eveloping a presentation is like building a house. Just as a building contractor frames out a house early in the building process, a speaker frames out a presentation by completing the first four stages of the speech preparation process—selecting and narrowing a topic, identifying a general and a specific purpose, determining a central idea, and generating main ideas. Framing completed, the contractor assembles all the materials needed for the house: windows, doors, cabinets, hardware, and flooring; the speaker finds and adds supporting material to the presentation "frame," the fifth stage of the process. Once the house is framed out and the building materials are ready, the contractor must organize the work of the electricians, plumbers, carpenters, and carpet layers. Similarly, the speaker must organize ideas and supporting material.

In this chapter, we will discuss strategies for organizing and outlining your presentation, and we will explore ways to introduce and conclude your presentation effectively. Grounded in the five communication principles for a lifetime with which you are now familiar, these suggestions and strategies will result in an essentially complete "house"—a presentation that is ready to be rehearsed and delivered.

ORGANIZING YOUR MAIN IDEAS

You have already completed the first five stages of audience-centered presentation preparation:

- Select and narrow a topic.
- Determine your purpose.
- Develop your central idea.
- Generate main ideas.
- Gather supporting material.

Now it is time to put your presentation together, organizing the ideas and information you have generated and discovered.

Verbal

Logical organization is one way you can communicate your verbal message effectively. A logically organized presentation has three major divisions—an introduction, a body, and a conclusion. The introduction catches the audience's attention and previews the body. The body presents the main content of the presentation. The conclusion summarizes the main ideas and provides memorable closure to the presentation.

Professional speaker Larry Tracy suggests a strategy he calls "3-1-2" for drafting the organization of a presentation.[1] It works like this:

1. Take a stack of 3X5 cards. Label one card "3" and write on it your "bottom line" message. This is the core of your conclusion.
2. Label another card "1" and write on it where the presentation will go—your preview.
3. Next, place the supporting points that flow from "1" to "3" on a series of cards marked "2a," "2b," "2c," etc. These will become the main ideas of the body of your presentation.

The advantage of the "3-1-2" strategy, says Tracy, is that it clarifies from the start of the drafting process where the presentation is going, ensuring more logical structure. He adds, "Just remember: You draft 3-1-2, but . . . you deliver 1-2-3."

Regardless of whether you use Tracy's drafting process, one recommended by your public speaking instructor, or one of your own devising, you will need to consider early on how best to organize your main ideas. Then you will organize your supporting material for maximum impact, and devise signposts to lead your audience through your presentation. Finally, you will need to develop an effective introduction and conclusion. Once you have made the necessary decisions about these component parts, you will be ready to outline the entire presentation.

If you intend to describe a series of different types of procedures in your presentation, you may find that it works well to organize your main ideas topically.

Organizing Ideas Chronologically

If you determine that you can best develop your central idea through a series of steps, you will probably organize those steps—your main ideas—chronologically. **Chronological organization** is based on sequential order, according to when each step or event occurred or should occur. If you are explaining a process, you will want to organize the steps of that process from first to last. If you are providing a historical overview of an event, movement, or policy, you might begin with the end result and trace its history backward in time.

Examples of topics that might lend themselves to chronological organization include the process for stripping and refinishing a piece of furniture, the four hurricanes that hit Florida in 2004, and the history of higher education for women.

Organizing Ideas Topically

If your main ideas are natural divisions of your central idea, you will probably arrange them according to **topical organization**. Topical organization may be simply an arbitrary arrangement of main ideas that are fairly equal in importance. For example, if you are giving an informative presentation on the various instrument families of the modern symphony orchestra, your main ideas will probably be strings, woodwinds, brass, and percussion. The order in which you discuss these instrument groups may not really matter.

At other times, topical organization is less arbitrary. The principle of **recency** suggests that audiences remember best what they hear last. If you want to emphasize the string section of an orchestra, you will purposefully place that family last in your presentation.

Another principle that can help guide your topical organization is the principle of **primacy**. Primacy suggests that you discuss your most convincing or least controversial idea first. To adapt to an audience who may be skeptical of some of your ideas, discuss first those points on which you all agree. If you are speaking to an anti–gun-control audience about ways to protect children from violence in schools, don't begin by advocating gun control. Instead, begin by affirming family values and education in the home, perhaps move on to the importance of small classes and adequate counseling in schools, and only then discuss gun control as a possible preventive measure.

One other type of topical organization is organization according to **complexity**, moving from simple ideas and processes to more complex ones. Many skills you have

chronological organization
Organization by time or sequence.

topical organization
Organization determined by the speaker's discretion or by recency, primacy, or complexity.

recency
The principle that audiences remember best what they hear last, which guides the arrangement of ideas from the least to the most important.

primacy
Arranging ideas from the strongest or least controversial to the weakest or most controversial.

complexity
Arranging ideas from simple to more complex.

learned in life have been taught by order of complexity. In first grade, you learned to read easy words first, then moved on to more difficult ones. In third grade, you learned single-digit multiplication tables before moving on to more complex double- and triple-digit multiplication problems. In junior high school, you learned to use the library's catalog before you began a research project. And in high school, you learned to drive by practicing simple maneuvers in the parking lot before going out on the highway. Similarly, if you are giving a presentation on how to trace your family's genealogy, you might discuss readily available, user-friendly Internet sources before explaining how to access old courthouse records or parish registries of births, deaths, and baptisms.

Organizing Ideas Spatially

"Go down the hill two blocks and turn left by the florist. Then go three blocks to the next stoplight and turn right. The place you're looking for is about a block farther, on your right." When you offer someone directions, you organize your ideas spatially. **Spatial organization** means arranging items according to their location, position, or direction.

Presentations that rely on description are good candidates for spatial organization. For example, discussions of the route taken by Sir Edmund Hillary and Tenzing Norgay when climbing Mt. Everest in 1953, and the molecular structure of DNA would lend themselves to spatial organization. Or, rather than organizing your presentation on Florida's 2004 hurricanes chronologically, you might choose to organize it spatially, according to where each hurricane made landfall.

Organizing Ideas to Show Cause and Effect

Cause-and-effect organization actually refers to two related patterns: identifying a situation and then discussing the resulting effects (cause–effect), and presenting a situation and then exploring its causes (effect–cause).

A speaker discussing the consequences of teenage pregnancy might use a cause–effect pattern, establishing first that teenage pregnancy is a significant social issue and then discussing various consequences or effects. On the other hand, a speaker who speaks on the same topic but who chooses to explore the reasons for the high rate of teen pregnancy will probably use an effect–cause pattern, discussing teenage pregnancy first as an effect and then exploring its various causes. As the recency principle would suggest, a cause–effect pattern emphasizes effects; an effect–cause pattern emphasizes causes.

Organizing Ideas by Problem and Solution

spatial organization
Organization according to location, position, or direction.

cause-and-effect organization
Organization by discussing a situation and its causes or a situation and its effects.

problem-and-solution organization
Organization by discussing first a problem and then various solutions.

If, instead of exploring causes or consequences of a problem or issue, you want either to explore how best to solve the problem or to advocate a particular solution, you will probably choose **problem-and-solution organization**. For example, if you were speaking on how listeners can protect themselves from mountain lion attacks in the American West, you might first establish that a significant problem exists, then talk about solutions to that problem. Or if you were talking about ending discrimination against overweight people, you could first establish that such discrimination exists and is harmful, then talk about the solutions. Although you can use problem-and-solution organization for either informative or persuasive presentations, you are more likely to use it when your general purpose is to persuade—to urge your audience to support or adopt one or more of the solutions you discuss.

Note that the topics in both of the above examples also lend themselves to organization by cause and effect. You could, for example, discuss mountain lion attacks as an effect and explore why the frequency of such attacks has increased in recent years (causes). Or you could talk about discrimination against the overweight as a cause and discuss the harmful effects of such discrimination. How do you decide which organizational pattern to use? Return to your specific purpose. If it is for your audience to be able to explain how best to guard against mountain lion attacks, select the problem-and-solution organizational strategy. If it is for your audience to be able to explain the harmful effects of discrimination against those who are overweight, use the cause-and-effect strategy of organization. Let both your general and your specific purpose continue to guide your presentation as you organize your main ideas.

RECAP

Organizing Your Main Ideas

Strategy	Description
Chronological	Organization by time or sequence
Topical	Arbitrary arrangement of topics or organization according to recency, primacy, or complexity
Spatial	Organization according to location or position
Cause-and-effect	Organization by discussing a situation and its causes, or a situation and its effects
Problem-and-solution	Organization by discussing a problem and then various solutions

ORGANIZING YOUR SUPPORTING MATERIAL

Once you have organized your main ideas, you are ready to organize the supporting material for each idea. Suppose that you find that you have two brief illustrations, a statistic, and an opinion in support of your first main idea. How should you organize these materials to communicate your verbal message most effectively?

The same organizational patterns you considered as you organized your main ideas can also help you organize your supporting material. For example, you might arrange a group of brief illustrations chronologically. At other times, you might find it more useful to organize supporting material according to the principle of recency, primacy, or complexity. You would employ the principle of recency if you saved your most convincing statistic for last. You would use primacy if you decided to present first the opinion with which you were certain your audience would agree. And you might arrange two explanations according to the principle of complexity, presenting the simplest one first and working up to the more complex one. Two additional principles that may help you organize supporting material are specificity and arrangement from "soft" to "hard" evidence.

Sometimes your supporting material includes both very specific illustrations and a more general explanation. The principle of **specificity** suggests that you group your specific information and either offer it first, followed by your general explanation; or make your general explanation first and then support it with your specific illustrations. In his speech on wearing ribbons to show support for a cause, Tony offers a series of brief illustrations first, followed by a more general explanation:

> Battling AIDS, surviving breast cancer, putting your life back together after 9/11, just being brave while your country is at war; all of these are situations that cause people to seek out support and comfort in others. We start looking for ways to connect with people around us, even total strangers. A simple way proven effective in the past and possible for the future is simply cutting off a ribbon and pinning it to your clothes.[2]

Another principle that can help you organize your supporting material is moving from "soft" evidence to "hard" evidence. Hypothetical illustrations, descriptions, explanations, definitions, analogies, and opinions are usually considered **soft evidence**. **Hard evidence** includes factual examples and statistics. Allie moves from soft evidence

specificity
Organization from specific information to a more general statement, or from a general statement to specific information.

soft evidence
Hypothetical illustrations, descriptions, explanations, definitions, analogies, and opinions.

hard evidence
Factual examples and statistics.

Diversity and Communication

Acknowledging Cultural Differences in Organizing Messages

*W*hat's the shortest distance between two points? Why, going in a straight line, of course. In organizing a message, it may seem that the most logical strategy is to develop a structure that moves from one idea to the next in a logical, "straight" way. But not every culture organizes ideas using that logic. In fact, each culture teaches its members unique patterns of thought and organization that are considered appropriate for various occasions and audiences. In general, U.S. speakers tend to be more linear and direct than do Semitic, Asian, Romance, or Russian speakers.[3] Semitic speakers support their main points by pursuing tangents that might seem "off topic" to many U.S. listeners. Asians may allude to a main point only through a circuitous route of illustrations and parables. And speakers from Romance and Russian cultures tend to begin with a basic principle and then move to facts and illustrations that only gradually are related to a main point. The models in Figure 12.1 illustrate these culturally diverse patterns of organization.[4] Of course, these are very broad generalizations. As an effective speaker who seeks to adapt to your audience, you should investigate and perhaps acknowledge or even consider adopting the customary organizational strategy of your particular audience. In addition, when you are listening to a presentation, recognizing the existence of cultural differences can help you appreciate and understand the organization of a speaker from a culture other than your own.

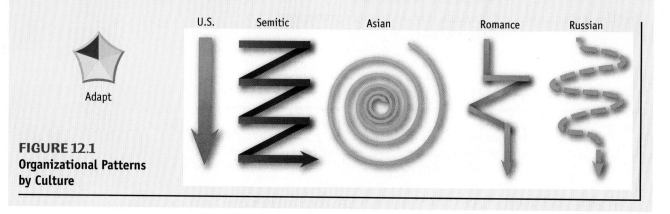

FIGURE 12.1
Organizational Patterns by Culture

Adapt

U.S.   Semitic   Asian   Romance   Russian

to a hard statistic as she discusses the widespread prescribing of selective serotonin re-uptake inhibitors, or SSRIs:

> The *PR Newswire* of April 14, 2003, explains that when people suffer from depression or an anxiety disorder, there could be a problem with their serotonin balance. Thus, it is unsurprising that SSRIs are frequently prescribed for a variety of mood disorders. *ABC News* of June 21, 2003, reports that one out of every eight Americans has been prescribed at least one SSRI.[5]

Developing Your Presentation
STEP BY STEP

Organize Your Speech

As he begins to integrate his supporting material in his speech on Coricidin abuse, Ben finds that he has four items to help him explain the ingredient in Coricidin that is the catalyst for abuse. He decides to arrange these four items in order of complexity—from stating where DXM can be found, to explaining its physical side effects:

1. DXM is found in over 100 cold medications, including those with "DM" or "Tuss" in their names.

2. Coricidin is the drug of choice because it's easier than swallowing several bottles of Robitussin.

3. As the National Institute on Drug Abuse indicates on *TheAntiDrug.com* Web site, last updated April 11, 2004, DXM closely resembles PCP, and when taken in excess, causes hallucinations.

4. According to *USA Today* of December 29, 2003, when abused, Coricidin can cause depressed breathing, an irregular heartbeat, seizures, coma, and even death.

RECAP

Organizing Your Supporting Material

Strategy	Description
Chronology	Organization by time or sequence
Recency	Most important material last
Primacy	Most convincing or least controversial material first
Complexity	From simple to more complex material
Specificity	From specific information to general overview or from general overview to specific information
"Soft" to "hard" evidence	From hypothetical illustrations and opinions to facts and statistics

ORGANIZING YOUR PRESENTATION FOR THE EARS OF OTHERS

You now have a fairly complete, logically organized plan for your presentation. But if you tried to deliver it at this point, your audience would probably become confused. What are your main ideas? How is one main idea related to the next? What supporting material develops which main idea? To adapt your logically organized message to your audience, you need to provide **signposts**, or organizational cues for their ears. You do this by adding previews, transitions, and summaries that allow you to move smoothly from one idea to the next throughout the presentation.

Adapt

Previews

A **preview** "tells them what you're going to tell them"—it is a statement of what is to come. Previews help your audience members anticipate and remember the main ideas of your presentation. They also help you move smoothly from the introduction to the body of your presentation and from one main idea to the next. The **initial preview** is usually presented in conjunction with, and sometimes as part of, the central idea. Note how Yarmela states her central idea and then previews her three main ideas near the end of the introduction to her presentation on genetic testing:

> Genetic testing is seen as the wave of the future, but too many Americans are putting their faith in these tests that simply are not adequate. In order to understand this problem, we will first examine the problems that are occurring with genetic testing, then look at the causes, and finally discuss the solutions that must occur in order to stop more tragedies from taking place.[6]

signpost
A verbal or nonverbal organizational signal.

preview
A statement of what is to come.

initial preview
First statement of the main ideas of a presentation, usually presented with or near the central idea.

Ethics and Communication

The Ethics of Primacy and Recency

Jessica knows that according to the principle of recency, she should discuss last what she wants her audience to remember best. However, in her presentation on the risk of counterfeit prescription drugs,

Jessica thinks that it may be more ethical to reveal immediately to her audience how costly the problem is in terms of both dollars and human lives. Is it ethical for Jessica to save that important statistic for last?

Canadian Prime Minister Jean Charest uses a nonverbal signpost to help listeners follow his transitions.

In addition to offering an initial preview, a speaker may also offer **internal previews** at various points throughout a presentation. These previews introduce and outline ideas that will be developed as the presentation progresses. Meleena provides an internal preview just before the final main idea of her presentation on sexual harassment in schools:

> Now . . . we can look at some things that we can all do, as parents, teachers, and students, to stop sexual harassment in our schools. There are two ways to prevent these causes from recurring. The first is education and the second is immediate action.[7]

When Meleena delivers this preview, her listeners know that she is going to talk about two possible solutions to the problem she has been discussing. Their anticipation increases the likelihood that they will hear and later remember these solutions.

Verbal and Nonverbal Transitions

A **transition** signals to an audience that a speaker is moving from one idea to the next. Effectively using verbal messages includes using **verbal transitions**, words or phrases that show relationships between ideas in your presentation. They include simple enumeration (*first, second, third*); synonyms or pronouns that refer to earlier key words or ideas (the word *they* at the beginning of this sentence refers to the phrase "verbal transitions" in the previous sentence); and words and phrases that show relationships between ideas (*in addition, not only . . . but also, in other words, in summary, therefore, however*). As you begin to rehearse your presentation, you might need to experiment with various verbal transitions to achieve coherence that seems natural and logical to you. If none of the verbal alternatives seems quite right, consider a nonverbal transition.

Nonverbal transitions are sometimes used alone and sometimes in combination with verbal transitions. An effective **nonverbal transition** might take the form of a facial expression, a pause, a change in vocal pitch or speaking rate, or movement. Most good speakers will use a combination of verbal and nonverbal transitions to help them move from one idea to the next throughout their presentations.

Summaries

Like previews, a **summary**—a recap of what has been said—provides an additional opportunity for the audience to grasp a speaker's most important ideas. Most speakers use two types of summaries: internal summaries and a final summary.

Internal summaries, like internal previews, occur within and throughout a presentation. You might want to use an internal summary after you have discussed two or

---

internal preview
Preview within the speech that introduces ideas still to come.

transition
A word, phrase, or nonverbal cue that indicates movement from one idea to the next or the relationship between ideas.

verbal transition
A word or phrase that indicates the relationship between two ideas.

nonverbal transition
Facial expression, vocal cue, or physical movement that indicates a speaker is moving from one idea to the next.

summary
A recap of what has been said.

internal summary
A recap of what has been said so far in the presentation.

three main ideas, to ensure that the audience keeps them firmly in mind as you move into another main idea. You can combine an internal summary with an internal preview. Rebecca clarifies what she has just discussed, as well as what she will discuss next, in this combined internal summary/preview from her presentation on Rohypnol, the so-called date-rape drug:

> Having examined the problem of Rohypnol and why it has become such a danger in today's society [summary], we can now explore solutions at the commercial and personal levels to purge this drug from our system [preview].[8]

You may also want to provide your audience with a final opportunity to hear and remember your main ideas, in the form of a **final summary** in your conclusion. While your initial preview gave your audience their first exposure to your main ideas, your final summary will give them their last exposure to those ideas. Near the end of Stephanie's presentation on cruise ship violence, she provides this final summary of her three main ideas:

> Today we outlined violence on cruise ships and the need for recourse; we then discussed the nature of these criminal environments and lack of laws; and finally, we explored solutions for handling or avoiding these crimes even if the authorities are not supportive.[9]

Adding previews, transitions, and summaries to your well-organized presentation applies the fundamental principles of using both verbal and nonverbal messages effectively and of adapting your message to others, increasing the likelihood that your audience will grasp your main ideas and the logic of your organizational strategy.

Verbal
Nonverbal
Adapt

INTRODUCING AND CONCLUDING YOUR PRESENTATION

At this point, you have pretty well developed the ideas and content of the body of your presentation, and you have strategies for organizing that material. But you have not yet given much thought to how you are going to begin and end the presentation. That's okay. Even though you will deliver it first, you usually plan your introduction last. You need to know first what you're introducing—especially your central idea and main ideas. Once you do, it is time to plan how you are going to introduce and conclude your presentation. While they make up a relatively small percentage of the total presentation, your introduction and conclusion provide your audience with first and final impressions of you and your presentation. They are important considerations in adapting your message to others.

Adapt

Introductions

Your **introduction** should convince your audience to listen to you. More specifically, it must perform five functions: get the audience's attention, introduce the topic, give the audience a reason to listen, establish your credibility, and preview your main ideas. Let's briefly consider each of these five functions.

Get the Audience's Attention   If an introduction does not capture the audience's attention, the rest of the presentation may be wasted on them. You have to use verbal messages effectively to wake up your listeners and make them want to hear more.

There are several good ways to gain an audience's attention. One commonly used and quite effective one is to open with an illustration. Tony opens his speech on forgiveness with a moving personal illustration:

> For my fifteenth birthday, my mother promised that we would spend the whole day together, and she would take me anywhere I wanted to go and buy me anything I wanted.

final summary
A recap of all the main points of a presentation, usually occurring just before or during the conclusion.

introduction
Opening lines of a presentation, which must catch the audience's attention and introduce the speaker's topic.

The 5th Wave

By Rich Tennant

© The 5th Wave, www.the5thwave.com.

You see, my mother was a single mom, and the true gift to me was just spending time with her; she was always at work. Well, I was so excited that the night before my birthday I couldn't sleep, and I woke up at dawn on my birthday, and I waited. And I waited, and I waited, and I waited. Well, 1:00 PM came around, and my mother was still sleeping. You see, I knew that she'd been up drinking all night the night before, and that she'd probably wake up angry at me if I was to wake her up. So I waited. And then 5:00 PM came around, and I gathered up the courage to wake her up. And when I did, she slapped me; she threw $60 at me and said, "Get out of my face."[10]

Other strategies are to ask a rhetorical question, relate a startling fact or statistic, quote an expert or a literary text, tell a humorous story, or refer to historical or recent events. Federal Reserve Chairman Alan Greenspan used humor to capture the attention of the 2005 graduating class of the Wharton School of the University of Pennsylvania:

I have more in common with you graduates than people might think. After all, before long, after my term at the Federal Reserve comes to an end, I too will be looking for a job.[11]

Eileen uses a historical reference to open her presentation on mental health privacy:

A bright political future loomed ahead of Thomas Eagleton in 1972. George McGovern had chosen him as his vice presidential running mate for the '72 elections, and his popularity was high among Americans. But then the press found out that Eagleton had received shock treatment for depression when he was younger. Eagleton was immediately dropped from the ticket and shunned from the political world.[12]

Still other speakers might get their audience's attention by referring to a personal experience, referring to the occasion, or referring to something said by a preceding speaker. While not all of these strategies will work for all presentations, at least one of them should be an option for any presentation you make. And with a little practice, you may find yourself being able to choose from several good possibilities for a single presentation.

Verbal

Introduce the Topic   Within the first few seconds of listening to you, your audience should have a pretty good idea of what your topic is. The best way to achieve this objective is to include a statement of your central idea in your introduction.

On the Web

We've emphasized the importance of catching your listeners' attention when you begin your presentation. The Internet can be a good place to find an attention-gaining quote, story, statistic, or illustration. Here are some Web addresses that may help you find what you need to begin your presentation in a memorable way:

- Famous Quotations
  dir.yahoo.com/Reference/quotations
- Humorous Quotations
  directory.google.com/Top/Recreation/Humor/Quotations
- Stories from Literature
  www.literature.org/Works
- Statistics from the U.S. Census Bureau
  www.census.gov

Give the Audience a Reason to Listen   Not only do you have to get your audience's attention and introduce your topic, you have to motivate your listeners to continue to listen. Show the audience how your topic affects them and those they care about. Catherine uses rhetorical questions to drive home to her audience the relevance and importance of her speech on a healthy diet:

What if I told you that, by decreasing one food item in your and your loved ones' diet, you could significantly lessen the chance for metabolic syndrome (or obesity); heart disease; coronary artery disease; osteoporosis due to calcium depletion; high blood pressure; colon, kidney, breast, prostate, and liver cancer? Would you change the menu at your and your loved ones' next meal?[13]

By the end of your introduction, your audience should be thinking, "This concerns *me*!"

Establish Your Credibility   A credible speaker is one whom the audience judges to be believable, competent, and trustworthy. Be aware of the skills, talents, and experiences you have had that are related to your topic. You can increase your credibility by telling your audience about your expertise. For example, in your introduction to a persuasive presentation on studying abroad, you might say:

> I know first-hand how studying abroad can broaden your worldview, increase your understanding of another culture, and enrich your academic studies. Last fall, I studied at the Sorbonne in Paris.

Preview Your Main Ideas   As we discussed above, you should provide an initial preview of your main ideas at or near the end of your introduction, to allow your listeners to anticipate the main ideas of your presentation.

Conclusions

While your introduction creates a critically important first impression, your **conclusion** leaves an equally important final impression. Long after you finish speaking, your audience will hear the echo of effective final words. An effective conclusion serves four functions: to summarize the presentation, to reemphasize the main idea in a memorable way, to motivate the audience to respond, and to provide closure. Let's consider each of these functions.

Summarize the Presentation   The conclusion offers a speaker a last chance to repeat his or her main ideas. Most speakers summarize their main ideas between the body of the presentation and its conclusion or in the first part of the conclusion.

Sarah Ferguson, Duchess of York, knows that a good conclusion is key to reinforcing the motivational purpose of her speech.

Reemphasize the Central Idea in a Memorable Way   The conclusions of many famous speeches contain many of the lines we remember best:

> . . . that government of the people, by the people, for the people, shall not perish from the earth. *(Abraham Lincoln)*[14]

> Old soldiers never die; they just fade away. *(General Douglas MacArthur)*[15]

> Free at last! Free at last! Thank God almighty, we are free at last! *(Martin Luther King Jr.)*[16]

Use your final verbal message effectively. Word your thoughts so that your audience cannot help but remember them.

Verbal

Motivate the Audience to Respond   Think back to your specific purpose. What do you want your audience to be able to do by the end of your presentation? If your purpose is to inform, you may want your audience to think about your topic or to seek more information about it. If your purpose is to persuade, you may want your audience to take some sort of action—to write a letter, make a phone call, or volunteer for a cause. Your conclusion is where you can motivate your audience to respond. Travis closes his presentation on sleep deprivation with this admonition:

> Before we are all, literally, dead on our feet, let's take the easiest solution step of all. Tonight, turn off your alarm, turn down your covers, and turn in for a good night's sleep.[17]

Provide Closure   You may have experienced listening to a presentation and not being certain when it was over. That speaker did not achieve the last purpose of an effective conclusion: providing **closure**, or a sense that the presentation is finished.

One good way to provide closure is to refer to your introduction by finishing a story, answering a rhetorical question, or reminding your audience of your introduc-

conclusion
Closing lines of a presentation, which leave a final impression.

closure
The sense that a presentation "sounds finished."

tion. Kyle had opened his presentation by quoting President Theodore Roosevelt, who declared in 1907 that depletion of America's natural resources would diminish the future prosperity of the country. Kyle provides closure to his presentation by referring again to Roosevelt's warning:

> If President Theodore Roosevelt were alive today, he'd certainly be concerned at the state and the future of our national forests. Therefore, it's so important that we heed his advice and we do everything that we can to protect our national forests—for our physical well-being, our financial well-being, and for the prosperity of future generations.[18]

Verbal
Nonverbal

You can also achieve closure by using verbal and nonverbal signposts. For example, you might use such transitions as "finally" and "in conclusion" as you move into your conclusion. You might pause before you begin the conclusion, slow your speaking rate as you deliver your final sentence, or signal by falling vocal inflection that you are making your final statement. Experiment with these strategies until you are certain that your presentation "sounds finished."

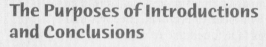

RECAP

The Purposes of Introductions and Conclusions

Your introduction should . . .

- Get your audience's attention.
- Introduce your topic.
- Give your audience a reason to listen.
- Establish your credibility.
- Preview your main ideas.

Your conclusion should . . .

- Summarize your presentation.
- Reemphasize your central idea in a memorable way.
- Motivate your audience to respond.
- Provide closure.

OUTLINING YOUR PRESENTATION

With your introduction and conclusion planned, you are almost ready to begin rehearsing your presentation. By this point, you should have your preparation outline nearly complete. A **preparation outline** is a fairly detailed outline of central idea, main ideas, and supporting material and may also include the specific purpose, introduction, and conclusion. A second outline, which you will prepare shortly, is a delivery outline, the notes from which you will eventually deliver your presentation.

Preparation Outline

Aware

Although few presentations are written in manuscript form, most speakers develop a fairly detailed preparation outline that helps them to ensure that their main ideas are clearly related to their central idea and are logically and adequately supported. A speaker who creates a preparation outline is applying the first fundamental principle of communication: becoming increasingly aware of his or her communication. In addition to helping the speaker judge the unity and coherence of the presentation, the preparation outline also serves as an early rehearsal outline and is usually the outline handed in as part of a class requirement.

Instructors who require students to turn in a preparation outline will probably have their own specific requirements. For example, some instructors ask you to include your introduction and conclusion as part of your outline, while others ask you to outline only the body of the presentation. Some ask that you incorporate signposts into the outline or write your specific purpose at the top of the outline. Be certain that you listen to and follow your instructor's specific requirements regarding which elements to include.

Almost certainly, your instructor will require that you use **standard outline format**. Standard outline format lets you become more aware of the exact relationships among various main ideas, subpoints, and supporting material in your presentation. Even if you haven't had much experience with formal outlines, the following guidelines can help you produce a correct outline.

Aware

Use Standard Numbering Outlines are numbered by using Roman and Arabic numerals and uppercase and lowercase letters followed by periods, as follows:

  I. First main idea
    A. First subdivision of I
    B. Second subdivision of I
      1. First subdivision of B
      2. Second subdivision of B
        a. First subdivision of 2
        b. Second subdivision of 2
  II. Second main idea

You will probably not need to subdivide beyond the level of lowercase letters in most presentation outlines.

Use at Least Two Subdivisions, if Any, for Each Point You cannot divide anything into fewer than two parts. On an outline, every I should have a II, every A should have a B, and so on. If you have only one subdivision, fold it into the level above it.

Line Up Your Outline Correctly Main ideas, indicated by Roman numerals, are written closest to the left margin. The *periods* following these Roman numerals line up, so that the first letters of the first words also line up:

  I. First main idea
 II. Second main idea
III. Third main idea

Letters or numbers of subdivisions begin directly underneath the first letter of the first *word* of the point above:

  I. First main idea
    A. First subdivision of I
    B. Second subdivision of I

preparation outline
Detailed outline of a presentation that includes main ideas, subpoints, and supporting material, and that may also include specific purpose, introduction, blueprint, internal previews and summaries, transitions, and conclusion.

standard outline format
Conventional use of numbered and lettered headings and subheadings to indicate the relationships among parts of a presentation.

If a main idea or subdivision takes up more than one line, the second line begins under the first letter of the first word of the preceding line:

I. First main idea
   A. A rather lengthy subdivision that
      runs more than one line
   B. Second subdivision

Within Each Level, Make the Headings Grammatically Parallel   Regardless of whether you write your preparation outline in complete sentences or in phrases, be consistent within each level. In other words, if I is a complete sentence, II should also be a complete sentence. If A is an infinitive phrase (one that begins with *to* plus a verb, such as "to guarantee greater security"), B should also be an infinitive phrase.

Following is a sample preparation outline for the presentation we've been watching Ben Johnson prepare in the Developing Your Presentation Step by Step feature.[19] Your instructor may give additional or alternate requirements for what your preparation outline should include or how it should be formatted.

SAMPLE PREPARATION OUTLINE

Writing the purpose statement at the top of the outline helps the speaker keep it in mind. But always follow your instructor's specific requirements for how to format your preparation outline.

Purpose
At the end of my presentation, the audience will take steps to end the abuse of the cold medication Coricidin.

Ben catches his reader's attention by opening his presentation with an illustration. Other strategies for effectively getting audience attention were discussed earlier in the chapter.

Introduction
Three days before Christmas, Jill and Jim Darling went to check on their daughter to make sure she was getting ready for school. When they opened the door to the bathroom, they found their daughter Jennifer unconscious on the floor. Jill frantically called 911, and then they waited helplessly for the paramedics. Only moments after the ambulance arrived, the high school senior was pronounced dead. The cause of Jennifer's death remained a mystery until investigators discovered a small plastic bag in her room containing 32 red pills. According to the January 27, 2003, issue of *University Wire*, the pills were an over-the-counter cold medication known as Coricidin. When used by adults, these pills are an effective method for decreasing the symptoms of the common cold, but in the hands of a child they become a dangerous hallucinogenic drug. These seemingly harmless pills are part of a new national epidemic of substance abuse by teenagers and children as young as 6.

Ben writes out and labels his central idea and preview. Again, follow your instructor's requirements.

Central Idea
We should take steps to end the abuse of the cold medication Coricidin.

Preview
For this reason we must first educate ourselves about the danger of Coricidin and the threat it poses for teens, and next uncover the cause for this growing trend, so that finally we may pose some viable solutions to safeguard our children's health.

Body Outline

The first main idea of the presentation is indicated by the Roman numeral I. This main idea has two subpoints, indicated by A and B.

  I. Coricidin abuse is rapidly becoming a significant problem.
    A. Coricidin contains the cough suppressant Dextromethorphan, or DXM.
      1. DXM is found in over 100 cold medications, including those with "DM" or "Tuss" in their names.

Subpoints 1, 2, 3, and 4 provide supporting material for A.

Ben's oral citation for this Web site is sufficient; he should also have the Web address available for his instructor or any other audience member who might want it.

2. Coricidin is the drug of choice because it's easier than swallowing several bottles of Robitussin.
3. As the National Institute on Drug Abuse indicates on *TheAntiDrug.com* Web site, last updated April 11, 2004, the drug closely resembles PCP, and when taken in excess, causes hallucinations.
4. According to *USA Today* of December 29, 2003, when abused, Coricidin can cause depressed breathing, an irregular heartbeat, seizures, coma, and even death.

B. Coricidin abuse is widespread.
   1. The American Association of Poison Control Centers told the *Boston Globe* of January 11, 2004, that there were over 14,000 calls to poison control centers last year to report the intentional overdose of cold medication.
   2. According to the January 29, 2004, Scripps Howard News Service, there were more than 3000 cases of Coricidin abuse in 2003 alone.
   3. A report by *CNN* on December 30, 2003, explains that overdoses tend to occur in clusters. A 13-year-old girl brought 80 Coricidin tablets to her middle school in Naples, Florida, and gave some to six of her friends. Each friend took at least five pills. The recommended dose for an adult is no more than one pill every six hours. The school was in chaos as three students lost consciousness and had to be rushed to the hospital. The girl who distributed the pills thought it would be "fun to feel messed up and act . . . drunk."

This signpost summarizes Ben's first main idea—that Coricidin abuse is significant—and previews his second main idea—why the problem has occurred.

Signpost: So if the drug poses such a threat, why has nothing been done to stop it? There are two main reasons that Coricidin has become such a problem. First, the pills and information on how to use them are widely available to teenagers. Second, there is a lack of awareness from parents and teachers.

II. Coricidin abuse has become a problem for two reasons.
   A. Coricidin is widely available to teenagers.
      1. *CBS News* reports on December 29, 2003, that some stores have begun keeping Coricidin behind the counter, but for the most part the pills are easily obtainable by teens.
      2. A box of 16 pills only costs about $5, and because the drug is safe when taken correctly, the Food and Drug Administration has made no move to regulate it. Jeff Hegelson, a 19-year-old abuser, told ABC's *20/20* on January 9, 2004, "As far as drugs go, you don't need to know a dealer. If you can find a Walgreen's or a grocery store, you're set."
      3. The Internet has contributed to the problem.
         a. The *Milwaukee Journal Sentinel* of October 24, 2003, explains that full-strength DXM can be purchased online. Two Wisconsin teens were arrested after purchasing a 50-gram bottle of DXM over the Internet and then reselling the pills.
         b. A simple Web search returns hundreds of sites giving detailed instructions on how many pills to take to get high.
         c. There are even recipes explaining how to extract DXM from Coricidin in order to achieve a more potent drug.
      4. In an interview with the previously cited *Boston Globe*, Dr. Michael Shannon, Chief of Emergency Medicine at Children's Hospital in Boston, says, "It's rampant. Look at who's taking it. These are kids who are unable to buy alcohol, unable to buy cigarettes . . . and now you've got something that you know is in many households. It's cheap, it's legal, and it's easy to obtain and nobody questions you if you have it in your backpack."

B. The attitudes of parents and teachers also complicate the problem.
1. Donna Oldham suspected that her son was abusing drugs, but she was shocked when she learned that he was getting his fix legally at the local pharmacy. Donna told the *Chicago Daily Herald* of September 8, 2003, "Most parents would have no idea their kids were doing this. It's not like pot or cocaine. It's this legal drug that a lot of people probably have in their own medicine cabinets. Unless you know what to look for, you're going to miss it."
2. The February 19, 2004, *Modesto Bee* explains that approximately 2/3 of teen drug abuse is from drugs found in the home or ones that you can get at the drugstore. Traditionally, parents and school officials watch out for illegal substances and alcohol. If a student were caught with a bottle of alcohol or marijuana, he or she would be suspended. But when a box of Coricidin is found in that student's backpack, school officials don't give it a second thought.

Having established the problem and discussed its causes, Ben turns to solutions.

Signpost: After exploring the problem and cause of this drug abuse, it's clear that Coricidin poses a threat, and something must be done to stop it.

III. Solutions at both the national and personal levels can ensure that no more harm is done.
A. On a national level, the use of Coricidin by minors needs to be regulated more carefully.
1. According to the *San Antonio Express News* of January 11, 2003, a bill was introduced in New Mexico making it illegal to sell products with DXM to minors and requiring stores to keep the pills behind the counter or in areas that require assistance. Other state governments need to follow suit.
2. Retailers can also help solve the problem. The previously cited *Chicago Daily Herald* reports that last year Wal-Mart started requiring customers to be at least 18 if they wanted to buy Coricidin, and they weren't allowed to purchase more than three boxes at a time.

A final signpost makes clear that Ben will talk about what individual audience members can do about Coricidin abuse.

Signpost: However, restrictions alone are not enough to stop this problem; action must be taken at the personal level as well.

B. We must begin to create awareness about the danger of Coricidin.
1. Parents should watch for boxes of the drug in their child's room or backpack and ask questions if they notice cold pills being used frequently.
2. Those people without children can log on to *Drugfreeamerica.org* or *TheAntiDrug.com* to learn more about drug prevention as well as additional ways to join the fight against this abuse.
   a. Donate time or money.
   b. Inform your friends and family about the dangers of Coricidin.

Aware that many of his listeners are not parents, Ben suggests appropriate actions for both groups.

Conclusion

In his conclusion, Ben returns to the illustration with which he began the presentation.

It's been a year since Jim and Jill Darling watched helplessly as their daughter died on the bathroom floor, but the drugs that took her life still pose a tremendous danger to children and teens across the country. Today we gained an understanding of the dangers of Coricidin, next uncovered the cause for this trend, and finally posed some viable solutions to safeguard our youth. Jim Darling said he "hopes his daughter's death has served as a wake-up call for law enforcement, teachers and parents." No parents should ever have to watch their child die, but as long as Coricidin remains easily available, the lives of our children will be at risk.

Delivery Outline

As you rehearse your presentation, you will find yourself needing to look at your preparation outline less and less. You have both the structure and the content of your presentation pretty well in mind. At this point, you are ready to develop a shorter delivery outline.

Your **delivery outline** should provide all the notes you will need to make your presentation as you have planned, without being so detailed that you will be tempted to read it rather than speak to your audience. Here are a few suggestions for developing a delivery outline:

- *Use single words or short phrases whenever possible.*
- *Include your introduction and conclusion in abbreviated form.* Even if your instructor does not require you to include your introduction and conclusion on your preparation outline, include an abbreviated version of them on your delivery outline. You might even feel more comfortable delivering the presentation if you have your first and last sentences written out in front of you.
- *Include supporting material and signposts.* Write out in full any statistics and direct quotations and their sources. Write your key signposts—your initial preview, for example—to ensure that you will not have to grope awkwardly as you move from one idea to another.
- *Do not include your purpose statement.* Because you will not actually say your purpose statement during your presentation, do not put it on your delivery outline.
- *Use standard outline form.* Standard outline form will help you find your exact place when you glance down at your speaking notes. You will know, for example, that your second main idea is indicated by II.

It might have been easier for this student to deliver an effective message if she had prepared a concise delivery outline on note cards.

delivery outline
Condensed and abbreviated outline of a presentation, from which speaking notes are developed.

Here is a delivery outline for Ben Johnson's presentation on the abuse of Coricidin.

SAMPLE DELIVERY OUTLINE

For the delivery outline, Ben does not need to write his purpose statement, as he will not actually state it in the presentation.

Ben writes his introduction as a bullet list so that he will be able to see each part at a glance.

Introduction

- 3 days before Christmas, Jill and Jim Darling check on daughter—find Jennifer unconscious on floor.
- 911—paramedics—dead.
- ? until small plastic bag of 32 red pills found.
- January 27, 2003, *University Wire*: over-the-counter cold medication Coricidin
- Adults—C. effective for decreasing cold symptoms.
- Child—C. dangerous hallucinogenic drug, part of ntl. epidemic of substance abuse by teens & children as young as 6.

Central Idea

We should take steps to end the abuse of the cold medication C.

Ben includes and labels his initial preview and signposts throughout the outline so that he can find them quickly.

Preview

1. Educate ourselves about the danger & threat of C.
2. Uncover cause for trend.
3. Pose viable solutions.

Body Outline

I. Significant problem.
  A. C. contains cough suppressant Dextromethorphan (DXM).
    1. DXM found in > 100 cold meds., incl. those w/"DM" or "Tuss" in name.
    2. C. the drug of choice because easier than swallowing several bottles of Robitussin.
    3. National Institute on Drug Abuse, *TheAntiDrug.com* Web site, last updated April 11, 2004—resembles PCP & when taken in excess causes hallucinations.
    4. *USA Today*, December 29, 2003—when abused, C. can cause depressed breathing, irregular heartbeat, seizures, coma, & death.
  B. Abuse widespread.
    1. American Ass. of Poison Control Centers told *Boston Globe*, January 11, 2004→ 14,000 calls to poison control centers last year.
    2. CNN, December 30, 2003—overdoses occur in clusters.
      a. 13-year-old girl brought 80 C. to middle school, Naples, Florida.
      b. Gave to 6 friends.
      c. Each took > 5.
      d. (Rec. adult dose = 1 pill/6 hrs.)
      e. Chaos: 3 lost consciousness & rushed to hospital.
      f. Girl thought it would be "fun to feel messed up and act . . . drunk."

Signpost: So if the drug poses such a threat, why has nothing been done to stop it? There are two main reasons that C. has become such a problem. First, the pills and information on how to use them is widely available to teenagers. Second, there is a lack of awareness from parents and teachers.

II. 2 reasons.
  A. Widely available to teenagers.
    1. *CBS News*, December 29, 2003—some stores keep C. behind counter, but usually easily obtainable by teens.
    2. Box of 16 pills = $5; Food & Drug Admin. has made no move to regulate. Jeff Hegelson, 19-year-old abuser, told ABC's *20/20*, January 9, 2004, "As far as drugs go, you don't need to know a dealer. If you can find a Walgreen's or a grocery store, you're set."
    3. Internet has contributed to problem.
      a. The *Milwaukee Journal Sentinel*, October 24, 2003—full-strength DXM can be purchased online; 2 Wis. teens arrested after purchasing 50-gram bottle of DXM over Internet and reselling pills.
      b. Web search = hundreds of sites w/detailed instructions on how many pills to take to get high.
      c. Recipes explaining how to extract DXM from C. in order to achieve a more potent drug.
    4. Interview w/*Boston Globe*, Dr. Michael Shannon, Chief of Emergency Medicine at Children's Hospital in Boston—"It's rampant. Look at who's taking it. These are kids who are unable to buy alcohol, unable to buy cigarettes . . . and now you've got something that you know is in many households. It's cheap, it's legal, and it's easy to obtain and nobody questions you if you have it in your backpack."
  B. Attitudes of parents & teachers complicate.
    1. Donna Oldham suspected son, but shocked to learn was getting fix legally @ local pharmacy. Donna told *Chicago Daily Herald*, Sept. 8, 2003, "Most parents would have no idea their kids were doing this. It's not like pot or cocaine. It's this legal drug that a lot of people probably have in their own

---

Although both main ideas and subpoints are shorter than in the preparation outline, source citations are still provided in full.

Part of the "shorthand" of the delivery outline may include such symbols as > or < for "greater than" or "less than"; @ for "at"; and w/ for "with." Ben also uses abbreviations in his delivery outline.

Ben lists the elements of the CNN illustration separately so he can quickly see any detail he needs.

To ensure that he quotes Jeff Hegelson and others accurately, Ben writes out their statements in full.

medicine cabinets. Unless you know what to look for, you're going to miss it."

    2. Feb. 19, 2004, *Modesto Bee*—approx 2/3 teen drug abuse from drugs found in home or drugstore. Parents & school officials watch for illegal substances & alcohol. Student w/bottle of alcohol or marijuana wd. be suspended. Box of C.: not a 2nd thought.

Signpost: After exploring the problem and cause of this drug abuse, it's clear that C. poses a threat, and something must be done to stop it.

  III. Ntl. & personal.
      A. Ntl.: C. regulated more carefully.
        1. *San Antonio Express News*, January 11, 2003—bill in N.M. makes it illegal to sell products with DXM to minors & requires stores to keep pills behind counter. Others need to follow suit.
        2. Retailers: *Chicago Daily Herald*—
          a. Wal-Mart started requiring customers to be > 18 to buy C.
          b. Not allowed to purchase > 3 boxes @ a time.

Signpost: However, restrictions alone are not enough to stop this problem; action must be taken at the personal level as well.

      B. Personal awareness
        1. Parents: Watch & ask?.
        2. No children—*Drugfreeamerica.org* or *TheAntiDrug.com* to learn about drug prevention & how to fight.
          a. Donate time or money.
          b. Inform friends & family.

Conclusion
- A yr. since Jim and Jill Darling watched daughter die.
- Drugs that took her life still pose tremendous danger to children & teens.
- Today,
    1. Understanding of dangers of C.
    2. Uncovered cause for trend.
    3. Posed viable solutions.
- Jim Darling said he "hopes his daughter's death has served as a wake-up call for law enforcement, teachers and parents."
- No parents should ever have to watch their child die, but as long as C. remains easily available, the lives of our children will be at risk.

Ben writes out his final sentence, to ensure that he can end his presentation fluently.

Although you may write the first version of your delivery outline on paper, eventually you will probably want to transfer it to note cards. They don't rustle as paper does, and they are small enough to hold in one hand. Two or three note cards will probably give you enough space for your delivery outline. Type or print neatly on one side only, making sure that the letters and words are large enough to read easily. Plan your note cards according to logical blocks of material, using one note card for your introduction, one or two for the body of your presentation, and one for your conclusion. Number your note cards to prevent getting them out of order while you are speaking.

A final addition to your note cards as you rehearse your presentation will be **delivery cues** such as "Louder," "Pause," or "Walk two steps left." These will remind you to communicate the nonverbal messages you have planned. Write your delivery cues in a different color ink so that you don't confuse them with your verbal content.

delivery cue
A reminder of how to speak or move during a presentation, which is often written on a speaker's note cards.

RECAP

Two Types of Presentation Outlines

Type	Purpose
Preparation Outline	Allows speaker to examine presentation for completeness, unity, coherence, and overall effectiveness. May serve as first rehearsal outline.
Delivery Outline	Serves as speaking notes; includes delivery cues.

PRINCIPLES FOR A LIFETIME: Enhancing Your Skills

Aware

Principle One: Be aware of your communication with yourself and others.
- Use the introduction of your presentation to help establish your own credibility: be aware of the skills, talents, and experiences you have that can enhance your credibility with your listeners.
- Use a preparation outline to demonstrate to yourself that your main ideas are clearly related to your central idea and are logically and adequately supported.

Verbal

Principle Two: Effectively use and interpret verbal messages.
- Organize your presentation logically to communicate your verbal message effectively.
- Use verbal transitions to show relationships between ideas in your presentation.
- Introduce your topic and preview your main ideas in your introduction.
- Use stories, examples, illustrations, statistics, a quotation, or other techniques to capture your listeners' attention when you begin your talk.
- In your conclusion, summarize your presentation and reemphasize your main idea in a memorable way.

Nonverbal

Principle Three: Effectively use and interpret nonverbal messages.
- Use nonverbal transitions—pauses, facial expression, altered vocal pitch or speaking rate, and movement—to indicate when you are moving from one idea to the next.
- Use nonverbal cues, such as pausing, slowing your rate of speech, and letting your vocal inflection fall, to signal that you are approaching the end of your presentation.
- Add delivery cues and reminders to your final delivery outline.

Listen and Respond

Principle Four: Listen and respond thoughtfully to others.
- As you listen to presentations, consider the cultural differences in the organization of speakers from cultures other than your own.

Principle Five: Appropriately adapt messages to others.
- Investigate and consider using the customary organizational strategy of your audience's culture.
- Discuss last the idea that you most want your audience to remember.
- If you know your audience will be skeptical of some of your ideas, first present ideas on which you can agree.
- Provide signposts as organizational cues for your audience.
- Use your introduction and conclusion to help adapt your presentation to your audience.

Adapt

SUMMARY

Once you have found supporting material, you are ready to organize your ideas and information. Depending on your topic, purpose, and audience, you can organize the main ideas of your presentation chronologically, topically, spatially, by cause and effect, or by problem and solution. You can sometimes organize supporting material according to one of these same patterns, or you can organize it according to the principles of recency, primacy, complexity, or specificity, or from soft to hard evidence.

With your presentation organized, you will want to add signposts—previews, transitions, and summaries—to make your organization clearly apparent to your audience. A carefully planned introduction will get your audience's attention, introduce your topic, give the audience a reason to listen, establish your credibility, and preview your main ideas. In an equally carefully planned conclusion, you can summarize your presentation, reemphasize the central idea in a memorable way, motivate your audience to respond, and provide closure.

A final step before beginning to rehearse your presentation is to prepare a detailed preparation outline and a delivery outline that eventually becomes your speaking notes.

Discussion and Review

1. List and explain five strategies for organizing the main ideas in a presentation.
2. List and explain five strategies for organizing supporting material in a presentation.
3. List and define three types of verbal signposts.
4. How can you make a nonverbal transition?
5. List and explain five functions of a presentation introduction.
6. How can you get your audience's attention in your introduction?
7. List and explain four functions of a presentation conclusion.
8. What is included on most preparation outlines? What are such outlines used for?
9. What is included on most delivery outlines? What are such outlines used for?

Putting Principles into Practice

1. Take notes as you listen to a presentation, either live or on audiotape or videotape. Then organize your notes into an outline that you think reflects both the speaker's organization and the intended relationship among ideas and supporting material.
2. Read one of the speeches in Appendix C. Answer the following questions:
   a. How are the main ideas organized?
   b. Look closely at the supporting materials. If two or more are used to support any one main idea, what strategy do you think the speaker used to organize them?
   c. Is there an initial preview statement? If so, what is it?
   d. Is there a final summary? If so, what is it?
   e. Find at least one example of each of the following:
      A transition word or phrase
      An internal preview
      An internal summary
3. Draft an introduction for a presentation on one of the following topics:
   Strategies for surviving a tornado
   Private-school vouchers
   Mars up close
   Celebrities and the press
   In addition to introducing the topic and previewing your main ideas, be sure to plan strategies for getting your audience's attention and giving them a reason to listen. Also devise a way to establish your own credibility as a speaker on that topic.
4. Miguel, who plays guitar in a mariachi band, plans to give an informative presentation on mariachi music. He wants to talk a little about the history of mariachi bands, the kind of music they play, and their role in Mexican and Mexican-American culture. In addition, he plans to introduce the instruments most commonly used in mariachi music: trumpet, guitar, and such percussion instruments as tambourines and maracas.
   Miguel asks you to help him develop a good introduction for the presentation. How do you think he might best introduce his presentation to achieve all five functions of a presentation introduction?

O the orator's joys! To inflate the chest, to roll the thunder of the voice out from the ribs and throat, to make the people rage, weep, hate, desire . . .

Walt Whitman

Jacob Lawrence, "The Life of Harriet Tubman, #21: Every antislavery convention held within 500 miles of Harriet Tubman found her at the meeting. She spoke in words that brought tears to the eyes and sorrow to the hearts of all who heard her speak of the suffering of her people." 1940. Casein tempera on hardboard, 17 7/8 × 12". © 2005 The Jacob and Gwendolyn Lawrence Foundation, Seattle/Artists Rights Society (ARS), New York. Photograph courtesy of Gwendolyn Knight Lawrence/Art Resource, NY.

Delivering Your Presentation

CHAPTER OUTLINE

Methods of Delivery

Effective Verbal Delivery

Effective Nonverbal Delivery

Effective Presentation Aids

Some Final Tips for Rehearsing and
Delivering Your Presentation

Summary

CHAPTER OBJECTIVES

After studying this chapter, you should be able to:

1. List and describe the four methods of delivery and provide suggestions for effectively using each one.

2. List and explain five criteria for using words well.

3. List and define three types of figurative language that can be used to make a presentation memorable.

4. Explain ways to create verbal drama and cadence in a presentation.

5. Identify and illustrate characteristics of effective delivery.

6. List 11 types of visual aids from which a speaker might select, and provide suggestions for using each type effectively.

7. Offer four general guidelines for preparing and using effective presentation aids.

Nonverbal

W hich is more important: the content of a presentation or the way it is delivered? Speakers and speech teachers have argued about the answer to this question for thousands of years. In the fourth century BC, the Greek rhetorician Aristotle declared delivery "superfluous." On the other hand, when his contemporary and fellow Athenian Demosthenes was asked to name the three most important elements for a speaker to master, he is reported to have replied, "Delivery, delivery, delivery."

The debate continues. Which is more important: content or delivery? It is clear that the way you deliver a speech influences the way listeners respond to you and to your message. In a now-classic study, Alan H. Monroe found that audience members equate effective presentational speaking with such nonverbal factors as direct eye contact, alertness, enthusiasm, a pleasant voice, and animated gestures.[1] Another researcher concluded that delivery was almost twice as important as content when students gave self-introduction presentations, and three times as important when students gave persuasive presentations.[2] Other scholars have found that delivery provides important information about a speaker's feelings and emotions and will in turn affect listeners' emotional responses to the speaker.[3] Most speech teachers today believe that both content and delivery contribute to the effectiveness of a presentation. As a modern speechwriter and communication coach suggests,

Aware
Verbal
Nonverbal
Listen and Respond
Adapt

> In the real world—the world where you and I do business—content and delivery are always related. And woe be to the communicator who forgets this.[4]

In this chapter, we will discuss how you can apply the five communication principles for a lifetime to delivery. We will talk about both verbal and nonverbal delivery skills. We will consider how important it is to be aware of the words you use and of such nonverbal cues as gestures, eye contact, and facial expression. We will discuss how to determine what presentation aids might be effective for your audience, and we'll offer guidelines for both the preparation and the use of various types of presentation aids.

METHODS OF DELIVERY

Audiences today generally expect speakers to use clear, concise, everyday language and conversational delivery style, as opposed to the flowery language and dramatic, choreographed gestures used by speakers a century ago. However, different audiences expect and prefer variations of this delivery style. For example, if you are using a microphone to speak to an audience of 1000 people, your listeners may expect a relatively formal delivery style. On the other hand, your communication class would probably find it odd if you delivered a formal oration to your 25 classmates.

People from different cultures also have different expectations of speakers' delivery. Listeners from Japan and China, for example, prefer subdued gestures to a more flamboyant delivery style. British listeners expect a speaker to stay behind a lectern and use relatively few gestures.

Speakers should consider and adapt to their audience's expectations, their topic, and the speaking situation as they select from four basic methods of delivery: manuscript speaking, memorized speaking, impromptu speaking, and extemporaneous speaking. Each is more appropriate to some speaking contexts and audiences than to others, and each requires a speaker to use a slightly different delivery style. Let's consider each of these four delivery methods in more detail.

Adapt

Manuscript Speaking

Perhaps you remember the first presentation you ever had to give—maybe as long ago as elementary school. Chances are that you wrote your speech out and read it to your audience.

Unfortunately, **manuscript speaking** is rarely done well enough to be interesting. Most speakers who rely on a manuscript read it in either a monotone or a pattern of vocal inflection that makes the presentation sound as if it were being read. They are so afraid of losing their place that they keep their eyes glued to the manuscript and seldom look at the audience. These challenges are significant enough that most speakers should avoid reading from a manuscript most of the time.

However, there are some exceptions. Sometimes effective verbal messages depend on careful and exact phrasing. For example, because an awkward statement made by the U.S. Secretary of State could cause an international crisis, he or she usually has remarks on critical issues carefully scripted. A company manager or administrator presenting a new, potentially controversial company policy to employees or customers might also deliver that announcement from a manuscript.

If you ever have to speak on a sensitive, critical, or controversial issue, you too might need to deliver a manuscript presentation. If so, consider the following suggestions:[5]

Verbal

- Type your manuscript in short, easy-to-scan phrases on the upper two-thirds of the paper so that you do not have to look too far down into your notes.
- Use appropriate nonverbal messages. Try to take in an entire sentence at a time so that you can maintain eye contact throughout each sentence.
- Do not read the manuscript too quickly. Use a slash mark (/) or some other symbol to remind you to pause in strategic places.
- Vary the rhythm, inflection, and pace of your delivery so that the presentation does not sound like it is being read.
- Use gestures and movement to add further nonverbal interest and emphasis to your message.

Nonverbal

Memorized Speaking

After that first speech you read in elementary school, you probably became a more savvy speaker, and the next time you had to give a speech, you decided to write it out and memorize it. You thought that no one would be able to tell you had written it out first. What you didn't know then, but probably do now, is that most **memorized speaking** sounds stiff and recited. In addition, you run the risk of forgetting parts of your speech and having to search awkwardly for words in front of your audience. And you forfeit the ability to adapt to your audience while you are speaking.

However, speaking from memory is occasionally justifiable. Memorized speaking might be appropriate in the same instances as manuscript speaking, when exact wording is critical to the success of the message, and when the speaker has time to commit the speech to memory. If you must deliver a short presentation within narrowly proscribed time limits, memorizing and rehearsing it will allow you to time it more accurately. Three guidelines can help you use nonverbal messages effectively when you deliver a presentation from memory:

- Do not deliver your memorized speech too rapidly.
- Avoid patterns of vocal inflection that make the speech sound recited. Focus on what you are saying, and let your voice rise and fall to emphasize key words and phrases and to reflect the structures of your sentences. Consider recording your presentation and listening to it to ensure that your vocal delivery sounds like a conversation rather than a recitation.
- Use gestures and movement to add interest and emphasis to your message.

Nonverbal

Impromptu Speaking

In September 1993, then-President Bill Clinton stood before a joint session of Congress to deliver an important speech about health-care reform. What happened during the first 9 minutes of that presentation has become what political advisor and commentator Paul Begala calls "part of the Clinton legend":

manuscript speaking
Reading a presentation from a written text.

memorized speaking
Delivering a presentation word for word from memory without using notes.

The teleprompter screens are whizzing forward and backwards with last year's speech, trying to find it, and finally, they killed it all together and reloaded it. Nine minutes the guy went without a note, and no one could tell.[6]

Although you can usually plan your presentations, there are times—as illustrated by Clinton's experience—when the best plans go awry. In other, more likely instances, you may be asked to answer a question or respond to an argument without advance warning or time to prepare a presentation. At such times, you will have to call on your skills in **impromptu speaking**, or speaking "off the cuff." Five guidelines can help you avoid fumbling for words or rambling:

Adapt

- Consider your audience. A quick mental check of who your audience members are and what their interests, expectations, and knowledge are can help ensure that your impromptu remarks are audience-centered.
- Be brief. As one leadership consultant points out,

   You're not the star—not this time, anyway. If you were the luminary, they would not have asked you to speak without warning. You're merely expected to hit a theme, say a few nice words, and then depart.[7]

One to three minutes is probably a realistic time frame for most impromptu presentations.

- Organize. Think quickly about an introduction, body, and conclusion. If you want to make more than one point, use a simple organizational strategy such as chronological order—past, present, and future. Or construct an alphabetical list, in which your main ideas begin with the letters A, B, and C.[8]
- Draw on your personal experience and knowledge. Audiences almost always respond favorably to personal illustrations, so use any appropriate and relevant ones.
- Use gestures and movement that arise naturally from what you are saying.
- Be aware of the potential impact of your communication. If your subject is at all sensitive or your information is classified, be noncommittal in what you say.

Aware
Nonverbal

Extemporaneous Speaking

We have saved for last the method of speaking that is the most appropriate choice for most circumstances: **extemporaneous speaking.** This is the speaking style taught today in most public speaking classes and preferred by most audiences. When you speak extemporaneously, you develop your presentation according to the various stages of the audience-centered public speaking model, stopping short of writing it out. Instead, you speak from an outline and rehearse the presentation until you can deliver it fluently. Your audience will know that you have prepared, but will also have the sense that the presentation is being created as they listen to it—and to some extent, it is. In short, the extemporaneous presentation is a well-developed and well-organized message delivered in an interesting and vivid manner. It reflects your understanding of how to use both verbal and nonverbal messages effectively and your ability to adapt these messages to your audience.

Although the presentational speaking chapters in this book offer numerous guidelines for extemporaneous speaking, consider these four when you reach the rehearsal and delivery stages:

Aware
Verbal
Nonverbal
Adapt

- Use a full-content preparation outline when you begin to rehearse your extemporaneous presentation. Be aware of your growing confidence in delivering it, and continue to decrease your reliance on your notes.
- Prepare an abbreviated delivery outline and speaking notes. Continue to rehearse, using this new outline.
- Even as you become increasingly familiar with your message, do not try to memorize it word for word. Continue to vary the ways in which you express your ideas and information.
- As you deliver your presentation, adapt it to your audience. Use gestures and movement that arise naturally from what you are saying.

impromptu speaking
Delivering a presentation without advance preparation.

extemporaneous speaking
Speaking from a written or memorized outline without having memorized the exact wording of the presentation.

RECAP

Methods of Delivery

Manuscript	Reading a presentation from a written text
Memorized	Giving a presentation word for word from memory without using notes
Impromptu	Delivering a presentation without advance preparation
Extemporaneous	Speaking from a written or memorized outline without having memorized the exact wording of the presentation

EFFECTIVE VERBAL DELIVERY

While you will not write out most presentations word for word, you will want to think about and rehearse words, phrases, and sentences that accurately and effectively communicate your ideas. At the same time, you will want to give your message a distinctive and memorable style. Let's examine some guidelines for effectively using and understanding words and word structures in a presentation.

Using Words Well

The most effective words are specific and concrete, unbiased, vivid, simple, and correct. Building on our discussion in Chapter 3 of the power of verbal messages, we'll examine each of these characteristics in turn.

Verbal

Specific, Concrete Words   A **specific word** refers to an individual member of a general class—for example, *ammonite* as opposed to the more general term *fossil*, or *sodium* as opposed to *chemical*. Specific words are often **concrete words,** appealing to one of the five senses and clearly communicating an image. For example, which of the following pairs of words creates a more specific mental picture: *Dog* or *poodle? Utensil* or *spatula? Toy* or *Lego?* In each case, the second word is more specific and concrete than the first and better communicates the image the speaker intends. For maximum clarity in your communication, use more specific, concrete words than general, abstract ones in your presentations.

Unbiased Words   **Unbiased words** are those that do not offend, either intentionally or unintentionally, any sexual, racial, cultural, or religious group—or any audience member who may belong to one of these groups. Although a speaker can fairly easily avoid overtly offensive language, it is more difficult to avoid language that more subtly stereotypes or discriminates. As we noted in Chapter 3, the once-acceptable usage of a masculine noun (*man, mankind*) to refer generically to all people may now be offensive to many audience members. Other words that reflect gender bias include *chairman, waiter,* and *congressman.* Even if you yourself do not consider these terms offensive, a member of your audience might. When possible, you should adapt to your audience by choosing instead such unbiased gender-neutral alternatives as *chairperson* or *chair, server,* and *member of congress.*

Vivid Words   **Vivid words** add color and interest to your language. Like concrete words, they help you communicate mental images more accurately and interestingly. Most speakers who try to make their language more vivid think first of adding adjectives to nouns—for example, *distressed oak table* instead of *table*, or *scruffy tabby cat* instead of *cat*. And certainly the first phrase of each example is more vivid. However, speakers less frequently consider the potential power of substituting vivid verbs for

specific word
A word that refers to an individual member of a general class.

concrete word
A word that refers to an object or describes an action or characteristic in the most specific way possible.

unbiased word
A word that does not stereotype, discriminate against, or insult any sexual, racial, cultural, or religious group.

vivid word
A colorful word.

© Reprinted with permission of King Features Syndicate.

"blah" verbs—for example, *sprout* instead of *grow*, or *devour* instead of *eat.* When searching for a vivid word, you might want to consult a **thesaurus,** or collection of synonyms. But do not feel that the most obscure or unusual synonym you find will necessarily be the most vivid. Sometimes a simple word can evoke a vivid image for your audience.

Simple Words   **Simple words** are generally an asset to a speaker. They will be immediately understandable to an audience. In his essay "Politics and the English Language," George Orwell includes this prescription for simplicity:

> Never use a long word where a short one will do. If it is possible to cut a word out, always cut it out. Never use a foreign phrase, a scientific word, or a jargon word if you can think of an everyday English equivalent.[9]

Selected thoughtfully, simple words can communicate with both accuracy and power.

Correct Words   Finally, and perhaps most obviously, you should use **correct words** when you speak. Grammatical and usage errors communicate a lack of preparation and can lower your credibility with your audience. Be aware of any errors you make habitually. If you are uncertain of how to use a word, look it up in a dictionary or ask someone who knows. If you are stumped by whether to say, "Neither the people nor the president *knows* how to solve the problem" or "Neither the people nor the president *know* how to solve the problem," seek assistance from a good English handbook. (By the way, the first sentence is correct!)

Aware

RECAP

Using Words Well

Use specific, concrete words to communicate clearly and specifically.

Use unbiased words to avoid offending any sexual, racial, cultural, or religious group.

Use vivid words to add color and interest to your language.

Use simple words to be understood readily.

Use correct words to enhance your credibility.

thesaurus
A list of synonyms.

simple word
A short word known to most people who speak the language.

correct word
A word that means what the speaker intends and is grammatically correct in the phrase or sentence in which it appears.

Crafting Memorable Word Structures

We have discussed the importance of using words that are concrete, unbiased, vivid, simple, and correct. Now we will turn our attention to word structures—phrases and

Verbal

Old Drum, the dog made famous by George Graham Vest's use of figurative language.

sentences that create the figurative language, drama, and cadences needed to make a presentation memorable.

Figurative Language One way to make your presentation memorable is to use **figurative language** or figures of speech, including **metaphors** (implied comparisons), **similes** (overt comparisons using *like* or *as*), and **personification** (the attribution of human qualities to nonhuman things or ideas). Such language is memorable because it is used in a way that is a little different from its ordinary, expected usage. Nineteenth-century Missouri Senator George Graham Vest used all three types of figurative language to good advantage in his short but memorable "Tribute to the Dog" (delivered in Warrensburg, Missouri, in 1870, and nominated by columnist William Safire as one of the greatest speeches of the Second Millennium).[10] Vest makes the abstract concept of malice more concrete with the metaphor "the stone of malice." He uses a simile to compare the dog's master to a prince: "He guards the sleep of his pauper master as if he were a prince." And he personifies death, which "takes [the dog's] master in its embrace." Vest's speech is memorable at least in part because of the figurative language he employs.

Drama Another way in which you can make your word structures more memorable is to use language to create **drama** in your presentation by phrasing something in an unexpected way. Three specific devices that can help you achieve verbal drama are omission, inversion, and suspension.

When you strip a phrase or sentence of nonessential words that the audience expects, or with which they are so familiar that they will mentally fill them in, you are using **omission**. A captain of a World War II Navy destroyer used omission to inform headquarters of his successful efforts at finding and sinking an enemy submarine. He cabled back to headquarters:

Sighted sub—sank same.

Inversion—reversing the normal order of words in a phrase or sentence—can also create drama in a presentation. John F. Kennedy inverted the usual subject–verb–object sentence pattern to object–subject–verb to make this brief declaration memorable:

This much we pledge. . . .[11]

A third way to create drama through sentence structures is to employ verbal **suspension**, saving a key word or phrase for the end of a sentence, rather than placing it at the beginning. Speaking to the Democratic National Convention in July 2004, former U.S. President Jimmy Carter used suspension to dramatize the importance of America's global role:

At stake is nothing less than our nation's soul.[12]

Advertisers use this technique frequently. Instead of saying, "Coke goes better with everything," one copywriter some years ago decided to make the slogan more memorable by suspending the product name until the end of the sentence. He wrote,

Things go better with Coke.

figurative language
Language that deviates from the ordinary, expected meaning of words to make a description or comparison unique, vivid, and memorable.

metaphor
An implied comparison between two things.

simile
An overt comparison between two things that uses the word *like* or *as*.

personification
The attribution of human qualities to inanimate things or ideas.

drama
Phrasing something in a way that differs from the way the audience expects.

omission
Leaving out a word or phrase the audience expects to hear.

inversion
Reversing the normal word order of a phrase or sentence.

suspension
Withholding a key word or phrase until the end of a sentence.

Maya Angelou mesmerizes her audiences with her extraordinary skill in the effective use of language.

Cadence   A final way to create memorable word structures is to create **cadence**, or language rhythm. A speaker does this, not by speaking in a singsong pattern, but by using such stylistic devices as parallelism, antithesis, repetition, and alliteration.

Parallelism occurs when two or more clauses or sentences have the same grammatical pattern. After the bitterly contested U.S. presidential election of 2000, George W. Bush used simple parallel structures to emphasize the importance of finding common ground and building consensus:

> Our future demands it, and our history proves it.[13]

Antithesis is similar to parallelism, except that the two structures contrast each other in meaning. Nobel Laureate Elie Wiesel used antithesis in his 1999 Millennium Lecture on "The Perils of Indifference":

> Indifference . . . is not only a sin, it is a punishment.[14]

Repetition of a key word or phrase can add emphasis to an important idea and memorability to your message. Note the repetition of the key phrase "It is a violation of human rights" in this excerpt from a speech by Hillary Rodham Clinton:

> It is a violation of human rights when babies are denied food, or drowned, or suffocated, or their spines broken, simply because they are born girls.
>   It is a violation of human rights when women and girls are sold into the slavery of prostitution.
>   It is a violation of human rights when women are doused with gasoline, set on fire, and burned to death because their marriage dowries are deemed too small.[15]

A final strategy for creating cadence is to use **alliteration**, the repetition of an initial consonant sound several times in a phrase, clause, or sentence. Kicking off the "space race" in 1962, John F. Kennedy coined this alliterative phrase:

> hour of change and challenge[16]

The repetition of the *ch* sound added cadence—and memorability—to the passage.

---

cadence
The rhythm of language.

parallelism
Using the same grammatical structure for two or more clauses or sentences

antithesis
A two-part parallel structure in which the second part contrasts in meaning with the first.

repetition
Emphasizing a key word or phrase by using it more than once.

alliteration
The repetition of a consonant sound (usually the first consonant) several times in a phrase, clause, or sentence.

RECAP

Crafting Memorable Word Structures

To make your message memorable, use . . .

Figurative Language

Metaphor	Making an implied comparison
Simile	Making a comparison using *like* or *as*
Personification	Attributing human qualities to nonhuman things or ideas

Drama

Omission	Leaving nonessential words out of a phrase or sentence
Inversion	Reversing the normal order of words in a phrase or sentence
Suspension	Withholding the key words in a phrase or sentence until the end

Cadence

Parallelism	Using two or more clauses or sentences with the same grammatical structure
Antithesis	Using a two-part parallel structure in which the second part contrasts in meaning with the first
Repetition	Using a key word or phrase more than once
Alliteration	Repeating a consonant sound

EFFECTIVE NONVERBAL DELIVERY

THE FAR SIDE®   By GARY LARSON

At this point, you know how important it is to deliver your presentation effectively and what delivery style most audiences today prefer. You are familiar with the four methods of delivery and know how to maximize the use of each one. And you have some ideas about how to use effective and memorable language. But you may still be wondering, "What do I do with my hands?" "Is it all right to move around while I speak?" "How can I make my voice sound interesting?" To help answer these and other similar questions, and to help you use nonverbal messages more effectively, we will examine five major categories of nonverbal delivery: eye contact, physical delivery, facial expression, vocal delivery, and personal appearance. This discussion further develops the fundamental principle of using and interpreting nonverbal messages that we introduced in Chapter 4.

"Hang him, you idiots! Hang him! ... 'String him up' is a figure of speech!"

Eye Contact

Of all the nonverbal delivery variables discussed in this chapter, the most important one in a presentational speaking situation for North Americans is **eye contact**. Eye contact with your audience lets them know that you are interested in them and ready to talk to them. It also permits you to determine whether they are responding to you. And most listeners will think that you are more capable and trustworthy if you look them in the eye. Several studies document a relationship between eye contact and speaker credibility, as well as between eye contact and listener learning.[17]

How much eye contact do you need to sustain? One study found that speakers with less than 50% eye contact are considered unfriendly, uninformed, inexperienced, and even dishonest by their listeners.[18] Is there such a thing as too much eye contact? Probably not, for North American audiences. Be aware, though, that not all people from all cultures prefer as much eye contact as North Americans do. Asians, for example, generally prefer less.

The following suggestions can help you use eye contact effectively when you speak in public:

- Establish eye contact with your audience before you say anything. Eye contact sends the message, "I am interested in you. I have something I want to say to you. Tune me in."
- Maintain eye contact with your audience as you deliver your opening sentence without looking at your notes.
- Try to establish eye contact with people throughout your audience, not just with the front row or only one or two people. Briefly look into the eyes of an individual, then transfer your eye contact to someone else. Do not look over your listeners' heads! They will notice if you do so and may even turn around to try to find out what you are looking at.

Physical Delivery

Gestures, movement, and posture are the three key elements of **physical delivery**. A good speaker knows how to use effective gestures, make meaningful movements, and maintain appropriate posture while speaking to an audience.

Gestures   The hand and arm movements you use while speaking are called **gestures**. Nearly all people from all cultures use some gestures when they speak. In

Adapt

Nonverbal

eye contact
Looking at an audience during a presentation.

physical delivery
A person's gestures, movement, and posture, which influence how a message is interpreted.

gestures
Movements of the hands and arms to communicate ideas.

By walking up close to her audience, this speaker establishes a connection with her listeners.

fact, research suggests that gesturing is instinctive and that it is intrinsic to speaking and thinking.[19] Yet even if you gesture easily and appropriately in the course of everyday conversation, you may feel awkward about what to do with your hands when you are in front of an audience. To minimize this challenge, consider the following guidelines:

Nonverbal

- Focus on the message you want to communicate. As in ordinary conversation, when you speak in public, your hands should help to emphasize or reinforce your verbal message. Your gestures should coincide with what you are saying.
- Again, as in conversation, let your gestures flow with your message. They should appear natural, not tense or rigid.
- Be definite. If you want to gesture, go ahead and gesture. Avoid minor hand movements that will be masked by the lectern or that may appear to your audience as accidental brief jerks.
- Vary your gestures. Try not to use the same hand or one all-purpose gesture all the time. Think of the different gestures you can use, depending on whether you want to enumerate, point, describe, or emphasize ideas.
- Don't overdo your gestures. You want your audience to focus not on your gestures, but on your message.
- Make your gestures appropriate to your audience and situation. When you are speaking to a large audience in a relatively formal setting, use bolder, more sweeping, and more dramatic gestures than when you are speaking to a small audience in an informal setting. Consider, too, the culture-based expectations of your audience. Americans in general tend to use more gestures than do speakers from other cultures. If you are speaking to a culturally diverse audience, you might want to tone down your gestures.

Adapt

Movement   Another element of physical delivery is **movement**. You may have wondered, "Should I walk around during my presentation, or should I stay in one place?" "Should I stay behind the lectern, or could I stand beside or in front of it?" "Can I move around among the audience?" The following criteria may help you to determine the answers to these questions:

Nonverbal

movement
Change of location during a presentation.

- Like gestures, any movement should be purposeful. It should be consistent with the verbal content of your message; otherwise it will appear to be aimless wandering. You might signal the beginning of a new idea or major point in your speech with

Diversity and Communication

The Academic Quarter

*W*hen speaking at a Polish university a few years ago, one of your authors expected to begin promptly at 11:00 AM, as announced in the program and on posters. By 11:10 it was clear that the speech would not begin on time, and your author began to despair of having any audience at all.

In Poland, it turns out, both students and professors expect to adhere to the "academic quarter." This means that most lectures begin at least 15 minutes, or a quarter of an hour, after the announced starting time.

If your author had asked a Polish professor about the audience's expectations, he would have known about this custom in advance. One way to avoid such misunderstandings is to talk with people you know who are familiar with the cultural expec-

tations. Try to observe other speakers presenting to similar audiences. And ask specific questions, including the following:

1. Where does the audience expect me to stand while speaking?
2. Do listeners expect direct eye contact?
3. When will the audience expect me to start and stop my talk?
4. Will listeners find movement and gestures distracting or welcome?
5. Do listeners expect presentation aids?

Keep cultural differences in mind as you rehearse and deliver presentations to diverse audiences.

---

movement. Or you might move to signal a transition from a serious idea to a more humorous one. The bottom line is that your use of movement should make sense to your listeners. No movement at all is better than random, distracting movement.

- If such physical barriers as a lectern, a row of chairs, or an overhead projector make you feel cut off from your audience, move closer to them. Studies suggest that physical proximity enhances learning.[20]
- Adapt to the cultural expectations of your audience. British listeners, for example, have commented to your authors that American lecturers tend to stand too close to an audience when speaking. If you think that movement will make your audience uncomfortable, stay in one carefully chosen spot to deliver your presentation.

Adapt

Posture **Posture** is the third element of physical delivery you should consider when delivering a presentation. One study suggests that your posture may reflect on your credibility as a speaker.[21] Another study suggests that "fear contagion," the spread of fear throughout a crowd, is largely a response to posture cues.[22] Certainly, slouching lazily across a lectern does not communicate enthusiasm for or interest in your audience or your topic. On the other hand, you should adapt your posture to your topic, your audience, and the formality or informality of the speaking occasion. For example, it may be perfectly appropriate, as well as comfortable and natural, to sit on the edge of a desk during a very informal presentation. In spite of the fact that few speech teachers or texts attempt to advocate specific speaking postures, speakers should observe some basic commonsense guidelines about their posture:

Nonverbal

- Avoid slouching, shifting from one foot to the other, or drooping your head.
- Unless you are disabled, do not sit while delivering a presentation. The exception might be perching on the edge of a desk or stool (which would still elevate you slightly above your audience) during a very informal presentation.

Adapt

Like your gestures and movement, your posture should not call attention to itself. It should reflect your interest in and attention to your audience and your presentation.

Facial Expression

Your **facial expression** plays a key role in expressing your thoughts, emotions, and attitudes.[23] Your audience sees your face before they hear what you are going to say, giving you the opportunity to set the tone for your message even before you begin speaking.

posture
A speaker's stance.

facial expression
Arrangement of the facial muscles to communicate.

Can you guess by his facial expression what message Bill Clinton may have been communicating to the graduating class?

On the Web

There are several sites on the Web where you can both see and hear famous speeches from the past and today.

C-SPAN Online
www.c-span.org/watch
History Channel Archive of Speeches
www.historychannel.com/speeches/index.html
U.S. Presidential Inaugural Speeches
www.bartleby.com/inaugural/
Michigan State University Vincent Voice Library
vvl.lib.msu.edu/index.cfm

Nonverbal

Adapt

vocal delivery
Nonverbal voice elements, including volume, pitch, rate, and articulation.

volume
The softness or loudness of a speaker's voice.

Social psychologist Paul Ekman has found that facial expressions of primary emotions are virtually universal, so even a culturally diverse audience will be able to read your facial expressions clearly.[24]

Throughout your presentation, your facial expression, like your body language and eye contact, should be appropriate to your message. Present somber news wearing a serious expression. Relate a humorous story with a smile. To communicate interest in your listeners, keep your expression alert and friendly. Consultants criticized both George W. Bush and John Kerry for their inappropriate facial expressions during the 2004 U.S. presidential debates, noting specifically that Bush needed to control his grimaces and smirks, and Kerry needed to develop a more natural, authentic smile.[25]

To help ensure that you are maximizing your use of this important nonverbal delivery cue, rehearse your presentation in front of a mirror; or better yet, videotape yourself rehearsing your presentation. Consider as objectively as possible whether your face is reflecting the emotional tone of your ideas.

Vocal Delivery

We have already discussed the importance of selecting words and word phrases that will most effectively communicate your ideas, information, and images. We referred to this element of delivery as verbal delivery. **Vocal delivery,** on the other hand, involves nonverbal vocal cues—not the words you say, but the way you say them. Effective vocal delivery requires that you speak so that your audience can understand you and will remain interested in what you are saying. Nonverbal vocal elements include volume, pitch, rate, and articulation.

Volume   **Volume** is the softness or loudness of your voice. It is the most fundamental determinant of audience understanding. If you do not speak loudly enough, even the most brilliant presentation will be ineffective, because the audience simply will not hear you. In addition, volume can signal important ideas in your presentation; you can deliver a key idea either more loudly or more softly than the level at which you have been speaking. Consider these guidelines to help you appropriately adapt the volume of your voice to your audience's needs:

- Speak loudly enough that the members of your audience farthest from you can hear you without straining. This will ensure that everyone else in the room can hear you, too.
- Vary the volume of your voice in a purposeful way. Indicate important ideas by turning your volume up or down.
- Be aware of whether you need a microphone to amplify your volume. If you do and one is available, use it.

There are three kinds of microphones, only one of which demands much technique. The *lavaliere microphone* is the clip-on type often used by news reporters and interviewees. Worn on the front of a shirt or a jacket lapel, it requires no particular care other than not thumping it or accidentally knocking it off.

The *boom microphone* is used by makers of movies and TV shows. It hangs over the heads of the speakers and is remote controlled, so the speakers need not be particularly concerned with it.

Developing Your Presentation

Rehearse Your Presentation

Ben begins to rehearse his presentation. From the beginning, he stands and speaks aloud, practicing gestures and movement that seem appropriate to his message.

At first, Ben uses his preparation outline (pp. 326–328). These early rehearsals go pretty well, but the speech runs a little long. Ben needs to edit it.

He wonders whether he can cut any of his plentiful supporting material. Examining his preparation outline again, he notes that he has two statistics to support the widespread abuse of Coricidin, one from the American Association of Poison Control Centers and another from the Scripps Howard News Service. The statistic from the American Association of Poison Control Centers seems more credible. He decides to cut the other statistic before he prepares his speaking notes and continues with his rehearsals.

The third kind of microphone, and the most common, is the *stationary microphone.* This is the type that is most often attached to a lectern, sitting on a desk, or standing on the floor. Generally, the stationary microphones used today are multidirectional. You do not have to remain frozen behind a stationary mike while speaking. However, you will have to keep your mouth about the same distance from the mike at all times to avoid distracting fluctuations in the volume of sound. You can turn your head from side to side and use gestures, but you will have to limit other movements.

Under ideal circumstances, you will be able to practice before you speak with the type of microphone you will use. If you have the chance, figure out where to stand for the best sound quality and how sensitive the mike is to extraneous noise. Practice will accustom you to any voice distortion or echo that might occur so that these sound qualities do not surprise you during your presentation.[26]

Pitch   While volume is the loudness or softness of your voice, **pitch** refers to how high or low your voice is. To some extent, pitch is determined by physiology. The faster the folds in your vocal cords vibrate, the higher the habitual pitch of your voice. In general, female vocal folds vibrate much faster than do those of males. However, you can raise or lower your habitual pitch within a certain range. Variation in pitch, called **inflection,** is a key factor in communicating the meaning of your words. You know that a startled "Oh!" in response to something someone has told you communicates something quite different than a lower-pitched, questioning, "Oh?" Your vocal inflection indicates your emotional response to what you have heard. Vocal inflection also helps to keep an audience interested in your presentation. If your pitch is a monotone, the audience will probably become bored quickly. To help you monitor and practice your pitch and inflection as you prepare to speak, record and play back your presentation at least once as you rehearse. Listen carefully to your pitch and inflection. If you think you are speaking in too much of a monotone, practice the presentation again with exaggerated variations in pitch.

Rate   Another vocal variable is **rate**, or speed. How fast do you talk? Most speakers average between 120 and 180 words per minute but vary their rate to add interest to their delivery and to emphasize key ideas. To determine whether your speaking rate is appropriate and purposeful, become consciously aware of your speaking rate. Record your presentation during rehearsal and listen critically to your speech speed. If it seems too fast, make a conscious effort to slow down. Use more **pauses** after questions and before important ideas. If you are speaking too slowly, make a conscious effort to speed up.

Articulation   **Articulation** is the enunciation of sounds. As a speaker, you want to articulate distinctly to ensure that your audience can determine what words you are using. Sometimes we fall into the habits of mumbling or slurring—saying *wanna*

pitch
How high or low a speaker's voice is.

inflection
Variation in vocal pitch.

rate
How fast or slowly a speaker speaks.

pause
A few seconds of silence during a presentation; can be used both to slow a fast pace and to signal a key idea.

articulation
The production of clear and distinct speech sounds.

instead of *want to*, or *chesterdrawers* instead of *chest of drawers*. Some nonstandard articulation may be part of a speaker's **dialect,** a speech style common to an ethnic group or a geographic region. One dialect with which most of us are probably familiar is the dialect of the southern United States, characterized by a distinctive drawl. Although most native speakers of English can understand English dialects, studies have shown that North American listeners assign more favorable ratings to, and can recall more information presented by, speakers with dialects similar to their own.[27] If your dialect is significantly different from that of your listeners, or if you suspect that it could be potentially distracting, you may want to work to improve or standardize your articulation. To do so, be aware of key words or phrases that you have a tendency to drawl, slur, or chop. Once you have identified them, practice saying them distinctly and correctly.

Appearance

Aware

Nonverbal

Adapt

What would you wear to deliver a presentation to your class? To address your city council? The fact that you probably would wear something different for these two occasions suggests that you are already aware of the importance of a speaker's **appearance.** There is considerable evidence that your personal appearance affects how your audience will respond to you and your message. If you violate your audience's expectations, you will be less successful in achieving your purpose. The following guidelines might help make your wardrobe selection a bit easier the next time you are called on to speak:

- Never wear anything that would be potentially distracting—for example, a T-shirt with writing on it. You want your audience to listen to you, not read you.
- Consider wearing appropriate clothing as a presentation aid. For example, if you are a nurse or emergency technician, wear your uniform when you speak about your profession. (We will discuss presentation aids in more detail shortly.)
- Take cues from your audience. If you know that they will be dressed in business attire, dress similarly. If anything, you want to be a bit more dressed up than members of your audience.
- When in doubt about what to wear, select something conservative.

dialect
A consistent style of pronunciation and articulation that is common to an ethnic group or geographic region.

appearance
A speaker's dress and grooming.

> **RECAP**
>
> ## Characteristics of Effective Nonverbal Delivery
>
> - **Gestures** should be relaxed, definite, varied, and appropriate to your audience and the speaking situation.
> - **Movement** should be purposeful.
> - **Posture** should feel natural and be appropriate to your topic, your audience, and the occasion.
> - **Eye contact** should be established before you say anything and sustained as much as possible throughout your presentation.
> - **Facial expression** should be alert, friendly, and appropriate to your message.
> - **Volume** should be loud enough that you can be easily heard, and should be purposefully varied.
> - **Pitch** should be varied so that the inflection in your voice helps to sustain your audience's interest.
> - **Rate** should be neither too fast nor too slow, and can be varied to add interest and emphasize key ideas.
> - **Articulation** should be clear and distinct.
> - **Appearance** should conform to what the audience expects.

Technology and Communication

Rehearsing on Videotape

*T*here is no feedback more total or more objective than feedback provided by videotape. First, it reproduces your total image, both visual and aural; and second, it lets you see for yourself. If friends or colleagues tell you that you are a good speaker, you may not respect their judgment, you may think they're being nice rather than honest, or you may think they're biased in your favor. Bruce, a pharmaceutical salesman, simply couldn't believe it when people told him he was a good speaker because an unpleasant high school speaking experience had convinced him he would never be able to speak well. Seeing himself on videotape was a revelation: He saw for himself how good he was. Another person could never have convinced him of it.

By the same token, if someone tells you your voice is too high, that you slouch, or that you need to loosen up your body, you may not be convinced. A videotape has the inherent reassurance of a machine: It has no ulterior motive, and it lets you see what others see.

People are constantly amazed when they see themselves on videotape—it's as if they were seeing and hearing themselves for the first time. They really see the extra 20 pounds they've been lugging for 10 years; they see the stiff way they stand; they hear the lack of energy in their voices, the *um*'s, the *you see*'s, the *you know*'s, the *like*'s.

Becoming aware of the kind of image you project is the first step toward controlling it or altering it.[28]

EFFECTIVE PRESENTATION AIDS

We have already discussed two elements of delivery: verbal delivery and nonverbal delivery. A third element used with increasing frequency in this era of sophisticated computer presentation software is the **presentation aid.** The term *presentation aid* refers to anything your audience can listen to or look at to help them understand your ideas. Charts, photographs, posters, drawings, graphs, videos, and CDs are some of the types of presentation aids frequently used by speakers.

Presentation aids can be invaluable to a speaker. They help you gain and maintain your audience's attention.[29] They communicate your organization of ideas. They illustrate sequences of events or procedures. And they help your audience understand and remember your message. In addition, chances are that, for at least one of the assignments in your communication class, you will be required to use a presentation aid. Because presentation aids are valuable supplements to your speeches and because students of communication are so often required to use them, let's discuss first the types of presentation aids that are available to you, including computer-generated ones. Then we will discuss guidelines for preparing presentation aids, and finally provide some general suggestions for using your presentation aids effectively.

Types of Presentation Aids

If you are required to use a presentation aid for an assignment, or if you think a presentation aid might enhance your message, you have a number of options from which to select. You might decide to use an object or a model; a person; such two-dimensional presentation aids as drawings, photographs, maps, charts, or graphs; or a videotape, CD-ROM, DVD, audiotape, or audio CD.

Objects The first type of presentation aid you ever used—perhaps as long ago as preschool "show and tell"—was probably an object. You took to school your favorite teddy bear or the new remote-control car you got for your birthday. Remember how the kids crowded around to see what you had brought? Objects add interest to a talk because they are real. Whether the members of your audience are in preschool or college, they like tangible, real things. If you use an object as a presentation aid, consider these guidelines:

presentation aid
Any tangible item used to help communicate ideas to an audience.

- Make certain the object can be handled easily. If it is too large, it may be unwieldy; if it is too small, your audience won't be able to see it.
- Don't use dangerous or illegal objects as presentation aids. They may make your audience members uneasy or actually put them at risk.

Models   If it is impossible to bring an object to class, you may be able to substitute a model. You cannot bring a 1965 Ford Thunderbird into a classroom, but you may be able to construct and bring a model. You could probably not acquire a dog's heart to bring to class, but you might be able to find a model to use for your explanation of how heartworms damage that vital organ. If you use a model as a presentation aid, be sure that the model is large enough to be seen by all members of your audience.

People   You might not think of people as potential presentation aids, but they can be. President George W. Bush has used ordinary people as visual aids for some of his most important speeches, "asking them to stand and then telling stories of their sacrifices or heroism . . . a way of coming down from the stage, as it were, and mingling with the crowd."[30] In other instances, people can model costumes, play a sport with you, or demonstrate a dance. Consider the following guidelines if you are going to ask someone to assist you by acting as a presentation aid for a speech:

- Rehearse with the person who will be helping you.
- Don't have the person stand beside you doing nothing. Wait until you need your presentation aid to have him or her come to the front.
- Don't let your presentation aid steal the show. Make his or her role specific and fairly brief. As the speaker, you should remain the "person of the hour."

Drawings   You can use simple drawings to help illustrate or explain ideas that you are talking about. For example, you could sketch the tunnels of a fire ant mound to show your audience why it is so difficult to eradicate an entire colony. You could sketch the plants and animals crucial to the life cycle of the Florida Everglades. If you use a drawing as a visual aid, consider these suggestions:

- Keep your drawings large and simple. Line drawings are often more effective than more detailed ones.
- Consider drawing or photocopying your drawing onto a sheet of overhead transparency film and using an overhead projector to show the drawing to your audience.
- Your drawing does not have to be original artwork. If you need help, you could ask a friend to help you prepare a drawing, or you could utilize computer software to generate a simple image. Just be sure to credit your source if you use someone else's sketch.

Photographs   If you are giving a speech on urban forestry, you might want to show your audience good color pictures of trees appropriate for urban sites in your area. In this case, photographs would show color and detail that would be nearly impossible to achieve with drawings. The biggest challenge to using photographs as presentation aids is size; most photos are simply too small to be seen clearly from a distance. If you want to use a photograph, you will usually have to enlarge it. Consider the following options for making photographs into viable presentation aids:

- Many copy centers or photo shops can produce poster-size color photocopies.
- Transfer your photograph to a slide and project it onto a screen.
- Store digital photos on a computer disk. Then, when you want the photos, you can bring them up on your computer screen and use a video projection system to enlarge them for your audience.

Maps   Like photographs, most maps are too small to be useful as presentation aids; you must enlarge them in some way. Consider these suggestions for using maps effectively in a presentation:

FIGURE 13.1
Chart

Population of the United States, by Age (Source: 2000 Census)	
Age	**Number**
0 to 9 years	40,000,000
10 to 19 years	41,000,000
20 to 34 years	59,000,000
35 to 54 years	83,000,000
55 to 64 years	24,000,000
over 64 years	35,000,000

- Enlarge your map by photocopying it or by transferring it to a slide. An outline map with few details can be copied or drawn on overhead transparency film.
- Highlight on your map the areas or routes you are going to talk about in your presentation.

Charts   Charts can summarize and organize a great deal of information in a small space. Consider using a chart any time you need to present information that could be organized under several headings or in several columns. The chart in Figure 13.1 displays 2000 United States census statistics on population age groups.[31] You can prepare charts quite easily by using the Table feature in your word-processing program. Keep in mind these guidelines:

- Whether you use a large flip chart, transfer your chart to an overhead transparency, or use a computer presentation program, be certain your chart is big enough to be seen easily.
- Keep your chart simple. Do not try to put too much information on one chart. Eliminate any unnecessary words.
- Print or type any lettering on a chart, instead of writing in script.

Graphs   Graphs are effective ways to present statistical relationships to your audience. They help to make data more concrete. You are probably already familiar with the three main types of graphs. A **bar graph** consists of bars of various lengths to represent percentages or numbers. It is useful for making comparisons. A round **pie graph** shows how data are divided proportionately. And a **line graph** can show both trends over a period of time and relationships among variables. Figure 13.2 illustrates all three types of graphs, displaying the statistics from the chart in Figure 13.1. All three graphs were generated by Microsoft Excel. The following guidelines will help you use graphs more effectively in your presentations:

- Make your graphs big, by drawing them on a large piece of paper, by drawing or copying them on an overhead transparency, or by putting them on a computer disk for projection.
- Keep your graphs simple and uncluttered.
- Remember that many computer programs will generate graphs from statistics. You don't usually need to draw your own.

bar graph
A graph consisting of bars of various lengths that represent numbers or percentages.

pie graph
A circular graph that shows how a set of data is divided proportionately.

line graph
A graph that shows trends over a period of time and relationships among variables.

FIGURE 13.2
Three Types of Graphs: Bar Graph, Line Graph, and Pie Graph

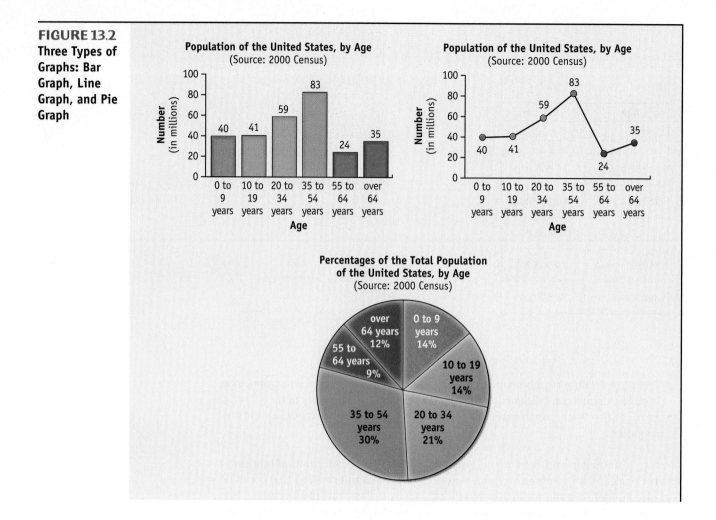

Videotapes   A VCR will allow you to show scenes from a movie, an excerpt from a training film, or a brief original video to an audience. Modern VCRs have good picture and sound quality and permit freeze-frame viewing. They also allow you to rewind and replay a scene several times if you want your audience to watch different specific elements of the film. If you plan to use a videotape in a presentation, consider these suggestions:

- If you have an audience of 25 to 30 people, you can use a 25-inch television screen. For larger audiences, you will need a large-screen projection TV or several monitors.
- Use only brief clips and excerpts. Video should always supplement, rather than take over for your speech.

CD-ROMs and DVDs   CD-ROMs and DVDs allow a speaker to retrieve audio and visual information easily and quickly. One CD-ROM can contain hundreds of words, pictures, or sounds. If you were talking about President Franklin Roosevelt's New Deal, you could click your mouse to let your audience hear Roosevelt speak. If you wanted to show various images of Monet's garden, you could retrieve and project those pictures with ease. Both CD-ROMs and DVDs can be used in combination with a large-screen video projector or a liquid crystal display (LCD) panel connected to an overhead projector. If you plan to use CD-ROM or DVD, remember these guidelines:

- Be certain that the equipment you will need will be available in the room in which you are going to speak.
- Have the equipment set up and ready to go before you speak.

Audiotapes and Audio CDs   If you want to supplement your speech with audio presentation aids—say, music or excerpts from speeches or interviews—you might want to use cassette audiotapes or audio CDs. Both are readily available, and their sound can be amplified to fill various size rooms. The advantage of a cassette tape is that you can tape and play back original material, such as an interview you did with the dean of students. A CD has better fidelity and can be more easily cued to begin in a specific place. If you use one of these audio presentation aids, consider these suggestions:

- Be certain that your tape or CD is amplified so that your audience can hear it without straining.
- Use audio presentation aids sparingly. You do not want them to engage the audience's attention to the point that they interfere with the speech.

Computer-Generated Presentation Aids

Not too many years ago, if you wanted to use a drawing or graph as a visual aid, you had to draw it by hand on a blackboard, flip chart, or overhead transparency. If you wanted to use a photograph or map, you had to have it professionally enlarged. While speakers still use overheads, blackboards, flip charts, and posters, today they also have another option: computer graphics programs. These programs, available for both Windows and Macintosh operating systems, can both create and present professional-looking visual aids inexpensively and easily.

Using a graphics program such as Microsoft's popular PowerPoint, you can develop a list of your main points that audience members can refer to as you speak, as illustrated in Figure 13.3. You can create graphs and charts. You can use clip art, or you can scan in photographs, maps, or drawings. You can even incorporate video and audio clips. If computer-projection equipment is available in the room in which you will speak, you can display your presentation by connecting a computer to a special large-screen projector or an LCD panel that fits on top of an overhead projector. You can then run your program with a keyboard or mouse, or even set it to run automatically. If you do not have access to such equipment, you can transfer the images you have created to slides, overhead transparencies, or paper.

FIGURE 13.3
PowerPoint Slide

Source: Photo of Paul Laurence Dunbar from the Ohio Historical Society, Dunbar House Web page. 14 January 2002 (9 July 2002): www.ohiohistory.org/places/dunbar

Steve Jobs, chief executive officer of Apple Computer, uses a large-screen projector to make sure his audience can see his PowerPoint presentation and the product he used to create it.

Among the advantages of learning to use computer graphics programs such as PowerPoint for classroom presentations is that they are an important way to adapt your message to audiences who increasingly expect sophisticated technical support. You will undoubtedly encounter and be expected to use these programs again in the business world. Gaining experience with them now can give you an edge in seeking employment and in making your earliest business presentation more effective.

However, such programs also have inherent risks. As one consultant points out,

When you darken the room and give the audience a preprogrammed, oh-so-beautiful, PowerPoint presentation, the audience will say, "I'm not part of this experience. That guy up there has done it all." The result: Your colleagues will mentally go on vacation. . . .[32]

The solution? As with other presentation aids we have discussed, don't let your PowerPoint slides become your presentation—use them to supplement it. Don't use too many slides. Make certain that the ones you do use contain significant information in a simple, uncluttered style. Don't overuse bulleted text. Instead, take advantage of the ease with which you can create and show such visual elements as graphs, charts, and photos on PowerPoint slides. Finally, practice with your PowerPoint slides so that you can time them to coincide with your oral presentation.

Guidelines for Preparing Presentation Aids

In addition to the specific guidelines for preparing and using various specific types of presentation aids that we have just discussed, four general guidelines can help you prepare all types of presentation aids more effectively.

Adapt

Select the Right Presentation Aids   As is evident from the above discussion, you have a number of options for presentation aids. If you are trying to decide which to use, consider these suggestions:

1. Adapt to your audience. Let their interests, experiences, and knowledge guide your selection of presentation aids. For example, an audience of accountants would readily understand arbitrage charts that might be incomprehensible to a more general audience. If you will be speaking to a large audience, be certain that everyone will be able to see or hear your presentation aid.
2. Be constantly aware of your specific purpose. Be certain that your presentation aid contributes to its achievement.
3. Consider your own skill and experience. Use equipment with which you have had experience, or allow yourself ample time to practice. It may be better to make an overhead transparency of your PowerPoint image if the alternative is to fumble with an unfamiliar computer and LCD projector.

Ethics and Communication

Profanity in an Audio Presentation Aid

Matt wants to talk to his college classmates about the use of profanity in rap music. He plans to play sound clips of several profane lyrics from current hits to illustrate his point. Should Matt play these songs, even though doing so might offend several members of his audience?

4. Take into account the room in which you will speak. If it has large windows and no shades, for example, do not plan to use a visual presentation aid that will require a darkened room. If you plan to run a PowerPoint presentation, be sure that both hardware and software are available and in good working order.

Make Your Presentation Aids Easy to See   You have probably experienced the frustration of squinting and straining to read a speaker's too-small presentation aid. If you are going to remember only one thing about using a presentation aid, remember this: Make it big!

Keep Your Presentation Aids Simple   Don't cram too much information on any single presentation aid. Limit text to key words or phrases. Leave plenty of white space.

Polish Your Presentation Aids   Especially in this day of readily available, professional-looking computer graphics, audiences have high expectations for the appearance of presentation aids. A sloppy, hand-drawn visual will detract from even the best verbal message. Prepare your presentation aids well in advance of your speaking date and make them as attractive and professional as possible. Even if you can't run a PowerPoint presentation in the room in which you are speaking, consider using such a program to produce your presentation aids.

Guidelines for Using Presentation Aids

Once you have prepared potentially effective presentation aids, you will want to utilize them effectively as well. In addition to the guidelines offered earlier in this chapter for using specific types of presentation aids, the following general suggestions will help you more effectively adapt various types of presentation aids to your audience.

Adapt

Rehearse with Your Presentation Aids   The day of your speech should not be the first time you deliver your presentation while holding up your chart, turning on your projector, or cueing your CD. Practice setting up and using your presentation aids until you feel at ease with them. Consider during rehearsal what you would do at various stages of the speech if you had to carry on without your presentation aid. Electricity fails, equipment fails to show up, and bulbs burn out. Have contingency plans.

Maintain Eye Contact with Your Audience, Not with Your Presentation Aids   You can glance at your presentation aids during your talk, but do not talk to them. Keep looking at your audience.

Explain Your Presentation Aids   Always talk about and explain your presentation aids. Do not assume that the audience will understand their relevance and how to interpret them.

Time the Display of Your Presentation Aids to Coincide with Your Discussion of Them   Don't put a presentation aid in front of your audience until you are ready to use it. Likewise, remove your presentation aid after you are finished with it. Keeping presentation aids in front of an audience before or after you use them will only serve to distract from your message.

Do Not Pass Objects, Pictures, or Other Small Items among Your Audience

Passing things around distracts audience members. People are either focused on whatever they are looking at, or they are counting the number of people who will handle the object before it reaches them. If the item is too small for everyone to see it when you hold it up, it is not a good presentation aid.

Use Handouts Effectively

Handing out papers during your presentation can also distract audience members. If possible, wait to distribute handouts until after you have spoken. If your audience needs to refer to the material while you're talking about it, go ahead and pass out the handouts; then, at various points in your presentation, tell audience members where in the handout they should focus.

Use Small Children and Animals with Caution

Small children and even the best-trained animals are unpredictable. In a strange environment, in front of an audience, they may not behave in their usual way. The risk of having a child or animal detract from your presentation may be too great to justify their use as presentation aids.

Use Technology Thoughtfully

Computer-generated graphics, LCDs, and DVDs have become increasingly common components of presentations as more and more classrooms and seminar rooms are equipped for them. However, resist the temptation to use them just because they are glitzy. One speechwriter and presentation coach warns against this bleak but all-too-common scenario:

> The presenter says, "And now, I'd like to talk about quality." And lo and behold . . . the word *quality* flashes on a screen. Now, folks, does this slide offer any new information? Does it clarify a complex point? Does it strengthen the bond between presenter and audience? You know the answer: a resounding "no."[33]

Be sure that the technology you use helps you communicate your message. And be sure that you know how to operate the hardware and that you rehearse with it.

RECAP

Preparing and Using Presentation Aids

Tips for Preparing and Using Specific Types of Presentation Aids

- Use **objects** that you can handle easily and that are safe and legal.
- Be sure that any **models** you use are large enough to be seen easily.
- Rehearse with **people** who will serve as presentation aids, and don't let them steal the show.
- Keep **drawings** simple and large.
- Be sure **photographs** are large enough to be seen easily.
- Highlight on a **map** the geographic areas you will discuss.
- Limit the amount of information you put on any single **chart**.
- Keep **graphs** simple and uncluttered.
- Use only brief excerpts and clips from **videotapes**.
- Have **CD-ROM, DVD,** or **VCR** equipment set up and ready to go before you speak.
- Amplify any **audiotapes** and **CDs** so they can be heard easily.

General Tips for Preparing and Using Presentation Aids

Preparing Presentation Aids
- Select the right presentation aid.
- Make your presentation aids easy to see.
- Keep your presentation aids simple.
- Polish your presentation aids.

Using Presentation Aids
- Rehearse with your presentation aids.
- Maintain eye contact with your audience, not with your presentation aids.
- Explain your presentation aids.
- Time the display of your presentation aids to coincide with your discussion of them.
- Do not pass objects, pictures, or other small items among your audience.
- Use handouts effectively.
- Use small children and animals with caution.
- Use technology thoughtfully.

SOME FINAL TIPS FOR REHEARSING AND DELIVERING YOUR PRESENTATION

Throughout this chapter, we have described and offered suggestions for effective verbal and nonverbal delivery and use of presentation aids. In addition to the tips offered throughout the chapter, the following suggestions will help you make the most of your rehearsal time and ultimately deliver your presentation successfully.

- Finish your preparation outline several days before you must deliver the presentation. Begin to rehearse from the preparation outline. Revise the presentation as necessary so that you can deliver it within your given time limits. Prepare your delivery outline and speaking notes. Continue to rehearse and to modify your speaking notes as necessary.
- Practice, practice, practice. Rehearse aloud as often as possible. Only by rehearsing will you gain confidence in both the content of the presentation and your delivery.
- Practice good delivery skills while rehearsing. Rehearse your presentation standing up. Pay attention to your gestures, posture, eye contact, facial expression, and vocal delivery, as well as the verbal message. Rehearse with your presentation aids.
- If possible, practice your presentation for someone. Seek and consider feedback from someone about both the content and your delivery.
- Tape record or videotape your presentation. Becoming more aware of your delivery can help you make necessary adjustments.
- Re-create the speaking situation in your final rehearsals. Try to rehearse in a room similar to the one in which you will deliver the presentation. Use the speaking notes you will use the day you deliver the presentation. Give the presentation without stopping. The more realistic the rehearsal, the more confidence you will gain.
- Get plenty of rest the night before you speak. Being well rested is more valuable than frantic, last-minute rehearsal.
- Arrive early. If you don't know for certain where your room is, give yourself plenty of time to find it. Rearrange any furniture or equipment and check and set up your presentation aids.

Listen and Respond

Aware

Developing Your Presentation
STEP BY STEP

Deliver Your Presentation

The long-awaited day of Ben's presentation has arrived at last. He got a full night's sleep last night and ate a light breakfast before setting out for class.

As he waits to speak, Ben visualizes himself delivering his speech calmly and confidently. When his name is called, he rises, walks to the front of the room, and establishes eye contact with his audience before he begins to speak.

During his speech, Ben focuses on adapting his message to his listeners. He looks at individual members of his audience, uses purposeful and well-timed gestures, and speaks loudly and clearly.

Even before he hears his classmates' applause, Ben knows that his presentation has gone well.

- Review and apply the suggestions offered in Chapter 11 for becoming a more confident speaker. As the moment for delivering your presentation nears, remind yourself of the effort you have spent preparing it. Visualize yourself delivering the presentation effectively. Silently practice your opening lines. Think about your audience. Breathe deeply, and consciously relax.
- After you have delivered your presentation, seek feedback from members of your audience. Use the information you gain to improve your next presentation.

PRINCIPLES FOR A LIFETIME: Enhancing Your Skills

Aware

Principle One: Be aware of your communication with yourself and others.
- If your subject is sensitive or your information classified, be cautious and noncommittal in any impromptu remarks you might be asked to make.
- As you feel increasingly comfortable rehearsing an extemporaneous presentation, you can decrease your reliance on your notes.
- Grammatical and usage errors communicate a lack of preparation. If you are uncertain of how to use a word or phrase, look it up or ask someone.
- Use a microphone if you need one and one is available. Be sure to rehearse with it.
- Be aware of your speaking rate, and adjust it if necessary.
- Identify key words or phrases that you have a tendency to drawl, slur, or chop. Practice saying them distinctly and clearly.
- Be certain that your presentation aids, including those that utilize technology, contribute to your specific purpose.
- Pay attention to your nonverbal delivery when you rehearse your presentation.
- During rehearsal, tape record or videotape your presentation; objectively and critically observe your gestures, posture, eye contact, facial expression, and vocal delivery, as well as your verbal message; and make necessary adjustments.
- When you deliver your presentation, apply the suggestions offered in Chapter 11 for becoming a more confident speaker.

Verbal

Principle Two: Effectively use and interpret verbal messages.
- Give a manuscript or memorized speech when exact wording is critical.
- Phrase your ideas so that they will be clear, accurate, and memorable.
- Do not try to memorize an extemporaneous presentation word for word; vary the ways in which you express ideas and information.
- Use words that are concrete, unbiased, vivid, simple, and correct.
- Make your presentation memorable with figurative images, drama, and cadence.

Nonverbal

Principle Three: Effectively use and interpret nonverbal messages.

- When you deliver a manuscript speech, try to look at an entire sentence at a time so that you can maintain eye contact throughout the sentence.
- Do not read a manuscript speech too rapidly; vary the rhythm, inflection, and pace of delivery so that the speech does not sound as though it were being read.
- Do not deliver a memorized speech too rapidly, and avoid patterns of vocal inflection that make the speech sound recited.
- Use gestures and movement to add interest and emphasis to both manuscript and memorized speeches.
- Use gestures to emphasize or reinforce your verbal message.
- Move during your presentation to signal the beginning of a new idea or major point, or to signal a transition from a serious idea to a humorous one or vice versa.
- To heighten your credibility and to increase listener learning, use eye contact to let your audience know that you are interested in them and ready to talk to them.
- Speak loudly enough to be heard easily by all members of your audience.
- Vary the volume of your voice to emphasize ideas and sustain the audience's interest.
- Vary your speaking rate to add interest to your delivery and to emphasize key ideas.
- Articulate your words clearly.

Listen and Respond

Principle Four: Listen and respond thoughtfully to others.

- Use eye contact to help you determine how your audience members are responding to you.
- If possible, rehearse your presentation for someone and seek feedback about both your content and your delivery.

Adapt

Principle Five: Appropriately adapt messages to others.

- Although audiences today generally expect speakers to use everyday language and a conversational delivery style, you will need to adapt your delivery to audiences of different sizes and from different cultures.
- Consider your audience and speaking context when you select a method of delivery.
- Consider your audience's interests, expectations, and knowledge to ensure that your impromptu presentation is audience centered.
- As you deliver an extemporaneous presentation, adapt it to your audience.
- Avoid any language that might be offensive to a member of your audience.
- Adapt your gestures to your audience. Use bolder, more sweeping, and more dramatic gestures with large audiences. Tone down gestures if you are speaking to a culturally diverse audience who might prefer a more subdued style.
- Adapt your movement during a presentation to the cultural expectations of your audience. Better to stay in one carefully chosen spot than to make your audience uncomfortable.
- Assume a posture that seems natural to you in light of your topic, your audience, and the formality of the occasion.
- Adapt the amount of eye contact you use to the expectations of your audience. North Americans prefer as much eye contact as possible; Asians generally prefer less.
- To communicate your interest in your listeners, keep your facial expression alert and friendly.
- Adapt the volume of your voice to your audience's needs.
- Adapt to your audience's expectations for your appearance.
- Let your audience's interests, experiences, and knowledge guide your preparation and selection of presentation aids.

SUMMARY

Once you have developed, supported, and organized your presentation, you are ready to begin to rehearse aloud in preparation for delivering it. The way in which you deliver your presentation will in large part determine your success as a speaker.

As you begin to consider how you will deliver your presentation, you will select from four methods of delivery: manuscript speaking, memorized speaking, impromptu speaking, or extemporaneous speaking. Extemporaneous speaking is the style taught today in most presentational speaking classes and preferred by most audiences.

Once you know what method of delivery you will use, you should begin to think about and rehearse words, phrases, and sentences that will best communicate your intended message and give it a distinct and memorable style. The most effective language is concrete, unbiased, vivid, simple, and correct. You can also make your presentation memorable by using figurative language and language that creates drama and cadence.

Nonverbal variables are also critical to effective delivery. Physical delivery includes a speaker's gestures, movement, and posture. Eye contact is perhaps the most important delivery variable, determining to a large extent your credibility with your audience. Facial expression plays a key role in expressing thoughts, emotions, and attitudes. Vocal delivery includes such elements as volume, pitch, rate, and articulation. And finally, your personal appearance can also affect how your audience responds to you and your message.

Presentation aids may not always be necessary, but they are used with increasing frequency. Presentation aids may include objects or models, people, drawings, photographs, maps, charts, graphs, videotapes, CD-ROMs, DVDs, audiotapes, and audio CDs. Today, many presentation aids can be created and displayed by computer graphics programs such as PowerPoint. Guidelines for using any type of presentation aid include selecting the right one for the audience, occasion, and room; and making the presentation aid simple, easy to see or hear, and polished. As you prepare to use any presentation aid, be sure that you rehearse with it, maintain eye contact with your audience, explain your presentation aid, time your use of your presentation aid, refrain from passing things around or using handouts indiscriminately, remember that small children and animals are unpredictable presentation aids, and use technology thoughtfully.

Final suggestions for rehearsing your presentation include allowing ample time for and conducting realistic rehearsals, audiotaping or videotaping your presentation, and practicing your presentation for someone who will offer feedback. Final tips for delivering your presentation include getting plenty of rest the night before you speak, arriving early, and applying the suggestions offered in Chapter 11 for becoming a more confident speaker.

Discussion and Review

1. In what way(s) does delivery contribute to the success of a presentation?
2. What delivery method is most commonly taught and used today?
3. Give an example of how culture can influence audience expectations for speaker delivery.
4. Under what circumstances might a speaker want to deliver a manuscript or memorized speech?
5. How does an extemporaneous presentation differ from an impromptu presentation?
6. List and explain five criteria for effectiveness of words in a presentation.
7. List and define three types of figurative language that can be used to make a presentation memorable.
8. How might you create verbal drama in a presentation?
9. What is cadence? Describe briefly four strategies for achieving it in a presentation.
10. List and define the three key elements of physical delivery and provide suggestions for effectively using each one.
11. What is the most important nonverbal delivery variable for most North American audiences?
12. What can facial expression communicate during a presentation?
13. List and define four nonverbal elements of vocal delivery, and provide suggestions for using each one effectively.
14. How should you dress when you are going to deliver a presentation?
15. List 11 types of presentation aids from which a speaker might select, and provide suggestions for effectively using each type.
16. Offer four general guidelines for preparing effective presentation aids.
17. Provide eight general guidelines for using presentation aids effectively in a presentation.
18. Offer nine general guidelines for rehearsing and delivering a presentation.

Putting Principles into Practice

1. Consult either a print thesaurus or the electronic thesaurus that is part of your word-processing program and find a more concrete or specific word to express each of the following:

go	happy
say	green
big	cat
dark	street
good	car

2. Listen to a political campaign speech in person or on television. Pay particular attention to the politician's delivery. Critique his or her use of gestures, movement, posture, eye contact, facial expression, vocal delivery, and appearance. What advice would you give this politician?

3. Videotape one of your presentations, during either rehearsal or delivery to your class. Analyze your strengths and weaknesses based on the principles and suggestions offered in this chapter.

4. You are a speech consultant to the superintendent of your local school district. She is about to begin working on her annual "State of the District" address, which she gives to an audience of about 250 teachers, parents, and community members. This year, she wants to enliven her presentation of enrollment statistics, student achievement facts, and the state of the physical plant with some presentation aids. Write an advisory memo to the superintendent in which you suggest types of presentation aids she might employ and ways of using each one effectively.

5. You will need the following materials to complete this assignment:

   One or two pieces of paper or poster board measuring at least 15 by 20 inches

   Felt-tipped markers or a set of marking pens in at least two different colors

   A ruler or straightedge

   A pencil with an eraser

   Three speech topics are listed below, each with a brief description and information that could be communicated with the help of a presentation aid. Design one or more presentation aids for one of the three speeches.

   a. A speech about various kinds of organizing tools that college students could use to help them keep track of assignments and projects. These tools include paper wall calendars, paper daytimers, personal information-management software, handheld electronic organizers, and Internet-based calendars.[34]

   b. A speech about the spread of AIDS. The number of new cases of HIV infection in 2004 on various continents are listed below.[35]

   North America: 44,000

   Caribbean: 53,000

   Latin America: 240,000

   Europe and Central Asia: 231,000

   North Africa and Middle East: 92,000

   Sub-Saharan Africa: 3.1 million

   East Asia: 290,000

   South and Southeast Asia: 890,000

   Oceania: 5,000

   c. A speech that discusses Web sites offering useful information about nutrition and diet. Sites might include the following:

   - www.mypyramid.gov/tips_resources/index.html provides tips and resources from the USDA to help you choose healthful food and physical activity

   - www.dietsite.com allows users to enter recipes to obtain a calorie count

   - www.mealsforyou.com offers thousands of healthful recipes

CHAPTER Fourteen

Diana Ong. "The Defense." © Diana Ong/SuperStock, Inc.

If you think knowledge is expensive, try ignorance.

Derek Bok

Speaking to Inform

CHAPTER OUTLINE

Types of Informative Presentations

Strategies for Organizing Your Informative Presentation

Strategies for Making Your Informative Presentation Clear

Strategies for Making Your Informative Presentation Interesting

Strategies for Making Your Informative Presentation Memorable

Summary

CHAPTER OBJECTIVES

After studying this chapter, you should be able to:

1. Explain the purpose of speaking to inform.

2. Describe and illustrate five types of informative presentations.

3. Identify and use appropriate strategies for organizing informative presentations.

4. Identify and use strategies for making informative presentations clear.

5. Identify and use strategies for making informative presentations interesting.

6. Identify and use strategies for making informative presentations memorable.

This is the information age. With the help of today's technology, we are immersed in facts, data, and words. The Internet is an overflowing fount of information on every conceivable topic. Information is a good thing: It is necessary to help us live our lives. But the volume of information may create a problem. There is often too much of a good thing. Trying to use and interpret all the information we encounter can be like trying to take a drink from a fire hose; the volume of information makes this nearly an overwhelming task.

Countless times each day, you are called on to share information with others. Whether it's directions to your house, the answer to a question from a teacher, or an update on a project at work, your competence as a communicator is often based on how clearly you can present information to others. One survey of both speech teachers and students who had taken a communication course found that the single most important skill taught in a presentational speaking class is how to give an informative presentation.[1] This is not surprising, given the importance of sending and receiving information in our lives.

The purpose of a message to **inform** is to share information with others to enhance their knowledge or understanding of the information, concepts, and ideas you present. When you inform someone, you assume the role of a teacher by defining, illustrating, clarifying, or elaborating on a topic.

Speaking to inform others can be a challenging task. The information you communicate to someone else is rarely, if ever, understood exactly as you intend it. As we have noted, we're each different from one another. We literally experience the world in different ways. As a student, you have firsthand experience that just because a teacher presents information, you don't always soak up knowledge like a sponge. Informing or teaching others is a challenge because of a simple fact: *Presenting information does not mean that communication has occurred.* Communication happens when listeners make sense of the information.

Another challenge of speaking to inform is to keep your informative message from becoming a persuasive one. It cannot be denied that informing and persuading are interrelated. Information alone may persuade someone to think or do something in a different way. However, if you intentionally try to change or reinforce your listeners' feelings, ideas, or behavior, your speech may become more persuasive than informative.

In this chapter, we will suggest ways to build on your experience and enhance your skill in informing others. We will examine different types of informative tasks and identify specific strategies to help you organize your messages and make them clear, interesting, and memorable. Throughout our discussion we will remind you of the five communication principles for a lifetime.

Aware
Verbal
Nonverbal
Listen and Respond
Adapt

TYPES OF INFORMATIVE PRESENTATIONS

When preparing an informative presentation, your first task, after considering the needs and backgrounds of your audience, is to select a topic. Although you may be assigned a topic based on your job, experience, or expertise, there are times (such as in a communication class) when you are given a free hand in determining what you will talk about. Identifying the type of informative presentation you will deliver can help you select and narrow your topic, organize your message, and select appropriate supporting material.

inform
To share information with others to enhance their knowledge or understanding of the information, concepts, and ideas you present.

Presentations about Objects

A speech about an object might be about anything tangible—anything you can see or touch. You may or may not show the actual object to your audience while you are talking about it. Objects that could form the basis of an interesting presentation might include these:

Objects from your own collection (antiques, compact discs, baseball cards)
The Eiffel Tower
Cellos
Digital cameras
The Roosevelt Memorial
Toys

The time limit for your speech will determine the amount of detail you can share with your listeners. Even in a 30- to 45-minute presentation, you cannot talk about every aspect of any of the objects listed. So you will need to focus on a specific purpose.

Presentations about Procedures

A presentation about a procedure discusses how something works (for example, how blood travels through the human circulatory system), or describes a process that produces a particular outcome (such as how grapes become wine). At the close of such a presentation, your audience should be able to describe, understand, or perform the procedure you have described. Here are some examples of procedures that could be the topics of effective informative presentations:

How to surf the Internet
How state laws are made
How to refinish furniture
How to select a personal digital assistant (PDA)
How to plant an organic garden
How to select and purchase a stock

Notice that all of these examples start with the word *how.* A presentation about a procedure usually focuses on how a process is completed or how something can be accomplished. Presentations about procedures are often presented in workshops or other training situations in which people learn skills. One good way to teach people a skill is to follow the acronym T-E-A-C-H, which stands for Tell-Example-Apply-Coach-Help.[2]

- *Tell:* Describe what you want your listeners to know.
- *Example:* Show them an example of how to perform the skill.
- *Apply:* Give them an opportunity to apply the knowledge by performing the skill.
- *Coach:* Provide positive coaching to encourage them.
- *Help:* Help them learn by correcting mistakes.

Many presentations about procedures include visual aids. Whether you are teaching people how to install a computer modem or how to give a presentation, showing them how to do something is almost always more effective than just telling them how to do it.

Presentations about People

A biographical presentation could be about someone famous or about someone you know personally. Most of us enjoy hearing about the lives of real people, whether famous or not, living or dead, who have some special quality. The key to making an effective biographical presentation is to be selective. Don't try to cover every detail of your subject's life. Relate the key elements in the person's career, personality, or other significant life features so that you build to a particular point, rather than just recite facts about an individual. Perhaps your grandfather was known for his generosity, for example. Mention some notable examples of his philanthropy. If you are talking about a well-known personality, pick information or a period that is not widely known, such as the person's private hobby or childhood. One speaker gave a memorable presentation about his friend:

> To enter Charlie's home was to enter a world of order and efficiency. His den reflected his many years as an Air Force officer; it was orderly and neat. He always knew exactly where everything was. When he finished reading the morning paper, he folded it so neatly by his favorite chair that you would hardly know that it had been read. Yet for all of his efficiency, you knew the minute you walked into his home that he cared for others, that he cared for you. His jokes, his stories, his skill in listening to others drew people to him. He never met a stranger. He looked for opportunities to help others.

Note how these details capture Charlie's personality and charm. Presentations about people should give your listeners the feeling that the person is a unique, authentic individual.

One specific type of presentation about a person is an introduction of another speaker and his or her topic. There are two cardinal rules for introducing another speaker: Be brief, and be accurate. Remember that the audience has come to hear the main speaker, not to listen to you. And be certain that you know how to pronounce the speaker's name and that you have accurate information about him or her.

Presentations about Events

Where were you on September 11, 2001, the day terrorists attacked the World Trade Center and the Pentagon? Chances are that you clearly remember where you were and what you were doing on that and other similarly fateful days. Major events punctuate our lives and mark the passage of time.

A major event can form the basis of a fascinating informative presentation. You can choose to talk about an event that you have either witnessed or researched. Your goal is to describe the event in concrete, tangible terms and to bring the experience to life for your audience. Have you experienced a major disaster such as a hurricane or a tornado? Have you witnessed the inauguration of a president, governor, or senator? Or you may want to re-create an event that your parents or grandparents lived through. What was it like to be at Pearl Harbor on December 7, 1941? How did people react when Neil Armstrong took his first steps on the moon on July 20, 1969?

Beetle Bailey

You may have heard a recording of the famous radio broadcast of the explosion and crash of the dirigible *Hindenburg.* The announcer's ability to describe both the scene and the incredible emotion of the moment has made that broadcast a classic. As that broadcaster was able to do, your purpose as an informative speaker describing an event is to make that event come alive for your listeners and to help them visualize the scene.

Presentations about Ideas

Presentations about ideas are by nature more abstract than the other types of presentations. The following principles, concepts, and theories might be topics of idea presentations:

Principles of time management
Freedom of speech
Evolution
Theories of communication
Buddhism
Animal rights

As you look at this list, you may think, "Those topics sure look boring." The key to gaining and maintaining interest in your presentation about an idea lies in your selection of supporting material. A good speaker selects illustrations, examples, and anecdotes that make an otherwise abstract idea seem both exciting and relevant to the audience.

Verbal

STRATEGIES FOR ORGANIZING YOUR INFORMATIVE PRESENTATION

As with any presentation, your audience will more readily understand your informative presentation if you organize your ideas logically. Regardless of the length or complexity of your message, you must follow a logical pattern in order to be understood.

Organizing Presentations about Objects

Presentations about objects may be organized topically; a topical pattern is structured around the logical divisions of the object you're describing. Here's a sample topical outline for a speech about an object—a nuclear power plant:

I. The reactor core
  A. The nuclear fuel in the core
  B. The placement of the fuel in the core
II. The reactor vessel
  A. The walls of a reactor vessel
  B. The function of the coolant in the reactor vessel
III. The reactor control rods
  A. The description of the control rods
  B. The function of the control rods

Presentations about objects may also be organized chronologically. A speaker might, for example, focus on the history and development of nuclear power plants; such a presentation would probably be organized chronologically. Or, depending on the speaker's specific purpose, the presentation could be organized spatially, describing the physical layout of a nuclear power plant.

When speaking about Native American rock art in Texas, this speaker may find it helpful to organize her speech either topically, spatially, or chronologically.

Organizing Presentations about Procedures

Speeches about procedures are usually organized chronologically, according to the steps involved in the process. Anita organized chronologically her explanation of how to develop a new training curriculum in teamwork skills:

I. Conduct a needs assessment of your department.
   A. Identify the method of assessing department needs.
   B. Implement the needs assessment.
II. Identify the topics that should be presented in the training.
   A. Specify topics that all members of the department need.
   B. Specify topics that only some members of the department need.
III. Write training objectives.
   A. Write objectives that are measurable.
   B. Write objectives that are specific.
   C. Write objectives that are attainable.
IV. Develop lesson plans for the training.
   A. Identify the training methods you will use.
   B. Identify the materials you will need.

Note that Anita grouped the tasks into steps. Her audience will remember the four general steps much more easily than they could have hoped to recall the curriculum development process if each individual task were listed as a separate step.

Organizing Presentations about People

One way to talk about a person's life is in chronological order—birth, school, career, family, professional achievements, death. However, if you are interested in presenting a specific theme, such as "Winston Churchill, master of English prose," you may decide instead to organize Churchill's experiences topically. You could first discuss Churchill's achievements as a brilliant orator whose words defied the German military machine in 1940, and then trace the origins of his skill to his work as a cub reporter in South Africa during the Boer War of 1899 to 1902.

Organizing Presentations about Events

Most speeches about an event follow a chronological arrangement. But a presentation about an event might also describe the complex issues or causes behind the event and be organized topically. For example, if you were to talk about the Civil War, you might choose to focus on the three causes of the war:

I. Political
II. Economic
III. Social

Adapt

   Although these main points are topical, specific subpoints may be organized chronologically. However you choose to organize your speech about an event, your goal should be to ensure that your audience is enthralled by your vivid description.

Organizing Presentations about Ideas

Most presentations about ideas are organized topically (by logical subdivisions of the central idea) or according to complexity (from simple ideas to more complex ones). The following example illustrates how Thompson organized a presentation about philosophy into an informative speech:

I. Definition of philosophy
   A. Philosophy as viewed in ancient times

    B. Philosophy as viewed today
II. Three branches of the study of philosophy
    A. Metaphysics
        1. The study of ontology
        2. The study of cosmology
    B. Epistemology
        1. Knowledge derived from thinking
        2. Knowledge derived from experiencing
    C. Logic
        1. Types of reasoning
        2. Types of proof

Thompson decided that the most logical way to give an introductory talk about philosophy was first to define it and then to describe three branches of philosophy. Because of time limits, he chose only to describe three branches or types of philosophy. He used a topical organizational pattern to organize his message.

RECAP

Organizing Informative Presentations

Presentation Type	Description	Typical Organizational Patterns	Sample Topics
Presentations about objects	Present information about tangible things	Topical Spatial Chronological	The Rosetta Stone MP3 players Space shuttle The U.S. Capitol

Presentations about procedures	Review how something works or describe a process	Chronological
		Topical
		Complexity
			How to . . .
			  Clone an animal
			  Operate a nuclear
			    power plant
			  Use a computer
			  Trap lobsters

Presentations about people	Describe either famous people or personal acquaintances	Chronological Topical	Rosa Parks Nelson Mandela Indira Gandhi Your grandmother Your favorite teacher
Presentations about events	Describe an actual event	Chronological Topical Complexity Spatial	Chinese New Year Inauguration Day Cinco de Mayo
Presentations about ideas	Present abstract information or information about principles, concepts, theories, or issues	Topical Complexity	Communism Economic theory Tao-Te Ching

STRATEGIES FOR MAKING YOUR INFORMATIVE PRESENTATION CLEAR

Think of the best teacher you ever had. He or she was probably a great lecturer with a special talent for making information clear, interesting, and memorable. Like teachers, some speakers are better than others at presenting information clearly. In this section, we will review some of the principles that can help you become the kind of speaker whose presentations are memorable.[3]

A message is clear when the listener understands it in the way the speaker intended. Phrased in baseball terminology, a message is clear when what I threw is what you caught. How do you make your messages clear to others? First, be aware (mindful) of what you intend to communicate. Is the message clear to you? Say to yourself, "If I heard this message for the first time, would it make sense to me?"

If the message makes sense to you, select appropriate words that are reinforced with appropriate nonverbal cues to express your ideas. If you detect that your listeners are puzzled by what you say, stop and try another way to express your ideas.

Adapt your message to your audience. Be audience centered. Keep your listeners in mind as you select and narrow a topic, fine-tune your purpose, and complete each preparation and presentation task. Here are several additional specific strategies to make your message clear.

Aware
Verbal
Nonverbal
Listen and Respond
Adapt

Simplify Ideas

Your job as a presentational speaker is to get your ideas over to your audience, not to see how much information you can cram into your speech. The simpler your ideas and phrases, the greater the chance that your audience will remember them.

Let's say you decide to talk about state-of-the-art personal computer hardware. Fine—but just don't try to make your audience as sophisticated as you are about computers in a 5-minute presentation. Discuss only major features and name one or two leaders in the field. Don't load your presentation with details. Edit ruthlessly.

Verbal

Pace Your Information Flow

Arrange your supporting material so that you present an even flow of information, rather than bunch up a number of significant details around one point. If you present too much new information too quickly, you may overwhelm your audience. Their ability to understand may falter.

You should be especially sensitive to the flow of information if your topic is new or unfamiliar to your listeners. Make sure that your audience has time to process any new information you present. Use supporting material to regulate the pace of your presentation.

Again, do not try to see how much detail and content you can cram into a presentation. Your job is to present information so that the audience can grasp it, not to show off how much you know.

Verbal
Adapt

Relate New Information to Old

Most of us learn by building on what we already know. We try to make sense out of our world by associating the new with the old. When you meet someone for the first time, you may be reminded of someone you already know. Your understanding of calculus is based on your knowledge of algebra.

When presenting new information to a group, help your audience associate your new idea with something that is familiar to them. Use an analogy. Tell bewildered college freshmen how their new academic life will be similar to high school and how it will be different. Describe how your raising cattle over the summer was similar to taking

Verbal

Diversity and Communication

Using an Interpreter

*I*t is quite possible that you may at some time be asked to speak to an audience that does not understand English. In such a situation, you will need an interpreter to translate your message so that your audience can understand you. When using an interpreter, consider the following tips:

1. Realize that a presentation that may take you 30 minutes to deliver without an interpreter will take at least an hour to present with an interpreter. Edit your message to make sure it fits within the time limit.

2. Even with an experienced interpreter, you'll need to slow your speaking rate a bit. Also, be sure to pause after every two or three sentences to give the interpreter time to translate your message.

3. Don't assume that your audience doesn't understand you just because you are using an interpreter. Don't say anything that you don't want your audience to hear.

4. If you have many facts, figures, or other detailed data, write this information down before you speak, and give it to your interpreter.

5. Humor often doesn't translate well. Be cautious of using a joke that was a real knee-slapper when you told it to your colleagues in your office; it may not have the same effect on people with a different cultural background and differ-

ent language. Also, even a very skilled interpreter may have difficulty communicating the intended meaning of your humor.

6. Avoid using slang, jargon, or any terms that will be unfamiliar to your listeners or interpreter.

7. When possible, talk with your interpreter before you deliver your presentation. Tell him or her the general points you will present. If possible, give the interpreter an outline or a transcript if you are using a manuscript.

care of any animal; they all need food, water, and shelter. By building on the familiar, you help your listeners understand how your new concept or information relates to their experience.

STRATEGIES FOR MAKING YOUR INFORMATIVE PRESENTATION INTERESTING

He had them. Every audience member's eyes were riveted on the speaker. It was as quiet as midnight in a funeral home. Audience members were also leaning forward, ever so slightly, not wanting to miss a single idea or brilliant illustration. No one moved. They hung on every word. How can you create such interest when *you* speak? Here are several strategies that can help you keep your audiences listening for more.

Relate to Your Listeners' Interests

Your listeners may be interested in your topic for a variety of reasons. It may affect them directly; it may add to their knowledge; it may satisfy their curiosity; or it may entertain them. These reasons are not mutually exclusive. For example, if you were talking to a group of businesspeople about the latest changes in local tax policies, you would be discussing something that would affect them directly, add to their knowledge, and satisfy their curiosity. But your listeners' primary interest would be in how the taxes would affect them. By contrast, if you were giving a lecture on 15th-century Benin sculpture to a middle-class audience at a public library, your listeners would be

Adapt

interested because your talk would add to their knowledge, satisfy their curiosity, and entertain them. Such a talk can also affect your listeners directly by making them more interesting to others. If your audience feels that they will benefit from your presentation in some way, your presentation will interest them.

Throughout this book, we have encouraged you to adapt to your communication partners—to develop an audience-centered approach to presentational speaking. Being an audience-centered informative speaker means that you are aware of information that your audience can use. Specifically, what factors help maintain audience interest? Consider the following strategies.[4]

- *Activity and movement:* We are more likely to listen to a story that is action-packed than to one that listlessly lingers on an idea too long.
- *Issues and events close to an audience:* To capture your listeners' attention, relate your information to what is happening in your school, community, or state. Not surprisingly, most people are interested in themselves. Therefore, one of the secrets to making a presentation interesting is to use examples to which your audience can relate. Make it personal. When appropriate, mention specific audience members' names.
- *Conflict:* Clashes of ideas; stories that pit one side against another; or opposing forces in government, religion, or interpersonal relationships grab attention. The Greeks learned long ago that the essential ingredient of any play, be it comedy or tragedy, is conflict.

Another way you can make your message interesting is to think about why you are interested in the topic. Once you are aware of your own interests and background, you can often find ways to establish common bonds with your audience.

Use Attention-Catching Supporting Material

Supporting material is effective if it both clarifies your ideas and keeps your listeners' attention. One classic type of supporting material often used in informative speaking is definition. But if you are trying to tell your listeners about a complex or abstract process, you will need more than definitions to explain what you mean. When describing abstract ideas or processes, it's usually more difficult to hold listeners' attention. Research suggests that you can demystify a complex process and increase audience interest if you first provide a simple overview of the process with an analogy, model, picture, or vivid description.[5]

Before going into great detail, first give listeners the "big picture" or convey the gist of the process. Analogies (comparisons) are often a good way to do this. For example, if you are describing how a personal computer works, you could say that it stores information the way a filing cabinet does or that computer software works like a piano roll on an old-fashioned player piano. In addition to using an analogy, consider using a model or other visual aid to show relationships among the steps of a complex process.

You can also describe the process, providing more detail than you do when you just define something. Descriptions answer questions about the *who, what, where, why,* and *when* of the process. Who is involved in the process? What is the process, idea, or event that you want to describe? Where and when does the process take place? Why does it occur, or why is it important to the audience? (Of course, not all of these questions apply to every description.)

The 5th Wave   By Rich Tennant

© The 5th Wave. www.the5thwave.com

Establish a Motive for Your Audience to Listen to You

Most audiences will probably not be waiting breathlessly for you to talk to them. You will need to motivate them to listen to you.

Some situations have built-in motivations for listeners. A teacher can say, "There will be a test covering my lecture tomorrow. It will count as 50% of your semester grade." Such threatening methods may not make the teacher popular, but they certainly will motivate the class to listen. Similarly, a boss might say, "Your ability to use these sales principles will determine whether you keep your job." Your boss's statement will probably motivate you to learn the company's sales principles. However, unlike a teacher or a boss, you will rarely have the power to motivate your listeners with such strong-arm tactics, and you will therefore need to find more creative ways to get your audience to listen to you.

One way to arouse the interest of your listeners is to ask them a question. Speaking on the high cost of tuition, you might ask, "How many of you are interested in saving tuition dollars this year?" You'll probably have their attention. Then proceed to tell them that you will talk about several approaches to seeking low-cost loans and grants. "Who would like to save money on their income taxes?" "How many of you would like to have a happier home life?" "How many of you would like to learn an effective way of preparing your next speech?" These are other examples of questions that could stimulate your listeners' interest and motivate them to give you their attention. Besides using rhetorical questions, you can begin with an anecdote, a startling statistic, or some other attention-grabbing device.

Don't assume that your listeners will be automatically interested in what you have to say. Pique their interest with a question. Capture their attention. Motivate them to listen to you. Tell them how the information you present will be of value to them. As the British writer G. K. Chesterton once said, "There is no such thing as an uninteresting topic; there are only uninterested people."

Use Word Pictures

Words have the power to create powerful images that can gain and hold an audience's attention. Consider using a word picture to make your message vivid and interesting. **Word pictures** are lively descriptions that help your listeners form a mental image by appealing to their senses of sight, taste, smell, sound, and touch. The following suggestions will help you construct effective word pictures:

- Form a clear mental image of the person, place, or object before you try to describe it.
- Describe the appearance of the person, place, or object. What would your listeners see if they were looking at it? Use lively language to describe the flaws and foibles, bumps and beauties of the people, places, and things you want your audience to see. Make your description an invitation to the imagination—a stately pleasure dome into which your listeners can enter and view its treasures with you.
- Describe what your listeners would hear. Use colorful, onomatopoetic words, such as *buzz, snort, hum, crackle,* or *hiss.* These words are much more descriptive than the more general term *noise.* Imitate the sound you want your listeners to hear with their "mental ear."

On the Web

The Internet is a vast resource of material for informative speeches. In addition to using search engines to perform keyword searches, you may want to take advantage of such resources as Web-based encyclopedias, almanacs, and statistical databases. Take a look at the following:

Infoplease provides access to a number of informative resources, including *The Columbia Electronic Encyclopedia,* 6th ed., and the *Information Please Almanac.*
www.infoplease.com

Factfinder is a user-friendly site that offers population, housing, economic, and geographic data from the U.S. Census Bureau.
factfinder.census.gov/

FedStats offers official statistical information from more than 100 federal government agencies.
www.fedstats.gov/

word picture
Vivid words that invite listeners to draw on their senses.

Colin Powell's use of memorable word pictures helps his audience visualize the images he talks about.

For example, instead of saying, "When I walked in the woods, I heard the sound of twigs breaking beneath my feet and wind moving the leaves above me in the trees," you might say, "As I walked in the woods, I heard the *crackle* of twigs underfoot and the *rustle* of leaves overhead."

- Describe smells, if appropriate. What fragrance or aroma do you want your audience to recall? Such diverse subjects as Thanksgiving, nighttime in the tropics, and the first day of school all lend themselves to olfactory imagery. No Thanksgiving would be complete without the rich aroma of roast turkey and the pungent, tangy odor of cranberries. A warm, humid evening in Miami smells of salt air and gardenia blossoms. And the first day of school evokes for many the scents of new shoe leather, unused crayons, and freshly painted classrooms. In each case, the associated smells greatly enhance the overall word picture.

- Describe how an object feels when touched. Use words that are as clear and vivid as possible. Rather than saying that something is rough or smooth, use a simile, such as "the rock was rough as sandpaper" or "the pebble was as smooth as a baby's skin." These descriptions appeal to both the visual and tactile senses.

- Describe taste, one of the most powerful of the senses, if appropriate. Thinking about your grandmother may evoke for you memories of her rich, homemade noodles; her sweet, fudgy, nut brownies; and her light, flaky, buttery pie crust. Descriptions of these taste sensations would be welcome to almost any audience, particularly your fellow college students subsisting mainly on dormitory food or their own cooking! More important, such description can help you paint an accurate, vivid image of your grandmother.

- Describe the emotion that a listener might feel if he or she were to experience the situation you relate. If you experienced the situation, describe your own emotions. Use specific adjectives rather than general terms such as *happy* or *sad*. One speaker, talking about receiving her first speech assignment, described her reaction with these words: "My heart stopped. Panic began to rise up inside. Me? . . . For the next five days I lived in dreaded anticipation of the forthcoming event."[6]

Note how effectively such words and phrases as "my heart stopped," "panic," and "dreaded anticipation" describe the above-mentioned speaker's terror at the prospect of giving a speech—much more so than if she had said simply, "I was scared." The more vividly and accurately you can describe emotion, the more intimately involved in your description the audience will become. One final word of caution: Don't describe horrific events too explicitly. You will risk alienating your audience, rather than engaging them.

Create Interesting Presentation Aids

Nonverbal

Research about learning styles suggests that many of your listeners are more likely to remember your ideas if you can reinforce them with presentation aids. Pictures, graphs, posters, and computer-generated graphics can help you gain and maintain audience members' attention, as well as increase their retention of the information you present. Today's audiences are exposed daily to a barrage of messages conveyed through highly visual electronic media—CD-ROM, DVD, the World Wide Web, and video. They have grown to depend on more than words alone to help them remember ideas and information. When you present summaries of data, a well-crafted line graph or colorful pie chart can quickly and memorably reinforce the words and numbers you cite.

Use Humor

"Humor is the spice of speeches," says comedian Michael Klepper. "Too little and your message may be bland or lifeless, too much and it can burn the mouth."[7] The challenge is to use just the right kind of humor in the right amounts. Use humor wisely by considering the following ideas:"[8]

- *Use humor to make a point:* Don't just tell jokes for the sake of getting a laugh. Make sure your story or punch line relates to your message. Here's an example of how a brief joke was used to make a point about the value of teamwork:

  > I read recently about a veterinarian and a taxidermist who decided to share a shop in a small town in Ohio. The sign in the front window read: "Either way, you get your dog back."
  >   There is an important lesson there. We need to work together to solve our problems. People from marketing need to work with operations people. Designers need to work with engineers. Then, when we find a problem that one part of the organization can't solve, someone else may suggest a solution. It doesn't matter who comes up with the solution. The important thing is to "get your dog back."[9]

- *Make yourself the butt of the joke:* Audiences love it when you tell a funny or embarrassing story about yourself. And if the joke's on you, you don't have to worry about whether you will offend someone else.
- *Use humorous quotations:* You don't have to be a comedy writer to be funny. Quote humorous lines of proverbs, poetry, or sayings from others. But remember, what may be funny to you may not be funny to your audience. Some people love the humor of George Carlin; some don't. Try out your quotes and jokes on others before you present them from behind the lectern. Also, don't try to pass off a quotation from someone else as one of your own; always give credit for quotations you use.
- *Use cartoons:* Using an overhead projector to display a cartoon or scanning a cartoon into your computer presentation may be just the right way to make your point. Make sure your cartoon is large enough to be seen by everyone in the audience. As with any humor, don't overdo your use of cartoons.

STRATEGIES FOR MAKING YOUR INFORMATIVE PRESENTATION MEMORABLE

If you've made your message clear and interesting, you're well on your way to ensuring that your audience members remember what you say. The goal is for your ideas to stick in your listeners' minds as if they were made of Velcro, rather than slide off as if they were made of Teflon. When you inform or teach, your job is to ensure as much retention of what you have conveyed as possible, by presenting the information as effectively as you can. People remember what is important to them. So one of the keys to making a message memorable is, again, to adapt your message to your listeners. Presenting a well-organized message will also go a long way toward helping your listeners remember what you say. Here are several strategies for making your presentation memorable.

Adapt

Build in Redundancy

It is seldom necessary for writers to repeat themselves. If readers don't quite understand a passage, they can go back and read it again. When you speak, however, it is useful to repeat key points. As we have noted before, audience members generally cannot stop you if a point in your presentation is unclear or if their minds wander; you need to build in redundancy to make sure that the information you want to communicate will get across. Most speech teachers advise their students to structure their presentations as follows:

Verbal

1. *Tell them what you're going to tell them.* In the introduction of your presentation, provide a broad overview of the purpose of your message. Identify the major points you will present.
2. *Tell them.* In the body of your presentation, develop each of the main points mentioned during your introduction.
3. *Tell them what you've told them.* Finally, in your conclusion, summarize the key ideas discussed in the body.

Use Adult Learning Principles

If your audience consists of adult listeners, you will need to ensure that you deliver your message in the way that adults learn best. **Adult learners** prefer the following.[10]

- To be given information they can use immediately
- To be involved actively in the learning process
- To connect their life experiences with the new information they learn
- To know how the new information is relevant to their busy lives
- To receive information that is relevant to their needs

Adapt

Most people who have office jobs have in-baskets (or simply "in-piles") on their desks, where they place work that needs to be done. Similarly, adult learners tend to have "mental in-baskets"; as audience members, they have mental agendas of what they want or need to gain from listening to a presentation. Remember the characteristics of adult learners, and don't forget about the important principle of adapting your message to others. You will make your message memorable and also have more success in informing your audience if you tailor your information to address *their* agenda.

Reinforce Key Ideas Verbally

Verbal

You can reinforce an idea by using such phrases as "This is the most important point" or "Be sure to remember this next point; it's the most compelling one." Suppose you have four suggestions for helping your listeners chair a meeting, and your last suggestion is the most important. How can you make sure your audience knows that? Just tell them: "Of all the suggestions I've given you, this last tip is the most important one. Here it is: Never fail to distribute an agenda before you chair any meeting." Be careful not to overuse this technique. If you claim that every other point is a key point, soon your audience will not believe you.

Reinforce Key Ideas Nonverbally

Nonverbal

You can also signal the importance of a point with nonverbal emphasis. Gestures serve the purpose of accenting or emphasizing key phrases, as italics do in written communication.

A well-placed pause can provide emphasis and reinforcement for a point. Pausing just before or just after you make an important point will focus attention on your thought. Raising or lowering your voice can also reinforce a key idea.

Movement can help emphasize major ideas. Moving from behind the lectern to tell a personal anecdote can signal that something special and more intimate is about to be said. Remember that your movement and gestures should be meaningful and natural, rather than seeming arbitrary or forced. Your need to emphasize an idea can provide the motivation to make a meaningful movement.

adult learners
Individuals who prefer practical, useful information that is relevant to their busy lives; they seek information that connects with their life experiences.

RECAP

Strategies for Making an Informative Presentation Clear, Interesting, and Memorable

Make Your Presentation Clear

Simplify ideas.

Pace the information flow.

Relate new information to old.

Make Your Presentation Interesting

Relate to your listeners' interests.

Use attention-catching supporting material.

Establish a motive for your audience to listen to you.

Use word pictures.

Use interesting presentation aids.

Use humor.

Make Your Presentation Memorable

Build in redundancy.

Use adult learning principles.

Reinforce key ideas verbally.

Reinforce key ideas nonverbally.

SAMPLE INFORMATIVE PRESENTATION

Alton Tisino
Texas State University–San Marcos

The Power of Music[11]

Alton establishes a motive for his audience to listen by referring to music experiences common to all people.

When I woke up this morning, one thing on my mind was music. I'm sure everyone wakes up with a certain tune or a favorite song in their head. Music is a treasured art form that we all share. Sometimes we can hear a song, and it will take us back to a significant time in our lives; or other times, a song can give us inspiration or motivate us to continue whatever it is we are doing. Whether it is in a car or at home, or at a restaurant or even in an elevator, music plays a big part in our daily lives and can bring us together like no other art form.

Alton further arouses the interest of his listeners by asking two rhetorical questions.

So why is music so powerful? What are the elements that make music so special? Some people say they like the beat of a song, some people say they like the melody in a song, while others simply enjoy the lyrics in a song. Well, according to world-famous composer Duke Ellington, there are three major elements in music: rhythm, melody, and harmony. In order for us to discover what makes music so special, we must first understand these terms, and then see how music itself is beneficial to us in our daily lives.

Alton previews the two main ideas of his presentation.

Alton uses both a definition and an explanation to clarify the role of rhythm in music.

The *Dictionary of Music* defines *rhythm* as "the division of impulses, sound, and accents or movement in musical time." There are many theories on how rhythm was transformed into music. But, I'd like to cite poet Langston Hughes and his explanation on how rhythm was transformed into music:

SAMPLE INFORMATIVE PRESENTATION (continued)

The rhythm of the heart is the first and most important rhythm in human life. Thousands of years ago men transformed the rhythm of the heartbeat into a drumbeat. And the rhythm of music began. They made a slow steady drumbeat to walk to or march to, a faster beat to sing to, and a changing beat to dance to. Rhythm is something we share in common. You and I, with all the plants and animals and people in the world and with all the stars and moon and sun and all the vast universe beyond this wonderful earth which is our home.[12]

Alton provides a signpost to summarize his first subpoint and preview the next one.

Now that we have found our rhythm, we must look further into the foundation of music and discover melody.

Melody is defined as "an arrangement of single tones in a meaningful sequence." A melody gives life to a song and is the root for every tune you will ever hear. We have now found our melody and now we're only missing one piece to the puzzle of music.

Harmony is defined as "the sound resulting from the simultaneous sounding of two or more tones consonant with each other." Rhythm and melody would not be complete without harmony.

This signpost signals Alton's move from his first main idea to his second main idea.

Now that we discovered the foundations of music, let me now explain to you how music is beneficial to us.

Many health experts believe music is good for the digestive system. According to researchers at the *Continuous Music Network*, slow music is better for your digestive system than no music at all. Clinical studies show that people take on average three mouthfuls when there's soothing music in the background, versus four mouthfuls when no tunes are played at all.

While music can help us relax at the dinner table, it can also help us go that extra mile when exercising. The music network *Galaxie* program director Mike Guinta stated that "Studies show men increase their workout time by 30 percent and women by 25 percent . . . ." Scientific studies have shown that music keeps your mind off the physical discomfort of a straining activity. I can personally recall a time I felt I could no longer go on with the strenuous activity of a workout. But somehow by listening to music on my headphones, it gave me an extra boost of energy.

Having offered statistical evidence that music is beneficial to exercise, Alton relates a brief personal anecdote.

Studies also have shown that unborn babies who listen to classical music in the mother's womb become smarter. Many therapists and psychiatrists have their patients listen to music to help them relax and deal with stress and depression. These are just a few of the many benefits that music has for us.

As part of the necessary built-in redundancy of informative presentations, Alton briefly summarizes his main ideas.

We have discovered the three major elements in music: rhythm, melody, and harmony. Whether it be the hard-hitting drums of rock, the melodic tunes of our favorite pop songs, or the harmonic, complex style of jazz, music is the universal language of the world because it can generate the feelings of human emotions—joy, sorrow, love, and pain—thus making it beneficial in our daily lives.

By explaining how the elements of music apply to everyone's life, Alton draws on the principles that adult learners prefer to connect their life experiences with the new information they have learned, and that they prefer relevant information.

The fact of the matter is we make our own music all the time. Now let me explain to you how we do this. Just by being alive, our heartbeat makes its own rhythm. We make melody by arranging our thoughts in a meaningful sequence. And we make the final stage of music, harmony, simply by interacting with each other. We all have rhythm, and we all have music, and with music we have good times.

Alton closes his presentation with a reference to George Gershwin's famous song "I Got Rhythm."

PRINCIPLES FOR A LIFETIME: Enhancing Your Skills

Aware

Principle One: Be aware of your communication with yourself and others.

- Be conscious of the type of informative message you are developing (presentation about an object, a procedure, a person, an event, or an idea), to help you determine how best to organize your message.
- Be consciously aware of using strategies that will make your informative messages clear, interesting, and memorable.

Verbal

Principle Two: Effectively use and interpret verbal messages.

- Use supporting material such as stories, examples, and illustrations to gain and maintain attention.
- Use word pictures to make images and stories interesting and memorable.
- Pace the flow of the information you present to enhance message clarity.
- Relate new information to old information to increase clarity and retention.
- Verbally reinforce ideas to help make your message memorable.
- Use simple ideas rather than complex ideas to make your message clear.
- Build in message redundancy to enhance message retention.

Nonverbal

Principle Three: Effectively use and interpret nonverbal messages.

- Use presentation aids to make messages clear, interesting, and memorable.
- Observe the nonverbal behavior of your audience to help you determine whether your message has been communicated clearly.
- Nonverbally reinforce ideas to make your message memorable.

Listen and Respond

Principle Four: Listen and respond thoughtfully to others.

- Before you deliver you presentation to an audience, talk and listen to audience members to help you customize your message for them.

Adapt

Principle Five: Appropriately adapt messages to others.

- Adapt the structure and flow of your presentation to your listeners to enhance message clarity.
- Adapt your examples and illustrations to your listeners to help gain and maintain interest and attention.
- Develop a motivation for your audience to listen to you.

SUMMARY

To inform is to teach someone something you know. In this chapter, you have studied the goals, principles, and strategies that presentational speakers use to inform others.

There are five basic types of informative presentations. Messages about ideas are often abstract and generally discuss principles, concepts, or theories. Messages about objects discuss tangible things. Messages about procedures explain a process or describe how something works. Messages about people can be about either the famous or the little known. Messages about events describe major occurrences or personal experiences.

Strategies for organizing your informative presentation will vary according to the type of informative presentation and your specific purpose. A presentation about an object may be organized topically, chronologically, or spatially. A presentation about a procedure will usually be organized chronologically. Presentations about either people or events are also usually organized chronologically but can be organized topically. And a presentation about an idea will probably be organized topically.

To make your message clear, use simple rather than complex ideas, pace the flow of your information, and relate new information to old ideas. In order to increase interest in your presentation, relate information to your listeners, find and use attention-catching supporting material, establish a motive for your audience to listen to you, use vivid word pictures, use humor appropriately, and create intriguing and clear presentation aids. Finally, to make messages memorable, build in some redundancy (tell them what you're going to tell them; tell them; tell them what you've told them), use principles of adult learning, and reinforce key ideas both verbally and nonverbally.

Discussion and Review

1. What is informative speaking?
2. What is the purpose of speaking to inform?
3. Describe the five types of informative speaking.
4. Explain how to organize each type of informative presentation.
5. What are three strategies to make your informative message clear?
6. Identify six strategies that can enhance interest in your informative talk.
7. What are four strategies that can make your presentation memorable?

Putting Principles into Practice

1. From the following list of suggested topics for an informative presentation, select five and develop a specific-purpose sentence for each. For one of those topics, identify two to four major ideas. Organize them topically, chronologically, or according to some other logical pattern of organization.

    How to get a better grade in your communication class
    The spread of terrorism in the world
    How the U.S. Constitution was written
    A historical person I wish I could meet
    What makes a good teacher
    The best way to lose weight
    How to buy a digital camera
    Surrogate parenthood
    Safe-driving principles
    How the stock market works
    Social Security

2. Replace each of the following words with a livelier one:

cat	work
airplane	light
house	eat
walk	study

3. Look up the origin of the following words in a comprehensive dictionary, such as the *Oxford English Dictionary* or the *Etymological Dictionary of Modern English*.

logic	teacher
pillow	dance
love	amateur
communication	disciple

4. Write a word picture—a vivid, colorful description that appeals to the senses—of one of the following scenes:

    Your first day learning how to drive
    Visiting your father or mother at work
    A holiday when you were six
    A visit to your grandparents' house
    Your first day at college
    Your most frightening experience
    Your most memorable birthday celebration

Give me the right word and the right accent and I will move the world.

Joseph Conrad

Edouard Pignon, "The Meeting," © 2005 Artists Rights Society (ARS), New York/ADAGP, Paris.
Photo credit: Reunion des Musées Nationaux/Art Resource, NY

Speaking to Persuade

CHAPTER OUTLINE

Persuasion Defined

Motivating Your Audience: The Psychology of Persuasion

Selecting and Narrowing Your Persuasive Topic

Identifying Your Persuasive Purpose

Developing Your Central Idea as a Persuasive Proposition

Supporting Your Presentation with Credibility, Logic, and Emotion

Organizing Your Persuasive Message

How to Adapt Ideas to People and People to Ideas

Summary

CHAPTER OBJECTIVES

After studying this chapter, you should be able to:

1. Define persuasion and describe four strategies for motivating listeners.

2. Define attitudes, beliefs, and values, and explain why a speaker should know which one he or she is targeting in a persuasive message.

3. Define and provide examples of propositions of fact, value, and policy.

4. Define credibility; analyze its three factors; and describe how to enhance initial, derived, and terminal credibility.

5. Define and provide an example of inductive, deductive, and causal reasoning and reasoning by analogy.

6. List and explain eight logical fallacies.

7. Explain three ways to make emotional appeals in a persuasive presentation.

8. List and explain four ways to organize a persuasive message.

9. List and explain the five steps of the motivated sequence.

10. Provide specific suggestions for adapting to receptive audiences, neutral audiences, and unreceptive audiences.

From ancient times to the present, the skill of persuasion has been highly valued. Consider:

- In ancient Greece, citizens accused of crimes would spend a tidy sum to hire skilled orators to argue their cases before a judge in hopes of gaining their freedom; today, skilled trial lawyers are still well paid, both for their knowledge of the law and for their persuasive skill.
- During the Super Bowl, advertisers spend thousands of dollars per second on TV commercials to persuade you to buy their products.
- It is estimated that during the 2004 U.S. presidential election, George W. Bush spent more than $345 million to persuade the citizens of the United States to vote for him.

But you don't have to be an attorney, an advertiser, or a politician to draw on the highly valued skill of persuasion. Whether you're asking your roommate to help you clean the kitchen, seeking an extension on your term paper, or trying to convince the school board not to raise taxes, you too will need to wield the power to persuade.

In 333 BC, Aristotle was among the first to write a comprehensive guide to persuasion. His work, *The Rhetoric*, was used by other Greek and Roman writers who sought to summarize principles and strategies of persuasion. The chapter you are reading draws on some of that more-than-2000-year-old classic advice and updates it with contemporary research. We first define persuasion, noting how it is similar to and different from informing others, and then describe how persuasion works by explaining how to motivate an audience. We'll also offer suggestions for developing a persuasive speech; present ideas to help you organize your persuasive message; and provide methods to help you move an audience with your credibility, use of logic, and use of emotional appeals. Finally, although we hope that all of the audiences you face are receptive to your persuasive speeches, we'll help you adapt your message not only to receptive audiences but also to those who are neutral or unreceptive.

PERSUASION DEFINED

Persuasion is the process of attempting to change or reinforce attitudes, beliefs, values, or behavior. When we persuade, we are inviting someone to modify or maintain the way he or she thinks, feels, or behaves.

In the previous chapter, we described strategies for informing others—presenting new information so that others will understand and remember what is communicated. Because informative speaking and persuasive speaking are related, we will build on the suggestions we offered for informing others. Like an informative presentation, a persuasive presentation needs to be well organized; to have a clear beginning, middle, and end; to use interesting supporting material; to have smooth transitions; and to be skillfully delivered. As a persuasive speaker, you will need to develop arguments supported with evidence. But in a persuasive presentation, the speaker invites the listener to make an explicit choice, rather than just offering information about the options. Also, when you persuade, you will do more than teach; you will ask your audience to respond thoughtfully to the information you present. Persuasive speakers intentionally try to change or reinforce their listeners' feelings, ideas, or behavior.

Coercive communication, unlike persuasive communication, takes away an individual's free choice. In the opening pages of this book we suggested that an effective communicator not only is understood and achieves his or her goal, but also is ethical. Using force to achieve your goal is **coercion**, not persuasion. Using weapons, threats, and other unethical strategies may momentarily achieve what you want, but it certainly is not appropriate or ethical to use such means. Efforts to persuade should be grounded in giving people options rather than forcing them to respond in a certain way.

persuasion
The process of attempting to change or reinforce a listener's attitudes, beliefs, values, or behavior.

coercion
The use of force to get another person to think or behave as you wish; coercion is unethical because it takes away free choice.

To be ethical, the persuader has an obligation to be honest and forthright in crafting messages.

Now that you have an understanding of what persuasion is and isn't, you undoubtedly have questions about how to begin to develop a persuasive message. You start your preparation for a persuasive presentation as you begin preparing for any speech, by considering the needs, interests, and background of your audience. Ethically adapting to listeners is important in any communication situation, but is especially important when persuading others.

The audience-centered model of public speaking, introduced in Chapter 11 and shown again in Figure 15.1, can help you design and deliver a persuasive presentation just as it can an informative one. Audience analysis is at the heart of the speech-making process; it affects every choice you make as a speaker. Before we talk about the nuts and bolts of developing a persuasive presentation, we'll describe the psychology of persuasion—what motivates an audience to respond to your persuasive appeal. Understanding how an audience is likely to respond to your message not only can help you to develop your presentation, but also can help you be a smarter consumer of persuasive messages that come your way.

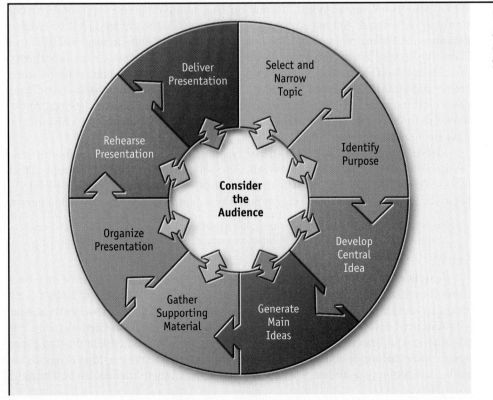

FIGURE 15.1
An Audience-Centered Model of the Presentational Speaking Process

What can you do to motivate your audience to act in a certain way? You might try to create cognitive dissonance, appeal to their needs or fears, or promise a positive result if they follow your advice.

MOTIVATING YOUR AUDIENCE: THE PSYCHOLOGY OF PERSUASION

How does persuasion work? What makes you dial the phone to have a piping hot cheese-and-pepperoni pizza delivered to your door after watching a television commercial for pizza? What motivates people to do things that they wouldn't do unless they were persuaded to do so? Let's look at four explanations of why people respond to efforts to persuade.

Motivating with Dissonance

When you are presented with information that is inconsistent with your current thinking or feelings, you experience a kind of mental discomfort called **cognitive dissonance**. For example, if you frequently drive while you are drowsy, and then you learn that drowsy driving is a major contributor to traffic accidents, dissonance theory predicts that you will experience cognitive dissonance. The incompatibility between your behavior and your new knowledge will make you feel uncomfortable. And your discomfort may prompt you to change your thoughts, likes or dislikes, feelings, or behavior so that you can restore your comfort level or sense of balance—in this case, by not driving when drowsy.

Skilled persuasive speakers know that creating dissonance and then offering their listeners a way to restore balance is an effective persuasive strategy. For example, Sean wants to persuade his listeners to take greater safety precautions in preparing food. He begins by focusing on the health threat posed by bacteria in even the cleanest kitchens:

Verbal

> Right now, as you sit and listen to me speak about kitchen bacteria, millions of them are probably reproducing in your kitchen, simply waiting for the perfect opportunity to join you for lunch.[1]

Sean is deliberately creating dissonance. He knows that his audience members value their health and that they have always assumed their kitchens to be relatively clean. His next task is to restore the audience's sense of balance. He assures them that solutions exist and that "they are simple and you can start them as early as today."[2] If the audience implements such simple actions as washing hands frequently, using paper towels, and washing sponges and dishcloths along with the dishes, then they can resolve their dissonance and once again feel secure about their kitchen safety. The need

cognitive dissonance
The sense of mental disorganization or imbalance that may prompt a person to change when new information conflicts with previously organized thought patterns.

to resolve dissonance provides one explanation of why people may respond to a speaker's attempts to persuade.

Motivating with Needs

Need is one of the best motivators. When you go shopping for a new pair of shoes because the heel has come off your old pair, you are much more likely to buy shoes than is someone who is just browsing. As a speaker, the better you understand what your listeners need, the better you can adapt to them and the greater the chances that you can persuade them to change an attitude, belief, or value, or get them to take some action.

Adapt

The classic theory that outlines our basic needs was developed by Abraham Maslow.[3] If you've taken a psychology course, you have undoubtedly encountered this theory, which has important applications for persuasion. Maslow suggested that a **hierarchy of needs** motivates the behavior of all people. Basic physiological needs (such as needs for food, water, and air) have to be satisfied before we attend to any other concern. Once our physiological needs are met, we think next about safety needs. We need to feel safe and to be able to protect those we love. Comfortable and secure, we attend next to social needs, including the needs to be loved and to belong to a group. The next level of need is the need for self-esteem, or to think well of ourselves. Finally, if these first four levels of need have been satisfied, we may attend to the need for self-actualization, or achieving our highest potential. Figure 15.2 illustrates Maslow's classic five levels of needs, with the most basic at the bottom.

As a persuasive speaker, understanding and applying the hierarchy of needs helps you to adapt to your audience. One practical application is to do everything in your power to ensure that your audience's physiological needs are met. For example, if your listeners are sweating and fanning themselves, they are unlikely to be very interested in whether Bigfoot exists or whether the city should re-open River Park. If you can turn on the air-conditioning or fans, you will stand a greater chance to persuade them.

Another way in which you can apply the need hierarchy is to appeal to an audience's basic needs. For example, Mike knows that most of his audience members have young friends or family members who routinely ride school buses. As he begins to talk about the problem of safety hazards on school buses, he appeals to the audience's need to protect those they love. Similarly, at one time the U.S. Army used the recruiting slogan "Be all that you can be" to tap into the need for self-actualization, or achievement of one's highest potential.

hierarchy of needs
Abraham Maslow's classic theory that humans have five levels of needs and that lower-level needs must be met before people can be concerned about higher-level needs.

FIGURE 15.2
Maslow's Hierarchy of Needs

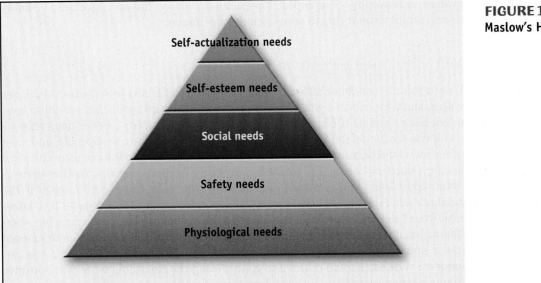

Motivating with Fear Appeals

Verbal

One of the oldest ways to convince people to change their minds or their behavior is by scaring them into compliance. Fear works. The appeal to fear takes the form of a verbal message—an "if-then" statement. *If* you don't do X, *then* awful things will happen to you. "If you don't get a flu shot, then you will probably catch the flu." "If you don't wear a seatbelt, then you are more likely to die in an automobile accident." "If you don't vote for me, then my opponent in this election will ruin the country." These are examples of fear appeals. A variety of research studies support the following strategies for effectively using fear as a motivator.[4]

- *A strong threat to a family member or someone whom members of the audience care about will often be more successful than a fear appeal directed at the audience members themselves.* Here's an example: "If your parents don't have a smoke alarm in their house, they are ten times more likely to die in a house fire."
- *The more respected the speaker, the greater the likelihood that the appeal to fear will work.* If you're trying to motivate your audience with fear, you may not have the credibility to convince them that the threat will harm them, but you could use the opinion of someone who is highly believable, competent, and trustworthy. Quoting a doctor if you're talking about a health issue, or an award-winning teacher if you're talking about an education issue, will probably be more effective than just stating your own opinion when trying to motivate with fear.
- *Fear appeals are more successful if you convince your audience that the threat is real and will affect them unless they take action.* In trying to convince her audience to eat less fat and exercise more, Doreen said, "An overly fatty diet coupled with lack of exercise is the primary cause of heart disease in the United States. Eat less fat and get more exercise, or you may die prematurely."
- *Increasing the intensity of a fear appeal increases the likelihood that the fear appeal will be effective; this is especially true if the listener can take the action the persuader is suggesting.*[5] Research findings suggest that the more fear and anxiety produced by a message, the more likely it is that the listener will respond. Strong, credible fear appeals seem to work better than mild fear appeals if evidence exists to support the claim.

Fear appeals work based on the theory of cognitive dissonance and Maslow's need theory. The fear aroused creates dissonance. Taking action reduces the fear and can meet a need—such as to live a long life, to be safe from harm, to have good friends, or to have a fulfilling career.

Of course, you have an ethical responsibility not to overstate your case or fabricate evidence when using a fear appeal. The persuader always has an ethical responsibility to be truthful when trying to arouse fear in the listener.

Motivating with Positive Appeals

Verbal

From a political candidate's TV ad: "Vote for me and you'll have lower taxes and higher wages, and your children will be better educated." Does this politician's promise have a familiar ring to it? It sounds like what most politicians offer—better days ahead if you'll vote for the person you see on your TV screen. Politicians, salespeople, and most other successful persuaders know that one way to change or reinforce your attitudes, beliefs, values, or behavior is to use a positive motivational appeal. Positive motivational appeals are verbal messages promising that good things will happen if the speaker's advice is followed. The key to using positive motivational appeals is to know what your listeners value. Most Americans value a comfortable, prosperous life; stimulating, exciting activity; a sense of accomplishment; world, community, and personal peace; and overall happiness and contentment. In a persuasive presentation, you can motivate your listeners to respond to your message by describing what good, positive things will happen to them if they follow your advice.

SELECTING AND NARROWING YOUR PERSUASIVE TOPIC

With a basic understanding of how persuasion works, we're ready to focus on the specifics of developing a persuasive talk. As with any presentation, after you've thought about your audience, the next step is to select and narrow your topic. In a communication class, you may be given some latitude in selecting your topic. The best persuasive topic is one about which you feel strongly. If your listeners sense that you are committed to and excited about your topic, the chances are greater that they will be interested and involved as well. In most nonclassroom persuasive-speaking situations, you probably won't be asked to pick a persuasive topic; your topic will stem from your personal convictions. When you have the flexibility of selecting your own topic, the principle of appropriately adapting messages to others can guide your choice. Know the local, state, national, and international issues that interest and affect your listeners. Should the city build a new power plant? Should convicted child molesters be permitted to live in any neighborhood they like? Should the United States drop economic sanctions against Cuba? These and other controversial issues make excellent persuasive speech topics. Avoid frivolous topics, such as "why you should make your own potholders," when so many important issues challenge the world and your listeners.

Aware
Adapt

Pay particular attention to print and electronic media so that you remain informed about important issues of the day. Daily newspapers and national weekly news magazines such as *Time, Newsweek,* and *U.S. News & World Report* can suggest potential persuasive topics. Another interesting source of controversial issues is talk radio; both local and national programs can provide ideas for persuasive topics. Chat rooms on the Internet and home pages of print and broadcast media can also provide ideas for persuasive presentations.

Verbal

After you have chosen a topic for your persuasive message, keeping up with the media can give you additional ideas for narrowing your topic and for finding interesting and appropriate supporting material for your presentation.

IDENTIFYING YOUR PERSUASIVE PURPOSE

Once you have a topic for your persuasive presentation, your next step is to identify both a general and a specific purpose. The general purpose is easy—to persuade. The specific purpose requires more thought. The way you word your specific purpose will help you focus your message. When your general purpose is to persuade, your specific purpose will target your audience's attitudes, beliefs, values, or behavior. You can, as you recall from our definition of persuasion, try to *reinforce* attitudes, beliefs, values, and behavior the audience already holds; or you can try to *change* their attitudes, beliefs, values, or behavior. Reinforcing what an audience already knows or thinks is relatively easy, but it is more of a challenge to change their minds. To increase your chances for success, it is important to be aware of the differences among attitudes, beliefs, and values and to know which one you are targeting in your specific purpose statement. Let's examine the terms *attitude, belief,* and *value* in more detail.

Aware

An **attitude** is a learned predisposition to respond favorably or unfavorably to something. In other words, attitudes represent likes and dislikes. Because many attitudes are formed quickly and often with little evidence, they are relatively susceptible to change if the person who holds them is exposed to additional evidence or gains more experience. For example, we may like a song we hear on the radio, then decide after we buy the single that we don't really like it so well after all. We may think that we don't like spinach, then discover that a friend's Florentine dip is delicious. As a persuasive speaker, you would probably have a good chance to succeed if your specific purpose targeted audience attitudes about the following issues:

attitude
A learned predisposition to respond favorably or unfavorably to something; a like or dislike.

- At the end of my presentation, the audience will favor making downtown streets one way to regulate traffic flow.
- At the end of my presentation, the audience will agree that the community needs a new elementary school.

A **belief** is the way in which we structure our perception of reality—our sense of what is true or false. Perhaps you believe that the earth is round, that God exists, and that your local bank is a financially sound institution. We base our beliefs on our own past experiences and on the experiences of other people. Beliefs are more difficult to alter than attitudes. If your audience were skeptical, you would need a great deal of evidence to succeed with these specific purpose statements:

- At the end of my presentation, the audience will testify that ghosts exist.
- At the end of my presentation, the audience will acknowledge that the increase in highway traffic deaths is related to the increase in the speed limit for large trucks.

A **value** is an enduring conception of right or wrong, good or bad. If you value something, you classify it as good or desirable and its opposite or its absence as bad or wrong. If you do not value something, you are indifferent to it. Values determine your behavior and goals. For example, because you value honesty, you refuse to cheat on a test. Because you value freedom, you support asylum for political refugees. Values are stable and deeply ingrained. Although it is not impossible to change the values of an audience, it is much more difficult than trying to change attitudes or beliefs. Political and religious points of view are especially difficult to modify. If you were speaking to a right-wing conservative Republican audience, you would find it difficult to achieve these specific purposes:

- At the end of my presentation, the audience will campaign for the Democratic ticket in the upcoming election.
- At the end of my presentation, the audience will support the right of art museums to show whatever kinds of art the museum directors deem appropriate.

Figure 15.3 illustrates that attitudes lie fairly close to the surface of our convictions, with values the most deeply ingrained in the center of the model. Be aware of whether your specific purpose aims to change or reinforce an attitude, a belief, a value, or a behavior, and be realistic in assessing what you will need to do in your presentation to effect change.

belief
A sense of what is true or false.

value
An enduring conception of right or wrong, good or bad.

FIGURE 15.3
Comparing Attitudes, Beliefs, and Values
Attitudes—our likes and dislikes—are more likely to change than are our beliefs or values. Our sense of what is right and wrong—our values—are least likely to change.

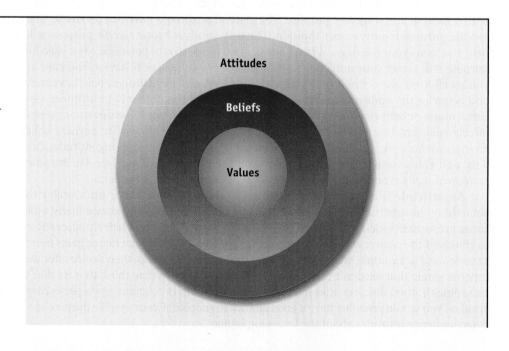

DEVELOPING YOUR CENTRAL IDEA AS A PERSUASIVE PROPOSITION

After clarifying their specific purpose, most persuasive speakers find it useful to cast their central idea as a **proposition**, or statement with which they want their audience to agree. A well-worded proposition is a verbal message that can help you further fine-tune your persuasive objective and develop strategies for convincing your audience that your proposition is true. There are three categories of propositions: propositions of fact, propositions of value, and propositions of policy. Let's examine each of these types in more detail.

Verbal

Propositions of Fact

Propositions of fact are claims that something is or is not the case or that something did or did not happen. A speaker who used a proposition of fact as the central idea of a persuasive presentation would focus on changing or reinforcing an audience's beliefs—what they think is true. Propositions of fact can become central ideas for persuasive speeches. Here are some examples:

> U.S. foreign embassies and consulates are vulnerable to terrorist attacks.
> Nuclear power plants are safe and efficient.
> People who were abused by their parents are more likely to abuse their own
>   children.

A speech based on one of these propositions would need to include credible evidence to support the accuracy of the conclusion.

Propositions of Value

As the word *value* suggests, **propositions of value** call for the listener to judge the worth or importance of something. A simple example would be "Tattoos are beautiful." Other value propositions compare two ideas, things, or actions and suggest that one is better than the other. Here are two examples:

> Small high schools are better than large high schools.
> Rock music is better than classical music.

Propositions of Policy

The third type of proposition, the **proposition of policy**, advocates a specific action—changing a regulation, procedure, or behavior. Propositions of policy include the word *should*. Here are some examples:

> All first-year college students should have their own laptop computers.
> The Honors Program should have a full-time faculty coordinator.
> The city should build a new public library.

The speaker who develops a proposition of policy is often likely to go one step beyond influencing an audience's attitudes, beliefs, and values, and urge them to take action.

With your specific purpose and central idea in hand, you are ready to move to the next stages in the presentational speaking process. In most cases, you can draw your main ideas from several *reasons* the persuasive proposition is true. Then you will be ready to begin gathering supporting material.

proposition
A claim with which you want your audience to agree.

proposition of fact
A claim that something is or is not the case or that something did or did not happen.

proposition of value
A claim that calls for the listener to judge the worth or importance of something.

proposition of policy
A claim advocating a specific action to change a policy, procedure, or behavior.

RECAP

Persuasive Propositions

Type of Proposition	Definition	Example
Proposition of Fact	A claim that something is or is not the case or that it did or did not happen	Asbestos exists in our elementary school.
Proposition of Value	A claim that calls for the listener to judge the worth or importance of something	Using calculators for elementary math is a good idea.
Proposition of Policy	A claim advocating a specific action to change a policy, procedure, or behavior	Casino gambling should be legalized in all states.

SUPPORTING YOUR PRESENTATION WITH CREDIBILITY, LOGIC, AND EMOTION

Aristotle defined *rhetoric* as the process of "discovering the available means of persuasion."[6] What are those "available means"? They are the various strategies you can use to support your message. Aristotle suggested three: (1) emphasizing the credibility or ethical character of a speaker (he called this **ethos**); (2) using logical arguments (**logos**); and (3) using emotional appeals to move an audience (**pathos**).

Ethos: Establishing Your Credibility

If you were going to buy a new computer, to whom would you turn for advice? Perhaps you would consult your brother, the computer geek, or your roommate, the computer science major. Or you might seek advice from *Consumer Reports*, the monthly publication of studies of various consumer products. In other words, you would turn to a source that you consider knowledgeable, competent, and trustworthy—a source you think is credible.

Credibility is an audience's perception of a speaker's competence, trustworthiness, and dynamism. It is not something a speaker inherently possesses or lacks; rather, it is based on the listeners' attitude toward the speaker. Your listeners, not you, determine whether you have credibility.

Teachers and researchers have for centuries sought to understand the factors audiences consider in deciding whether a speaker is credible. Aristotle thought that a public speaker should be ethical, possess good character, display common sense, and be concerned for the well-being of his audience. Quintilian, a Roman teacher of public speaking, advised that a speaker should be "a good man speaking well." These ancient speculations about the elements that enhance a speaker's credibility have been generally supported by modern research.

One clear factor in credibility is **competence**. A speaker should be informed, skilled, or knowledgeable about the subject he or she is discussing. You will be more persuasive if you can convince your listeners that you know something about your topic. How? You can use verbal messages effectively by talking about relevant personal experience with the topic. If you have taken and enjoyed a cruise, you can tell your audience about the highlights of your trip. You can also cite evidence to support your ideas. Even if you have not taken a cruise yourself, you can be prepared with information about what a good value a cruise is—how much it costs and what is included, versus how much the same tour would cost if one were to travel by air and stay and eat in hotels.

ethos
The credibility or ethical character of a speaker.

logos
Logical arguments.

pathos
Emotional appeals.

credibility
An audience's perception of a speaker's competence, trustworthiness, and dynamism.

competence
An aspect of a speaker's credibility that reflects whether the speaker is perceived as informed, skilled, and knowledgeable.

Bono uses his charismatic speaking style to help persuade his audience to support his cause.

A second factor in credibility is **trustworthiness**. While delivering a speech, you need to convey honesty and sincerity to your audience. You can't do this simply by saying, "Trust me." You have to earn trust. You can do so by demonstrating that you are interested in and experienced with your topic. Again, speaking from personal experience makes you seem a more trustworthy speaker. Conversely, having something to gain by persuading your audience may make you suspect in their eyes. That's why salespeople and politicians often lack credibility. If you do what they say, they will clearly benefit by earning sales commissions or being elected to public office.

A third factor in credibility is a speaker's **dynamism**, or energy. Dynamism is often projected through delivery. Applying the communication principle of effectively using and understanding nonverbal messages, a speaker who maintains eye contact, has enthusiastic vocal inflection, and moves and gestures purposefully is likely to be seen as dynamic. **Charisma** is a form of dynamism. A charismatic speaker possesses charm, talent, magnetism, and other qualities that make the person attractive and energetic. President Franklin Roosevelt and Diana, Princess of Wales, were considered charismatic speakers by many people.

trustworthiness
An aspect of a speaker's credibility that reflects whether the speaker is perceived as believable and honest.

dynamism
An audience's perception that a speaker is energetic.

charisma
Talent, charm, and attractiveness.

Diversity and *Communication*

"Elementary Reasoning, My Dear Watson"

Although we often use the word *diversity* to refer to readily discernible differences in sex, race, culture, and age, *diversity* can also refer to differences in perspective or point of view. As the following narrative shows, people may draw different conclusions from the same evidence.

Sherlock Holmes and Dr. Watson went on a camping trip. After a good meal and a bottle of wine, they lay down for the night and went to sleep. Some hours later, Holmes awoke and nudged his faithful friend.

"Watson, look up at the sky and tell me what you see."

Watson replied, "I see millions and millions of stars."
"What does that tell you?" inquired Holmes.

Watson pondered for a minute. "Astronomically, it tells me that there are millions of galaxies and potentially billions of planets. Astrologically, I observe that Saturn is in Leo. Horologically, I deduce that the time is approximately a quarter past three. Theologically, I can see that God is all powerful and that we are small and insignificant. Meteorologically, I suspect that we will have a beautiful day tomorrow. What does it tell you?"

Holmes was silent for a minute, then spoke. "Watson, you idiot! Someone has stolen our tent!"

Nonverbal

Adapt

Verbal
Nonverbal
Listen and Respond

A speaker has opportunities throughout a presentation to enhance his or her credibility. The first such opportunity results in **initial credibility**. This is the impression of your credibility your listeners have even before you begin speaking. They grant you initial credibility based on such factors as your appearance and your credentials. Dressing appropriately and having a brief summary of your qualifications and accomplishments ready for the person who will introduce you are two strategies for enhancing your initial credibility.

The second credibility-building opportunity yields **derived credibility**. This is the perception your audience forms as you deliver your presentation. If you appropriately adapt your message to your audience, you will enhance your derived credibility. Specific strategies include establishing common ground with your audience, supporting your arguments with evidence, and presenting a well-organized message.

The last form of credibility, called **terminal credibility**, is the perception of your credibility your listeners have when you finish your presentation. A thoughtfully prepared and well-delivered conclusion can enhance your terminal credibility, as can maintaining eye contact through and even after your closing sentence. Also, apply the communication principle of listening and responding thoughtfully to others. Be prepared to answer questions after your presentation, regardless of whether a question-and-answer period is planned.

RECAP

Enhancing Your Credibility

Enhancing Your Initial Credibility: Before You Speak
- Dress appropriately.
- Have a brief summary of your qualifications and accomplishments ready for the person who will introduce you.

Enhancing Your Derived Credibility: As You Speak
- Establish common ground with your audience.
- Support your arguments with evidence.
- Present a well-organized message.

Enhancing Your Terminal Credibility: After You Speak
- Prepare your conclusion, and deliver it well.
- Maintain eye contact through and even after your closing sentence.
- Be prepared to answer questions after your presentation.

initial credibility
The impression of a speaker's credibility that listeners have before the speaker begins to speak.

derived credibility
The impression of a speaker's credibility based on what the speaker says and does during the presentation.

terminal credibility
The final impression listeners have of a speaker's credibility after the presentation has been concluded.

proof
Evidence plus reasoning.

evidence
Material used to support a point or premise.

reasoning
The process of drawing a conclusion from evidence.

Logos: Using Evidence and Reasoning

In addition to being considered a credible speaker, you will gain influence with your audience if you can effectively use logically structured arguments supported with evidence. As we noted earlier, Aristotle called logical arguments *logos*, which, translated from Greek, means "the word." Using words effectively to communicate your arguments to your listeners is vital to persuading thoughtful and informed listeners. The goal is to provide logical **proof** for your arguments. Proof consists of both evidence and reasoning. **Evidence** as another word for the illustrations, definitions, statistics, and opinions that are your supporting material. **Reasoning** is the process of drawing conclusions from your evidence. There are three major ways to draw logical conclusions: inductively, deductively, and causally.

Inductive Reasoning

Reasoning that arrives at a general conclusion from specific instances or examples is known as **inductive reasoning**. You reason inductively when you claim that a conclusion is probably true because of specific evidence. For example, if you were giving a speech attempting to convince your audience that Hondas are reliable cars, you might use inductive reasoning to make your point. You have a 1994 Honda Civic that has 140,000 miles on it and has required little repair other than routine maintenance. Your brother has a Honda Accord and has driven it twice as long as any other car he has ever owned. Your mom just returned from a 3000-mile road trip in her Honda Odyssey minivan, which performed beautifully. Based on these specific examples, and bolstered by statistics from many other Honda owners, you ask your audience to agree that your general conclusion is probable: Hondas are reliable cars.

Reasoning by analogy is a special type of inductive reasoning. An analogy demonstrates how an unfamiliar idea, thing, or situation is similar to something the audience already understands. If you develop an original analogy, rather than quote one you find in a printed source, you are reasoning inductively. Here's an example of reasoning by analogy: The new mandatory rear seatbelt laws that were enacted in Missouri saved lives; Kansas should also develop mandatory rear seatbelt laws. The key to arguing by analogy is to claim that the two things you are comparing (such as driving habits in Missouri and Kansas) are similar, so that your argument is a sound one. Here's another example: England has a relaxed policy toward violence being shown on television and has experienced no major rise in violent crimes; the United States should therefore relax its policy on showing violence on TV.

Deductive Reasoning

Reasoning from a general statement or principle to reach a specific conclusion is called **deductive reasoning**. Deductive reasoning can be structured as a **syllogism**, a three-part argument that consists of a major premise, a minor premise, and a conclusion. In a message in which you are attempting to convince your audience to vote for an upcoming school bond issue, your syllogism might look like this:

MAJOR PREMISE: Keeping schools in good repair extends the number of years that the buildings can be used.

MINOR PREMISE: The proposed school bond issue provides money for school repairs.

CONCLUSION: The proposed school bond issue will extend the number of years that we can use our current buildings.

Contemporary logicians note that when you reason deductively, your conclusion is certain rather than probable. The certainty of the conclusion rests primarily on the validity of the major premise and secondarily on the truth of the minor premise. If you can prove that keeping schools in good repair extends the useful life of the buildings, and if it is true that the proposed bond issue provides money for school repairs, then your conclusion will be certain.

Causal Reasoning

You use **causal reasoning** when you relate two or more events in such a way as to conclude that one or more of the events probably caused the others. For example, you might argue that public inoculation programs during the twentieth century eradicated smallpox.

As we noted when we discussed cause-and-effect as a persuasive organizational strategy, there are two ways to structure a causal argument. One is by reasoning from cause to effect, or predicting a result from a known fact. You know that you have had an inch of rain over the last few days, so you predict that the aquifer level will rise. The inch of rain is the cause; the rising aquifer is the effect. The other way to structure a causal argument is by reasoning from a known effect to the cause. National Transportation Safety Board accident investigators

Verbal

inductive reasoning
Using specific instances or examples to reach a probable general conclusion.

reasoning by analogy
A special kind of inductive reasoning that draws a comparison between two ideas, things, or situations that share some essential common feature.

deductive reasoning
Moving from a general statement or principle to reach a certain specific conclusion.

syllogism
A three-part way of developing an argument; includes a major premise, a minor premise, and a conclusion.

causal reasoning
Relating two or more events in such a way as to conclude that one or more of the events caused the others.

Holocaust survivor, author, and human rights activist Elie Wiesel uses the rhetorical devices of evidence and reasoning to appeal to his audiences.

reason from effect to cause when they reconstruct airplane wreckage to find clues to the cause of an air disaster.

The key to developing any causal argument is to be certain that a causal relationship actually exists between the two factors you are investigating. A few summers ago, a young science student was involved in a project involving counting chimney swifts in a given area just before sunset. He counted the most swifts on the Fourth of July. However, it would not have been valid to argue that fireworks (or watermelon or hot dogs or anything else connected with the Fourth of July) caused an increase in the number of chimney swifts seen in the area. The Fourth of July holiday and the bird count were not related by cause and effect.

Trying to establish a causal link where none exists is one type of **logical fallacy**. Unfortunately, not all people who try to persuade you will use sound evidence and reasoning. Some will try to develop arguments in ways that are irrelevant or inappropriate. To be a better-informed consumer, as well as a more ethical persuasive speaker, you should be aware of some of the following common logical fallacies.

Aware

RECAP

Inductive, Deductive, and Causal Reasoning

Type of Reasoning	Reasoning begins with . . .	Reasoning ends with . . .	Conclusion is . . .	Example
Inductive	specific examples	a general conclusion	probable or not probable	Dell, Gateway, and IBM computers are all reliable. Therefore, PCs are reliable.
Deductive	a general statement	a specific conclusion	certain or not certain	All professors at this college have advanced degrees. Tom Bryson is a professor at this college. Therefore, Tom Bryson has an advanced degree.
Causal	something known	a speculation about causes or effects of what is known	likely or not likely	The number of people with undergraduate degrees has risen steadily since 1960. This increasing number has caused a glut in the job market for people with degrees.

logical fallacy
False reasoning that occurs when someone attempts to persuade without adequate evidence or with arguments that are irrelevant or inappropriate.

causal fallacy
Making a faulty cause-and-effect connection between two things or events.

Causal Fallacy   Trying to link the Fourth of July with the chimney swift count is an example of a **causal fallacy**, or, to use its Latin term, *post hoc, ergo propter hoc* ("after this; therefore, because of this"). Simply because one event follows another does not mean that the two are related.

Bandwagon Fallacy   "Jumping on the bandwagon" is a colloquial expression for thinking or doing something just because everybody else is. Someone who argues that "everybody thinks that, so you should too" is using the **bandwagon fallacy**. Speakers using the bandwagon fallacy often use the word *everybody:*

> Everybody knows that taxes are too high.
> Everybody agrees that the government should support a
> strong military.

Either-Or Fallacy   "Either we support the bond issue, or we end up busing our students to another school district!" shouts Lupe in a moment of heated debate among the members of the school board. This **either-or fallacy** ignores the fact that there may be other solutions to the district's problem of dilapidated buildings (for example, purchasing portable classroom buildings or drawing new attendance zones within the district).

Hasty Generalization   A person who tries to draw a conclusion from too little evidence or nonexistent evidence is making a **hasty generalization**. For example, one person's failing a math test does not necessarily mean that the test was too difficult or unfair.

Personal Attack   Using a **personal attack** as a substitute for a refutation of issues is a logical fallacy. This approach is also known as an *ad hominem* argument, a Latin phrase that means "to the man." "The HMO bill is a bad idea because it was proposed by that crazy senator" is an example of a personal attack. Don't dismiss an idea solely because you have something against the person who presents it.

Red Herring   Someone who argues against an issue by bringing up irrelevant facts or arguments is using a **red herring**. This fallacy takes its name from the old trick of dragging a red herring across a trail to distract dogs who are following a scent. Speakers use a red herring when they want to distract an audience from certain issues. For example, a congressional representative who has been indicted for misuse of federal funds calls a press conference and spends most of the time talking about a colleague's sexual indiscretions.

Appeal to Misplaced Authority   When advertisers trot out baseball players to endorse breakfast cereal and movie stars to pitch credit cards, they are guilty of an **appeal to misplaced authority**. Although baseball players may know a great deal about the game of baseball, they are no more expert than most of us about cereal. Movie stars may be experts at acting but probably are not in the field of personal finance.

Non Sequitur   If you argue that students should give blood because it is nearly time for final exams, you are guilty of a **non sequitur** (Latin for "it does not follow"). Your reason has nothing to do with your argument.

Persuasive speakers who provide logical proof (evidence and reasoning) for their arguments and who avoid logical fallacies heighten their chances for success with their audience. But good speakers know that evidence and reasoning are not their only tools. Emotion is another powerful strategy for moving an audience to support a persuasive proposition.

Pathos: Using Emotion

People often make decisions based not on logic but on emotion. Advertisers know this. Think of the soft-drink commercials you see on television. There is little rational reason

On the Web

Besides teaching you how to become more persuasive, one of our goals in this chapter is to help you become a better consumer of persuasive messages that come your way. One of the most important skills a consumer of persuasive messages can have is the ability to spot poorly constructed persuasive arguments. Being able to identify faulty reasoning is especially important. On the following Web site, you'll find several reasoning fallacies, along with examples to help you identify them:

www.philosophypages.com/lg/index.htm

bandwagon fallacy
Suggesting that because everyone believes something or does something, it must be valid, accurate, or effective.

either-or fallacy
Oversimplifying an issue as offering only two choices.

hasty generalization
Reaching a conclusion without adequate supporting evidence.

personal attack
Attacking irrelevant personal characteristics of someone connected with an idea, rather than addressing the idea itself.

red herring
Irrelevant facts or information used to distract someone from the issue under discussion.

appeal to misplaced authority
Using someone without the appropriate credentials or expertise to endorse an idea or product.

non sequitur
Latin for "it does not follow"; an idea or conclusion that does not logically follow the previous idea or conclusion.

that people should spend any part of their food budget on soft drinks. They are "empty calories." So soft-drink advertisers turn instead to emotional appeals, striving to connect feelings of pleasure with their product. Smiling people, upbeat music, and good times are usually part of the formula for selling soft drinks.

Verbal

One way to make an emotional appeal is with emotion-arousing verbal messages. Words such as *mother, flag, freedom,* and *slavery* trigger emotional responses in listeners. Patriotic slogans, such as "Remember the Alamo" and "Give me liberty, or give me death," are examples of phrases that have successfully aroused emotions in their listeners.

Another way to appeal to emotions is by using concrete illustrations and descriptions. Although illustrations and descriptions are themselves types of evidence or supporting material, their impact is often emotional, as in the following example:

> Michelle Hutchinson carefully placed her three-year-old daughter into her child safety seat. She was certain that Dana was secure. Within minutes Michelle was involved in a minor accident, and the seat belt that was never designed to hold a child safety seat allowed the seat to lunge forward, crushing the three-year-old's skull on the dash. Dana died three days later. . . .[7]

Nonverbal

Effective use of nonverbal messages can also appeal to an audience's emotions. Visual aids—pictures, slides, or video—can provide emotion-arousing images. A photograph of a dirty, ragged child alone in a big city can evoke sadness and pain. A video clip of an airplane crash can arouse fear and horror. A picture of a smiling baby makes most of us smile, too. As a speaker, you can use visual aids to evoke both positive and negative emotions.

When you use emotional appeals, you do have an obligation to be ethical and forthright. Making false claims, misusing evidence or images, or relying exclusively on emotion without any evidence or reasoning violates standards of ethical presentational speaking.

RECAP

Tips for Using Emotion to Persuade

- Use emotion-arousing words.
- Use concrete illustrations and descriptions to create emotional images.
- Use visual aids to evoke both positive and negative emotions.
- Be ethical and forthright. Avoid making false claims, misusing evidence or images, or relying exclusively on emotion.

ORGANIZING YOUR PERSUASIVE MESSAGE

Adapt

You already know that how you organize a presentation can have an impact on your listeners' response to your message. Some speakers gather stories, examples, facts, and statistics to achieve their persuasive goal and then develop an organizational structure for these materials. Other speakers organize the presentation first and then collect supporting material. In reality, the organization of your presentation usually emerges after you have done at least some initial research and thinking about both your message and your audience. An audience-centered speaker adapts the organizational structure of the presentation based on the needs, attitudes, beliefs, behaviors, and background of the audience. Most persuasive presentations are organized according to one of four strategies: problem and solution, cause and effect, refutation, or the motivated sequence—a special variation of the problem-and-solution format.

Problem and Solution

Problem-and-solution organization is the most basic organizational pattern for a persuasive presentation. The problem-and-solution strategy works best when a problem can be clearly documented and a solution or solutions proposed to deal with the evils of the problem.

When you use problem-and-solution organization, apply the principle of appropriately adapting messages to others. If you are speaking to an apathetic audience or one that is not even aware that a problem exists, you can emphasize the problem portion of the message. If your audience is already aware of the problem, you can emphasize the solution or solutions. In either case, your challenge will be to provide ample evidence that your perception of the problem is accurate and reasonable. You'll also need to convince your listeners that the solution or solutions you advocate are the most appropriate ones to solve the problem.

Note how Nicholas organizes his presentation, "The Death of Reading," in a problem-and-solution pattern:[8]

I. PROBLEM: Reading is a dying activity.
  A. Each year more than 500 courts hear arguments to ban books.
  B. Since 1990, more than 2000 libraries across America have closed.
  C. Leisure reading has decreased more than 50% since 1975.
II. SOLUTIONS:
  A. Teach children that reading as an activity has worth and beauty.
  B. Teach children that books in and of themselves only express ideas and should not be banned.
  C. Support programs such as "One City, One Book" that encourage community involvement and literary discussion.
  D. Give books as gifts.
  E. Allow others to see you read.

The persuasive presentation at the end of this chapter offers an example of a message organized by first stating the problem and then presenting some specific solutions.

Cause and Effect

A speaker who employs **cause-and-effect organization** can either identify a situation and then discuss the resulting effects (cause-effect), or present a situation and then explore its causes (effect-cause).

Regardless of which variation you choose, you should apply the fundamental principle of being aware of your communication with yourself and others. Specifically, you must analyze and then convince your listeners of the critical causal link. An effect may have more than one cause. For example, standardized test scores may be low in your state both because of low per-pupil expenditures and because of a lack of parental involvement in the schools. To argue that only one of the two factors causes the low test scores would not be accurate. It is also possible for two situations to coexist but not be causally related. Perhaps standardized test scores are indeed low in your state, and your state has a lottery. Both situations exist, but one does not cause the other. However, if two or more situations are causally related, a cause-and-effect strategy can work well for a persuasive presentation. Here is an example of a persuasive outline organized from cause to effect:[9]

I. CAUSE: The foster care system is in crisis.
  A. Since 1987, there has been a 90% increase in the number of children placed in foster care nationally.
  B. During that same time, there has been a 3% decrease in the number of licensed foster homes.
II. EFFECT: Children in foster care are at risk.

Adapt

Aware

problem-and-solution organization
Organization by discussing first a problem and then its various solutions.

cause-and-effect organization
Organization by discussing a situation and its causes, or a situation and its effects.

A. Children in the foster care system are five times more likely to die as a result of abuse than children in the general population.
B. 80% of federal prisoners spent time in the nation's foster care system as children.

Refutation

A third way to organize your efforts to persuade an audience is especially useful when you are facing an unreceptive audience—one that does not agree with your point of view or your specific proposition. **Refutation** is an organizational strategy by which you identify objections to your proposition and then refute those objections with arguments and evidence. You will be most likely to organize your persuasive message by refutation if you know your listeners' chief objections to your proposition. In fact, if you do not acknowledge such objections, the audience will probably think about them during your presentation anyway. Credible facts and statistics will generally be more effective than emotional arguments in supporting your points of refutation.

Suppose, for example, that you plan to speak to a group of junior high school teachers, advocating a school reconfiguration that would eliminate the junior high and send the teachers either to middle school or to high school. They would undoubtedly have some concerns about their own welfare and that of their students, as well as issues of loyalty to their present administrators. You could organize your presentation to this group according to those three issues. Your major points could be as follows:

I. The school reconfiguration will not jeopardize any of your jobs or programs.
II. The school reconfiguration will actually benefit students by requiring fewer changes in schools during their critical pre-adolescent years.
III. Principals and lead teachers will be reassigned at their same levels in the schools to which they will move.

Utilizing refutation as your organizational strategy is one way to adapt your message to your audience.

The Motivated Sequence

The **motivated sequence**, devised by Alan Monroe, is a five-step organizational plan that integrates the problem-and-solution organizational method with principles that have been confirmed by research and practical experience.[10] The five steps involved are attention, need, satisfaction, visualization, and action.

Attention   Your first task in applying the motivated sequence, and the first stage in appropriately adapting your message to others, is to get your listeners' attention. You already know attention-getting strategies for introductions: rhetorical questions, illustrations, startling facts or statistics, quotations, humorous stories, and references to historical or recent events. The attention step is, in essence, your application of one of these strategies.

Sherry begins her presentation about reforming sex offender registries with this attention-catching illustration:

> Maureen Kanka felt her neighborhood was like any other. She never knew danger lurked across the street from her house until her 7-year-old daughter, Megan, disappeared. Megan's body was later found dumped in a nearby park. A puppy had been used to lure Megan into a neighbor's house where she was raped, strangled, and suffocated.[11]

Need   After getting your audience's attention, establish why your topic, problem, or issue should concern your listeners. Tell your audience about the problem. Adapt your message to them by convincing them that the problem affects them directly. Argue that there is a need for change. During the need step (which corresponds to the prob-

Adapt

Adapt

refutation
Organization according to objections your listeners may have to your ideas and arguments.

motivated sequence
Alan H. Monroe's five-step plan for organizing a persuasive message: attention, need, satisfaction, visualization, and action.

lem step in a problem-and-solution strategy), you should develop logical arguments backed by evidence. It's during the need step that you create dissonance or use a credible fear appeal to motivate listeners to respond to your solution. Sherry develops her need step as follows:

> State and local authorities are dismally failing to keep track of convicted child molesters, meaning that thousands of perpetrators like Megan's killer are unidentified, putting millions of children at risk. Problems in sex offender registries are allowing thousands of sexual predators to roam unchecked.[12]

In the final step of Monroe's motivated sequence, the speaker calls for the audience to take action.

Satisfaction   After you explain and document a need or problem, identify your plan (or solution) and explain how it will satisfy the need. You need not go into painstaking detail. Present enough information so that your listeners have a general understanding of how the problem may be solved. Sherry suggests two legislative solutions in her satisfaction step:

> At the government level, federal coordination is a must. A truly national registry needs to be created. However, a national registry alone will not fix the problem. Thus, a second piece of legislation should put coded notations onto sex offenders' driver's licenses and require the licenses to be presented for annual routine automobile registration. Furthermore, license bureaus would be required to contact police when offenders change addresses.[13]

Visualization   Now you need to give your audience a sense of what it would be like if your solution were adopted or, conversely, if it were not adopted. **Visualization**—a word picture of the future—applies the fundamental principle of effectively using and understanding verbal messages. An appropriate presentation aid can also help your audience visualize the implications of your persuasive message. With a **positive visualization** approach, you paint a rosy picture of how wonderful the future will be if your satisfaction step is implemented. With a **negative visualization** approach, you paint a bleak picture of how terrible the future will be if nothing is done; you use a fear appeal to motivate your listeners to do what you suggest to avoid further problems. Or you might combine both approaches: The problem will be solved if your solution is adopted, but things will get increasingly worse if it is not. An ethical speaker takes care to ensure that the positive or negative visualization message is accurate and not overstated. Sherry offers negative visualization to drive home the urgency of her message:

> It is too late to save Megan Kanka. Her parents will never again be met by the joy of her smile and the contributions she could have made to our society will never be fulfilled.[14]

Action   The final step of the motivated sequence requires that you adapt your solution to your audience. Offer them some specific action they can take to solve the problem you have discussed. Identify exactly what you want them to do. Give them simple, clear, easy-to-follow steps. Provide a phone number to call for more information, an address to which they can write a letter of support, or a petition to sign at the end of your presentation. Sherry suggests a specific action step her listeners can take to solve the problem she has identified:

> On a personal level, we can help police follow up on offenders missing from the registry by being on guard and watching for signs of abuse among children in our families and neighborhoods.[15]

The action step is your conclusion. You remind your audience of the problem (need step), give them the solution (satisfaction step), and remind them what great things will happen if they follow your advice (positive visualization) or what bad things will hap-

Verbal

Adapt

visualization
A word picture of the future.

positive visualization
A word picture of how much better things will be if a solution is implemented.

negative visualization
A word picture of how much worse things will be if a solution is not implemented; a fear appeal.

Adapt

pen if they don't do what you say (negative visualization). Finally, unless they are unreceptive to your ideas, tell them what they need to do next (action step).

You can adapt the motivated sequence to your topic and the needs of your audience. For example, if you are speaking to a knowledgeable, receptive audience, you do not need to spend a great deal of time on the need step. Your listeners already know that the need is serious. They may, however, feel helpless to do anything about it. Clearly, you would want to emphasize the satisfaction and action steps.

On the other hand, if you are speaking to a neutral or apathetic audience, you will need to spend time getting their attention and proving that a problem exists, that it is significant, and that it affects them personally. You will emphasize the attention, need, and visualization steps. In the final section of this chapter, we will offer additional strategies for persuading receptive, unreceptive, and neutral audiences.

Is there one best way to organize a persuasive message? The answer is no. The organizational strategy you select must depend on your audience, your message, and your desired objective. What is important is that you remember that your decision can have a major effect on your listeners' response to your message.

HOW TO ADAPT IDEAS TO PEOPLE AND PEOPLE TO IDEAS

Donald C. Bryant's definition of rhetoric emphasizes the principle of appropriately adapting a message to an audience: "Rhetoric" he said, "is the process of adjusting ideas to people and people to ideas."[16] And with this thought we've come full circle in the process of developing a persuasive message. As we have emphasized throughout our discussion of presentational speaking, analyzing your audience and adapting to them is at the heart of the speech-making process; it's one of the fundamental communication principles for a lifetime. In a persuasive presentation, that adaptation begins with identifying your specific purpose and understanding whether you are trying to change or reinforce attitudes, beliefs, values, or behavior. It continues with your selection of an organizational strategy. For example, if your audience members are unreceptive toward your ideas, you might choose to organize your speech by refutation, addressing the audience's objections head-on. Both research studies and experienced speakers can offer other useful suggestions to help you adapt to your audience. Let's look at some specific strategies for persuading receptive, neutral, and unreceptive audiences.

The Receptive Audience

It is usually a pleasure to address an audience that already supports you and your message. You can explore your ideas in depth and can be fairly certain of a successful appeal to action if your audience is receptive.

RECAP

Organizational Patterns for Persuasive Presentations

Organizational Pattern	Definition	Example
Problem and Solution	Organization by discussing a problem and then its various solutions	I. Tooth decay threatens children's dental health. II. Inexpensive, easy to apply sealants make teeth resistant to decay.
Cause and Effect	Organization by discussing a situation and its causes, or a situation and its effects	I. Most HMOs refuse to pay for treatment they deem "experimental." II. Patients die who might have been saved by "experimental" treatment.
Refutation	Organization according to objections your listeners may have to your ideas and arguments	I. Although you may think that college football players get too much financial aid, they work hard for it, spending 20 to 30 hours a week in training and on the field. II. Although you may think that college football players don't spend much time on academics, they have 2 hours of enforced study every weeknight.
Motivated Sequence	Alan H. Monroe's five-step plan for organizing a persuasive message; the five steps are attention, need, satisfaction, visualization, and action	I. Attention: "An apple a day keeps the doctor busy." What has happened to the old adage? Why has it changed? II. Need: Pesticides are poisoning our fresh fruits and vegetables. III. Satisfaction: Growers must seek environmentally friendly alternatives to pesticides. IV. Visualization: Remember the apple poisoned by Snow White's wicked stepmother? You may be feeding such apples to your own children. V. Action: Buy fruits and vegetables raised organically.

Adapt

One suggestion that may help you make the most of such a speaking opportunity is to identify with your audience. Emphasize your similarities and common interests. The introduction of your message may be a good place in which to do this.

Another suggestion is to be overt in stating your speaking objective, telling your audience exactly what you want them to do, and asking audience members for an immediate show of support. If your audience is already receptive, you need not worry that being overt will antagonize them. Rather, it will give you more time to rouse them to passionate commitment and action.

A third suggestion for persuading a receptive audience is to use emotional appeals. If your audience already supports your position, you can spend less time providing detailed evidence. Rather, you can focus on moving your receptive audience to action with strong emotional appeals.

The Neutral Audience

Many audiences will fall somewhere between being wildly enthusiastic and being hostile. They will simply be neutral. Their neutrality may take the form of indifference: They know about the topic or issue, but they don't see how it affects them, or they can't make up their minds about it. Or their neutrality may take the form of ignorance: They just don't know much about the topic. Regardless of whether your neutral audience is indifferent or ignorant, your challenge is to get them interested in your message.

One way to get a neutral audience interested is to "hook" them with an especially engaging introduction or attention step. Brian provided such an introduction to his persuasive presentation about the number of Americans who live with chronic pain:

> "I can't shower because the water feels like molten lava. Every time someone turns on a ceiling fan, it feels like razor blades are cutting through my legs. I'm dying." Meet David Bogan, financial advisor from Deptford, New Jersey; Porsche, boat, and home-owner; and a victim of a debilitating car accident that has not only rendered him two years of chronic leg pain, but a fall from the pinnacle of success. Bogan has nothing now. Life to him, life with searing pain, is a worthless tease of agony and distress.[17]

Another strategy for persuading neutral audiences is to refer to universal beliefs or common concerns. Protecting the environment and having access to good health care might fall in the latter category.

A third strategy for neutral audiences is to show how the topic affects not only them but also people they care about. For example, parents will be interested in issues and policies that affect their children.

Finally, be realistic about what you can accomplish. People who are neutral at the beginning of your presentation are unlikely to change in just a few minutes to having strong opinions. Persuasion is unlikely to occur all at once or after one presentation of arguments and issues.

The Unreceptive Audience

One of your biggest challenges as a speaker is to persuade audience members who are unreceptive toward you or your message. If they are unreceptive toward you personally, your job is to seek ways to enhance your credibility and persuade them to listen to you. If they are unreceptive toward your point of view, several strategies may help.

First, don't immediately announce your persuasive purpose. Immediately and explicitly telling your listeners that you plan to change their minds can make them defensive. Focus instead on areas of agreement. As you would with a neutral audience, refer to universal beliefs and concerns. Instead of saying to your unreceptive audience, "I'm here this morning to convince you that we should raise city taxes," you might say, "I think we can agree that we have an important common goal: achieving the best quality of life possible here in our small community."

Second, if you think your audience may be unreceptive, advance your strongest arguments first. This strategy is the principle of primacy. If you save your best argument for last (the recency principle), your audience may already have stopped listening.

Third, acknowledge the opposing points of view that members of your audience may hold. Summarize the reasons they may oppose your point of view; then cite evidence and use arguments to refute the opposition and support your conclusion. In speaking to students seeking to hold down tuition costs, a dean might say, "I am aware that many of you struggle to pay for your education. You work nights, take out loans, and live frugally." Then the dean could go on to identify how the university could provide additional financial assistance to students.

Finally, as with a neutral audience, don't expect a major shift in attitude from an unreceptive audience. Set a realistic goal. It may be enough for an 8- to 10-minute presentation just to have your listeners hear you out and at least think about some of your arguments.

RECAP

Adapting Ideas to People and People to Ideas

Persuading the Receptive Audience	Persuading the Neutral Audience	Persuading the Unreceptive Audience
• Identify with your audience. • Emphasize common interests. • Provide a clear objective; tell your listeners what you want them to do. • Appropriately use emotional appeals.	• Gain and maintain your audience's attention. • Refer to beliefs and concerns that are important to listeners. • Show how the topic affects people your listeners care about. • Be realistic about what you can accomplish.	• Don't tell listeners that you are going to try to convince them to support your position. • Present your strongest arguments first. • Acknowledge opposing points of view. • Don't expect a major shift in attitudes or behavior.

SAMPLE PERSUASIVE PRESENTATION

William Stephens
Sheridan College

Cruisin' Out of Control[18]

William captures the attention of his listeners with a startling statistic about the number of people who go on cruises annually. His use of the first person ("we") helps him establish common ground with his listeners.

William previews his speech.

William's analogy of a cruise ship as "a floating city" helps listeners comprehend the daily waste that such a ship produces.

William turns next to the harm—the effects—caused by the pollution he has documented.

Each year more than twelve million vacationers pack their bags, head for ocean ports, and embark on cruises. We love the sumptuous banquets, the impeccable service, and especially the pristine scenery. Unfortunately, as the October 2001 *Natural Life* reported, the trips we take are "endangering the very ecosystems [we're] so keen to observe." According to Ross Klein's book *Cruise Ship Blues*, pollution by hundreds of luxury liners sailing the seas is fouling the world's oceans and beaches, destroying vast food supplies on which we depend, threatening endangered species, and spreading deadly diseases.

Today we'll expose the dirty underside of the cruise ship industry, explore reasons these liners continue to pollute our oceans and coastlines, and examine some steps we must take to remedy this shameful situation. Think of a cruise ship—the largest of which carry 5,000 passengers—as a floating city. Each day people shower and flush toilets; crews launder tons of linens; staffs prepare 20,000 meals and dispose of the scraps; photo labs, dry cleaners, and beauty parlors use and toss tanks of toxic chemicals. At the same time, clean-up crews collect countless plastic containers, cardboard boxes, batteries, burned-out fluorescent and mercury vapor light bulbs, and medical wastes. We may assume that this mass of toxic trash is stored in holding bins and processed when the vessels return to port. But according to Oceana, an environmental protection group, we'd be wrong. Why? As the group stated in a February 1, 2003, article, "unlike cities . . . cruise ships are exempt from the . . . Clean Water Act." That means they are virtually free to dump these wastes and pollute at will. And pollute they do! In his book, Klein estimates that each day a large cruise ship produces 500,000 gallons of wastewater and 50,000 gallons of sewage. Ships may discharge gray water from showers, laundry, and dishwashing virtually anywhere. The Environmental Protection Agency discovered that some gray water actually had "higher levels of disease-causing bacteria than raw sewage." The reason? Cruise ships often combine chemical wastes and sewage with the gray water to circumvent regulations about dumping the most harmful products.

In May 2002, the Ocean Conservancy reported that because cruise ships use less water per flush, sewage on cruise ships is more concentrated than that from cities. An October 2003 report jointly published by Blue Water Network and Ocean Advocates confirmed that more than 98% of cruise ships discharge effluents that would be illegal on land. The Conservancy reveals that ballast water, used to stabilize the ship and control its buoyancy, poses another problem. Ships can suck up to thirty tanker trucks of ballast, including marine plants and animals, transport this biological soup thousands of miles, and discharge it, releasing non-native plants and animals to compete with and harm local species. Ballast water also carries diseases like cholera into clean areas.

Every day a cruise ship produces seven tons of garbage and solid waste, which workers often dump directly into the ocean. The damages from such practices are legion. First, according to the Smithsonian Institution's *Ocean Planet*, the polluted coastal water destroys shellfish beds and contaminates oysters, clams, and lobsters. Our next seafood platter may be palatable but poisonous. Second, Smithsonian says the sewage-polluted waters carry viral hepatitis, cholera, typhoid fever, and intestinal diseases. In one recent year, 2,400 United States beaches were temporarily closed because of bacteria. Unfortunately, some coastal states do not even monitor the water quality, and no federal laws require notifying the public of the pollution. Third, *Americas* of July/August 2003 explains that the raw sewage promotes massive growth of algae, which rob the water of oxygen and thus kill fish and other marine

Notice the use of a rhetorical question to provide a transition into William's next main idea.

life. Recently such a huge "dead zone" has developed in the Gulf of Mexico. In addition, Oceana confirms that sewage has destroyed almost 90% of Caribbean coral reefs. Fourth, endangered species are succumbing to cruise ship pollution. For example, the *Anchorage Daily News* of July 22, 2001, reports that such pollutants are killing orcas, or killer whales, in Alaskan waters. In 2000, the orcas monitored were some of the most contaminated marine mammals ever measured. Some contained more than 500 times the level of contaminants considered safe.

How has such a devastating situation evolved? A number of factors have come together to create the disaster. First, laws governing the dumping of waste are inadequate. *Americas* of July/August 2003 reports that international laws are largely non-existent. U.S. laws are weak and applicable only to a narrow band of water along the U.S. coasts. For example, cruise ships may legally dump treated sewage 3 miles off the U.S. coast, but the definition of "treated" is so vague that ships often get away with dumping untreated sewage anywhere. Beyond 12 miles, ships can legally discharge raw sewage, which tides return to soil our shores. Second, the July 12, 2001, *Christian Science Monitor* reveals that most cruise lines register their fleets in foreign countries, exempting themselves from most U.S. laws and taxes. Such avoidance means that you and I, not the polluters, pay the bill for coastal clean-up.

Third, cruise ships openly violate the few laws and voluntary agreements that supposedly regulate them. One of the worst is Royal Caribbean Cruise Lines. Save Our Shores Foundation reports that this giant company's claim to be pro-environment is only a public relations ploy. In reality the line has been fined more than $30 million for illegally discharging oil, garbage, and sewage—and then falsifying its records as a cover-up. Royal Caribbean merely writes off these fines as business expenses and continues to pollute. And because so many regulations are non-binding agreements called Memoranda of Understanding, the October 2003 report *The Cruise Industry and Environmental History and Practice* tells us that the cruise lines feel free to violate them, claiming they are not breaking any laws but merely breaking their word. Rarely are violating ships caught. In fact, companies give financial bonuses to officers who routinely dump their wastes to save disposal and water treatment costs and so return from cruises under budget. Fourth, according to the General Accounting Office, the ships get away with illegal dumping because our Coast Guard, the agency responsible for monitoring compliance and conducting inspections, is so hopelessly over-extended that it can't do an adequate job. It uses less than 1 percent of its resources to monitor cruise ships. In addition, the Guard often schedules its inspections, allowing ships time to conceal illegal activities and falsify logs.

William uses negative visualization of the future as larger and larger cruise ships are launched.

Unfortunately, without extensive reform, the situation will get worse as cruise ships become bigger and more numerous. *The New York Times* of February 1, 2004, reports that the *Queen Mary 2* completed its maiden voyage on January 26. As long as the Empire State Building is high and twenty-three stories tall, the ship is the largest ocean liner yet built. But it won't hold that title for long. *CNN* of January 26, 2004, tells us that Royal Caribbean has ordered an even larger cruise ship scheduled for delivery in two years. *Americas* estimates that in the next 7 years the cruise business will double. Oceana reports that between 2001 and 2005 cruise lines expect to add 36 new ships, increasing the industry's capacity by 45%. What will our coastal waters be like then? Studies published by Bluewater Network and Ocean Advocates in October 2003 reveal that some ship-polluted Alaskan waters already have fecal bacteria levels 100,000 times the allowable standards.

Another rhetorical question serves as a transition to the satisfaction step of the presentation.

So what can we do to remedy this ever-growing threat? Obviously the government must replace the non-binding Memoranda of Understanding with much stricter regulations about cruise ship discharges, especially raw sewage. The *Congressional Record* of April 2, 2004, tells us that Representative Sam Farr of California has just introduced the "Clean Cruise Ship Act of 2004," which closes some of the loopholes in federal law that have allowed cruise lines to escape prosecution for some

SAMPLE PERSUASIVE PRESENTATION (Continued)

William includes himself and his listeners as potential cruise ship passengers who can and should take action. "This concerns you" is his underlying message.

discharges of polluted water. If it can survive the expected powerful lobbying from the cruise industry, its impact could be significant. The bill requires cruise ships operating in U.S. waters to install the latest technology for treating emissions. Some devices, now available and reasonably priced, leave water cleaner than the natural ocean. Oceana estimates that companies could equip their ships with these devices for about $1.50 per passenger per day — about the price of a soft drink.

In addition, Congress must extend the Coast Guard's authority randomly to inspect the cruise ships and their logs. Of course, this extension means that the Guard must increase its budget and employ more inspectors. By levying stiffer fines for the violations, Congress can fund these additional services. You and I also have a part to play. As most of us will someday take a cruise, we must make sure we support responsible cruise lines, not those that repeatedly violate existing laws. In addition, we should support those few cruise lines actually registered in the United States who pay taxes to finance the monitoring and maintenance of coastal waters. According to a personal correspondence from Ross Klein on February 16, 2004, those are Cruise West, Glacier Bay, and American Safari. On board, we should watch for illegal dumping. We can videotape violations and even earn rewards for reporting violators. The *Juneau Empire* carried the story of an engineer who did just that. He reported a Holland American ship for dumping polluted bilge water in Alaska's Inside Passage and earned a half million dollar reward for his vigilance. As U. S. citizens, who comprise 82% of cruise passengers, we can pressure the cruise lines to clean up their act.

Finally, William summarizes his main points as he concludes his presentation.

Today we've exposed the dirty underside of the cruise ship industry, explored some reasons this nasty situation has developed, and finally examined several steps we must take to remedy this dangerous situation. For too long we've allowed the cruise ship industry to make their fortunes at the expense of our environment. It's time we told the cruise lines to shape up or ship out.

PRINCIPLES FOR A LIFETIME: Enhancing Your Skills

Aware

Principle One: Be aware of your communication with yourself and others.

- Know whether your specific purpose is to change or reinforce an attitude, a belief, a value, or a behavior, and be realistic in assessing what you will need to do in your presentation to effect change.
- When you use cause-and-effect organization, you must analyze and then convince your listeners of the critical causal link.
- Relate personal experience to make you seem a more competent and trustworthy speaker.
- Have a brief summary of your qualifications and accomplishments ready for the person who will introduce you, to help enhance your initial credibility.
- To be a better informed consumer of persuasive messages, as well as a more ethical persuasive speaker, be aware of and avoid using common logical fallacies.

Verbal

Principle Two: Effectively use and interpret verbal messages.

- To create negative visualization, describe in detail how bleak or terrible the future will be if your solution is not implemented.
- To create positive visualization, describe in detail how wonderful the future will be if your solution is implemented.
- To select and narrow a topic for a persuasive presentation, pay attention to print and electronic media to help keep you current on important issues of the day.
- Word your central idea as a proposition to help you fine-tune your speaking objective and develop strategies for persuading your listeners.

- To make yourself seem more competent to your audience, cite evidence to support your ideas.
- Prepare a thoughtful conclusion to enhance your terminal credibility.
- Provide logical proof (evidence and reasoning) for your arguments and avoid logical fallacies to heighten your chances for success with your audience.
- Use emotion-arousing words to appeal to an audience's emotions.
- Use concrete illustrations and descriptions to appeal to an audience's emotions.

Nonverbal

Principle Three: Effectively use and interpret nonverbal messages.
- Maintain eye contact, use enthusiastic vocal inflection, and move and gesture purposefully to increase the likelihood that your audience will view you as dynamic.
- Dress appropriately to enhance your credibility.
- Maintain eye contact through and even after your closing sentence to enhance your terminal credibility.
- Use presentation aids to help evoke both positive and negative emotions as well as positive and negative visualization.

Listen and Respond

Principle Four: Listen and respond thoughtfully to others.
- Be prepared to answer questions after your presentation, regardless of whether there is a planned question-and-answer period.

Adapt

Principle Five: Appropriately adapt messages to others.
- Do everything possible to ensure that your audience's physiological and safety needs are met.
- To motivate an audience, appeal to their basic needs.
- If you are speaking to an apathetic audience or one that is not even aware that a problem exists, emphasize the problem portion of your problem-and-solution presentation.
- If your audience is aware of the problem you are discussing, emphasize the solution or solutions in your problem-and-solution presentation.
- Acknowledge and then refute the opposing points of view held by an unreceptive audience.
- In the need step of your motivated-sequence presentation, establish why your topic, problem, or issue should concern your listeners. Convince your audience that the problem affects them directly.
- In the action step of the motivated sequence, offer your audience members specific action they can take to solve the problem you have discussed.
- If you are speaking to a knowledgeable, receptive audience, do not spend a great deal of time on the need step of the motivated sequence; instead, emphasize the satisfaction and action steps.
- If you are speaking to a neutral audience, emphasize the attention, need, and visualization steps of the motivated sequence.
- Establish common ground with your audience.
- Consider the background and cultural expectations of your listeners as you develop your persuasive purpose.
- Make the most of your opportunity to speak to a receptive audience by identifying with them.
- If your audience is receptive, state your speaking objective overtly, tell your audience exactly what you want them to do, and ask audience members for an immediate show of support.
- Use emotional appeals with a receptive audience.
- Appeal to universal beliefs and concerns to persuade a neutral audience.
- Show a neutral audience how your topic affects both them and those they love.
- Be realistic about what you can accomplish with neutral and unreceptive audiences.
- Focus on areas of agreement with an unreceptive audience.
- If your audience is unreceptive, advance your strongest arguments first.

SUMMARY

Persuasion is the process of attempting to change or reinforce attitudes, beliefs, values, or behaviors. Several theories suggest how persuasion works—how listeners may be motivated to respond to a persuasive message. Cognitive dissonance is a sense of mental disorganization or imbalance that arises when new information conflicts with previously organized thought patterns. Cognitive dissonance may prompt a person to change attitudes, beliefs, values, or behavior. Maslow's classic hierarchy of needs is another approach that attempts to explain why people may be motivated to respond to persuasive appeals to various levels of need. Both fear appeals and positive motivational appeals can also motivate listeners to respond to your persuasive message.

Preparing and presenting a persuasive message require the same general approach as preparing any other kind of presentation. When you have a choice of persuasive topics, select a topic that is of interest to you and your listeners. Your specific purpose will target your audience's attitudes, beliefs, values, or behavior. Attitudes are learned predispositions to respond favorably or unfavorably toward something. A belief is one's sense of what is true or false. Values are enduring conceptions of right or wrong, good or bad. Of the three, attitudes are most susceptible to change; values are least likely to change. After clarifying your specific purpose, you can word your central idea as a proposition of fact, value, or policy.

Ways to organize your persuasive message include problem and solution, cause and effect, refutation, and the motivated sequence. The motivated sequence includes five steps: attention, need, satisfaction, visualization, and action.

A key to persuading others is to establish your credibility as a speaker. Credibility is an audience's perception of a speaker's competence, trustworthiness, and dynamism. Enhancing your initial credibility (what you do before you speak), your derived credibility (what you do during your presentation), and your terminal credibility (what you do after your presentation) will help you improve your overall credibility as a presentational speaker.

Reasoning, the process of drawing a conclusion from evidence, is integral to the persuasive process. The three primary types of reasoning are inductive, deductive, and causal. You can also reason by analogy. You can be an effective and ethical persuader by avoiding reasoning fallacies such as the causal fallacy, the bandwagon fallacy, the either-or fallacy, hasty generalization, personal attack, red herring, appeals to misplaced authority, and non sequiturs.

In addition to persuading others because of who you are (ethos) or how well you structure your logical arguments (logos), you can also move an audience to respond by using emotional appeals (pathos).

Finally, be prepared to adapt your persuasive messages to receptive, neutral, and unreceptive audiences. Throughout the persuasive speaking process, being aware of your messages and others' messages, effectively using verbal and nonverbal messages, listening and responding to your audience, and adapting to your listeners can enhance your skill as a persuasive speaker.

Discussion and Review

1. Where might you turn if you needed ideas for a topic for a persuasive presentation?
2. Define attitudes, beliefs, and values. Why is it important that a persuasive speaker know which one he or she is targeting in a persuasive presentation?
3. What is a proposition of fact? Give one original example.
4. What is a proposition of value? Give one original example.
5. What is a proposition of policy? Give one original example.
6. List and explain four ways to organize a persuasive presentation.
7. When would you be most likely to organize a presentation by refutation?
8. List and explain the five steps of the motivated sequence.
9. What is credibility?
10. Define initial, derived, and terminal credibility, and explain how to enhance each one.

11. Define and provide an example of inductive reasoning.
12. How is reasoning by analogy different from using an analogy as supporting material?
13. Define and provide an example of deductive reasoning.
14. Define and provide an example of causal reasoning.
15. List and explain eight logical fallacies.
16. How can you appeal to your listeners' emotions in a persuasive presentation?
17. What is cognitive dissonance? How can you apply the theory in a persuasive presentation?
18. List and explain the five levels of Maslow's hierarchy of needs. How can you apply the theory in a persuasive presentation?
19. Provide specific suggestions for adapting to receptive audiences, neutral audiences, and unreceptive audiences.

Putting Principles into Practice

1. Watch a C-SPAN, CNN, or network news broadcast of a politician arguing for or against a particular proposition. Decide whether it is a proposition of fact, value, or policy. Identify the organizational pattern and the persuasive strategies the speaker uses.

2. Identify three nationally or internationally known speakers whom you consider to be credible. Analyze why these speakers are credible, according to the three components of credibility.

3. Identify the logical fallacy in each of the following arguments:

   - We must raise taxes to finance the construction of new streets. Otherwise, we will have to rely on four-wheel-drive vehicles to get around.
   - Breaking that mirror this morning was the reason I did so poorly on my history test.
   - Everybody knows that you can't get a decent summer job around here.
   - You should be concerned about your grade in that class because your new part-time job pays well.
   - Jane grew up in a state that spends less money on education than any state in the United States; she could not possibly have any useful ideas about how to improve our children's test scores on standardized tests.

4. Develop a specific purpose statement and central idea for a persuasive message. Describe strategies you would use if you were to give this presentation to a receptive audience. Identify strategies you would use if you were to give this presentation to a neutral audience. Finally, suggest strategies you would use if you were to give this presentation to an unreceptive audience.

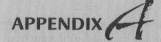

Interviewing

APPENDIX A OUTLINE

The Nature and Types of Interviews

Interview Structure

How to Be Interviewed for a Job

How to Be Interviewed in an Information-Gathering Interview

The Responsibilities of the Interviewer

Summary

APPENDIX A OBJECTIVES

After studying this appendix, you should be able to:

1. Describe what an interview is.

2. Identify five different kinds of interview goals.

3. Identify and discuss the important elements of being interviewed for a job.

4. Develop a clear, well-worded resumé.

5. Identify and discuss the important elements of participating in an information-gathering interview.

6. Explain how to conduct an interview.

The stakes are often high when you participate in an interview. If you are interviewing for a job, your career and perhaps your future rest on the impression you make. If someone is interviewing you to gather information, the accuracy of what you say can have a powerful impact on others. Or if you are the person who is conducting the job interview, you have much to gain or lose; your choice of a new employee will affect the success of the organization. If you're interviewing someone to gather information, your credibility is at stake if you pass on or publish information that later proves to be false or inaccurate.

In this introduction to interviewing, we'll discuss communication strategies that can enhance your job interview skills and offer tips about how to participate in an information-gathering interview. We conclude the appendix by identifying strategies that can help you polish your talents if you are the person interviewing others. Whether you are a recent high school graduate or have been in the work force for several years and have come back to school to finish your degree and pursue a new career, the principles for a lifetime that we've emphasized in this book can help you enhance your interviewing skills.

THE NATURE AND TYPES OF INTERVIEWS

An **interview** is a form of oral interaction structured to achieve a goal, which often involves just two people, but could include more than two people, who take turns speaking and listening. An effective interview is not a random conversation but occurs when the person conducting the interview has carefully framed the objectives of the interview and developed a structured plan for achieving the objectives. The person being interviewed should also prepare by considering the kinds of questions he or she may be asked and being ready to give appropriate responses.

When many people think of the term *interview*, the most common image that comes to mind is a job interview. Yet interviews can also be means of gathering information, sharing job performance feedback, solving problems, and persuading others. Even though we are focusing primarily on employment and information-gathering interviews, the strategies we present can help you with *any* interview situation.

Information-Gathering Interview

Information-gathering interviews, just as the name suggests, are designed to seek information from the person being interviewed. Public-opinion polls are one type of information-gathering interview. When you leave an organization, you may be asked to participate in an exit interview, an interview designed to assess why you are leaving the company. A reporter for a newspaper, radio, or TV station interviews people to gather information for a story or broadcast.

Those most skilled at conducting information-gathering interviews do their homework before the interview. They come prepared with specific questions and have already conducted background research. In addition to preparing questions, a skilled information-gathering interviewer listens and develops questions that stem from the information that is shared during the interview.

Appraisal Interview

An **appraisal interview,** sometimes called a performance review, occurs when a supervisor or employer shares information with you about your job performance. Such an interview enables you to see how others perceive your effectiveness and helps you determine whether you are likely to get a promotion or a "pink slip." During an appraisal interview you can typically express your observations about the organization and your goals for the future. Usually a supervisor begins by preparing a written report summarizing your strengths and weaknesses, then meets with you to review it.

When receiving feedback from a supervisor, the best approach is to listen and gather as much objective information about his or her perceptions as possible. In an evaluation situation, especially if the feedback is negative, it is easy to become defensive; try to manage your emotions and use the information to your benefit instead. If you disagree with your supervisor's evaluation, consider using the conflict management skills we discussed in Chapter 8. In addition, provide specific examples to support your position. Just saying you don't like the review is likely to do more harm than good.

Problem-Solving Interview

A **problem-solving interview** is designed to resolve a problem that affects one or both parties involved in the interview. A disciplinary interview to consider corrective action toward an employee or students is one type of problem-solving interview. Grievance interviews are also problem-solving interviews; one person brings a grievance or complaint against another person, and solutions are sought to resolve the problem or conflict.

---

interview
A form of oral interaction structured to achieve a goal; it involves two or more people, who take turns speaking and listening.

information-gathering interview
An interview, such as an opinion poll, whose purpose is to seek information from another person.

appraisal interview
An interview during which a supervisor or employer shares information with an employee about his or her job performance.

problem-solving interview
An interview such as a grievance or disciplinary interview that is designed to solve a problem.

By using all the communication skills you have learned in this course, you just might land that all-important first job.

The strategies for structuring a problem-solving group discussion that we presented in Chapter 10 can also help you organize a problem-solving interview. Before seeking to solve or manage a problem, first define the issues, and then analyze the causes, history, and symptoms of the problem. Rather than focusing on only one solution, brainstorm several possible solutions and then evaluate the pros and the cons of the potential solutions before settling on a single solution.

Persuasion Interview

During a **persuasion interview,** one person seeks to change or reinforce the attitudes, beliefs, values, or behavior of another person. The sales interview is a classic example of an interview in which the goal is to persuade. A political campaign interview is another example of a persuasion interview.

Our discussion in Chapter 15 of the principles and strategies of persuading others can help you prepare for a persuasion interview. The advantage of trying to persuade someone during an interview rather than in a speech is the size of the audience; during a persuasive interview, you may have an audience of one. It is especially important to analyze and adapt to your listener when seeking to persuade.

Job Interview

A **job interview** is a focused, structured conversation whose goal is to assess the credentials and skills of a person for employment. The job interview may involve elements of each of the types of interviews we've already discussed. Information is both gathered and shared; it will certainly solve a problem if you're the one looking for a job and you are hired. Elements of persuasion are also involved in a job interview. If you are seeking a job, you're trying to persuade the interviewer to hire you; if you are the interviewer and you're interviewing an exceptionally talented person, your job is to persuade the interviewee to join your organization.

The planned or structured nature of an interview sets it apart from other communication situations. Yet interviews may sometimes include elements of interpersonal, group, and presentational communication. Interviews embody interpersonal communication in that there are two or more people participating in the interview who must establish a relationship. If the goal of the interview is to find a solution to a vexing prob-

persuasion interview
An interview that attempts to change or reinforce attitudes, beliefs, values, or behavior, such as a sales interview.

job interview
A focused, structured conversation whose goal is to assess the credentials and skills of a person for employment.

lem, the interview may resemble elements of a group discussion in which a problem is defined and analyzed and solutions are generated, evaluated, and then implemented. Preparing for a job interview is like a public speaking situation; you focus on your audience (the interviewer), keep your purpose in mind as you research the company you're interviewing with, organize your ideas, and even rehearse your responses to questions you think you may be asked.

Regardless of the purpose or format of an interview, the five communication principles for a lifetime that we've used to organize our discussion of interpersonal, group and team, and presentational communication situations will serve you well when you participate in an interview. Whether you are the interviewer or the interviewee, it is important to be aware of how you are coming across to others. Using and interpreting verbal and nonverbal messages are critical to participating in a successful interview. In our definition of an interview, we noted that all individuals involved both talk and listen. Unless you can adapt your messages to others, you won't be successful. Effective interview participants are able to listen, respond, and speak extemporaneously, rather than delivering overly scripted, planned messages. Adapting to others is essential.

Aware
Verbal
Nonverbal
Listen and Respond
Adapt

INTERVIEW STRUCTURE

Just as a speech or term paper has a beginning, middle, and end, so does a well-structured interview. Most interviews have three phases:

1. *The opening:* The interviewer tries to put the interviewee at ease and presents an overview of the interview agenda.
2. *The body:* During the longest part of an interview, the interviewer asks questions, and the interviewee listens and responds. The interviewee may also ask questions.
3. *The conclusion:* The interviewer summarizes what will happen next and usually gives the interviewee an opportunity to ask any final questions.

It is the responsibility of the person leading the interview to develop a structure for the interview. But it's helpful for the interviewee to understand the overall structure of an interview in advance in order to know what to expect both before and during the interview. So, whether you're the interviewer (regardless of the type of interview) or the interviewee, understanding the interview structure we discuss should be of value to you.

The Opening

The opening of any interview is crucial because it creates a climate for positive and open communication. When interviewing someone, you should strive to establish rapport and clarify the goals of the interview.

To establish rapport, start the conversation with something that will put the interviewee at ease. The discussion could be about something as simple as the weather, recent events both of you attended, or other light topics. Making direct eye contact, smiling appropriately, and offering a firm handshake all help establish a warm atmosphere.

Besides making the interviewee comfortable, the interviewer should clarify the goals of the interview by explicitly stating the general purpose for the meeting. After the opening conversation, it may be helpful to provide a general overview of the nature and purpose of the interview and an estimate of how long the interview will last. Clarifying a meeting's purpose helps both parties get their bearings and check their understanding. A good interviewer makes sure that everyone is on the same wavelength before the actual questioning begins.

Arrive for the interview a few minutes ahead of the scheduled hour. Be prepared, however, to wait patiently, if necessary. If you are the interviewer and have decided to use a recorder, set it up. You may keep it out of sight once the interviewee has seen it, but *never* try to hide a recorder at the outset—such a ploy is unethical and illegal. If you are going to take written notes, get out your paper and pen. Now you are ready to begin asking your prepared questions.

The Body: Asking Questions

Once the interviewee is at ease during the opening of the interview, the bulk of the interview will consist of the interviewer asking the interviewee questions. If an interviewer has done a good job of identifying and clarifying his or her objectives and gathering information, the key questions to be asked usually are fairly obvious. But what kinds of questions are they?

Question Types   An interview is conducted as a series of questions and responses. Even though both parties listen and speak, the interviewer has the primary responsibility for questioning. Interview questions fall into one of four categories: open, closed, probing, or hypothetical.[1] A typical interview usually includes some of each type.

Open Questions   **Open questions** are broad and basically unstructured. Often they indicate only the topic to be considered and allow interviewees considerable freedom to determine the amount and kind of information they will provide.

Because they encourage the interviewee to share information almost without restriction, open questions are useful to determine opinions, values, and perspective. Such questions as "What are your long- and short-term career goals?" or "Why do you seek employment here?" or "How do you feel about gun control?" prompt personal and wide-ranging responses.

Closed Questions   **Closed questions** limit the range of possible responses. They may ask for a simple yes or no—"Do you enjoy working in teams?"—or they may allow interviewees to select responses from a number of specific alternatives: "How often do you go to the movies? (1) Less than once a month, (2) Once a month, (3) Twice a month, (4) Once a week." Closed questions enable the interviewer to gather specific information, by restricting interviewees' freedom to express personal views or elaborate on responses. Closed questions are most often used when an interviewer is trying to obtain a maximum amount of information in a short period of time.

Probing Questions   **Probing questions** encourage interviewees to clarify or elaborate on partial or superficial responses. Through the use of these questions, interviewers attempt to clarify or direct responses. Such questions as "Could you elaborate on your coursework in the area of communication?" "Do you mean to say that you already own three vacuum cleaners?" and "Will you tell me more about your relationship with your supervisor?" call for further information in a particular area. Often spontaneous, probing questions follow up on the key questions that interviewers have prepared in advance.

Hypothetical Questions   Interviewers use **hypothetical questions** to describe a set of conditions and ask interviewees what they would do if they were in those situations. Such questions are generally used either to gauge reactions to emotion-arousing or value-laden circumstances or to reveal on interviewee's likely responses to real situations. A police officer might ask an eyewitness to a murder, "What if I told you that the man you identified as the murderer in the line-up was the mayor?" During an exit interview, a personnel manager might ask, "If we promoted you to Chief Sanitary Engineer and paid you $4 an hour more, would you consider staying with Bob's Landfill and Television Repair?"

open question
Question that is broad and unstructured and that allows the respondent considerable freedom to determine the amount and kind of information provided.

closed question
A question that limits the range of possible responses and requires a simple, direct, and brief answer.

probing question
A question that encourages the interviewee to clarify or elaborate on partial or superficial responses and that usually directs the discussion in a desired direction.

hypothetical question
A question used to gauge an interviewee's reaction to an emotion-arousing or value-laden situation or to reveal an interviewee's likely reactions to a real situation.

RECAP

Types of Interview Questions

	Uses	Example
Open Question	Prompts wide-ranging responses. Answers reveal interviewee's opinions, values, perspectives.	Tell me about your previous job duties. How would you describe your son's problems in school?
Closed Question	Requests simple yes or no response or forces interviewee to select a response from limited options.	Have you been skiing in the past month? Which one of the following drinks would you buy? (a) Coke (b) Pepsi (c) 7-Up
Probing Question	Encourages clarification of or elaboration on previous responses. Directs responses in a specific direction.	Would you tell me more about the pain in your side? We've talked about your mother. Can you describe how you felt about your father's long absences from home when you were a child?
Hypothetical Question	Gauges reactions to emotional or value-laden situations. Elicits response to a real or imaginary situation.	How would you support your opponent if she were elected chair of the board? What would you do if your secretary lost an important file?

Questioning Sequences   Open, closed, probing, and hypothetical questions may be used in any combination, as long as their sequence is thoughtfully planned. Depending on the purpose, these questions may be arranged into three basic sequences: funnel, inverted funnel, and tunnel.

The Funnel Sequence   The **funnel sequence** begins with broad, open questions and proceeds to more closed questions (see Figure A.1). The advantage of this format is that it allows an interviewee to express views and feelings without restriction, at least early in an interview. For example, it may be more useful to begin a grievance interview with the question, "How would you describe your relationship with your supervisor?" instead of asking, "What makes you think your supervisor treats you like an idiot?" The first question allows the free expression of feelings, while the second question clearly reflects an interviewer's bias, immediately forcing the discussion in a negative direction. The following series of questions provides an example of a funnel sequence that might be used for an information-gathering interview.

1. Why do you find communication interesting?
2. What area of communication are you primarily interested in?
3. How long have you studied interpersonal communication?

funnel sequence
A questioning sequence that begins with broad, open questions and proceeds toward more closed questions.

FIGURE A.1
The Funnel Sequence

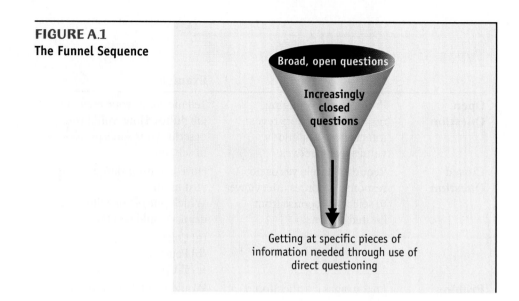

Broad, open questions

Increasingly closed questions

Getting at specific pieces of information needed through use of direct questioning

4. Why do you think interpersonal attraction theory is useful?
5. What would you do to test interpersonal attraction theory?

Notice that the questions start by asking for general information and then focus on more specific ideas.

The Inverted Funnel Sequence   Just the opposite of the funnel sequence, the **inverted funnel sequence** begins with closed questions and proceeds to more open questions (Figure A.2). An interview designed to gather information about a worker grievance might be based on the inverted funnel and might include the following series of questions:

1. Do you believe that your supervisor wants to fire you?
2. What makes you think you'll be fired soon?
3. What do you think has caused this problem between you and your supervisor?
4. How has this problem affected your work?
5. How would you describe the general working climate in your department?

The relatively closed questions that begin the inverted funnel sequence are intended to encourage an interviewee to respond easily, because they require only brief answers (yes or no, short lists, and the like). As the sequence progresses, the questions become more open and thus require more elaborate answers and greater disclosure.

The inverted funnel sequence is appropriate when an interviewer wants to direct the interview along specific lines and encourage an interviewee to respond with short, easily composed answers. An interviewer can follow up with more general questions to provide increasingly broad information—the "big picture," so to speak.

The Tunnel Sequence   Finally, the **tunnel sequence** consists of a series of related open or closed questions or a combination of the two; the sequence is intended to gather a wide range of information. This sequence does not include probing questions; it goes into less depth than the other three sequences. An interviewer may use the tunnel sequence to gather information about attitudes and opinions without regard for the reasons behind an interviewee's answers or the intensity of his or her feelings. The following is a typical tunnel sequence:

1. What are the three major issues in the presidential campaign this year?
2. Which candidate would you vote for if the election were held today?

inverted funnel sequence

A questioning sequence that begins with closed questions and proceeds to more open questions, intended to encourage an interviewee to respond easily early in the interview.

tunnel sequence

A way of structuring interview questions so that parallel open or closed questions (or a combination of open and closed questions) are asked to gather a large amount of information in a short amount of time; no probing questions are asked.

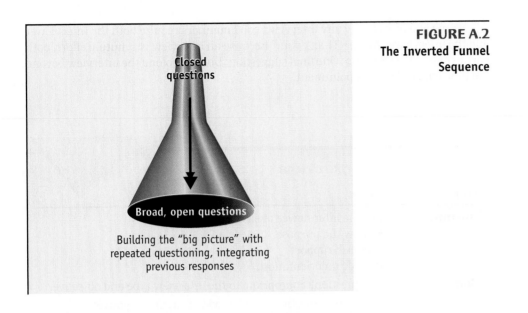

FIGURE A.2
The Inverted Funnel Sequence

Closed questions

Broad, open questions

Building the "big picture" with repeated questioning, integrating previous responses

3. For whom do you think you will vote in the race for U.S. Senator?
4. Are you a registered voter in this state?
5. What do you think of the proposition to set up a nuclear waste dump in this state?

The tunnel sequence is most appropriate when an interviewer wants some general information on a variety of topics in a relatively short period of time.

Although these sequences have been discussed as if they were independent and easily distinguishable, good questioning strategy will probably combine one or more question sequences. The key to effective interviewing is to prepare a set of questions that will get the needed kinds and amount of information. An interviewer should remain flexible enough to add, subtract, and revise questions as a discussion proceeds. Such an approach ensures that the objectives of the interview will be accomplished.

As you conduct the interview, use the questions you have prepared as a guide but not a rigid schedule. If the person you are interviewing mentions an interesting angle you did not think of, don't be afraid to pursue the point. Listen carefully to the person's answers, and ask for clarification of any ideas you don't understand.

The Conclusion

Opinion polls, marketing surveys, and sales pitches often end rather abruptly with a "Thank you for taking the time to help me out." Many other kinds of interviews require follow-up meetings or some form of future contact, however. For this reason, and for reasons of common courtesy, the conclusion of an interview is very important.

A primary function of the conclusion is to summarize the proceedings. All parties should be aware of and agree on what happened during the meeting. To ensure understanding and agreement, an interviewer summarizes the highlights of the discussion, asking for and offering clarification, if necessary.

Another function of the conclusion is to encourage continued friendly relations. The positive communication climate developed during the interview should be carried into the conclusion. You may need to establish interpersonal harmony if you asked questions that resulted in conflict or made the interviewee uncomfortable. Comments such as "I'm glad we had a chance to talk about this problem" or "Thank you for sharing and listening" enable both parties to feel that they have had a positive and productive encounter. An interviewer can tell the other person when to expect further contact or action, if appropriate. A job applicant wants to know when to expect a phone call about a follow-up interview or a job offer. An expert, interviewed by a journalist, wants to know what will be done with her comments and when the story is likely to be published.

At the end of virtually any interview, good manners require both the interviewer and the interviewee to say "Thank you." Because an interview is a mutual effort, both parties deserve recognition. One final suggestion: Do not prolong the interview beyond the time limits of your appointment.

RECAP

Organizing an Interview

Step	Goals
Opening	Put the interviewee at ease. Review the purpose. Establish rapport. Provide an orientation.
Body	Use questions appropriate to the interview type and objective. • Use open questions to elicit wide-ranging responses. • Use closed questions to get specific responses. • Use probing questions to seek clarification or elaboration. • Use hypothetical questions to gauge a reaction to an imaginary situation. Design questioning sequences appropriate to the interview purpose. • Use the funnel sequence to elicit general comments first and specific information later. • Use the inverted funnel sequence to elicit specific information first and more general comments later. • Use the tunnel sequence to gather lots of information without probing too deeply.
Conclusion	Summarize the proceedings. Encourage friendly relations. Arrange further contact(s). Exchange thank-yous.

HOW TO BE INTERVIEWED FOR A JOB

It's been said that a major element in being successful in life is just showing up—but we suggest that you do more than just show up for a job interview. Giving a speech involves considerable preparation. Like a speech, a successful job interview involves thoughtful preparation and careful planning.

Be Aware of Your Skills and Abilities

Aware

The first communication principle we introduced in this book is to be aware of your communication. Before you interview for a job, it is important to be aware not only of your communication as you interact with others, but also of your unique skills, talents, and abilities. Many people select a career because they think they might like to *be* a lawyer, doctor, or teacher. But rather than thinking about what you want to be, we suggest considering what you like to *do*. Ask yourself these questions:

- What do I like to do in my free time?
- What are my best skills and talents?
- What education and training do I have?
- What experiences or previous jobs have I had?

In addition to these questions, write down responses to complete this statement: "I can . . . ." For example, you might respond: "I can cook, write, relate well to others." List as many answers as possible. Here's another statement to complete: "I have . . . ." "I have traveled, worked on a farm, sold magazine subscriptions." Responding to the "I can" and "I have" statements will help you develop an awareness of your skills and experiences that will help you respond readily when you are asked about them during the interview. Reflecting on your interests can help you decide which career will best suit your talents; you will also be able to develop a resumé that reflects your best abilities.

Verbal

Prepare Your Resumé

A **resumé** is a written, concise, well-organized description of your qualifications for a job. How long should a resumé be? Many employers don't expect a resumé to be longer than two pages; some will look only at a one-page resumé. (Resumés of experienced career professionals may be longer than two pages, however.) Although your resumé is important in helping you land a job, its key function is to help you get an interview—it's how you perform in the interview that determines whether you get the job. Employers rarely hire someone based only on a resumé. Most employers spend less than a minute—and some only a few seconds—looking at each resumé. Therefore, your resumé should be clear and easy to read and should focus on the essential information an employer seeks.

Most employers will be looking for standard information on your resumé. Study the sample resumé that appears in this chapter.[2] Here's a list of the essential pieces of information that should be included on your resume.

- *Personal information:* Employers will look for your name, address, phone numbers, e-mail address, and a Web page address (if you have one). Provide phone numbers where you can be reached during both the day and the evening.
- *Career objective:* Many employers will want to see your career objective. Make it brief, clear, and focused. You may need to customize your career objective for the different positions you seek.
- *Education:* Include your major, your degree, your graduation date, and the institution you attended.
- *Experience:* Describe your relevant work experience, listing your most recent job first. Include the names of employers, dates when you worked, and a very brief description of your duties.
- *Honors and special accomplishments:* List any awards, honors, offices held, or other leadership responsibilities.
- *Optional information:* If you have volunteer experience, have traveled, or have computer skills or other pertinent experience, be sure to include it if it is relevant to your objective and the job.
- *References:* List the names, phone and fax numbers, and e-mail addresses of people who can speak positively about your skills and abilities. Or you may indicate that your references are available on request.

When developing your resumé, be sure to use specific action verbs to describe your experience. Also use these action words during your interview. Rather than using a general verb such as "I *worked* on a project," use more descriptive action words that clarify the role you assumed. Consider using some of the following words when listing or describing your activities or accomplishments:

resumé
A written, concise, well-organized description of a person's qualifications for a job.

SAMPLE RESUMÉ

MARK SMITH
3124 West Sixth Street
San Marcos, TX 78666
(512)555-0102
(512)555-0010

PROFESSIONAL OBJECTIVE:
Seeking a position in human resources as a training specialist.

EDUCATION:
Bachelor of Arts degree
Major: Communication Studies
Minor: English
Texas State University–San Marcos
Graduation date: May 20XX

PROFESSIONAL EXPERIENCE:
20XX–Present, Intern, GSD&M, Austin, Texas.
Assisted in creating a leadership training program. Wrote copy for flyers and display ads. Made cold calls to prospective clients. Position required extensive use of desktop publishing programs.

20XX–August 20XX, Intern, Target Market, Houston, Texas.
Developed sales training seminar. Coordinated initial plan for writing advertising copy for Crest Inc.'s advertising campaign.

20XX–20XX, Supervisor, S&B Associates, San Marcos, Texas.
Supervised three employees editing training materials.

20XX–20XX, Advertising Sales and Reporter, *University Star*, San Marcos, Texas. Sold ads for university paper and worked as social events reporter.

OTHER EXPERIENCES:
20XX–20XX, Summer jobs and part-time work.

SKILLS:
20XX–20XX, Team Leadership, Photography, Computer Proficiency, Research and Analysis, Public Speaking, Customer Service.

ACCOMPLISHMENTS AND HONORS:
Paid for majority of my college education while maintaining a 3.5 grade point average, Presidential Scholarship, Vice President of Texas State University Communication Club, Editor/Historian of MortarBoard, John Marshall High School Vice President of Junior Class, Yearbook Coordinator.

PROFESSIONAL ORGANIZATIONS:
Lambda Pi Eta, American Society for Training and Development, Communication Club, National Communication Association.

INTERESTS:
Photography, tennis, softball, theatre.

REFERENCES:
Available at your request.

accelerated	evaluated	planned
accepted	expanded	promoted
accomplished	expedited	proposed
achieved	facilitated	provided
adapted	found	recommended
administered	generated	reduced
analyzed	guided	researched
approved	improved	resulted in
built	increased	reviewed
completed	influenced	revised
conceived	initiated	selected
conducted	instructed	solved
controlled	interpreted	stimulated
coordinated	maintained	structured
created	managed	supervised
delegated	mastered	tested
demonstrated	motivated	trained
designed	negotiated	translated
developed	operated	traveled
directed	organized	updated
effected	originated	utilized
eliminated	participated	won

Identify the Needs of Your Employer

After you have analyzed your skills and abilities and prepared a well-crafted resumé, you need to be audience centered, to anticipate the needs and goals of your potential employer. A good interviewee adapts his or her message to the interviewer.

Adapt

How do you find out information about an organization that will help you adapt your message to fit the needs of the organization? In a word, research. Gather as much information as you can about not only the person who will interview you but the needs and goals of the organization or company where you seek a job. Most libraries include books and articles about organizations both large and small. Typical library resources that include information about major corporations include:

- *The Information Please Business Almanac and Sourcebook*
- *Louis Rukeyser's Business Almanac*
- *Standard and Poor's Register of Corporations, Directors, and Executives*
- *The Job Vault: The One-Stop Job Search Resource*

Virtually every organization these days has a Web page. Explore the information available on the Web. Do more than just look at the organization's home page; explore the various hyperlinks that help you learn about what the organization does.

What determines whether you are hired for the job? The short answer to this question is "the way you communicate." By the time you get to an interview, your interviewer has already determined that you have at least minimum qualifications for the job. Your ability to apply the communication principles for a lifetime that we've reiterated throughout the book is key to making a good impression on your interviewer. In Chapter 1, when discussing why it's important to learn about communication, we noted the key factors that employers look for in a job applicant; the top three factors focus on your communication skill.[3] Your ability to listen, respond, and relate to your interviewer is one of the best predictors of whether you will be hired for a job.

As you prepare for the interview, don't forget about the power of nonverbal messages in making a good impression, which we discussed in Chapter 4. Dressing for success is important. Most experts suggest you dress conservatively and give special attention to your grooming. For most professional positions, men will be expected to

Nonverbal

wear a coat and tie or a suit and well-polished shoes. Women will be expected to wear a dress, suit, or other coordinated attire.

Besides assessing your appearance and your ability to communicate, interviewers consider several other traits

Listen and Respond

- *Self-expression:* Are you clear or vague when you respond to questions? Do you have effective eye contact? Do you talk too much or too little?
- *Maturity:* Are you likely to make good judgments and effective decisions?
- *Personality:* What's your overall style of relating to people? Are you outgoing, shy, quiet, overbearing, enthusiastic, warm, friendly?
- *Experience:* Can you do the job? Do you have a track record that suggests you can effectively do what needs to be done?
- *Enthusiasm:* Do you seem interested in this job and the organization? Do you seem to be genuine and authentic, or is your enthusiasm phony?
- *Goals:* Where are you heading in life? Are your short-term and long-term goals compatible with the needs of the organization?

Listen, Respond, and Ask Appropriate Questions

Listen and Respond

Because an interview is a structured, planned discussion, it is important to demonstrate effective listening and responding skills. Stay focused on what your interviewer is asking you. Remember to stop, look, and listen for both the details of the questions and the major points of the questions.

When you respond to questions, you should project genuine enthusiasm and competence. Don't put on an act: be yourself while being professional. Be friendly and pleasant without being overly effusive or giddy.

One of the best ways to prepare for an interview is to anticipate the interviewer's questions. Table A.1 lists typical questions that may be asked during an interview. We don't recommend that you memorize "canned" or overly rehearsed answers, but it may be helpful to think about possible responses to these questions. Also be prepared to answer questions about your unique experiences, such as military service, vocational training, membership on sports teams, and the like.

It is also important to be sure to get a good night's sleep before the interview and to eat sensibly (don't skip breakfast; don't stuff yourself at lunch) so that you can stay alert. Long interviews can be physically demanding.

Consider the interview an opportunity to ask questions as well as to answer them; most interviewers will give you an opportunity to ask whatever questions you'd like toward the end of an interview. Asking questions about an organization is a way to display enthusiasm for the job, as well as a means of assessing whether you really want to join the organization. You will want to know the following:

- Will there be any job training for this position?
- What are the opportunities for advancement?
- What is the atmosphere like in the work place? (You will also be able to observe this during the interview.)
- What hours do people work?
- Is there flexibility in scheduling the work day?
- When do you anticipate making a decision about this position?

The very first question you ask should *not* be, "How much does this job pay?" Usually the interviewer will discuss salary and benefits with you during the interview. If this is a preliminary interview and there is a chance you will be called back for another visit, you may want to defer questions about salary and benefits until you know that the organization is seriously considering you for the position.

During the interview, maintain eye contact and speak assertively. The goal in an interview is to project a positive attitude to the interviewer. As motivational speaker Zig Ziglar once noted, "Your attitude, not your aptitude, will determine your altitude."

TABLE A.1
Typical Questions Asked during a Job Interview.[4]

I. Education

1. Why did you select your major area of study?
2. Why did you select your college/university?
3. If you were starting college again, what would you do differently? Why?
4. What subjects were most and least interesting? Useful? Why?
5. Other than the courses you studied, what is the most important thing you learned from your college experience?
6. How did you finance your college education?

II. Experience

7. What do you see as your strengths as an employee?
8. You say that a strength you have is _____. Give me some indication, perhaps an example, that illustrates this strength.
9. What special skills would you bring to this position?
10. Describe your last few work experiences. Why did you leave each one?
11. What were the best and worst aspects of your last job?
12. What were some of your achievements and disappointments in your last job?
13. Do you see yourself as a leader/manager of people? Why?
14. What kinds of work situations would you like to avoid? Why?
15. What frustrations have you encountered in your work experience? How have you handled these frustrations?
16. What do you look for in a boss?
17. Most employees and bosses have some disagreements. What are some things that you and your boss have disagreed about?

III. Position and Company

18. Why did you select this company?
19. Why did you decide to apply for this particular position?
20. How do you see yourself being qualified for this position?
21. Are you willing to relocate?

IV. Self-Evaluation

22. Tell me a little bit about yourself. Describe yourself.
23. What do you see as your personal strengths? Talents? How do you know that you possess these? Give examples of each.
24. What do you see as your weak points? Areas for improvement? Things you have difficulty doing? What have you done to deal with these?
25. Describe a specific work problem you had. Tell what you did to solve this problem.
26. What do you consider to be your greatest work achievement? Why?

V. Goals

27. Where do you see yourself being in your profession in five years? In ten years? How did you establish these goals? What will you need to do to achieve these goals?
28. What are your salary expectations for this position? Starting salary? Salary in five years?

Follow Up after the Interview

After the interview, it is wise to write a brief letter to thank the interviewer and to provide any additional information that he or she requested. You may also want to send a thank-you note to others in the organization, such as a secretary or administrative

Technology *and* Communication

Tips for E-Resumés

An **e-resumé** is a resumé that is submitted in an electronic form via the Internet. Given the dramatic growth in the number and popularity of e-resumés, chances are that you will send an e-resumé to a prospective employer rather than mailing or hand-delivering a "hard copy."[5] An e-resumé has several advantages:

- You can send your resumé to many people in a short amount of time.
- You can easily customize your resumé for different prospective employers, emphasizing the particular skills that the employer is seeking.
- You can showcase your computer and graphic skills if the job you are applying for requires those skills.[6]

When you develop your e-resumé, you have some decisions to make. First, do you use a "plain text" file, which does not permit you to enhance your resumé with such formatting such as boldface, italics, or underlining but only uses unadorned words to sell your credentials? A plain text file is also called an ASCII file. It has the advantage of being easily distributed to many employers but it can be viewed by anyone, including your current employer whom you may not want to know that you are job hunting.[7] If you use an HTML resumé, which is basically a Web page, you can provide more formatting information and direct your resumé to a specific person or organization. Most consultants recommend an HTML format.[8]

Another decision to make is how widely you should distribute your e-resumé. Because it only takes a click of a mouse to send your resumé, you may be tempted to submit it to prospective employers whose job offerings are not quite a match for your skills. Resist this temptation. Because of the ease of submitting e-resumés, employers have been inundated with them, making it a challenge to sort through all of the resumés they receive. As in any communication situation, be audience centered. Send your resumé only to those you think are interested in someone with your credentials.

Most employers won't take the time to read attachments that you send along with your resumé. Rather than using attachments to your resumé to showcase work that you've done in the past, many experts recommend that you use a **hyperlink** to lead the e-resumé reader to your work samples. A hyperlink is simply the connector between one page and another on the World Wide Web.[9]

Although e-resumés have many advantages, you may still want to follow up with more personal approaches to the job search. Some employers specifically state that they do not want calls or visits, but unless you are prohibited from making follow-up contacts, it can be helpful to support your e-contact with a personal contact between you and your prospective employer.

---

e-resumé
A resumé that is submitted in an electronic form via the Internet.

hyperlink
An electronic connector between one page and another on the World Wide Web.

assistant, for helping you arrange the interview. If the interviewer asked for references, make sure you contact your references quickly and ask them to send letters of recommendation to the organization. Expedite this process by providing addressed, stamped envelopes and a copy of your resumé so that they can personalize their letters with specific information.

Is it appropriate to call the person who interviewed you to ask when a decision will be made about hiring someone? Some employers abide by the philosophy "Don't call us, we'll call you." But many others would interpret your call as a sign of your interest in the position and a testament to your ability to follow through. You may want to take the direct approach and simply ask your employer toward the end of the interview, "Would it be all right if I called you in a few days to see if you have made a decision or if you need additional information?" If the interviewer tells you a decision will be made by a certain date and that date passes by, it is probably okay to call and find out whether

Frank and Ernest

they've offered the job to someone else and to express your continued interest in the position if it hasn't been filled.

HOW TO BE INTERVIEWED IN AN INFORMATION-GATHERING INTERVIEW

The bulk of the responsibility for an effective information-gathering interview falls on the shoulders of the person who is doing the interviewing. If you are the interviewer in an information-gathering interview, review the suggestions we offered earlier in this appendix for structuring the interview; most information-gathering interviews follow the general structure we outlined.

If you are the person being interviewed, however, your primary responsibilities are to be prepared, to listen carefully, and to respond appropriately to questions. In addition, a good interviewee knows what to expect in an information-gathering interview. You should prepare responses to anticipated questions, pay close attention to requests for specific information, and answer questions directly and accurately.

Prepare for the Interview

In most cases, interviewees have some advance knowledge of the purpose and objective of interviews, especially if someone is seeking specific information or advice. You can therefore anticipate probable topics of discussion. If you are uncertain what the interview is about, it is appropriate to ask the person who will interview you how to best prepare for the questions he or she plans to ask you. Yes, sometimes news programs have an interviewer pop up in an office, thrust a microphone in an interviewee's face, and ask a pointed question; in most cases, however, Mike Wallace of *60 Minutes* fame (or his equivalent) is not going to ambush you.

Depending on the nature of the interview, you may want to brush up on the facts you may be asked about. Jot down a few notes to remind you of names, dates, and places. In some cases, you may want to do some background reading on the topic of the interview.

Finally, think about not only what you will say in the interview but how you will respond nonverbally. Be on time. Maintain an attitude of interest and attentiveness with eye contact, attentive body positions, alert facial expressions, and an appropriately firm handshake.

Listen Effectively

Interviewing situations require you to listen to determine the amount and depth of information desired. If your responses are to be appropriate and useful, you must know what is being requested. If questions are unclear, ask for clarification or elaboration. By doing so, you can respond more fully and relevantly.

Successful interviewees also practice empathy. Interviewers are people, and interviewing situations are interpersonal encounters. Effective interviewees consider situations from interviewers' points of view, listen "between the lines" of what someone says to focus on underlying emotions, and watch for nonverbal cues. When interviewees listen to all facets of the communication, they can better adapt to the situation.

Listen and Respond

Respond Appropriately

Just as questioning is the primary responsibility of an interviewer, responding is the primary responsibility of an interviewee. Keep answers direct, honest, and appropriate in depth and relevance. For example, in response to the question "How would you describe the quality of your relationship with your family?" don't give a 15-minute speech

Verbal

On the Web

about your problems with your ex-spouse, keeping the children in clothes, and finding dependable home care for your aging parents. To make sure that you give the best possible answer, listen carefully when a question is posed and, if necessary, take a few moments to think before you answer. A response that is well thought out, straightforward, and relevant will be much more appreciated than one that is hasty, evasive, and unrelated to the question.

Using language and vocabulary appropriate to the situation is also important. The use of too much slang or technical terminology in an attempt to impress an interviewer can easily backfire by distracting the interviewer or distorting communication. Direct and simple language promotes understanding.

Finally, be adaptable and flexible to the needs of the interviewing situation. Some interviewers will ask questions to throw you off guard. When this happens, take a moment to think before you respond. Try to discover the reason for the question and respond to the best of your ability. Listen carefully for content *and* intent of questions so that you provide the information requested, especially when the interviewer changes topics. Flexibility and adaptability depend on good listening, empathy, accurate reading and interpretation of nonverbal communication, and practice. Just remember, "engage brain before opening mouth."

THE RESPONSIBILITIES OF THE INTERVIEWER

So far we've emphasized how to behave when you are the person being interviewed. As you assume leadership positions in your profession and community, you will undoubtedly be called on to interview others. In addition to knowing how to structure the opening, body, and conclusion of an interview, which we discussed earlier, there are several other characteristics of effective interviewers, whether you are seeking a future employee or simply gathering information.

Knowing how to conduct an effective interview will help you determine if an applicant will be right for the job.

Be Aware of Biases and Prejudices

First and foremost, an interviewer must be aware of his or her own biases and prejudices. Each person has a set of experiences, beliefs, attitudes, and values that influence how that person receives, interprets, and evaluates incoming stimuli. If accurate and useful information is to be shared in an interview, an interviewer must be aware of his or her own perceptual processes in order to make accurate and objective interpretations. An otherwise qualified candidate for a job shouldn't be eliminated from consideration just because the interviewer has a bias against redheads, for example.

Adapt to an Interviewee's Behavior

Adapt

Skilled interviewers observe, evaluate, and adapt to the communication behavior of their interviewees. Because no two interviews—and no two interviewees—are exactly alike, interviewers adapt their communication behavior accordingly. A flexible communication style is a necessity. Interviewers should have predetermined plans, but they should not be thrown off balance if an interviewee suddenly turns the tables and asks, "How much money do *you* make for *your* job?"

Adaptability also includes the use of appropriate language and vocabulary. You should consciously choose language and vocabulary that interviewees will understand. Little is gained by the use of technical, ambiguous, or vague terms. Words should be straightforward, simple, and specific, but not so simple that interviewees feel "talked down" to. Empathy is important in determining the most appropriate language and vocabulary.

Deal Wisely with Sensitive Content

Verbal

When planning questions for an interview, consider possible sensitive topics and topics to be avoided. A question such as "Why were you fired from your last job?" will provoke a defensive reaction in a grievance interview.

Good judgment and choice of words play crucial roles. One ill-chosen question can destroy the positive and open communication developed in an opening. Effective interviewers avoid potentially troublesome topics and attempt to put interviewees at ease. They discuss sensitive issues *if and only if* they are related to the purpose of the interviews. When a sensitive subject must be discussed, experienced interviewers choose their words carefully; thus, the question, "Why were you fired?" might be rephrased as "How would you describe your relationship with your previous supervisor?"

Listen Effectively

Listen and Respond

The admonition to listen effectively has appeared frequently in this appendix. Effective listening is at the heart of any interview. No matter how well interviewers have prepared, the time will have been wasted if they are poor listeners. They need strong listening skills to make sure that they are receiving the kind and amount of information they need. They must be able to identify partial or irrelevant responses.

Highly developed listening skills also increase the ability to accurately perceive and interpret unintentional messages and beliefs, attitudes, and values. Interviewers learn a great deal from nonverbal, as well as verbal, communication.

Record Information

The information accumulated from an interview is useless if it is not recorded completely and accurately. A partial or inaccurate report can lead to poor decisions and mistaken actions. Take appropriate, legible written notes. If you use a tape or digital recorder, ask in advance for permission to use it.

Verbal

Ask Appropriate Questions

The success of most interviews will be determined by the quality of the questions asked during the conversation. Think of questions as "mental can openers" designed to reveal how the other person thinks and behaves. Earlier we discussed question types (open, closed, probing, and hypothetical) and question sequences (funnel, inverted funnel, and tunnel). Some of your questions should be planned. Other questions may evolve from the discussion. Famed TV interviewer Larry King suggests that the best questions during an interview emerge from simply listening to what the other person is saying and then probing or following up on information and ideas verbalized.

If you are interviewing a job applicant, you should be aware that there are certain questions that you should *not* ask. These are questions that are inappropriate because they ask for information that either laws or court interpretations of laws suggest could lead to illegal discrimination. Here's a list of topics you should not bring up during an employment interview when you're asking the questions.[10]

arrest records	insurance claims
less-than-honorable discharges	judgments
gender and marital status	citizenship or national origin
maiden name	mother's maiden name
number of children	place of birth
ages of children	disabilities
number of preschool children	handicap
spouse's name	illnesses or accidents
spouse's education	hospitalizations
spouse's income	current or prior medication/treatment
form of birth control	workers' compensation claims
family plans	weight
child care arrangements	religion
car accidents	church affiliation
lawsuits	social organizations
legal complaints	loans
ownership of home	wage assignments or garnishments
rental status	bankruptcy
length of residence	credit cards
date of high school graduation	form of transportation
age	ownership of car
sexual orientation	

PRINCIPLES FOR A LIFETIME: Enhancing Your Skills

Aware

Principle One: Be aware of your communication with yourself and others.

- Take inventory of your skills and abilities to help you determine the job opportunities and careers that are best for you.
- Use your analysis of your talents to help you develop your resumé.
- During an interview, monitor your messages to ensure you are communicating clearly and effectively.

Verbal

Principle Two: Effectively use and interpret verbal messages.
- Speak clearly and respond to each question you are asked during an interview.
- Use action-oriented words on your resumé and during an interview to describe your accomplishments.
- Organize your resumé to include key elements of your education, experience, and special qualifications.
- Don't ask illegal or unethical questions during an employment interview.

Nonverbal

Principle Three: Effectively use and interpret nonverbal messages.
- Pay special attention to your appearance when you interview for a job; dress conservatively and appear neat and well groomed.
- Speak with confidence, use appropriate eye contact, and communicate interest and enthusiasm during the interview.
- When you interview someone, monitor your interviewee's nonverbal messages for clues about the individual's personality and ability to work with people.
- Skilled interviewers observe, evaluate, and then appropriately adapt to the communication behavior of interviewees.

Listen and Respond

Principle Four: Listen and respond thoughtfully to others.
- When you are interviewed for a job, be sure to stop, look, and listen to the questions and comments of the interviewer.
- Listen for both the details of the message and the major points or key ideas.
- When interviewing others, among your most important tasks is to listen.

Adapt

Principle Five: Appropriately adapt messages to others.
- Learn as much as you can about any prospective employer so that you can describe how your abilities best fit with the needs of the organization to which you are applying.

SUMMARY

An interview is a form of oral interaction structured to achieve a goal and involving two or more people who take turns speaking and listening. In this appendix, we have focused on tips and strategies for being interviewed and offered strategies for interviewing others. The five types of interview situations we've identified include the information-gathering interview, the appraisal interview, the problem-solving interview, the persuasion interview, and the job interview. This appendix focused primarily on job interviews and information-gathering interviews.

All interviews have an opening, in which the interviewee is put at ease; a body, during which questions are asked and answered; and a conclusion, which brings the interview to a comfortable close.

When you are seeking employment, start by becoming aware of your skills and abilities, and use your personal inventory to help you develop a well-written resumé. Focus on the needs of your prospective employer: Research the organization to which you are applying for a job. During the interview, listen carefully to the questions asked by the interviewer and respond appropriately. After the interview, it may be appropriate to send a thank-you note to the interviewer.

When preparing to be interviewed for an information-gathering interview, remember three primary tasks. First, prepare for the interview by reviewing information you think the interviewer will ask you about. Second, listen closely to the questions that you are being asked. Finally, respond appropriately by keeping answers direct and honest. Don't ramble. Observe the nonverbal responses of the interviewer to determine whether you are appropriately answering the questions.

We concluded this appendix by summarizing the essential requirements when you interview others. Don't let your own biases and prejudices interfere with your job of listening and responding to the interviewee. Although it's useful to have a prepared list of questions to ask, be prepared to adapt to the interviewee's behavior. The best interviews have a spontaneous flow rather than a rigid structure. Don't ask illegal questions during a job interview, and handle sensitive questions with tact and diplomacy. Listening well is the hallmark of an effective interviewer. Develop a strategy to record the information you gather from the interview. Finally, the key to any interview is the quality of the questions asked. As the interviewer, you have prime responsibility for asking clear, appropriate, and answerable questions.

Communication and Technology

APPENDIX B OUTLINE

Technology and Interpersonal
    Communication

Technology and Group
    Communication

Technology and Presentational
    Communication

Summary

APPENDIX B OBJECTIVES

After studying this appendix, you should be able to:

1. Discuss ways that technological innovations have affected the formation, development, and maintenance of interpersonal relationships.

2. Explain new ways that technology can allow people to participate in groups.

3. Define teleconferencing and describe the three primary forms of teleconferencing.

4. Discuss the pros and cons of teleconferencing as a form of group communication.

5. Describe the main effects of technology on group interaction.

6. Explain why speakers should exercise caution when using Internet sources of supporting material.

7. Describe the main concerns for speakers when they employ technological innovations in presentation aids.

8. Discuss how technology can help a speaker improve delivery.

What happens when the power goes out? Probably all of us have been in a severe storm or other circumstance that caused our electric service to be disrupted. Were you prepared—meaning did you have candles or flashlights on hand? Had you saved whatever you were doing on your computer before you lost power? Did you have a battery-operated radio so that you could get weather updates? Or did you just sleep through the whole thing?

At times like these, when severe storms or other problems cause a power outage, we realize how pervasively technology (and the electricity that powers most of it) affects our lives. We realize the need for such simple things as batteries, flashlights and matches, canned food and a manual can opener, and a regular or cell phone (instead of a cordless one that has to be plugged into a socket to function). We may also wish we knew the names of our neighbors.

Many people are concerned about the world's seeming obsession with technology, because it seems that we become enamored with the technology before we stop to think: Is this really the best thing for my life? for my relationships with other people? for society? for future generations?[1]

No one doubts the wonders of technology and the many ways in which technological advances have improved everyday life. We have almost stopped marveling at how quickly a meal can be prepared, a document can be written and edited, and a message can travel around the world. We can be exposed to and learn about other cultures around the globe, so technology helps us embrace diversity. In this appendix we explore some positive effects of technology on the three main contexts for communication we have focused on in this text: interpersonal relationships, group communication, and presentational communication. But we also pause to consider the effect of "instant everything" on our relationships and communication with other people. Our main point is this: Technology is part of modern life in much of the world, and technological advances will keep on coming. But before we become completely dazzled by the next innovation, we should apply our critical thinking powers to consider whether the innovation is positive or negative, healthy or harmful for our lives, our relationships, and the culture in which we function.

TECHNOLOGY AND INTERPERSONAL COMMUNICATION

Is technology bringing people together or pulling them apart? Does technology make communication with others easier and faster or more difficult and time-consuming?

An Impersonal Technological Innovation

When was the last time you called a government agency, a utility company, or a bank and a real, live human being answered the phone? Most often, we hear something like this: "Welcome to _____'s automated customer service system. This call is being monitored so that we can improve our service. Please listen to the following menu of items before selecting an option. For _____, press 1; for _____, press 2," and so forth. Then, when you make your selection from the opening menu, you'll likely hear something like this: "Thank you for your selection. For current account information, press 1; for inquiries about _____, press 2"—another set of menu options. The very last option, if it's an option at all, is usually, "To speak to a service representative, please stay on the line and your call will be answered in the order it was received." You can grow old on that line.

If this sounds painfully familiar, then you have probably already wondered whether this particular technological advance, **interactive voice response,** is a good thing or not. On the plus side, use of such menus reduces labor costs and may allow customers 24-hour access to information. However, market research shows that when customers encounter this technology, their satisfaction decreases in proportion to the length of the list of menu choices.[2] Some of you reading this are too young to know this, but many of us remember a time when you could dial a company (dial, rather than push buttons on a telephone) and actually speak to someone. Perhaps things were slower and less efficient then, but it did seem somehow more personal, even more enjoyable to have a real person attend to your concerns.

Enter technological innovation: the **chatterbot.** In a newspaper article describing this device, a journalist begins by explaining, "People find Alice easy to talk to. She listens more than she speaks. She says she likes dining by candlelight. She reads newspapers and news magazines, so she is up on popular culture. But Alice's favorite topic of conversation is robots. That's because she is one."[3] Reading further, we discover that Alice (full name: Artificial Linguistic Computer Entity) is a computer software program that simulates conversations with humans. Chatterbots are being developed to act as

interactive voice response
A recorded menu of options that callers encounter in many phone systems.

chatterbot
A robot in the form of a computer software program that simulates a human voice and can respond to questions placed by online users.

customer service representatives, information deliverers, and even "potential companions for human surfers in the sometimes lonely world of the Web."[4] A person asks a question of a chatterbot, which searches for word clues in the question and matches them to its vast database of English words. It then attempts to offer a helpful response, even a personalized one by inserting the name of the questioner into the response. Chatterbots are but one form of artificial intelligence that attempts to make machines operate like people.

What are the pros and cons of such a device? On the pro side, we can see an advantage to having a human-like response to a question instead of a recording, words on a computer screen, or dead air. The news article gives as an example someone entering an online music store, conversing with a chatterbot about musical tastes, and receiving the chatterbot's recommendations for artists the consumer may not have heard of. But just like the menu approach to customer service calls, chatterbots simply can't deal with some questions or concerns. Chatterbots may also give those "lonely surfers" described in the article a false sense of a social connection—a feeling that a human-to-human conversation has occurred when it actually has not. What about the ethics involved? What if someone thinks she or he is chatting with a person (perhaps named Alice), but instead is chatting with a machine? In computer applications, such programs are clearly identified as artificial intelligence or human simulation devices, but it's possible such devices could be used by the unscrupulous to dupe the public.

"On the Internet, nobody knows you're a dog."

One of the most obvious technological advances to affect human relationships is the ability to communicate in cyberspace. Just what is cyberspace? One interesting description of *cyberspace* is "the diverse experiences of space associated with computing and related technologies."[5] Most of us who communicate in cyberspace do so through that technological marvel known as the Internet. The Internet has become an invaluable tool for accomplishing a variety of tasks—e-mailing, instant messaging, downloading music, conducting research, and buying products and services. Estimates indicate that over 600 million people worldwide use these types of Internet services, and that yearly business transactions conducted online number in the trillions. Research has determined that 72% of Americans go online at least once a month. A fairly recent development that is gaining popularity is "blogging," short for Web logging—live journaling on the Internet. Many Web sites include blogging spaces now, which offer forums for free expression to all visitors to the site. Over 500,000 people are estimated to be active "bloggers."[6] In the next few pages, we explore online tools for initiating relationships and connecting people; then we discuss the role of computer-mediated communication in ongoing relationships.

The Role of Technology in Relationship Initiation

In Chapter 7 we discussed interpersonal communication and the initiation of relationships. How has technology helped and hurt these processes? First, our Principle One, of being aware of your communication with yourself and others, is affected by technology. We've described how important it is to know yourself, to develop your self-concept and monitor what affects your self-esteem as you form relationships—friendships, dating or romantic relationships, and workplace connections. But what about relationships that develop only in cyberspace? Do cyber-relationships have as much potential impact on one's self-concept as other relationships?

One of the more interesting opportunities that Internet relationships afford is the ability to alter and expand one's identity.[7] Some researchers describe identity in the vir-

This Marine Corps medic uses his blog "Doc in the Box" to communicate vital information about members of his unit.

Verbal

synchronous time
Online communication in which there is little to no lag time between comments; sometimes referred to as "real time."

asynchronous time
Online communication in which messages posted at one time are read at another time.

newsgroup
A group of online users interested in a common topic or who belong to an organization; postings go out to all members, who then can respond with their own postings.

tual world as "fluid," meaning that we don't really know who we're chatting with online, who their families are, where they're located, and so forth. Our chatting partners don't know much about us either. In such a virtual world, power and status are equalized and minimized, but the potential for deception is expanded.[8] We're not advocating that you deceive people when chatting online or e-mailing, because that's unethical. It can also lead to potential abuse and disastrous consequences, as evidenced in stories about young children who pretend to be adults online and form connections with highly disturbed people, such as sexual predators. But apart from these extreme cases, the opportunity exists to experiment with your identity online and note the response you get from others. You can test untapped parts of your personality, perhaps by being more bold or more sensitive than you normally are in your face-to-face relationships. You can expand who you are and adjust who you want to become based on others' reactions.

We're all probably aware of the increase in people's use of verbal communication skills (Principle Two) to make connections with others via the Internet. Online users can communicate in **synchronous time,** meaning that there is little to no lag time between comments. Such Internet tools as IRC (Internet Relay Chat) allow users to read and respond to others' comments on a computer screen as the remarks are being generated. It's as close to in-person chatting in real time as is possible on a computer, given the current technology. In recent years, instant messaging, sometimes in the form of text messaging via cell phones or personal computers, has become an increasingly popular method of communicating, especially among teens and young adults. Devices such as Blackberries and PDAs (personal data assistants), which offer a combination of services such as cell phone and e-mail options, are extremely popular and are becoming more affordable. However, there can be a downside to the use of such technology: Blackberries are occasionally referred to as "crackberries" because they can become addictive for users. The temptation to use one's instant messaging device during class or work hours can be irresistible, but doing so creates a distraction. Another negative result of the use of such devices may be that more communication occurs through computer-mediated channels than face-to-face.[9] Others prefer to converse in **asynchronous time,** meaning that messages posted at one time are read at another time. Many asynchronous online users belong to a **newsgroup** in which postings by subscribers go out to all members, who then can respond with their own postings.

However, involvement in newsgroups, which is one of the oldest components of the Internet, dating back to 1979, has seriously declined. The decline is primarily related to *spam* (electronic garbage or junk mail) and to spammers' increasingly sophisticated means of disguising themselves as newsgroup subscribers, all the while clogging newsgroups as they hawk their products and services.[10] Similar to the newsgroup is the **listserv**, which involves a "host" and software that facilitates discussions by linking people who share common interests.[11] Yet another option is the **electronic bulletin board** that anyone, not just a subscriber, can access.[12]

Perhaps you've made friendships with people you've never met in person, and these virtual friendships have become just as valuable as your face-to-face friendships. You may even be one of those brave souls who has made a "love connection" over the Internet.[13] Online dating services such as Yahoo personals, Match.com, and eharmony.com have experienced record success in recent years. While online dating may have once been seen as a refuge for social misfits, it is now a booming business, as sites have improved security measures and as more romantic "success stories" receive publicity.[14] One study found that relationships established online were just as satisfying to the partners participating in the study as those that were established the "old-fashioned way" through nonmediated channels.[15]

What makes virtual relationships attractive? Many users enjoy the freedom of getting to know other people without some of the nonverbal dimensions that give us pause in face-to-face interaction, primarily the dimension of physical attractiveness.[16] As Annette Markham explains in her fascinating book *Life Online: Researching Real Experience in Virtual Space*, some people feel trapped by their offline selves—both their bodies and the roles they play. As their online selves, they can transcend the trappings of physicality. One user Markham interviewed in her research felt that her appearance was a hindrance when she met people face-to-face. She was much more confident of her ability to connect with people through her use of language because, as the user put it, "eloquence makes me beautiful online."[17]

Nonverbal

A second reason people are drawn to electronic communication as a means of establishing relationships relates to the ability to edit one's messages—a form of adaptation (Principle Five) not easily managed in face-to-face communication. In Chapter 3 on verbal communication, we discussed something most of us have experienced—saying the wrong thing to someone and then trying to take it back or undo the damage we've caused. In such instances we wish we could have a chance to change our inane or hurtful comment. Electronic communication provides this editing opportunity, unless you hit "enter" too quickly.

Verbal
Adapt

Another aspect of cyber-relating that is attractive, but also disturbing to many people (particularly people in committed, monogamous relationships) is the potential to stray from one's committed partner by making virtual connections. This trend has called into question the concept of fidelity; it's hard to determine if developing emotionally intimate relationships online with someone other than one's partner is a form of cheating.[18] Many believe that there is a clear difference between establishing emotionally supportive relationships online and developing sexual relationships online. But might both be considered a breach of faith by one's partner?

Robert Weiss, Director of the Sexual Recovery Institute of Los Angeles, remarked, "This [Internet usage] totally reinvents adultery. If you have a totally cyber-sexual intimacy with someone you've never met, have you had an affair?"[19] While some believe online flirtations are harmless, like office flirtations that don't escalate into romantic relationships or affairs, others see online relationships as outgrowths of a problem within the primary relationship. Energy that once might have been directed toward the primary relationship now becomes directed to virtual relationships.

The Role of Technology in Relationship Maintenance

One of the most obvious positive uses of electronic communication is the ability to keep up with people who live long distances from us. E-mail, instant messaging, and

listserv
A computer service that involves a "host" and software that facilitates discussions by linking people who share common interests.

electronic bulletin board
An online group service in which anyone, not just a subscriber, can access and read postings.

online chatting are more economical ways to maintain relationships than carrying on long-distance telephone service or traveling to be together. For many people, online communication doesn't replace the good old personal letter delivered via "snail mail," but it is much faster and more immediate, in that you can transmit what you're thinking and get a rapid response. Some online users develop virtual communities, like **MUDs** (Multi-User Dimensions or Dungeons) or **MOOs** (MUD Object Oriented), for such purposes as generating political activism, exploring common interests, collaborating on projects, and socializing.[20] According to MUD users, these virtual communities can be just as supportive and sustaining as any in-person community established on campus or in a neighborhood.[21] So, in a sense, technology has brought us closer together as a nation and a world, because we can communicate quickly, regularly, and economically across great distances.

However, some argue that electronic communication, among other forms of technological innovation, actually pulls people apart more than it brings them together. According to this view, something is wrong when we converse regularly across the world with people we're not likely to meet but do not know or socialize with our neighbors down the hall or across the street. Some people rely too heavily on e-mail because it lets them avoid nerve-wracking or uncomfortable in-person conversation.[22]

The question is, which community is more "*real*"—the in-person one or the virtual one? Electronic communication can create a false sense of community, because computer users who interact across the globe most often do so alone, in the small spaces of their private existences. Likewise, the rising popularity of the home office connected to a virtual world has the potential to diminish the social or communal impact of the workplace.[23]

Many people actually prefer computer-mediated intimacy to in-person intimacy. Some prefer it to the point of becoming **cyber-addicts,** meaning that they spend all of their free time surfing the Net and making online connections. Some cyber-addicts jeopardize their jobs or school performance because they spend so much time online. The Sexual Recovery Institute published a checklist to help people determine if they or someone they know has reached the stage of cyber-addiction. Some warning signs include (1) spending increasing amounts of online time focused on sexual or romantic intrigue or involvement; (2) not considering online sexual or romantic affairs to be a possible violation of one's commitment to one's spouse or partner; (3) online use interfering with work, in that the user is tired or late to work because of the previous night's use; and (4) online use interfering with primary relationships, because users minimize or lie to partners about online activities and spend less time with family or partners.[24]

As a communication channel, e-mail is better for some relationships than others. It's a great way to communicate information, check perceptions, and stay in touch with busy colleagues and friends, both near and far. But close or intimate relationships—family relationships, friendships, and romantic relationships—typically require more than just e-mail to maintain closeness. E-mail is also better for some topics than others. In close relationships, e-mail tends to work best for quick updates or brief expressions of affection and to make plans or share ideas. The reply function in e-mail software serves our Principle Four, that of listening and responding. Once you've read an e-mail message, the most expedient thing to do is to use the reply function and generate an immediate response. But what about self-disclosure, communication described in Chapter 7 as critical to the development of trust and intimacy in relationships? Self-disclosing in an electronic format has pros and cons. On the pro side: In some circumstances you might decide to electronically share information that you deem safe—meaning that it isn't too personal but it is still self-disclosure. Some research shows that self-disclosure occurs earlier and is more intimate between persons developing their relationship online than between those developing their relationship through more conventional methods. The difference mostly relates to anonymity. Since anonymity is possible in computer-mediated relationships, participants feel more free to disclose about themselves. In contrast, the lack of anonymity in face-to-face en-

Listen and Respond

MUD
Multi-User Dimensions or Dungeons; virtual communities that form for such purposes as generating political activism, exploring common interests, collaborating on projects, and socializing.

MOO
A MUD that is Object Oriented; users connect because of interest in a common subject or focal point.

cyber-addict
Someone who spends all of his or her free time surfing the Net and making online connections, possibly jeopardizing job or school performance.

counters can create psychological discomfort and a need to protect oneself. Thus, face-to-face self-disclosure often develops more slowly and requires repeated exposure to one's partner and a gradual increase in trust.[25] Perhaps the best aspect of electronic self-disclosure is its potential effect on reciprocity. While the recipient of your electronic disclosure might choose not to reply quickly and in kind, the technology makes it easy to reciprocate if he or she so desires.

On the con side, remember that e-mail messages generated at work or school aren't your private property. Be careful what you disclose online, because people other than the person you intend to receive the message could learn this information about you. There are computer programs that will keep e-mail generated from one's personal computer completely private, meaning that once a message has been sent and read, it can be completely erased from a computer's memory and hard drive. However, most of us don't own such a program. So even a deleted message can be retrieved by an expert or hacker.

Self-disclosure may also work better when communicated in person because of the tendency for the discloser to feel vulnerable. Although some avid online users disagree, face-to-face communication involves more channels of information than e-mail. In face-to-face encounters we call on all our verbal and nonverbal communication skills to self-disclose to another person in an appropriate manner.[26] We also need to be able to see and hear the other person's reactions—to our disclosure—verbal and nonverbal—to determine the effects on our relationship. In Chapter 4 we provided a list of "emoticons," symbols people often use to convey emotions or to add a more human expression to their e-mail messages. But these can only go so far; they are generally ineffective when personal information and serious emotions are involved.

Verbal
Nonverbal

This information relates to our Principle Five, adaptation, because it's important to learn to adapt your message to your receivers, but also to adapt by selecting the most appropriate channel for communication. One suggestion particularly relevant to our discussion is this: Never communicate anything electronically that you would not say in person. If you would have trouble conveying something in person, don't fall prey to the false sense of anonymity or face-saving attributes of e-mail to bail you out of a difficult conversation.[27] Think long and hard about which channel of communication you should use for certain kinds of information and in certain relationships. First consider what the relationship means to you; then put yourself in your relational partner's shoes and think about the way you'd prefer to receive the information.

Adapt

TECHNOLOGY AND GROUP COMMUNICATION

Technology not only has a pervasive effect on how people interact one-on-one, it has had an impact on the way groups form and function, as we explain in this section.

The Technological Formation of Small Groups

How has technology affected group communication? First, it has affected the way we even conceptualize a group. As we discussed in Chapter 9, a small group consists of from three to fifteen people who share a common purpose, feel a sense of belonging to the group, and exert influence on each other. After reading this definition, most of us picture a cluster of people in a room, sitting around a table, discussing some task. But do people necessarily have to be in the same location to be considered a group?

Think about study groups that form at your institution; perhaps you're a member of one. Members of these kinds of groups typically meet in person to work on class projects and study for exams. But with the level of activity of today's average college student—full class loads, work responsibilities, family commitments—many students find that they just don't have the time to meet in person with classmates. Do they abandon this important activity? No—they meet in cyberspace. Through the use of such

A video conference is an improvement over a phone conference because the participants can see visual nonverbal cues as well as hear the conversation.

computer software as Web CT and Course Compass, instructors create cybergroups so that they and their students can discuss course topics and assignments. Study groups, collaborative work groups, and people with common majors or interests use technology to accomplish their goals. The frequency of information exchange and the amount of information that circulates among members of a virtual group are likely to be much greater than in groups who meet face-to-face once a month or every so often.

However, one frustration reported by members of virtual groups is that, in essence, there are no group meetings. Research has determined that identification—a sense of connectedness and similarity with group members—is weaker among groups who conduct electronic meetings than among those who meet face-to-face.[28]

Teleconferencing

Widgit Incorporated is having a problem with its newest product and it's causing sales and stock values to dip. The idea people think it's a production problem, the production people think it's a design flaw, and the marketing people don't know what to think—except that somebody better do something, and fast. In the past, corporate executives would gather to address the problem and create a workable solution. Nowadays these executives put their corporate heads together and do the same thing—just not in person. **Teleconferencing** allows people who are geographically separated to meet together through the wonders of technology, saving a great deal of time and money.[29]

Three primary forms of teleconferencing currently exist. **Audio conferencing** occurs when groups of people or individuals at different locations gather around a telephone and hold a joint discussion. On the plus side, audio conferencing saves time and money. Like other forms of electronic communication, it is an efficient way to accomplish tasks.[30] It also embodies the adage that "two heads are better than one"; in fact, organizations that conduct regular teleconferences report much greater attendance compared to face-to-face meetings.[31] However, teleconferencing may not be ideal for building solidarity, if that is one goal of the company or entity setting up the conference. By its very nature it segments groups into subgroups, which can create divisiveness and competition. Participants also experience a negative side effect similar to the use of e-mail and other forms of electronic communication: a loss of nonverbal in-

teleconferencing
Meeting by means of electronic technology with people who are geographically distant.

audio conferencing
Meeting by telephone with groups of people or individuals at different locations.

formation. While teleconferencing retains properties of the voice, participants lose the ability to detect such things as eye contact, facial expressions, gestures, and body positions of group members.[32]

A second, increasingly popular form of teleconferencing is **video conferencing.** In these situations, through the use of satellite technology, video cameras broadcast visual images of colleagues or conference participants to one another's sites. Video conferences may involve small groups of people who gather to focus on a specific task, or they may be a means of broadcasting large conferences to numerous sites. Video conferencing tends to be more expensive than audio conferencing, and its cost is prohibitive for many organizations. But with rising costs of travel and accommodations, video conferencing is becoming more economical than sending a team of participants to a conference or to meet with long-distance clients.

One advantage of video conferencing over audio conferencing is that it includes more channels of nonverbal communication, transmitting a more complete and understandable message. More interaction is generated because participants can both hear and see one another, which leads to better organized and more productive meetings.[33] One drawback is the ever-present concern about equipment failures at any of the sites involved. And often, if attendance at a conference is large, on-site attendees' questions are more likely to receive responses than participants who call or e-mail in from off-site.

Nonverbal

A third form of teleconferencing is **computer conferencing,** which allows multiple participants to exchange a sequence of e-mail messages.[34] Individuals at their own computer terminals can participate in brainstorming sessions by viewing responses of all other participants simultaneously. Authors of comments are not revealed, which encourages participants to be more engaged, to overcome status concerns (like fear of openly disagreeing with the boss's idea), and to focus on the quality of ideas, not on who produced the ideas.[35] Less advanced programs require participants to author a complete message before they can interact with other conferees. Other advantages of this approach are its similarity to face-to-face interaction, the potential for producing higher-quality decisions, and its relatively inexpensive cost.[36]

The Effects of Technology on Group Interaction

In groups we tend to speak to specific members rather than to the group as a whole. We also direct more of our communication toward the leaders or higher-status persons in the group, as well as to people we like. In some groups, everyone talks to everyone else. In other groups, cliques or subgroups form, which can be either beneficial or detrimental to group interaction and functioning. What happens to these interaction patterns when technology facilitates the meeting, as in the case of teleconferencing?

For one thing, the formation of cliques or subgroups whose members communicate privately, out of earshot or the view of other group members, can be quite detrimental. Not only can it be distracting (because it makes it harder to hear interaction from other sites and concentrate on the focus of attention), it can lead to distrust. If several individuals or small groups of colleagues teleconference in an effort to solve problems, generate creativity, or discuss critical issues, then interaction that pulls people away from the primary discussion will likely be perceived negatively and deter success.

Verbal

What can enhance the success of teleconferences? It is important to set, announce, and enforce time limitations for participation. If certain members dominate the interaction or deliver prepared remarks without concern for how much time they're taking, group cohesiveness and progress will be impeded. A facilitator—ideally, the group's most effective communicator (not necessarily the person who is the most adept with technology)—should attempt to do the following: orient participants as to the purpose of the conference, provide guidelines for participation, keep the group on task through the use of an agenda, moderate interaction so as to avoid over-talking or lack of participation by individual members, mediate any conflicts that arise, and bring the session to closure by summarizing key ideas or recapping progress.[37]

video conferencing
Meeting in the presence of video cameras, which, through the use of satellite technology, broadcast visual images of participants to distant sites.

computer conferencing
Meeting by using computer programs that allow multiple participants to exchange a sequence of e-mail messages.

TECHNOLOGY AND PRESENTATIONAL COMMUNICATION

At various points throughout the five chapters on presentational communication in this text, we explored applications of technology to this context of communication. We won't repeat that information here, but we do want to offer a few reminders or cautions about the effects of technology on presentational speaking.

Source Material for Presentations

Times have changed. Instead of combing through dusty volumes in musty library stacks, most students who seek information simply type on a keyboard and click a mouse, and the information they seek appears on a computer screen. We also realize that, as college students, you're encouraged to employ your powers of critical thinking to assess the validity and usefulness of information before you use it in a speech or paper. But we have come to detect, through many semesters of teaching presentational speaking and conducting our own research, a sense among students that computers embody what can only be described as a "mystical" quality. Just as people decades ago believed that everything that appeared in print in the town newspaper just had to be true, many people believe that if it's on the computer screen, it counts as legitimate information. What we want to make sure you realize is that anyone with access to a computer and half a brain can learn to create a Web site. Just because something appears on a Web site doesn't mean it is necessarily reliable, legitimate, true, or useful.

Many Web sites are advocacy-based, meaning that they present only one side or a slanted view of an issue—the side they want to persuade you to agree with. Others are more even-handed, presenting multiple perspectives and allowing the reader to decide for herself or himself. It's acceptable to incorporate some of this kind of material into a presentation, but, at present, this information does not carry the same level of legitimacy that published research carries.

A related caution pertains to your ethical responsibility as a public speaker. You are expected to present the best information you can find—not the best information you can find the most quickly. Take time to hunt for the best information. Also realize that commonly used search engines, such as Yahoo!, Google, and Lycos, only catalog about 16% of the estimated 800 million Web pages that currently exist.[38] The research process is tedious and time-consuming, and computers have helped streamline it by a tremendous amount. However, the computer is but one tool to help you locate pertinent information. Other tools may take more time to use, but you may find that they provide more information of varying types than you could access via computer. You may also find yourself researching a topic that pre-dates the computerization of information. In a case like this, you don't want to discover that you've lost your library research skills because you constantly turn to a computer.

Technological Innovations and Presentation Aids

In Chapter 13 we provided information about a range of presentation aids, including computer-generated visual aids, that can be used to enhance a presentation. We also discussed some guidelines for using these aids, including this one: "Use technology thoughtfully." You want to avoid deciding to use technology to support a speech just because it will "wow" an audience. Keep in mind that there is nothing inherently dazzling about technology itself; it's all in how you *use* the technology.

In a presentational context, programs that generate images and text, such as Microsoft's PowerPoint®, may or may not help you get your message across to the audience.[39] We've seen presentations in which the technology outshone the speaker and overwhelmed the audience. And if your room isn't conducive to the technology, you may have to speak in the dark so that the presentation aids can be seen. This can also be a problem for speakers who rely on overhead projectors. A darkened room is not the best environment for a speaker, because you run the risk of losing some of your audience's attention. Also, some people (especially those who are quite nervous in speaking situations) let the darkness shield them and the presentation aids supplant their speech content. Remember that all presentation aids should *aid* the speaker; they should not *replace* the speaker.

Technology and Enhanced Speech Delivery

When we hear a recording of ourselves, most of us respond with "That's not my voice; I don't sound like that." The truth is, recording technology today is so sophisticated that it can capture sounds quite accurately—so indeed, you actually *do* sound like that. The way you hear your voice in your head is distorted, compared to the way others hear it when you speak. So if you want to know how you will sound when making a presentation, tape yourself and force yourself to listen to the playback, just as we advised in Chapter 13. This is one of the best ways to improve a speech—its content, organization, and delivery. But try not to be overly critical of yourself when you listen, as many of us tend to be. You want to note if you use too many filler sounds or words, such as "uh," "er," "okay," "you know," and "like" (our personal favorite). You want to attempt to slow down if you hear yourself rushing on the recording; you want to develop vocal variety so you don't speak in a monotone. But realize that you're developing a delivery style that is unique to you; don't try to change too much or you'll likely make yourself unduly nervous when you actually present the speech.

Aware

If you're really daring, need an extra dose of reality, or are a narcissist, videotape yourself rehearsing or performing your speech. Of course, we're kidding when we say that, but we know that most people aren't thrilled with the thought of being videotaped. Most of us are thrilled even less with the thought of having to watch ourselves on tape. But, as we indicated in Chapter 13, a videotape of yourself is the absolute best form of pre- or post-speech feedback you can use as a tool to improve your speaking abilities. If you don't own a video camera, most colleges and universities have media centers that give students access to video equipment.

Verbal

Nonverbal

When you watch the tape, imagine yourself as an audience member, sitting in the room listening to you speak. Are you bored by yourself as a speaker? Do you make yourself laugh? Are you understandable? Are you persuaded by you, if that's the goal? You might want to assess your presentation using the same criteria your instructor will use when you give the speech in class. As you watch, first note things you did well; then note those things you want to change. Try not to be overly harsh or distracted by such unchangeable things as your physical characteristics and appearance. Concentrate on the speech—how well it was organized; whether you cited your supporting materials adequately; whether you handled your note cards smoothly; whether you need to alter delivery elements like voice, eye contact, and movement; and whether the speech fit the specified time frame. It may be a humbling experience to watch your presentation on tape, but it will teach you a great deal.

Adapt

PRINCIPLES FOR A LIFETIME: Enhancing Your Skills

Aware

Principle One: Be aware of your communication with yourself and others.

- Technological innovations, such as Internet chat rooms, allow you to explore your identity and note the responses you get from other online users.
- Audiotaping or videotaping yourself making a presentation and then listening to or viewing the playback are excellent ways to become more aware of how you communicate as a speaker.

Verbal

Principle Two: Effectively use and interpret verbal messages.

- Some people have better verbal communication skills online than in face-to-face interaction.
- Edit electronic messages; don't say something in an e-mail message or as a comment in a chat room that you would not say to someone in person.
- Be careful when self-disclosing via an electronic channel; e-mail isn't necessarily private, and self-disclosure may be more effectively communicated in person.
- A facilitator is recommended for teleconferencing, to orient participants to the group's purpose, agenda, and interaction rules, and to moderate interaction.
- Audiotaping or videotaping presentations and listening to or watching the playback is an excellent strategy to help speakers improve their use of language.

Nonverbal

Principle Three: Effectively use and interpret nonverbal messages.

- Some people enjoy the freedom of getting to know people online, without the constraints of nonverbal dimensions, such as appearance and physical attractiveness.
- Be careful when self-disclosing over an electronic channel, because self-disclosure is more effectively accomplished when nonverbal cues accompany verbal ones.
- Emoticons are keyboard symbols that help convey nonverbal elements of an electronic message, such as tone of voice and emphasis.
- Participants in audio conferencing can use vocal cues to help interpret messages but do not have the benefit of visual cues, such as eye contact and facial expressions.
- Video conferencing is preferable to audio conferencing because more nonverbal information is available.
- Audiotaping or videotaping presentations and listening to or watching the playback is an excellent strategy to help speakers improve their nonverbal delivery.

Listen and Respond

Principle Four: Listen and respond thoughtfully to others.

- One advantage of e-mail and other forms of electronic communication is the potential for an immediate response; learn to use the reply function.

Adapt

Principle Five: Appropriately adapt messages to others.

- One advantage of electronic communication is the ability to edit your message and adapt it to receivers *before* you communicate it.
- Learn to adapt your message as well as the channel for your message. If you have bad news or negative information to relate to someone, in-person communication is preferable to electronic communication.
- When viewing a videotape of your presentation, imagine yourself as an audience member; then adapt the presentation to make the best impression possible on listeners.

SUMMARY

In this appendix we explored the effects of technology on human communication. We focused on three primary contexts for communication: interpersonal, group, and presentational communication. Interpersonal relationships that form in cyberspace offer particular challenges. While you can experiment with your online identity and explore parts of your personality, there is the potential for unethical behavior in misrepresenting yourself to another online user. Relationships can form and be maintained via technology such as e-mail; however, for some forms of interpersonal communication and some relationships, cyber-channels are inappropriate. E-mail and other online channels of communication such as electronic bulletin boards, listservs, and newsgroups, allow rapid communication with distant partners, but some scholars worry that these forms of technology are segmenting our culture, rather than uniting us.

The second context, group communication, is affected by technology in interesting ways. There are pros and cons to conducting online meetings and group discussions. A popular form of cyber-group communication is the teleconference. Three primary forms of teleconferencing currently exist: audio conferencing, video conferencing, and computer conferencing. Of these three forms, video conferencing provides the most information and aids receivers in interpreting messages because it can transmit both verbal and nonverbal messages.

Finally, we explored the effects of technology on presentational speaking. Speakers need to use caution when accessing source material for speeches from the Internet; some sources are more reliable than others. Computer searching should supplement, not replace, traditional library methods of research. Technology is improving our methods of generating and using presentation aids, but we warned about overusing or relying too heavily on technology. Aids simply help the speaker; they do not replace the speaker. Current technology can help speakers improve their delivery, especially through the use of audiotaped and videotaped speech rehearsals.

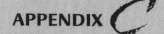
Sample Speeches for Discussion and Evaluation

INFORMATIVE SPEECH

Taming Hostile Audiences: Persuading Those Who Would Rather Jeer than Cheer

Larry Tracy[1]

Delivered to the Washington, D.C., Chapter of the National Speakers Association, Washington, D.C. January 8, 2005

Thank you, Sylvia, for that fine introduction. As professional speakers, we know how a poor introduction can be deflating. Sylvia, on the other hand, was somewhat inflating in her kind remarks.

I am frequently asked how I got into the field of presentations coaching after being a colonel in the U.S. Army. The first time that question was asked of me, my answer, I'm afraid, was a bit flippant. After reflection, however, I decided it was indeed quite accurate. I said that early in my career, I concluded (as did my superiors, I believe) that I could talk better than I could shoot. From that time on, I seemed to become the duty briefer no matter what my primary assignment. Ultimately, as Sylvia mentioned in her introduction, I was selected to head the Pentagon's top briefing team, responsible for daily intelligence presentations to the Chairman of the Joint Chiefs of Staff and the Secretary of Defense.

My experience with hostile and difficult audiences came later when the Department of State requested the Army to assign me to the Department for the specific task of speaking and debating controversial foreign policy issues throughout the U.S. and abroad. Initially, I found it flattering that State Department officials believed I was qualified to take on this task, but after the first few "confrontations," I realized these officials had decided it was better to place an Army colonel in jeopardy than a promising diplomat.

In all seriousness, however, that assignment was a wonderful life-changing experience. The almost 400 presentations, debates, and panels in which I participated caused me to enter the field of speech training as my post-Army career. I knew that few people in this field had the "real-world" experience I had gained and could now pass on to others.

Let me say something that may offend some of you. Although you are all professional speakers, I submit that you are not a true professional if you are only capable of speaking to groups that agree with you. The true professional speaker can deal with the jeers as well as the cheers. The true professional knows how to persuade the "nonpersuadable," not just preach to the choir.

There is no greater challenge in the field of speaking than the task of bringing around to your position audience members who are initially opposed to what you are advocating. Many people are inclined to take a fatalistic position at the prospect of dealing with such an audience. But that attitude is self-defeating. Bringing such an audience to your side by the lucidity of your reasoning, the coherence of your message, and the excellence of your presentation skills will indeed make you a complete speaker. As you have no doubt discovered, speakers in today's world must blend substantive mastery, focused structure, and stylistic elegance to a degree not required previously.

In today's contentious business and government climate, adversarial panels, debates, and presentations on controversial issues are more the rule rather than the exception. I want to divide today's presentation into two parts. In Part One, I'll emphasize the importance of mastering the fundamentals of the speaking art. In Part Two, I'll show how to apply these fundamentals to persuading audiences inclined to disagree with you.

Part One: The Fundamentals of the Speaking Art

I know that some of you are thinking "Hold on, we're professional speakers. We don't need any advice on "fundamentals." Just get to the good stuff—how to tame hostile audiences." Well, I disagree with those of you thinking that way. I have given over 3000 presentations, and I always review the fundamentals. Let me use a sports analogy to emphasize this point. By doing so, I am departing from the advice I teach in my workshops—"Men, go easy on the sports metaphors; you run the risk of alienating people in your audience who are not sports nuts." So please indulge me this one time, as the comparison is so apt.

Professional football players are superb athletes, who, in their games, employ complex formations, options, and plays. Yet, when they report to training camp, they initially practice only football fundamentals—blocking, tackling, running, passing, and catching. Only after honing these skills do these athletes move to their complex formations and plays.

Professional speakers should do no less. It is especially important when you are preparing to face a demanding audience. You may get by with a less-than-polished presentation when you are addressing people who agree with you and only wish to have their views reinforced. It is, however, sheer folly to speak to an audience opposed to you without a strict adherence to the fundamentals of the speaking art.

Now, just what am I referring to with the word *fundamentals*? I don't mean just the platform skills of body language, eye contact, gestures, and vocal inflection. They are indeed important tools for the speaker, but I mean something deeper. If your presentation does not take into consideration the objections, questions, and other obstacles to understanding, it is unlikely the audience will accept and act upon your message.

Don't think of a presentation as merely a series of words strung together, any more than a bridge is merely wires and steel haphazardly connected. Just as there are sound engineering principles in bridge construction that take into consideration soil composition, prevailing winds, stress and strain, etc., there are sound principles which must be followed in the construction of a presentation.

Your mission as a speaker, to either a supportive or nonsupportive audience, is to provide maximum information in minimum time in the clearest possible manner. Keep in mind that every presentation is actually four presentations: (1) the one you plan to deliver, (2) the one you actually deliver, (3) the one your audience hears you deliver, and (4) the one you wish you had delivered. I hope my presentation today will help you to deliver as you have planned and practiced, be on the same page as the audience, and have fewer of those "I wish I had said it this way" moments.

A motto of the National Speakers Association of a few years ago very elegantly described professional speakers as enjoying "The privilege of the platform." As a speaker, you have the rare opportunity to "write on the brains" of the people in your audience. Never undertake a presentation without that thought uppermost in your own mind.

To communicate effectively and persuasively with any audience, you need "actionable intelligence" on these people. Note that I do not use the term "audience analysis," which is a favorite phrase of most of my colleagues in the field of presentations training. That phrase reminds me of high school students dissecting a frog. When addressing an audience, you are dealing with living, breathing human beings with beliefs, attitudes, biases, prejudices, etc. Into that mix you will be adding new information. You must know their "what's in it for me" button, the pushing of which will cause them to listen to your message. You must know what problems these people have, so that your presentation can provide the information to solve these problems. This information must be delivered so it will be received by audience members. You must, in short, open the minds of these audience members.

So just how do you open the minds of an audience so your facts will be heard and accepted? You do so by going back to the teaching of history's greatest speech coach—Aristotle. He considered "Ethos," which we would call "source credibility," the most important part of a speaker's means of persuasion. He wrote in *The Rhetoric*, the seminal work on public speaking, that an audience which knew nothing of the subject being addressed would accept the position being advocated by the speaker if that person was considered to have "Ethos."

Moving that Aristotelian precept to our times, we base our view of whether a speaker has credibility on three elements:

1. Expertise
2. Believability
3. Likability

Your audience members want to know that you bring to the table information that will shorten their learning curve, that you have the credentials to speak on this issue, that you are telling the truth, not merely a glib speaker selling snake oil. Finally, they must like you. We all tend to accept information from people we like, and we reject it from people we do not like. Interpersonal skills are intimately connected to speaking skills.

Credibility is subjective. No one in this room, including me, can say "I have credibility to speak on my specialty." Your audience members will decide if you are credible. If they do so, you are in a position to bring them to your point of view. If they do not, you are wasting your time speaking to them.

With all that in mind, I want to show you a systematic way of following the fundamentals of speaking. It is what I call the S3P3 system, the heart of my executive workshops. It has worked for me, and it works for my clients who, for the most part are not nearly as experienced in speaking as you are. Therefore, I know it will work for you. Let me again ask you to open your mental PowerPoint, this time visualizing a pyramid supported by three pillars. The levels of the pyramid are, from base to apex, Planning, Practicing, and Presenting. The pillars are Substance, Structure, and Style.

Substance is the content of the presentation. Always remember that the purpose of a presentation is to convey information from speaker to audience. Style refers to how you look, how you sound, your choice of words—all those attributes we ascribe to a good public speaker. Substance without style is a dry and boring recitation of data. Style without substance is shallow and meaningless. Structure is the skeletal outline, or scaffolding, of the presentation. That's the word a young British Army lieutenant named Winston Churchill used in the title of a brilliant essay written in 1897, "The Scaffolding of Rhetoric." The future British Prime Minister emphasized that audience members needed a guide to show them where the speaker and they were going on this joint journey. A reading of Churchill's memorable World War Two speeches, [which were said to have] "marched the English language into battle," demonstrates that he followed the advice he developed in his youth.

Such organization is vital for an oral presentation. A written memo can have faulty structure, but can be reread. There is no instant replay of the oral presentation. Some examples of this structure are problem-solution, cause and effect, chronological. The presentation must have a beginning, a middle, and an end. It must also have transitions which send signals to the audience that new elements will be discussed.

Now, let's look at that pyramid, starting with that wide base. In Planning, you must develop a concrete objective, aimed at intersecting with the problems, needs, wants, and concerns of your audience. This is always important, but especially so when facing a demanding audience. Know specifically what you wish to have this audience do with the information you are providing. It is here where you draft your presentation, and this can best be done, in my opinion, by following my 3-1-2 system. While this system is counterintuitive, it virtually guarantees that you will have both focus and theme, vital for an oral presentation.

Take a stack of 3×5 cards. Mark one with a "3" and place on it the "bottom line" message you wish to impart to your audience. In front of these words, put "In summary," "In conclusion," or some other phrase signaling the end of your presentation. You now have your conclusion, as well as a mini-presentation, especially beneficial when making a business or sales presentation when time for the presentation is reduced at the last minute. Take another card, mark it with "1" and use it to tell the audience where you are taking them on this oratorical journey. Next, place the supporting points that flow from "1" to "3" on a series of cards marked "2A," "2B," "2C," etc.

Using the 3-1-2 system will enable you to present maximum relevant content within the limited amount of time your audience may have to listen to you. You'll have more focus, because you will know when you start drafting where you are going in the presentation. Most importantly, audience members will see a structure to your presentation, enabling them to follow and, in the best of cases, ultimately agree with your argument. Just remember: you draft 3-1-2, but when you have the allotted time, you deliver 1-2-3.

Now to Practicing, something many of us find rather odious. It is, however, vitally important, especially when preparing to face a difficult audience. Thorough practice will permit you to hone your presentation skills, anticipate questions, and it will certainly build your confidence.

I teach my clients a three-step practice process. First, practice by yourself, with a tape recorder and, if possible, a video camera. You are at your weakest at this stage and do not want anyone criticizing your performance. Listen for your "uh's" and "y'knows." The [fewer] of those abominations you utter, the less you will irritate your audience. Men, listen for a droning monotone. Ladies, listen for a high pitch. Next, ask a colleague to be your "audience." This should be a person who can offer constructive criticism and comments. The third stage is to convene a "Murder Board," a realistic simulation with colleagues role-playing your prospective audience. I'll cover this in more detail in just a few minutes when we focus on communicating with a demanding audience.

Finally, you reach that apex: Presenting. This is when you put voice to thought within a structure that facilitates audience comprehension and agreement with the position you are advocating, done with the style most appropriate to make your presentation memorable and successful. Eye contact, purposeful gestures, pleasant vocal inflection, skillful answering of questions, are all part of the presentation. If you have practiced well, you will present well.

For those of us who deliver similar presentations over and over, the challenge is to keep your material fresh. To do so, take a tip from the theatre. Actors who play the same role night after night refer to this as "creating the illusion of the first time." As speakers, you can add new material, and you can concentrate on getting yourself "pumped." Your obligation is to not be boring to members of your audience who are hearing your words for the first time.

Part Two: Persuading Hostile Audiences

Now let's see how we can apply these fundamentals to communicate with, and perhaps persuade, people who are adamantly opposed to our position.

We live in an increasingly high-tempo, fast-moving, information-laden, real-time age, and the pace is picking up. Audiences are knowledgeable, critical, impatient, and demanding. Public debates and panels on controversial issues are becoming common. Perhaps it has been the institutionalization of presidential and other political debates over the last several years that has led to this state of affairs. Perhaps there is a "Super Bowl" desire deep in our national psyche that craves the clash of ideas, issues, and rivals. A debate or confrontational panel means sharing the platform with a person or persons opposed to you, perhaps with an audience acting as cheerleader for these opponent(s). You will then know how the Christians in the Roman Coliseum felt as they looked at the hungry lions.

To be an effective presenter under such circumstances, a flexible "blueprint" must be developed for transferring information and perceptions from the speaker's mind to the minds of audience members. When facing a skeptical or hostile audience, you must keep in mind that the information you are presenting is probably at variance with the preconceived opinions and biases of audience members. Anticipating how audience members will react and what lines of attack any opponent(s) will follow is an absolute necessity. Knowing your vulnerabilities and developing responses/counterattacks will enable you to snatch victory from the jaws of defeat, if I may use an overdone cliché.

I'll illustrate how failure to develop an effective counterattack had profound consequences for one of our political leaders several years ago. To make this interesting, I'd like to make a wager with you that in a few minutes, as I recount this story, some of you will be able to repeat, almost verbatim, something you saw and heard on television about 16 years ago. Any takers?

I didn't think there would be. Let me tighten the focus. It's a cool October evening in 1988, and two Senators are in the vice-presidential debate. They are Lloyd Bentsen and Dan Quayle.

I'm starting to see some knowing nods. I told you you'd remember.

Quayle had been a controversial choice to be on the Republican ticket, due to his relative youth. To counter this perception, his campaign compared his age, and his time in the Congress, to that of the late President John F. Kennedy. In his memoirs, Quayle says that his "handlers," as he derisively referred to his debate prep team, feared Bentsen would turn the tables and make an unfavorable comparison of Quayle to Kennedy. They advised him to avoid any mention of Kennedy so Bentsen would not have an opportunity to skewer him. This was foolish advice, because in a debate one has no control over the questions. Quayle attempted to avoid the Kennedy comparison, but eventually, in response to a reporter's question, said he was the same age as Kennedy was in 1960, and had served the same number of years in the Congress as had the late president.

Now I see a lot of knowing smiles, and I would venture more than half of you know what happened next. Senator Bentsen said—and repeat after me—"Senator, I knew Jack Kennedy. Jack Kennedy was a friend of mine. Senator, you are no Jack Kennedy." What was Quayle's response? "That was uncalled for."

The remark by Bentsen, and Quayle's stunned reaction, was the most devastating and best-remembered exchange in the history of American political debates. Dan Quayle's image was permanently damaged, even though the Bush–Quayle ticket went on to win the November 1988 election.

The Bentsen–Quayle debate provides an excellent lesson for all presenters. You must seek to anticipate the most daunting objections and questions your audience will raise. Failure to do so could result in public humiliation, the fate suffered by then-Senator Quayle. Despite the fact that Quayle was, by all accounts, an effective Vice President, he never recovered from the Bentsen broadside. His every gaffe of the next four years was exaggerated by the media and TV comedians because it fit the image of the youthful, bumbling, politician established in the debate.

Could Quayle have neutralized Bentsen's broadside? Yes, with an intensive "Murder Board," which I've mentioned in passing and will discuss in a few minutes. Had Quayle and his advisers decided to act on their worst fears, rather than put their heads in the sand and hope for the best, think how effective this response to Bentsen would have been: "Senator, if you want to say who is not a John F. Kennedy, I would suggest you look at your running mate. The only thing Governor Dukakis and JFK have in common is the state of Massachusetts." Such a response would have taken little imagination to devise. A lemon could have been turned into lemonade by luring Bentsen into an "ambush," as a means of guaranteeing the hit on Dukakis. Quayle's risk-averse coaches, however, took the cautious approach, hoping to deny Bentsen the chance to launch the attack they feared. Quayle and the Republican Party were ill-served by such incompetence. If Quayle had delivered such a response, his supporters in the audience would have responded with robust applause, Bentsen's comment would not have captured the headlines, and Quayle would have been credited with a quick-thinking comeback. The exchange would probably have been forgotten, and Quayle, who did well in the rest of the debate, would have possibly been viewed as the winner, or at worst the debate would have been judged a draw. Instead, he was considered the clear loser.

Now let's move away from recent history and back to today. A presenter can connect with even a skeptical audience by showing that he or she shares certain views with members of the audience. You must develop rapport and seek to establish common ground with the audience. If you don't, there is no chance of success in bringing these people to your side. You simply must, at the outset, open the minds of audience members. Let me illustrate once again with a visual image. Imagine a car that is out of gas at point A. This is your prospective audience, which lacks the vital information you will be imparting. You wish to drive this car to point B—acceptance of your information. If the gas cap—the minds of audience members—is closed, any "gas" you pour will wind up on the ground. So how do you get that "gas cap" open? You can do so by getting audience members to like or respect you. You can establish personal contact, perhaps by phone, with key members of the audience well before the presentation. In so doing, you'll not only establish that needed "human connection," you'll also gain additional intelligence on why these people are opposed to you.

Arrive early so you can have conversations with people who are opposed to you. Learn more about their concerns, and why they are opposed to the position you are advocating. Perhaps you will learn who will be the troublemakers. You can speak with them in a nonconfrontational way. These people, in turn, may now see you more as a human being, not a remote corporate figure. During the actual presentation, mention the names of the people with whom you have conferred. Nothing is so sweet to the human ear as the sound of his or her name, especially if it is mentioned positively before others. These people that you mention will probably be less inclined to ask tough questions, as it could appear less than gracious after your kind remarks. Next, find that necessary common ground by emphasizing areas where you and the audience agree, even at a high level of abstraction. This at least puts you and the audience on the same page, even if it is a small page. After establishing that there are points of agreement, you can then move to the arguments supporting your position.

A technique I used in facing audiences initially opposed to the position I was advocating was to acknowledge that we in Washington had done a poor job of articulating our policy, and I could therefore understand why so many people in the audience were opposed to this policy. I would then say I hoped to fill in some of those gaps with my presentation. In this way, I was providing audience members with the opportunity to "save face," perhaps even [become] willing to change their mind as a result of the new information I was about to present. Remember that people don't want to admit they were wrong, and you cannot persuade people to change their mind; they must persuade themselves.

Now, let's look at three tactics for dealing with demanding audiences. First, The Murder Board: The term "Murder Board" comes from military briefings. It is a rigorous practice, a simulation of the actual presentation to be made. It consists of colleagues role-playing the actual audience, asking the type of questions this audience is likely to ask. As its rather macabre name implies, the Murder Board is intended to be more difficult and demanding than the actual presentation. In football terms, it is a full-pads scrimmage. This realistic practice session is the most effective shortcut to speaking excellence. It allows you to make your mistakes when they don't count. It allows you to be exposed to those tough questions, leading to focused research, which enables you to provide succinct, accurate answers in the actual presentation. In sum, the Murder Board increases the odds that you will shine. When faced with the audience inclined more to jeer than cheer, it is essential to have such rigorous preparation—unless you take some perverse joy in public humiliation.

Next, stay within your evidence: During the give-and-take of a presentation with a demanding audience, you may be tempted to go beyond the hard, factual evidence that is the underpinning of your argument. An analogy or metaphor may be stretched beyond its limits, or a conclusion stated that is simply not supported by the facts. This can destroy the credibility you have established up to that point and provide a lucrative target for those strongly opposed to you. Credibility lost is difficult to regain.

Finally, you simply must maintain your composure in the face of hostility: It is quite natural to let your emotions take over if a person in the audience starts to harangue you. Natural, but a recipe for disaster if you lose your temper. Audiences will adopt an "us against the speaker" attitude if you respond in kind to a heckler or a person making obnoxious remarks.

I'll illustrate with an example from my own speaking experience when I was called a liar by an audience member. I was on a panel at a major university, addressing U.S. Latin American policy. The three other members of the panel were professors from the university, all opposed to that policy. The audience was composed primarily of students, who, in the Q&A session, were aggressive but fair. Then a man in his 40s rose, asked a question to which I responded. This was then followed by two more, which were loud personal attacks against my honesty. I felt my Irish temper starting to boil. My instinct was to lash back. Fortunately, for reasons I still don't understand, I did not. Instead, I said, "Look, everybody in this auditorium wants to give me a hard time, and I just can't let you have all the fun." I broke eye contact, but he kept shouting.

At that point, another person shouted at the questioner "Will you sit down and shut up? We want to get at him too." That struck me as funny—perhaps I have a perverted sense of humor—and I laughed. The audience joined in, and even my adversaries on the panel laughed. We then had a fairly civil discussion of policy issues.

What would have happened if I had succumbed to the temptation of responding sharply to this man's accusations? The audience would have sided with him, I would have been booed, and the evening would have been quite unpleasant. The moral of this story? Keep your cool, no matter how provoked you may be. Your audience will respect you and may turn on the heckler who is taking up their time. I fortuitously learned a valuable lesson that day.

Let me make some final observations about our profession. Emotions do indeed play an important role with any audience, but it is still verifiable, factual data that persuades reasonable people to come to your side. Above all, remember that you cannot persuade an audience; audience members must persuade themselves. Never tell them that you are going to persuade, sell, or convince them. Do so and you are dead in the water. Allow audience members to "save face" by providing backing for your position with oral footnotes and with information they did not have prior to listening to you. Remember to maintain your composure, avoid personal attacks, and always keep in mind what you want your audience to do as a result of listening to your argument.

I think a fitting way to conclude may be with one of my favorite quotations about the true purpose of speaking to any group. It comes from the birthplace of speech training and the art of persuasion, ancient Greece. The people of Athens, although admiring the speaker with the stentorian voice, dramatic gesture, and clever turn of phrase, nevertheless realized the purpose of any presentation was to cause audience members to take the action the speaker wished them to take. So it was said, in comparing the greatest speaker of the day with one who had lived many years before: "When Demosthenes speaks, people say 'how well he speaks'. But when Pericles spoke, people said, 'Let us march.'"

Thank you, and good luck in all your speaking ventures, to friend and foe alike.

PERSUASIVE SPEECH

Blinded by the Light

Erica Radcliffe[2]

On June 14, 2003, Bishop Thomas O'Brien was on his way home from celebrating mass. During his routine drive home, he heard a loud noise on the passenger side of his car and noticed his windshield had been damaged by what he thought was a rock. It wasn't until two days later that, according to *CNN.com* March 19, 2004, Bishop O'Brien was arrested by police, not for a cracked windshield, but rather for having struck and killed 43-year-old Jim Reed. In *The Washington Post* of February 10, 2004, Bishop O'Brien contends he never saw Reed in the roadway. The cause of his temporary blindness: the glare from streetlamps and headlights of oncoming traffic.

But this growing epidemic of excessive artificial nighttime lighting, better known as light pollution, isn't confined to this one tragic incident. According to an AAA publication of March 2003, nighttime glare from excessive lighting on roadways and from headlights is responsible for an average of 38,000 traffic accidents each year. But the effects of untamed illumination do more than put us at risk behind the wheel. Since *The New York Times* of August 30, 2003, reports that the United States wastes as much as 2 billion tax dollars every year in bad lighting, and because 99% of Americans live in areas tainted by light pollution, we must first look at the problems it creates, next investigate the causes, before finally figuring out some solutions that will help us flick the switch fueling light pollution.

Although often underestimated, excessive nighttime lighting can produce a plethora of safety, health, and environmental impacts. First, while bright light after dark may seem like a safety precaution, it can actually be a safety hazard. According to *The Santa Fe New Mexican* of July 27, 2003, too much lighting on sidewalks or in alleyways creates shadows, making unsuspecting passersby more susceptible to crime. Here we see a woman walking on what appears to be a well-lit sidewalk. However, in this photo she's gone, but she didn't go far; in fact, she only moved 4 feet to her left—now well hidden by the shadows created from the excessive lighting.

Light pollution also affects our safety on the road. According to *The Vail Daily* of September 25, 2003, after a nighttime fill-up, it takes our eyes 10 minutes to readjust from unnecessary lighting at gas stations once we're back on the road. And a study presented at the 2003 meeting of the National Transportation Research Board confirmed that only 5% of drivers recognized a pedestrian on a road with glare.

Light pollution not only affects our safety, but also has a direct impact on our health. *Discover Magazine* of July 2003 explains that light pollution can "trigger deadly hormonal imbalances." According to *ABC Science Online* of February 18, 2003, the increased and unnatural levels of light we are exposed to after dark is likely raising the risk of cancers. And an August 22, 2003, article by the Harvard Center for Cancer Prevention reports that nighttime light exposure may significantly increase the risk of breast and colon cancer. According to *Life Extension Magazine* of January 2004, light from sources as small as a night-light or television inhibits cancer-fighting melatonin production, compromising our immune systems, making us more susceptible to any number of diseases.

And if your eyesight is not as good as it used to be, recent studies have found that light pollution also affects our vision. *CNN.com*, updated daily and last accessed March 23, 2004, revealed that 55% of children who slept with a light on before the age of 2 were diagnosed with myopia, or nearsightedness, 30% more than those that slept in complete darkness, leading to increased risk of glaucoma, retinal detachment, and macular degeneration in old age. Finally, light pollution is leaving its mark on the environment. *The Norfolk Eastern Daily Press* of September 15, 2003, warns that every 100-watt bulb left on during the hours of darkness all year releases a quarter of a ton of carbon dioxide into the atmosphere, contributing significantly to global warming.

All of us are plagued by the three biggest causes of light pollution: industrialization, commercial competition, and our growing fear of the dark. Due to urban sprawl, the *Audubon Magazine* Web site accessed March 13, 2004, and updated monthly reveals that only 10% of us live in an area where we can see all the stars that should be visible under normal nighttime conditions. According to *The Providence Journal-Bulletin* of August 3, 2003, astronomers at Kitte Peak National Observatory have been complaining about the lights from Phoenix, an area that lies over 120 miles away.

Commercial competition is also responsible. The *Progressivegrocer.com,* updated daily and last accessed March 3, 2004, explains that many small businesses are now forced to expand their hours due to competition from larger chain stores. This rising need for 24-hour service only leads to more unnecessary excess lighting. Advertisements are also a problem. *American Demographic* of December 1, 2003, explains that outdoor advertising is a 6-billion-dollar industry on the rise; over the past 10 years, spending on outdoor ads has risen 97%. According to the February 10, 2004, *Pittsburgh Post-Gazette,* billboards "ruin drivers' night vision" as they use excessive lighting to get consumers' attention quickly on highways or busy city streets.

Finally, it's our own age-old fear of the dark. According to the previously cited *New York Times,* recent studies have found that contrary to popular belief, over-lighting does not reduce crime, but instead, as we saw earlier, merely alleviates our fear of crime, creating a dangerous false sense of security. So maybe it's time we conquered this fear, and we can start by looking at some solutions.

Although the problem seems glaring, it is one of the most easily curable forms of pollution, but must be addressed on a community, industry, and an individual level. The previously cited *Norfolk Eastern Daily Press* explains that the Norfolk city government now requires that white bulbs in street lamps be replaced with low-light-polluting orange bulbs. Road signs and billboards should be replaced with prismatic material, explains *The Pasadena Citizen* of September 16, 2003. This new, highly reflective material eliminates the need for overhead lighting on all road signs because it uses a car's headlights to light up the signs, illuminating them only when needed.

Businesses must also do their part. *The New Haven Register* of September 24, 2003, explains large light-emitting commercial buildings should surround their properties with fences and trees, reducing light pollution from the site. To eliminate unnecessary overnight light pollution, the previously cited *Vail Daily* explains that in that part of Colorado, business lights must be shut off 1 hour after closing. According to the May 17, 2003, *ABC News.com,* by going dark at night, some office buildings and school systems are saving as much as 1 million dollars every year.

But you can start fighting light pollution right now. The AAA Foundation for Traffic Safety offers tips to handle glare for safer driving at night. Please feel free to take one. And as soon as you get home, replace those 200-watt bulbs with 100s and turn out the lights when you leave a room. If you have a nightlight, place it low on a wall facing away from you and keep it as dim as possible. If you tend to fall asleep with the TV on, many sets can now be programmed to shut off after a certain period of time. And according to the Home Depot Web site, last accessed March 23, 2004, you can purchase a Motion Sensor Security Light that only turns on when needed for as little as $12.97.

Today, we have seen the problems, looked at the causes, and finally, viewed some solutions to help us fight light pollution. Bishop Thomas O'Brien served Phoenix's 480,000 Catholics for 21 years. He now owns the title of the first-ever felony conviction for a U.S. Roman Catholic bishop. This is clearly one time Bishop O'Brien would have given anything not to be blinded by the light.

Notes

CHAPTER 1

1. E. T. Klemmer and F. W. Snyder, "Measurement of Time Spent Communicating," *Journal of Communication* 20 (June, 1972): 142.

2. F. E. X. Dance and C. Larson, *Speech Communication: Concepts and Behavior* (New York: Holt, Rinehart and Winston, 1972).

3. Dance and Larson, *Speech Communication*.

4. J. T. Masterson, S. A. Beebe, and N. H. Watson, *Invitation to Effective Speech Communication* (Glenview, IL: Scott, Foresman, 1989).

5. M. Gladwell, *Blink: The Power of Thinking without Thinking* (New York: Little Brown and Company, 2005).

6. This section is based on J. T. Masterson, S. A. Beebe, and N. H. Watson. We are especially indebted to J. T. Masterson for this discussion.

7. See R. P. Wolff, *About Philosophy* (Upper Saddle River, NJ: Prentice Hall, 2000), 308–335.

8. C. S. Lewis, *The Abolition of Man* (New York: Macmillan, 1947); also see A. M. Nicholi, Jr., *The Question of God: C. S. Lewis and Sigmund Freud Debate God, Love, Sex, and the Meaning of Life* (New York: The Free Press, 2002).

9. C. Christians and M. Traber, *Communication Ethics and Universal Values* (Beverly Hills, CA: Sage, 1997); also see S. Bok, *Common Values* (Columbia, MO: University of Missouri Press, 2002).

10. Christians and Traber, *Communication Ethics and Universal Values*.

11. For an excellent discussion of comparative religions and the common principle of being other oriented see W. Ham, *Man's Living Religions* (Independence, MO: Herald Publishing House, 1966), 39–40.

12. For additional discussion of the ethical values taught in the world's religions, see H. Smith, *The World's Religions* (San Francisco: HarperSanFrancisco, 1991).

13. National Communication Association, "NCA Credo for Communication Ethics," 1999 (June 27, 2001) <http://www.natcom.org/conferences/Ethics/ethicsconfcredo99.htm>.

14. We thank Tom Burkholder, University of Nevada, Las Vegas, for this idea.

15. D. Quinn, *My Ishmael* (New York: Bantam Books, 1996).

16. V. Marchant, "Listen Up!" *Time* (June 28, 1999): 72.

17. A. Vangelisti and J. Daly, "Correlates of Speaking Skills in the United States: A National Assessment," *Communication Education* 38 (1989): 132–143.

18. M. Cronin, ed., "The Need for Required Oral Communication Education in the Undergraduate General Education Curriculum," unpublished paper, 1993, available from the National Communication Association, Washington, D.C.

19. J. Ayres and T. S. Hopf, "The Long-Term Effect of Visualization in the Classroom: A Brief Research Report," *Communication Education* 39 (1990): 75–78.

20. See J. C. McCroskey and M. Beatty, "The Communibiological Perspective: Implications for Communication in Instruction," *Communication Education* 49 (2000): 1. Also see J. C. McCroskey, J. A. Daly, M. M. Martin, and M. J. Beatty, eds., *Communication and Personality: Trait Perspectives* (Cresskill, NJ: Hampton Press, 1998).

21. J. H. McConnell, *Are You Communicating? You Can't Manage Without It* (New York: McGraw-Hill, 1995).

22. J. L. Winsor, D. Curtis, and R. D. Stephens, "National Preferences in Business and Communication Education: A Survey Update," *Journal of the Association of Communication Administration 3* (1997): 170–179.

23. Winsor, Curtis, and Stephens, "National Preferences in Business and Communication Education."

24. K. E. Davis and M. Todd, "Assessing Friendship: Prototypes, Paradigm Cases, and Relationship Description." In *Understanding Personal Relationships*, edited by S. W. Duck and D. Perlman (London: Sage, 1985); B. Wellman, "From Social Support to Social Network." In *Social Support: Theory, Research and Applications*, edited by I. G. Sarason and B. R. Sarason (Dordrecht, Netherlands: Nijhoff, 1985); R. Hopper, M. L. Knapp, and L. Scott, "Couples' Personal Idioms: Exploring Intimate Talk," *Journal of Communication* 31 (1981): 23–33.

25. M. Argyle and M. Hendershot, *The Anatomy of Relationships* (London: Penguin Books, 1985), 14.

26. D. Goleman, "Emotional Intelligence: Issues in Paradigms Building." In *The Emotionally Intelligent Workplace*, edited by C. Cherniss and D. Goleman (San Francisco: Jossey Bass, 2001), 13.

27. V. Satir, *Peoplemaking* (Palo Alto, CA: Science and Behavior Books, 1972).

28. M. Argyle, *The Psychology of Happiness* (London: Routledge, 2001).

29. J. J. Lynch, *The Broken Heart: The Medical Consequences of Loneliness* (New York: Basic Books, 1977).

30. D. P. Phillips, "Deathday and Birthday: An Unexpected Connection." In *Statistics: A Guide to the Unknown*, edited by J. M. Tanur (San Francisco: Holden Day, 1972). Also see F. Korbin and G. Hendershot, "Do Family Ties Reduce Mortality? Evidence from the United States 1968," *Journal of Marriage and the Family 39* (1977): 737–746; K. Heller and K. S. Rook, "Distinguishing the Theoretical Functions of Social Ties: Implications of Support Interventions." In *Handbook of Personal Relationships* 2e, edited by S. W. Duck, K. Dindia, W. Ickes, R. Milardo, R. S. L. Mills, and B. R. Sarason (Chichester: Wiley, 1997); B. R. Sarason, I. G. Sarason, and R. A. R. Gurung, "Close Personal Relationships and Health Outcomes: A Key to the Role of Social Support." In *Handbook of Personal Relationships*, Duck et al., eds. Also see S. Duck, *Relating to Others* (Buckingham, England: Open University Press, 1999), 1.

31. H. Lasswell, "The Structure and Function of Communication in Society." In *The Communication of Ideas*, edited by L. Bryson (New York: Institute for Religious and Social Studies, 1948), 37.

32. See V. E. Cronen, W. B. Pearce, and L. M. Harris, "The Coordinated Management of Meaning: A Theory of Communication." In *Human Communication Theory: Comparative Essays*, edited by F. E. X. Dance (New York: Harper & Row, 1982), 61–89.

33. L. Barker, R. Edwards, C. Gaines, K. Gladney, and F. Holley, "An Investigation of Proportional Time Spent in Various Communication Activities of College Students," *Journal of Applied Communication Research 8* (1981): 101–109.

34. See D. Barnlund, *Interpersonal Communication: Survey and Studies* (Boston: Houghton Mifflin Company, 1968).

35. See C. R. Berger and J. J. Bradac, *Language and Social Knowledge: Uncertainty in Interpersonal Relations* (London: Arnold, 1982).

36. O. Wiio, *Wiio's Laws—and Some Others* (Espoo, Finland: Welin-Goos, 1978).

37. T. Watzlawick, J. B. Bavelas, and D. Jackson, *The Pragmatics of Human Communication* (New York: W. W. Norton, 1967).

38. S. B. Shimanoff, *Communication Rules: Theory and Research* (Beverly Hills: Sage, 1980).

39. For an excellent review of intrapersonal communication theory and research, see D. Voate, *Intrapersonal Communication: Different Voices, Different Minds* (Hillsdale, NJ: Lawrence Erlbaum, 1994).

40. Quinn, *My Ishmael*.

41. Barker et al., "An Investigation of Proportional Time Spent in Various Communication Activities of College Students."

42. We appreciate and acknowledge our friend and colleague M. Redmond for his contributions to our understanding of interpersonal communication. For more information, see S. A. Beebe, S. J. Beebe, and M. V. Redmond, *Interpersonal Communication: Relating to Others* 4e (Boston: Allyn & Bacon, 2005).

43. For an excellent discussion of the power of dialogue to enrich the quality of communication, see D. Yankelovich, *The Magic of Dialogue: Transforming Conflict into Cooperation* (New York: Simon & Schuster, 1999).

44. S. A. Beebe and J. T. Masterson, *Communicating in Small Groups: Principles and Practices* 8e (Boston: Allyn & Bacon, 2006).

45. For a discussion of group size, see Beebe and Masterson, *Communicating in Small Groups*.

CHAPTER 2

1. L. Garcia, "Dating Service Founder's Goal: Love That Lasts," *Dallas Morning News* (March 21, 2005): 1E, 4E; R. Konrad, "Dating Site Gets Patent: EHarmony Pushes Its Method for Love," *Corpus Christi Caller Times* (May 28, 2004): A2.

2. S. R. Covey, *The Seven Habits of Highly Effective People* (New York: Simon & Schuster, 1989), 67.

3. R. A. Baron, D. Byrne, and N. R. Branscombe, *Social Psychology* 11e (Boston: Allyn & Bacon, 2005).

4. K. Horney, *Neurosis and Human Growth* (New York: W. W. Norton & Co., 1950), 17.

5. B. Goss, *Processing Communication* (Belmont, CA: Wadsworth, 1982), 72.

6. J. T. Masterson, S. A. Beebe, and N. H. Watson, *Invitation to Effective Speech Communication* (Glenview, IL: Scott, Foresman and Company, 1989).

7. W. James, *Principles of Psychology* (New York: Henry Holt and Company, 1890).

8. M. Beck, "Makeover Madness," *O: The Oprah Winfrey Magazine* (April, 2005): 175–178; A. Botta, "Television Images and Adolescent Girls' Body Image Disturbance," *Journal of Communication* 49 (1999): 22–37; M. Wiederman and S. R. Hurst, "Body Size, Physical Attractiveness, and Body Image among Young Adult Women: Relationships to Sexual Experience and Sexual Esteem," *Journal of Sex Research* 35 (1998): 272–281; N. Wolf, *The Beauty Myth: How Images of Beauty Are Used against Women* (New York: William Morrow, 1991).

9. D. M. Garner, "The 1997 Body Image Survey Results," *Psychology Today* (January/February, 1997): 30–44, 74–75, 78, 80, 84.

10. T. Spiker, "How Men Really Feel About Their Bodies," *O: The Oprah Winfrey Magazine* (August, 2003): 150–151, 181–182; G. B. Forbes, L. E. Adams-Curtis, B. Rade, and P. Jaberg, "Body Dissatisfaction in Women and Men: The Role of Gender-Typing and Self-Esteem," *Sex Roles* 44 (2001): 461–484.

11. A. N. Markham, *Life Online: Researching Real Experience in Virtual Space* (Walnut Creek, CA: AltaMira Press, 1998), 135; 202–203.

12. C. H. Cooley, *Human Nature and the Social Order* (New York: Scribner's, 1912).

13. G. H. Mead, *Mind, Self, and Society* (Chicago: University of Chicago Press, 1934).

14. J. Stewart, K. E. Zediker, and S. Witteborn, *Together: Communicating Interpersonally* 6e (Los Angeles: Roxbury, 2005).

15. D. K. Ivy and P. Backlund, *GenderSpeak: Personal Effectiveness in Gender Communication* 3e (New York: McGraw-Hill, 2004).

16. J. C. Pearson, L. Turner, and W. T. Mancillas, *Gender & Communication* 3e. (Dubuque, IA: William C. Brown, 1995).

17. J. E. Stake, "Gender Differences and Similarities in Self-Concept within Everyday Life Contexts," *Psychology of Women Quarterly* 16 (1992): 349–363.

18. G. Steinem, *Revolution from Within: A Book of Self-Esteem* (Boston: Little, Brown and Company, 1993), 26.

19. Ivy and Backlund, *GenderSpeak*.

20. See C. Gilligan, *In a Different Voice: Psychological Theory and Women's Development* (Cambridge, MA: Harvard University Press, 1982); P. Orenstein, *Schoolgirls: Young Women, Self-Esteem, and the Confidence Gap* (New York: Doubleday, 1994); R. A. Josephs, H. R. Markus, and R. W. Tafarodi, "Gender and Self-Esteem," *Journal of Personality and Social Psychology* 63 (1991): 391–402.

21. American Association of University Women, *Shortchanging Girls, Shortchanging America* (Washington, DC: AAUW Educational Foundation, 1991).

22. M. Sadker and D. Sadker, *Failing at Fairness: How America's Schools Cheat Girls* (New York: Charles Scribner's Sons, 1994), 77.

23. G. J. Carter, "The New Face: As Women's World Cup Soccer Kicks Off This Weekend, Girls around the Globe Finally Get the Role Model They Deserve: Mia Hamm," *USA Weekend* (June 18–20, 1999): 6–7.

24. "Shot of Brandi Lifts U.S.," *Corpus Christi Caller Times* (July 11, 1999): B1, B9.

25. L. Festinger, "A Theory of Social Comparison Processes," *Human Relations* 2 (1954): 117–140.

26. J. S. Phinney, C. L. Cantu, and D. A. Kurtz, "Ethnic and American Identity as Predictors of Self-Esteem Among African American, Latino, and White Adolescents," *Journal of Youth and Adolescence* 26 (1997): 165–185.

27. G. Flynn, "Self-Hate Crime: Misogynistic Makeover Show *The Swan* Is One Ugly Duckling," *Entertainment Weekly* (April 23, 2004): 69.

28. M. M. Martin and J. W. Gentry, "Stuck in the Model Trap." In *Taking Sides: Clashing Views on Controversial Issues in Mass Media and Society* 8e, edited by A. Alexander and J. Hanson (Dubuque, IA: McGraw-Hill/Dushkin, 2005), 52–61.

29. M. Cottle, "Turning Boys into Girls." In *Taking Sides*, Alexander and Hanson, eds.

30. J. Hattie, *Self-Concept* (Hillsdale, NJ: Lawrence Erlbaum, 1992).

31. A. Chatham-Carpenter and V. DeFrancisco, "Pulling Yourself Up Again: Women's Choices and Strategies for Recovering and Maintaining Self-Esteem," *Western Journal of Communication* 61 (1997): 164–187.

32. Goss, *Processing Communication*.

33. L. C. Lederman, "The Impact of Gender on the Self and Self-Talk." In *Women and Men Communicating: Challenges and Changes* 2e, edited by L. P. Arliss and D. J. Borisoff (Prospect Heights, IL: Waveland, 2001), 78–89; J. R. Johnson, "The Role of Inner Speech in Human Communication," *Communication Education* 33 (1984): 211–222; C. R. Streff, "The Concept of Inner Speech and Its Implications for an Integrated Language Arts Curriculum," *Communication Education* 33 (1984): 223–230; J. L. McFarland, "The Role of Speech in Self-Development, Self-Concept, and Decentration," *Communication Education* 33 (1984): 231–236; J. Ayres, "The Power of Positive Thinking," *Communication Education* 37 (1988): 289–296.

34. C. J. Mruk, *Self-Esteem: Research, Theory, and Practice* (New York: Springer, 1995).

35. See J. Ayres and T. S. Hopf, "The Long-Term Effect of Visualization in the Classroom: A Brief Research Report," *Communication Education 39* (1990): 75–78; J. Ayres and T. S. Hopf, "Visualization: Is It More Than Extra-Attention?" *Communication Education 38* (1989): 1–5.

36. J. Ayres, T. S. Hopf, and D. M. Ayres, "An Examination of Whether Imaging Ability Enhances the Effectiveness of an Intervention Designed to Reduce Speech Anxiety," *Communication Education 43* (1994): 252–258.

37. Covey, *The Seven Habits of Highly Effective People*, 105.

38. P. R. Hinton, *The Psychology of Interpersonal Perception* (New York: Routledge, 1993).

39. U. Neisser, *Cognition and Reality: Principles and Implications of Cognitive Psychology* (San Francisco: W. H. Freeman and Company, 1976).

40. D. J. Schneider, A. H. Hastorf, and P. C. Ellsworth, *Person Perception* 2e (Reading, MA: Addison-Wesley, 1979).

41. D. T. Kenrick, S. L. Neuberg, and R. B. Cialdini, *Social Psychology: Unraveling the Mystery* 3e (Boston: Allyn & Bacon, 2004).

42. C. N. Macrae, G. V. Bodenhausen, A. B. Milne, and J. Jetten, "Out of Mind but Back in Sight: Stereotypes on the Rebound," *Journal of Personality and Social Psychology 67* (1994): 808–817.

43. Macrae et al., "Out of Mind," 808.

44. This chapter benefited from the fine scholarship and work of M. V. Redmond, coauthor of *Interpersonal Communication: Relating to Others* 4e (Boston: Allyn & Bacon, 2005).

CHAPTER 3

1. S. Friess, "Yo, can u plz help me write English?: Parents Fear Online Chatting Ruins Kids' Language Skills," *USA Today* (April 1, 2003).

2. J. Scott, "I Feel," *Bitch: Feminist Response to Pop Culture* (Spring, 2003): 25.

3. "College Graduates Aren't Ready for the Real World," *The Chronicle of Higher Education* (February 18, 2005): B11.

4. B. Spitzberg and J. P. Dillard, "Social Skills and Communication." In *Interpersonal Communication Research: Advances Through Meta-Analysis*, edited by M. Allen, R. W. Preiss, B. M. Gayle, and N. Burrell (Mahwah, NJ: Lawrence Erlbaum, 2002), 89–107.

5. D. Spender, *Man Made Language* 2e (London: Routledge & Kegan Paul, 1985).

6. B. L. Whorf, "Science and Linguistics." In *Language, Thought, and Reality*, edited by J. B. Carroll (Cambridge: Massachusetts Institute of Technology Press, 1956).

7. W. Johnson, *People in Quandaries: The Semantics of Personal Adjustment* (New York: Harper & Row, 1946).

8. *Oxford Desk Dictionary and Thesaurus, American Edition* (New York: Oxford University Press, 1997).

9. A. G. Smith, ed., *Communication and Culture* (New York: Holt, Rinehart, & Winston, 1966).

10. D. K. Ivy and P. Backlund, *GenderSpeak: Personal Effectiveness in Gender Communication* 3e (New York: McGraw-Hill, 2004).

11. A. Ellis, *A New Guide to Rational Living* (North Hollywood, CA: Wilshire Books, 1977).

12. C. Peterson, M. E. P. Seligman, and G. E. Vaillant, "Pessimistic Explanatory Style Is a Risk Factor for Physical Illness: A 35-Year Longitudinal Study," *Journal of Personality and Social Psychology 55* (1988): 23–27.

13. J. Barlow, "E-Mail Etiquette Has Its Own Rules," *Houston Chronicle* (March 11, 1999): C1.

14. D. A. Lieberman, *Public Speaking in the Multicultural Environment* 2e (Boston: Allyn & Bacon, 1997), 34–35.

15. *Newsweek* (November 20, 1995): 81.

16. "Y? The National Forum on People's Differences," *Entertainment Weekly* (July 12, 1999): 30.

17. L. Pitts, "African-American? Hispanic? Indian? Does It Really Matter What We Call Ourselves?" *Corpus Christi Caller Times* (May 25, 2003): A15.

18. See J. K. Swim, R. Mallett, and C. Stangor, "Understanding Subtle Sexism: Detection and Use of Sexist Language," *Sex Roles 51* (2004): 117–128; J. Briere and C. Lanktree, "Sex-Role Related Effects of Sex Bias in Language," *Sex Roles 9* (1983): 625–632; L. Brooks, "Sexist Language in Occupational Information: Does It Make a Difference?" *Journal of Vocational Behavior 23* (1983): 227–232; A. Stericker, "Does This 'He or She' Business Really Make a Difference? The Effect of Masculine Pronouns as Generics on Job Attitudes," *Sex Roles 7* (1981): 637–641.

19. H. S. O'Donnell, "Sexism in Language," *Elementary English 50* (1973): 1067–1072, as cited by J. C. Pearson, L. Turner, and W. Todd Mancillas, *Gender & Communication* 3e (Dubuque, IA: William C. Brown, 1995).

20. See J. L. Stinger and R. Hopper, "Generic *He* in Conversation?" *Quarterly Journal of Speech 84* (1998): 209–221; J. Gastil, "Generic Pronouns and Sexist Language: The Oxymoronic Character of Masculine Generics," *Sex Roles 23* (1990): 629–641; D. K. Ivy, L. Bullis-Moore, K. Norvell, P. Backlund, and M. Javidi, "The Lawyer, the Babysitter, and the Student: Inclusive Language Usage and Instruction," *Women & Language 18* (1994): 13–21; W. Martyna, "What Does 'He' Mean? Use of the Generic Masculine," *Journal of Communication 28* (1978): 131–138.

21. L. Madson and R. M. Hessling, "Does Alternating between Masculine and Feminine Pronouns Eliminate Perceived Gender Bias in a Text?" *Sex Roles 41* (1999): 559–576; D. Kennedy, "Review Essay: She or He in Textbooks," *Women and Language 15* (1992): 46–49.

22. See R. Maggio, *The Nonsexist Word Finder: A Dictionary of Gender-Free Usage* (Boston: Beacon, 1988); C. Miller, K. Swift, and R. Maggio, "Liberating Language," *Ms.* (September/October, 1997): 50–54.

23. *Fox News* Broadcast, May 6, 2003.

24. C. H. Palczewski, " 'Tak[e] the Helm,' Man the Ship . . . and I Forgot My Bikini! Unraveling Why Woman Is Not Considered a Verb," *Women & Language 21* (1998): 1–8; Maggio, *The Nonsexist Word Finder*.

25. A. Walker, as cited in A. Bilger, "The Common *Guy*: One Seemingly Benign Phrase Makes a Man Out of All of Us," *Bitch: Feminist Response to Pop Culture* (Fall, 2002): 87.

26. Ivy and Backlund, *GenderSpeak*.

27. J. S. Seiter, J. Larsen, and J. Skinner, " 'Handicapped' or 'Handicapable'? The Effects of Language about Persons with Disabilities on Perceptions of Source Credibility and Persuasiveness," *Communication Reports 11* (1998): 21–31.

28. D. O. Braithwaite and C. A. Braithwaite, "Understanding Communication of Persons with Disabilities as Cultural Communication." In *Intercultural Communication: A Reader* 10e, edited by L. A. Samovar and R. E. Porter (Belmont, CA: Wadsworth, 2002), 136–145.

29. J. R. Gibb, "Defensive Communication," *Journal of Communication 11* (1961): 141–148. Also see R. Bolton, *People Skills* (New York: Simon & Schuster, 1979), 14–26; O. Hargie, C. Sanders, and D. Dickson, *Social Skills in Interpersonal Communication* (London: Routledge, 1994); O. Hargie, ed., *The Handbook of Communication Skills* (London: Routledge, 1997).

30. M. V. Redmond, "The Functions of Empathy (Decentering) in Human Relations," *Human Relations 42* (1993): 593–606.

CHAPTER 4

1. L. E. Boone and D. L. Kurtz, *Contemporary Business* (New York: Dryden Press, 1997); V. Quercia, *Internet in a Nutshell* (Cambridge, MA: O'Reilly, 1997).

2. A. Mehrabian, *Nonverbal Communication* (Chicago: Aldine-Atherton, 1972).

3. R. L. Birdwhistell, *Kinesics and Context* (Philadelphia: University of Pennsylvania Press, 1970).

4. J. H. Bert and K. Piner, "Social Relationships and the Lack of Social Relations." In *Personal Relationships and Social Support*, edited by S. W. Duck with R. C. Silver (London: Sage, 1989).

5. W. E. Chaplin, J. B. Phillips, J. D. Brown, N. R. Clanton, and J. L. Stein, "Handshaking, Gender, Personality, and First Impressions," *Journal of Personality and Social Psychology* 79 (2000): 110–117.

6. J. K. Burgoon, L. A. Stern, and L. Dillman, *Interpersonal Adaptation: Dyadic Interaction Patterns* (Cambridge, England: Cambridge University Press, 1995).

7. P. Ekman, "Communication through Nonverbal Behavior: A Source of Information about an Interpersonal Relationship." In *Affect, Cognition, and Personality*, edited by S. S. Tomkins and C. E. Izard (New York: Springer, 1965).

8. M. Argyle, *Bodily Communication* (New York: Methuen & Company, 1988).

9. P. Ekman and W. V. Friesen, "Constants across Cultures in the Face and Emotion," *Journal of Personality and Social Psychology 17* (1971): 124–129; Argyle, *Bodily Communication*, 157; I. Eibl-Eibesfeldt, "Similarities and Differences between Cultures in Expressive Movements." In *Nonverbal Communication*, edited by R. A. Hinde (Cambridge, England: Royal Society and Cambridge University Press, 1972); P. Collett, "History and Study of Expressive Action." In *Historical Social Psychology*, edited by K. Gergen and M. Gergen (Hillsdale, NJ: Lawrence Erlbaum, 1984); E. T. Hall, *The Silent Language* (Garden City, NY: Doubleday, 1959); R. Shuter, "Proxemics and Tactility in Latin America," *Journal of Communication 26* (1976): 46–55; E. T. Hall, *The Hidden Dimension* (New York: Doubleday, 1966).

10. R. E. Porter and L. A. Samovar, "An Introduction to Intercultural Communication." In *Intercultural Communication: A Reader* 10e, edited by L. A. Samovar and R. E. Porter (Belmont, CA: Wadsworth, 2002).

11. J. Douglas, Jr., "Outside Texas, 'Hook 'em Horns' Gesture Has Different and Unflattering Meanings," *Fort Worth Star Telegram* (January 23, 2005): 2A.

12. "Watch Your Tongue; This Isn't Tibet," *Fort Worth Star Telegram* (October 10, 2004): 2A; E. Adams, "Manners Can Sink International Business Dealings," *Corpus Christi Caller Times* (November 2, 2003): K2.

13. See J. K. Burgoon and S. B. Jones, "Toward a Theory of Personal Space Expectations and Their Violations," *Human Communication Research 2* (1976): 131–146. For recent applications of expectancy violations theory, see S. Campo, K. A. Cameron, D. Brossard, and M. S. Frazer, "Social Norms and Expectancy Violation Theories: Assessing the Effectiveness of Health Communication Campaigns," *Communication Monographs 71* (2004): 448–470; L. A. Erbert and K. Floyd, "Affectionate Expression as Face-Threatening Acts: Receiver Assessments," *Communication Studies 55* (2004): 254–270; J. L. Bevan, "General Partner and Relational Uncertainty as Consequences of Another Person's Jealousy Expression," *Western Journal of Communication 68* (2004): 195–218; J. L. Bevan, "Expectancy Violation Theory and Sexual Resistance in Close, Cross-Sex Relationships." *Communication Monographs 70* (2003): 68–82; W. A. Afifi and J. K. Burgoon, "The Impact of Violations on Uncertainty and the Consequences for Attractiveness," *Human Communication Research 26* (2000): 203–233.

14. J. Fast, *Body Language* (New York: M. Evans, 1970).

15. P. Ekman and W. V. Friesen, "The Repertoire of Nonverbal Behavior: Categories, Origins, Usage, and Coding," *Semiotica 1* (1969): 49–98.

16. E. Tenner, "Political Timber: Glitter, Froth, and Measuring Tape," *The Chronicle of Higher Education* (October 1, 2004): B12–B13.

17. G. Montell, "Do Good Looks Equal Good Evaluations?" *The Chronicle of Higher Education: Career Network* (October 15, 2003) <http://chronicle.com>.

18. G. B. Forbes, L. E. Adams-Curtis, B. Rade, and P. Jaberg, "Body Dissatisfaction in Women and Men: The Role of Gender-Typing and Self-Esteem," *Sex Roles 44* (2001): 461–484; R. A. Botta, "Television Images and Adolescent Girls' Body Image Disturbance," *Journal of Communication 49* (1999): 22–37; M. Wiederman and S. Hurst, "Body Size, Physical Attractiveness, and Body Image among Young Adult Women: Relationships to Sexual Experience and Sexual Esteem," *Journal of Sex Research 35* (1998): 272–281.

19. E. Hatfield and S. Sprecher, *Mirror, Mirror . . .: The Importance of Looks in Everyday Life* (Albany: SUNY Press, 1986); C. M. Marlowe, S. L. Schneider, and C. E. Nelson, "Gender and Attractiveness Biases in Hiring Decisions: Are More Experienced Managers Less Biased?" *Journal of Applied Psychology 81* (1998): 11–21; W. R. Zakahi, R. L. Duran, and M. Adkins, "Social Anxiety, Only Skin Deep? The Relationships between Ratings of Physical Attractiveness and Social Anxiety," *Communication Research Reports 11* (1994): 23–31; L. A. Zebrowitz, *Reading Faces: Window to the Soul?* (Boulder, CO: Westview, 1997).

20. J. Gorham, S. H. Cohen, and T. L. Morris, "Fashion in the Classroom III: Effects of Instructor Attire and Immediacy in Natural Classroom Interactions," *Communication Quarterly 47* (1999): 281–299; K. D. Roach, "Effects of Graduate Teaching Assistant Attire on Student Learning, Misbehaviors, and Ratings of Instruction," *Communication Quarterly 45* (1997): 125–141; S. E. White, "A Content Analytic Technique for Measuring the Sexiness of Women's Business Attire in Media Presentations," *Communication Research Reports 12* (1995): 178–185; J. M. Townsend and G. D. Levy, "Effects of Potential Partners' Costume and Physical Attractiveness on Sexuality and Partner Selection," *Journal of Psychology 124* (1990): 371–389; F. B. Furlow, "The Smell of Love." In *The Nonverbal Communication Reader: Classic and Contemporary Readings* 2e, edited by L. K. Guerrero, J. DeVito, and M. L. Hecht (Prospect Heights, IL: Waveland, 1999), 118–125; R. K. Aune, "The Effects of Perfume Use on Perceptions of Attractiveness and Competence." In Guerrero, *The Nonverbal Communication Reader*, 126–132.

21. J. T. Molloy, *New Dress for Success* (New York: Warner Books, 1988); J. T. Molloy, *New Woman's Dress for Success Book* (New York: Warner, 1996).

22. L. Averyt, "Casual-Attire Fridays Are Spreading to Rest of Week in Many Companies," *Corpus Christi Caller Times* (August 31, 1997): A1, A6; M. G. Frank and T. Gilovich, "The Dark Side of Self- and Social Perception: Black Uniforms and Aggression in Professional Sports," *Journal of Personality and Social Psychology 54* (1988): 74–85; P. A. Andersen, *Nonverbal Communication: Forms and Functions* (Mountain View, CA: Mayfield, 1999); V. Santos-Garza, "School Code Is Dressed in Stress," *Corpus Christi Caller Times* (August 1, 2004): C1; O. Garcia Hunter, "Goodbye Grunge," *Corpus Christi Caller Times* (July 18, 2004): A1, A8.

23. N. Armstrong and M. Wagner, *Field Guide to Gestures: How to Identify and Interpret Virtually Every Gesture Known to Man* (Philadelphia: Quirk Books, 2003).

24. Birdwhistell, *Kinesics and Context*; D. G. Leathers, *Successful Nonverbal Communication: Principles and Applications* 3e (Boston: Allyn & Bacon, 1997).

25. Ekman and Friesen, "The Repertoire of Nonverbal Behavior."

26. G. Beattie and H. Shovelton, "Mapping the Range of Information Contained in the Iconic Hand Gestures That Accompany Spontaneous Speech," *Journal of Language & Social Psychology 18* (1999): 438–462; J. Streeck, "Gesture as Communication I: Its Coordination with Gaze and Speech," *Communication Monographs 60* (1993): 275–299.

Notes 459

27. W. G. Woodall and J. P. Folger, "Nonverbal Cue Context and Episodic Memory: On the Availability and Endurance of Nonverbal Behaviors as Retrieval Cues," *Communication Monographs 52* (1985): 320–333; A. A. Cohen and R. P. Harrison, "Intentionality in the Use of Hand Illustrators in Face-to-Face Communication Situations," *Journal of Personality and Social Psychology 28* (1973): 276–279.

28. C. Darwin, *Expression of Emotions in Man and Animals* (London: Appleton; reprinted University of Chicago Press, 1965).

29. E. McClure and K. Pope, "Facial Expression Recognition in Adolescents with Mood and Anxiety Disorders," *Journal of Psychology 160* (2003): 1172–1175; V. Lee and H. Wagner, "The Effect of Social Presence on the Facial and Verbal Expression of Emotion and the Interrelationships among Emotion Components," *Journal of Nonverbal Behavior 26* (2002): 3–23; P. Gosselin, M. Perron, M. Legault, and P. Campanella, "Children's and Adults' Knowledge of the Distinction between Enjoyment and Nonenjoyment Smiles," *Journal of Nonverbal Behavior 26* (2002): 83–107; L. Goos and I. Silverman, "Sex Related Factors in the Perception of Threatening Facial Expressions," *Journal of Nonverbal Behavior 26* (2002): 27–41; M. Thunberg and D. Dimberg, "Gender Differences in Facial Reactions to Fear-Relevant Stimuli," *Journal of Nonverbal Behavior 24* (2000): 44–50; D. LaPlante and N. Ambady, "Multiple Messages: Facial Recognition Advantage for Compound Expressions," *Journal of Nonverbal Behavior 24* (2000): 211–221.

30. L. A. Renninger, T. J. Wade, and K. Grammer, "Getting That Female Glance: Patterns and Consequences of Male Nonverbal Behavior in Courtship Contexts," *Evolution and Human Behavior 25* (2004): 416–431; D. Singh, "Mating Strategies of Young Women: Role of Physical Attractiveness," *Journal of Sex Research 41* (2004): 43–54; K. Grammer, K. Kruck, A. Juette, and B. Fink, "Nonverbal Behavior as Courtship Signals: The Role of Control and Choice in Selecting Partners," *Evolution and Human Behavior 21* (2000): 371–390; M. F. Abrahams, "Perceiving Flirtatious Communication: An Exploration of the Perceptual Dimensions Underlying Judgments of Flirtatiousness," *Journal of Sex Research 31* (1994): 283–292; K. Grammer, "Strangers Meet: Laughter and Nonverbal Signs of Interest in Opposite-Sex Encounters," *Journal of Nonverbal Behavior 14* (1990): 209–235.

31. M. M. Moore, "Nonverbal Courtship Patterns in Women: Context and Consequences," *Ethology and Sociobiology 6* (1985): 237–247; D. Knox and K. Wilson, "Dating Behaviors of University Students," *Family Relations 30* (1981): 255–258.

32. D. D. Henningsen, "Flirting with Meaning: An Examination of Miscommunication in Flirting Interactions," *Sex Roles 50* (2004): 481–489; M. M. Moore, "Courtship Communication and Perception," *Perceptual and Motor Skills 94* (2002): 97–105; E. Koukounas and N. M. Letch, "Psychological Correlates of Perception of Sexual Intent in Women," *Journal of Social Psychology 141* (2001): 443–456; A. Abbey, "Sex Differences in Attributions for Friendly Behavior: Do Males Misperceive Females' Friendliness?" *Journal of Personality and Social Psychology 42* (1982): 830–838; L. B. Koeppel, Y. Montagne, D. O'Hair, and M. J. Cody, "Friendly? Flirting? Wrong?" In Guerrero, *The Nonverbal Communication Reader*, 290–297.

33. A. Abbey, T. Zawacki, and P. O. Buck, "The Effects of Past Sexual Assault Perpetration and Alcohol Consumption on Reactions to Women's Mixed Signals," *Journal of Social and Clinical Psychology 24* (2005): 129–157; H. J. Delaney and B. A. Gluade, "Gender Differences in Perception of Attractiveness of Men and Women in Bars," *Journal of Personality and Social Psychology 16* (1990): 378–391.

34. A. E. Scheflen, "Quasi-Courtship Behavior in Psychotherapy," *Psychiatry 28* (1965): 245–257; K. Grammer, K. B. Knuck, and M. S. Magnusson, "The Courtship Dance: Patterns of Nonverbal Synchronization in Opposite Sex Encounters," *Journal of Nonverbal Behavior 22* (1998): 3–25.

35. J. A. Daly, E. Hogg, D. Sacks, M. Smith, and L. Zimring, "Sex and Relationship Affect Social Self-Grooming," *Journal of Nonverbal Behavior 7* (1983): 183–189.

36. M. L. Knapp and J. A. Hall, *Nonverbal Communication in Human Interaction* 5e (Fort Worth, TX: Harcourt Brace, 2002), 390–391.

37. S. A. Beebe, "Eye Contact: A Nonverbal Determinant of Speaker Credibility," *Speech Teacher 23* (1974): 21–25.

38. M. G. Frank and T. H. Feeley, "To Catch a Liar: Challenges for Research in Lie Detection Training," *Journal of Applied Communication Research 31* (2003): 58–75; D. Goleman, "Can You Tell When Someone Is Lying to You?" In Guerrero, *The Nonverbal Communication Reader*, 358–366; T. H. Feeley and M. A. deTurck, "The Behavioral Correlates of Sanctioned and Unsanctioned Deceptive Communication," *Journal of Nonverbal Behavior 22* (1998): 189–204; L. A. Zebrowitz, L. Voinescu, and M. A. Collins, "'Wide-Eyed' and 'Crooked-Faced': Determinants of Perceived and Real Honesty across the Life Span," *Personality and Social Psychology Bulletin 22* (1996): 1258–1269.

39. D. G. Leathers, L. Vaughn, G. Sanchez, and J. Bailey, "Who Is Lying in the Anita Hill–Clarence Thomas Hearing?: Nonverbal Communication Profiles." Paper presented at the meeting of the Speech Communication Association, October, 1992.

40. P. Ekman and W. Friesen, *Unmasking the Face* (Englewood Cliffs, NJ: Prentice-Hall, 1975).

41. Ekman and Friesen, *Unmasking the Face.*

42. Lee and Wagner, "The Effect of Social Presence on the Facial and Verbal Expression of Emotion and the Interrelationships among Emotion Components"; M. T. Motley, "Facial Affect and Verbal Context in Conversation," *Human Communication Research 20* (1993): 3–40; D. S. Berry, "Accuracy in Social Perception: Contributions of Facial and Vocal Information," *Journal of Personality and Social Psychology 61* (1991): 298–307.

43. Ekman and Friesen, *Unmasking the Face.*

44. P. M. Cole, "Children's Spontaneous Control of Facial Expression," *Child Development 57* (1986): 1309–1321.

45. S. Dang, "Abused Kids More Sensitive to Anger: Study Shows Victims Identify More Faces as 'Angry' Than Non-Abused," *Corpus Christi Caller Times* (June 23, 2002): A26.

46. S. E. Jones and A. E. Yarbrough, "A Naturalistic Study of the Meanings of Touch," *Communication Monographs 52* (1985): 19–56.

47. A. Montague, *Touching: The Human Significance of the Skin* (New York: Harper & Row, 1978).

48. M. S. Remland, T. S. Jones, and H. Brinkman, "Proxemic and Haptic Behavior in Three European Countries," *Journal of Nonverbal Behavior 15* (1991): 215–231; M. S. Remland, T. S. Jones, and H. Brinkman, "Interpersonal Distance, Body Orientation and Touch: Effect of Culture, Gender, and Age," *Journal of Social Psychology 135* (1995): 281–295; S. M. Jourard, "An Exploratory Study of Body-Accessibility," *British Journal of Social and Clinical Psychology 26* (1966): 235–242; D. C. Barnlund, "Communicative Styles in Two Cultures: Japan and the United States." In *Organization of Behavior in Face-to-Face Interaction*, edited by A. Kendon, R. M. Harris, and M. R. Key (The Hague: Mouton, 1975).

49. M. A. Beres, E. Herold, and S. B. Maitland, "Sexual Consent Behaviors in Same-Sex Relationships," *Archives of Sexual Behavior 33* (2004): 475–486; J. W. Lee and L. K. Guerrero, "Types of Touch in Cross-Sex Relationships between Coworkers: Perceptions of Relational and Emotional Messages, Inappropriateness, and Sexual Harassment," *Journal of Applied Communication Research 29* (2001): 197–220; M. S. Remland, *Nonverbal Communication in Everyday Life* (Boston: Houghton Mifflin, 2000); J. D. Murphy, D. M. Driscoll, and J. R. Kelly, "Differences in the Nonverbal Behavior of Men Who Vary in the Likelihood to Sexually Harass," *Journal of Social Behavior and Personality 14* (1999):

113–128; D. K. Ivy and S. Hamlet, "College Students and Sexual Dynamics: Two Studies of Peer Sexual Harassment," *Communication Education* 45 (1996): 149–166.

50. L. M. Kneidinger, T. L. Maple, and S. A. Tross, "Touching Behavior in Sport: Functional Components, Analysis of Sex Differences, and Ethological Considerations," *Journal of Nonverbal Behavior* 25 (2001): 43–62; L. K. Guerrero and P. A. Andersen, "Public Touch Behavior in Romantic Relationships between Men and Women." In Guerrero, *The Nonverbal Communication Reader*, 202–210; S. E. Jones, "Sex Differences in Touch Communication," *Western Journal of Speech Communication* 50 (1986): 227–241; A. Hall and E. M. Veccia, "More 'Touching' Observations: New Insights on Men, Women, and Interpersonal Touch," *Journal of Personality and Social Psychology* 59 (1990): 1155–1162; F. N. Willis, Jr., and L. F. Briggs, "Relationship and Touch in Public Settings," *Journal of Nonverbal Behavior* 16 (1992): 55–63; B. Major, A. Schmidlin, and L. Williams, "Gender Patterns in Social Touch: The Impact of Setting and Age," *Journal of Personality and Social Psychology* 58 (1990): 634–643.

51. L. L. Hinkle, "Perceptions of Supervisor Nonverbal Immediacy, Vocalics, and Subordinate Liking," *Communication Research Reports* 18 (2001): 128–136.

52. T. DeGroot and S. J. Motowidlo, "Why Visual and Vocal Interview Cues Can Affect Interviewers' Judgments and Predict Job Performance," *Journal of Applied Psychology* 84 (1999): 986–993; L. L. Carli, S. J. LaFleur, and C. C. Loeber, "Nonverbal Behavior, Gender, and Influence," *Journal of Personality and Social Psychology* 68 (1995): 1030–1041; N. Christenfeld, "Does It Hurt to Say Um?" *Journal of Nonverbal Behavior* 19 (1995): 171–186; J. K. Burgoon, T. Birk, and M. Pfau, "Nonverbal Behaviors, Persuasion, and Credibility," *Human Communication Research* 17 (1990): 140–169; R. L. Street, Jr., R. M. Brady, and R. Lee, "Evaluative Responses to Communicators: The Effects of Speech Rate, Sex, and Interaction Context," *Western Journal of Speech Communication* 48 (1984): 14–27.

53. K. Tracy, *Everyday Talk: Building and Reflecting Identities* (New York: Guilford Press, 2005).

54. C. A. Braithwaite, "Cultural Uses and Interpretations of Silence." In Guerrero, *The Nonverbal Communication Reader*, 163–172.

55. M. L. Knapp and A. L. Vangelisti, *Interpersonal Communication and Human Relationships* 5e (Boston: Allyn & Bacon, 2005); A. Jaworski, "The Power of Silence in Communication." In Guerrero, *The Nonverbal Communication Reader*, 156–162.

56. D. D. Henningsen, D. Dryden, M. G. Cruz, and M. C. Morr, "Pattern Violations and Perceptions of Deception," *Communication Reports* 13 (2000): 1–10; M. A. deTurck, T. H. Feeley, and L. A. Roman, "Vocal and Visual Cue Training in Behavioral Lie Detection," *Communication Research Reports* 14 (1997): 249–259; T. H. Feeley and M. A. deTurck, "Global Cue Usage in Behavioral Lie Detection," *Communication Quarterly* 43 (1995): 420–430.

57. S. J. Baker, "The Theory of Silence," *Journal of General Psychology* 53 (1955): 145–167.

58. J. Sandberg, "Want to Know Someone's Job Status? Look at Desk Location," *Corpus Christi Caller Times* (March 2, 2003): D4.

59. D. R. Peterson, "Interpersonal Relationships as a Link between Person and Environment." In *Person–Environment Psychology*, edited by W. B. Walsh, K. H. Craig, and R. H. Price (Hillsdale, NJ: Lawrence Erlbaum, 1991), 154.

60. A. Rapoport, *The Meaning of the Built Environment: A Nonverbal Communication Approach* (Beverly Hills: Sage, 1982).

61. A. H. Maslow and N. L. Mintz, "Effects of Esthetic Surroundings: I," *Journal of Psychology* 41 (1956): 247–254.

62. M. H. Eaves and D. G. Leathers, "Context as Communication: McDonald's vs. Burger King," *Journal of Applied Communication Research* 19 (1991): 263–289; E. J. Langan, "Environmental Features in Theme Restaurants." In Guerrero, *The Nonverbal Communication Reader*, 255–263.

63. Hall, *The Hidden Dimension*.

64. R. Sommer, "Studies in Personal Space," *Sociometry* 22 (1959): 247–260; L. Smeltzer, J. Waltman, and D. Leonard, "Proxemics and Haptics in Managerial Communication." In Guerrero, *The Nonverbal Communication Reader*, 184–191.

65. J. A. Hall, *Nonverbal Sex Differences: Communication Accuracy and Expressive Style* (Baltimore: Johns Hopkins University Press, 1984); P. A. Bell, L. M. Kline, and W. A. Barnard, "Friendship and Freedom of Movement as Moderators of Sex Differences in Interpersonal Distancing," *Journal of Social Psychology* 128 (1998): 305–310; M. Remland, T. S. Jones, and H. Brinkman, "Interpersonal Distance, Body Orientation and Touch: Effect of Culture, Gender, and Age," *Journal of Social Psychology* 135 (1995): 281–295.

66. S. M. Lyman and M. B. Scott, "Territoriality: A Neglected Sociological Dimension." In Guerrero, *The Nonverbal Communication Reader*, 175–183.

67. A. L. S. Buslig, "'Stop' Signs: Regulating Privacy with Environmental Features." In Guerrero, *The Nonverbal Communication Reader*, 241–249.

68. R. L. Paetzold and A. M. O'Leary-Kelly, "Organizational Communication and the Legal Dimensions of Hostile Work Environment Sexual Harassment." In *Sexual Harassment: Communication Implications*, edited by G. L. Kreps (Cresskill, NJ: Hampton Press, 1993), 63–77.

69. Mehrabian, *Nonverbal Communication*. For interesting applications of Mehrabian's immediacy principle to the instructional context, see S. D. Johnson and A. N. Miller, "A Cross-Cultural Study of Immediacy, Credibility, and Learning in the U.S. and Kenya," *Communication Education* 51 (2002): 280–292; M. A. Jaasma and R. J. Koper, "Out-of-Class Communication between Female and Male Students and Faculty: The Relationship to Student Perceptions of Instructor Immediacy," *Women's Studies in Communication* 25 (2002): 119–137; J. L. Chesebro and J. C. McCroskey, "The Relationship of Teacher Clarity and Immediacy with Student State Receiver Apprehension, Affect, and Cognitive Learning," *Communication Education* 50 (2001): 59–68; P. L. Witt and L. R. Wheeless, "An Experimental Study of Teachers' Verbal and Nonverbal Immediacy and Students' Affective and Cognitive Learning," *Communication Education* 50 (2001): 327–342; D. K. Baringer and J. C. McCroskey, "Immediacy in the Classroom: Student Immediacy," *Communication Education* 49 (2000): 178–186; J. W. Neuliep, "A Comparison of Teacher Immediacy in African-American and Euro-American College Classrooms," *Communication Education* 44 (1995): 267–277; J. F. Andersen, "Teacher Immediacy as a Predictor of Teaching Effectiveness." In *Communication Yearbook 3*, edited by D. Nimmo (New Brunswick, NJ: Transaction Books, 1979), 543–559.

70. Argyle, *Bodily Communication*.

71. Andersen, *Nonverbal Communication*.

72. K. McGinty, D. Knox, and M. E. Zusman, "Nonverbal and Verbal Communication in 'Involved' and 'Casual' Relationships among College Students," *College Student Journal* 37 (2003): 68–71; C. C. Weisfeld and M. A. Stack, "When I Look into Your Eyes: An Ethological Analysis of Gender Differences in Married Couples' Nonverbal Behaviors," *Psychology, Evolution, and Gender* 4 (2002): 125–147; B. Le Poire, A. Duggan, C. Shepard, and J. Burgoon, "Relational Messages Associated with Nonverbal Involvement, Pleasantness, and Expressiveness in Romantic Couples," *Communication Research Reports* 19 (2002): 195–206.

73. M. S. Mast and J. A. Hall, "Who Is the Boss and Who Is Not? Accuracy of Judging Status," *Journal of Nonverbal Behavior* 28 (2004): 145–165; M. Helweg-Larsen, S. J. Cunningham, A. Carrico, and A. M. Pergram, "To Nod or Not to Nod: An Observational Study of Nonverbal Communication and Status in Female and Male College Students," *Psychology of Women Quarterly* 28 (2004): 358–361; L. Z. Tiedens and A. R. Fragale, "Power Moves:

Complementarity in Dominant and Submissive Nonverbal Behavior," *Journal of Personality and Social Psychology 84* (2003): 558–568; H. Aguinis and C. A. Henle, "Effects of Nonverbal Behavior on Perceptions of a Female Employee's Power Bases," *Journal of Social Psychology 141* (2001): 537–549; J. A. Hall, L. S. LeBeau, J. G. Reinoso, and F. Thayer, "Status, Gender, and Nonverbal Behavior in Candid and Posed Photographs: A Study of Conversations between University Employees," *Sex Roles 44* (2001): 677–692; Mehrabian, *Nonverbal Communication*.

CHAPTER 5

1. L. Barker, et al., "An Investigation of Proportional Time Spent in Various Communication Activities of College Students," *Journal of Applied Communication Research 8* (1981): 101–109.

2. J. Brownell, "Perceptions of Effective Listeners: A Management Study," *The Journal of Business Communication* (Fall, 1990): 401–415; D. A. Romig, *Side by Side Leadership* (Austin, TX: Bard, 2001).

3. Adapted from the International Listening Association's definition of listening, which may be found on their Web site <http://www.listen.org>.

4. K. W. Watson, L. L. Barker, and J. B. Weaver, *The Listener Style Inventory* (New Orleans: SPECTRA, 1995).

5. M. D. Kirtley and J. M. Honeycutt, "Listening Styles and Their Correspondence with Second Guessing," *Communication Research Reports 13* (1996): 174–182.

6. S. L. Sargent and J. B. Weaver, "Correlates Between Communication Apprehension and Listening Style Preferences," *Communication Research Reports 14* (1997): 74–78.

7. Sargent and Weaver, "Correlates Between Communication Apprehension and Listening Style Preferences."

8. C. Y. Cheng, "Chinese Philosophy and Contemporary Communication Theory." In *Communication Theory: Eastern and Western Perspectives*, edited by D. L. Kincaid (New York, 1987).

9. T. S. Lebra, *Japanese Patterns of Behavior* (Honolulu: University Press of Hawaii, 1976).

10. A. Yugi, (trans. N. Chung), *Ilbon-in ye usik koo-jo (Japanese Thought Patterns)* (Seoul: Baik Yang Publishing Co. [in Korean], 1984).

11. J. O. Yum, "The Impact of Confucianism on Interpersonal Relationships and Communication Patterns in East Asia." In *Intercultural Communication: A Reader*, edited by L. A. Samovar and R. E. Porter (Belmont, CA: Wadsworth Publishing Company, 2000), 86.

12. W. Winter, A. J. Ferreira, and N. Bowers, "Decision-Making in Married and Unrelated Couples," *Family Process 12* (1973): 83–94.

13. R. Montgomery, *Listening Made Easy* (New York: AMACOM, 1981). Also see O. Hargie, C. Sanders, and D. Dickson, *Social Skills in Interpersonal Communication* (London: Routledge, 1994); O. Hargie, ed., *The Handbook of Communication Skills* (London: Routledge, 1997).

14. R. G. Owens, "Handling Strong Emotions." In *The Handbook of Communication Skills*, edited by O. Hargie (London: Croom Helm/New York University Press, 1986).

15. D. Goleman, *Emotional Intelligence: Why It Can Matter More Than IQ* (New York: Bantam Books, 1995). Also see D. Goleman, "Emotional Intelligence: Issues in Paradigms Building." In *The Emotionally Intelligent Workplace*, edited by C. Cherniss and D. Goleman (San Francisco: Jossey Bass, 2001), 13.

16. J. L. Gonzalez-Balado, ed., *Mother Teresa: In My Own Words* (New York: Gramercy Books, 1997).

17. R. G. Nichols, "Factors in Listening Comprehension," *Speech Monographs 15* (1948): 154–163; G. M. Goldhaber and C. H. Weaver, "Listener Comprehension of Compressed Speech When the Difficulty, Rate of Presentation, and Sex of the Listener Are Varied," *Speech Monographs 35* (1968): 20–25.

18. M. Fitch-Hauser, D. A. Barker, and A. Hughes, "Receiver Apprehension and Listening Comprehension: A Linear or Curvilinear Relationship?" *Southern Communication Journal* (1988): 62–71.

19. Fitch-Hauser et al., "Receiver Apprehension and Listening Comprehension."

20. K. Watson, L. Barker, and J. Weaver, "The Listening Styles Profile (LPP16): Development and Validation of an Instrument to Assess Four Listening Styles," *Journal of the International Listening Association* (1995). Research cited on *20/20*, ABC television network, September 1998.

21. A. Carruthers, "Listening, Hearing and Changing." *Business Communicator 5* (2004): 3.

22. I. W. Johnson, C. G. Pearce, T. L. Tuten, and L. Sinclair, "Self-Imposed Silence and Perceived Listening Effectiveness," *Business Communication Quarterly 66* (2003): 23–45.

23. M. V. Redmond, "The Functions of Empathy (Decentering) in Human Relations," *Human Relations 42* (1993): 593–606.

24. A. Mehrabian, *Nonverbal Communication* (Chicago: Aldine Atherton, 1970). A. Mehrabian, *Silent Messages* (Belmont, CA: Wadsworth, 1981). Also see D. Lapakko, "Three Cheers for Language: A Closer Examination of a Widely Cited Study of Nonverbal Communication," *Communication Education 46* (1997): 63–67.

25. M. Argyle and M. Cook, *Gaze and Mutual Gaze* (Cambridge, MA: Cambridge University Press, 1976).

26. Hargie et al., *Social Skills in Interpersonal Communication*; Hargie, *The Handbook of Communication Skills*.

27. For a review of the literature on gender, listening, and communication see D. K. Ivy and P. Backlund, *GenderSpeak* (New York: McGraw-Hill, 2005).

28. S. L. Sargent, "Listening Styles: Sex Differences in Perceptions of Self and Others," *International Journal of Listening 17* (2003): 5–18.

29. C. G. Pearce, I. W. Johnson, and R. T. Barker, "Assessment of the Listening Styles Inventory," *Journal of Business & Technical Communication 17* (2003): 84–113.

30. M. K. Johnston, J. B. Weaver, K. W. Watson, and L. L. Barker, "Listening Styles: Biological or Psychological Differences?" *International Journal of Listening 14* (2000): 32–46.

31. J. Silverman, "Attentional Styles and the Study of Sex Differences." In *Attention: Contemporary Theory and Analysis*, edited by D. I. Mostofsky (New York: Appleton-Century-Crofts, 1970): 61–79.

32. See R. G. Nichols and L. A. Stevens, "Listening to People," *Harvard Business Review 35* (September–October, 1957): 85–92.

33. K. K. Halone and L. L. Pecchioni, "Relational Listening: A Grounded Theoretical Model," *Communication Reports 14* (2001): 59–71.

34. Pearce et al., "Assessment of the Listening Styles Inventory."

35. Pearce et al., "Assessment of the Listening Styles Inventory."

36. J. B. Weaver and M. B. Kirtley, "Listening Styles and Empathy," *The Southern States Communication Journal 60* (1995): 131–140.

37. Goleman, "Emotional Intelligence."

38. Goleman, "Emotional Intelligence."

39. H. J. M. Nouwen, "Listening as Spiritual Hospitality." In *Bread for the Journey* (New York: HarperCollins, 1997).

40. J. C. McCroskey and M. J. Beatty, "The Communibiological Perspective: Implications for Communication in Instruction," *Communication Education 49* (2000): 1–6; M. J. Beatty and J. C. McCroskey, "Theory, Scientific Evidence and the Communibiological Paradigm: Reflections on Misguided Criticism," *Communication Education 49* (2001): 36–44.

41. Goleman, "Emotional Intelligence."

42. "Personality Typing," *Wired* (July, 1999): 71.

43. "Personality Typing."

44. Hargie et al., *Social Skills in Interpersonal Communication*; R. Boulton, *People Skills* (New York: 1981). We also acknowledge others who have presented excellent applications of listening and responding skills in interpersonal and group contexts: D. A. Romig

and L. J. Romig, *Structured Teamwork (D Guide)* (Austin, TX: Performance Resources, 1990); S. Deep and L. Sussman, *Smart Moves* (Reading, MA: Addison-Wesley, 1990); P. R. Scholtes, *The Team Handbook* (Madison, WI: Joiner Associates, 1988); Hargie et al., *Social Skills in Interpersonal Communication*; Hargie, *The Handbook of Communication Skills*.

45. L. B. Comer and T. Drollinger, "Active Empathic Listening and Selling Success: A Conceptual Framework," *Journal of Personal Selling & Sales Management* 19 (1999): 15–29; S. B. Castleberry, C. D. Shepherd, and R. Ridnour, "Effective Interpersonal Listening in the Personal Selling Environment: Conceptualization, Measurement, and Nomological Validity," *Journal of Marketing Theory and Practice* (Winter, 1999): 30–38.

46. F. C. B. Hansen, H. Resnick, and J. Galea, "Better Listening: Paraphrasing and Perception Checking—A Study of the Effectiveness of a Multimedia Skills Training Program," *Journal of Technology in Human Services* 20 (2002): 317–331.

47. Pearce et al., "Assessment of the Listening Styles Inventory."

CHAPTER 6

1. Research documents several culture-based differences in communication, including approaches to leadership, deception, and conflict management styles. See N. Ensari and S. E. Murphy, "Cross-Cultural Variations in Leadership Perceptions and Attribution of Charisma to the Leader," *Organizational Behavior and Human Decision Processes* 92 (2003): 52–66; M. K. Lapinski and T. R. Levine, "Culture and Information Manipulation Theory: The Effects of Self-Construal and Locus of Benefit on Information Manipulation," *Communication Studies* 5 (2000): 55–73; D. Cai and E. L. Fink, "Conflict Style Differences Between Individualists and Collectivists," *Communication Monographs* 69 (2002): 67–87.

2. S. Roberts, *Who We Are Now: The Changing Face of America in the Twenty-First Century* (New York: Henry Holt, 2004).

3. M. E. Ryan, "Another Way to Teach Migrant Students," *Los Angeles Times* (March 31, 1991): B20, as cited by M. W. Lustig and J. Koester, *Intercultural Competence: Interpersonal Communication across Cultures* (New York: HarperCollins, 1999), 11.

4. U.S. Census Bureau. <http:www.prb.org/AmeristatTemplate>. Accessed December 17, 2001.

5. G. Chen and W. J. Starosta, "A Review of the Concept of Intercultural Sensitivity," *Human Communication* 1 (1997): 7.

6. Lustig and Koester, *Intercultural Competence*.

7. *Newsweek* (July 12, 1999): 51.

8. U.S. Census Bureau, *Statistical Abstract of the United States: 1996*, 116e (Washington, DC, 1996), as cited by Lustig and Koester, *Intercultural Competence*, 8.

9. U.S. Census Bureau Report 1999, as reported in R. E. Schmid, *Austin-American Statesman* (September 17, 1999): A20.

10. "One Nation, One Language?" *U.S. News & World Report* (September 25, 1995): 40, as cited by Lustig and Koester, *Intercultural Competence*, 10.

11. Roberts, *Who We Are Now*, 122

12. Roberts, *Who We Are Now*, 122; A. Caldwell, "Census: More Than Half of Texans Are Minorities," *Austin-American Statesman* (August 11, 2005): 1B.

13. Roberts, *Who We Are Now*, 126.

14. Adapted from *Information Please Almanac* (Boston: Houghton Mifflin, 1990) and *World Almanac and Book of Facts* (New York: World Almanac, 1991), as cited by Lustig and Koester, *Intercultural Competence*, 11.

15. T. Friedman, *The World Is Flat: A Brief History of the Twenty-First Century* (New York: Farrar, Straus and Giroux, 2005).

16. Friedman, *The World Is Flat*, 10.

17. A. G. Smith, ed., *Communication and Culture* (New York: Holt, Rinehart & Winston, 1966).

18. E. T. Hall, *Beyond Culture* (Garden City, NY: Doubleday, 1976).

19. For example, see A. V. Matveeve and P. E. Nelson, "Cross Cultural Competence and Multicultural Team Performance: Perceptions of American and Russian Managers," *International Journal of Cross Cultural Management* 4 (2004): 253–270.

20. G. Hofstede, *Culture's Consequences: International Differences in Work-Related Values* (Beverly Hills: Sage, 1980); G. Hofstede, *Cultures and Organizations: Software of the Mind* (London: McGraw-Hill, 1991).

21. See J. B. Walter, "Interpersonal Effects in Computer-Mediated Interaction: A Relational Perspective," *Communication Research* 19 (1992): 52–90; J. B. Walter, "Relational Aspects of Computer-Mediated Communication: Experimental and Longitudinal Observations," *Organizational Science* 6 (1995): 186–203; J. B. Walther, J. F. Anderson, and D. Park, "Interpersonal Effects in Computer-Mediated Interaction: A Meta-Analysis of Social and Anti-Social Communication, *Communication Research* 21 (1994): 460–487.

22. C. Ward, S. Bochner, and A. Furnham, *The Psychology of Culture Shock* (Hove, England: Routledge, 2001).

23. For an excellent discussion of worldview and its implications for intercultural communication, see C. H. Dodd, *Dynamics of Intercultural Communication* (New York: McGraw Hill, 1998).

24. Hall, *Beyond Culture*.

25. L. A. Samovar, R. E. Porter, and L. A. Stefani, *Communication between Cultures* (Belmont, CA: Wadsworth, 1998).

26. Hofstede, *Culture's Consequences*. For an excellent summary of Geert Hofstede's cultural values, see Lustig and Koester, *Intercultural Competence*, 111–125.

27. H. C. Triandis, "The Many Dimensions of Culture," *Academy of Management Executive* 18 (2004): 88–93.

28. M. Voronov and J. A. Singer, "The Myth of Individualism-Collectivism: A Critical Review," *Journal of Social Psychology* 142 (2002): 461–480.

29. For an excellent review of Hofstede's work, see J. W. Bing, "Hofstede's Consequences: The Impact of His Work on Consulting and Business Practices," *Academy of Management Executive* 18 (2004): 80–87.

30. Hofstede, *Culture's Consequences*; Hofstede, *Cultures and Organizations*.

31. W. B. Gudykunst, *Bridging Differences: Effective Intergroup Communication* (Newbury Park, CA: Sage, 1998).

32. Gudykunst, *Bridging Differences*.

33. Hofstede, *Culture's Consequences*; Hofstede, *Cultures and Organizations*.

34. Hofstede, *Culture's Consequences*; Hofstede, *Cultures and Organizations*.

35. Hofstede, *Culture's Consequences*; Hofstede, *Cultures and Organizations*.

36. G. Hofstede, "Cultural Dimensions in Management and Planning," *Asia Pacific Journal of Management* (January, 1984): 81–98; Hofstede, *Cultures and Organizations*.

37. J. Cloud, "Sex and the Law," *Time* (March 23, 1998): 48–54.

38. W. W. Neher, *Organizational Communication: Challenges of Change, Diversity, and Continuity* (Boston: Allyn & Bacon, 1997).

39. E. E. Maccoby, "Gender and Relationships: A Developmental Account," *American Psychologist* 45 (1990): 513–520.

40. J. Gray, *Men Are from Mars, Women Are from Venus* (New York: Harper Collins, 1992).

41. D. K. Ivy and P. Backlund, *GenderSpeak: Personal Effectiveness in Gender Communication* 3e (New York: McGraw Hill, 2004); D. J. Canary and T. R. Emmers-Sommer, *Sex and Gender Differences in Personal Relationships* (New York, Guilford, 1997).

42. D. Tannen, *You Just Don't Understand* (New York: William Morrow, 1990).

43. T. Parsons and R. F. Bales, *Family, Socialization, and Interaction Processes* (New York: Free Press of Glencoe, 1955). Also see D. Bakan, *The Duality of Human Existence* (Chicago: McNally, 1966).

44. A. C. Selbe, *Are You from Another Planet or What?* Workshop presented at the Joint Service Family Readiness Matters Conference, Phoenix, AZ, July, 1999.

45. R. B. Rubin, E. M. Perse, and C. A. Barbato, "Conceptualization and Measurement of Interpersonal Communication Motives," *Human Communication Research 14* (1988): 602–628; D. Tannen, *That's Not What I Meant!* (London: Dent, 1986).

46. See L. Davis, "Domestic Violence," in *Encyclopedia of Social Work*, vol. 1 (Washington, DC: National Association of Social Work: 780–789; Federal Bureau of Investigation, *Violence against Women: Estimates from the Redesigned Survey*, August, 1995 <http://www.ojp.usdoj.gov>; L. K. Hamberger, D. G. Saunders, and M. Hovey, "The Prevalence of Domestic Violence in Community Practice and Rate of Physician Inquiry," *Family Medicine 24* (1992): 283–287; Women's Action Coalition, *WAC Stats: The Facts about Women* (New York: The New Press, 1993).

47. J. W. Neuliep, "Assessing the Reliability and Validity of the Generalized Ethnocentrism Scale," *Journal of Intercultural Communication Research 31* (2002): 201–215. For additional research on the role of ethnocentrism in communication, see Y. Lin, A. Rancer, and A. Sunhee Lim, "Ethnocentrism and Intercultural Willingness to Communicate: A Cross-Cultural Comparison between Korean and American College Students," *Journal of Intercultural Communication Research 32* (2003).

48. See Ensari and Murphy, "Cross-Cultural Variations in Leadership Perceptions and Attribution of Charisma to the Leader"; Lapinski and Levine, "Culture and Information Manipulation Theory"; Cai and Fink, "Conflict Style Differences Between Individualists and Collectivists."

49. C. Kluckhohn and S. Murray, 1953, as quoted by J. S. Caputo, H. C. Hazel, and C. McMahon, *Interpersonal Communication* (Boston: Allyn & Bacon, 1994), 304.

50. D. E. Brown, "Human Universals and Their Implications." In *Being Humans: Anthropological Universality and Particularity in Transdisciplinary Perspectives*, edited by N. Roughley (New York: Walter de Gruyter, 2000). For an applied discussion of these universals, see S. Pinker, *The Blank Slate: The Modern Denial of Human Nature* (London: Penguin Books, 2002).

51. D. W. Kale, "Ethics in Intercultural Communication." In *Intercultural Communication: A Reader* 6e, edited by L. A. Samovar and R. E. Porter (Belmont, CA: Wadsworth, 1991).

52. L. A. Samovar and R. E. Porter, *Communication Between Cultures* (Stamford, CT: Wadsworth and Thomson Learning, 2001), 29.

53. C. S. Lewis, *The Abolition of Man* (New York: Macmillan Publishing Company, 1944).

54. As reported by M. Obernauer, "Lessons on Values to Go Beyond Schools," *Austin-American Statesman* (March 30, 2005): B1, B5.

55. Obernauer, "Lessons on Values to Go Beyond Schools."

56. M. Gladwell, *Blink: The Power of Thinking Without Thinking* (New York: Little Brown, 2005).

57. S. Kamekar, M. B. Kolsawalla, and T. Mazareth, "Occupational Prestige as a Function of Occupant's Gender," *Journal of Applied Social Psychology 19* (1988): 681–688.

58. Eleanor Roosevelt, as cited by Lustig and Koester, *Intercultural Competence.*

59. W. B. Gudykunst and Y. Kim, *Communicating with Strangers* (New York: Random House, 1984); Gudykunst, *Bridging Differences.*

60. For a classic discussion of egocentrism and ethnocentrism, see T. W. Adorno, E. Frenkel-Brunswik, D. J. Levinson, and R. N. Sanford, *The Authoritarian Personality* (New York: Harper & Brothers, 1950).

61. Neuliep, "Assessing the Reliability and Validity of the Generalized Ethnocentrism Scale"; Lin, "Ethnocentrism and Intercultural Willingness to Communicate."

62. S. DeTurk, "Intercultural Empathy: Myth, Competency, or Possibility for Alliance Building?" *Communication Education 50* (2001): 374–384.

63. M. V. Redmond, "The Functions of Empathy (Decentering) in Human Relations," *Human Relations 42* (1993): 593–606. Also see M. V. Redmond, "A Multidimensional Theory and Measure of Social Decentering," *Journal of Research in Personality* (1995); for an excellent discussion of the role of emotions in establishing empathy, see D. Goleman, *Emotional Intelligence* (New York: Bantam, 1995).

64. See B. J. Broome, "Building Shared Meaning: Implications of a Relational Approach to Empathy for Teaching Intercultural Communication," *Communication Education 40* (1991): 235–249. Much of this discussion is based on the treatment of social decentering and empathy in S. A. Beebe, S. J. Beebe, and M. V. Redmond, *Interpersonal Communication: Relating to Others* 4e (Boston: Allyn & Bacon, 2005).

65. For an excellent discussion of empathy as it relates to intercultural communication, see D. W. Augsburger, *Pastoral Counseling Across Cultures* (Philadelphia: The Westminister Press, 1986), 28–30.

66. H. J. M. Nouwen, *Bread for the Journey* (New York: HarperCollins, 1997).

67. L. J. Carrell, "Diversity in the Communication Curriculum: Impact on Student Empathy," *Communication Education 46* (1997): 234–244.

68. R. H. Farrell, ed., *Off the Record: The Private Papers of Harry S. Truman* (New York: Harper & Row, 1980), 310.

CHAPTER 7

1. See S. B. Barnes, *Computer-Mediated Communication: Human-to-Human Communication across the Internet* (Boston: Pearson, 2003); L. C. Tidwell and J. B. Walther, "Computer-Mediated Communication Effects on Disclosure, Impressions, and Interpersonal Evaluations: Getting to Know One Another a Bit at a Time," *Human Communication Research 28* (2002): 317–348; J. B. Walther, C. L. Slovacek, and L. C. Tidwell, "Is a Picture Worth a Thousand Words? Photographic Images in Long-Term and Short-Term Computer-Mediated Communication," *Communication Research 28* (2001): 105–134; J. T. Hancock and P. J. Dunham, "Impression Formation in Computer-Mediated Communication Revisited: An Analysis of the Breadth and Intensity of Impressions," *Communication Research 28* (2001): 325–347.

2. K. M. Galvin and C. Wilkinson, "The Communication Process: Impersonal and Interpersonal." In *Making Connections: Readings in Relational Communication*, edited by K. M. Galvin and P. Cooper (Los Angeles, CA: Roxbury, 1996): 4–10; Y. Abraham, "Aspiring Doctors Have a New Exam to Pass: Bedside Manner 101," *Corpus Christi Caller Times* (July 20, 2003): A14.

3. E. Berscheid, "Interpersonal Attraction." In *The Handbook of Social Psychology*, edited by G. Lindzey and E. Aronson (New York: Random House, 1985), 413–484, as reported in J. A. Simpson and B. A. Harris, "Interpersonal Attraction." In *Perspectives on Close Relationships*, edited by A. L. Weber and J. H. Harvey (Boston: Allyn & Bacon, 1994), 45–66.

4. W. Stoebe, "Self-Esteem and Interpersonal Attraction." In *Theory and Practice in Interpersonal Attraction*, edited by S. Duck (London: Academic Press, 1977).

5. See D. T. Kenrick, S. L. Neuberg, and R. B. Cialdini, *Social Psychology: Unraveling the Mystery* 3e (Boston: Allyn & Bacon, 2004); L. K. Guerrero, P. A. Andersen, and W. A. Afifi, *Close Encounters: Communicating in Relationships* (New York: McGraw-Hill, 2001); E. Berscheid and H. T. Reis, "Attraction and Close Relationships," In *The Handbook of Social Psychology* 4e, Vol. 2, edited by D. T. Gilbert, S. T. Fiske, and G. Lindzey (New York: Oxford University Press, 1998): 193–281; V. Sharma and T. Kaur, "Interpersonal Attraction in Relation to Similarity and Help," *Psychological Studies 39* (1995): 84–87; T. Shaikh and S. Kanakar, "Attitudinal Similarity and Affiliation Need as Determinants of Interperson-

al Attraction," *Journal of Social Psychology 134* (1994): 257–259; S. S. Brehm, R. Miller, D. Perlman, and S. M. Campbell, *Intimate Relationships* 3e (New York: McGraw-Hill, 2001); M. Sunnafrank, "Interpersonal Attraction and Attitude Similarity: A Communication-Based Assessment." In *Communication Yearbook 14*, edited by J. A. Andersen (Newbury Park, CA: Sage, 1991): 451–483; J. E. Lydon, D. W. Jamieson, and M. Zanna, "Interpersonal Similarity and the Social and Intellectual Dimensions of First Impressions," *Social Cognition 6* (1988): 269–286.

6. K. Y. A. McKenna, A. S. Green, and M. E. J. Gleason, "Relationship Formation on the Internet: What's the Big Attraction?" *Journal of Social Issues 58* (2002): 9–31.

7. B. R. Burleson, A. W. Kunkel, and J. D. Birch, "Thoughts about Talk in Romantic Relationships: Similarity Makes for Attraction (and Happiness, Too)," *Communication Quarterly 42* (1994): 259–273; A. E. Varnadore, S. C. Howe, and S. Brownlow, "Why Do I Like You? Students' Understanding of the Impact of the Factors That Contribute to Liking." Paper presented at the meeting of the Southeastern Psychological Association, March, 1994.

8. D. Garner, "Harmless Crushes Can Be Uplifting," *Corpus Christi Caller Times* (December 3, 1996): H1, H4.

9. Sunnafrank, "Interpersonal Attraction and Attitude Similarity."

10. J. H. Harvey and A. L. Weber, *Odyssey of the Heart: Close Relationships in the 21st Century* 2e (Mahwah, NJ: Lawrence Erlbaum, 2002); Kenrick et al., *Social Psychology*; M. L. Knapp and J. A. Hall, *Nonverbal Communication in Human Interaction* 5e (Belmont, CA: Wadsworth, 2002); M. Crawford and R. Unger, *Women and Gender: A Feminist Psychology* 4e (New York: McGraw-Hill, 2003).

11. A. Cooper and L. Sportolari, "Romance in Cyberspace: Understanding Online Attraction," *Journal of Sex Education and Therapy 22* (1997): 7–14; McKenna, "Relationship Formation on the Internet."

12. A. Cooper, I. P. McLoughlin, and K. M. Campbell, "Sexuality in Cyberspace: Update for the 21st Century," *Cyberpsychology & Behavior 32* (2000): 521–536.

13. Guerrero, *Close Encounters*, 59.

14. A. Feingold, "Gender Differences in Effects of Physical Attractiveness on Romantic Attraction: A Comparison across Five Research Paradigms," *Journal of Personality and Social Psychology 59* (1990): 981–993.

15. <http://www.wildxangel.com>; <http://www.bol.ucla.edu>; <http://www.thirdage.com>; <http://www.onlinedatingmagazine.com>.

16. See A. Botta, "Television Images and Adolescent Girls' Body Image Disturbance," *Journal of Communication 49* (1999): 22–37; M. Wiederman and S. R. Hurst, "Body Size, Physical Attractiveness, and Body Image among Young Adult Women: Relationships to Sexual Experience and Sexual Esteem," *Journal of Sex Research 35* (1998): 272–281; L. Lazier and A. Gagnard Kendrick, "Women in Advertisements: Sizing Up the Images, Roles, and Functions." In *Women in Mass Communication* 2e, edited by P. Creedon (Newbury Park, CA: Sage, 1993), 199–219; A. Gagnard, "From Feast to Famine: Depiction of Ideal Body Type in Magazine Advertising: 1950–1984." In *Proceedings of the Nineteen Eighty-Six Conference of the American Academy of Advertising*, edited by E. F. Larkin (Charleston, SC: American Academy of Advertising, 1986), R46–R50; B. Silverstein, L. Perdue, B. Peterson, and E. Kelly, "The Role of Mass Media in Promoting a Thin Standard of Bodily Attractiveness for Women," *Sex Roles 14* (1986): 519–532.

17. S. W. Duck, *Personal Relationships and Personal Constructs: A Study of Friendship Formation* (New York: John Wiley & Sons, 1973).

18. E. H. Walster, V. Aronson, D. Abrahams, and L. Rottmann, "Importance of Physical Attractiveness in Dating Behavior," *Journal of Personality and Social Psychology 4* (1966): 508–516; V. B. Hinsz, "Facial Resemblance in Engaged and Married Couples," *Journal of Social and Personal Relationships 6* (1989): 223–229.

19. Guerrero, *Close Encounters*; Kenrick, *Social Psychology*; Knapp and Hall, *Nonverbal Communication in Human Interaction*.

20. K. R. Van Horn, A. Arnone, K. Nesbitt, L. Desilets, T. Sears, M. Giffin, and R. Brudi, "Physical Distance and Interpersonal Characteristics in College Students' Romantic Relationships," *Personal Relationships 4* (1997): 15–24; M. E. Rohlfing, "'Doesn't Anybody Stay in One Place Anymore?' An Exploration of the Understudied Phenomenon of Long-Distance Relationships." In *Understudied Relationships: Off the Beaten Track*, edited by J. T. Wood and S. Duck (Thousand Oaks, CA: Sage, 1995), 173–196; L. Stafford and J. R. Reske, "Idealization and Communication in Long-Distance Premarital Relationships," *Family Relations 39* (1990): 274–279; T. Stephen, "Communication and Interdependence in Geographically Separated Relationships," *Human Communication Research 13* (1986): 191–210.

21. Brehm, *Intimate Relationships*.

22. E. R. Merkle and R. A. Richardson, "Digital Dating and Virtual Relating: Conceptualizing Computer-Mediated Relationships," *Family Relations 49* (2000): 187–196.

23. Guerrero, *Close Encounters*; Brehm, *Intimate Relationships*.

24. W. Schutz, *FIRO: A Three-Dimensional Theory of Interpersonal Behavior* (New York: Holt, Rinehart, and Winston, 1960).

25. A. Mehrabian, *Nonverbal Communication* (Chicago: Aldine-Atherton, 1972).

26. J. A. Daly, E. Hogg, D. Sacks, M. Smith, and L. Zimring, "Sex and Relationship Affect Social Self-Grooming." In *The Nonverbal Communication Reader: Classic and Contemporary Readings* 2e, edited by L. K. Guerrero, J. DeVito, and M. L. Hecht (Prospect Heights, IL: Waveland, 1999), 56–61.

27. M. T. Whitty, "Cyber-Flirting: An Examination of Men's and Women's Flirting Behaviour Both Offline and on the Internet," *Behaviour Change 21* (2004): 115–126.

28. Merkel and Richardson, "Digital Dating and Virtual Relating," 190.

29. For research on initial interaction in online relationships, see A. Ramirez, Jr. and J. K. Burgoon, "The Effect of Interactivity on Initial Interactions: The Influence of Information Valence and Modality and Information Richness on Computer-Mediated Interaction," *Communication Monographs 71* (2004): 422–447; J. B. Walther and M. R. Parks, "Cues Filtered out, Cues Filtered in: Computer-Mediated Communication and Relationships." In *Handbook of Interpersonal Communication* 3e, edited by M. L. Knapp and J. A. Daly (Thousand Oaks, CA: Sage, 2002): 529–563; J. A. McCown, D. Fischer, R. Page, and M. Homant, "Internet Relationships: People Who Meet People," *Cyberpsychology & Behavior 4* (2001): 593–596; McKenna, "Relationship Formation on the Internet."

30. C. R. Berger and R. J. Calabrese, "Some Explorations in Initial Interaction and Beyond: Toward a Developmental Theory of Interpersonal Communication," *Human Communication Research 1* (1975): 99–112; C. R. Berger and J. J. Bradac, *Language and Social Knowledge: Uncertainty in Interpersonal Relations* (Baltimore: Edward Arnold, 1982).

31. McCown, "Internet Relationships."

32. McKenna, "Relationship Formation on the Internet."

33. Merkle and Richardson, "Digital Dating and Virtual Relating," 191.

34. A. N. Joinson and B. Dietz-Uhler, "Explanations for the Perpetration of and Reactions to Deception in a Virtual Community," *Social Science Computer Review 20* (2002): 275–289; D. Knox, V. Daniels, L. Sturdivant, and M. E. Zusman, "College Student Use of the Internet for Mate Selection," *College Student Journal 35* (2001): 158–160; McCown, "Internet Relationships."

35. C. L. Kleinke, F. B. Meeker, and R. A. Staneski, "Preference for Opening Lines: Comparing Ratings by Men and Women," *Sex Roles 15* (1986): 585–600.

36. E. Weber, *How to Pick Up Girls!* (New York: Bantam Books, 1970).

37. For research on sex roles and interaction, see P. A. Mongeau, M. C. M. Serewicz, and L. F. Therrien, "Goals for Cross-Sex First Dates: Identification, Measurement, and the Influence of Contextual Factors," *Communication Monographs* 71 (2004): 121–147; C. L. Clark, P. R. Shaver, and M. F. Abrahams, "Strategic Behaviors in Romantic Relationship Initiation," *Personality and Social Psychology Bulletin* 25 (1999): 707–720; A. E. Lindsey and W. R. Zakahi, "Perceptions of Men and Women Departing from Conversational Sex Role Stereotypes during Initial Interaction." In *Sex Differences and Similarities in Communication*, edited by D. J. Canary and K. Dindia (Mahwah, NJ: Lawrence Erlbaum, 1998), 393–412; A. E. Lindsey and W. R. Zakahi, "Women Who Tell and Men Who Ask: Perceptions of Men and Women Departing from Gender Stereotypes during Initial Interaction," *Sex Roles* 34 (1996): 767–786; L. A. McCloskey, "Gender and Conversation: Mixing and Matching Styles." In *Current Conceptions of Sex Roles and Sex Typing: Theory and Research*, edited by D. B. Carter (New York: Praeger, 1987), 139–153; J. Coates, *Women, Men, and Language* 3e (New York: Pearson, 2004); V. Derlega, B. Winstead, P. Wong, and S. Hunter, "Gender Effects in an Initial Encounter: A Case Where Men Exceeded Women in Disclosure," *Journal of Social and Personal Relationships* 2 (1985): 25–44; R. Lakoff, *Language and Woman's Place* (New York: Harper & Row, 1975); P. M. Fishman, "Interaction: The Work Women Do," *Social Problems* 25 (1978): 397–406; J. D. Davis, "When Boy Meets Girl: Sex Roles and the Negotiation of Intimacy in an Acquaintance Exercise," *Journal of Personality and Social Psychology* 36 (1978): 684–692.

38. A. L. Vangelisti, M. L. Knapp, and J. A. Daly, "Conversational Narcissism," *Communication Monographs* 57 (1990): 251–274.

39. C. Derber, *The Pursuit of Attention: Power and Ego in Everyday Life* (New York: Oxford University Press, 2000).

40. J. Holmes, "Complimenting—A Positive Politeness Strategy." In *Language and Gender: A Reader*, edited by J. Coates (Malden, MA: Blackwell, 1998), 100–120.

41. E. M. Doohan and V. Manusov, "The Communication of Compliments in Romantic Relationships: An Investigation of Relational Satisfaction and Sex Differences and Similarities in Compliment Behavior," *Western Journal of Communication* 68 (2004): 170–194.

42. S. Jourard, *The Transparent Self* (Princeton, NJ: Van Nostrand, 1971); J. C. Pearson, *Interpersonal Communication: Concepts, Components, and Contexts* 2e (New York: McGraw-Hill, 1990).

43. Harvey and Weber, *Odyssey of the Heart*, 105–106.

44. S. Petronio, "The Boundaries of Privacy: Praxis of Everyday Life." In *Balancing Secrets of Private Disclosure*, edited by S. Petronio (Mahwah, NJ: Lawrence Erlbaum, 2000), 37–49; L. B. Rosenfeld, "Overview of the Ways Privacy, Secrecy, and Disclosure Are Balanced in Today's Society." In Petronio, *Balancing Secrets of Private Disclosure*, 3–17; C. A. Wilkinson, "Expressing Affection: A Vocabulary of Loving Messages." In Galvin and Cooper, *Making Connections*, 150–157; Guerrero, *Close Encounters*.

45. M. L. Rasmussen, "The Problem of Coming Out," *Theory into Practice* 43 (2004): 144–151; T. W. Harrison, "Adolescent Homosexuality and Concerns Regarding Disclosure," *Journal of School Health* 73 (2003): 107–119; R. Galatzer and B. J. Cohler, "Making a Gay Identity: Coming Out, Social Context, and Psychodynamics," *Annual of Psychoanalysis* 30 (2002): 256–286.

46. C. A. Vanlear, Jr., "The Formation of Social Relationships: A Longitudinal Study of Social Penetration," *Human Communication Research* 13 (1987): 299–322.

47. Harvey and Weber, *Odyssey of the Heart*.

48. J. Fine, "Intimacy," *O: The Oprah Winfrey Magazine* (October, 2001), 225.

49. For research on the role of self-disclosure in relationship development, see M. Kito, "Self-Disclosure in Romantic Relationships and Friendships Among American and Japanese College Students," *Journal of Social Psychology* 145 (2005): 127–140; J. H.

Berg, "Responsiveness and Self-Disclosure." In *Self-Disclosure: Theory, Research, and Therapy*, edited by V. Derlega and J. Berg (New York: Plenum, 1987); J. Honeycutt, "A Model of Marital Functioning Based on an Attraction Paradigm and Social-Penetration Dimensions," *Journal of Marriage and the Family* 48 (1986): 651–667; G. J. Chelune, E. Waring, B. Yosk, F. Sultan, and J. Ogden, "Self-Disclosure and Its Relationship to Marital Intimacy," *Journal of Clinical Psychology* 40 (1984): 216–219; M. Knapp and A. L. Vangelisti, *Interpersonal Communication and Human Relationships* 5e (Boston: Allyn & Bacon, 2005); C. R. Berger and J. J. Bradac, *Language and Social Knowledge: Uncertainty in Interpersonal Relations* (London: Edward Arnold, 1982); S. S. Hendrick, "Self-Disclosure and Marital Satisfaction," *Journal of Personality and Social Psychology* 40 (1981): 1150–1159; G. J. Chelune and associates, *Self-Disclosure: Origins, Patterns, and Implications of Openness in Interpersonal Relationships* (San Francisco: Jossey-Bass, 1979); G. R. Miller and M. Steinberg, *Between People: A New Analysis of Interpersonal Communication* (Chicago: Science Research Associates, 1975); G. Levinger and D. Senn, "Disclosure of Feelings in Marriage," *Merrill-Palmer Quarterly* 13 (1967): 237–249.

50. D. Borisoff, "The Effect of Gender on Establishing and Maintaining Intimate Relationships." In *Women and Men Communicating: Challenges and Changes* 2e, edited by L. P. Arliss and D. J. Borisoff (Prospect Heights, IL: Waveland, 2001), 15–31; K. Galvin and C. Bylund, "First Marriage Families: Gender and Communication." In Arliss and Borisoff, *Women and Men Communicating*, 132–148; H. T. Reis, "Gender Differences in Intimacy and Related Behaviors: Context and Process." In Canary, *Sex Differences and Similarities in Communication*, 203–231; J. T. Wood and C. C. Inman, "In a Different Mode: Masculine Styles of Communicating Closeness," *Journal of Applied Communication Research* 21 (1993): 279–295; K. Dindia and M. Allen, "Sex Differences in Self-Disclosure: A Meta-Analysis," *Psychological Bulletin* 112 (1992): 106–124.

51. D. Scott, "Marriage Online: Saying 'I Do' by a Virtual Waterfall, Moving into a Virtual House," *Corpus Christi Caller Times* (March 7, 1999): H1, H3.

52. S. Winston, "Cyberlove: Florida Man Gives On-Line Advice for the Lovelorn," *Corpus Christi Caller Times* (May 28, 1995): G1, G7.

53. D. J. Canary and T. M. Emmers-Sommer, with S. Faulkner, *Sex and Gender Differences in Personal Relationships* (New York: Guilford, 1997).

54. E. L. Paul and K. M. White, "The Development of Intimate Relationships in Late Adolescence," *Adolescence* 25 (1990): 375–400; J. M. Reisman, "Intimacy in Same-Sex Friendships," *Sex Roles* 23 (1990): 65–82; S. Swain, "Covert Intimacy in Men's Friendships: Closeness in Men's Friendships." In *Gender in Intimate Relationships: A Microstructural Approach*, edited by B. Risman and P. Schwartz (Belmont, CA: Wadsworth, 1989), 71–86; R. J. Barth and B. N. Kinder, "A Theoretical Analysis of Sex Differences in Same-Sex Friendships," *Sex Roles* 19 (1988): 349–363; B. A. Winstead, "Sex Differences in Same-Sex Friendships." In *Friendship and Social Interaction*, edited by V. J. Derlega and B. A. Winstead (New York: Springer-Verlag, 1986), 81–99.

55. W. K. Rawlins, "Times, Places, and Social Spaces for Cross-Sex Friendship." In Arliss and Borisoff, *Women and Men Communicating*, 93–114.

56. Wood and Inman, "In a Different Mode."

57. I. Altman and D. Taylor, *Social Penetration: The Development of Relationships* (New York: Holt, Rinehart and Winston, 1973); Brehm. *Intimate Relationships*: B. M. Montgomery, "Communication in Close Relationships." In Weber, *Perspectives on Close Relationships*, 67–87.

58. J. Luft, *Group Process: An Introduction to Group Dynamics* (Palo Alto, CA: Mayfield, 1970).

59. P. Mehta and M. S. Clark, "Toward Understanding Emotions in Intimate Relationships." In Weber, *Perspectives on Close Relationships*, 88–109.

60. A. Hochschild, "The Economy of Gratitude." In *The Sociology of Emotions: Original Essays and Research Papers*, edited by D. Franks and E. D. McCarthy (Greenwich, CT: JAI Press, 1989), 95–113.

61. E. R. McDaniel, "Nonverbal Communication: A Reflection of Cultural Themes." In *Intercultural Communication: A Reader* 8e, edited by L. A. Samovar and R. E. Porter (Belmont, CA: Wadsworth, 1997), 256–265.

62. P. M. Cole, "Children's Spontaneous Control of Facial Expression," *Child Development* 57 (1986): 1309–1321.

63. R. W. Simon and L. E. Nath, "Gender and Emotion in the United States: Do Men and Women Differ in Self-Reports of Feelings and Expressive Behavior?" *American Journal of Sociology* 109 (2004): 1137–1176; L. K. Guerrero and R. L. Reiter, "Expressing Emotion: Sex Differences in Social Skills and Communicative Responses to Anger, Sadness, and Jealousy." In Canary, *Sex Differences and Similarities in Communication*, 321–350; Canary, *Sex and Gender Differences in Personal Relationships*.

64. Jourard, *The Transparent Self*.

65. B. B. Burleson, "Introduction to the Special Issue: Psychological Mediators of Sex Differences in Emotional Support," *Communication Reports* 15 (2002): 1–4; W. E. Snell, R. S. Miller, and S. S. Belk, "Development of the Emotional Self-Disclosure Scale," *Sex Roles* 18 (1988): 59–73.

66. W. Pollack, *Real Boys: Rescuing Our Sons from the Myths of Boyhood* (New York: Owl Books, 1999); O. Silverstein and B. Rashbaum, *The Courage to Raise Good Men* (New York: Penguin, 1995); V. Monroe, "How to Raise the Men We'd Want to Marry," *O: The Oprah Winfrey Magazine* (June, 2003): 163, 203; P. C. McGraw, "Dr. Phil's MANual," *O: The Oprah Winfrey Magazine* (June, 2003): 46–50; P. C. McGraw, "Dr. Phil: Who *Is* That Masked Man?" *O: The Oprah Winfrey Magazine* (March, 2005): 52, 56.

67. Galvin, "First Marriage Families"; F. Dickson-Markman, "How Important Is Self-Disclosure in Marriage?" *Communication Research Reports* 1 (1984): 7–14.

68. A. L. Vangelisti, "Communication Problems in Committed Relationships: An Attributional Analysis." In *Attributions, Accounts, and Close Relationships*, edited by J. H. Harvey, T. L. Orbuch, and A. L. Weber (New York: Springer-Verlag, 1992), 144–164.

69. This chapter benefited from the fine scholarship and work of M. Redmond, coauthor of *Interpersonal Communication: Relating to Others* 4e (Boston: Allyn & Bacon, 2005).

CHAPTER 8

1. W. Rawlins, *Friendship Matters: Communication, Dialectics, and the Life Course* (Hawthorne, NY: Aldine de Gruyter, 1992); W. J. Dickens and D. Perlman, "Friendship over the Life-Cycle." In *Personal Relationships 2: Developing Personal Relationships*, edited by S. W. Duck and R. Gilmour (London: Academic Press, 1981).

2. R. Blieszner, "Close Relationships over Time," as reported in J. A. Simpson and B. A. Harris, "Interpersonal Attraction." In *Perspectives on Close Relationships*, edited by A. L. Weber and J. H. Harvey (Boston: Allyn & Bacon, 1994), 1–18.

3. J. Yager, *Friendshifts: The Power of Friendship and How It Shapes Our Lives* (Stamford, CT: Hannacrois Creek Books, 1999); W. Rawlins, "Being There for Friends." In *Making Connections: Readings in Relational Communication*, edited by K. M. Galvin and P. Cooper (Los Angeles: Roxbury, 1996), 258–260; R. Blieszner and R. Adams, *Adult Friendships* (Newbury Park, CA: Sage, 1992).

4. A. J. Johnson, E. Wittenberg, M. M. Villagran, M. Mazur, and P. Villagran, "Relational Progression as a Dialectic: Examining Turning Points in Communication among Friends," *Communication Monographs* 70 (2003): 230–249.

5. P. M. Sias and D. J. Cahill, "From Coworkers to Friends: The Development of Peer Friendships in the Workplace," *Western Journal of Communication* 62 (1998): 273–299; G. A. Fine, "Friendships in the Workplace." In Galvin and Cooper, *Making Connections*, 270–277.

6. M. Hughes, K. Morrison, and K. J. K. Asada, "What's Love Got to Do with It? Exploring the Impact of Maintenance Rules, Love Attitudes, and Network Support on Friends with Benefits Relationships," *Western Journal of Communication* 69 (2005): 49–66.

7. T. A. Lambert, A. S. Kahn, and K. J. Apple, "Pluralistic Ignorance and Hooking Up," *Journal of Sex Research* 40 (2003): 129–133; E. L. Paul and K. A. Hayes, "The Casualties of 'Casual' Sex: A Qualitative Exploration of the Phenomenology of College Students' Hookups," *Journal of Social and Personal Relationships* 29 (2002): 639–661; E. L. Paul, B. McManus, and K. A. Hayes, "'Hookups': Characteristics and Correlates of College Students' Spontaneous and Anonymous Sexual Experiences," *Journal of Sex Research* 37 (2000): 76–88; W. A. Afifi and S. L. Faulkner, "On Being 'Just Friends': The Frequency and Impact of Sexual Activity in Cross-Sex Friendships," *Journal of Social and Personal Relationships* 17 (2000): 205–222.

8. Hughes et al., "What's Love Got to Do With It?"

9. M. Monsour, *Women and Men as Friends: Relationships across the Life Span in the 21st Century* (Mahwah, NJ: Lawrence Erlbaum, 2002).

10. D. Carnegie, *How to Win Friends and Influence People* (New York: Simon & Schuster, 1937).

11. K. Galvin and C. Bylund, "First Marriage Families: Gender and Communication." In *Women and Men Communicating: Challenges and Changes* 2e, edited by L. P. Arliss and D. J. Borisoff (Prospect Heights, IL: Waveland, 2001), 132–148; V. Satir, "The Rules You Live By." In Galvin and Cooper, *Making Connections*, 168–174; S. S. Brehm, R. Miller, D. Perlman, and S. M. Campbell, *Intimate Relationships* 3e (New York: McGraw-Hill, 2001).

12. *The Miami Herald* (July 9, 1982): 12A.

13. M. Coleman, M.A. Fine, L. H. Ganong, K. J. M. Downs, and N. Pauk, "When You're Not the Brady Bunch: Identifying Perceived Conflicts and Resolution Strategies in Stepfamilies," *Personal Relationships* 8 (2001): 55–73; D. O. Braithwaite, L. N. Olson, T. D. Golish, C. Soukup, and P. Turman, "'Becoming a Family': Developmental Processes Represented in Blended Family Discourse," *Journal of Applied Communication Research* 29 (2001): 221–247; J. D. Teachman, L. M. Tedrow, and K. D. Crowder, "The Changing Demography of America's Families," *Journal of Marriage and the Family* 62 (2000): 1234–1246; J. Hauser, "Communication in the Stepfamily: Transitions Bring Challenges." In Arliss and Borisoff, *Women and Men Communicating*, 149–167; K. M. Galvin and B. J. Brommel, "Communication within Stepfamily Systems." In Galvin and Cooper, *Making Connections*, 239–246.

14. M. M. Kern, "Fighting the Fight." In Galvin and Cooper, *Making Connections*, 247–249.

15. J. Koesten, "Family Communication Patterns, Sex of Subject, and Communication Competence," *Communication Monographs* 71 (2004): 226–244.

16. V. Satir, *The New Peoplemaking* (Mountain View, CA: Science & Behavior Books, 1988), 4.

17. *Contexts: A Publication of the American Sociological Association* 3 (2004), retrieved from <www.contextsmagazine.org>; AFL-CIO, *National Study of the Changing Workforce* (2002), retrieved from <www.aflcio.org>.

18. National Association of Colleges and Employers, "Job Outlook 2005" (2005) <http://www.jobweb.com>; M. S. Peterson, "Personnel Interviewers' Perceptions of the Importance and Adequacy of Applicants' Communication Skills," *Communication Education* 46 (1997): 287–291.

19. H. Mintzberg, "The Manager's Job: Folklore and Fact," *Harvard Business Review* 53 (1975): 26–41.

20. J. H. Harvey and A. L. Weber, *Odyssey of the Heart: Close Relationships in the 21st Century* 2e (Mahwah, NJ: Lawrence Erlbaum, 2002); L. K. Guerrero, P. A. Andersen, and W. A. Afifi, *Close Encounters: Communicating in Relationships* (New York: McGraw-Hill 2001); M. L. Knapp and A. Vangelisti, "Relationship Stages: A Communication Perspective." In Galvin and Cooper, *Making Connections*, 134–141; M. L. Knapp and A. L. Vangelisti, *Interpersonal Communication and Human Relationships* 5e (Boston: Allyn & Bacon, 2005); S. A. Welch and R. B. Rubin, "Development of Relationship Stage Measures," *Communication Quarterly 50* (2002): 24–40.

21. A. L. Busboom, D. M. Collins, M. D. Givertz, and L. A. Levin, "Can We Still Be Friends? Resources and Barriers to Friendship Quality after Romantic Relationship Dissolution," *Personal Relationships 9* (2002): 215–223.

22. S. W. Duck, "A Topography of Relationship Disengagement and Dissolution." In *Personal Relationships 4: Dissolving Relationships*, edited by S. W. Duck (New York: Academic Press, 1982); Guerrero, *Close Encounters.*

23. M. L. Knapp, *Social Intercourse: From Greeting to Goodbye* (Boston: Allyn & Bacon, 1978).

24. Duck, "A Topography of Relationship Disengagement and Dissolution."

25. Retrieved February 12, 2004 from <cnn.com>.

26. For research on relationship termination, see S. A. Jang, S. W. Smith, and T. R. Levine, "To Stay or to Leave? The Role of Attachment Styles in Communication Patterns and Potential Termination of Romantic Relationships Following Discovery of Deception," *Communication Monographs 69* (2002): 236–252; S. Metts, "Face and Facework: Implications for the Study of Personal Relationships." In *Handbook of Personal Relationships: Theory, Research, and Interventions*, edited by S. Duck (Chicester, UK: Wiley, 1997), 373–390; B. M. Phillips and J. T. Wood, "The Deterioration Stages in Human Relationships." In Galvin and Cooper, *Making Connections*, 213–218; L. A. Baxter, "Accomplishing Relational Disengagement." In *Understanding Personal Relationships: An Interdisciplinary Approach*, edited by S. Duck and D. Perlman (London: Sage, 1985), 243–265; L. A. Baxter, "Trajectories of Relationship Disengagement," *Journal of Social and Personal Relationships 1* (1984): 29–48; L. A. Baxter, "Strategies for Ending Relationships: Two Studies," *Western Journal of Speech Communication 46* (1982): 223–241; T. L. Morton, J. F. Alexander, and I. Altman, "Communication and Relationships Definition." In *Explorations in Interpersonal Communication*, edited by G. R. Miller (Newbury Park, CA: Sage, 1976), 105–125.

27. L. Stafford, S. L. Kline, and J. Dimmick, "Home E-Mail: Relational Maintenance and Gratification Opportunities," *Journal of Broadcasting & Electronic Media 43* (1999): 659–669.

28. F. S. Christopher and S. Sprecher, "Sexuality in Marriage, Dating, and Other Relationships: A Decade Review." In *Speaking of Sexuality: Interdisciplinary Readings*, edited by J. K. Davidson, Sr., and N. B. Moore (Los Angeles: Roxbury, 2005): 54–71.

29. K. Y. A. McKenna, A. S. Green, and P. K. Smith, "Demarginalizing the Sexual Self," *Journal of Sex Research 38* (2001): 302–316; A. Cooper, I. P. McLoughlin, K. M. Campbell, "Sexuality in Cyberspace: Update for the 21st Century," *Cyberpsychology & Behavior 3* (2000): 521–536.

30. McKenna et al., "Demarginalizing the Sexual Self."

31. P. C. McGraw, "Couples Combat: The Great American Pastime," *O: The Oprah Winfrey Magazine* (August, 2002): 42–43.

32. S. Ting-Toomey and L. Chung, *Understanding Intercultural Communication* (Los Angeles: Roxbury, 2003); S. Ting-Toomey and J. G. Oetzel, *Managing Intercultural Conflict Effectively* 2e (Newbury Park, CA: Sage, 2001); S. Ting-Toomey, "Managing Intercultural Conflicts Effectively." In *Intercultural Communication: A Reader* 8e, edited by L. A. Samovar and R. E. Porter (Belmont, CA: Wadsworth, 1997), 392–404.

33. M. Deutsch, *The Resolution of Conflict* (New Haven: Yale University Press, 1973).

34. W. W. Wilmot and J. L. Hocker, *Interpersonal Conflict* 6e (New York: McGraw-Hill, 2001).

35. C. R. Berger, "Social Power and Interpersonal Communication." In *Explorations in Interpersonal Communication.*

36. Brehm, *Intimate Relationships.*

37. P. J. Kalbfleisch and M. J. Cody, eds., *Gender, Power, and Communication in Human Relationships* (Hillsdale, NJ: Lawrence Erlbaum, 1995); L. P. Arliss, "When Myths Endure and Realities Change: Communication in Romantic Relationships." In Arliss and Borisoff, *Women and Men Communicating*, 115–131; F. E. Millar and L. E. Rogers, "Relational Dimensions of Interpersonal Dynamics." In *Interpersonal Process: New Directions in Communication Research*, edited by M. E. Roloff and G. R. Miller (Newbury Park, CA: Sage, 1987), 117–139.

38. D. A. Infante and A. S. Rancer, "Argumentativeness and Verbal Aggressiveness: A Review of Recent Theory and Research," *Communication Yearbook 19* (1996): 319–351; D. A. Infante, B. L. Riddle, C. L. Horvath, and S. A. Tumlin, "Verbal Aggressiveness: Messages and Reasons," *Communication Quarterly 40* (1992): 116–126; D. A. Infante, K. C. Hartley, M. M. Martin, M. A. Higgins, S. D. Bruning, and G. Hur, "Initiating and Reciprocating Verbal Aggression: Effects on Credibility and Credited Valid Arguments," *Communication Studies 43* (1992): 182–190; D. A. Infante, T. C. Sabourin, J. E. Rudd, and E. A. Shannon, "Verbal Aggression in Violent and Nonviolent Marital Disputes," *Communication Quarterly 38* (1990): 361–371; D. A. Infante and C. J. Wigley III, "Verbal Aggressiveness: An Interpersonal Model and Measure," *Communication Monographs 53* (1986): 61–69. For extensions of this line of research on verbal aggression, see K. A. Rocca, "College Student Attendance: Impact of Instructor Immediacy and Verbal Aggression," *Communication Education 53* (2004): 185–195; T. R. Levine, M. J. Beatty, S. Limon, M. A. Hamilton, R. Buck, and R. M. Chory-Assad, "The Dimensionality of the Verbal Aggressiveness Scale," *Communication Monographs 71* (2004): 245–268; R. M. Chory-Assad, "Effects of Television Sitcom Exposure on the Accessibility of Verbally Aggressive Thoughts," *Western Journal of Communication 68* (2004): 431–453; A. D. Heisel, B. H. La France, and M. J. Beatty, "Self-Reported Extraversion, Neuroticism, and Psychoticism as Predictors of Peer Rated Verbal Aggressiveness and Affinity-Seeking Competence," *Communication Monographs 70* (2003): 1–15; G. H. Sherwin and S. Schmidt, "Communication Codes among African American Children and Youth: The Fast Track from Special Education to Prison?" *Journal of Correctional Education 54* (2003): 45–52; P. Schrodt, "Students' Appraisals of Instructors as a Function of Students' Perceptions of Instructors' Aggressive Communication," *Communication Education 52* (2003): 106–121; C. K. Atkin, S. W. Smith, A. J. Roberto, T. Fediuk, and T. Wagner, "Correlates of Verbally Aggressive Communication in Adolescents," *Journal of Applied Communication Research 30* (2002): 251–268; S. A. Myers and K. A. Rocca, "Perceived Instructor Argumentativeness and Verbal Aggressiveness in the College Classroom: Effects on Student Perceptions of Climate, Apprehension, and State Motivation," *Western Journal of Communication 65* (2001): 113–137.

39. Wilmot and Hocker, *Interpersonal Conflict.*

40. C. M. Carey and P. A. Mongeau, "Communication and Violence in Courtship Relationships." In *Family Violence from a Communication Perspective*, edited by D. D. Cahn and S. A. Lloyd (Hillsdale, NJ: Lawrence Erlbaum, 1996), 127–150.

41. P. Yelsma, "Couples' Affective Orientations and Their Verbal Aggressiveness," *Communication Quarterly 43* (1995): 100–114.

42. T. C. Sabourin, "The Role of Negative Reciprocity in Spousal Abuse: A Relational Control Analysis," *Journal of Applied Communication Research 23* (1995): 271–283.

43. Infante et al., "Verbal Aggressiveness."

44. L. N. Olson, "Exploring 'Common Couple Violence' in Heterosexual Romantic Relationships," *Western Journal of Communication 66* (2002): 104–128; T. C. Sabourin and G. H. Stamp, "Communication and the Experience of Dialectical Tensions in Family Life: An Examination of Abusive and Nonabusive Families," *Communication Monographs 62* (1995): 213–242; J. W. White and J. A. Humphrey, "Women's Aggression in Heterosexual Conflicts," *Aggressive Behavior 20* (1994): 195–202.

45. M. M. Martin, C. M. Anderson, and C. L. Horvath, "Feelings about Verbal Aggression: Justifications for Sending, and Hurt from Receiving, Verbally Aggressive Messages," *Communication Research Reports 13* (1996): 19–26; D. Cloven and M. E. Roloff, "The Chilling Effect of Aggressive Potential on the Expression of Complaints in Intimate Relationships," *Communication Monographs 60* (1993): 199–219.

46. Satir, *The New Peoplemaking;* Wilmot and Hocker, *Interpersonal Conflict.*

47. L. L. Putnam and C. E. Wilson, "Communicative Strategies in Organizational Conflicts: Reliability and Validity of a Measurement Scale." In *Communication Yearbook 6,* edited by M. Burgoon (Beverly Hills: Sage, 1982).

48. Cloven and Roloff, "The Chilling Effect of Aggressive Potential on the Expression of Complaints in Intimate Relationships"; Wilmot and Hocker, *Interpersonal Conflict.*

49. M. A. Gross, L. K. Guerrero, and J. K. Alberts, "Perceptions of Conflict Strategies and Communication Competence in Task-Oriented Dyads," *Journal of Applied Communication Research 32* (2004): 249–270.

50. R. Fisher, W. Ury, and B. Patton, *Getting to Yes: Negotiating Agreement without Giving In* 2e (New York: Penguin Books, 1991).

51. This information is based on several excellent discussions of conflict management skills. We acknowledge W. R. Cupach and D. J. Canary, *Competence in Interpersonal Conflict* (Long Grove, IL: Waveland, 2000); D. Borisoff and D. A. Victor, *Conflict Management: A Communication Skills Approach* 2e (Boston: Allyn & Bacon, 1999); D. Yankelovich, *The Magic of Dialogue: Transforming Conflict into Cooperation* (New York: Simon & Schuster, 1999); Wilmot and Hocker, *Interpersonal Conflict;* O. Hargie, ed., *The Handbook of Communication Skills* (London: Routledge, 1997); O. Hargie, C. Saunders, and D. Dickson, *Social Skills in Interpersonal Communication* 3e (London: Routledge, 1994); W. A. Donohue, with R. Holt, *Managing Interpersonal Conflict* (Newbury Park, CA: Sage, 1992); D. A. Romig and L. J. Romig. *Structured Teamwork© Guide* (Austin: Performance Resources, 1990); S. Deep and L. Sussman, *Smart Moves* (Reading, MA: Addison-Wesley, 1990); Fisher, *Getting to Yes;* M. D. Davis, E. L. Eshelman, and M. McKay, *The Relaxation and Stress Reduction Workbook* (Oakland, CA: New Harbinger, 1982); R. Boulton, *People Skills* (New York: Simon & Schuster, 1979).

52. J. B. Rubin, "Stand Back from the Rope!" *O: The Oprah Winfrey Magazine* (March, 2005): 193–194, 197.

53. B. M. Gayle and R. W. Preiss, "Language Intensity Plus: A Methodological Approach to Validate Emotions in Conflicts," *Communication Reports 12* (1999): 43–50; Wilmot and Hocker, *Interpersonal Conflict.*

54. A. Ellis, *A New Guide to Rational Living* (North Hollywood, CA: Wilshire Books, 1977).

55. L. C. Lederman, "The Impact of Gender on the Self and Self-Talk." In Arliss and Borisoff, *Women and Men Communicating,* 78–89; Ellis, *A New Guide to Rational Living.*

56. S. R. Covey, *The Seven Habits of Highly Effective People* (New York: Simon & Schuster, 1989), 67.

57. Fisher, *Getting to Yes.*

CHAPTER 9

1. R. K. Mosvick and R. B. Nelson, *We've Got to Start Meeting Like This!* (Glenview, IL: Scott, Foresman, 1987).

2. Mosvick and Nelson, *We've Got to Start Meeting Like This!*

3. K. W. Hawkins and B. P. Fillion, "Perceived Communication Skill Needs for Work Groups," *Communication Research Reports 16* (1999): 167–174; also see S. Burkhalter, J. Gastil, and T. Kelshaw, "A Conceptual Definition and Theoretical Model of Public Deliberation in Small Face-to-Face Groups," *Communication Theory 12* (2002): 398–422.

4. S.A. Beebe and J.T. Masterson, *Communicating in Small Groups: Principles and Practices* 8e (Boston: Allyn and Bacon, 2006).

5. N. Katz and G. Koenig, "Sports Teams as a Model for Workplace Teams: Lessons and Liabilities," *Academy of Management Executive 15* (2001): 56–67.

6. Our discussion of teams and teamwork is from Beebe and Masterson, *Communicating in Small Groups.*

7. A. G. Sheard and A. P. Kakabadse, "From Loose Groups to Effective Teams: The Nine Key Factors of the Team Landscape," *Journal of Management Development 21* (2002): 133–151.

8. See F. C. Broadbeck and T. Breitermeyer, "Effects of Individual versus Mixed Individual and Group Experience in Rule Induction on Group Member Learning and Group Performance," *Journal of Experimental Social Psychology 36* (2002): 621–648.

9. S. B. Shimanoff, *Communication Rules: Theory and Research* (Beverly Hills: Sage, 1980).

10. M. Hoegl, "Goal Setting and Team Performance in Innovative Projects: On the Moderating Role of Teamwork Quality," *Small Group Research 34* (2003): 3–19.

11. F. LaFasto and C. Larson, *Teamwork* (Thousand Oaks, CA: Sage, 2001).

12. A. T. Pescosolido, "Group Efficacy and Group Effectiveness: The Effects of Group Efficacy over Time on Group Performance and Development," *Small Group Research 34* (2003): 20–43.

13. B. Bell and S. W. J. Kozlowski, "A Typology of Virtual Teams: Implications for Effective Leadership," *Group & Organization Management 27* (2002): 14–49; A. Thatcher, "Small Group Decision-Making in Face-to-Face and Computer-Mediated Environments: The Role of Personality," *Behavior & Information Technology 22* (2003): 203–218; D. R. Lemus, D. R. Seibold, A. J. Flanagin, and M. J. Metzger, "Argument and Decision Making in Computer-Mediated Groups," *Journal of Communication 54* (2004): 302–320; E. V. Hobman, P. Bordia, B. Irmer, and A. Chang, "The Expression of Conflict in Computer-Mediated and Face-to-Face Groups," *Small Group Research 33* (2002): 439–464; R. Benbunan-Fich, S. R. Hiltz, and M. Turoff, "A Comparative Content Analysis of Face-to-Face vs. Asynchronous Group Decision Making," *Decision Support Systems 34* (2002): 457–469.

14. K. D. Benne and Paul Sheats, "Functional Roles of Group Members," *Journal of Social Issues 4* (1948): 41–49. For a good review of role development in groups, see A. P. Hare, "Types of Roles in Small Groups: A Bit of History and a Current Perspective," *Small Group Research 25* (1994): 433–438; A. J. Salazar, "An Analysis of the Development and Evolution of Roles in the Small Group," *Small Group Research 27* (1996): 475–503.

15. R. F. Bales, *Interaction Process Analysis* (Chicago: University of Chicago Press, 1976).

16. Shimanoff, *Communication Rules.*

17. M. Shaw, *Group Dynamics: The Psychology of Small Group Behavior* (New York: McGraw-Hill, 1981), 281.

18. J. I. Hurwitz, A. F. Zander, and B. Hymovitch, "Some Effects of Power on the Relations among Group Members." In *Group Dynamics: Research and Theory,* edited by D. Cartwright and A. Zander (New York: Harper & Row, 1953), 483–492; D. C. Barnlund and C. Harland, "Propinquity and Prestige as Determinants of Communication Networks," *Sociometry 26* (1963): 467–479; G.

C. Homans, *The Human Group* (New York: Harcourt Brace and World, 1992); H. H. Kelly, "Communication in Experimentally Created Hierarchies," *Human Relations 4* (1951): 36–56.

19. M. R. Singer, *Intercultural Communication: A Perceptual Approach* (Englewood Cliffs, NJ: Prentice-Hall, 1987), 118.

20. J. R. P. French and B. H. Raven, "The Bases of Social Power." In Cartwright and Zander, *Group Dynamics*, 607–623.

21. D. Neumann, "Small Group Cohesion and Frequency of Idiom Use." Paper presented at the annual meeting of the National Communication Association, Chicago, IL, November, 2004.

22. Adapted from E. G. Bormann and N. C. Bormann, *Effective Small Group Communication* (Minneapolis: Burgess, 1980), 70–72.

23. N. Katz, D. Lazer, H. Arrow, and N. Contractor, "Network Theory and Small Groups," *Small Group Research 35* (2004): 307–332.

24. S. Wheelan, B. Davidson, and F. Tilin, "Group Development Across Time: Reality or Illusion?" *Small Group Research 34* (2003): 223–245; S. Furst, M. Reeves, B. Rosen, and R. S. Blackburn, "Managing the Life Cycle of Virtual Teams," *Academy of Management Executive 18* (2004): 6–22.

25. B. A. Fisher, "Decision Emergence: Phases in Group Decision-Making," *Speech Monographs 37* (1970): 60.

26. For a discussion of primary tension and group phases, see E. Bormann, *Discussion and Group Methods* (New York: Harper & Row, 1975).

27. M. A. Von Glinow, D. Shapiro, and J. Brett, "Can We Talk, and Should We? Managing Emotional Conflict in Multicultural Teams," *Academy of Management Review 29* (2004): 578–592.

28. S. A. Wheelan and T. Williams, "Mapping Dynamic Interaction Patterns in Work Groups," *Small Group Research 34* (2003): 433–467; Wheelan, "Group Development Across Time."

29. M. S. Poole, "Decision Development in Small Groups III: A Multiple Sequence Model of Group Decision Development," *Communication Monographs 50* (1983): 321–341; also see C. Pavitt and K. Kline Johnson, "Scheidel and Crowell Revisited: A Descriptive Study of Group Proposal Sequencing," *Communication Monographs 69* (2002): 19–32.

30. G. Hofstede, *Culture's Consequences: International Differences in Work-Related Values* (Beverly Hills: Sage, 1980): G. Hofstede, *Cultures and Organizations: Software of the Mind* (London: McGraw-Hill, 1991).

31. Adapted from J. Mole, *Mind Your Manners: Managing Business Cultures in Europe* (New York: Nicholas Brealey Publishing, 1995).

32. Beebe and Masterson, *Communicating in Small Groups*.

33. Beebe and Masterson, *Communicating in Small Groups*.

34. Beebe and Masterson, *Communicating in Small Groups*.

CHAPTER 10

1. See N. R. F. Maier, "Assets and Liabilities in Group Problem Solving: The Need for an Integrative Function," *Psychological Review 74* (1967): 239–249; M. Argyle, *Cooperation: The Basis of Sociability* (London: Routledge, 1991); H. A. M. Wilke and R. W. Meertens, *Group Performance* (London: Routledge, 1994).

2. Maier, "Assets and Liabilities in Group Problem Solving"; Argyle, *Cooperation*; Wilke and Meertens, *Group Performance*.

3. R. Y. Hirokawa, "Discussion Procedures and Decision-Making Performance: A Test of a Functional Perspective," *Human Communication Research 12* (1985): 203–224.

4. R. Y. Hirokawa, "Why Informed Groups Make Faulty Decisions: An Investigation of Possible Interaction-Based Explanations," *Small Group Behavior 18* (1987): 3–29.

5. R. Y. Hirokawa and K. Rost, "Effective Group Decision-Making in Organizations: Field Test of the Vigilant Interaction Theory," *Management Communication Quarterly 5* (1992): 267–288; Hirokawa, "Why Informed Groups Make Faulty Decisions"; R. Y. Hirokawa, "Group Communication and Decision-Making Performance: A Continued Test of the Functional Perspective," *Human*

Communication Research 14 (1988): 487–515; M. O. Orlitzky and R. Y. Hirokawa, "To Err Is Human, to Correct for It Divine: A Meta-Analysis of Research Testing the Functional Theory of Group Decision-Making Effectiveness." Paper presented at the meeting of the National Communication Association, Chicago, IL, November, 1997.

6. Hirokawa, "Discussion Procedures and Decision-Making Performance."

7. C. E. Larson and F. M. J. LaFasto, *Teamwork: What Must Go Right/What Can Go Wrong* (Beverly Hills: Sage, 1989). Also see D. D. Chrislip and C. E. Larson, *Collaborative Leadership* (San Francisco: Jossey-Bass, 1994); D. A. Romig, *Breakthrough Teamwork: Outstanding Results Using Structured Teamwork* (Chicago: Irwin, 1996); M. A. Marks, J. E. Mathieu, and S. J. Zaccaro, "A Temporally Based Framework and Taxonomy of Team Processes," *Academy of Management Review 26* (2001): 356–376; N. Katz, "Sports Teams as a Model for Workplace Teams: Lessons and Liabilities," *Academy of Management Executive 15* (2001): 56–67.

8. Larson and LaFasto, *Teamwork*; Chrislip and Larson, *Collaborative Leadership*; Romig, *Breakthrough Teamwork*.

9. Larson and LaFasto, *Teamwork*.

10. O. S. Chernyshenko, A. G. Miner, M. R. Baumann, and J. A. Sniezek, "The Impact of Information Distribution, Ownership, and Discussion on Group Member Judgment: The Differential Cue Weighting Model," *Organizational Behavior and Human Decision Processes 91* (2003): 12–25.

11. Orlitzky and Hirokawa, "To Err Is Human, to Correct for It Divine."

12. Orlitzky and Hirokawa, "To Err Is Human, to Correct for It Divine"; B. L. Smith, "Interpersonal Behaviors That Damage the Productivity of Creative Problem Solving Groups," *Journal of Creative Behavior 27* (1993): 171–187.

13. A. B. Henley and K. H. Price, "Want a Better Team? Foster a Climate of Fairness," *Academy of Management Executive 16* (2002): 153–155.

14. From a discussion in S. A. Beebe and J. T. Masterson, *Communicating in Small Groups: Principles and Practices* 8e (Boston: Allyn & Bacon, 2006), 16–17.

15. See A. B. VanGundy, *Techniques of Structured Problem Solving* (New York: Van Nostrand Reinhold Company, 1981), 4; Romig, *Breakthrough Teamwork*.

16. Beebe and Masterson, *Communicating in Small Groups*; VanGundy, *Techniques of Structured Problem Solving*.

17. J. K. Brilhart and L. M. Jochem, "Effects of Different Patterns on Outcomes of Problem-Solving Discussion," *Journal of Applied Psychology 48* (1964): 174–179; W. E. Jurma, "Effects of Leader Structuring Style and Task Orientation Characteristics of Group Members," *Communication Monographs 49* (1979): 282–295; S. Jarboe, "A Comparison of Input–Output, Process–Output, and Input–Process–Output Models of Small Group Problem-Solving Effectiveness," *Communication Monographs 55* (1988): 121–142; VanGundy, *Techniques of Structured Problem Solving*.

18. D. M. Berg, "A Descriptive Analysis of the Distribution and Duration of Themes Discussed by Task-Oriented Small Groups," *Speech Monographs 34* (1967): 172–175; E. G. Bormann and N. C. Bormann, *Effective Small Group Communication* 2e (Minneapolis: Burgess, 1976), 132; M. S. Poole, "Decision Development in Small Groups III: A Multiple Sequence Model of Group Decision Development," *Communication Monographs 50* (1983): 321–341.

19. J. Dewey, *How We Think* (Boston: D. C. Heath, 1910).

20. This discussion of the journalist's six questions is based on a discussion by J. E. Eitington, *The Winning Trainer* (Houston: Gulf Publishing, 1989), 157.

21. Based on the research of K. Lewin, "Frontiers in Group Dynamics," *Human Relations 1* (1947): 5–42.

22. M. Gladwell, *Blink: The Power of Thinking Without Thinking* (New York: Little, Brown and Company, 2005).

23. See S. Taggar, "Individual Creativity and Group Ability to Utilize Individual Creative Resources: A Multilevel Model," *Academy of Management Journal* 45 (2002): 315–330; C. E. Johnson and M. A. Hackman, *Creative Communication: Principles and Applications* (Prospect Heights, IL: Waveland Press, 1995).

24. A. F. Osborn, *Applied Imagination* (New York: Scribner's, 1962).

25. A. L. Delberg, A. H. Van de Ven, and D. H. Gustason, *Group Techniques for Program Planning: A Guide to Nominal Group and Delphi Processes* (Glenview, IL: Scott, Foresman, 1975), 7–16.

26. M. C. Roy, S. Gauvin, and M. Limayem, "Electronic Group Brainstorming: The Role of Feedback on Productivity," *Small Group Research* 27 (1996): 215–247.

27. K. L. Dugosh, P. B. Paulus, E. J. Roland, and H. C. Yang, "Cognitive Stimulation in Brainstorming," *Journal of Personality and Social Psychology* 79 (2000): 722–735.

28. J. J. Sosik, B. J. Avolio, and S. S. Kahai, "Inspiring Group Creativity: Comparing Anonymous and Identified Electronic Brainstorming." *Small Group Research* 29 (1998): 3–31; W. H. Cooper, R. B. Gallupe, S. Pollard, and J. Cadsby, "Some Liberating Effects of Anonymous Electronic Brainstorming," *Small Group Research* 29 (1998): 147–177.

29. D. Straker, *Rapid Problem Solving with Post-It® Notes* (Tucson: Fisher Books, 1997).

30. M. A. Roberto, "Strategic Decision-Making Processes: Beyond the Efficiency–Consensus Trade-Off," *Group & Organizational Management* 29 (2004): 625–658.

31. R. Y. Hirokawa, D. S. Gouran, and A. Martz, "Understanding the Sources of Faulty Group Decision Making: A Lesson from the *Challenger* Disaster," *Small Group Behavior* 19 (1988): 411–433.

32. R. K. M. Haurwitz, "Faculty Doubted Bonfire's Stability," *Austin-American Statesman* (December 10, 1999), A1, A2.

33. D. Jehl, "Panel Unanimous: 'Groupthink' Backed Prewar Assumptions, Report Concludes," *New York Times* (July 10, 2004): 1; also see *The 9/11 Commission Report: Final Report of the National Commission on Terrorist Attacks Upon the United States* (Washington, DC: National Commission on Terrorist Attacks, 2004).

34. J. F. Veiga, "The Frequency of Self-Limiting Behavior in Groups: A Measure and an Explanation," *Human Relations* 44 (1991): 877–895.

35. I. L. Janis, *Victims of Groupthink* (Boston: Houghton Mifflin, 1973).

36. See B. M. Bass, *Stodgill's Handbook of Leadership* (New York: The Free Press, 1981).

37. G. J. Galanes, "In Their Own Words: An Exploratory Study of Bona Fide Group Leaders," *Small Group Research* 34 (2003): 741–770.

38. R. White and R. Lippitt, "Leader Behavior and Member Reaction in Three 'Social Climates'." In *Group Dynamics* 3e, edited by D. Cartwright and A. Zander (New York: Harper & Row, 1968), 319.

39. M. Van Vugt, S. F. Jepson, C. M. Hart, and D. De Cremer, "Autocratic Leadership in Social Dilemmas: A Threat to Group Stability," *Journal of Experimental and Social Psychology* 40 (2004): 1–13.

40. S. Halverson, S. E. Murphy, and R. E. Riggio, "Charismatic Leadership in Crisis Situations: A Laboratory Investigation of Stress and Crisis," *Small Group Research* 35 (2004): 495–514.

41. S. S. K. Lam, X. P. Chen, and J. Schaubroeck, "Participative Decision Making and Employee Performance in Different Cultures: The Moderating Effects of Allocentrism/Idiocentrism and Efficacy," *Academy of Management Journal* 45 (2002): 905–914.

42. P. Hersey, K. H. Blanchard, and D. E. Johnson, *Management of Organizational Behavior: Leading Human Resources* (New Delhi: Prentice-Hall of India, 2004), 175.

43. Hersey, *Management of Organizational Behavior.*

44. Hersey, *Management of Organizational Behavior.*

45. F. Fiedler, *A Theory of Leadership Effectiveness* (New York: McGraw-Hill, 1967), 144.

46. B.M. Bass and M.J. Avolio, "Transformational Leadership and Organizational Culture," *International Journal of Public Administra-* *tion 17* (1994): 541–554. Also see F. J. Yammarino and A. J. Dubinsky, "Transformational Leadership Theory: Using Levels of Analysis to Determine Boundary Conditions," *Personnel Psychology 47* (1994): 787–809.

47. P. M. Senge, "The Leader's New Role: Building Learning Organizations," *Sloan Management Review 32*, no. 1 (1990).

48. For a discussion of monochronic and polychronic time, see E. T. Hall, *The Silent Language* (New York: Doubleday, 1959).

49. Hall, *The Silent Language.*

50. Hall, *The Silent Language.*

51. M. J. Waller, M. E. Zellmer-Bruhn, and R. C. Giambatista, "Watching the Clock: Group Pacing Behavior Under Dynamic Deadlines," *Academy of Management Journal 45* (2002): 1046–1055.

52. D. I. Jung and J. J. Sosik, "Transformational Leadership in Work Groups: The Role of Empowerment, Cohesiveness, and Collective Efficacy on Perceived Group Performance," *Small Group Research 33* (2002): 313–336; also see T. Dvir, D. Eden, B. J. Avolio, and B. Shamir, "Impact of Transformational Leadership on Follower Development and Performance: A Field Experiment," *Academy of Management Journal 45* (2002): 735–744; C. L. Hoyt and J. Blascovich, "Transformational and Transactional Leadership in Virtual and Physical Environments," *Small Group Research 34* (2003): 678–715.

53. V. U. Druskat and J. V. Wheeler, "Managing From the Boundary: The Effective Leadership of Self-Managing Work Teams," *Academy of Management Journal 46* (2003): 435–457.

54. For an excellent discussion of transformational leadership applied to teams, see S. D. Dionne, F. J. Yammarino, L. E. Atwater, and W. D. Spangler, "Transformational Leadership and Team Performance," *Journal of Organizational Change Management 17* (2004): 177–193.

55. J. A. Raelin, "Don't Bother Putting Leadership Into People," *Academy of Management Executive 18* (2004): 131–135; M. W. McCall, "Leadership Development Through Experience," *Academy of Management Executive 18* (2004): 127–130; J. Conger, "Developing Leadership Capability: What's Inside the Black Box?" *Academy of Management Executive 18* (2004): 136–139; D. Vera and M. Crossan, "Strategic Leadership and Organizational Learning," *Academy of Management Review 29* (2004): 222–239.

56. D. Barry, *Dave Barry Turns 50* (New York: Ballantine Books, 1998), 182.

57. R. K. Mosvick and R. B. Nelson, *We've Got to Start Meeting Like This!* (Glenview, IL: Scott, Foresman, 1987).

58. Suggestions about organizing meeting agendas are based on M. Doyle and D. Straus, *How to Make Meetings Work* (New York: Playboy Press, 1976); Mosvick and Nelson, *We've Got to Start Meeting Like This!*; G. Lumsden and D. Lumsden, *Communicating in Groups and Teams: Sharing Leadership* (Belmont, CA: Wadsworth, 1993); D. B. Curtis, J. J. Floyd, and J. L. Winsor, *Business and Professional Communication* (New York: HarperCollins, 1992); D. Romig, *Breakthrough Teamwork* (Chicago: Irwin, 1996); T. A. Kayser, *Mining Group Gold* (El Segundo, CA: Serif Publishing, 1990); J. E. Tropman and G. Clark Morningstar, *Meetings: How to Make Them Work for You* (New York: Van Nostrand Reinhold, 1985): 56; Beebe and Masterson, *Communicating in Small Groups.*

59. J. E. Tropman, *Making Meetings Work* (Thousand Oaks, CA: Sage, 1996).

60. See D. S. Gouran, "Variables Related to Consensus in Group Discussions of Questions of Policy," *Speech Monographs 36* (1969): 385–391; T. J. Knutsun, "An Experimental Study of the Effects of Orientation Behavior on Small Group Consensus," *Speech Monographs 39* (1972): 159–165; J. A. Kline, "Orientation and Group Consensus," *Central States Speech Journal 23* (1972): 44–47.

61. Mosvick and Nelson, *We've Got to Start Meeting Like This!*

62. Beebe and Masterson, *Communicating in Small Groups.*

63. D. W. Johnson and F. P. Johnson, *Joining Together* (Englewood Cliffs, NJ: Prentice-Hall, 1975), 114.

64. S. A. Beebe and J. K. Barge, "Evaluating Group Discussion." In *Small Group Communication: Theory & Practice*, edited by R. Y. Hirokawa, R. S. Cathcart, L. A. Samovar, and L. D. Henman (Los Angeles, CA: Roxbury, 2003).

CHAPTER 11

1. J. Fitzgerald, "Metcalfe to MIT Geeks: Get to Writin'," *The Boston Herald* (April 28, 2005).
2. The sample presentation that is developed in this chapter is adapted from B. Johnson, "Coricidin: No Prescription Needed," *Winning Orations 2004* (Mankato, MN: Interstate Oratorical Association, 2004), 56–58.
3. S. B. Butterfield, "Instructional Interventions for Situational Anxiety and Avoidance," *Communication Education 37* (1988): 214–223.
4. Survey conducted by R. H. Bruskin and Associates, *Spectra* 9 (December, 1973): 4.
5. L. Fletcher, *How to Design & Deliver Speeches* (New York: Longman, 2001), 3.
6. K. Savitsky and T. Gilovich, "The Illusion of Transparency and the Alleviation of Speech Anxiety," *Journal of Experimental Social Psychology 39* (2003): 618–625.
7. K. Dwyer and D. Fus, "Perceptions of Communication Competence, Self-Efficacy, and Trait Communication Apprehension: Is There an Impact on Basic Course Success?" *Communication Research Reports 19* (2002): 29–37.
8. J. Ayres, "Speech Preparation Processes and Speech Apprehension," *Communication Education 45* (1996): 228–235.
9. P. Addison, E. Clay, S. Xie, C. Sawyer, and R. Behnke, "Worry as a Function of Public Speaking State Anxiety Type," *Communication Reports 16* (2003): 125–131.
10. J. Ayres and B. Huett, "An Examination of the Long-Term Effect of Performance Visualization," *Communication Research Reports 17* (2000): 229–236.
11. J. Ayres and B. Huett, "An Examination of the Impact of Performance Visualization," *Communication Research Reports 16* (1999): 29–39; Ayres and Huett, "An Examination of the Long-Term Effect of Performance Visualization."
12. L. Tracy, "Taming Hostile Audiences," *Vital Speeches of the Day 71.10* (March 1, 2005).
13. J. Humphrey, "Taking the Stage: How Women Can Achieve a Leadership Presence," *Vital Speeches of the Day* (May 1, 2001): 437.
14. Data provided by Center for Defense Information, "Chronology of Major Terrorist Attacks against U.S. Targets," *CDI Terrorism Project* (June 27, 2002) <http://www.cdi.org/terrorism/chronology-pr.html>; "September 11 Fatalities Make 2001 the Worst Year," *Airwise News* January 4, 2002 (June 27, 2002) <http://news.airwise.com/stories/2002/01/1010177858.html>.
15. W. Mossberg, "Product Review: Vertical Search Sites Promising," *Tucson Citizen*, April 6, 2005 (May 24, 2005) <www.tucsoncitizen.com/index.php?page=business&story_id=040605d1_vertical&toolbar=print_story>.
16. F. Fox, "Google or Yahoo?" *Bookmarks: Alkek Library (Texas State University–San Marcos) News 1* (2004), 2.
17. These criteria for evaluating Web resources are adapted from E. Kirk, "Practical Steps in Evaluating Internet Resources," May 7, 2001 (May 22, 2001) <http://Milton.mse.jhu.edu:8001/research/education/practical.html>.
18. J. Heffernan et al., *Writing: A College Handbook*, 5e. (New York: Norton, 2001), 53–54.
19. P. Gorski, "A Multicultural Model for Evaluating Educational Web Sites," December 1999 (May 22, 2001) <curry.edschool.Virginia.edu/go/multicultural/net/comps/model.html>; "Section 508," August 15, 2002 (May 26, 2005) <www.section.508.gov/index.cfm?FuseAction=Content&ID=11>.

20. "Section 508," August 15, 2002 (May 26, 2005) <www.section508.gov/index.cfm?FuseAction=Content&ID=11>.
21. M. Mirapaul, "Making Federal Web Sites Friendly to Disabled Users," *The New York Times* (June 11, 2001): B2.
22. U.S. Government Printing Office, "National Bibliography Program," *GPO Access*. May 9, 2005 (May 24, 2005) <www.access.gpo.gov/su_docs/fdlp/cip/index.html>.
23. B. Obama, speech delivered to the 2004 Democratic National Convention, July 2004. Available *America 2004: The Democratic National Convention*. (May 26, 2005) <www.dems2004.org/site/apps/nl/content3.asp?c=lu2LaPYG&b=131063&ct=158769>.
24. J. Potter, untitled speech. In *Winning Orations 2000* (Mankato, MN: Interstate Oratorical Association, 2000), 40.
25. M. Sanchez, "Diplomatic Immunity Unjustified." In *Winning Orations 1996* (Mankato, MN: Interstate Oratorical Association, 1996), 66.
26. M. Limon and D. Kazoleas, "A Comparison of Exemplar and Statistical Evidence in Reducing Counter-Arguments and Responses to a Message," *Communication Research Reports 21* (2004): 291–298.
27. S. Gomes, "Toxic Noise." In *Winning Orations 2000*, 28.
28. A. Hickman, "Race Against Time." In *Winning Orations 1997* (Mankato, MN: Interstate Oratorical Association, 1997), 102.
29. J. A. Dick, "The Dangers of Oral Polio Vaccination." In *Winning Orations 1997*, 89.
30. K. Clanton, "African American History." In *Winning Orations 2000*, 55.
31. R. Lamm, "How to Make an Environmentalist," *Vital Speeches of the Day 71.10* (March 1, 2005).
32. J. Celoria, "The Counterfeiting of Airline Safety: An Examination of the Dangers of Bogus Airline Parts." In *Winning Orations 1997*, 79.
33. N. Tremel, "The New Wasteland: Computers." In *Winning Orations 2000*, 37.
34. M. Curtin, "Importance of Language Education," *Vital Speeches of the Day 71.8* (February 1, 2005).
35. J. Pruitt, "College Credit Card Crisis." In *Winning Orations 1996*, 26.
36. Curtin, "Importance of Language Education."
37. L. Altman, "Wider Student Use Is Urged for New Meningitis Vaccine," *The New York Times* (May 27, 2005): A14.
38. J. T. Masterson and N. Watson, "The Effects of Culture on Preferred Speaking Style." Paper presented at the meeting of the Speech Communication Association, November, 1979.
39. See D. A. Lieberman, *Public Speaking in the Multicultural Environment* 2e (Boston: Allyn & Bacon, 1997).
40. The World's Easiest Quiz? Joke-of-the-Day.com (February 25, 1998) <http.www.joke-of-the-day.com> Copyright 1997/1998 JOKE-OF-THE-DAY.com/TWT. All rights reserved. Permission is granted to reprint or distribute Joke-of-the-Day's jokes as long as this full copyright notice is included, including the subscription information. To get a joke every day, e-mail us at <Subscribe@joke-of-the-day.com>.
41. W. W. Braden, *Abraham Lincoln, Public Speaker* (Baton Rouge: Louisiana State University Press, 1988), 90.

CHAPTER 12

1. L. Tracy, "Taming Hostile Audiences," *Vital Speeches of the Day 71.10* (March 1, 2005).
2. T. Martinet, "Ribbons: Function or Fashion." In *Winning Orations 2004* (Mankato, MN: Interstate Oratorical Association, 2004), 79.
3. D. A. Lieberman, *Public Speaking in the Multicultural Environment* 2e (Boston: Allyn & Bacon, 1997), 23.
4. Lieberman, *Public Speaking in the Multicultural Environment*.

5. A. Lee, untitled speech. In *Winning Orations 2004*, 19.

6. Y. Pavlovic, "Genetic Testing: Medical Miracle or Health Hazard?" In *Winning Orations 2000* (Mankato, MN: Interstate Oratorical Association, 2000), 111.

7. M. Erikson, "See Jane, See Jane's Dilemma." In *Winning Orations 1997* (Mankato, MN: Interstate Oratorical Association, 1997), 63.

8. R. A. Dankleff, "Rohypnol—The Date-Rape Drug of the Nineties." In *Winning Orations 1997*, 87.

9. S. Hamilton, "Cruise Ship Violence." In *Winning Orations 2000*, 95.

10. T. Longoria, "Let Go of Anger and Forgive." (Texas State University–San Marcos, 2005).

11. A. Greenspan, commencement address delivered to the Wharton School of the University of Pennsylvania, May 15, 2005 (May 24, 2005) <www.federalreserve.gov/boarddocs/speeches/2005/20050515/default.htm>.

12. E. Monaghan, "Mental Health Privacy." In *Winning Orations 2000*, 117.

13. C. Reed, "Decreasing Red Meat in Your Diet." (Texas State University–San Marcos, 2005).

14. A. Lincoln, "Gettysburg Address," delivered at Gettysburg, PA, November 19, 1863. Available Douglass Archives of American Public Address. August 19, 1998 (July 12, 1999). <http://douglass.speech.nwu.edu/linc_b33.htm>.

15. D. MacArthur, "Farewell to the Cadets," address delivered at West Point, May 12, 1962. Reprinted in *Contemporary American Speeches* 7e, edited by R. L. Johannesen, R. R. Allen, and W. A. Linkugel (Dubuque, IA: Kendall/Hunt, 1992), 393.

16. M. L. King Jr., "I Have a Dream," delivered in Washington, D.C., August 28, 1963. Reprinted in Johannesen et al., *Contemporary American Speeches*, 369.

17. T. Kirchhefer, "The Deprived." In *Winning Orations 2000*, 151.

18. K. Morris, "National Forests: For Ourselves and Our Posterity." (Texas State University–San Marcos, 2005).

19. The preparation outline on pages 326–328 and the delivery outline that appears on pages 329–331 were adapted from a speech by B. Johnson, "Coricidin: No Prescription Needed." In *Winning Orations 2004*, 56–58.

CHAPTER 13

1. A. H. Monroe, "Measurement and Analysis of Audience Reaction to Student Speakers' Studies in Attitude Changes," *Bulletin of Purdue University Studies in Higher Education 22* (1937).

2. P. Heinbert, "Relationship of Content and Delivery to General Effectiveness," *Speech Monographs 30* (1963): 105–107.

3. A. Mehrabian, *Nonverbal Communication* (Hawthorne, NY: Aldine, 1972).

4. J. Detz, "Delivery Plus Content Equals Successful Presentation," *Communication World 15* (1998): 34.

5. Adapted from R. Ailes, *You Are the Message* (New York: Doubleday, 1989), 37–38.

6. P. Begala, "Flying Solo." PBS, *The Clinton Years: Anecdotes*. 2000 (July 14, 2002) <http://www.pbs.org/wgbh/pages/frontline/shows/clinton/anecdotes/#5>.

7. J. Wareham, "Doing It Off-the-Cuff," *Across the Board 35* (1998): 49–50.

8. Wareham, "Doing It Off-the-Cuff."

9. G. Orwell, "Politics and the English Language," reprinted in *About Language*, edited by W. H. Roberts and G. Turgeson (Boston: Houghton Mifflin, 1986), 282.

10. W. Safire, "Faithful, Even in Death," *The New York Times Magazine* (April 18, 1999): 72–74. Quotes from Vest's speech are from the text reprinted in this article.

11. J. F. Kennedy, inaugural address (January 20, 1961). In *Speeches in English*, edited by B. Aly and L. F. Aly (New York: Random House, 1968), 272.

12. J. Carter, address to the Democratic National Convention (July 2004). (August 1, 2004) <www.dems2004.org/site/pp.asp?c=1u12LAPYG&b=92959>.

13. G. W. Bush, Presidential victory speech, delivered at Austin, Texas, December 13, 2000. (December 14, 2000) <http://dailynews.yahoo.com/h/ap/20001214/el/recount_bush_text_1.html>.

14. E. Wiesel, "The Perils of Indifference," delivered at the White House, April 12, 1999 (July 1, 1999) <http://www.historyplace.com/speeches/wiesel.htm>.

15. H. R. Clinton, "Women's Rights Are Human Rights," delivered to the United Nations Fourth World Conference on Women, Plenary Session in Beijing, China, September 5, 1995 (July 1, 1999) <http://douglass.speech.nwu.edu/clin_a64.htm>.

16. J. F. Kennedy, "Address at Rice University on the Space Effort," delivered at Rice University, September 12, 1962 (July 1, 1999) <http://riceinfo.rice.edu/Fondren/Woodson/speech.html>.

17. S. A. Beebe, "Eye Contact: A Nonverbal Determinant of Speaker Credibility," *Speech Teacher 23* (1974): 21–25; S.A. Beebe, "Effects of Eye Contact, Posture and Vocal Inflection Upon Credibility and Comprehension," *Australian Scan Journal of Nonverbal Communication 7–8* (1979–80): 57–70; M. Cobin, "Response to Eye Contact," *Quarterly Journal of Speech 48* (1963): 415–419.

18. Beebe, "Eye Contact."

19. E. Adler, "Gestures May Give You a Hand with Speaking," *Austin American-Statesman* (November 25, 1998): E6.

20. J. C. McCroskey, V. P. Richmond, A. Sallinen, J. M. Fayer, and R. A. Barraclough, "A Cross-Cultural and Multi-Behavioral Analysis of the Relationship between Nonverbal Immediacy and Teacher Evaluation," *Communication Education 44* (1995): 281–290.

21. M. J. Beatty, "Some Effects of Posture on Speaker Credibility," library paper, Central Missouri State University, 1973.

22. R. Schmid, "Study: Posture Able to Communicate Fear," The Associated Press. November 16, 2004 (November 16, 2004) <news.yahoo.com>.

23. P. Ekman, W. V. Friesen, and S. S. Tomkins, "Facial Affect Scoring Technique: A First Validity Study," *Semiotica 3* (1971).

24. P. Ekman and W. Friesen. *Unmasking the Face* (Englewood Cliffs, NJ: Prentice-Hall, Inc., 1975).

25. "Bush's Smirk and Kerry's Smile Send the Wrong Message, Say Experts," The Associated Press. October 1, 2004 (October 1, 2004) <news.yahoo.com>.

26. Adapted from S. A. Beebe and S. J. Beebe, *Public Speaking: An Audience-Centered Approach* 5e. (Boston: Allyn & Bacon, 2003), 292–293.

27. M. M. Gill, "Accents and Stereotypes: Their Effect on Perceptions of Teachers and Lecture Comprehension," *Journal of Applied Communication Research 22* (1994): 348–361.

28. Adapted from S. Linver, *Speak Easy: How to Talk Your Way to the Top* (New York: Summit Books, 1978), 204–205.

29. E. Bohn and D. Jabusch, "The Effect of Four Methods of Instruction on the Use of Visual Aids in Speeches," *Western Journal of Speech Communication 46* (1982): 253–265.

30. A. Wilson, "In Defense of Rhetoric," *The Toastmaster 70.2* (2004): 11.

31. U.S. Census Bureau, "Profile of General Demographic Characteristics: 2000," *American FactFinder*. December, 2004 (June 7, 2005) <factfinder.census.gov/>.

32. P. S. Sochaczewski, "How Can We Put Intimacy into Presentations?" *Consulting to Management 12* (2001): 37–38.

33. Detz, "Delivery Plus Content Equals Successful Presentation."

34. R. Raskin, "Have Your Calendar Call Mine," *Family PC* (June/July, 1999): 21–26.

35. UNAIDS, *AIDS Epidemic Update 2004*, December, 2004 (June 7, 2005) <www.unaids.org/wad2004/report_pdf.html>.

CHAPTER 14

1. J. R. Johnson and N. Szczupakiewicz, "The Public Speaking Course: Is It Preparing Students with Work-Related Public Speaking Skills?" *Communication Education 36* (1987): 131–137.
2. For an excellent discussion about teaching someone to perform a skill, especially a social skill, see M. Argyle, *The Psychology of Interpersonal Behavior* (London: Penguin, 1990).
3. For an excellent discussion of strategies for informing others see K. E. Rowan, "A New Pedagogy for Explanatory Public Speaking: Why Arrangement Should Not Substitute for Invention," *Communication Education 44* (1995): 236–250.
4. For an excellent discussion of factors affecting audience attention in public speaking, see D. Ehninger, B. E. Gronbeck, R. E. McKerrow, and A. H. Monroe, *Principles and Types of Speech Communication* (Glenview, IL: Scott, Foresman, 1986), 43.
5. This suggestion is based on an excellent review of the literature found in Rowan, "A New Pedagogy for Explanatory Public Speaking."
6. M. Groover, "Learning to Communicate: The Importance of Speech Education in Public Schools." In *Winning Orations 1984* (Mankato, MN: Interstate Oratorical Association, 1984), 7.
7. M. Klepper and R. Gunther, *I'd Rather Die than Give a Speech* (New York: Carol Publishing Group, 1995).
8. Our discussion of using humor is adapted from Klepper and Gunther, *I'd Rather Die than Give a Speech.*
9. Klepper and Gunther, *I'd Rather Die than Give a Speech.*
10. M. Knowles, *Self-Directed Learning* (Chicago: Follett Publishing, 1975).
11. A. Tisino, "The Power of Music" (Texas State University–San Marcos, 2005).
12. L. Hughes, *The First Book of Rhythms* (New York: Franklin Watts, 1954).

CHAPTER 15

1. S. McLaughlin, "The Dirty Truth about Your Kitchen: Using Common Sense to Prevent Food Poisoning." In *Winning Orations 1996* (Mankato, MN: Interstate Oratorical Association, 1996), 73.
2. McLaughlin, "The Dirty Truth about Your Kitchen," 75.
3. A. Maslow, "A Theory of Human Motivation." In *Motivation and Personality* (New York: Harper & Row, 1954), Chapter 5.
4. See I. L. Janis and S. Feshback, "Effects of Fear Arousing Communications," *Journal of Abnormal and Social Psychology 48* (1953): 78–92; F. A. Powell and G. R. Miller, "Social Approval and Disapproval Cues in Anxiety Arousing Situations," *Speech Monographs 34* (1967): 152–159; and K. L. Higbee, "Fifteen Years of Fear Arousal: Research on Threat Appeals, 1953–1968," *Psychological Bulletin 72* (1969): 426–444.
5. P. A. Mongeau, "Another Look at Fear-Arousing Persuasive Appeals." In *Persuasion: Advances through Meta-Analysis,* edited by M. Allen and R. W. Preiss (Cresskill, NJ: Hampton Press, 1998), 65.
6. Aristotle, *Rhetoric* (L. Cooper, trans.). (New York: Appleton-Century-Crofts, 1960).
7. A. Bogeajis, "The Danger of Child Safety Seats: Why Aren't They Safe?" In *Winning Orations 1996,* 10.
8. N. Barton, "The Death of Reading." In *Winning Orations 2004* (Mankato, MN: Interstate Oratorical Association, 2004), 33–35.
9. S. Groom, "Hope for Foster Care." In *Winning Orations 2004,* 60–62.
10. D. Ehninger, B. Gronbeck, R. McKerrow, and A. Monroe, *Principles and Types of Speech Communication* (Glenview, IL: Scott, Foresman, 1986), 15.
11. S. Nay, "Sex Offender Registries: A Call for Reform." In *Winning Orations 2004,* 87.
12. Nay, "Sex Offender Registries: A Call for Reform," 87.

13. Nay, "Sex Offender Registries: A Call for Reform," 88.
14. Nay, "Sex Offender Registries: A Call for Reform," 89.
15. Nay, "Sex Offender Registries: A Call for Reform," 89.
16. D. C. Bryant, "Rhetoric: Its Functions and Its Scope," *Quarterly Journal of Speech 39* (1953): 26.
17. B. Sosnowchick, "The Cries of American Ailments." In *Winning Orations 2000* (Mankato, MN: Interstate Oratorical Association, 2000), 114.
18. W. Stephens, "Cruisin' Out of Control." In *Winning Orations 2004,* 103–105.

APPENDIX A

1. Our discussion of interview questions is based on J. T. Masterson, S. A. Beebe, and N. Watson, *An Invitation to Effective Speech Communication* (Glenview, IL: Scott Foresman and Company, 1989). We especially acknowledge the contributions of Norm Watson to this discussion.
2. This resumé and our suggestions for developing a resumé are based on the 2005 *Texas State University Career Services Manual* (San Marcos, TX: Office of Career Services, 2005).
3. J. L. Winsor, D. B. Curtis, and R. D. Stephens, "National Preferences in Business and Communication Education: A Survey Update," *Journal of the Association for Communication Administration 3* (1997): 174.
4. Adapted from M. S. Hanna and G. Wilson, *Communicating in Business and Professional Settings* (New York: McGraw-Hill, 1991), 263–265.
5. S. Armour, "Employers: Enough Already with the E-Resumés," *USA Today* (July 15, 1999): B1.
6. "Advantages of Web Resumés." April 2, 2005. <http://www.eresumeiq.com/web-resume-advantages.html>.
7. "Advantages of Web Resumés."
8. "Advantages of Web Resumés."
9. "Advantages of Web Resumés."
10. 2005 *Texas State University Career Services Manual.*

APPENDIX B

1. R. D. Gratz and P. J. Salem, "Technology and the Crisis of Self," *Communication Quarterly 32* (1984): 98–103.
2. M. S. Hanna and G. L. Wilson, *Communicating in Business and Professional Settings* 4e (New York: McGraw-Hill, 1998).
3. D. Pescovitz, "Software Robots Simulate Real Conversations," *Corpus Christi Caller Times* (March 21, 1999): D1, D4.
4. Pescovitz, "Software Robots Simulate Real Conversations."
5. L. Strate, "The Varieties of Cyberspace: Problems in Definition and Delimitation," *Western Journal of Communication 63* (1999): 382–412.
6. W. Rousch, "The Internet Reborn." In *Taking Sides: Clashing Views on Controversial Issues in Mass Media and Society* 8e, edited by A. Alexander and J. Hanson (Dubuque, IA: McGraw-Hill/Dushkin, 2005), 224–229; J. J. Jordan, "(Ad)Dressing the Body in Online Shopping Sites," *Critical Studies in Media Communication 20* (2003): 248–268; S. Morreale, "Morreale's Mailbag: 'Blogging' on the Web," *Spectra* (April, 2003): 9.
7. S. Turkle, *Life on the Screen: Identity in the Age of the Internet* (New York: Simon & Schuster, 1995).
8. R. Lee and S. Wahl, "Justifying Surveillance: An Ideological Analysis of the Journalistic Framing of Pedophiles and the Internet." Paper presented at the meeting of the National Communication Association, November, 2003; J. A. McCown, D. Fischer, R. Page, and M. Homant, "Internet Relationships: People Who Meet People," *Cyberpsychology & Behavior 4* (2001): 593–596; J. K. Seale & R. Pockney, "The Use of the Personal Home Page by Adults with Down Syndrome as a Tool for Managing Identity and

Friendship," *British Journal of Learning Disabilities 30* (2002): 142–148.

9. *The Washington Post* (September 29, 2004): A1, as cited in S. Morreale, "Morreale's Mailbag," *Spectra* (November, 2004): 3; J. Wagman, "No LOL Matter: Peer Pressure Pops Up with Instant Messaging," *Corpus Christi Caller Times* (June 22, 2003): A19.

10. M. A. Banks, "Filtering the Net in Libraries." In Alexander and Hanson, *Taking Sides,* 224–229.

11. C. A. Hult and T. N. Huckin, *The New Century Handbook* (Boston: Allyn & Bacon, 1999).

12. T. A. Doyle, *Allyn & Bacon Quick Guide to the Internet for Speech Communication* (Boston: Allyn & Bacon, 1998).

13. K. Y. A. McKenna, A. S. Green, and M. E. J. Gleason, "Relationship Formation on the Internet: What's the Big Attraction?" *Journal of Social Issues 58* (2002): 9–31. For interesting newspaper discussions of cyber-relationships, see "Female Inmates Making Connections—For Good or Ill—On Internet," *Corpus Christi Caller Times* (July 11, 1999): C7; D. Scott, "Marriage Online: Saying 'I Do' By a Virtual Waterfall, Moving into a Virtual House," *Corpus Christi Caller Times* (March 7, 1999): H1, H3; S. Winston, "Cyberlove: Florida Man Gives On-Line Advice for the Lovelorn," *Corpus Christi Caller Times* (May 28, 1995): G1, G7.

14. *New York Times* News Service, "Online Dating No Longer Loser Central," *Corpus Christi Caller Times* (June 29, 2003): A2; Associated Press, "EHarmony Patents Its Formula for Romance," *Corpus Christi Caller Times* (May 30, 2004): A2; R. Konrad, "Dating Site Gets Patent," *Corpus Christi Caller Times* (May 28, 2004): A2; C. Hinojosa, "Couples Say That the Sites Gave Them Time to Learn about Each Other," *Corpus Christi Caller Times* (February 8, 2004): H1, H4.

15. J. Walther and L. Tidwell, "When Is Mediated Communication Not Interpersonal?" In *Making Connections: Readings in Relational Communication,* edited by K. M. Galvin and P. Cooper (Los Angeles: Roxbury, 1996), 300–307.

16. A. Cooper, J. P. McLoughlin, and K. M. Campbell, "Sexuality in Cyberspace: Update for the 21st Century," *Cyberpsychology & Behavior 3* (2000): 521–536.

17. A. N. Markham, *Life Online: Researching Real Experience in Virtual Space* (Walnut Creek, CA: AltaMira Press, 1998), 203.

18. D. Fiely, "Cyber-Infidelity: Internet Access Implicated in Growing Number of Divorces," *The Columbus Dispatch,* Health and Medicine Week [Electronic Version] (2003); "Mental Health: Cybersex Is More Damaging to Relationships Than Pornography," *Cyberpsychology & Behavior 6* (2003): 553; E. R. Merkle and R. A. Richardson, "Digital Dating and Virtual Relating: Conceptualizing Computer-Mediated Romantic Relationships," *Family Relations 9* (2000): 187–196; K. Y. A. McKenna, A. S. Green, and P. K. Smith, "Demarginalizing the Sexual Self," *Journal of Sex Research 38* (2001): 302–316.

19. L. Averyt, "Caught in Adultery's New 'Net,'" *Corpus Christi Caller Times* (September 21, 1997): A1, A10.

20. Hult and Huckin, *The New Century Handbook;* S. McRae, "Coming Apart at the Seams: Sex, Text, and the Virtual Body." In *Wired Women: Gender and New Realities in Cyberspace,* edited by L. Cherny and L. R. Weise (Seattle: Seal Press, 1996), 242–263; L. Kendall, "MUDder? I Hardly Know 'Er! Adventures of a Feminist MUDder." In Cherny and Weise, *Wired Women,* 207–223.

21. H. Rheingold, "The Virtual Community." In Galvin and Cooper, *Making Connections,* 295–299.

22. J. Mahoney, "The E-Mail Explosion: Computer Messaging System Spawns Cultural Revolution," *Austin American-Statesman* (October 11, 1999): A1, A6.

23. Gratz and Salem, "Technology and the Crisis of Self."

24. Averyt, "Caught in Adultery's New 'Net'."

25. D. K. Wysocki, "Let Your Fingers Do the Talking: Sex on an Adult Chatline," *Sexualities 1* (1998): 425–452; Merkle and Richardson, "Digital Dating and Virtual Relating."

26. Walther and Tidwell, "When Is Mediated Communication Not Interpersonal?"

27. J. Barlow, "E-Mail Etiquette Has Its Own Rules," *Houston Chronicle* (March 11, 1999): C1.

28. C. R. Scott and J. C. Fontenot, "Multiple Identifications During Team Meetings: A Comparison of Conventional and Computer-Supported Interactions," *Communication Reports 12* (1999): 91–100.

29. G. J. Galanes and J. K. Brilhart, *Communicating in Groups: Applications and Skills* 2e (Madison, WI: Brown & Benchmark, 1994).

30. L. Sproull and S. Kiesler, *Connections: New Ways of Working in the Networked Organization* (Cambridge, MA: MIT Press, 1991).

31. Aslib Electronics Group News, "Have You Tried Teleconferencing?" <http://www.aslib.co.uk>.

32. J. F. Coates and J. Jarratt, "Managing Effectively in the Emerging Electronic Communications Environment." In Galvin and Cooper, *Making Connections,* 308–314.

33. M. Desmond, "Video Conferencing: Coast to Coast and Face-To-Face," *PC World* (March, 1994): 177–186.

34. G. M. Santoro, "The Internet: An Overview," *Communication Education 43* (1994): 73–86.

35. Hanna and Wilson, *Communicating in Business and Professional Settings.*

36. Galanes and Brilhart, *Communicating in Groups.*

37. L. L. Barker, K. J. Wahlers, K. W. Watson, and R. J. Kibler, *Groups in Process: An Introduction to Small Group Communication* 3e (Englewood Cliffs, NJ: Prentice-Hall, 1987); R. J. Johansen, J. Vallee, and K. Spangler, *Electronic Meetings: Technical Alternatives and Social Choices* (Reading, MA: Addison-Wesley, 1979).

38. "Search Us," *Entertainment Weekly* (September 13, 1999): 17.

39. J. Downing and C. Garmon, "Teaching Students in the Basic Course How to Use Presentation Software," *Communication Education 50* (2001): 218–229; R. W. Bly, "The Case Against PowerPoint," *Successful Meetings 50* (2001): 51–52; T. A. Stewart, "Ban It Now! Friends Don't Let Friends Use PowerPoint," *Fortune 143* (2001): 210; T. Simons, "The Least We Can Do Is Allow PowerPoint to Die in Peace," *Presentations 16* (2002): 6; D. G. Levasseur, "Pedagogy Meets PowerPoint: A Research Review on the Effects of Computer-Generated Slides in the Classroom." Paper presented at the meeting of the National Communication Association, November, 2004; "Honk If You Hate PowerPoint," *PR Newswire,* November, 2004, <http://www.biz.yahoo.com/prnews>.

APPENDIX C

1. L. Tracy, "Taming Hostile Audiences," *Vital Speeches of the Day,* 71.10 (March 1, 2005).

2. E. Radcliffe, "Blinded by the Light." In *Winning Orations 2004* (Mankato, MN: Interstate Oratorical Association, 2004), 91–93.

Index

Ability
    awareness of, 420–421
    language bias and, 71
Abolition of Man, The (Lewis), 152
Abstract meaning, 62
Academic quarter, 345
Academic Search Premier, 301
Action-oriented listeners, 110
Action words, 421, 423
Active listening, 122
Active strategy, for reducing uncertainty, 176
Acton, Lord, 150
Adapt, 21, 159–160
Adapting
    and approaches to communication, 148
    to audience, 404–405
    barriers to, 149–154
    ethics in, 137
    in family relationships, 195
    to interviewee's behavior, 429
    to others different from you, 154–160
Adaptors, 90
Adult learners, 376
Advanced search, 298
Advertising, motivated sequence in, 402
Affect displays, 90
Affection, 173
Age, and biased language, 71
Agenda, 268–271
    hidden, 385
Aggressive communication, 206–208
Alcoholics Anonymous, 225
Alice (Artificial Linguistic Computer Entity), 434
All-channel network, in group communication, 235–236
Alliteration, 342
Allness, 67
Alta Vista, 297, 298
Altman, Irwin, 182
Ambiguity, tolerance for, 156
American Association of University Women, 39
Analogy, 305, 370, 372
Andersen, Peter, 100
Androgynous, 146
Angelou, Maya, 342
Antithesis, 342
Appeal to misplaced authority, 397
Appeals to invitation, 90
Appearance, 88, 348
Appraisal interview, 413

Appropriateness, in self-disclosure, 180–181
Aristotle, 25, 192, 336, 384, 392, 394, 448
Armstrong, Nancy, 89
Arousal, 100
Articulation, 347
Artifacts, 88
Artificial Linguistic Computer Entity (Alice), 434
Asada, Kelli Jean, 193
Ascribed identity, 36
Assertive communication, 206–208
Assumed roles, 37
Asynchronous time, 436–437
Attending, 108
Attention, 47, 116, 400
Attitude, 32, 81–82, 389–390, 424
Attraction, 169–173
Attractiveness, physical, 40, 437
Audience, 288, 354
    attention of, 321–322
    diverse, 307
    focus on, 286
    hostile, 446–453
    motivating, 386–388
    and motive for listening, 373
    neutral, 404
    receptive, 404
    unreceptive, 404–405
Audience-centered model of presentational speaking, 283, 284, 385
Audience-centered purpose, 293
Audio CDs, 353
Audio conferencing, 440–441
Audio presentation, profanity in, 354
Audiotapes, 353
Authoritarian leader, 263, 264, 267
Avowed identity, 36
Awareness, 50–51, 420–421

Back-channel cues, 95
Baggage, 45
Baker, Sidney, 95
Bandwagon fallacy, 397
Bandwidth, 64
Bar graph, 351, 352
Barker, Larry, 110
Barlow, Jim, 64
Barnlund, Dean, 16
Barry, Dave, 267
Beamer, Todd, 306
Begala, Paul, 337
Beliefs, 32, 390

Benne, Kenneth, 228
Bentsen, Lloyd, 450, 451
Berger, C. R., 175
Bias
    of interviewer, 429
    in language, 66–72
Black English, 66
Blackberry, 436
Blanchard, Kenneth, 265
Blink: The Power of Thinking without Thinking (Gladwell), 153
Blogging, 435
Bodenhausen, Galen, 52
Body Language (Fast), 87
Body movement, 88–89, 344–345
Bok, Derek, 362
Bono, 393
Books, as supporting material, 300
Boolean search, 298
Boom microphone, 346
Bradac, J. J., 175
Brainstorming, 255
    electronic, 256
    silent, 255, 272, 288–289
Braithwaite, Charles, 95
Brehm, Sharon, 172
Brooks, Garth, 75
Brothers, Joyce, 104
Brown, Donald, 151
Bryant, Donald C., 404
Buddhism, 6
Burgoon, Judee, 85, 86
Bush, George W., 66, 85, 342, 346, 350, 384
Business Index Backfile, 301
Bypassing, 61

Cadence, in language, 342
Calabrese, R. J., 175
Call number, 300
Card catalog, 300
Carell, Lori, 160
Carlin, George, 375
Carnegie, Dale, 183
Carrey, Jim, 92
Carter, Jimmy, 341
Cartoons, in informative presentations, 375
Causal fallacy, 396
Causal reasoning, 395
Cause-and-effect organization, 316, 399
CD-ROM, as presentation aid, 352
Central idea, in presentational speaking, 292–294
Chain network, in group communication, 235, 236

Channel, 11–12
Chaplin, William, 83
Character education, 152
Charest, Jean, 320
Charisma, 393
Chart, as presentation aid, 351
Chatterbot, 434–435
Cheng, C. Y., 111
Chesterton, G. K., 373
Christianity, 6
Christians, Clifford, 5, 6
Chronological organization, 315
Churchill, Winston, 73, 284, 368, 448, 449
Class, and biased language, 71
Classification, 304
Clinton, Bill, 71, 337, 346
Clinton, Hillary Rodham, 342
Clique, 236, 441
Closed question, 416
Closure, 48, 323–324
Clothing
    for job interview, 423–424
    as nonverbal communication, 88
Co-culture, 65, 140, 146, 155
Coercion, 384
Coercive power, 233
Cognitive dissonance, 386–387
Cohesiveness, of group, 234
Collaborative learning, 225
Colleagues, 196–197
Collectivism, groups and teams and, 239
Collectivistic culture, 142–144, 204
Communication
    aggressive, 206–208
    assertive, 206–208
    characteristics of, 15–17
    computer-mediated, 34
    defensive, 73
    defined, 2–4
    and enhancement of perceptual
        accuracy, 49–53
    and enhancement of self-esteem, 42–46
    gender and, 146–148
    group, 24–25
    impersonal, 23, 167
    intercultural, 140
    interpersonal, 23–24
    intrapersonal, 19, 42–43
    mediated, 23, 25
    models of, 10–15
    other-oriented, 156–157
    presentational, 25
    reasons for studying, 8–10
    unmediated, 23
Communication competence, 4–7
Communication Ethics and Universal Values
    (Christians and Traber), 5–6
Communication interaction pattern,
    235–236
Communication models, 10–15
Communication principles for a lifetime, 2,
    17–23, 26, 30, 53, 58, 76, 80, 101,
    107, 129, 136, 161, 166, 186–187,
    195, 196, 214–215, 240, 274, 309,
    332, 358–359, 379, 408–409,
    430–431, 444

Communication triage, 115
Competence, of speaker, 392
Complementarity, 173
Complementary relationship, 206
Complexity, 315–316
Compliments, 179
Computer conferencing, 441
Computer-generated presentation aids,
    353–354
Computer-mediated communication, 34
Computer-mediated relationship, 435–439
Computers
    empathic listening by, 127
    simulated conversation with, 434–435
Computing, 209
Conclusion, 323–324
Concrete meaning, 62
Concrete word, 339
Conditional language, 74
Confidential information, 365
Conflict, interpersonal, 202–208
Conflict management
    in groups and teams, 259
    skills for, 210–214
    styles of, 208–209
Conflict phase, in group development,
    237–238
Confrontational style, 209
Connotative meaning, 62
Conrad, Joseph, 382
Consensus, 257–258
Constructive conflict, 203–204, 205
Content, 17
Content dimension, of message, 148
Content-oriented listeners, 110, 111
Context, 12, 63
Context barriers, to listening, 116–117
Control, 73–74, 173
Conversation, 174–179
    computer-simulated, 434–435
    with people of opposing views, 451
Conversational narcissism, 178
Cooley, Charles Horton, 35
Cooperative style, 209, 212
Correct word, 340
Cottle, Michelle, 40
Couric, Katie, 284
Courtship readiness, 90
Covey, Stephen, 30, 45, 212
Coworkers, as friends, 193
Creativity, 254–255
Credibility, of speaker, 323, 392–394, 448,
    452
Credo for Communication Ethics, 6
Criteria, 253
Criticism, as listening barrier, 114–115
Crushes, 170
Cultural contexts, 141–145
Cultural values, 141–145
Culture
    audience and, 307, 345
    and barriers to adapting to others,
        149–154
    clothing and, 88
    collectivistic, 142–144
    defined, 139–141
    delivery expectations and, 336

and electronic communication, 140
    expressing emotion and, 184–185
    eye contact and, 119
    feminine, 145
    gender roles and, 37, 146–148
    gestures and, 89
    globalization and, 138–139
    high-context, 141, 142
    individualistic, 142–144
    and language, 65, 155
    low-context, 141, 142, 156
    masculine, 145
    meaning of silence and, 95
    nonverbal communication and, 85
    organizing messages and, 318
    spatial zones and, 96, 97
    touching and, 94
    and universal norms, 5–7
    word meanings and, 62–63
Culture shock, 140
Curtin, Mike, 306
Cyber-addict, 438
Cyber selves, 36
Cybersex, 201
Cyberspace, 435

Dalai Lama, 6
Darwin, Charles, 90
De Saint-Exupery, Antoine, 125
Decentering, social, 118–119, 157
Deception, 92
Declarative sentence, 294
Decoding, 11
Deductive reasoning, 395
Deep-breathing techniques, 287
Defensive communication, 73
Definition, 304
De-intensification stage, of relationship,
    200
Delivery, of speech, 357–358
    effective verbal, 339–342
    methods of, 336–338
    nonverbal, 343–349
    physical, 343–345
    technology and enhancement of, 443
    vocal, 346–348
Delivery cues, 331
Delivery outline, 329–331, 338
Democratic leader, 263–264, 267
Demosthenes, 336, 453
Denotative meaning, 62
Derived credibility, 394
Descriptions, 303
Destructive conflict, 204–205
Dewey, John, 252
Dialect, 348
Diana, Princess of Wales, 393
Direct perception checking, 52
Directory, 297
Disciplinary interview, 413
Dissonance, as motivator, 386–387
Distracting, as conflict-management style,
    208–209
Diversity
    almanac of, 138
    in attraction, 171
    in audience expectations, 345

in audiences, 307
communication principles for a lifetime and, 22
in conflict management, 204
and individualism and collectivism, 239
in listening styles, 111, 120
in meaning of silence, 95
and patterns of organization, 318
of perspective, 393
in self-esteem and ethnicity, 39
and use of interpreter, 371
in use of time, 266
in word usage, 61
Diversity backlash, 138
Dodd, Charley, 141
Dominance cues, 100–101
Dr. Phil, 203
Drama, in speech presentation, 341
Drawings, as presentation aid, 350–351
Duck, Steve, 200
Dukakis, Michael, 451
DVD, as presentation aid, 352
Dyad, 24
Dynamism, 393

E. T. the Extra Terrestrial, 158
Eagleton, Thomas, 322
Ebonics, 66
E-brainstorming, 256
Egocentric, 157
eharmony.com, 437
Either-or fallacy, 397
Ekman, Paul, 88, 92, 346
Electronic brainstorming, 256
Electronic bulletin board, 437
E-mail
conveying emotions using, 82
cultural differences in, 140
etiquette in, 64
in relationship maintenance, 437, 438, 439
Emblems, 89
Emergence phase, of group development, 238
Emerson, Ralph Waldo, 164
Emoticon, 82, 174, 439
Emotional intelligence, 114, 125
Emotional Intelligence (Goleman), 114
Emotional noise, 113–114
Emotions
in conflict management, 210–211
in decision making, 397–398
expressing, 184–186
masking of, 93
nonverbal cues of, 90
paraphrasing of, 127–129
Empathy, 74, 121, 124–129, 158–159, 160, 427, 429
Employability, communication skills and, 8–9
Employer, identifying needs of, 423–424
Encoding, 11
Environment, 96
E-resumé, 426, 428
Ethics, 5–7
in achievement of team goal, 225

and adapting communication to others, 137, 160
and confidential or potentially dangerous information, 365
of conflict management, 259
of crushes, 170
of cyber selves, 36
ebonics and, 66
hidden agenda and, 385
of honest listening, 126
and interactions on Internet, 36
lie detectors and, 91
of online breakup, 200
of primacy and recency, 319
of profanity in audio presentation aid, 354
sources of, 7
of speechwriting, 301
of stereotyping others, 153
and touch, 93
Ethnicity. *See also* Culture
and language bias, 67–68
self-esteem and, 40
Ethnocentrism, 150
Ethos, 392–394, 448
Events, presentations about, 366–367, 368
Evidence, 394
Exclusive language, 68
Expanded Academic Index, 301
Expectancy violations model, 85–86
Expert power, 233
Expert testimony, 306
Explanation, 304
Exploration stage, of relationship development, 198
Expressive orientation, 148
Extelligence Creative Word Dictionary, 75
Extemporaneous speaking, 338
Eye contact, 91–92, 343
with audience, 355
in interview, 415
listening and, 119, 120

Face-to-face (FtF) communication, 167
Facial expression, 92–93, 119, 345–346
Factfinder, 373
Failing at Fairness: How America's Schools Cheat Girls (Sadker and Sadker), 39
Fallacy
bandwagon, 397
causal, 396
either-or, 397
logical, 396
Family, 194–195
communication within, 9
pluralistic, 195
as primary group, 224
Fast, Julius, 87
Fear, as motivator, 388
Fed Stats, 373
Feedback, 12
Feelings
language and, 73
nonverbal communication and, 81–82
of partner, 125
Feingold, Alan, 171
Felt, Mark, 306

Feminine culture, 145
Ferguson, Sarah, 323
Fidelity, Internet and, 437
Field Guide to Gestures (Armstrong and Wagner), 89
Fighting. *See* Conflict, interpersonal
Figurative analogy, 305
Figurative language, 341
Final summary, 321
Fine, Jeffrey, 181
Fisher, Andrew, 236
Flirting, 90, 174, 437
Focus group, 226
Force field analysis technique, 254
Formal presentation, 22
Foxworthy, Jeff, 51
Friedman, Thomas, 139
Friends with benefits relationship, 193
Friendship, 10, 182, 192–194, 437
Friesen, Wallace, 88, 92
Frost, Robert, 98
Full-text databases, 301
Functional approach
to group communication, 247
to leadership, 262
Funnel sequence, for interview questions, 417–418

Gamblers Anonymous, 225
Gang language, 65
Gatekeeper, 263, 271
Gates, Bill, 41
Gender
and approaches to communication, 147–148
attraction and, 171
defined, 38
and expression of emotions, 185
importance in culture of, 146–148
language bias and, 68–70
listening differences and, 120
online communication and, 175
self-disclosure and, 181–182
self-esteem and, 38–40
Gender-neutral term, 69
General purpose, of presentation, 291
Generic language, 68
Gestures, 89, 119, 343–344
Gibb, Jack, 72, 73
Gide, André, 154
Gladwell, Malcolm, 153
Globalization, 139
Goal
of group, 247
interpersonal conflict and, 212–213
Goldberg, Whoopi, 68
Goleman, Daniel, 114, 125, 289
Google, 297, 298, 301, 442
Government documents, 302
Graphs, as presentation aid, 351–352
Gray, John, 147
Greenspan, Alan, 322
Grievance interview, 413, 417
Group, 24. *See also* Team
association with, and self-concept, 36–37

Group *(Cont.)*
   cohesiveness in, 234
   communication interaction pattern in, 235–236
   defined, 220–222
   and differences in use of time, 266
   effective members of, 246–250
   effects of technology on, 441
   enhancing meetings of, 267–273
   impact of individualism and collectivism on, 239
   norms of, 231
   phases of development of, 236–240
   power in, 232–233
   problem solving in, 251–261
   roles in, 227–228, 229–230
   status in, 231–232
   types of, 224–226, 439
   virtual, 226, 440
   when to avoid working in, 250–251
Group communication, 24–25
Group deviate, 235
Groupthink, 258–260
Gudykunst, William, 156
Gunny-sacking, 75, 211

Habituation, 286
Hall, Edward T., 96, 97, 139, 141
Handouts, 356
Handshake, 83
Haptics, 93
Hard evidence, 317–318
Harvey, John, 180
Hasty generalization, 397
Hawking, Stephen, 114
Health, communication and, 9–10
Hearing, 107
Helical model of communication, 15, 16
Hersey, Paul, 265
Heterosexist language, 68, 71
Hidden agenda, 385
Hierarchy of needs, 387
High-context culture, 141, 142
Hill, Anita, 92
Hillary, Sir Edmund, 316
Hinduism, 6
Hirokawa, Randy, 247
Hits, 298
Hocker, Joyce, 205
Hofstede, Geert, 139, 142, 143, 144
Holmes, Janet, 179
Homophobic language, 68
Honest listening, 126
Honesty, 7, 32, 36, 44
Hookup, 193
Hoover, J. Edgar, 65
Horney, Karen, 32
How to Pick Up Girls!, 177
How We Think (Dewey), 252
Hughes, Mikayla, 193
Human communication, 3
Humor, 375
Humphrey, Judith, 292
Hyperlink, 299, 426
Hypothetical illustrations, 303
Hypothetical question, 416–417

"I" language, 212
"I" message, 272
Ideas, presentations about, 367, 368
Identity, 36
Illusion of transparency, 285
Illustrations, 303
Illustrators, 89–90
Immediacy, 99–100, 174
Impersonal communication, 23, 167
Impromptu speaking, 337–338
Inclusion, 173
Indeed.com, 297
Indirect perception checking, 52
Individual role, 227–228, 230
Individualism, 143, 239
Individualistic culture, 142–144, 204
Individualization stage, of relationship de-escalation, 200
Inductive reasoning, 395
Infante, Dominic, 207
Infinite interpretation, 111
Inflection, 347
Info Trac, 301
Infoplease, 373
Inform, 364
Information-gathering interview, 413, 417, 427
Information overload, 115
Information-processing rate, 115
Informative presentation
   organizing, 367–369
   sample of, 377–378
   strategies for, 370–377
   types of, 364–367
Ingham, Harry, 183
Initial credibility, 394
Initial preview, 319
Initiation stage, 198
Inner speech, 42
Instant messaging, 436, 437
Instrumental orientation, 148
Intensification stage, 198
Interactive strategy, 176
Interactive voice response, 434
Intercultural communication, 140
Interlibrary loan, 302
Internal preview, 320
Internal summary, 320–321
Internet, 34, 167, 435. *See also* Web resources
Internet relationship, 435–439. *See also* Online relationship
Internet Relay Chat (IRC), 436
Interpersonal attraction, 169–173
Interpersonal communication, 23–24, 167–169, 197
Interpersonal conflict, 202–208. *See also* Conflict management
Interpersonal power, 205–206
Interpretation, 48–49
Interpreter, 371
Interview
   nature and types of, 413–415
   preparation for job, 420–427
   structure of, 415–420
Interviewer, 428–430

Intimacy, gender and, 181–182
Intimacy stage, 198
Intimate space, 96, 97
Intrapersonal communication, 19, 42–43
Introduction, 321–323
Inversion, 341
Inverted funnel sequence, for interview questions, 418–419
IRC, 436
Islam, 6

Jackson, Jesse, 66
James, William, 33
Jefferson, Lisa, 306
Job interview, 414–415
   follow-up after, 425–427
   listening and responding skills in, 424–425
   preparation for, 420–424
Jobs, Steve, 354
Johari Window, 183–184
Johnson, Ben, 284, 301, 318, 326, 329, 347, 358
Jones, Paula, 71
Jordan, Barbara, 59
Jourard, Sidney, 185
Journalist's Six Questions method, 253
Judaism, 6

Kale, David, 152
Keenan, Mabel A., 28
Keller, Helen, 71
Kennedy, Florynce R., 312
Kennedy, John F., 92, 94, 284, 341, 342, 450, 451
Kenrick, Douglas, 51
Kerry, John, 346
Kinesics, 89
King, Martin Luther Jr., 94, 323
Klepper, Michael, 375
Kluckhohn, Clyde, 150
Knapp, Mark, 199

LaFasto, Frank, 223
Laissez-faire leader, 264, 267
Lamm, Richard, 305
Language, 19
   bias in, 66–72
   culture and, 155
   exclusive, 68
   figurative, 341
   focus on, 59–60
   gang, 65
   generic, 68
   heterosexist, 68, 71
   homophobic, 68
   in job interview, 428
   nature of, 60–63
   as reflection of culture, 65
   in relationships, 65–66
   sexist, 68–70
Lao Tsu, 267
Larson, Carl, 223
Lasswell, Harold, 11, 12
Lavaliere microphone, 346
Lavigne, Avril, 58

Lay testimony, 306
Leadership
    functional approach to, 262
    situational approach to, 264–265
    styles approach to, 263–264
    trait approach to, 262
    transformational, 266–267
Lebra, T. S., 111
Lee, Toby, 303
Legitimate power, 232
Leno, Jay, 121, 284
Lewis, C. S., 5, 134, 136, 152
LEXIS/NEXIS, 301
Library, 299–300
Library of Congress classification system,
    300
Lie detectors, 91
Lieberman, Devorah, 65
*Life Online: Researching Real Experience in
    Virtual Space* (Markham), 34, 437
Lincoln, Abraham, 323
Line graph, 351, 352
Lippman, Walter, 237
Listeners, styles of, 110, 111
Listening, 21
    in adapting to others, 155–156
    barriers to, 112–117
    by computers, 127
    in conflict management, 212
    defined, 107
    honest, 126
    improving skills in, 118–123
    in interview, 424, 427
    by interviewer, 429
    process of, 107–109
Listening style, 109–110, 111
Listserv, 437
Literal analogy, 305
Literary quotations, 306
Logical fallacy, 396
Logos, 392, 394–397
Long-term maintenance attraction, 170
Low-context culture, 141, 142, 156
Luft, Joe, 183
Lycos, 442
Lying, 175, 176

MacArthur, Douglas, 323
Main ideas
    organization of, 314–317
    for presentational speaking, 294–296
Manuscript speaking, 336–337
Maps, as presentation aid, 350–351
Markham, Annette, 34, 437
Masculine culture, 145
Masculinity, 143
Maslow, Abraham, 31, 387
Mass communication, 25
Match.com, 437
Matching hypothesis, 172
Material self, 33–34
McConnell, John H., 8
McGovern, George, 322
McGraw, Phillip, 203
Mead, George Herbert, 35
Mead, Margaret, 222, 244

Meaning, 3, 61, 62
Mediated communication, 23, 25
Mediation services, 211
Meeting
    agenda for, 268–271
    managing interaction in, 271–273
    virtual, 269
Mehrabian, Albert, 81, 82, 99, 100
Memorized speaking, 337
Memory, short-term, 109
Men Are from Mars, Women Are from Venus
    (Gray), 147
Message, 4–7, 11, 12–15
    nonverbal, 83–84
Metadiscussion, 271
Metaphors, 341
Metcalf, Bob, 282
Microphone, 346–347
Microsoft Excel, 351
Mind, Self, and Society (Mead), 35
Mindful communicator, 156
Mintzberg, Harvey, 196
Models, as presentation aids, 350
Monochronic, 266
Monroe, Alan H., 336, 400, 401
*Monthly Catalog of U.S. Government
    Publications*, 302
MOOs, 438
Moral code, 6
Morrison, Kelly, 193
Mosvic, Roger, 273
Motivated sequence, 400–402
Movement, and speech delivery, 88–89,
    344–345
MUDs, 438
Multitasking, 116
Murray, Henry, 150
MySpeechLab, 325

Nass, Clifford, 127
National Association for Self-Esteem
    (NASE), 38
*National Bibliography of U.S. Government
    Publications*, 302
National Communication Association, 6
National Forum on People's Differences, 68
National Newspaper Index, 302
National Speakers Association, 448
Nationality, 67–68. *See also* Culture
Needs, 400
    of employer, 423–424
    Maslow's hierarchy of, 387
Negative visualization, 401
Nelson, Robert, 273
Neutral audience, 404
Newsgroup, 436–437
Newspaper index, 302
Newspaper Source, 301, 302
Newspapers, 302
Nixon, Richard, 92
Noise, 12, 116–117
Nominal group technique, 255
Non sequitur, 397
Nonconfrontational style, 208–209
Nonverbal communication, 20
    appearance as, 88, 348

    in attraction, 174
    body movement, gestures, and posture
        as, 88–91, 343–345
    in conflict management, 211
    defined, 80
    eye contact as, 91–92, 343
    facial expressions as, 92–93, 345–346
    interpreting, 98–101
    as listening barrier, 119
    nature of, 84–87
    physical environment, space, and
        territory as, 95–98
    reasons to study, 81–84
    touch as, 93–94
    in videoconferencing, 441
    voice as, 94–95, 346–348
Nonverbal delivery, 343–349
Nonverbal reinforcement, 376
Nonverbal symbols, 4
Nonverbal transition, 320
Norgay, Tenzing, 316
Norms, of group or team, 231
Note cards, 331
Nouwen, Henri J. M., 125, 158

Obama, Barack, 303
Objective self-awareness, 31
Objects
    as presentation aids, 349–350
    presentations about, 364–365, 367
O'Brien, Conan, 284
O'Brien, Thomas, 453, 454
Old Drum, 341
Omission, 341
Online dating service, 437
Online relationship, 174, 175, 176, 200,
    435–439
Open question, 416
Operational definition, 304
Opinions, 305–306
Oprah Winfrey Show, The, 36
Oral citation, 306
Organization, 48
    cause-and-effect, 316, 399
    chronological, 315
    cultural differences in, 318
    of informative presentations, 367–369
    of main ideas, 314–317
    motivated sequence and, 400–402
    of presentation, 319–321
    problem-and-solution, 316–317, 399
    refutation as, 400
    spatial, 316
    of supporting material, 317–319
    topical, 315–316
Organizational cues, 319
Orientation phase, of group development,
    237
Other-oriented speaker, 4, 21, 156–157
Outline
    delivery, 329–331
    preparation, 324–328
Outlining software, 325

Paralanguage, 94
Parallel relationship, 206

Parallelism, 342
Paraphrasing, 126–129
Passive strategy, for reducing uncertainty, 176
Pathos, 392, 397–398
Pauling, Linus, 218
Pause, 347
PDA (personal digital assistant), 436
Peer pressure, 36
People
    as presentation aids, 350
    presentations about, 366, 368
People-oriented listeners, 110, 111
Perception
    enhancing accuracy of, 49–53
    process of, 46–49
Perception checking, 52–53, 86, 196, 212
Performance review, 413
Performance visualization, 287
Pericles, 453
Periodical index, 300–301
Periodicals, 300–301
Personal attack, 397
Personal space, 86, 96, 97
Personification, 341
Perspective, 393
Persuasion. See also Persuasion interview;
        Persuasive presentation
    defined, 384–385
    identifying purpose of, 389–390
    motivating audience with, 386–388
    narrowing topic for, 389
    as proposition, 391
Persuasion interview, 414
Persuasive presentation. See also Persuasion
    organizing, 398–403
    sample, 406–408, 453–454
Photographs, as presentation aids, 350
Physical attraction, 171–172
Physical attractiveness, 40, 437
Physical delivery, 343–345
Physical environment, 96
Pie graph, 351, 352
Pitch, of voice, 347
Pitts, Leonard, 68
Placating response, 208
Platinum Rule, 125
Pluralistic family, 195
Point of view, 393
Polarization, as barrier to communication, 65–66, 69
Political campaign interview, 414
Political correctness, 66
Polychronic, 266
Porter, Richard, 85, 152
Positional cues, 90
Positive appeals, as motivator, 388
Positive people, 44–45
Positive visualization, 401
Post-interaction stage, of relationship de-escalation, 200
Posture, 119, 345
Powell, Colin, 373
Power
    in group or team, 232–233
    interpersonal, 205–206
Power distribution, 143, 144

PowerPoint, 353, 442
Preening behaviors, 90
Pre-interaction awareness stage, of
        relationship escalation, 198
Prejudice, 153, 154, 429
Preparation outline, 324–328, 338
Presentation aids, 374
    computer-generated, 353–354
    guidelines for preparing, 354–355
    guidelines for using, 355–356
    technological innovations and, 442–443
    types of, 349–353
Presentational communication, 25
Presentational speaking, 43, 282. See also
        Informative presentation; Persuasion;
        Persuasive presentation
    developing central idea for, 292–294
    effective nonverbal delivery in, 343–349
    effective verbal delivery in, 339–342
    gathering supporting material for,
        296–308, 442
    generating main ideas for, 294–296
    identifying purpose of, 290–293
    introducing and concluding, 321–324
    methods of delivery for, 336–338
    organizing main ideas in, 314–317
    organizing supporting material for,
        317–319
    outlining, 324–332
    overview of process of, 283–284
    and presentation aids, 349–356
    rehearsing and delivering, 357–358
    selecting and narrowing topic of,
        287–290
    speaker anxiety and, 284–287
    and use of signposts, 319–321
Preview, 319–320
Primacy, 315, 319
Primary group, 224
Primary tension, 237
Probing question, 416
Problem, managing, in interpersonal
        conflict, 213–214
Problem-and-solution organization,
        316–317, 399
Problem solving, in groups and teams,
        225–226, 251–261
Problem-solving group, 225–226,
        251–261
Problem-solving interview, 413–414
Procedures, presentations about, 365, 368
Process functions, of leaders, 263
Profanity, in presentation aid, 354
Proof, 394
Proposition, 391
    of fact, 391
    of policy, 391
    of value, 391
Proxemics, 96
Proximity, 172
Public Affairs Information Service (P.A.I.S.)
        Bulletin, 301
Public space, 96, 97
Public speaking, 282. See also
        Presentational speaking
Purpose, in presentational speaking,
        290–293

Quasi-courtship behavior, 90
Quayle, Dan, 450, 451
Questions
    in adapting to others, 155–156
    anticipating, 450–451
    asking appropriate, 125–126
    in conversations, 178–179
    in job interview, 424–425, 430
    sequence of, in interview, 417–419
    types of, in interview, 416–417
Quinn, Daniel, 8, 19
Quintilian, 392
Quorum, 270
Quotations
    attention-getting, 322
    humorous, 375
    literary, 306

Race, 67–68. See also Culture
Radcliff, Erica, 453–454
Rapport
    with audience, 451
    in interview, 415
Rate, of vocal delivery, 347
Reader's Guide to Periodical Literature, The,
        301
Reasoning, 394, 395
Reasoning by analogy, 395
Receiver, 11
Receiver apprehension, 115–116
Recency, 315, 319
Receptive audience, 404
Reciprocal borrowing privileges, 302
Reciprocity, 180
Red herring, 397
Redmond, Mark, 157, 197
Redundancy, 376
Reed, Jim, 453
Reeves, Byron, 127
Reference resources, 302
References, for interview, 426
Referent power, 233
Reflective thinking, 252
Reframing, 44
Refutation, 400
Regulators, in nonverbal communication,
        90
Rehearsal
    of presentation, 347, 357–358, 449
    with presentation aids, 355
    on videotape, 349, 443
Reinforcement phase, of group
        development, 238
Relational de-escalation, 199–202
Relational dimension, of message, 148
Relational escalation, 198–199
Relationship
    with colleagues, 196–197
    communication in, 9
    complementary, 206
    conflict in, 203–208
    with family, 194–195
    with friends, 192–194
    honest, 44
    initiating, 169–179, 435–437
    interpersonal communication and,
        168–169

maintaining, 179–186, 437–439
nonverbal messages and, 82–83
online, 174, 175, 176, 200, 435–439
parallel, 206
role of language in, 65–66
stages of development in, 197–202
supportive, 72–75
symmetrical, 206
Relationship dimension, of message, 17
Relationship of choice, 168
Relationship of circumstance, 168
Religion
  language bias and, 67–68
  and moral code, 6
Remembering, 109
Repetition, 342
Responding, 109
  with empathy, 124–129
  in job interview, 424
Responding skills, 123–124
Response latency, 95
Results-driven structure, 248
Resumé, 421–423
  electronic, 426, 428
Revolution from Within: A Book of Self-Esteem
  (Steinem), 38
Reward power, 233
Rhetoric, 25, 392, 404
Rhetoric, The (Aristotle), 25, 384, 448
Rice, Condoleezza, 263
Role
  assumed, 37
  in group or team, 227–228, 229–230
  individual, 227–228, 230
  task, 227, 229
Romantic relationship, 171, 172, 206
Roosevelt, Eleanor, 154
Roosevelt, Franklin D., 280, 393
Roosevelt, Theodore, 324
Rubin, Jeffrey, 210
Rule, 17
  of group or team, 228, 231
  in nonverbal communication, 85–86

Sadker, David, 39
Sadker, Myra, 39
Safire, William, 341
Sales interview, 414
Samovar, Larry, 85, 152
Sapir, Edward, 60, 78
Sapir-Whorf hypothesis, 60
Sarget, Stephanie, 120
Satir, Virginia, 9, 195
Schutz, Will, 173
Search engine, 297, 442
Secondary tension, 237
Second-guessing, 110
Seinfeld, Jerry, 43
Selecting, 47, 107–108
Selection, 47, 107–108
Self, 32
  as barrier to listening, 112–115
  material, 33–34
  social, 34–35
  spiritual, 35
Self-absorbed communicator style, 178, 179
Self-awareness, 30, 31–32, 115, 119, 288

Self-concept, 32–37
Self-disclosure, 180–182
  Johari Window model of, 183–184
  social penetration model of, 182–183
  in virtual communication, 438–439
Self-esteem
  communication and enhancement of,
    42–46
  ethnicity and, 40
  gender and, 38–40
  self-expectations and, 41
  social comparisons and, 40–41
Self-expectations, 41
Self-focus, 112–113
Self-fulfilling prophecy, 41
Self-image, 32
Self-labels, 37
Self-reflexiveness, 37
Self-talk, 42–43, 114, 156, 211
Self-worth, 38. *See also* Self-esteem
Senge, Peter, 266
Sensitivity, 21, 249
Separation stage, in relational de-
  escalation, 200
Seven Habits of Highly Effective People, The
  (Covey), 30, 212
Sex, 38. *See also* Gender
Sexist language, 68–70
Sexual attraction, 171–172
Sexual harassment, 98
Sexual liaisons, 193
Sexual orientation, language and, 70–71
Sexual Recovery Institute, 438
Shakespeare, 33, 64
Shannon, Claude, 11, 12
Sheats, Paul, 228
Shimanoff, Susan, 17
Short-term initial attraction, 170
Short-term memory, 109
Shyness, 45
Sign language, 80, 85
Signpost, 319
Silence, 95, 118, 125
Silent brainstorming, 255, 272, 288–289
Similarity
  in adapting to others, 150–151
  in attraction, 170
Similes, 341
Simple word, 340
Situational approach to leadership,
  264–265
Slang, 58, 428
Small group, 221–222, 439–440
Small group communication, 24, 222
Social Cognition Laboratory, 52
Social comparison, 39–41
Social decentering, 118–119, 157
Social group, 226
Social penetration, 182–183
Social role, 227, 229–230
Social self, 34–35
Social space, 96, 97
Social support, 9, 10
Soft evidence, 317–318
Software, outlining, 325
Source, of communication, 11
Space, zones of, 96–97

Spam, 437
Spatial organization, 316
Speaker anxiety, 284–287
Speaking. *See also* Presentational speaking
  audience-centered model of, 385
  extemporaneous, 338
  impromptu, 337–338
  manuscript, 336–337
  memorized, 337
  public, 282
Specific purpose, 291–292, 293
Specific word, 339
Specificity, 317
Spender, Dale, 60
Spiritual self, 35
Springer, Jerry, 113
Stacks, 300
Stagnation, in relational de-escalation, 200
Standard outline format, 325–326
Stationary microphone, 347
Statistics, 305
Status, in group or team, 231–232
Steinem, Gloria, 38
Stereotype, 51–52, 120, 152–153, 155
Stewart, John, 35, 36
Streisand, Barbra, 285
Structure, in group or team discussion, 251
Study group, 224–225, 439
Styles approach to leadership, 263–264
Subjective self-awareness, 31
Summary, 320–321
Supporting material, 296
  acknowledgment of, 306–308
  attention-catching, 372
  organizing, 317–319
  sources of, 297–302
  types of, 302–306
Supportive communication, 73
Suspension, 341
Suswein, Ruth, 306
Syllogism, 395
Symbolic self-awareness, 31
Symbols, 3
  words as, 61
Symmetrical relationship, 206
Sympathy, 158
Synchronous time, 436
Systematic desensitization, 287

Tannen, Deborah, 147
Tao, 152
Tape recorder, 449
Task functions, of leaders, 262
Task role, 227, 229
Taylor, Dalmas, 182
T-chart, 260, 261
Team, 24–25. *See also* Group
  characteristics of members of, 223–224
  cohesiveness in, 234
  communication interaction pattern in,
    235–236
  defined, 222
  dynamics of, 227–236
  goals of, 225
  norms of, 231
  phases of development of, 236–240
  power in, 232–233

Team (*Cont.*)
    virtual, 226
    Web resources about, 222
Team ground rules, 228
Technology
    and adapting to cultural differences, 140
    brainstorming using, 256
    conveying emotions through, 82
    and cybersex, 201
    effect of on group interaction, 441
    and electronic thesaurus, 374
    and e-mail etiquette, 64
    and emotion-emulating software, 127
    and e-resumé, 426, 428
    exploring self-concept through, 34
    and gender gap, 175
    and group decision making, 226
    impersonal innovations in, 434–435
    and outlining software, 325
    presentational communication and, 442–443
    rehearsal using, 349
    and relationships, 201, 435–439
    and search engines, 297
    in small group formation, 439–440
    and teleconferencing, 440–441
    use of by virtual group or team, 226
Teleconferencing, 440–441
Ten Commandments, 6
Teoma, 298
Teresa, Mother, 114
Terminal credibility, 394
Territorial markers, 97–98
Territoriality, 97–98
Text messaging, 436
Therapy group, 225, 227
Thesaurus, 340
    electronic, 374
Thomas, Clarence, 67, 92
Time
    asynchronous, 436–437
    as listening barrier, 116
    in meeting interactions, 272
    synchronous, 436
    use of by group or team, 266
Time-oriented listeners, 110
Ting-Toomey, Stella, 204
Tolstoy, Leo, 192
Topic, 293, 287–290
Topical organization, 315–316
Touch, 93–94
Touch ethic, 93
Traber, Michael, 6
Tracy, Larry, 314, 446–453
Trait approach to leadership, 262
Transformational approach to leadership, 266–267
Transgender individuals, 70
Transition, 320
Trigger words, 72
Truman, Harry, 160
Trustworthiness, of speaker, 393

Tunnel sequence, for interview questions, 418–419
Turmoil stage, in relational de-escalation, 199–200
Twain, Mark, 56, 153

Unbiased word, 339
Uncertainty, 16, 144
    reducing, 175–179
Uncertainty avoidance, 143, 144
Uncertainty-reduction theory, 175
Understanding, 5, 108–109
Universal ethical code, 5
Unmediated communication, 23
Unreceptive audience, 405
URL, 298

Values, 32–33, 36, 152, 390
Van Gundy, Arthur, 251
Verbal abuse, 207
Verbal aggression, 207
Verbal delivery, 339–342
Verbal transition, 320
Vertical search engines, 297
Vest, George Graham, 341
Videoconferencing, 440, 441
Videotape
    as presentation aid, 352
    of presentation, 357
    rehearsal using, 349, 443, 449
Vigilant thinkers, 247
Virtual friendship, 437
Virtual group, 226, 440
Virtual Meeting Assistant, 269
Virtual team, 226
Visualization, 43–44, 401
Vivid word, 339
Vocabulary, Web resources for, 60
Vocal delivery, 346–348
Vocalics, 94
Voice, 94–95, 346–348
Volume, 346

Wagner, Melissa, 89
Walker, Alice, 70
Wallace, Mike, 427
Watson, Kitty, 110
Weaver, James, 110
Weaver, Warren, 11, 12
Web directories, 289
Web logging, 435
Web pages, 289, 298
    of potential employers, 423
Web resources
    for e-resumés, 428
    evaluation of, 442
    Extelligence Creative Word Dictionary as, 75
Web resources
    on facial expressions, 92
    for famous speeches, 346
    for improvement of listening skills, 127
    for informative speeches, 373

    intercultural communication and, 145
    for mediation services, 211
    National Forum on People's Differences as, 68
    for profession of communication, 8
    for quotes, 322
    for romantic relationships, 172
    self-disclosure using, 181
    on self-esteem, 38
    on shyness, 45
    on small group communication, 239
    for speech topic, 289
    on stereotyping and perception, 52
    for team information, 222
    for virtual meeting information, 269
    for vocabulary, 60
Web sites, 298
Weber, Ann, 180
Weight Watchers, 225
Weiss, Robert, 437
Wells, H. G., 306
Welty, Eudora, 190
We've Got to Start Meeting Like This! (Mosvic and Nelson), 273
Wheel network, in group communication, 235, 236
Whitman, Walt, 334
Whorf, Benjamin Lee, 60
Wiesel, Elie, 342, 395
Wiio, Osmo, 16
Wilmot, William, 205
Winfrey, Oprah, 284
Withdrawing, 209
Word pictures, 303, 373–374
Word structures, 340–342
Words, 59, 60
    action, 421, 423
    allness and, 67
    concrete, 339
    correct, 340
    effective use of, 339–340
    to establish supportive relationships, 72–75
    meanings of, 61–63
    power of, 63–66
    simple, 340
    specific, 339
    as symbols, 61
    trigger, 72
    unbiased, 339
    vivid, 339
Working with Emotional Intelligence (Goleman), 289
World Wide Web, 297–299, 302. *See also* Web resources
Worldview, 140

Yahoo!, 297, 298, 442
Yahoo personals, 437
"You" message, 272

Ziggs (search engine), 297
Ziglar, Zig, 424

Credits